Third Edition

LANGUAGE DEVELOPMENT
An Introduction

ROBERT E. OWENS, JR.
State University of New York
Geneseo, New York

Merrill, an imprint of
Macmillan Publishing Company
New York

Maxwell Macmillan Canada
Toronto

Maxwell Macmillan International
New York   Oxford   Singapore   Sydney

Cover art: Antonio Gore; Southeast School, Columbus, Ohio
Editor: Ann Castel
Production Editor: Mona M. Bunner
Art Coordinator: Peter A. Robison
Production Buyer: Patricia A. Tonneman

This book was set in Zapf Book and Univers by Carlisle Communications, Ltd. and was printed and bound by R. R. Donnelley & Sons Company.
The cover was printed by New England Book Components.

Macmillan Publishing Company
866 Third Avenue
New York, NY 10022

Macmillan Publishing Company is part of the
Maxwell Communication Group of Companies.

Maxwell Macmillan Canada, Inc.
1200 Eglinton Avenue East, Suite 200
Don Mills, Ontario M3C 3N1

Library of Congress Cataloging-in-Publication Data

Owens, Robert E.
    Language development : an introduction / by Robert E. Owens, Jr.
    3rd ed.
        p.   cm.
    Includes bibliographical references and index.
    ISBN 0-02-390181-0
    1. Language acquisition.   I. Title.
    P118.093   1992
    401'.93—dc20   91—22117
                                                                CIP

Printing: 3 4 5 6 7 8 9   Year: 2 3 4 5

Photo credits: Sandra Anselmo/Macmillan Publishing, p. 134; Andrew Brunk/Macmillan Publishing, pp. 74, 288, 430; Robert Finken, p. 408; Kevin Fitzsimons/Macmillan Publishing, pp. 148, 254, 458; Jean Greenwald/Macmillan Publishing, p. 352; Larry Hamill/Macmillan Publishing, p. 167; Lloyd Lemmerman/Macmillan Publishing, p. 416; Robert Meir/Sunrise Photos, p. 114; Macmillan Publishing, p. 68; Timothy O'Leary, p. 242; Harvey R. Phillips, p. 9; Michael Siluk, p. 210; Jan Smyth/Macmillan Publishing, p. 460; and Gale Zucker, pp. xiv, 26, 61, 122, 201, 250, 312, 396, 426.

Mommy, say that again. I didn't hear you. I was listening to my toast.

Jessica Owens, age four

To Jason, Todd, and Jessica, who have learned more about language in their few short years than we could possibly describe in only a few hundred pages, and to Tom, who taught me more about myself than I would ever have known.

Preface

There is no single way in which children learn to communicate. Each child follows an individual developmental pattern. Still, it is possible to describe a pattern of general communication development and of English specifically. This text attempts such descriptions but emphasizes individual patterns.

In recognition of the tremendous variation across children and languages, the third edition of *Language Development* devotes much more space to developmental differences. In addition, the sections on dialects and bilingualism have been expanded to reflect more accurately the realities of everyday life in the United States. Discussion of other cultures has also been included in the text wherever possible.

Other improvements in the third edition are the inclusion of a new chapter on language research, stressing the methods and issues in collection and analysis of data. This chapter also includes actual transcripts of child language with descriptive analysis. Instructors will also note that the chapters have been rearranged somewhat from the second edition. This change is based on the advice of those using the text who felt that it was better to introduce students to learning principles and techniques prior to a discussion of development. Finally, in an attempt to make the text more readable, I have rewritten it throughout. Many quotations have been removed, reworded, or shortened to make the flow more even.

Those students who will one day become parents should appreciate the value of this text as a guideline to development. Most college students, however, do not take courses in order to prepare for parenthood. Students who plan to work with disordered or delayed populations will find that normal development can provide a model for evaluation and intervention. The developmental rationale can be used to decide upon the targets for training and to determine the overall remedial approach.

In recognition of the importance of the developmental rationale as a tool and of the changing perspectives in child language development, the third edition offers expanded coverage of preschool and school-age language development. Pragmatics receives increased attention, as do the conversational context within which most language and the development of narration occur. Prospective speech-language pathologists will find these developmental progressions valuable when making decisions concerning materials for use with disordered or delayed populations. As consumers of educational and therapeutic products, educators and speech pathologists must be especially sensitive to the philosophy that governs the organization of such materials. While a developmental intervention rationale is only one of several possible approaches, it is generally the most widely accepted. Unfortunately, many educational materials claim to be developmental in design but are not. I recall opening one such book to find *please* and *thank you* as the first two phrases to be taught to a deaf child. These words violate many of the characteristics of first words in general.

The experienced teacher, psychologist, or speech pathologist need not rely on prepackaged materials if he or she has a good base in communication development. An understanding of the developmental process and the use of a problem-solving approach can be a powerful combination in the hands of a creative clinician.

Finally, as in the other editions, I have varied the sex of the child by chapter. This is an attempt at fairness and has not been without its detractors. I apologize to those who find the sex change confusing and hope that they too can appreciate my desire not to devalue girls and women.

With these considerations in mind, I have created what I hope to be a useful text for future parents, educators, and speech pathologists.

ACKNOWLEDGMENTS

A volume of this scope must be the combined effort of many people fulfilling many roles, and this one is no exception.

My first thanks must go to all those professionals, too numerous to mention, who have corresponded or conversed with me on the need for such a text. The overall organization of this text reflects the general organization of my own communication development course and that of those professionals with whom I have been in contact.

The professional assistance of Brenda Rogerson and Kathy Jones has been a godsend. In addition to being knowledgeable, each has been a true friend. Brenda has been my sounding board and critic for longer than I can remember. I am thrilled with the return of Kathy Jones to SUNY Geneseo. Her expertise and, more important, her warmth are welcome. I would also like to thank my current department chair, Linda House, who has helped to create an environment in which I enjoy working.

I have also had the assistance of an able group of distinguished reviewers. I would especially like to thank Thomas Klee, University of Wyoming; Roberta Wacker-Mundy, SUNY at Plattsburg; and Frank Kersting, Western Kentucky University.

A special note of thanks goes to two people, Christina Payne and Antonio Gore. Christina and her mother, Linda, allowed me to include the story *Tow Forg* in the chapter on school-age language development. Antonio is a talented artist who has been commissioned to paint the covers for both this text and its companion, *Language Disorders*.

Finally, I would like to express my love and appreciation to my kids, Jason, Todd, and Jessica, who are as beautiful as young adults as they were as children, and to Tom, my partner, who has had to endure the frustrations of having a textbook author in the house. His encouragement, patience, and kindness, not to mention faithful doing of the dishes and laundry when I'm too busy, are greatly appreciated. I love all four of you.

Contents

1 The Territory

CHAPTER OBJECTIVES

Before we can discuss language development, we need to agree on a definition of language—what it is and what it is not. As a user of language, you already know a great deal about it. This chapter will organize your knowledge and provide some labels for the many aspects of language you know. When you have completed this chapter, you should understand

- the difference between speech, language, and communication.
- the difference between nonlinguistic, paralinguistic, and metalinguistic aspects of communication.
- the main properties of language.
- the five components of language and their descriptions.
- terms that will be useful later in the text:

antonyms	paralinguistic codes
bound morphemes	phonemes
cognitive knowledge	phonology
communication	pragmatics
communicative competence	psycholinguistics
dialects	selection restrictions
episodic memory	semantic features
free morphemes	semantic knowledge
grammars	semantic memory
language	semantics
linguistic competence	sociolinguistics
linguistic performance	speech
metalinguistic cues	speech act
morphemes	suprasegmental devices
morphology	synonyms
nonlinguistic cues	syntax

L ANGUAGE AND THE LINGUISTIC process are so complex that many specialists devote their lives to investigating them. These specialists, called *linguists*, try to determine the language rules that individual people use to communicate. The linguist deduces the rules of language from the regularities or patterns demonstrated when we, as users of the language, communicate with one another. In a sense, each child is a linguist who must deduce the rules of his own native language. Unlike the linguist, however, the child does not yet have a mature language of his own to use in understanding another person.

To understand some of the complexity of the language system, let's reverse the linguist's procedure for a moment. Assume that you've been commissioned to create a large force of humanlike computers for interplanetary exploration. These humanoids must communicate using American English. As you imagine writing the computer's program, you may begin to appreciate the intricate process that underlies language use. First, the computer must be able to encode and decode. Some method of transmission must be found. If you choose speech transmission, you must program all possible English sounds. Once the sounds are programmed, each must be modified to accommodate the minute variations that are the result of sound combinations. And you must determine which sounds go together in English and which ones can never be used in combination. No English words begin with *bn*, for example.

Second, you must create a storage bank of words that can be produced by using the sounds and sound combinations already programmed. To produce smooth, efficient humanlike speech, you will have to program intonation and stress patterns, too. These allow the speaker to differentiate between the noun *record* and the verb *record*. In addition, each word must be stored under the appropriate category for easy reference and retrieval. Thus, *record* would be stored under both the action verb and object noun categories. Definitions must be programmed for each word.

Categorical classification can be best understood if we examine some of the simple rules for combining words. You can begin to program word combinations with rules like the following:

Sentence = Noun + Verb

No one would argue with this rule. Examples are as follows:

Girl run.
Boy eat.

It is immediately obvious that this rule creates some problems. The sentences seem awkward or incorrect. You must modify your rule slightly so that with singular nouns an *s* is added at the end of the verb and with plural nouns an *s* is added to the noun. What would you do with a sentence such as "Chair jumps"? This sentence requires another rule change to ensure that meaningless sentences will not be produced. How could you avoid the creation of such sentences as "Chair jumps," "Desk walks," and "House flies"? You could delete all possible nonsense combinations, but this process would be very time-consuming. It would be more efficient to write a rule, but what rule could you write that would encompass all possibilities? Are the categories for *house* and *girl* different? On what variables do they differ? Add to these decisions all the rules you would need to create for other categories, such as articles, adjectives, and adverbs, and for verb tenses, plurals, possessives, questions, imperatives, and so on. It might be easier to dismember your humanoid force, bid family and friends farewell, and explore the solar system yourself.

Our little experiment may seem trivial or overly tedious. You may even think it's unfair to ask you to state the rules of American English, especially in the first few pages of a language development textbook. You might even claim that you don't know the rules—or at least not all of them. I'll let you in on a secret: Neither do linguists. Their task, like that of the very young child, is to deduce the language rules from the language used around them. Yet the linguist, the child, you, and I, as users of American English, demonstrate daily that we clearly know what the rules are. Forcing you to think about the rules is not unfair; expecting you to program a humanoid for human communication is. In fact, even with linguists' knowledge, no one has been able to create a computerized spoken version of American English that has the complexity, the richness, or the flow of human communication (McDermott, 1983). This puzzle is all the more interesting when we realize that most 4-year-old children have deciphered American English and have well-developed speech, language, and communication skills. This feat is truly remarkable, given the complexity of the task. You probably recall little of your own language acquisition process. One statement is probably true: Unless you experienced difficulty, there was no formal instruction. Congratulations are in order because you probably did most of it on your own.

To appreciate the task involved in language learning, you need to be familiar with some of the terminology that is commonly used in the field. The remainder of this chapter is devoted to an explanation of these terms. First, we must distinguish three often confused terms: *speech*, *language*, and *communication*. Then we will look at some special qualities of language itself.

SPEECH, LANGUAGE, AND COMMUNICATION

Child development professionals study the changes that occur in speech, language, and communication as children grow and develop. To the nonprofessional, these three terms are often interpreted as having similar meanings or as being identical. Actually, the terms are very different and denote different aspects of development and use.

Speech

Speech* is a verbal means of communicating or conveying meaning. The result of specific motor behaviors, speech is a process that requires very precise neuromuscular coordination. Speech sounds or **phonemes** are combined in various ways to form the language units that will be used for verbal communication. Each spoken language has specific sounds and sound combinations that are characteristic of that language. In addition, speech involves other components, such as voice quality, intonation, and rate. These components enhance the meaning of the message. Speech is not the only means of human communication. We also use gestures, facial expressions, and body posture to send messages. When speaking on the phone, we rely on the speech modality to carry our message. In face-to-face conversation, more emphasis is placed on nonverbal means. It has been estimated that up to 60% of the information in face-to-face conversation may be transmitted through nonspeech means. Other ways of communicating include writing, drawing, and manual signing.

Humans are not the only animals to make sounds, though no other species can match the variety and complexity of human speech sounds. These qualities are the result of the unique structures of the human vocal tract, a mechanism that is functional months before the first words appear. Children spend much of their first year experimenting with the vocal mechanism and producing a variety of sounds. Gradually these sounds come to reflect the language of the child's environment. Meaningful speech, however, must await the development of some linguistic rules.

Language

Without attached meaning, speech sounds are only grunts and groans or meaningless strings of sounds. The relationship between all the linguistic forms—individual sounds, meaningful units, and the combination of these units—is specified by the rules of language. **Language** can be defined as a socially shared code or conventional system for representing concepts through the use of arbitrary symbols and rule-governed combinations of those symbols. English is a language, as is Spanish or Navajo. Each has its own unique symbols and rules for symbol combination. **Dialects**† are subcategories of the parent language that use similar but not identical rules. All users of a language follow certain dialectal rules that differ from an idealized standard. For example, I sometimes find myself reverting to former dialectal usage in saying "*across* the street" and "*um*brella."

Although all the languages noted so far can be transmitted via speech, speech is not an essential feature of language. American Sign Language, which is transmitted via a manual or signing mode, is not a mirror of American English but is a separate language with its own rules for symbol combinations.

---

*Words found in boldface in the text are defined in the Glossary at the end of this book.
†Dialects and bilingualism are discussed in more detail in Chapter 11.

Mathematics is another language, but a more precise one than those previously mentioned. Mathematical symbols have exact values and represent specific quantities and relationships. For example, 8 is greater than 2, and the relationship between 8 and 2 can be stated in a variety of ways.

$$8 = 4(2) \qquad 8 = 4 \times 2 \qquad 8 = 2^3 \qquad 8 = 6 + 2$$

The two numbers represent definite quantities. Compare this precision to that of the English word *group*. In *group,* quantity is inherent but not specified. How many people or things form a group? Most users of English would recognize *group* as more than *couple* but less than *crowd*. The word *women* represents more quantity than *woman* but could refer to any quantity of more than one.

Following is the American Speech-Language-Hearing Association definition of language (Committee on Language, 1983). Like the proverbial camel who is the result of a committee trying to design a horse, this definition has a little of everything, but it also is very thorough.

> Language is a complex and dynamic system of conventional symbols that is used in various modes for thought and communication.
>
> - Language evolves within specific historical, social and cultural contexts;
> - Language, as rule governed behavior, is described by at least five parameters—phonologic, morphologic, syntactic, semantic, and pragmatic;
> - Language learning and use are determined by the intervention of biological, cognitive, psychosocial, and environmental factors;
> - Effective use of language for communication requires a broad understanding of human interaction including such associated factors as nonverbal cues, motivation, and sociocultural roles.

Languages exist because users have agreed on the symbols to be used and the rules to be followed. This agreement is demonstrated through language usage. Thus, languages exist by virtue of social agreement or convention. Just as users agree to follow the rules of a language system, they can agree to change the rules. For example, the *th* found as an ending on English verbs in the King James Version of the Bible has disappeared from use. New words can be added to a language; others fall into disuse. For example, we are adding new scientific terminology almost daily; such words as *laser* and *byte* were uncommon just a few years ago. In addition, users of one language can borrow words from another. For instance, despite the best efforts of the French government, its citizens seem to prefer the English word *jet* to the more difficult, though lyrical, *avion de reaction.*

The conventional or socially shared code of language allows the listener and speaker or writer and reader of the same language to exchange information. Internally, each uses the same code. The shared code is a device that enables each to represent one thing with another. More precisely, the code allows each user "to represent an object, event or relationship without reproducing it" (Bloom & Lahey, 1978, p. 5). Let's see how this is done. Close your eyes for a few seconds and concentrate on the word *ocean*. You may have a visual image of surf and sand. The concept was transmitted to you and decoded without your having to be transported physically to the coast. In a conversation, listener and speaker switch from encoding to decoding and back again without difficulty.

Each user encodes and decodes according to his concept of a given object, event, or relationship; the actual object, event, or relationship does not need to be present. Let's assume that you encounter a priest. From past experience, you recognize his social role. Common elements of these experiences are *Catholic, male, clergy.* As you pass, you draw on the appropriate symbol and encode "Morning, Father." This representational process is presented in Figure 1.1. The common word *father* may denote or signify a male family member to both speaker and listener, but the word may connote or suggest a very different meaning, depending upon the experiences of each party. Let's assume for a moment that your biological father is an Episcopal priest. You see him on the street and say "Good morning, Father." A passer-by, unaware of your relationship, will assume something very different from the meaning that you and your father share. Coding is a factor of the speaker's and listener's shared meanings, the linguistic skills of each, and the context in which the exchange takes place.

Languages evolve; they grow and change. Those that do not become obsolete. Sometimes for reasons other than linguistic ones, languages either flourish or wither. At present, for example, fewer than 100 individuals fluently speak Seneca, a western New York Native American language. How sad that it may soon be gone as a spoken language offering its unique perspective on our world.

Individual linguistic units communicate little in isolation. Most of the meaning or information is contained in the way symbols are combined. For example, "Teacher Jim a is" seems a meaningless jumble of words. By shifting a few words,

---

FIGURE 1.1   Symbol-Referent Relationship
The concept is formed from the common elements of past experiences. The common elements of these experiences form the core of the concept. When a referent is experienced, it is interpreted in terms of the concept and the appropriate symbol applied.

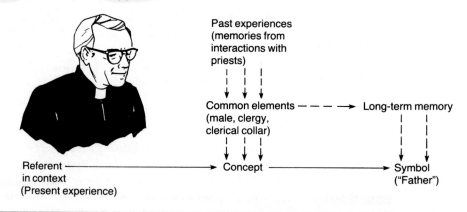

---

however, we can create "Jim is a teacher." Another modification could produce "Is Jim a teacher?", a very different sentence. Language specifies a system of relationships among its parts (Dever, 1978). The rules for these relationships give language order and allow users to predict which units or symbols will be used. In addition, the rules permit language to be used creatively. A *finite* set of symbols and a *finite* set of rules governing symbol combinations can be employed to create an *infinite* number of utterances. Language should not be seen, though, merely as a set of static rules. It is a process of use and modification within the context of communication. It is a tool for social use.

Communication

Both speech and language are parts of the larger process of communication. In fact, "communication is the primary function of language" (Muma, 1978, p. 118). Communication is the process of exchanging information and ideas between participants. The process is an active one that involves encoding, transmitting, and decoding the intended message. It requires a sender and a receiver, and each communication partner must be alert to the informational needs of the other to ensure that messages are conveyed effectively and that intended meanings are preserved. For example, a speaker must identify a specific female for the listener prior to using the pronoun *she*. The probability of message distortion is very high, given the number of ways a message can be formed and the past experiences and perceptions of each participant. The degree to which a speaker is successful in communicating, measured by the appropriateness and effectiveness of the message, is called **communicative competence** (Dore, 1986; Hymes, 1972). The competent communicator is able to conceive, formulate, modulate, and issue messages and to perceive the degree to which intended meanings are successfully conveyed (Muma, 1978).

Speech and language are only a portion of communication. Figure 1.2 illustrates this relationship. Other aspects of communication that may enhance or change the linguistic code can be classified as paralinguistic, nonlinguistic, and metalinguistic. **Paralinguistic codes** include intonation, stress or emphasis, speed or rate of delivery, and pause or hesitation superimposed on speech to signal attitude or emotion. All components of the signal are integrated to produce the totality of the meaning. Intonation, or the linguistic use of pitch, is the most complex of all paralinguistic codes and is used to signal the mood of an utterance. For example, falling or rising pitch alone can signal the pragmatic function of an utterance, as in the following example:

You're coming, aren't you. ↓   (Telling)
You're coming, aren't you? ↑   (Asking)

A rising pitch contour can change a statement into a question. Pitch can signal emphasis, asides, emotions, importance of the information conveyed, and the role and status of the speaker.

FIGURE 1.2   Relationships of Speech, Language, and Communication

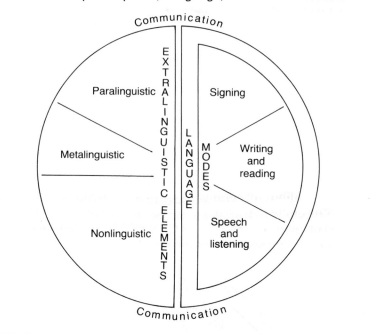

Stress is employed for emphasis. Each of us remembers hearing an insistent mother bellow, "You *will* clean your room!", to which you may have responded, "I *did* clean my room!" Rate varies with the speaker's state of excitement, familiarity with the content, and perceived comprehension of the listener. In general, we tend to talk faster if we are more excited, more familiar with the information being conveyed, or more assured that our listener understands our message. Pauses may be used to emphasize a portion of the message or to replace the message. Even young children recognize that a short maternal pause after a child's request usually signals a negative reply. Remember asking "Can Chris sleep over tonight?" A long silence meant that your plans were doomed.

Pitch, rhythm, and pauses may be used to mark syntactic divisions between phrases and clauses. Combined with loudness and duration, pitch is used to give prominence to certain syllables and to new information.

Paralinguistic mechanisms are called **suprasegmental devices** because they can change the form and meaning of a sentence by acting across elements, or segments, of a sentence. For example, a rising pitch can change a declarative sentence to an interrogative or question form without altering the arrangement of words. Similarly, "I did my homework" and "I *did* my homework" convey different emotions across words that signal the same information.

Nonlinguistic cues include gestures, body posture, facial expression, eye contact, head and body movement, and physical distance or proxemics. The effectiveness of these devices varies with users and between users. We all know someone who seems to gesture too much or to remain too close while communicating. Some nonlinguistic messages, such as a wink, a grimace, a pout, or folded arms, can convey the entire message, with no need to rely on speech or language.

Metalinguistic cues signal the status of the transmission or the success of communication. Metalinguistic skills are the abilities to talk about language, analyze it, think about it, see it as an entity separate from its content, and judge it. For example, learning to read and write depends on metalinguistic awareness of the component units of language—sounds, words, phrases, sentences. In metalinguistics, language is abstract. Forming a sentence using *has been* takes certain metalinguistic skills because it is out of context. A preschooler may not be able to accomplish this task correctly but within the context of *The Three Bears* may be able to state, "Someone *has been* sleeping in my bed." Metalinguistic skills are

Communication is accomplished through a linguistic code and many means of transmission, such as speech, intonation, gestures, and body language.

used to judge the correctness or appropriateness of the language we produce and receive.

With all the communication devices available, it is almost impossible not to communicate. If you tried not to communicate, your accompanying behavior alone would communicate your negative choice.

ASPECTS OF LANGUAGE

Linguistics is the scientific study of language, and linguists are the theoreticians. Linguists describe language units and theorize about the manner in which these units interact. As a result, linguists attempt to develop theories that characterize particular languages or to describe cross-language phenomena. Two specialized areas of linguistics—psycholinguistics and sociolinguistics—combine the study of language with other disciplines. **Psycholinguistics** is the study of the way in which people acquire and process language. Of particular interest is the relationship of language to thought or of language to attention, perception, storage, and retrieval. **Sociolinguistics** is the study of language and cultural or situational influences. Context, both situational and linguistic, determines the language user's communication options. In developmental studies the sociolinguist focuses on caregiver–child interactions and on the early social uses of language.

Properties

Several linguists have attempted to describe the general properties or characteristics of all languages (Bolinger, 1975; Hockett, 1960). In general, language is a social interactive tool, that is, both rule governed and generative, or creative.

Language as a Social Tool

It does little good to discuss language outside of the framework provided by communication. While language is not essential for communication, the reverse is not true. Even long extinct languages are studied for what they can communicate to us about ancient peoples.

Language is a shared code that enables users to transmit ideas and desires to one another. It is shared by these language users because they wish to communicate. No one in his right mind would devise or learn such a complex system without some purpose in mind. In short, language has but one purpose: to serve as the code for transmissions between people.

As such, language is influenced by its environment and, in turn, influences that environment. Overall, language reflects the collective thinking of its societal base and influences that thinking. In the United States, for example, certain words, such as *democracy*, reflect certain meanings and emotions and influence our concepts of other forms of government. The ancient Greek notion of democracy was somewhat different and influenced the Greeks' thinking similarly.

Likewise, at any given moment, language in use is influenced by what precedes it and influences what follows. The utterance "And how's my little girl feeling this morning?" only fits certain situations that define the appropriate language use. It would not be wise to use this utterance when meeting the Queen of England for the first time. In turn, the sick child to whom this is addressed has only limited options that she can use to respond. Responses such "Go directly to jail; do not pass 'Go' " and "Mister Speaker, I yield the floor to the distinguished senator from West Virginia," while perfectly correct sentences, just don't fit. The reason is that they do not continue the communication, but rather cause it to break down.

To consider language without communication is to assume that language occurs in a vacuum. It is to remove the very *raison d'etre* for language in the first place.

A Rule-Governed System

The relationship between meaning and the symbols employed is an arbitrary one (Hockett, 1960), but the arrangement of the symbols in relation to one another is nonarbitrary (Bolinger, 1975). This nonarbitrary organizational feature of language demonstrates the presence of underlying rules or patterns that occur repeatedly. These systems of rules are called **grammars.** Do not confuse the linguistic term *grammar* with the study of "parts of speech" that most of us endured in elementary school grammar lessons. Rather, a grammar is a finite set of underlying operational principles or rules that describe the relationships between symbols that form the structure of a language. As such, grammars describe the relationships between sounds, between words and smaller units such as plural *s*, between words and meaning, and between words and communicative intent or purpose. These shared rule systems allow users of a language to comprehend and to create messages. Language is "the product of grammar" (Muma, 1978, p. 17), but language and grammar are not the same. Language includes not only the rules, but also the process of rule usage and the resulting product. For example, we know the rule that a sentence is made up of a noun plus a verb, but that tells us nothing about the process of noun and verb selection or the infinite number of possible combinations using these two categories.

A language user's underlying knowledge about the system of rules is called his **linguistic competence.** His knowledge of the operating principles is essential for him to be a user of a language. The specific rules a language user knows are called his *intuitive grammar.* Even though he can't state the rules, his behavior demonstrates his adherence to them. The linguist observes human behavior in an attempt to determine these rules or operating principles. The results of such studies are called *formal grammars*, precise statements of the linguistic rules. To date, we still do not have a complete formal grammar for English.

If you have ever listened to an excited speaker or a heated argument, you know that speakers do not always observe the linguistic rules. In fact, much of what we, as mature speakers, say is ungrammatical. Imagine that you have just returned from the New Year's celebration at Times Square. You might say the following:

> Oh, wow, you should have . . . you wouldn't be-believe all the . . . I've never seen so many people. We were almost . . . ah, trampled. And when the ball came down . . . fell, all the . . . Talk about yelling, you've never heard so much noise. We made a, the mistake of . . . can you imagine anything as dumb as . . . well, it was crazy to drive.

Linguistic knowledge in actual usage is called **linguistic performance.** The linguist can explore and analyze linguistic competence only through observing linguistic performance. Thus, the linguist's formal grammar must be deduced from linguistic performance.

There are many reasons for the discrepancy between competence and performance in normal language users. Some constraints are long-term, such as ethnic background, socioeconomic status, and region of the country. These account for dialects and regionalisms. We are all speakers of some dialectal or regional variations, but most of us are still competent in the standard dialect. Dialectal speakers, even those with relatively nonstandard dialects, do not have a language disorder. Other long-term constraints, such as mental retardation and language-learning disability, may result in a language disorder. Short-term constraints on nondisordered performance include physical state changes within the individual, such as intoxication, fatigue, distraction, and illness; and situational variations, such as the role, status, and personal relations of the speakers.

Even though much that is said is ungrammatical, native speakers have relatively little difficulty decoding messages. If a native speaker knows the words being used, he can apply the rules he knows in order to understand almost any sentence encountered. In actual communication, comprehension is influenced by the available shared meanings, the linguistic complexity of the utterance, the intent of the speaker, and the context (Bloom, 1974; Bransford & Johnson, 1972; Ingram, 1974b; G. Lakoff, 1972; Schank, 1972; Winograd, 1972). Even preschoolers know virtually all the rules of language except for some subtleties (McNeill, 1970). Children learn the rules by actually using the language to encode and decode. The rules learned in school are "arbitrary finishing touches of embroidery on a thick fabric of language that each child weaves for herself before arriving in the English teacher's classroom" (Moskowitz, 1978, p. 93). A child demonstrates by the way he uses words that he knows what a noun—or any class or category of words—is long before he can define the term.

On one family trip, we passed the time with a word game. My 5-year-old daughter was asked to provide a noun. Immediately, she inquired, "What's that?" Patiently I explained that a noun was a person, place, or thing. She replied, "Oh." After some prodding, she stated, "Then my word is 'thing.' " Despite her inadequate understanding of the formal definition of a noun, my daughter demonstrated in actual use that she knew how to use nouns.

Knowing the rules enables us to predict which symbols will come next. The following blank sentence will demonstrate this ability. Let's see how well you can identify the part of speech and the actual words in a sentence.

—————— —————— —————— —————— —————— —————— ——————

Above each blank, write the part of speech that will go into that blank; below the blank, write the actual word. Do one word at a time and then check your answer before going to the next.

- I'll help on the first word. It's an article. Can you guess which one? It's *the*. That's a clue to the second word. Try to predict the part of speech and the actual word.
- *Second word:* It could be a noun or an adjective; it's the latter. The word is *young*.
- *Third word:* You should get this one: a noun. What might the word be? It's *boy*. *Girl* or several others were equally likely.
- *Fourth word:* I hope you chose a verb. The word is *runs*. Boys can do lots of activities, such as eat, drink, jump, or walk. Thus, you may have missed the exact word.
- *Fifth word:* This one should be easy. It's a preposition, and the word is *to*.
- *Sixth word:* This word is also a noun. You may have missed the word, since boys usually run in the opposite direction of the one I've chosen. The word is *school*.
- *Seventh word:* One last chance. The part of speech is adverb. The word is *quickly*.

In this exercise, rarely does someone select all the correct parts of speech, and no one ever gets all the specific words. Almost everyone, however, does better than chance alone would predict. This sentence could have included any number of possibilities. As a child, you learned symbols, or words, such as *boy, girl, cat*, and *dog*, and hypothesized as to the classes or categories of these words, such as nouns, based on use. The relationships between words are specified in the rules or grammars for these word classes. For example, nouns can be made plural; verbs cannot.

A sentence such as "Chairs sourly young up swam" is ungrammatical. It violates the rules for word order. Native speakers notice that the words do not fall into predictable patterns. When rearranged, the sentence reads "Young chairs swam sourly up." This is now grammatical in terms of word order but meaningless; it doesn't make sense. Other rules allow language users to separate sense from nonsense and to determine the underlying meaning. Although "Dog bites man" and "Man bites dog" are very similar, in that each uses the same words, the meanings of the two sentences are very different. Only one will make a newspaper headline. Likewise, a single sentence may have two meanings. For example, the sentence "The shooting of the hunters was terrible" can be taken two ways: either they shot poorly or someone shot them. Language users must know several sets of rules to make sense of what they hear or read.

A Generative System

Language is a generative system. The word *generative* has the same root as *generate*, which means to produce, create, or bring into existence. Thus, language is a productive or creative tool. A knowledge of the rules permits speakers to generate, or form, meaningful utterances. From a finite number of words and a finite set of rules, speakers can create an almost infinite number of sentences. This creativity is provided because words can refer to more than one thing or referent. Referents can also be called by more than one name. Think of all the possible sentences you could create by combining all the nouns and verbs you know. When this task is completed, you could modify each sentence by adding adverbs and adjectives, articles and prepositions, and by combining sentences or creating questions. The possibilities for creating new sentences are virtually endless. Consider the following novel sentence:

Large elephants danced gracefully beneath the street lights.

Even though you have probably never seen this utterance before, you understand its meaning because you know the linguistic rules. Try to create your own novel utterance. The process will seem difficult, and yet you form novel utterances every day and are not consciously aware of using any effort. In fact, most of what you have said today was novel or new. You didn't learn those specific utterances. As a young child, you deduced the rules for forming these types of sentences. Of course, I do not mean to imply that sentences are never repeated. Polite social communication is often repetitious. How frequently have you said the following sentences?

How are you?
Thank you very much.
I'm fine.
Can I, Mom, please?
See you soon.

You have probably repeated each one more often than you care to recall.

In summary, native speakers of a language do not learn all possible word combinations. Instead, they learn rules that govern these combinations. Knowing the linguistic rules allows each language user to understand and create an infinite variety of sentences.

Components or Functions of Language

Language is a very complex system that can best be understood by breaking it down into its functional elements or components (Figure 1.3). Language can be divided into three major, although not necessarily equal, components: form, content, and use (Bloom & Lahey, 1978). Form includes syntax, morphology, and phonology, the components that connect sounds or symbols with meaning. Traditionally, the study of language has been equated with form only. Content encompasses meaning or semantics, and use includes pragmatics. These five

FIGURE 1.3   Components of Language

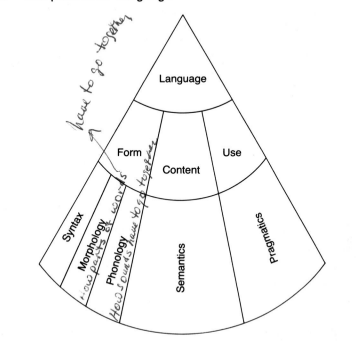

components—syntax, morphology, phonology, semantics, and pragmatics—are the basic rule systems found in language.

As each of us uses language, we code ideas (*semantics*); that is, we use a symbol—a sound, a word, and so forth—to stand for an actual event, object, or relationship. To communicate these ideas to others, we use certain forms, which include such important elements as the appropriate sound units (*phonology*), the appropriate word order (*syntax*), and the appropriate word beginnings and endings (*morphology*) to clarify meaning more specifically. Speakers use these components to achieve certain communication ends or goals, such as gaining information, greeting, or responding (*pragmatics*). Let's examine the five components of language in more detail.

Syntax

The form or structure of a sentence is governed by the rules of **syntax.** These rules specify word order, sentence organization, and the relationships between words, word classes, and other sentence elements. Sentences are organized according to their overall function; declaratives, for example, make statements, and interrogatives form questions. The main elements, or constituent parts, of a sentence are noun and verb phrases, each composed of various word classes or word types (such as nouns, verbs, adjectives, and the like).

Syntax specifies which word combinations are acceptable, or grammatical, and which are not. As we have seen, word sequences are not random but follow definite word order rules. In addition to these word order rules, syntax specifies which word classes appear in noun and verb phrases and the relationship of these two types of phrases. Each sentence must contain a *noun phrase* and a *verb phrase*. The mandatory features of noun and verb phrases are a noun and a verb, respectively. The short biblical verse "Jesus wept" is a perfectly acceptable English sentence: it contains both a noun phrase and a verb phrase. The following, however, is not a complete sentence, even though it is much longer:

> The grandiose plan for the community's economic revival based upon political cooperation of the inner city and the more affluent suburban areas

This example contains no verb and thus no verb phrase; therefore it does not qualify as a sentence.

Within the noun and verb phrases, certain word classes combine in predictable patterns. For example, articles appear before nouns and adverbs modify verbs. Some words may function in more than one word class. The linguistic context of the sentence clarifies any ambiguity. For example, the word *dance* may be a noun or a verb. Yet there is no confusion between the following sentences:

> The *dance* was attended by nearly all the students.
> The children will *dance* to earn money for charity.

The linguistic context of the sentence specifies the word class of *dance* in each sentence—a noun in the first and a verb in the second.

Syntax can be conceptualized as a tree diagram or a hierarchy (Figure 1.4). Each noun phrase or verb phrase included in a sentence contains, in turn, constituent word classes. In a given phrase, word classes may be deleted or added. As long as the noun and verb remain, a sentence is produced. This hierarchical structure permits boundless elaboration within the confines of the syntactic rules. Words may be used within each word class to create an endless variety of sentences.

Languages can be divided into those with so-called free word order and those with word order rules (Goodluck, 1986). The Australian aboriginal language Warlpiri has a relatively free word order. The same sentence may be expressed in several different word orders. Word order rules fall into three classes based on the order of the subject, the verb, and the object. English is an example of the basic subject-verb-object (SVO) word order (*She eats cookies*). In contrast, Dutch and Japanese have a basic verb-final form (SOV). The third type, represented by Irish, is verb-subject-object (VSO).

Morphology

Morphology is concerned with the internal organization of words. Words consist of one or more smaller units called *morphemes*. A **morpheme** is the smallest grammatical unit and is indivisible without violating the meaning or producing mean-

FIGURE 1.4   Hierarchical Sentence Structure
Within the noun and verb phrases, a number of different word classes can be arranged to form a variety of sentences. Many words could be used within each word class to form sentences such as "The young man ate his hamburger quickly" or "The mad racer drove his car recklessly."

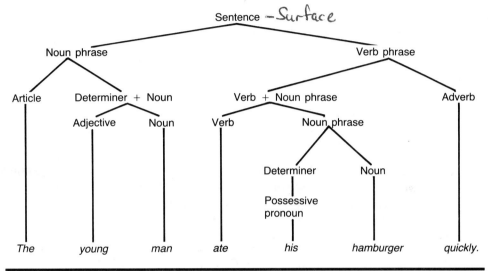

ingless units. Therefore, *dog* is a single morpheme because *d* and *og* are meaningless alone. If we split the word into *do* and *g*, we have a similar situation: *do* violates the meaning of *dog* because there is nothing in *dog* that includes the meaning of *do*, and *g* is meaningless alone. Most words in English consist of one or two morphemes. In contrast, Mohawk, a northern New York and southern Quebec Native language, constructs words of several morphemes strung together.

Morphemes are of two varieties, free and bound (Figure 1.5). **Free morphemes** are independent and can stand alone. They form words or parts of words. Examples of free morphemes are *toy, big,* and *happy.* **Bound morphemes** are grammatical tags or markers that cannot function independently. They must be attached to free morphemes or to other bound morphemes. Examples include *-s, -est, un-,* and *-ly,* meaning plural, most, negative, and manner, respectively. By combining the free and bound morphemes mentioned above, we can create *toys, biggest,* and *unhappily.* Bound or grammatical morphemes are attached to words in the noun, verb, and adjective classes to accomplish changes in meaning.

Furthermore, bound morphemes can be either *derivational* or *inflectional* in nature. Derivational morphemes include both prefixes and suffixes. Prefixes precede the free morpheme, and suffixes follow. Derivational morphemes change whole classes of words. For example, *-ly* may be added to most adjectives to create an adverb, and *-ness* may be added to an adjective to create a noun: *mad,*

FIGURE 1.5   Morpheme Classes and Examples

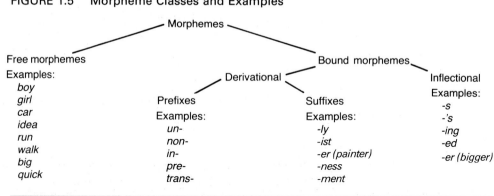

madly, madness. Inflectional morphemes can be suffixes only. They change the state or increase the precision of the free morpheme. Inflectional morphemes include tense markers (such as *-ed*), plural markers, and the third-person singular present tense verb ending *-s*. Since all these modulations operate within the syntactic constraints of sentences, some linguists consider the morphological rules to be a subset of the syntactic rules.

Languages differ in their relative dependence on the syntactic and morphological components. Latin, for example, changes meaning through the use of many morphological endings. In contrast, English uses word order more than morphological additions to convey much of the meaning of the utterance.

Phonology

The aspect of language concerned with the rules governing the structure, distribution, and sequencing of speech sounds is **phonology.** Each language employs a variety of speech sounds or **phonemes.** A phoneme is the smallest linguistic unit of sound that can signal a difference in meaning. English has approximately 45 phonemes, give or take a few for dialectal variations. (See Appendix A.) Phonemes are actually families of very similar sounds. Individual members of these families of sounds differ slightly from one another, but not enough to sound like another phoneme and thus modify the meaning of a word. If you repeat the /p/ sound 10 times, each production will vary slightly for a number of physiological reasons. In addition, the /p/ sound in *pea* differs from that in *poor* or *soup*, because each is influenced by the surrounding sounds. Even so, each /p/ sound is similar enough so as not to be confused with another phoneme. Thus /p/ is a distinct English phoneme.[‡] There is an obvious difference in the initial sounds in *pea* and *see* because each begins with a different pho-

---

[‡]Transcriptions of phonemes are placed within slashes, such as /p/. This book uses the notation of the International Phonetic Alphabet, as will be discussed in more detail in Appendix A.

neme. Likewise, the /d/ and /l/ sounds are different enough to be considered as different phonemes. Each can signal a different meaning if applied to other sounds. For example, the meanings of *dog* and *log* are very different, as are those of *dock* and *lock*, and *pad* and *pal*. Phonemes are classified by their acoustic or sound properties, as well as by the way they are produced (how the air stream is modified) and their place of production (where along the vocal tract the modification occurs).

Phonological rules govern the distribution and sequencing of phonemes within a language. This organization is not the same as speech, which is the actual mechanical act of producing phonemes. Without the phonological rules, the distribution and sequencing of phonemes would be random. Distributional rules describe which sounds can be employed in various positions in words. For example, in English the *ng* sound, which is found in *ring* and is considered to be a single phoneme (/ŋ/), can never appear at the beginning of a word. In contrast, sequencing rules determine which sounds may appear in combination. The sequence *dn*, for example, may not appear back-to-back in the same syllable in English. Sequencing rules also address the sound modifications made when two phonemes appear next to each other. For example, the past *-ed* in *jogged*, pronounced as /d/, is different from the *-ed* in *walked*, which is pronounced as /t/. On other occasions, the distributional and sequencing rules both apply. The combination *nd*, for example, may not begin a word but may appear elsewhere, as in *window*. The word *stew* is perfectly acceptable in English. *Snew* is not an English word but would be acceptable; *sdew*, however, could never be acceptable because in English words cannot begin with *sd*.

Semantics

This section might be subtitled "What do you mean?" because the answer to that question forms the basis of semantics. **Semantics** is a system of rules governing the meaning or content of words and word combinations. Meaning is an arbitrary classification system for dividing reality into smaller categories and units (Bolinger, 1975). These smaller units allow language users to group similar objects, actions, and relationships and to distinguish dissimilar ones. Some units are mutually exclusive, such as *man* and *woman*; a human being is not usually classified as both. Other units overlap somewhat, such as *female, woman*, and *lady*. Not all females are women, and even fewer could be called ladies. When we consider the similarities and differences between these words and between word combinations, we are in the realm of semantics. Semantics is concerned with the relationship of language form to our perceptions of objects, events, and relationships or to cognition and thought (Bowerman, 1976). The actual words or symbols used represent not reality but rather ideas or concepts about reality.

A person's knowledge about reality can be called **cognitive knowledge** (Wells, 1974). Experiences and perceptions are categorized, organized, and related to one another in order to form concepts. This information is generally stored in each person's memory.

It is useful at this point to make a distinction between *episodic* and *semantic* memory (Tulving, 1972). **Episodic memory** refers to an individual's autobiographical and experiential memory of particular events. In contrast, **semantic memory** contains word and symbol definitions; it is primarily verbal. Semantic memory "is a mental thesaurus, organized knowledge a person possesses about words and other verbal symbols, their meaning and referents, about relations among them, and about rules, formulas, and algorithms for the manipulation of these symbols, concepts, and relations" (Tulving, 1972, p. 386)

The two types of memory are related because semantic memory is usually based on information stored in episodic memory (Lindsay & Norman, 1977). Conceptual or episodic memory is a generalized concept formed from several particular events. Thus, your concept of *dog* has been formed from several encounters with different types of dogs. These events become somewhat generalized, or separated from the original context, and are, therefore, more broadly useful than context-bound experiences would be (Kintsch, 1974). With more experience, knowledge becomes more general, less dependent upon particular events. The resultant generalized episodes or scripts form the conceptual base for semantic knowledge. Therefore, concept formation would seem to be the primary cognitive process, with linguistic relations having a secondary role. Research has shown that very "young children's memory is all episodic and only later develops a semantic component" (Nelson, 1978, p. 239). Language meaning is based on what we, as individuals, know.

According to this model, a concept is related to a whole class of experiences rather than to any single one. As an adult, you have experienced many very different creatures that can be classified as *dog*, yet your concept of *dog* is not limited to any one example. In general, all canines have enough in common to allow inclusion in the general concept of *dog*. Word meaning relates to this core concept. When the concept is paired with a linguistic unit or word, we can speak of **semantic knowledge**. Therefore, words do not refer directly to an object, event, or relationship but to a concept, which is the result of a cognitive categorization process, as in the previous example of the father (Figure 1.1). Concept development results in increased validity, increased status, and increased accessibility (Flavell, 1970). *Validity* is the amount of agreement between a language user's concept and the shared concept of the language community. *Status* refers to the addition of alternative referents: for example, *canine* can be substituted easily for the concept *dog*, and *dog* can be used to refer to the dry, hot, dog days of summer, to a dog-eared book, or to being dog tired. *Accessibility* relates to the ease of retrieval from memory and use of the concept.

Each word meaning contains two portions—semantic features and selection restrictions—drawn from the core concept (Katz, 1966). **Semantic features** are aspects of the meaning that characterize the word. For example, the semantic features of *mother* include parent and female. One of these features is shared with *father*, the other with *woman*, but neither word contains both features. **Selection restrictions** are based on these specific features and prohibit certain word combinations as meaningless. For example, *male mother* is meaningless, because one word has the feature male and the other the feature female; *female mother* is redundant, because biological mothers are female, at least for the foreseeable future. It should be noted that a male is perfectly capable of fulfilling the mothering or nurturing role, although not the physical act of birthing. In addition to this denotative meaning of objective features, there is a connotative meaning of subjective features or feelings. Thus, whereas the semantic knowledge of the features of *dog* may be similar, I may have encountered several large, vicious examples that you have not and may therefore be more fearful of dogs than you. Throughout life, language users acquire new features, delete old features, and reorganize the remainder to sharpen word meanings.

Word meanings are only a portion of semantics, however, and are not as important as the relationships between symbols. One important relationship is that of common or shared features. The more features two words share, the more alike they are. Words with almost identical features are **synonyms**. Some examples are *abuse* and *misuse*, *dark* and *dim*, *heat* and *warmth*, and *talk* and *speak*.

Antonyms are words that differ only in the opposite value of a single important feature. Examples include *up* and *down*, *big* and *little*, and *black* and *white*. (*Big* and *little*, for example, both describe size but are opposite extremes.)

Knowledge of semantic features provides a language user with a rich vocabulary of alternative words and meanings. To some extent, this knowledge is more important than the overall number of words in a language user's vocabulary. Because words may have alternative meanings, users must rely upon additional cues for interpretation of messages, including selection restrictions, linguistic context, and nonlinguistic context (R. Brown, 1958a; D. Olson, 1970, 1971). Sentence meanings are more important than individual word meanings because sentences represent a meaning greater than the sum of the individual words. A sentence represents not only the words that form that sentence but also the relationships between those words. Mature language users generally recall the overall sentence meaning rather than the particular sentence form (Sachs, 1967).

Pragmatics

When we use language to affect others or to relay information, we make use of pragmatics. **Pragmatics** is a set of sociolinguistic rules related to language use within the communicative context. That is, pragmatics is concerned with the way language is used to communicate rather than with the way language is structured.

Every speech utterance is called a **speech act**. In order to be valid, each speech act must meet certain conditions. It must involve the appropriate persons and circumstances, be complete and correctly executed by all participants, and contain the appropriate intentions of all participants (Searle, 1972). "May I have a donut, please" is valid only when speaking to a person who can actually get you one and in a place where donuts are found. If you just said "May I" without nonlinguistic communication, the speech act would be incomplete and incorrect. Finally, the utterance encodes my intention, which is to get a donut. Some acts, called *performatives*, are actually performed by the very act of saying them. Each of the following is a performative:

> I *apologize* for my behavior.
> I *christen this ship the U.S.S. Schneider.*
> I *now pronounce* you husband and wife.

Again, certain conditions must be met, however, before each is valid. For someone to apologize when he's feeling overjoyed by another's discomfort, or for a child or nondesignated adult to pronounce a couple husband and wife, invalidates the act.

Not all speech acts are performatives. For example, saying "John should apologize for his behavior" doesn't make the apology. In this case, the act is an expression of opinion.

Speech acts may be *direct* or *indirect.* Direct speech acts are reflected in their syntactic form. "Answer the phone" is a direct order or request to perform that act. The form is imperative. On the other hand, the syntactic form of an indirect speech act does not reflect the intention. For example, "Could you answer the phone?" is an indirect way of requesting you to answer the ringing telephone. You know that the expected outcome of the question is for you to answer the phone, not to respond to the question with a "yes." If the question seems to merit action rather than a verbal response, then the speech act is probably indirect. Indirect forms are generally used for politeness.

Speech acts may also be *literal* or *nonliteral.* In a literal speech act, the speaker means what he says. After a 10-mile hike, you might exclaim, "My feet really hurt," and no doubt they do. In contrast, the nonliteral speech act does not mean what the speaker has said. Upon discovering that transportation home has not arrived, the same tired hiker might state, "Just what I need, more walking."

There are three general categories of sociolinguistic rules (Ervin-Tripp, 1971). These are rules of alternation, co-occurrent constraint, and sequence. The *alternation* rules relate to the selection of alternative linguistic forms. Social variables influence the choice between "Gimme a cookie" and "May I have one, please," or between a direct and an indirect speech act. One choice may work with a school friend, whereas the other is best with the teacher. Rules for *co-occurrent constraint* limit the forms that may be used when speakers assume roles or use another dialect. For example, if you are in a less dominant role, you are more likely to be polite. *Sequential* rules regulate the use of certain ritualized sequences in various social situations. We can all recall an occasion when we felt close to death and yet responded, "I'm fine! How are you?" —a response that has become ritualized in casual greetings.

There are two aspects of use: (1) linguistic selection, or the choice of codes to be used, and (2) language functions, or the reasons for communicating (Bloom & Lahey, 1978). The choice of codes is determined primarily by the speaker's intent (I. Schlesinger, 1971) but also by the speaker's perceptions of the listener and the situation. Listener characteristics that influence speaker behaviors are sex, age, race, style, dialect, social status, and role. For example, an older, technically trained woman might assume that a young female from a minority group shares very little of her technical knowledge; she may thus modify her language by using lengthy explanations. In contrast, close friends in a familiar situation may say very little because so much information is shared common knowledge. In addition, the listener attempts to keep the speaker informed of the status of the communication. If the listener doesn't understand or is confused, he might assume a quizzical expression or say "Huh?"

Conversation is governed by the "cooperation principle" (Grice, 1975): conversational participants cooperate with each other. The four maxims of the cooperation principle relate to quantity, quality, relation, and manner. Quantity is the informativeness of each participant's contribution: no participant should provide too little or too much information. In addition, the quality of each contribution should be governed by truthfulness and based on sufficient evidence. The maxim of relation states that a contribution should be relevant to the topic of conversation. Finally, each participant should be reasonably direct in manner and avoid vagueness, ambiguity, and wordiness.

Since language is transmitted primarily via the speech mode, pragmatic rules govern a number of social interactions: sequential organization and coherence of conversations, repair of errors, role, and speech acts (Rees & Wollner, 1981). Organization and coherence of conversations include turn taking; opening, maintaining, and closing a conversation; establishing and maintaining a topic; and making relevant contributions to the conversation. Repair includes giving and receiving feedback and correcting conversational errors. Role skills include establishing and maintaining a role and switching linguistic codes for each role. In some conversations you are dominant, as with a small child, and in others you are not, as with your professor, and you adjust your language accordingly. Finally, speech acts include coding of intentions relative to the communicative context. For example, the form of your utterance will differ depending on whether your intention is to gain information or to influence someone's behavior.

Relationship of Language Components

Traditionally, linguists have viewed the five aspects of language—syntax, morphology, phonology, semantics, and pragmatics—as of equal importance (Figure 1.6). Increasingly, however, theoreticians are consigning a more important role to pragmatics. Reasoning that language is heavily influenced by context and that a need to communicate exists prior to the selection of content and form, these theoreticians, called *functionalists,* see pragmatics as the overall organizing principle of language. According to functionalist reasoning, it is only when the child desires a cookie that he employs the rules of syntax, morphology, phonology, and semantics in order to form his request.

FIGURE 1.6   Comparison of Formalist and Functionalist Models of Language

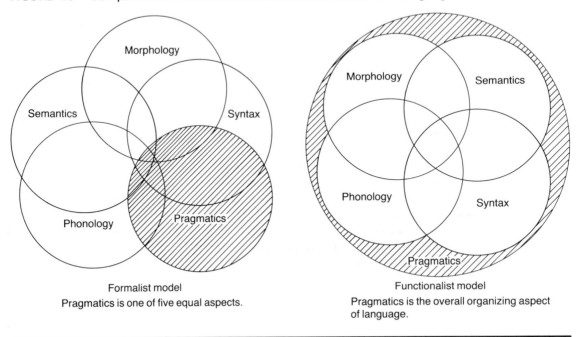

Formalist model
Pragmatics is one of five equal aspects.

Functionalist model
Pragmatics is the overall organizing aspect
of language.

CONCLUSION

Language is a very complex system of symbols and rules for using those symbols. The native speakers of a language must be knowledgeable about the symbols employed and the acceptable usage rules, including concept, word, morpheme, and phoneme combinations.

Humans may be the only animals with a productive communication system that gives them the ability to represent reality symbolically without dependence on immediate context support (R. Brown, 1973). Although animals clearly communicate at some level, this communication is limited in topic and scope and is dependent on the context. For example, bees have an elaborate system of movements for conveying information, but it is extremely iconic (it looks like what it conveys) and unitopical (the topic is always where to find nectar) (Von Frisch, 1950). Whether or not higher mammals, such as chimpanzees and other primates, are capable of complex symbolic communication will be discussed in the next chapter. In any case, it is only after intensive, long-term training that these animals learn what the human infant acquires in a few short months with little or no training.

REFLECTIONS

1. Speech, language, and communication are different aspects of the same process. Can you contrast all three?
2. Not all of the message is carried by the linguistic code. How do the other aspects of communication contribute?
3. Language is both rule governed and generative. Explain these two properties.
4. Language consists of five interrelated components. Describe these components, as well as the units of morpheme, phoneme, and speech act.

2 Language Development Models

CHAPTER OBJECTIVES

Models of language development help us understand the developmental process by bringing order to our descriptions of this process and providing answers to the questions *how* and *why.* Of the many linguistic theories proposed, we will examine four that have had the greatest impact on language development study. Each contains a core of relevant information, and the overall evolution reflects our changing view of language and child development. When you have completed this chapter, you should understand

- the language development process described in the behavioral theory.
- the two rule systems employed in the psycholinguistic-syntactic model of linguistic processing and their sources.
- the advances of government-binding theory.
- the contributions of the semantic revolution.
- the relationship between cognition and semantics.
- the context in which language is said to develop in the sociolinguistic model.
- the following terms:

case	phrase structure rules
cognitive determinism	primitive speech act (PSA)
deep structure	propositional force
extinction	punishment
government-binding theory	reinforcement
illocutions	rich interpretation
illocutionary forces	segmentation
joint (shared) reference	surface structure
locutions	topic-comment
noun phrases	transactional model
operant conditioning	transformational rules
perlocutions	verb phrases

T HE STUDY OF LANGUAGE and language development has interested inquiring persons for thousands of years. Herodotus, a historian in ancient Greece, reported that Psammetichus I, an Egyptian pharoah of the seventh century B.C., conducted a child language study to determine the "natural" language of humans. Two children were raised with sheep and heard no human speech. Needless to say, they did not begin to speak Egyptian or anything else that approximated human language. In the Middle Ages, St. Augustine discussed his language development in *The Confessions*. Charles Darwin, the father of modern evolutionary theory, published a narrative of his son's development, noting language learning. Several modern researchers have devoted their professional careers to the study of child development.

People study language development for a variety of reasons. First, interest in language development represents part of a larger concern for child development. People who specialize in early childhood education are eager to learn about this developmental process in order to facilitate child behavior change. Special educators and speech-language pathologists study child language to increase their insight into normal and other-than-normal processes. A second reason for studying language development is that it is interesting and can help us understand our own behavior. There is a slightly mystical quality to language development related to the complexity of language. The developmental process has been called "mysterious" (Gleitman & Wanner, 1982) and "magic" (Bloom, 1983). As mature language users, we cannot state all the rules we use; yet, as children, we deciphered and learned these rules within a few years. Few of us, though, can fully explain the development of our language expertise. It just seemed to happen. Finally, language development studies can probe the relationship between language and thought. Language development is parallel to cognitive development. Hopefully, the study of language development may enable language users to understand the underlying cognitive processes to some degree.

Since language and language development are so complex, professionals are often at odds as to which approach provides the best description.

- The linguist is primarily concerned with describing language symbols and stating the rules these symbols follow to form language structures. The psycholinguist is interested in the psychological processes and constructs underlying language. The psychological mechanisms that let language users produce and comprehend language are of particular concern.
- The sociolinguist studies language rules and use as a function of role, socioeconomic level, and linguistic or cultural context. Dialectal differences and social–communicative interaction are important.
- The behavioral psychologist minimizes language form and emphasizes the behavioral context of language. The behaviorist is concerned with eliciting certain responses and determining how the number of these responses can be increased or decreased.

- The speech-language pathologist concentrates on disordered communication. Of most interest are the causes of disorder, the evaluation of the extent of the disorder, and the remediation process.

The study of how children learn language is like many other academic pursuits in that different theories that attempt to explain the phenomenon compete for acceptance. Occasionally one theory predominates, but generally portions of each are used to explain different aspects. Part of the problem in designing an overall theory is the complexity of both language and communication behavior. In recent years, four theoretical approaches to language development have evolved and become predominant—behavioral, syntactic, semantic/cognitive, and sociolinguistic. In this chapter we shall explore these four approaches, examining their overall theories, limitations, and contributions.

BEHAVIORAL THEORY

At the turn of the twentieth century, the study of language development emphasized language form. Much of the information was anecdotal, data collection was inconsistent, and many important aspects of development were overlooked. In general, language forms were identified and classified into categories related to sentence types, parts of speech, and so on.

By the 1930s and 1940s, data collection had become more formalized. Researchers were interested in observable behaviors. Many of the child language studies of the period are called *count studies* because they cataloged and made distributional measurements of many language behaviors. M. Smith (1933), McCarthy (1954), Templin (1957), and others observed regularities in language behavior that they accepted as evidence of underlying language knowledge.

During this period, the major influences on the psychological study of language were information theory and learning theory. Both approaches were concerned with the probability of production of a response or response unit, such as a word. According to information theory, the linguistic and nonlinguistic contexts determined the probability of a response being produced (Shannon & Weaver, 1949). Thus, some information theorists suggested that the occurrence of an individual word is determined by the immediately preceding word or phrase. Critics countered that there is no intrinsic order to words and that a given word can be followed by many different words (Lashley, 1951). The word order is governed by the speaker's intention to convey a certain message. Thus, the organization of the message involves larger units than words and follows a generalized pattern.

Learning theorists, such as Mowrer (1954), Skinner (1957), and Osgood (1963), considered language a subset of other learned behaviors. Language, as a set of associations between meaning and word, word and phoneme, and statement and response, is learned or conditioned through association between a stimulus and the following response. The strength of the stimulus–response bond determines the probability of occurrence of a certain response. Complex linguistic behaviors represent chains or combinations of various stimulus–response sequences.

Operant Conditioning

The most widely known proponent of language as a learned behavior is the psychologist B. F. Skinner. According to Skinner and his followers, all behavior is learned or operant. Behavior is modified or changed by the events that follow or are contingent upon that behavior. Any event that increases the probability of occurrence of a preceding behavior is said to be a **reinforcer** of that behavior. Any event that decreases the probability is said to be a **punisher.** The resultant behavior change is called *learning* or **operant conditioning.** Complex behaviors are learned by chaining or by shaping. In chaining, a sequence of behaviors is trained in such a way that each step serves as a stimulus for the next. In shaping, a single behavior is gradually modified by reinforcement of ever-closer (successive) approximations of the final behavior. Thus, language results from the active role of the environment. The learner herself is secondary to the process.

In 1957 Skinner published a classic language text, *Verbal Behavior.* Minimizing linguistic form, Skinner described language as a set of use or functional units. Traditional linguistic units, such as syntactic forms, are irrelevant. Instead, language is viewed as something we do (Lee, 1981). The "how" of language use takes precedence over the "what" of language form. Thus, language is defined as a verbal behavior, a learned behavior subject to all the rules of operant conditioning. As such, verbal behavior is modified by the environment or "reinforced through the mediation of other persons" (Skinner, 1957, p. 14). A child acquires language or verbal behavior, stated Skinner, "when relatively unpatterned vocalizations, selectively reinforced, gradually assume forms which produce appropriate consequences in a given verbal community" (p. 31). According to the theory, parents provide modeling and reinforcement and, as a result, establish the child's repertoire of sounds. For example, an infant produces many sounds that do not appear in the language she will use later. At 4 months of age, the infant gives little or no indication of her parent language. By 9 months, however, she vocalizes primarily the sounds she will later use in speech. In the interim, parents have reinforced only those sounds used in the native language. Reinforcement has included soothing the child, feeding and handling, and attending to the child when she produces sounds of the parent language. Once acquired, a behavior requires only occasional reinforcement to be strengthened and maintained. Speech sounds that are ignored are produced less frequently and eventually disappear. This process of decreasing a behavior without punishment is called **extinction.**

Word learning is more complex. When the child says "mama" in her mother's presence, she is reinforced with attention or some other reinforcer. Should she say "mama" when her mother is not present, she will not be reinforced. Thus, the presence of her mother becomes a stimulus that evokes or elicits the verbal response "mama." Mother has become a *discriminative stimulus (S^D),* a stimulus in the presence of which "mama" will be reinforced. Therefore, a bond is built between the referent "mother" and the word *mama*. Meaning is attached to the speech sound. Obviously, other word–referent associations would be more elaborate because some other mature language user must be present in order for any word to be reinforced. According to Skinner, the child hears a word, such as *horsie*, in the presence of many examples of *horse*. Extracting similar attributes from each example of *horse*, the child associates these common attributes with the word *horsie*. The child's initial imitative attempts to say *horsie* will be reinforced by language users in the environment.

More complex responses are learned through successive approximation. Skinner (1957) summarized this process as follows: "Any response which vaguely resembles the standard behavior of the community is reinforced. When these begin to appear frequently, a closer approximation is insisted upon. In this manner very complex verbal forms may be reached" (pp. 29–30). Mature language users provide a model of the standard behaviors. For example, the child hears "I want a cookie, please" and produces the imitation "Want cookie." Initially this response is acceptable, but the adults require gradual modifications that more closely approximate the adult model. Eventually the child will produce the full adult form. Thus, language learning is based on modeling, imitation, practice, and selective reinforcement.

Longer sentences are also learned through imitation and chaining. By hearing and imitating enough examples, the child learns word associations rather than grammatical rules.

According to Skinner, individual verbal behaviors fulfill one of several language functions, defined in terms of their effect. Skinner calls these functions mand, echoic, intraverbal, tact, and autoclitic. A *mand* is a verbal behavior that specifies its reinforcer, such as "Want cookie." In general, mands include behaviors known variously as commands, demands, and requests. The form of the utterance may vary, but the goal of "May I have a cookie, please" and "Gimme cookie" is similar. In contrast, *echoic* responses are imitative. *Intraverbal* responses include social small talk and rituals, verbal responses with no one-to-one correspondence with the verbal stimuli that evoke them. For example, when I say that I went to New York for the weekend, you might reply, "Oh, I love the Metropolitan Museum." My initiating statement requires no reply, nor was the form of your utterance specified by my utterance. Conversations depend on intraverbal responses in which participants reply without a direct request to do so. A *tact* is used in response to a nonverbal stimulus, to the things and events that speakers discuss. Tacts fill the function of naming, labeling, or commenting. Finally, *autoclitic* responses are those that are influenced by, or influence, the behavior of the speaker. In addition, the autoclitic function includes frames for the ordering of words, such as subject-verb-object. A child acquires grammar by learning these frames or chains, in which each word acts as a stimulus for the next. Thus, grammatical units are controlled by surrounding words. Grammar develops through the learning of structured phrases and sentence frames. Syntactic and semantic "slots" within each frame are filled by substituting words or phrases that fulfill the same requirements. The child can comprehend or produce novel phrases and sentences by substituting units within these frames. Simply put, the child learns "I eat cookie" by chaining, with *I* acting as the stimulus for *eat*, which in turn is a stimulus for *cookie*. Gradually the child learns that *mommy, daddy*, and other words can be substituted for *I*; that *cut, drink*, and so on can replace *eat*; and that *meat, juice*, and others can replace *cookie* in the frame. Thus, word ordering is learned as adults reinforce chains of symbols that are increasingly more adultlike. Early language behavior is not rule governed but rather shaped by the contingencies of the environment.

Limitations

There are several inadequacies in a strict behavioral theory of language acquisition. Perhaps these limitations were delineated best by psycholinguistic theorists. Noam Chomsky, a leading psycholinguist of the late 1950s and 1960s, summarized many of these inadequacies in his 1959 review of Skinner's *Verbal Behavior*. Specifically, Chomsky addressed the issues of reinforcement, imitation, and syntactic development.

"I have been able to find no support whatsoever," Chomsky (1959) stated, "for the doctrine . . . that slow and careful shaping of verbal behavior through differential reinforcement is an absolute necessity" (p. 42). In fact, parents of young language-learning children directly reinforce only a small percentage of their children's utterances. Parents of young children tend to ignore grammatical errors and to reinforce for truthfulness of utterances (R. Brown & Hanlon, 1970). Thus, the 2-year-old girl who says "That bes a horsie" while pointing to a cow will be corrected. If she is pointing to a horse, however, her parent will probably respond with "Yes, that's a horsie." Chomsky also faulted Skinner for attempting to explain the process of acquisition while ignoring the content being learned. He continued, "There is little point in speculating about the process of acquisition without much better understanding of what is acquired" (p. 55).

Likewise, imitation may account for little syntactic learning. The value of imitation as a language-learning strategy has been questioned because of its infrequent use by children above age 2 (Moerck, 1974; Nelson, 1973b; Owens & MacDonald, 1982). When children do imitate, they correctly imitate structures they have produced without imitation on a previous occasion (Bloom, Hood, & Lightbown, 1974). In general, imitation is reserved for learning new words and stabilizing forms the child already produces. An overall imitative language acquisition strategy would be of little value, according to Chomsky (1957) and McNeill (1970), because adult speech provides a very poor model. Adult-to-adult speech is characterized by false starts and revisions, dysfluencies or breaks in speech flow, and slips of the tongue. In addition, imitation cannot account for common child language structures, such as "I eated," that are presumably absent from adult speech.

Finally, the autoclitic function provides an insufficient explanation of complex syntactic development. The child could not possibly learn through imitation all the sentences she has the potential of producing later. Nor could the child experience all possible sentences in order to become aware of successive word associations, as Skinner suggested. In general, behavioral theory fails to explain the generative aspect of language, the ability to create novel utterances. The generative quality of language suggests underlying rules of language formation. Rather than learning specific sentences through imitation, the child learns rules that can be used for comprehension and production. Thus, children frequently produce the full form "Mommy is eating" before the contracted "Mommy's eating," though adults prefer to use the contracted form (R. Brown, 1973). Chomsky (1959) dismissed operant learning by stating: "The fact that all normal children acquire essentially comparable grammars of great complexity with remarkable rapidity suggests that human beings are somehow specially designed to do this" (p. 57).

In conclusion, Chomsky criticized Skinner's explanation as superficial because it did not consider what the child brings to the learning task. By emphasizing production, Skinner minimized comprehension and underlying cognitive processes. Chomsky summarized this point as follows:

> The magnitude of the failure of this attempt to account for verbal behavior serves as a kind of measure of the importance of the factors omitted from consideration, and an indication of how little is really known about this remarkably complex phenomenon. . . . The questions to which Skinner has addressed his speculations are hopelessly premature. It is futile to inquire into the causation of verbal behavior until much more is known about the specific character of this behavior. (pp. 28, 55)

Contributions

The behavioral explanation of language development should not be dismissed entirely. Theorists such as Skinner have attempted to explain a complex process within the environmental context in which that process occurs. In that sense, behavioral notions have influenced later sociolinguistic theories. Chomsky may have been correct in stating that Skinner's efforts were premature. In subsequent years, we have learned much about language structure. This learning has provided new categories for our use in analysis of development within the social environment of the child who is learning language. In addition, environmental input is now recognized as critical to language development.

Behaviors identified by Skinner and other operant psychologists have also proven very useful in language training. Today, structured behavioral techniques provide a basis for most remedial programs used with children who have delayed or disordered language.

PSYCHOLINGUISTIC THEORY: A SYNTACTIC MODEL

In contrast to the behavioral emphasis on language use, psycholinguistic theorists of the late 1950s and 1960s stressed language form and the underlying mental processes these forms represent. The linguistic structures, it was reasoned, are a key to the methods employed by language users to understand and generate language. The leading proponent of psycholinguistic theory was Noam Chomsky, who defined sentence elements, described their relationships, and explained the formation of different sentence types. Chomsky tried to describe language from a scientific perspective and thus to create a theoretical explanation for the manner in which humans create and make judgments about language. He attempted to provide simplified operating principles that explained both the similarities and the differences within human languages.

Biological Basis

Chomsky and his peers reasoned that there must be some universality or commonality to the rules followed in the diverse languages of humans. For example, all languages make temporal or time distinctions, have some means of negating a proposition, require both a subject and a predicate for correct sentence formation, and so on. Of central importance is the fact that some form of language is common to almost all human beings. "Anyone concerned with the study of human nature and capabilities," explained Chomsky (1968), "must somehow come to grips with the fact that all humans acquire language" (p. 59). Even humans with very limited mental abilities can communicate following simple conventional linguistic rules (Lenneberg, 1967). The differences between humans are differences in degree of acquisition. But are humans the only species to use linguistic systems? Lenneberg, a colleague of Chomsky, asserted (1964) that "there is no evidence that any nonhuman form has the capacity to acquire even the most primitive stages of language development" (p. 67). Since Lenneberg made that assertion, however, a number of studies have questioned his conclusions.

B. Gardner and R. Gardner (1969, 1971, 1975) trained Washoe, a chimpanzee, to communicate using American Sign Language. Washoe performed at a level equivalent to the expressive linguistic abilities of a 12- to 24-month-old child (R. Brown, 1973). All previous primate language studies had failed because they attempted to train speech. The vocal mechanism of a chimpanzee is not capable of the great variety of human speech sounds. Although she was able to learn approximately 130 signs and to create new words, such as *water-bird* for *duck*, Washoe seemed incapable of learning other than a very simple word order. Premack (1970, 1971, 1972), in a separate study, trained a chimpanzee named Sarah to communicate using colored plastic shapes. Like Washoe, Sarah was capable of using very simple symbol-order rules expressively. For example, Sarah produced "Randy give banana Sarah" (although this example may be a lexical substitution, as she had previously learned "Randy give *apple* Sarah"). Success seemed to be based on matching the abilities of these chimpanzees with a mode of communication. "The primary issue is one of matching the topography of the task with the performance capabilities of the primate" (Schiefelbusch, 1979, p. 5).

Critics were quick to note that this language use occurred only after an extraordinary training effort, which does not occur in human language acquisition. Several authors have questioned the conclusions of the primate language studies (R. Brown, 1973; Fodor, Bever & Garrett, 1974). Much of the reported success, for example, may have been due to trainer prompting and to imitation (Terrance, Pettito, Saunder, & Bever, 1979).

Much of the negative reaction may be the result of the overblown early claims of success. The more recent studies with Koko (the mountain gorilla best known for her adoption of a kitten she named "All-ball") and with other primates have caused a reevaluation of earlier conclusions. Controversy often results from linguists' definition of language and from the results of specific methods of training, such as the use of imitation (Premack, 1986). Although primates appear to be capable of creating sentences, they have failed so far to master the more difficult task of conversation. It is possible that conversational dialogue is a distinctly human behavior that must be examined separately from the issue of learning language.

Since complex language and its use seems specific to the human species and nearly universal, the early psycholinguists reasoned that it must be biologically based. In other words, humans possess a specific, innate capacity for language. But even though language use is nearly universal, it doesn't follow that underlying language rules are also universal. Human languages seem to be very diverse. Chomsky found that human languages differ only superficially but that underlying principles are more uniform. These underlying principles are based on two types of universal features, substantive and formal. *Substantive universals* are rules that relate to a particular element, such as the rules related to noun and verb use. In contrast, *formal universals* are general rules related to linguistic forms, such as passive sentences. Chomsky proposed to describe these linguistic universals.

Prior to the publication of Chomsky's *Syntactic Structures* in 1957, linguistics had been primarily a "classificatory science" (Searle, 1972). Chomsky described language from the psychological perspective of the capacity of a language user to produce and comprehend language. Thus, Chomsky concentrated on the linguistic process instead of the grammatical products. He was interested in a theory of the universal grammatical rules of language.

Linguistic Processing

Chomsky proposed two levels of linguistic processing. The initial level operates using phrase structure rules; the second employs transformational rules. **Phrase structure rules** delineate the basic relationships underlying all sentence organization, regardless of the language being used; they are universal. **Transformational rules,** on the other hand, govern the rearrangement of phrase structure elements based on a specific language and are not universal.

The units within each sentence are known as **constituents,** and a description of sentence units is called a *constituent analysis.* Sentence constituents can be nominal, verbal, adverbial, or adjectival. Nominal constituents, or **noun phrases,** consist of a single word or phrase that can act as a noun, such as *he, the* *boy,* or *the nearly 1,000 college graduates.* Several different types of words can form a noun phrase, but the only obligatory word is the noun; without it there is no noun phrase. Verbal constituents, called **verb phrases,** must include the verb plus any additional words or phrases that might be needed to complete the verb. For example, some verbs, such as *walk,* may be used without a direct object, whereas others, such as *sell,* need a direct object to be complete. Thus a verb phrase might include a noun phrase also, as in *sells used cars.* Adverbial constituents serve the function of an adverb, thus marking the manner, place, or time of an action. For example, a word such as *easily* or *late* or a phrase such as *in the gymnasium* may serve as an adverbial constituent. Finally, adjectival constituents serve as an adjective to modify a noun and may be a word, such as *big, handsome,* or *inarticulate,* or a phrase, such as *in sheep's clothing.* Each of these constituents may be combined with or embedded within the others.

Sentence constituents or elements are organized hierarchically, which means that each, in turn, may be broken into its constituent parts, as in Figure 2.1. Chomsky's phrase structure rules begin with the sentence as the basic unit. A rule common to all languages is that each sentence must contain at least a noun and a verb. Thus, the Bible's shortest verse, "Jesus wept," is a perfectly acceptable sentence. Most sentences, however, contain longer phrases and more modifiers. The basic relationship is written as follows:

$$S \rightarrow NP + VP$$

This formula is read as "A sentence can be rewritten as a noun phrase and a verb phrase." (Remember, however, that only the noun and the verb are mandatory.)

Phrase structure rules may be successively rewritten because each symbol to the left of the arrow can be replaced by the symbol(s) to the right. In the final step, actual words may be selected for each constituent, as in Figure 2.1. For example, a noun phrase may be rewritten as

$$NP \rightarrow Det + (Adj) + N$$

In this rule, the noun phrase is rewritten as a determiner, an optional adjective (as noted by the parentheses), and a noun. Determiners can be further rewritten as articles (*the, a*), demonstratives (*these, those*), or possessive pronouns (*his, her, their*). Constituents can be added or deleted to form a variety of noun phrase types. For example, under this phrase structure rule, we can form *the big hat, those red apples, his car, the baby, my yellow shirt,* and so on.

Likewise, verb phrases can be subjected to the same element or constituent analysis. For example,

$$VP \rightarrow VI$$

$$VP \rightarrow VT + NP$$

These rules are interpreted to mean that a verb phrase may be rewritten as an intransitive verb (VI) or a transitive verb (VT) with a direct object, which is a noun phrase. Intransitive verbs, such as *walk* and *look,* do not act upon another noun.

FIGURE 2.1   Phrase Structure Hierarchical Rules

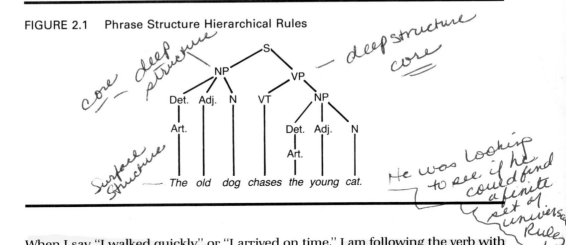

core — deep structure *— deep structure core*

Surface Structure

He was looking to see if he could find a finite set of universal Rules

When I say "I walked quickly" or "I arrived on time," I am following the verb with an adverb of manner (*quickly*) or an adverbial phrase of manner (*on time*). In contrast, transitive verbs, such as *buy, give,* or *eat,* act upon a noun. Thus, we say "I bought a new car" or "She is eating ice cream." *Car* and *ice cream* are nouns used as direct objects. They answer the questions "What did I buy?" and "What is she eating?" Transitive verbs occasionally have indirect objects, so another variation of the rule might read

So that you could produce any sentence you want.

$$VP \rightarrow VT + (NP) + NP$$

The noun phrase in parentheses is optional and represents an indirect object. An example might be *bought me a car.* The *me* is not necessary for a complete verb phrase, but it is needed to understand for whom the car was bought. These noun phrases might be analyzed further into their constituent parts. Thus, as before, each noun phrase might be rewritten as determiner, adjective, and noun. The verb phrase might now result in *bought his old uncle the antique automobile.*

In this manner, Chomsky attempted to provide a finite set of universal rules from which language users of all languages generate an almost infinite number of sentences. By rearranging the rules, we can construct a tree diagram, such as the one in Figure 2.1. Each rule previously formed can be seen by reading down the tree diagram from one level to the related constituents on the next lower level. Once a terminal category has been delineated, the variety of sentences that can be produced is limited only by the number of words available for each constituent. For example, for the rule given in Figure 2.1, let's assume that available nouns include *man, woman, dog,* and *cat* and that verbs include *chases* and *sees.* We can now construct numerous sentence variations; several examples are:

> The old dog chases the young cat.
> The old man chases the young dog.
> The old cat chases the young woman.
> The old woman chases the young woman.
> The old man sees the young cat.

> The old dog sees the young dog.
> The old woman sees the young man.

The particular constituent structure presented in Figure 2.1 will result in 32 different sentences if four nouns and two verbs are available. If the adjectives *young* and *old* are used interchangeably, 128 sentences can be produced. Should we expand the article constituent to include both *a* and *the*, then 512 sentences are possible. It is easy to see how humans can theoretically create millions of sentences when over 500 are possible from one constituent structure using four noun choices, two verbs, two adjectives, and two articles. While our examples have been in English, keep in mind that Chomsky was interested in universal rules. Therefore, we would actually be operating at a conceptual level, not at a spoken word level.

Although the phrase structure rules can be used to construct many sentences, the rules do not apply to all sentence types. For example, phrase structure rules are of only limited use for interpreting ambiguity or for explaining the similar meanings found in very different sentences. Ambiguous sentences have two different possible meanings. The sentence "They are arresting officers" can be interpreted in two ways. The ambiguity can be resolved by assigning different constituent structures to the sentence. The word *arresting* may be a verb or an adjective, thus modifying the sentence's interpretation. But not all ambiguity can be resolved this easily. In a second example, the sentences "The dog chased the cat" and "The cat was chased by the dog" are very different but have the same meaning. The phrase structure rule for both is NP + VT + NP. In addition, the form "The cat was chased by the dog" is not universal but represents English syntax, so it is not found in the phrase structure rules.

Theoretical inadequacies such as these are addressed in a second set of rules called *transformations*. These are language-specific syntactic rules that rearrange the structure of the basic phrase structure sentence. By operating on the phrase structure frame, transformational rules create general sentence types, such as questions, negatives, passives, and imperatives, and more complex sentences, such as those with embedded or subordinate clauses. These sentences cannot be formed by phrase structure rules because of the interrelated operations needed and because the forms used to make questions, negatives, and the like are not universal, as are the phrase structure rules. For example, selection of the correct verb form depends on the number and person of the noun and on the temporal or time aspect of the sentence. In the sentence "Mark was late last evening," the verb form *was* agrees with the singular noun and with the notion of time past. Transformational rules are an attempt to describe this contextual relatedness. To change one element causes changes in the sentence, as in the following examples:

> Mark and Ray *were* late last evening.
> Mark *will be* late tomorrow.

In addition, the verb form used and the manner of use are English based, not universal.

Using a combination of the universal phrase structure rules and the transformational rules for English, Chomsky tried to explain the human ability to create all possible sentences. Although transformational rules are specific to each language, the operations they describe are common to all languages, such as replacing one element with another or changing the location of one element. These operations are written as rules or formulas for changing the basic phrase structure of the sentence. For example, a transformational rule for passive sentences in English might be as follows:

$$NP_2 + be + V + \text{-}ed + by + NP_1$$

This rule can be read as "Noun phrase two followed by the verb *to be*, followed by the verb plus *-ed*, followed by *by*, followed by noun phrase one." This rule is a transformation of the phrase structure rule NP + VT + NP. The two noun phrases have been redesignated as one and two, respectively. Applying the rule, the sentence "The boy likes the girl" becomes "The girl is liked by the boy."

The boy likes the girl.

$$(NP_1 + VT + NP_2)$$

becomes
The girl is liked by the boy.

$$(NP_2 + be + V + \text{-}ed + by + NP_1)$$

The process seems quite simple, but if we modify the sentence slightly, the rule does not apply:

Cindy drives horses.
becomes
The horses are drived by Cindy.

A related but separate rule is needed in which *-en* is added to the verb instead of *-ed*.

These theoretical constructs need some psychological model within which to operate. Chomsky has proposed a two-tier mental model that includes a deep structure and a surface structure (Figure 2.2). Each sentence has both structures. The **deep structure**, found in the brain, is generated by the phrase structure rules and as such contains the basic meaning of the sentence. All the syntactic relationships needed to express the meaning correctly are present. The basic concept relationship "Mother eat something," for example, is universal. As speakers of English, however, we know that most sentences we produce are more complex and interrelated than those that are possible using only the phrase structure rules. An actual sentence that we produce is called the **surface structure**, and the form is determined by the constituent elements of the deep structure. Thus the deep structures of an active sentence, such as "Mother ate something," and a passive sentence, such as "Something was eaten by Mother," are the same. The

FIGURE 2.2   Syntactic Psycholinguistic Language-Processing Model

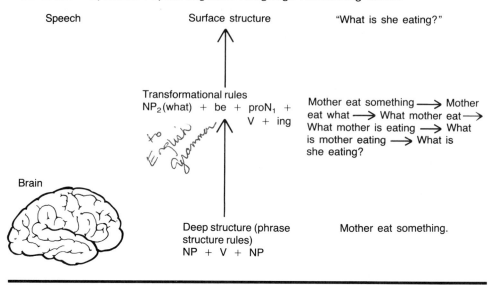

meanings of the two sentences do not differ, and the basic relationships are maintained in the surface structure.

The relationship between the deep and surface structures is expressed in the transformational rules. The transformational operations are performed on the deep structures. By changing, reordering, and modifying the deep structure elements, transformational operations create the surface structure. For example, the deep structure elements "John open gift" must be modified for the present progressive verb tense by the transformational rule $NP_1 + be + V + \text{-}ing + NP_2$, resulting in "John is opening the gift." As surface structure complexity increases, more transformational operations must be performed and the relationship between the deep and surface structures becomes less obvious. In the example in Figure 2.2, the phrase structure rule $NP_1 + V + NP_2$ is changed by the transformational rule NP_2 (*What*) $ + be + \text{pro } N_1 + V + \text{-}ing$. There may be several steps, as suggested by the changes at the transformational rule level.

In *Aspects of the Theory of Syntax* (1965), Chomsky stated that a complete grammar must have three parts—syntax, phonology, and semantics. Syntax is the most important element, according to Chomsky, because it enables language users to generate sentences. Phonology and semantics are purely "interpretive." The syntactic element specifies a deep structure that determines the semantic interpretation and a surface structure that determines the phonetic interpretation. Thus the transformational rules link semantics and phonology.

In addition, transformational rules specify an underlying relationship, not only between surface and deep structures but also between various surface structures. Thus, the transformational rules help language users recognize the close meanings of sentences with shared constituents. For example, there is a meaningful relationship between all of the following sentences:

> The woman drove the car.
> Did the woman drive the car?
> Who drove the car?
> What did the woman drive?
> The car was driven by the woman.
> Was the car driven by the woman?

The interrelatedness can be explained in terms of the underlying phrase structure rule system.

Language Acquisition

Since transformational grammar is concerned with underlying grammatical knowledge, it seems reasonable that Chomsky's theory could be used to explain the process of child language acquisition. The child learning language is similar to a linguist in the field (McNeill, 1970). Presented with a finite set of examples, the child must form hypotheses about the underlying rules and test these hypotheses in actual use.

With each child acting as a linguistic theorist, we would expect to see very different patterns of language development. Yet there appear to be similarities in development within and between languages. For example, the sequence of development seems to be invariant. Children progress from single to multiword utterances of the subject-verb-object type and then begin to modify these structures. These modifications or transformations are a limited set of universal syntactic operations. In addition, the developmental milestones are very similar across children. Most children say their first word at about 1 year of age. At around 18 months, two-word utterances appear. These utterances are so predictable that children must be using some common method of analysis and generation, linguists concluded.

The early psycholinguists assumed that the biological basis for language, its universality, and the developmental similarities across children pointed to an innate or inborn language acquisition mechanism. Chomsky called this mechanism the *language acquisition device*, or *LAD*. The LAD contains universal underlying linguistic principles or phrase structure rules. Thus the infant is "prewired" for linguistic analysis, for she possesses knowledge of the "basic grammatical categories and relationships and the fact that sentences represent on two levels—deep and surface structure" (Edmonds, 1976, p. 180). In other words, the LAD contains both substantive and formal universals in the form of a catalog of semantic or meaning classes and the rules for generating sentences. These universals form a primitive theory for any potential natural language. The LAD enables each child to process incoming language and to form hypotheses based on the regularities found in that language. Through hypothesis testing, the child derives an accurate concept of the syntactic rules of her native language.

Although the LAD is innate, linguistic input is needed to activate the analysis mechanism. Hypotheses are formulated on the basis of the speech the child hears. Often ungrammatical, this linguistic input cannot serve as a complete model for language learning. However, it is regular enough to enable the child to extract linguistic rules based on her innate knowledge.

If the innateness theory is correct, then we would expect the child first to use the phrase structure rules and only later to use the transformational rules. Since the universal features of the deep structure are not learned but already exist in each normal infant, they should be evident in early child speech. In fact, the early multiword utterances of children do consist primarily of simple constituent strings similar to the phrase structure rules. Transformations appear later, it is reasoned, because they are peculiar to specific languages and must be deduced by the child using the phrase structure rules.

Child language, however, is not a mirror of adult language. It has some unique qualities of its own. "The child does not merely speak a garbled version of the adult language around him but . . . rather, he speaks his own language, with its own characteristic patterns" (Dale, 1976, p. 2).

Chomsky's delineation of adult generative rules sparked an interest in describing the operating rules of child language. Initially, child language was described as "telegraphic speech" (R. Brown and Bellugi, 1964) — "Throw ball me" or "Airplane up," for example — reflecting a lack of sophisticated rehearsal and memory strategies, which prevent the child from exhibiting more mature memory performance. This model is inadequate because it offers only a superficial description of child language. It does not explore word relationships or provide an explanation of language acquisition. At this point, child development experts and linguists began to study the organization of child language in earnest.

Limitations

Transformational grammar emphasizes syntactic structures but virtually ignores the contributions of phonetics, semantics, and pragmatics. This approach fails to recognize the underlying semantic structures upon which language form is heavily dependent (C. Fillmore, 1968). A linguistic theory that ignores semantics cannot adequately explain why a syntactically correct sentence such as "Lively tables leap narrowly under the ceiling" does not make sense.

In addition, a syntax-based model seems inappropriate for describing single-word and two-word levels of development. The organization of these structures seems to be governed by semantic relationships and to be devoid of syntactic processes (Bowerman, 1976; R. Brown, 1973). Nor does later language learning follow transformational models (Menyuk, 1969). Children do not use one transformational rule, followed by two, and so on until multiple transformations are accomplished.

The inadequacies of transformational grammar as an explanation for language development stem from the nature of that grammar. Chomsky's theoretical grammar is based on adult data. Difficulty arises when this preconceived adult model is imposed upon child language, which is different from adult language.

> When imposing a classification scheme on data, there is the risk of losing other important variables and interactions that are not included in the original scheme. . . . In the course of development, children are not learning adult "parts of speech," and descriptions of the words that children use in terms of adult parts of speech can be misleading. . . . It is more important, for both description and explanation of children's language, that the children have learned words that represent certain aspects of experience and have learned something of how such words can be combined in sentences, rather than that they have learned words that are nouns or verbs. (Bloom & Lahey, 1978, pp. 37–39)

Looking for mature structures in child speech may result in missing important structures and underevaluating children's knowledge and capabilities.

The theory also negates the uses of language by children. Children use language to describe and to accompany their experiences. Unfortunately, the theory deemphasizes the importance of the environment and of early social and cognitive growth. Chomsky did concede that children gain language through exposure to "scraps" of adult language, but he and his peers have described a process that occurs independently of cognitive development (I. Schlesinger, 1977). While Chomsky and his followers concentrated on innate syntactic knowledge, they neglected innate cognitive abilities (Sinclair-DeZwart, 1973).

The issue of innateness is the weakest aspect of Chomsky's theory. The notion of a language acquisition device is too simplified and provides an inadequate explanation. To assume that the ability to use language is innate does little to facilitate our understanding of the actual process of language development.

Contributions

It would be a great disservice to Chomsky to dismiss his linguistic contributions because of the inadequacies of his developmental explanations. In Chomsky's defense, we must note that he did not set out to describe language acquisition. Rather, his goal was to describe and explain linguistic processing.

Chomsky redefined linguistic behavior in psychological terms that were quite different from the older syntactic structural models. "The difference in Chomsky's case is that, because he explicitly emphasized the generative feature of grammars, he was led to formulate his own grammatical rules in a radically novel way" (Greene, 1972, p. 27). His main concern was process or linguistic competence, not product or linguistic performance. Chomsky noted that operating rules exist and that some are universal. By carefully examining the constituents, we can discover the underlying transformational rules.

In redefining linguistic units, Chomsky also offered a different view of human beings than that presented by the behaviorists and learning theorists. Chomsky's human organism is psychologically active and linguistically creative. Language is not externally imposed but develops from internal processing mechanisms and is used in a generative fashion.

Government-Binding Theory

It is only fair that we update Chomsky somewhat and not leave him in the late 1960s. In recent years, Chomsky (1981) has modified his theory to account more for language rules and well-formedness and for language learnability. The result, called **government-binding theory,** attempts to describe the way in which the human mind represents the autonomous system of language. His goal was to present a theory that could account for the great diversity in human languages and that could explain the development of grammars by children on the basis of limited input (Leonard & Loeb, 1988). The resultant principles Chomsky calls *universal grammar.*

Universal grammar consists of four levels—D-structure, S-structure, phonetic form, and logical form—and several subtheories. D-structures consist of sentence formation rules and the lexicon or personal dictionary. The lexicon specifies meaning but, more importantly, the manner in which each word is to be treated syntactically. For example, the word *see* should be followed by a noun phrase, as in *see the dog.* More complex terms such as *before* might be followed by a noun phrase (*before school*) or a clause (*before I had eaten*). D-structures are formed by placing the lexical items in the appropriate sentence forms.

Unlike phrase structure rules, however, D-structures are expanded to explain other sentence forms, such as questions. Phrase structure rules have been rewritten as follows:

$$S \rightarrow COMP + S$$
$$S \rightarrow NP + INFL + VP$$

A COMP or complementizer, such as *that* or *what*, is assumed to be contained in every sentence, whether stated or not. In addition, every verb is assumed to contain an INFL or inflection, such as a tense marker or auxiliary verb. The formation of questions would involve the use of the COMP and/or INFL, unavailable under the older phrase structure rules of $S \rightarrow NP + VP$.

S-structures are derived from D-structures by the *move alpha rule,* a single movement of sentence elements that replaces the separate transformational rules. Thus, the sentence "Joell can throw [what]" becomes "What can Joell throw?" The object noun phrase is moved to the initial position and replaced by the COMP, as in Figure 2.3.

Obviously, it is still possible to produce ungrammatical and nonsensical sentences. Phonetic form rules include phonological rules and the use of inflections (INFL). Logical form rules govern the sense making of sentences. These two

FIGURE 2.3   Sentence Formation Applying the Rules of Government-Binding Theory

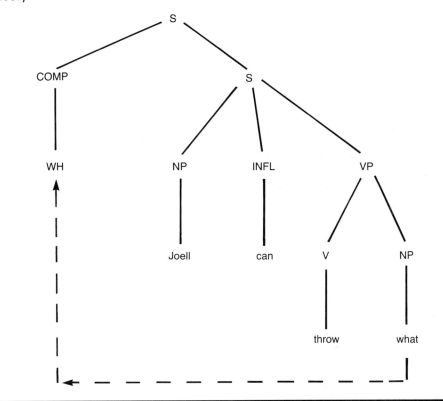

alone, however, cannot handle potential confusions and ambiguities. For example, the sentence "Mary could not decide what she should do" is well formed and makes sense, but the word *she* might refer to Mary or another female mentioned outside of this sentence.

Chomsky expands well beyond his previous theories to offer more constraints on the rather open-ended sentence forms he has proposed so far. He reasons that the universal rules, by their very simplicity, can result in so many different sentences that children could never learn language in the short time in which they do. Therefore, he proposes several subtheories: bounding theory, government theory, case theory, binding theory, θ-theory, and control theory (Leonard & Loeb, 1988).

Bounding theory states that no constituent can be moved out of both the noun phrase and the clause. Too many movements disrupt the relationships between elements, as demonstrated here:

> Model: With great relief, all participants received the peace proposal made by the French delegation.
> 1. All participants received with great relief the peace proposal made by the French delegation.   (*Acceptable*)
> 2. All participants received by the French delegation the peace proposal made with great relief.   (*Unacceptable*)

The first version is acceptable because *with great relief* remains with the verb phrase and describes the manner of acceptance. In the second version, *with great relief* moves to another verb phrase, as does *by the French delegation*, which previously was part of the verb phrase including *made*.

Government theory describes the privileged relations of some constituents that govern which other constituents will be used. For example, prepositional phrases, by their nature, dictate the use of a preposition and a noun phrase. Elaborate tree diagrams can be constructed to establish dominance and control by certain sentence constituents.

Case theory is concerned with semantic case. It is assumed that certain constituents govern the assignment of case. For example, a verb governs the assignment of objective case to the noun phrase it governs. For example, in the sentences "I walk home" and "I bought a home," the verb determines that the first *home* is a location, while the second is an object. Cases will be discussed in more detail in the next section.

Binding theory concerns coreference, or the conditions under which a noun phrase refers to the same entity as another noun phrase. Some noun phrases, such as reflexives (*herself*) and reciprocals (*another one*), refer to another noun phrase, while others, such as pronouns may (Mary saw *him* leave) or may not (Mary knew *she* could do it). Finally, referential noun phrases are free and do not refer to other noun phrases. The three following examples illustrate the difference:

> Jean saw *herself* in the dream.   (Refers back to the noun phrase *Jean*)
> Jean saw *her* in the dream.   (Independent of the noun phrase in this sentence)
> Jean saw *Harriet* in the dream.   (Independent of any noun phrase)

θ-*theory* or thematic theory is concerned with the assignment of roles such as goal-of-action and so on. The type of verb decides the other structures that will accompany it by the roles assigned. For example, a verb such as *stack* might take a noun phrase and also a prepositional phrase as in *stack the dishes in the cupboard.*

Finally, *control theory* determines the reference for pronouns and pronounlike words. A sentence such as "Mary had cared for her mother and she was ill" leaves some question as to the referent of *she*.

Mature speakers, according to Chomsky, use all of these processes to encode and decode the language around them, confounding the universal grammar with the peculiarities of their individual languages.

It should be noted that although he tries to incorporate many aspects of language, Chomsky's primary interest is still language form. Nor have we come any closer to explaining language development. As before, Chomsky assumes that the universal grammar is innate and that the child acquires the peripheral structures of her own language by using the universal grammar to decode her language experience.

PSYCHOLINGUISTIC THEORY:
A SEMANTIC/COGNITIVE MODEL

As early as 1963, the syntax-only theory of language processing was questioned (J. Katz & Fodor). It was argued that a full account of language must include meanings, or semantics. These meanings should not be limited to individual words but should include the meanings expressed through syntactic relations as well. Although Chomsky discussed meaning at the deep structure level, he minimized the contribution of semantics to syntactic processes. It is inadequate to say merely that a certain position in a sentence can be filled by any noun or by the subject of the sentence. Consider the vacancy in the subject position of the following sentence, for example:

The [noun] pushed the door angrily.

Only certain nouns can fill the vacancy. Inanimate nouns, such as *ball, door,* and *shoe,* though grammatically correct, do not make sense. Semantics helps us distinguish sense from nonsense. To have a generative language system, we must appreciate the semantic characteristics of each word. The word *mother* contains the semantic characteristics of being animate, human, female, parental, and so on. Such features govern the selection of appropriate verbs, pronouns, adjectives, and other words that are related in some way. Interpretation of any utterance must include the *referential context,* or its underlying semantic features and relationships.

Case Grammar

C. Fillmore's (1968) case grammar is a generative system that attempts to explain the influence of semantics on the syntactic structure of language. It presents the language user's distinction between sense and nonsense, just as Chomsky distinguished what is grammatical from what is not.

Fillmore proposed that there is an underlying level of the deep structure that is conceptually more fundamental than the syntactic constituents. This level consists of a set of universal semantic concepts that specify the relationships of nouns to verbs. These semantic concepts are distinct from syntactic relations and from the form of the surface structure. They are not innate rules found in a language acquisition device, but are the events and relationships found in the environment or in human genetic coding and are therefore universal (Chafe, 1970).

According to Fillmore, the constituents of a sentence are modality and proposition. *Modality* includes such aspects as tense, mood, interrogation, and negation. More basic to semantic theory is the *proposition*, or noun–verb relationship, which defines the meaning or concept underlying a particular utterance. As a group, propositions represent a set of sentence types defined as a verb plus a case or set of nouns. Particular verbs require specific cases. A **case** is a distinct semantic role or function for a certain noun phrase. In the previous example, "The [noun] pushed the door angrily," only nouns of a certain case, those that cause action, can be employed.

A case consists of the case marker (K) plus the noun phrase (NP). English subject and object nouns do not have special case markers. Their function is marked by word order in the typical subject-verb-object sentence.

Fillmore's cases, definitions, and examples are listed in Table 2.1. The seven major universal cases are agentive (A), dative (D), experiencer (E), factitive (F), instrumental (I), locative (L), and objective (O). Each case has certain semantic features that mark it. For example, agentive and dative case nouns must be animate or alive. Instrumental case nouns must be inanimate. In our previous example, "The [noun] pushed the door angrily," an instigator of action—that is, an agentive noun—is required. If the sentence had read "The boy pushed the [noun] angrily," the choice of noun would have been an objective case noun. With the objective case, almost any noun whose role fits the verb may be used. Therefore, the blank could be filled with *ball, girl* or *bicycle, chair,* but not with *skyscraper* or *airport*. The verb *push* implies movement or the possibility of movement, so *skyscraper* would not fit the role needed (unless we lived in a world inhabited by Saturday morning TV superheroes). The difference between agentive and dative case nouns is one of performing an action as opposed to being affected by an action. Agentive case nouns are used with *listen* and *look,* dative ones with *hear* and *see.* The dative case suggests a more passive state. Verbs used with the dative case cannot be used in the progressive form (verb + -*ing*) or in the imperative or command form. "I am seeing television" and "Hear your mother" sound awkward; "I am looking at television" and "Listen to your mother" are much better.

In general, cases are not exclusive, and a noun may be used in all cases in which it meets the criteria. The verb that is employed determines the case of the noun. Thus, Fillmore (1968) and Chafe (1970) have accounted for structure through the semantic functions of nouns in relation to verbs.

Fillmore's general rule for surface structure is that "if there is an A [agent], it becomes the subject; otherwise, if there is an I [instrument], it becomes the subject; otherwise, the subject is O [objective]" (p. 33). This rule is dependent upon the type of verb employed, although some verbs, like *give*, are exceptions. In the following examples, the subject changes according to the case:

> The *boy* used a screwdriver to open the door.
> (agentive)   (instrumental)   (objective)
> The *screwdriver* was used to open the door.
> (instrumental)   (objective)

The *door* opened easily.
(objective)
The door was opened by the *boy* with his screwdriver.
(objective)   (agentive)   (instrumental)

Unlike other languages, English has few case markers other than position. Outside of the subject position, cases are marked by prepositions. (See Table 2.1.)

TABLE 2.1   Case Relationships

Case Name	Definition	Example
Agentive (A)	The perceived instigator of action; typically animate with own motivation	*Mike* threw the ball. The ball was thrown by *Mike*.
Dative (D)	The animate being affected by the state or action named by the verb	Mother gave *Joe* a big hug. The clown gave a flower to *Grandma*.
Experiencer (E)	The animate being who experiences a given event, action, or mental disposition	*Mother* heard Stan. *Jeff* wanted a new car above all else.
Factitive (F)	The object or being resulting from the action or state of the verb	Father built a *treehouse*. Joyce wrote a *poem*.
Instrumental (I)	The inanimate object or force involved in a causal manner in the state or action named by the verb; the object brings about the process but is not the instigator	Lee battered the door with his *axe*. Martin ate peas with a *spoon*.
Locative (L)	The place, locus, or spatial orientation of the state, action, or process of the verb	The dog is in his *house*. *Seattle* is very humid. The game was played in the *stadium*.
Objective (O)	The animate or inanimate noun whose role in the state or action named by the verb depends on the meaning of the verb; the most semantically neutral case	Dad threw the *ball* to me. Mother heard *Tom* come in late.

Source: Based on C. Fillmore, "The Case for Case," in E. Bach & R. Harmas (Eds.), *Universals in Linguistic Theory*, New York: Holt, Rinehart & Winston, 1968; and on W. Chafe, *Meaning and the Structure of Language*, Chicago: University of Chicago Press, 1970.

Agentive case nouns take *by* in a passive sentence. For example, the sentence "Todd ate the hamburger" becomes "The hamburger was eaten by Todd." The instrumental case takes *by* or *with*, depending on the presence of an agentive case noun. If an agentive case noun is not present, the instrumental case takes *by*. In the example "The church was struck *by* lightning," there is no instigator of action (divine guidance aside). Later, "The sexton inspected the damage *with* a flashlight." In this example, the agent is clearly present in the form of the church sexton. The dative case takes *to* when not in the subject position, as in the sentence "She gave the money *to* me." Finally, the locative takes the appropriate preposition for the spatial relation expressed, such as *in*, *on*, or *under*. The factitive and objective cases generally do not take prepositions.

Much like Chomsky's transformational grammar, case grammar is an attempt to describe a generative system based on usage rules. These universal semantic cases form a structure that underlies, and provides a basis for, syntax.

The Semantic Revolution

Following the lead of other linguists, Lois Bloom attempted to apply a syntactic analysis technique to child language in the late 1960s. She analyzed the language of three children at an early multiword stage. Bloom applied a reduction transformation process in which, presumably, the children know the underlying adult structure but delete certain elements. Thus, Bloom assumed that children have both a deep and a surface structure. Since children can process only a limited number of constituents at a given time, some must be omitted from the surface structure. Adult linguistic processing does not require this reduction because adults have greater memory and processing skills. Assuming that underlying meaning would help her analysis, Bloom recorded the verbal and nonverbal contexts of each child utterance. She was interested in the ongoing event and the communication partners. This information is very important, since most early child language is directly related to the immediate context.

Although Bloom was able to ascertain the children's meanings from the context, she found that syntactic rules were inadequate for describing these different meanings. In fact, without consideration of semantics, many of the syntactic relationships were missed. For example, on two occasions, Bloom's subject Kathryn said "Mommy sock." The contexts were very different. Once she said "Mommy sock" while picking up her mother's stocking; on the other occasion, she said those same words while her mother was putting the child's sock on Kathryn. The child's intended meaning was very different, but the surface structure was unchanged. Bloom (1970) therefore concluded that "generative transformational grammar could be used in a more powerful way to account for children's language than it has been if semantic information were available in order to make inferences about underlying structure" (p. 9).

Bloom found that children's speech contains consistent relationships among entities in the children's world and that these relationships are expressed by simple word-order rules. For example, one relationship is between the agent performing the action and the action itself. This is expressed as agent followed by action (agent + action), as in "Dad throw" or "Doggie run." The relationship of anything to its location is the entity followed by the location (X + location), as in "Go bed," "Throw me," or "Mommy car." Bloom assumed that word order marks semantic relationships that are expressed syntactically in later development.

With the publication of *Language Development: Form and Function of Emerging Grammars* in 1970, Bloom presented the conclusions of her study. Her results signaled the beginning of a new era in child language study. This move from a syntactic-transformational to a semantic analysis has been aptly dubbed the *semantic revolution.* Child language structure began to be examined in relation to the intended meaning of the speaker. The child's intended meaning was interpreted from both nonlinguistic and linguistic contexts. Such analysis is called a rich interpretation because it goes beyond the words of the speaker to attain the fuller meaning. "Baby bed," for example, may mean quite different things in different contexts. The child may be providing information while the baby sleeps or pointing to an empty crib. In the first instance, she may be telling her listener where the baby sleeps; in the second, she may be signaling ownership.

It was hypothesized that the underlying semantic basis of language developed prior to syntax (Chafe, 1970; G. Lakoff, 1971; Leech, 1970). Researchers began to analyze child language for early examples of the case relationships identified by C. Fillmore (1968) and Chafe (1970).

Three other linguists, I. M. Schlesinger, Roger Brown, and Dan Slobin, reached the same general conclusions simultaneously with Bloom. Going beyond Bloom, Schlesinger (1971) proposed that child grammar is semantic, not syntactic. Semantic relations are expressed by simple rules, such as "agent precedes action," rather than through abstract syntactic categories such as subject and verb. Schlesinger went on to identify the major semantic relationships of early child speech. Unlike Fillmore, whose case grammar expressed semantic relationships in many syntactic forms, Schlesinger, Brown, and (later) Bloom described early child language as a one-to-one relationship. The semantic relationships are expressed very clearly in the word order of the child's utterance. As the child develops, word-order rules give way to the syntactic devices adults use to signal case relationships. For example, possession is originally signaled by word order, then by addition of the more mature possessive *'s*. Thus, the word-order possessives "Mommy sock" and "Baby hat" become "Mommy's sock" and "Baby's hat." There is a continuity through child and adult language structure. Following the lead of Brown and others, Greenfield and Smith (1976) found that semantic grammars could be used to describe children's initial, single-word utterances as well. Thus, the semantic approach assumes that content or meaning precedes language form. When the child acquires syntactic forms, they are used to express older semantic functions, as in the possession example (Slobin, 1973). It is important to note that children have a range of semantic functions and can use a single-word utterance to express a number of meanings. For example, the questions "What's that?" and "Where's cookie?" require a name and a location answer, respectively, yet both could receive the single-word reply "Table." Therefore, *table* can signify the inanimate thing (an objective case) or a place (a locative).

To many readers of introductory language development texts, the semantic–syntactic distinction may seem akin to the medieval argument over the number of angels who could sit on the head of a pin. Yet to describe a child utterance such as "Mommy sleep" as "noun plus verb" is to do a disservice to children. Consider the following utterances:

A	B
Mommy eat	Eat cookie
Daddy throw	Throw ball
Baby drink	Drink milk

List A consists of "noun plus verb" sentences; list B, "verb plus noun" sentences. If children are just stringing two syntactically different types of words together, the order should be of no importance. Yet a reversal of the word order results in sentences that do not make sense or are awkward, such as "Throw Daddy" and "Cookie eat." There is a distinct difference between the nouns in lists A and B: those in the first list are agentive, and those in the second are objective, case. It is important to note that young children have learned this distinction and can use it.

In addition to providing a new direction in child language study, the semantic revolution weakened the notion of the innateness of language rules. According to the semantic hypotheses, meaning, or semantics, is a method of representing mental experience. It follows, then, that experience, not innate rules, must be the basis for early language. In her 1970 book, Bloom concluded that

> it appears that the results of this study would cast some doubt on the view of language development as some innately preprogrammed behavior. . . . The syntactic difference among . . . children must reflect the importance of individual differences in the interaction between cognitive function and experience. (p. 277)

Support for the semantic structuring of early child language came from cross-cultural studies (Bowerman, 1973a; R. Brown, 1973; Slobin, 1973). Results suggested that the early semantic rules are universal. Brown concluded that "a rather small set of operations and relations describe all the meanings expressed in the early multimorphemic utterances of . . . children, whatever the language they are learning" (p. 198). Unlike Chomsky, these semanticists assumed that the common rules represent a general pattern of cognitive development, not innate structure. Stated another way, "a universality of semantic intent implies that most children, regardless of their language or culture, operate from a similar 'view of the world'" (McLean and Snyder-McLean, 1978, p. 6). Children learn basic relationships between entities within the environment, and these relationships are reflected in the semantic structures produced by the child. Information about entities is communicated by marking the relationships of those entities

(K. Nelson, 1974). These relationships form a general structure of language that children learn to express by actively attending to the linguistic environment, especially to the language addressed to them. Children begin to use language expressively to talk about the things they know. In other words, thought precedes language. "Representation starts with just those meanings that are most available to it, propositions about action schemas involving agents and objects, assertions of nonexistence, recurrence, location and so on" (R. Brown, 1973, p. 200). Language is grafted onto existing knowledge about the world and serves as a means of representing the world. According to the Swiss educator Jean Piaget, language is only one of several methods of representing reality, one aspect of a general symbolic function.

The developmental order of language encoding of semantic relationships reflects the order of development of cognitive structures. This concept has been termed **cognitive determinism.** Several studies have demonstrated that the semantic concepts that children express are present in their thoughts and actions (Gilmore, Suci, & Chan, 1974; Golinkoff, 1975; Golinkoff & Kerr, 1978; McHale, 1973; Robertson & Suci, 1980). For example, children demonstrate a concept of object permanence, or of the existence of an object that cannot be seen, before they express relationships such as appearance, disappearance, and nonexistence in their speech (Bloom, 1973; R. Brown, 1973; E. Clark, 1973a; Kahn, 1975; Nelson, 1974). Thus, early utterances represent children's understanding and overall cognitive processing (Bruner, 1975). Linguistic- and cognitive-processing patterns reflect an organization based on the relationships within children's environments (Nelson, 1974, 1977). Children do not learn language and then use it to express relationships; rather, they learn entity relationships and express that knowledge in the language they learn subsequently.

Language Development

In some ways, the semantic/cognitive description of language development is a return to the earlier mentalistic approaches of the late 1800s, in which language was viewed as a key to the child's mind. By the very nature of the cognitive hypothesis, language development is rooted in early cognitive development, prior to the appearance of the first word. A particular level of cognitive achievement is necessary before language can be used expressively. Piaget described a general symbolic function that must be attained before language, a form of symbolic behavior, can develop.* There are several cognitive factors that must be present for a child to acquire language (Bowerman, 1974):

1. Ability to represent objects and events not perceptually present.
2. Development of basic cognitive structures and operations related to space and time, classification of types of action, embedding of action

---

*Piaget's theories of cognitive development are discussed in depth in Chapter 5.

patterns within each other, establishment of object permanence and constancy, relationships between objects and action, and construction of a model of one's own perceptual space.

3. Ability to derive linguistic-processing strategies from general cognitive structures and processes.

4. Ability to formulate concepts and strategies to serve as structural components for the linguistic rules.

These cognitive abilities develop during the first year of life. The newborn is primarily a sensory detector. With maturity she begins to act upon the world, to explore, and to manipulate. The child's early sensorimotor interactions form a process that helps her organize the incoming stimuli from the real world.

Several language development specialists believe that symbolic functioning is rooted in imitation (Bates, Benigni, Bretherton, Camaioni, & Volterra, 1979; Piaget, 1952; Sinclair-DeZwart, 1973). The child learns to imitate or re-present her own motor behaviors and those of others. Later, the child imitates without an immediate model. In a play mode, this nonimmediate or deferred imitation behavior lets the child represent reality through play, or play symbolically. For example, a piece of paper can be used to represent a blanket. The child has presumably internalized the original behavior or referent in some symbolic storage mode. With language the child is able to represent the referent with an arbitrary symbol or word.

The child also uses sensorimotor behaviors to manipulate objects and explore their functions. The child groups these functional use features into classes—such as the category of things that cause action—to form the basis for early definitions (Nelson, 1974).

Finally, with the development of the concept of object permanence, the child can represent entities that are not present in the immediate context. Presumably the child has indexed or stored the image of the object symbolically. If an object stills exists, even though removed from the child's immediate perception, the child can cause it to recur by evoking the symbol for it.

Imitation, functional use, and object permanence can account for development of the young child's general ability to use symbols, but they are not directly translatable into semantic relationships (Rice, 1984). It is hypothesized that the child must have a concept of object permanence in order to develop semantic notions of appearance, disappearance, and recurrence. Other early cognitive relationships can also be seen in the presymbolic behavior of children.

Children are able to attend visually to location at 5 months of age (Robertson, 1975). By 9 months, children begin to discriminate between different agents and react to any change of agents in a situation. Children can discriminate between different actions by 1 year of age. This ability is an important prerequisite to classifying verbs for making case decisions.

Young children can distinguish between the agent and the object (Golinkoff, 1975; McHale, 1973). In studies that concentrated on both functions, children attended more to the agent in visual action sequences (Robertson & Suci, 1980).

Their rule seems to be "Once the action begins, attend to the agent" (Grace & Suci, 1985, p. 3). By age 2, most children do not expect inanimate objects to move on their own. This finding is in harmony with observations that agents in early multiword utterances are primarily animate.

The receptive abilities of young children also suggest underlying relationships. A number of studies have shown that children who produce predominantly one- and two-word utterances use an agent-action-object strategy to comprehend unfamiliar sentences (Bever, 1970; Chapman & Miller, 1975; de Villiers & de Villiers, 1973; Strohner & Nelson, 1974; Wetstone & Friedlander, 1973). Children at the single-word production level comprehend the possessive word order of possessor-possessed object used in children's later two-word utterances (Golinkoff & Markessini, 1980). The inference is that children use those linguistic forms of which they have prior knowledge.

Although single-word utterances are basically structure-free, they still demonstrate some of the underlying cognitive concepts. Nomination, or naming, is signaled by words such as *see*, *this*, and *that*. Recurrence is marked by *more* and *'nuther*. Nonexistence markers are phrases such as *all gone*, *no more*, and *no*. These words are later joined in longer utterances that signal semantic intent, or meaning.

Early two-word combinations are not just random sequences of words. Meaning is signaled by word order, one of the simpler means of consistent marking (R. Brown, 1973). Specific word orders fulfill specific functions. For example, the possessive function is marked by the possessor plus the possessed object. Obviously, there can be many different possessors and many different objects, but most follow the same rule, as in "Mommy car" and "Baby bed." Other relationships depend primarily on one or two words that signal the semantic function. The recurrence function, for example, is marked by a recurrent word followed by an object or a location. The recurrent word is usually *more* or *'nuther*, as in "more milk" or "'nuther cookie." Approximately 70% of the two-word utterances of children who are learning language can be described by a few simple word-order rules. These rules are listed in Table 8.7 (p. 278) and will be discussed in detail in Chapter 8. Syntactic markers are later applied to the basic word-order rules to form more mature sentences and to mark semantic functions that do not comply with word order. Semantics, however, remains the key to sentence production and comprehension.

At higher language levels, cognitive development still precedes linguistic development, although the relationship is not clear-cut (Rice, 1984). For example, children gain concepts of time and place before they begin to use the prepositions that mark these concepts. Likewise, sequential knowledge and increased memory are required before a child can use the linguistic relationships of *why* and *because*.

It has been recognized recently that conceptual knowledge is only a portion of what the child needs to know. The competent communicator has conceptual knowledge of persons, social categories, and events (Rice, 1984). Person knowledge involves knowing that certain features of persons and things are constant and that each individual has a unique perspective on the world. Constant features of persons include their identity, their perceptual fields and emotional states, their intention to communicate, and the like. Social category knowledge includes recognition of situational similarities and understanding of social relational terms, such as *mother* and *parent*. Event knowledge is an understanding of sequentially organized events and routines, such as a telephone conversation or a conversational opener, and of accompanying scripts, such as "Hi, how are you?" Thus, a cognitive basis for language presupposes more than mere knowledge of the concepts behind words. "As children acquire the system of language-based knowledge . . . , they draw upon the totality of their experiences" (Rice, 1984, p. 178).

The semantic/cognitive hypothesis of language acquisition can be summarized as follows (McLean and Snyder-McLean, 1978):

1. Children's early language utterances appear to be expressions of perceived *semantic* relationships as opposed to being expressions of innate preprogrammed syntactic relationships among language elements.
2. Semantic relationships necessarily reflect the perception and understanding of certain relationships between and among the entities and the actions which are present in a child's environment.
3. Such perception and the subsequent development of an understanding of these relationships [are] products of the cognitive domain of human functioning.
4. The products of the cognitive domain in the form of the perception and understanding of relationships among elements in the environment can be considered to be a child's *knowledge* of [the] world.
5. Therefore, a child's language utterances reflect . . . knowledge of the relationships among and between the entities and the actions which make up [the child's] world.
6. Thus, language "maps" onto or encodes a child's existing knowledge. (p. 22)

The semantic/cognitive hypothesis is characterized by an "information-processing approach" (Reber, 1973). The child must abstract basic relationships from the physical environment and rules from the linguistic environment. This information is internalized and categorized to appear later in the child's expressive language. Language input is interpreted using linguistic rules that reflect these cognitive relationships. Language development is a product of the strategies and processes of general cognitive development, though not a direct manifestation of it.

Limitations

Noam Chomsky (1969) claimed that the semantically based notion of linguistic processing is merely a "notational variation" on his transformational theory. To dismiss the semantic/cognitive hypothesis so easily is to miss the psychological and developmental implications.

The semantic/cognitive hypothesis has highlighted at least one prerequisite to language acquisition, though cognition alone is an inadequate explanation of the process. Some children with normal cognitive abilities do not acquire language. In addition, there is evidence that cognition does not always influence language. At around age 3 or 4, there seems to be a crossover period in which language is equally likely to influence thought (Bloom, 1975). Some aspects of linguistic development cannot be explained without reference to earlier linguistic input (I. Schlesinger, 1977).

Presumably, young children are exposed to and process linguistic input in the same relational terms that are later evident in their linguistic production. These semantic relationships, which seem to explain the construction of early utterances, may be more "psychologically real" to the child than Chomsky's syntactic constituents (Bowerman, 1974). As with transformational grammar, however, the semantic relationships represent an adult perspective. Although these semantic rules can be used to describe most child utterances, they do not necessarily explain linguistic processing or language acquisition.

The greatest limitation of the semantic/cognitive hypothesis is found in the how and why of language acquisition. The link between cognitive abilities and language acquisition is not adequately explained. The hypothesis does not explain why the child's cognitive concepts and relationships become linguistically coded because it ignores the contribution of early communication. An adequate description of language acquisition "must also include the basic nature and purpose of children's communicative transactions within the social context in which they reside or function" (McLean and Snyder-McLean, 1978, p. 41). In other words, "in order to communicate successfully, a child must be able to produce and comprehend utterances on the basis of social appropriateness as well as grammatical well-formedness and referential accuracy" (Rice, 1984, p. 143).

Contributions

The semantic/cognitive hypothesis has helped explain many of the phenomena of language acquisition. The hypothesis offers a description of child language that seems to represent more closely the reality of the child and to offer a clear relationship between child and adult language. Case grammar is particularly well adapted to the simple structure found in early multiword utterances.

In addition, the semantic/cognitive hypothesis presents a notion of language acquisition against the backdrop of general child development. Without certain cognitive attainments, the child could not ascertain the transformational rules of her language or make the required behavioral associations found in the behavioral and earlier syntactic theories of language acquisition.

SOCIOLINGUISTIC THEORY

To view language from either a syntactic or a semantic perspective is to concentrate on the structural aspect of language. Although the structural units and rules differ, syntax and semantics are interdependent and tend to focus on discrete "bits" of language rather than larger, less finite units. Sociolinguistic analysis centers on the communication unit required to convey information. This unit could just as easily be an entire conversation as a word phrase or sentence. The single word *yes*, for example, can convey much information. In contrast, the lengthy speech of a politician might convey only "vote for me," even though those actual words are not spoken.

A structure-only approach also removes language from its communicative context, thus ignoring language's primary function. According to sociolinguistic thought, language is used to communicate and does not occur in a vacuum. Only rarely is language the end in itself. Usually language serves as a means for accomplishing some end within the communicative context.

Theorists who adhere to a sociolinguistic model concentrate on the underlying reasons or social/communicative functions of language. According to the sociolinguistic model, language *use* in communication is central to the linguistic process and to development. An utterance should be judged not "in terms of . . . well-formedness . . . of grammatical rules, but rather in terms of its effectiveness in achieving the speaker's intention" (Bruner, 1975, p. 3). Thus, the social/communicative context is essential to the process of conveying meaning.

According to the sociolinguistic approach, the overriding motivation for language and language acquisition is effective communication. The speaker chooses the form and content that will best fulfill her intentions based on her perception of the communication situation. Thus, the form of the speaker's utterance is controlled by her knowledge of, and her assumptions about, the listener's knowledge of the referent; and by the communicative context, which consists of the relative status, roles, and previous history of the participants, along with the social setting. "Rules of grammar do not operate independently of the context; a rule operates in conjunction with constraints in the linguistic and nonlinguistic environment" (Bloom & Lahey, 1978, p. 60). Thus, the speaker decides what to say, how to say it, and when to say it. Pragmatic rules govern the alternation of speech and language styles and symbols and the sequencing of utterances. It is only within context that we can interpret an utterance. Thus, "all semantics is *essentially* pragmatic in nature" (Bates, 1976b, p. 426). Meaning is inherent not in words but in the linguistic and referential contexts of those words. In short, speakers are "co-constructing events with others by negotiating their word meanings for their situations on hand" (Dore, 1986, p. 7).

Speech Act Theory

There are two broad pragmatic functions of language, *intrapersonal* and *interpersonal* (Muma, 1978). The intrapersonal or *ideational* function (Halliday, 1975b) is found in the internal language used for memory, problem solving, and concept development. The interpersonal function of language is communication. One unit for analysis of this communicative function is called a **speech act.** A speech act is "a unit of linguistic communication, which is expressed according to grammatical and pragmatic rules and which functions to convey a speaker's conceptual representations and intentions" (Dore, 1974, p. 344). The speech act is a larger conceptual unit than the syntactic and semantic units discussed in previous theories and can thus be divided into other elements.

The **propositional force** of a speech act consists of the conceptual content of the utterance, or its meaning. The speaker's attitude toward the proposition, which is called her *intention,* is found in the **illocutionary force.** For example, the one-word proposition *candy* can be altered in several ways with gestures and intonation. A rising intonation and a quizzical look might convey a question, whereas pointing might signify a labeling type of utterance. Reaching while whining the word *candy* might be considered a demand or request for the item. Thus an utterance with fixed form and semantic content can fulfill several intentions. The reverse is also possible; several different forms or propositions can fulfill a single intention or function. For example, you can ask for the salt using many different forms, including:

> Please pass the salt.
> May I have the salt, please.
> Salt please.
> Does this dish taste like it needs more salt?
> Is that the salt over there?

The particular form of the speech act is somewhat dependent upon the communicative context.

The concept of *speech act* was first introduced by John Austin (1962). He theorized that discourse is composed not of words or sentences but of speech acts. Searle (1965) strengthened this point by stating, "it is the . . . performance of the speech act that constitutes the basic unit of linguistic communication" (p. 222). According to Austin, each speech act can be analyzed into three parts: **locutions,** or propositions; **illocutions,** or intentions; and **perlocutions,** or the listener's interpretation.

Searle (1965) further clarified the work begun by Austin and redefined Austin's illocutions, or illocutionary acts. He proposed speech act categories including the following:

- Representatives—Statements that convey a belief or disbelief in some proposition, such as an assertion.
- Directives—Attempts to influence the listener to do something, such as a demand or command.
- Commissives—Commitments of self to some future course of action, such as a vow, promise, or swear.
- Expressives—Expressions of a psychological state, such as thanking, apologizing, or deploring.
- Declaratives—Statements of fact that presume to alter a state of affairs, such as "I confer upon you."

Both Austin and Searle were primarily concerned with adult speech.

The speech act approach to the study of language acquisition has been fruitful because "the uses of language are . . . crucial to an understanding of how language is acquired" (Bruner, 1975, p. 1). Several investigators have reported that initial child utterances can be categorized roughly into classes approximating Searle's representatives and directives. Others have found early prelinguistic cognitive precursors to speech acts and social-gestural precursors.

Two investigators, Michael Halliday and John Dore, have developed separate child-based speech act taxonomies. Halliday (1975a) concluded, after a longitudinal study of his son, Nigel, that a child emerges with limited adult functional abilities around age 2, enabling the speaker to have multiple purposes within a single utterance.

Dore (1974) was primarily interested in preverbal or one-word communicative functions. The basic unit of Dore's taxonomy is the **primitive speech act** (PSA). A PSA is "an utterance, consisting formally of a single act or a single prosodic sound-intonation pattern which functions to convey the child's intention before he acquires sentences" (p. 345). Not merely truncated adult forms, PSAs are qualitatively different, composed of only some of the features of adult speech acts. Each PSA contains a lexical/semantical component and an illocutionary force or intention. The illocutionary component, the speaker's intention, is usually exhibited in intonational patterns. Thus, as described earlier, a word such as *candy* can be a request for action when the child wants candy, a request for an answer when the child is unsure of the name, or an answer to an adult question. Dore described nine categories of PSAs: labeling, repeating, answering, requesting action, requesting answer, calling, greeting, protesting, and practicing (see Table 8.1). The components of these PSAs eventually develop into adultlike speech acts as the child's pragmatic intentions gradually become governed by syntactic and semantic structures. In short, "language is preceded by, and possibly evolves from, a well integrated nonverbal communication system" (Mahoney & Seely, 1976, p. 94).

In summary, the sociolinguistic model considers the communication effectiveness of language within the linguistic and nonlinguistic contexts. Language use is central to linguistic coding, which is determined by speaker knowledge and perceived listener knowledge. From a developmental perspective, therefore, the role of the child's communication partners is crucial. The language development process is "made possible by the presence of an interpreting adult who operates not so much as a corrector or reinforcer but rather as a provider, an expander and idealizer of utterances while interacting with the child" (Bruner, 1975, p. 17). This notion contrasts with Chomsky's, in which the adult provides only scraps of language for the child. Language acquisition, therefore, is a process of socialization. It follows a **transactional model** of child–caregiver give-and-take in which the child learns to understand the rules of dialogue, not of syntax or semantics (Bruner, 1977a). A communication base is established first; language is then mapped on this base to express verbally those intentions or functions that the child previously expressed nonverbally. Social interactions and social rela-

Sociolinguistic theory considers the communication context within which language development occurs.

tionships provide the needed framework that enables the child to decode and encode language form and content.

Language Acquisition

Within the sociolinguistic model of language acquisition, the primary communication context of interest is the child–mother or child–caregiver pair. The interactions that occur within this context are thought to be "the originating force as well as the conditions for language learning" (Rees, 1978, p. 238). As caregivers respond to their infants' early reflexive behaviors, the infants learn to communicate their intentions. Gradually, the infants refine these communication skills through repeated interactions.

The process is not one-sided, however; the direction of communication is more circular than caregiver-to-child models suggest (K. Bell, 1968; Moerk, 1972). Within the first few months of life, infants are able to discriminate contrasting phonemes, different intonational patterns, and speech from nonspeech (Eimas,

1974; Hirschman & Katkin, 1974; Kearsley, 1973; Moffitt, 1971; Turnure, 1971). Infants are also able to discriminate voices and to demonstrate a preference for the human face and human speech sounds (Richards, 1974). These discriminations and preferences provide the bases for early communication.

Parents or caregivers respond differentially to these infant behaviors and treat them as meaningful social communication. In other words, "It is the infant's mother who . . . endows his behavior with meaning" (Dore, 1986, p. 17). Therefore, the infant receives input and confirmation of her own communication attempts. The degree of parental responsiveness appears to be positively correlated with later language abilities (S. Bell & Ainsworth, 1972). In addition, parental responsiveness forges an attachment bond between the infant and the parent that fosters communication (Ainsworth, Bell, & Slayton, 1974; Blehar, Lieberman, & Ainsworth, 1977). By 3 to 4 months, interactions are regulated by eye gaze and form an early dialogue that evolves into vocalization patterns and later into conversational exchanges. Infants engage in selective listening; by 3 months of age, they can distinguish and attend to utterances addressed to them (Lewis & Freedle, 1973).

These dialogues alone do not explain the language acquisition process. Children receive highly selective language input within the routines of child–parent interactions, such as shared or joint action and joint reference (Bruner, 1975). Within joint action routines or dialogues, such as "peekaboo" and "this little piggy," children learn turn-taking skills. Mothers provide a consistent set of behaviors that enable their children to predict the outcome and later to anticipate. Children learn to signal their intention to play. Bruner (1975) summarized the relationship between play and language rules:

> Elaborating rule structures in communication . . . is inherent in play, particularly in the mutual play between mother and infant. . . . Elaborative play involves complex role shifting between partners as with peek-a-boo . . . and also ritualized and repeated play on objects as with pushing a ball back and forth. (p. 10)

There are parallels between the attributes of these routines and early semantic relationships seen in child language. For example, the caregiver interacts with a ball in a certain ritualized way that helps the child learn that it can appear, disappear, reappear, and be acted upon.

Within joint action sequences, caregivers systematically train children to differentiate between objects, a process called *joint reference* (Bruner, 1974/1975). Joint (or **shared**) reference is the achievement of a common referent or the focusing of joint attention on an object or event. Mothers construct elaborate routines to establish joint reference, beginning with eye contact in the first few months and extending to calling the child, pointing, and naming an object. Children progress from following gestural to following vocal-only cues for the referent. Once the referent has been established, mothers provide linguistic input. A joint reference sequence might be as follows:

MOTHER:	Gerry, see doggie. (Points.)
CHILD:	(Looks at dog.)
MOTHER:	Big doggie. Doggie bark.

The establishment of a joint or shared referent and the subsequent maternal verbalizations are important for early meaning development (Wells, 1974). Maternal speech is modified systematically so that it is comprehensible at the assumed level of the child (Mahoney, 1975; Snow, 1977a, 1977b).

The social interaction surrounding language input makes language acquisition possible (Ninio & Snow, 1988). One of the most important aspects of this input is the high degree of form–function relationship (Shatz, 1975). Many maternal utterances are function-specific. In other words, they serve a single function and are used repeatedly for that function. Thus, it is possible that the child's own intentions arise from maternal input. The mother's pragmatically specific and predictable utterances may well provide a base from which the child can begin to decipher semantic and syntactic categories.

For their part, children evolve from using reflexive, nonintentional communication to expressing conventional verbal intentions in the second year of life. Bates (1976a) has identified three developmental stages of early communication functions: the prelocutionary, in which children's behaviors are undifferentiated; the illocutionary, in which children use conventional gestures and vocalization to express intent; and the locutionary, in which words convey children's intentions. Thus, communication functions or intentions are well established before the child acquires linguistic structures (Bruner, 1974/1975; Lewis & Freedle, 1973).

Before she expresses her first meaningful word or shortly thereafter, a child is able to express a range of early intentions (Dore, 1974; Owens, 1978). Language structure is acquired as a more efficient means of communicating these intentions. Bruner (1974/75) has explained this motivation:

> Neither the syntactic nor the semantic approach to language acquisition takes sufficiently into account what the child is trying to do by communicating. As linguistic philosophers remind us, utterances are used for different ends and use is a powerful determinant of rule structures. (p. 283)

The structure of these early utterances seems to be governed by the nonlinguistic context and by the assumptions of both communication partners (Moerk, 1977). Syntactic correctness appears to have very little influence on the form of the young child's productions.

Children's utterances are produced to accompany joint action or to establish joint reference, and the form reflects these purposes. Thus, the child produces utterances within the very sequences her caregiver has employed for selective language input. There are two possible toddler generative systems: segmentation of action sequences and topic-comment. In **segmentation,** children structure their utterances to encode the changing elements of a situation. While the father throws a ball, the child might say "Throw ball," "Daddy throw," "Daddy ball," "Ball go," or "Go up." By contrast, in **topic-comment** structure, children establish the topic and then provide information on some element of that topic (Gruber, 1967). Having established the topic *doggie,* the child might elaborate to form "Doggie big," "Doggie bite," "Doggie bed," and so on. Obviously, the processes of segmentation of action and topic-comment can occur together.

The earliest one-word utterances are purely functional. Many of the first words of children perform some function, such as *bye-bye,* and *hi,* or are names of persons to request attention or of objects to request those objects. Even two-word combinations may be more pragmatically based than semantic. The semantic rules described in this chapter do not account for all two-word combinations. In addition, utterances categorized as *Recurrent + Head* ("More juice," "'Nuther cookie") fulfill a requesting function almost exclusively.

Borrowing somewhat from Chomsky, we can posit a similar model of communication (Ninio & Snow, 1988). The deep structure would include the purpose or the intent of the speaker. There are limited ways in which to express this intention. For example, if a speaker desires something, there is a restricted set of language options that will satisfy this intention. Although "May I have X, please," "X, please" or "Give me X" fulfills this intention, many other forms do not. The speaker selects the appropriate symbols and form to express this intention. The speaker must determine which elements of the deep structure or intent to encode.

Parents respond to a child's early utterances by expanding the form or extending the meaning of the utterance, by offering a reply or comment, by imitating, or by giving feedback. In addition, parents continue to provide a simplified model of adult speech (Broen, 1972; Garnica, 1977; Snow, 1972). As children begin using new structures, parents systematically modify their language model. Children continue to learn those structures that most effectively encode their intentions. In short, the child's language acquisition is embedded in, and dependent upon, the child's social context. Development reflects the child's communication needs and her knowledge and expectations of that context (Snow, 1984). Thus, the language development process is a reciprocal one involving the language-developing child and a "socializer-teacher-nurturer" who is a competent language user (Holzman, 1984). The caregiver's modeling and feedback differ with the language level of the child.

Limitations

Like the other theoretical approaches, the sociolinguistic position alone does not adequately explain language acquisition. Although the evidence of early communication is great, this evidence still does not explain how the child associates symbol and referent or how language structure is acquired. If, in fact, the child learns language to express intentions, there must be some underlying process by which intentions are linked to language form and content.

In addition, sociolinguistics, as a field of study, is so new that scholars have not had sufficient time to agree on a classification system. It is difficult to describe how a certain category of utterances developed when linguists cannot agree on the existence of that category of behavior.

Contributions

With the sociolinguistic approach, the study of child language has come almost full circle historically and theoretically. The sociolinguistic approach emphasizes language use or functions, similar to Skinner's functional analysis (Moerk, 1977). Language is employed to attain extralinguistic ends, and this attainment reinforces the linguistic behavior. The reinforcement in the sociolinguistic approach is qualitatively different, however, from that hypothesized by Skinner. Skinner envisaged a more direct type of reinforcement. In fact, the reinforcement process is more subtle and is grounded in the child–parent relationship. In most instances, the act of communication itself is reinforcing. The reinforcement may consist of closeness, caring, and needs fulfillment.

In addition to highlighting the social aspect of language learning, the sociolinguistic approach specifies the contribution of environmental linguistic input and the role of caregiver modeling and feedback. All of these contributions to children's learning are aspects of a general communication background established well before children begin to use language expressively.

The major conclusions of sociolinguistic thought are as follows (McLean and Snyder-McLean, 1978):

> Language is acquired because, and only if, the child has a reason to talk. This, in turn, assumes that he has become "socialized" . . . and has learned that he can affect his environments through . . . communication.
>
> Language is first acquired as a means of achieving already existing communicative functions . . . directly related to the . . . pragmatic aspect of later language.
>
> Linguistic structure is initially acquired through the process of decoding and comprehending incoming linguistic stimuli. . . .
>
> Language is learned in dynamic social interactions involving the child and the mature language users in his environment. The mature language users facilitate this process. . . .
>
> The child is an active participant in this transactional process and must contribute to it a set of behaviors which allow him to benefit from the adult's facilitating behaviors. (p. 78)

In short, the sociolinguistic approach minimizes language structure by distinguishing "between the meaning in the message and the meaning of the message" (Bloom & Lahey, 1978, p. 48). Most other aspects of this theoretical position stem from this distinction.

One outgrowth of this theory is the realization that speech, language, and communication differences among children are just that, differences, and not disorders or improper usage. Communication effectiveness must be judged within the context in which it occurs. The question is, Does the communication work?

Child language behavior is now being examined using the same criteria, and there is a new appreciation for individual and cultural-ethnic-regional differences.

CONCLUSION

Within the past several decades, four major theories of language acquisition have been proposed—behavioral, psycholinguistic-syntactic, psycholinguistic-semantic/cognitive, and sociolinguistic. They are compared and contrasted in Table 2.2. Of course, there are hazards inherent in any summary table. These theoretical positions are much more complex than the table indicates. It reduces the linguistic theories to their most general common bases and ignores many minor differences. Such a summary can nevertheless be helpful.

Most linguists do not adhere strictly to one theoretical construct but prefer to position themselves somewhere between. This apparent fence straddling reflects the complexity of language and language acquisition.

R. Brown (1956) has stated that initial language learning is "a process of cognitive socialization" (p. 247). The child's own meanings and uses become integrated with those of the child's environment through interaction. This integrative model assumes that language is interrelated with, but separate from,

TABLE 2.2   Comparisons and Contrasts of Four Language Development Models

	Behavioral	Psycholinguistic-syntactic	Psycholinguistic-semantic/cognitive	Sociolinguistic
Language Form	Functional units (mands, tacts)	Syntactic units (nouns, verbs)	Semantic units (agents, objects)	Functional units: speech acts (requesting, commenting)
Method of Acquisition	Selective reinforcement of correct form	Language Acquisition Device (LAD) contains universal phrase structure rules used to decipher the transformational rules of language	Universal cognitive structures help child establish nonlinguistic relationships later expressed as semantic relations	Early communication established through which child expresses intentions preverbally; language develops to express early intentions
Environmental Input	Reinforcement and extinction; parental modeling	Minimal	Cognitive relationships established through active involvement of child with environment	Communicative interaction established first; parental modeling and feedback

social and cognitive development (Vygotsky, 1962). As the child matures, there is a gradual delineation of these separate aspects of development. As McLean and Snyder-McLean (1978) concluded:

> By nature of its content, language carries within it the products of the cognitive developmental domain; by nature of its function, language carries within it the products of human social development; by nature of its form, language carries within it the complex products of all of the inputs identified . . . plus the effect of the nature and functions of the human physiological and neurological systems. (p. 43)

It is quite possible that for each child the relative contribution of each of these aspects will differ greatly. Their contributions may also differ with the developmental level of the child. Indeed, there is evidence that at certain stages of development the relationships between the linguistic, social, and cognitive domains differ.

Finally, we must face the possibility that none of the descriptive units used within the four theoretical models has any reality for children. In each case, linguists have imposed adult classification models upon child language. Children may be organizing their worlds in very nonadult ways as they play and explore, as they fantasize and create, and as they think and speak.

REFLECTIONS

1. Explain the several limitations of the behavioral model that are addressed within the psycholinguistic-syntactic model.
2. Describe how a sentence is produced using the two rule systems of the psycholinguistic-syntactic model.
3. The psycholinguistic-syntactic model also demonstrates some limitations when applied to child language. Explain this inadequacy and the way it is addressed by the psycholinguistic-semantic model.
4. Describe the main features of the government-binding theory.
5. Part of the appeal of the psycholinguistic-semantic theory is the relationship between cognition and semantics. Explain this relationship.
6. In what way does the sociolinguistic model differ from the two psycholinguistic models?
7. Can you explain the relationship between deep structure and surface structure? The benefit of a rich interpretation and its relationship to child-based semantics?

3 Child Development

CHAPTER OBJECTIVES

Language is only one aspect, although a very important and complex one, of child development. To understand language development and keep it in perspective, we should have some knowledge of the overall development of the child. In this chapter we will explore this development, with special emphasis on the development of speech. When you have completed this chapter, you should understand

- the major patterns of development. ✓
- the sources of speech production. ✓
- the major reflexes of the newborn relative to oral movement. → *including crying*
- the characteristics of babbling and vocal play. ✓
- the general behaviors of 2-, 3-, 4-, and 5-year-olds.
- the overall conclusions of several studies of speech sound development.
- the general changes that occur in the development of the school-aged child.
- the following terms:

Do these

- articulation
- babbling
- cephalocaudal
- convergent semantic production
- echolalia
- figurative language
- fully resonant nuclei (FRN)
- idioms
- jargon
- larynx
- lexicon
- metaphors
- myelination
- nasal cavity

- neonate
- oral cavity
- pharynx
- phonation
- phonetically consistent forms (PCFs)
- quasi-resonant nuclei (QRN)
- reduplicated babbling
- reflexes
- resonation
- respiration
- similes
- variegated babbling
- vocal folds

W HEN STUDYING LANGUAGE DEVELOPMENT, we can easily forget that children are also developing in many other ways. Far from being static and unchanging, children are growing and learning continually. We must understand children's growth and development to appreciate fully the behavioral changes associated with language.

In addition, students of language acquisition should remind themselves of the joy and wonder of childhood. Dry academic study can cause us to forget such youthful inquiries as the following from my daughter:

> Daddy, do you think that maybe the trees are moving and that we're standing still? Maybe we just think that we're moving because the trees are.

Language is used by all of us to describe, explain, and inquire about the world around us. For children, this world is a fascinating wonder that often is controlled by unseen forces that we adults can only imagine.

DEVELOPMENTAL PATTERNS

Development is more than a cumulative list of changes and accomplishments. Each individual's growth reveals certain patterns. Several generalizations or principles are evident:

1. Development is predictable.
2. Developmental milestones are attained at about the same age in most children.
3. Developmental opportunity is needed.
4. Children go through developmental phases or periods.
5. Individuals differ greatly.

Developmental Predictability

The developmental pattern is predictable in character. There is an orderly sequence. For example, motor development proceeds from the head down. This progression is called **cephalocaudal**. Thus, a child is able to hold his head up before he can sit unsupported. In addition, he usually crawls prior to walking. Language development also follows a predictable pattern: initially a child babbles, then says individual words, then sentences.

Developmental Milestones

In general, children attain certain skills or abilities at predictable ages. Although there is some individual variation, most nonhandicapped children reach such milestones as walking and talking at about the same age. For example, somewhere around the first birthday, a child will take his first unaided step and say his first meaningful word.

Developmental Opportunity

Although much development is the result of maturation, learning is also important. The opportunity for learning must be present in order for the child to develop. Walking will not occur on schedule without an opportunity to practice the needed prerequisite skills. A corollary to this principle is that opportunity is wasted if the child has not attained the required maturational level. A 6-month-old child does not have the intellectual and physical abilities to read, and no amount of practice can compensate for these deficits.

In general, a child practices through play, an active, pleasurable involvement with the environment. Play is a nonserious, self-contained activity motivated by sheer enjoyment (Dearden, 1967). Play is spontaneous and voluntary and has no goals beyond pleasure. Within play, a child imitates others or himself in endless repetition until a skill is perfected.

Developmental Phases or Periods

Development does not occur as a straight line. There are orderly, predictable phases in which certain areas of development are emphasized. For example, there are two phases of rapid physical growth: from prenatal development to about 6 months, and from age 10 or 12 years to about 15 or 16. As expected, nutritional needs are greatest during these periods. During other periods, the rate of growth is greatly decelerated. Within the first year of life, a child approximately triples his weight. If this rate of growth were to continue, he would weigh over 1,240,000 pounds by age 11. In fact, the typical 11-year-old weighs approximately 70 to 80 pounds. General height and weight data are presented in Table 3.1. Note the amount of change relative to the child's last height and weight. Phases of physical growth do not necessarily coincide with other phases of development, such as cognition or socialization. Each area has its own developmental cycle.

TABLE 3.1   Height and Weight Ranges of Developing Children

Age	Height	Weight
Newborn	17–21 inches	6–8 pounds
4 months	23–24 inches	12–16 pounds
8 months	26–28 inches	
12 months	28–30 inches	26–30 pounds
2 years	32–34 inches	
5 years	40–42 inches	3–5 pounds/year
5 years–puberty	3 inches/year	

Even within a given developmental area, the type of development changes as a child matures. For example, initial language development emphasizes vocabulary growth, which decelerates as syntactic growth is stressed. Physical growth of body parts also varies with the developmental level. Each part reaches maturity at its own rate, with its own growth phases; thus, the physical growth pattern is *asynchronous*. Some organs, such as the inner ear, the eyes, and the brain, reach mature size very early. Other parts of the body, such as the limbs, reach mature size only at the conclusion of puberty. This asynchronous growth is also reflected in the amount of development within different body parts. The head increases to twice its size from birth to maturity, whereas the torso increases to three times its birth size and the limbs four to five times their size. As body proportions change, so does weight distribution. The brain, which accounts for 1/8th of total body weight at birth, equals only 1/40th by maturity. The greatest gain in brain weight is within the first 2 years.

Individual Differences

Even though there are predictable stages and ages for development, the range of normality is broad. No individual child should be expected to conform to all of the averages or milestones presented. Mean ages, weights, or heights do not describe any given child but rather some fictitious "average" child, who is a combination of all children. A child who exceeds the norms may be experiencing a momentary acceleration or delay or may be proceeding at his own pace. Even a severely retarded child is a developing being; his personal schedule may be delayed beyond the normal period, but development proceeds nonetheless.

Normative data are meant as a guide. Beginning students of child development should avoid the pitfall of using this information as a diagnostic tool. Concerned parents must be cautious of normative data as well. Child–parent interactions do not need the increased anxiety of slavish adherence to some normative timetable.

Individual development depends on many factors, including genetic inheritance, nutrition, sex, intelligence, overall emotional and physical health, socioeconomic level, ethnicity, and prenatal conditions. Other conditions being equal—which they never are—a child can be expected to develop more quickly if he has good nutrition, a high IQ, good overall health, a high socioeconomic status, and good prenatal conditions. The effects of these factors vary with age, and most of these factors are interrelated.

THE DEVELOPING CHILD

The remainder of this chapter presents a general child development chronology, with emphasis on four related, but separate, developmental areas: physical, cognitive, socioemotional, and communicative growth.

Physical development refers to physical growth and motor control. Here several related hierarchies apply: cephalocaudal, proximodistal, and gross-to-fine development. Cephalocaudal, or head-to-foot, development was discussed earlier. Proximodistal development is from the center out and is related to the gross-to-fine hierarchy. We will be concerned with the proximodistal progression when we discuss the development of control of the speech mechanism. In addition, development proceeds from gross motor to fine motor control. Gross motor, or large muscle, movements are those of the head, torso, and limbs. These movements are used in walking, running, throwing, head turning, and so on. Most children have attained gross motor control by age 4 or 5. Fine motor, or small muscle, control involves the eyes, hands, fingers, and so on. Much of this control is gained during the early school years. By age 12, a child has adultlike control of the arms, wrists, and shoulders. Adultlike finger control is gained later, though a child can write, draw, and perform other fine motor behaviors before adolescence. The muscular control needed for both types of movement depends, in part, on neural or central nervous system maturation. At birth, the spinal cord is more mature than the higher centers of the brain. The senses send a signal to the spinal column, brain stem, or midbrain, and an immediate response is returned to the affected muscles. Thus reflexes predominate. As a child matures, the higher portions of the brain develop, and the child attains increased control over finer and finer muscle movement.

Cognitive development is intellectual growth. Beyond physical growth and internal development of the central nervous system, cognitive development also involves the methods a child uses to organize, store, and retrieve information for problem solving and generalization. Each child perceives the world differently and must interpret incoming stimuli in light of his past experiences. Thus, even reception of new stimuli is not a passive process but involves interpretation and organization. As a child matures, he organizes incoming stimuli in different ways. His memory also increases. Part of this change is due to increased brain weight. Other changes can be attributed to learning. By age 8, the brain is nearly mature in size but not in structure. Further development concentrates on internal growth and maturation.

Socioemotional development is closely related to the other three areas. Physical size and prowess, intellectual growth, and communication abilities all contribute to a child's perceptions of himself and others. As a child matures, he becomes less egocentric and more social. By comparison, the extreme egocentrism of the autistic child stands out. Although humans are social beings, each must learn social behaviors and the social rules and customs of his society.

Finally, communicative development is also related to the other developmental areas. The development and use of linguistic symbols depends upon attaining certain cognitive, social, and motor skills. Speech requires the physical growth of certain neuromuscular structures and motor control of their functions.

The human body is, among other things, a sound production source. As with any sound source, there must be power to move or drive the mechanism, and there must be a vibrating body. In speech, humans produce a great variety

Children follow similar but individually different patterns of growth within the several interrelated developmental areas. Speech and language use and development are related to the physical, cognitive, and socioemotional growth of the child.

of sounds, so the human body must also be capable of modifying or resonating the vibrations produced.

The source of energy is compressed air in the lungs. Adults exchange this air with air in the environment approximately 12 times each minute. This process of inhaling and exhaling air, and the resultant gas exchange in the lungs, is called **respiration**. Air expelled from the lungs passes between the **vocal folds**, located in the **larynx** (Figure 3.1). In speech, the air may vibrate the vocal folds rapidly in a process called **phonation**, resulting in a series of short puffs of air that occur so rapidly that they are perceived as a sustained, low-pitched buzz or tone. Above the level of the larynx, in the vocal tract, this tone is modified by the joint processes of **resonation** and **articulation**. The vocal tract consists of the throat, or **pharynx**; the mouth, or **oral cavity**; and the **nasal cavity**. By varying the shape of the vocal tract, the speaker changes the resonating characteristics of the laryngeal tone. The resulting acoustic signals are perceived as speech sounds.

The following sections examine the different stages of a child's growth, with emphasis on the four types of development—physical, cognitive, socioemotional, and communicative—and the relationships among them.

FIGURE 3.1   The Speech Mechanism

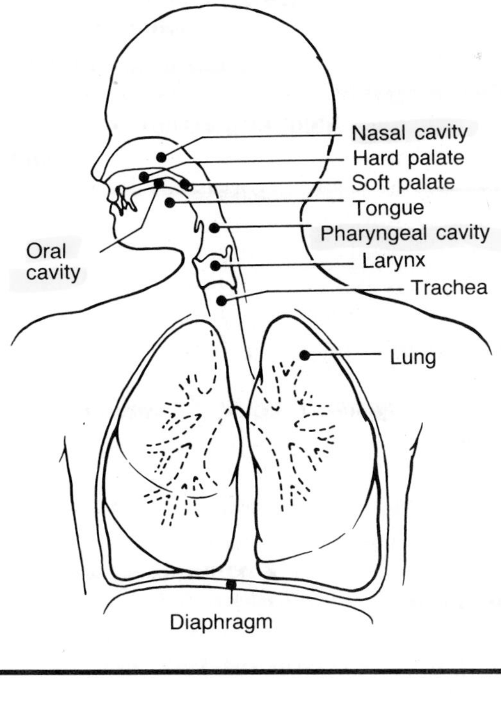

The New Kid in Town: Age Birth–1 Month

The newborn, or **neonate**, is hardly the "thing of beauty" that most people expect. Most neonates are very different from the plump, active, gregarious infants seen a few months later. Usually the skin is red and wrinkled and covered with a white, waxy material called *vernix*. This covering protects the newborn's skin and helps him slip through the birth canal. This passage may have left the newborn's face bluish and puffy, with his ears pressed against the sides of his head. Frequently the top of the head is swollen and misshapen from the pressure of passage. The head is a third to a quarter of the total body length, as opposed to an eighth for adults, and makes the neonate appear top-heavy and awkward. In fact, the area above his eyes is much greater in relation to the total head size than the proportions found in adults. His head may be bald or covered by hair that may fall out later. His torso is small in comparison to his head, and the limbs are even more so. The newborn has narrow shoulders and a bulky middle, and a fine matte of hair called *lanugo* may cover his entire body.

Soon after birth, the newborn falls into a deep sleep of 14 to 18 hours to conserve energy for stabilizing such body functions as the rates of circulation and respiration and the process of digestion. At birth he is generally unable to maintain homeostasis, a relatively stable condition of temperature, functioning, and chemical composition. In general, he breathes twice as fast as an adult, and his heart beats at 120 times per minute versus 70 for an adult. Frequently he is unable to digest milk for a few days, so his fatty reserves must sustain him.

The newborn is unable to control motor behavior smoothly and voluntarily. Instead, his behaviors consist of twitches, jerks, and random movements, most of which involve automatic, involuntary motor patterns called **reflexes**. There are two general types of reflexes, mass activity and specific activity. Mass activity occurs when the whole body responds to stimulation of one part, such as to temperature, light, and sound changes. Specific activity involves stimulation and response within a specific muscle group or portion of the body. The primary reflexes of the newborn are listed in Table 3.2. "Babies' reflex actions allow them to react to things in their world as they're learning to control their bodies themselves" (Braga & Braga, 1975, p. 39). In addition, reflexes help to ensure survival by protecting vital systems. For example, the gag reflex protects the lungs from inhalation of ingested fluids. Even smiling is reflexive in the newborn, occurring when the cheek or lips are touched (Tanternannova, 1973). Although some reflexes, such as gagging, coughing, yawning, and sneezing, remain for life, most disappear or are modified by 6 months of age. This disappearance is related to the rapid rate of brain growth and to myelination. The rate of brain growth is greatest immediately following birth; in fact, no other body system develops as rapidly. **Myelination** is the development of a protective myelin sheath or sleeve around the cranial nerves. When myelination is complete, the organism has the capacity for full neural functioning.

The phasic bite and the rooting reflex are present at birth but disappear by 3 months of age. The phasic bite reflex is a bite-release action that occurs when the

TABLE 3.2   Reflexes of the Newborn

Reflex Name	Stimulation	Response
Babinski	Stroking side of foot from heel to toe	Big toe lifts and other toes spread out
Babkin	Applying pressure on both palms while child is lying on back	Eyes close, mouth opens, and head turns toward the midline
Biceps	Tapping tendon of bicep	Short contraction of the bicep
Blink	Flashing light	Both eyelids close
Doll's eye	Turning head slowly with hand	Eyes stay fixed instead of moving with head
Galant	Stroking back to one side of spine	Trunk arches toward side on which stroked
Knee jerk or patellar tendon	Tapping on tendon below patella or knee cap	Kick or quick extension of lower leg
Moro	Making a sudden loud noise or jarring; dropping head a few inches; or dropping baby a few inches	Arms extend and then come together as hands open and then clench; spine and legs extend
Palmar or automatic hand grasp	Pressing infant's palm	Fingers grasp object
Perez	Stroking baby's spine from tail toward head	Cry and head extension
Phasic bite	Touching or rubbing the gums	Bite-release mouth pattern
Plantor or toe grasp	Applying pressure to balls of feet	Toes flex
Rooting	Stroking cheek at corner of mouth	Head turns toward side being stroked; mouth begins sucking movements
Stepping	Holding infant supported with feet touching level surface; moving infant forward	Rhythmic stepping movements
Sucking	Inserting finger or nipple into mouth	Rhythmic sucking
Withdrawal	Pricking sole of foot with pin	Knee and foot flex

newborn's gums receive tactile stimulation. The rooting reflex results from tactile stimulation of the cheek near the mouth. In response, the newborn's lips, tongue, and jaw all move toward the area of stimulation. This reflex is often seen during nursing.

The reflex of most interest for speech development is the rhythmic suck-swallow pattern, which is first established at 6 months postconception, 3 months before birth. Like other reflexes, sucking is a subcortical behavior involving the midbrain and brain stem. At birth, sucking is primarily accomplished by up-and-down jaw action. Within a few weeks, the newborn develops more lateral movement. Back-and-forth jaw movement appears at about 1 month. In order to suck, the neonate uncouples, or seals off, the nasal cavity by raising the velum, or soft palate; he can then create a vacuum in the mouth, or oral cavity, by lowering his mandible, thus increasing the volume of the space. To swallow, the neonate opens his mouth slightly and protrudes and then retracts his tongue. Although this action is greatly reduced by 3 months of age, it is not until around 3 years of age that independent swallowing appears. To complete a swallow, the neonate must also close, or abduct, his vocal folds to protect the lungs.

The newborn is not totally helpless, however, but instead possesses many skills (Table 3.3). Shortly after birth he is able to breathe on his own and ingest food, coordinating the two to ensure that the food passes down the appropriate tube. In addition, the newborn is able to process ingested fluids, usually milk, and to eliminate waste. He can turn his head from side to side and signal distress by crying.

Newborns produce predominantly reflexive sounds, such as fussing and crying, and vegetative sounds, such as burping and swallowing. Reflexive sounds

TABLE 3.3   The Newborn's Behaviors

Motor	Cognition	Socialization	Communication
Makes reflexive movements of head and limbs	Sees best at 7½ inches; is sensitive to brightness and color; can follow a moving object; visually prefers movement, sharp contours, and contrasts	Recognizes nipple	Cries
Makes nonspecific, random, nonreflexive movements,		Is comforted by sound of human voice	Makes noncrying speechlike sounds, usually when feeding
Exhibits mass response to sudden changes		Sleeps about 70% of the day	
Moves head side to side when on back	Is sensitive to volume, pitch, and duration of sound (slight hearing loss until middle ear clear); discriminates sound sources; prefers hearing human voice	Smiles reflexively	
Cannot raise head when on stomach			
Eyes frequently do not converge	Is sensitive to temperature changes		
	Discriminates smells and tastes		
	Screens out stimuli		
	Is alert less than 5% of the day		

are primarily produced on exhalation and consist of relatively lengthy voiced sounds of a vowellike nature (Stark, 1986). In contrast, vegetative sounds, associated with activity and management of nutrients, are produced equally on inhalation and exhalation, voiced or voiceless, consonant- and vowellike, and of brief duration.

Some vegetative sounds, such as coughing, belching, and sneezing, which persist into adulthood, are defenses against penetration by substances that might choke the infant. Other sounds, such as gulping and clicking, result from unstable positioning of the vocal mechanism and from adaptations to oral reflexes and to swallowing.

Infant crying has been the subject of much study because of its early communication value. "Crying is one of the first ways in which the infant is able to communicate with the world at large" (Ostwald & Peltzman, 1974, p. 85). Initially the newborn cries on both inhalation and exhalation, but there are many individual variations. The expiration phase of breathing gradually increases with crying (Langlois & Baken, 1976). The relative amount of crying also varies with the time of day. Crying is most frequent before feeding and bed. Although it has been claimed that a newborn's cries are reflexive and undifferentiated, four basic cries have been identified (Wasz-Hockert, Lind, Vuorenkoski, Partanen, & Valanne, 1968; Wolff, 1969). The first cry heard, of course, is the birth cry, consisting of two gasps followed by a wail that lasts for 1 second, with a flat, falling tone. Later, three cries can be differentiated: the basic or hunger cry, the pain cry, and the temper cry. The basic or hunger cry consists of a rhythmic pattern of loud crying, silence, whistling inhalation, and rest. During the rest, the infant may emit the sucking response. The pain cry, a loud, shrill cry, consists of one long cry followed by a long breath-holding silence and a series of short whimpers. Frequently, this cry is accompanied by tense facial muscles, frowns, and clenched fists. Finally, the anger cry is an exasperated sound because of the greater volume of air expended. By the end of the first month, the mother or the primary caregiver can usually ascertain the reason for the cry by its sound pattern. Crying helps the child become accustomed to air flow across his vocal folds and to modified breathing patterns. Since speech sounds originate at the level of the larynx, this early stimulation is important. The modified breathing will progress to the lengthened exhalations of speech.

Usually other, noncrying sounds accompany feeding or are produced in response to smiling or talking by the mother. These noncrying vowellike sounds with brief consonantal elements have been characterized as **quasi-resonant nuclei (QRN)**. QRN are "vocalizations which include normal phonation, but which possess no consonants and lack full vocalic resonance of vowels" (Oller, 1978, p. 534). In other words, the sounds contain phonation, or vibration at the larynx, but the child does not have sufficient control of the vocal mechanism to produce or resonate consonants or full vowels. Resonation, you will recall, is a modification of the vibratory pattern of the laryngeal tone through changes in the size and configuration of the vocal tract, which consists of the nasal cavity; the oral cavity, or mouth; and the pharynx, or throat. QRN are probably the result of opening the mouth less than an adult would when resonating a sound. Considerable air is emitted via the nasal cavity, and the resultant sounds range from partial nasal consonants to a nasalized high-to-mid vowel. Initially, production of these sounds is caused accidentally by chance movements of the vocal folds. QRN tend to be individual sounds. Later these sounds become sound sequences. The amounts of time spent in crying and cooing are inversely related: as vocal behaviors increase, crying decreases.

The vocal tract of the neonate resembles those of nonhuman primates more closely than that of an adult human (Figure 3.2). Thus, the noncrying sounds tend to be nasalized because of the relative height of the larynx and the close proximity of the larynx and the nasopharynx (Kent, 1981). During crying, the lower jaw and tongue are dropped and the soft palate and pharyngeal wall move rearward, resulting in the vowellike quality of distress sounds. At other times, the tongue is in close proximity to or touching the soft palate. Thus, many of the comfort sounds have a nasal consonantlike character (Stark & Nathanson, 1974).

The newborn also has perceptual skills of some magnitude, especially in sight and hearing. Nearsighted at birth, he can best see things about 7 ½ inches

FIGURE 3.2   Comparison of the Oral Structures of the Infant and Adult
In part, the differences in the sounds of infants and adults can be explained by the physical differences of the two. In this schematic, the infant has been enlarged to the approximate size of an adult.

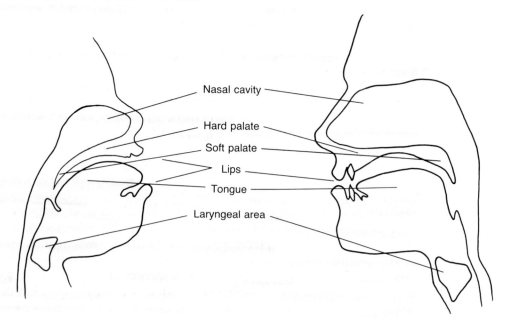

away (Haynes, White, & Held, 1965). Still, he is sensitive to both brightness and color, and he will close his eyes to a very intense light. Although he can follow a moving object visually from side to side, his eyes don't always converge on the object. Generally, convergence is confined to nonmoving objects.

Short-term visual memory is present in the newborn but is limited to recognition when the object reappears within 2 ½ seconds. Within limits, the newborn learns to distinguish some people and objects. Newborns tend to rely on patterns for recognition, with special emphasis on high-contrast areas (Appleton, Clifton, & Goldberg, 1975). For example, newborns concentrate on such features as the hairline when viewing the face. Concentration on high-contrast areas is an effective visual strategy when full field focus is unavailable. It is not until about 4 months of age, when he gains full field vision and better eye control, that the infant prefers the complexity of a whole object (Appleton et al., 1975). Prior to this age, the infant prefers to concentrate on particular parts or "attractive elements" (Salapatek & Kessen, 1966).

At birth the newborn scans the environment visually during only about 5% of his waking hours. This amount increases to 35% by the 10th week (White, 1971). The newborn becomes "stuck" on any visually interesting object that comes to view (Bruner, 1969). Not until about 4 or 5 months does the infant gain sufficient ocular control to move smoothly from object to object, thus gaining control over attending.

In general, the newborn attends to objects of interest and has definite preferences. He prefers objects that move, have sharp contours, or have contrasts of light and dark (Kagan, 1972). These preferences change with visual abilities. According to Haith (1976), the infant is attracted by visual stimuli that can activate his current level of neural activity. For example, the 2-month-old infant has certain short-term mental images, or schema, for common objects in his environment. He will attend to objects that differ slightly from the mental image he already has (Kagan, 1972).

In addition to visual skills, the newborn possesses auditory abilities. The middle and inner ears reach their adult size at 20 weeks of fetal development and, therefore, are ready to function at birth. The auditory cortex is not mature, however, and the middle ear is filled with fluid. The immaturity of the cortex and the lack of internal coordination of the brain's hemispheres make it difficult for the newborn to integrate sounds (Dreyfus-Brisac, 1966). In addition, the middle ear is not as sensitive to sound as it will be within 2 weeks after birth, when the fluid is absorbed. Despite these limitations, the newborn can distinguish loudness or intensity and duration of sound (Hirschman & Katkin, 1974). The newborn blinks, jerks, draws in a breath, and increases his heart and respiration rates in response to sounds. Within the first 4 days, the infant can discriminate between different sounds (Morse, 1979).

Infant and adult perceptual skills with phonetic contrasts are very similar. The only exception is the distinction between /f/ and the voiceless th (/θ/), which is difficult for children until about 5 years of age. Since infant perception studies use a constant phonetic context in which contrasted sounds always appear with the same adjacent sounds, as in *pet* and *bet*, it is not clear whether newborns are able to identify the same phoneme in different phonetic environments, as in *pet* and *poor*.

It must be stressed that discrimination of speech sounds is not the same as linguistic perception (Ferguson, 1978; Ingram, 1976). Speech sound discrimination does not involve sound–meaning relationships. The infant has only limited memory. Young infants cannot make sound discriminations if there is a 30-second delay between sounds (Morse, 1979). In order to develop spoken language, the child must be able to store sounds, to use this information for later comparison and identification, and to relate these sounds to meaning.

The newborn has auditory as well as visual preferences. Above all, he seems to prefer the sound of the human voice. In general, a voice has a quieting effect on the newborn.

Although vision and audition will be very important for later communication development, they are not the only sensory abilities of the newborn. He can sense body temperature changes and respond accordingly. Within 55 hours of birth, he can differentiate smells. Finally, newborns can discriminate different tastes and prefer sweet tastes to sour ones (Desor, Maller, & Andrews, 1975).

At birth, the child is not the active, outgoing infant we will see later. He already has the abilities, however, to respond to the world. In the next few months he will begin to explore the physical and social worlds around him.

The Examiner: Age 1–6 Months

During the first 6 months of life (Table 3.4, pp. 84–85), the child gains voluntary muscle control rapidly and begins to examine objects, people, and events that occur close at hand. Increased motor abilities enable the infant to sit, thus freeing his hands for object appraisal. Vision and reach become coordinated, and the infant is able to reach and grasp. Social behaviors also increase as the child gains the ability to recognize and respond to familiar faces and situations.

The big events of the first 6 months are those that accompany the downward progression of large muscle control and the further maturation of the brain. The infant goes from reflexive and random behaviors to rolling and creeping. Better control accompanies firmer muscles and bones and the building of new neural connectors. Initially, the infant gains control of his large head, lifting and then being able to hold it steady. This positioning provides a new perspective, albeit prone, from which to examine the environment. At about the same time, approximately 3 months of age, the infant gains full focus, which enables him to appreciate all the new visual stimuli available. Head and neck control is followed by trunk control and sitting. In the upright position, the infant's hands are free to examine small objects placed in front of him. He is able to grasp voluntarily at 2 months of age but cannot control his reach. Increasing arm control enables the infant to hit, then reach for, and finally grasp objects. It is not unexpected, then, that toy or object play should begin shortly after some measure of hand control is achieved. Grasping is still somewhat primitive, however, with the fingers generally undifferentiated, as in a mitten. Most objects are brought to the mouth, a very sensitive and highly developed area, for tactile examination and identification. As early as 2 months, the infant develops distinct nutritive and nonnutritive sucking behaviors. By 4 months of age, the infant engages in up to 4 hours per day of nonnutritive sucking of fingers and objects and of examining his face and mouth.

Neuromuscular control moves forward from the back of the oral cavity, reflecting the progression of myelination in the primary motor cortex (Salus & Salus, 1974; Whitaker, 1973) and the proximodistal hierarchy. With greater control of the tongue, the infant exhibits tongue bowling and strong tongue projection. If you have ever attempted to spoon-feed a 4- to 6-month-old, you will recall the difficulty of inserting the spoon because the infant protrudes the tongue. Food constantly reappears on the infant's lips and chin. In sucking, the infant is also able to use the intrinsic muscles of the tongue rather than a whole-jaw movement.

The infant's bite is more volitional, and he does not rely on tactile stimulation before moving his mouth. He can place his lips around a spoon and use them to ingest the contents.

Toward the end of the first half year, large muscle control has progressed so that the infant can crouch on his hands and knees and can roll over and creep, two early forms of locomotion. When creeping, the infant keeps his stomach on the floor while pushing with his feet and steering with his outstretched arms. Since the muscles for forward movement are not as strong as those for backward movement, the infant often goes in reverse. Small muscle development enables the child to hold his own bottle and to feed himself with his hands, though most of the food is smeared across his face.

Reaching and object examination become increasingly directed by vision, which now can focus on the hands at different distances. Even so, reaching seems to require his total concentration.

The increased visual abilities used for directing reach also aid the infant's social development. As early as the first month, the infant becomes excited when he sees objects and people. Visual recognition is not a factor, however, because the infant does not respond differentially. By the second month, periods of responsiveness expand to up to 20 minutes. They are accompanied by arching, turning, twisting, and kicking. Certain people become associated with particular behaviors. For example, the infant's mother becomes associated with feeding, and the infant will begin a sucking response when he sees her. This recognition of familiar people, plus the infant's rapid habituation to, or boredom with, other visual stimuli, signify an increase in visual memory. By 3 months of age, the infant is able to discriminate different people visually and to respond accordingly. This change is reflected in stages of smile development (T. Bower, 1977; Sroufe & Waters, 1976; Trevarthen, 1979). At the end of the first month the infant's smile becomes less automatic, but it is still unselective. The infant will respond to both people and objects with a whole body movement that includes limb and trunk activation and vocalizations. During the third month, as the child becomes more

TABLE 3.4   The Examiner: 1–6 Months

Age (Months)	Motor	Cognition	Socialization	Communication
1	Moves limbs reflexively Lifts head while on stomach but cannot support head while body held upright Has coordinated side-to-side eye movement; stares but does not reach	Cries from distress Prefers visual patterns Remembers an object that reappears within 2½ seconds	Establishes eye contact with mother Quiets when held; adjusts body to person holding Follows own sleep schedule Smiles spontaneously	Responds to human voice, which usually has quieting effect Cries for assistance Makes pleasure sounds, quasi-resonant nuclei
2	Moves arms in circle smoothly; swipes at objects Holds head up briefly while on stomach; raises head while sitting supported but head bobs	Visually prefers face to objects, regards own hands, and follows in a circle Repeats own actions Excites in anticipation of objects	Excites when sees people; has unselective social smile Quiets self with sucking Prefers touch and oral stimulation to social stimulation Sleeps on schedule closer to rest of household	Distinguishes different (speech) sounds Makes more guttural or "throaty" gooing
3	Controls body voluntarily Lifts head and chest while prone; holds head up with minimum bobbing while sitting supported Can swallow voluntarily Reaches and grasps; keeps hands open frequently	Attains full focus; can glance smoothly between objects Visually searches for sounds Begins exploratory play; explores own body	Exhibits gregarious behavior Visually discriminates different people and things; recognizes mother Has selective social smile Sleeps most of the night	Coos single syllable (consonant-vowel) Turns head when hears a voice Responds vocally to speech of others Makes predominately vowel sounds

TABLE 3.4 *continued*

Age (Months)	Motor	Cognition	Socialization	Communication
4	Can turn head in all directions whether body is prone or seated Still has inaccurate reach Occasionally opposes thumb and fingers, as a mitten; grasps small objects put in hand; brings objects to mouth	Localizes to sound Stares at place from which object is dropped Remembers visually for 5–7 seconds	Pays selective attention to faces: Looks longer at joyful versus angry face; discriminates different faces Looks in direction of person leaving room Smiles at notice of another baby Anticipates being lifted; laughs when played with	Babbles strings of consonants Varies pitch Imitates tones Smiles at person speaking to him
5	Sits supported for up to half an hour Rolls from stomach to back Can be easily pulled to stand Has partial thumb apposition; swaps objects from hand to hand	Begins to play Visually follows a vanishing object; recognizes familiar objects; anticipates whole object after seeing a part; is capable of 3-hour visual memory Explores objects by mouthing and touching Remembers own actions in immediate past	Reacts differently to smiling and scolding Discriminates parents and siblings from others Imitates some movements of others Frolics when played with	Vocalizes to toys Discriminates angry and friendly voices Experiments with sounds Imitates some sounds Responds to name Smiles and vocalizes to image in mirror
6	Turns head freely Sits straight when slightly supported or in chair Balances well Reaches with one arm, grasps, and brings to mouth Holds bottle Turns and twists in all directions Creeps	Looks and reaches smoothly and quickly Inspects objects Reaches to grab dropped objects	Differentiates social responses Prefers people games, such as "peek-a-boo" Feeds self finger food Explores face of person holding him	Varies volume, pitch, and rate Vocalizes pleasure and displeasure: squeals with excitement, intones displeasure

responsive to people, he smiles less at objects. In turn, his smile becomes more social and physically broader, with a crinkling around the eyes. This responsiveness is reflected in the infant's selective attention at 4 months of age to specific individuals and to joyful expressions longer than to angry ones (LaBarbera, Izard, Vietze, & Parisi, 1976). Although the infant learns to suck and look simultaneously by 4 months of age, often he will ignore feeding in order to concentrate on "people watching." Such visual attending also reflects increased visual memory, which, by 5 months of age, has expanded to 3 hours, unless there are competing visual stimuli (Fagan, 1973). By 6 months the infant is very social. He smiles and vocalizes, examines faces visually and tactilely, and responds differentially. He cries or draws back from unfamiliar faces.

Visual responsiveness and memory are also reflected in increased communication skills. The 2-month-old will search visually for his mother's voice but will avert his gaze from the direction of strange voices. Although the 2-month-old infant can discriminate speech sounds, he will not be able to produce these different sounds willfully for some time (Eimas, Siqueland, Jusczyk, & Vigorito, 1971). For example, the 2-month-old infant can discriminate between /p/, which is made at the lips, and /g/, which is produced in the throat, but he cannot discriminate between /p/ and /b/, both made at the lips.

By 2 months of age, the infant has developed oral muscle control to stop and start movement definitively, though tactile stimulation is still needed. This stage is characterized by laughter and nondistress "gooing" (Laufer & Morii, 1977; Stark, 1978). Oller (1978) described gooing as "vocalizations in which QRN occur in the same breath group with a velar to uvular closure or near closure" (p. 534). Thus, the infant produces back consonant and middle and back vowel sounds with incomplete resonance. The consonant sounds consist of velar or soft palate fricatives similar to /s/ and incomplete velar plosives similar to /k/ and /g/.

The infant does control the timing of his vocalizations, and it is this timing that demonstrates his responsiveness. By 3 months of age, he vocalizes in response to the speech of others. An infant is most responsive if his caregivers respond to him. As the infant's repertoire of responses expands, the amount of his crying and vegetative sounds decreases markedly. By 16 weeks, sustained laughter, characterized by a rapid alternation of voiced and voiceless sounds, emerges.

At 5 months an infant is able to imitate a few general sounds, usually vowels, immediately following a vocal model. He is even better at imitating tone and pitch signals. Most of the infant's imitative and nonimitative vocalizations are single-syllable units of consonant-vowel or vowel-consonant construction. These sound units and the early strings of sounds that begin at 4 months are called **babbling**. Vocalizing for attention, the infant will vary the volume, pitch, and rate of babbling. He will stop to listen to other sounds, especially to his mother's voice.

With maturity, longer sequences and prolonged individual sounds evolve. Production is characterized by high and low pitches and glides between the two, growling and gutteral sounds, some friction sounds—produced by passing air through a narrow constriction—nasal /m/ and /n/, and a greater variety of vowels

(Stark, 1986). The child produces increasingly more c̲...
these features and conversational units in which the v̲...
highly variable and often very long (Oller, 1976).

The infant is capable of fully resonating the laryngeal tone...
resonant nuclei (FRN), vowellike sounds similar to /a/ (Oller, 197...
abilities become more mature in the forward portion of the mou...
months labial or lip sounds predominate. The resultant sounds may b...
but more often they are vibratory, such as the "raspberries" or "Bronx...
Gutteral sounds, such as growling, tend to disappear when the range of so...
expands to labials (Nakazima, 1962). Increase in the size of the oral cavity a...
further development of discrimination to touch, pressure, and movement in the...
tongue tip and lips result in the increased variety of sounds heard (Bosma, 1975).

Babbling is random sound play of an almost infinite variety. Even the deaf
infant babbles, which indicates the minimal effect of environmental auditory
input upon babbling. Hearing loss does, however, affect the repertoire of consonants in the prespeech vocalizations of infants (Stoel-Gammon, 1988). In general,
hearing-impaired infants have a smaller repertoire than hearing infants, and a
greater proportion of labial sounds and prolongable consonants such as nasals
(/m, n, ŋ/), glides (/w, j/), and fricatives (i.e., /f, v, s, z/).

During the babbling period, the infant experiments with sound production.
Often the sounds he produces do not appear in, or differ in some way from, those
of his native language. Ferguson (1978) has offered three explanations for this
difference. First, the vocal tract of the infant differs in size and configuration from
that of the adult. Therefore, laryngeal tones and subsequent resonated frequencies will differ. Second, the infant has not gained basic motor control for programming and sequencing the entire speech mechanism. Third, the infant has
not acquired the phonological patterns of the surrounding language, such as
sequencing and distribution of sounds. Despite these limitations, infants tend to
produce sounds from the surrounding language more frequently than other
speech sounds (Cruttenden, 1970; Rees, 1972).

Linguists have argued for years about the relationship between babbling
and later speech. One group, represented by the views of Jakobson, has claimed
that babbling has little, if any, effect on phonological development. There is a
sharp break, or discontinuity, they contend, between the infant's random vocalizations and his later, more limited (albeit more structured) speech production.
The contrasting view maintains that babbling sounds are gradually shaped toward the surrounding language. Children use adults as speech models. Both
hypotheses have limitations.

Although there appears to be little connection between the order of babbled
sounds and the later order of correct phoneme production, this fact should not
obscure other relationships. The frequency of consonant appearance in babbling
seems to be reflected in the order of speech sound acquisition (Menyuk, 1977).
The more frequent sounds contain features that are produced correctly at an
earlier age than those contained in less frequent sounds. To assume discontinuity is also to ignore the direction of babbling development. With age, the child's

ıdult speech, especially in syllable structure and ıplications of later babbling often continue as the ...erguson & Garnica, 1975; Oller, Wieman, Doyle, & ...e, as Halliday (1975b) contended, that "the lan- ...age owes nothing at all to the adult language that ...9).

...assumes that the infant's babbling is shaped ...ent. Yet there is very little evidence that parents ...s that are used in their language. Even if parents ...lts might be unforeseen. Although social and ...the frequency or amount of babbling (Rhein- ...& Palmer, 1968), reinforcement used to modify ...le effect except to increase the overall amount ...g (Dodd, 1972; Nakazima, 1962). Furthermore, some qualities, such as the rate and pattern of development, depend upon maturational factors (J. de Villiers & P. de Villiers, 1979). More research is needed before we can definitively state the relationship between babbling and speech production.

Within 6 months the infant is able to examine with his hands and vision and to remember familiar persons and objects. He is very social and will respond to smiles and vocalizations. Within limits, he can make his wants known and influence his environment.

The Experimenter: Age 7–12 Months

The second 6 months of life are filled with new methods of locomotion and new abilities (Table 3.5, pp. 90–91). In addition, the infant experiments with speech and problem solving. Faced with a desired item, he will use a trial-and-error approach to achieve it. By 12 months of age, the infant begins to walk, to speak, and to use tools.

As the infant demonstrates increasing versatility in oral movements, his speech progresses to repetitive syllable production and takes on more of the qualities of the surrounding language.

By approximately 6 months of age, the infant is able to pout and draw his lips in without moving his jaw. Within 2 more months he can keep his lips closed while chewing and swallowing semiliquids. At the same time, his chewing changes from vertical to a more rotary pattern, reflecting changes in tongue movement control. At 8 months the extension-retraction pattern of the tongue changes gradually to a lateral, or sideways, movement. As a result, food is moved to the side for better mastication. In addition, the tongue can remain elevated, independent of jaw movement. By 11 months the infant has the neuromuscular control to elevate his tongue tip and to bite soft solid foods with some control. He can draw his lips and cheeks in during chewing and close his lips when swallowing liquids.

The downward bodily progression of motor skills continues during the second 6 months. The infant learns to sit unaided and to creep forward and back, then crawl, and finally walk. During the seventh month the infant sits, creeps, and begins experimenting with standing. Within a month, standing has improved greatly but descent to the floor still needs practice. By 10 months the infant is able to push to a stand from a crawl and sit on the floor again. In the meantime, crawling speed and style improve. Two months later, the infant may walk unsupported for a few steps but still crawl when in a hurry. While walking, the infant extends his arms for balance. He stops by falling or grabbing nearby furniture or people. Both the unaided sitting and the crawling and walking expand the infant's range of exploration.

While sitting, the infant is free to examine and manipulate objects with his hands and to experiment with uses. His index finger probes incessantly. He experiments with sounds and reactions. For example, he may clear his highchair tray of all food and utensils while his horrified caregiver looks on. In addition, he is adept at emptying drawers and rearranging furniture. At 8 months the infant begins to experiment with perspective by shaking his head from side to side and looking upside down, thus noting the constancy of object shapes. The knowledge of object functions and characteristics gained from such experiments is important for early concept and definition development.

The infant also acquires the ability to search physically for a missing object. This skill depends on physical and cognitive development. In order to search, the infant must be able to remember the object while searching and be able to reach for it. During the second 6 months of life, searching progresses from a short glance for a missing object to a brief physical search. By his first birthday, the infant can reach while looking away. Physical search problem solving leads to the early trial-and-error methodology that begins to develop at 10 months. At this age, the trial-and-error approach is used only with physical problems. For example, the infant must determine, through experimentation, the best method for attaining a toy that is on the floor on the other side of the coffee table. Only a physical attempt can result in success or nonsuccess. The infant is not capable of solving the problem through reasoning alone.

Toward the end of the second 6 months of life, the infant is also capable of solving problems by imitation, first direct and then indirect, or deferred. Imitation is an important learning strategy and requires a degree of representational thought. The infant develops the ability to remember a behavior in order to reproduce it. In addition, imitation is important for social interaction. At about 9 months, the infant becomes an active game player and performer. He loves to play peekaboo and patty-cake, anticipating the end. Later he anticipates other routines and experiments with attempts to influence the outcome. He anticipates leaving and waves bye-bye, anticipates his mother's or father's arrival, and shows excitement. The infant also gains some measure of independence with self-help, such as feeding and dressing, but he becomes very attached to his mother, usually the primary caregiver.

The infant's increasing social and representational behavior is reflected most clearly in his communication. At about 6 or 7 months, his babbling begins to change. He enters a brief stage of **reduplicated babbling**. Even though he still produces single-syllable sounds, he begins to experiment with long strings of consonant-vowel syllable repetitions or self-imitations, such as "ma-ma-ma-ma-ma." Development of glottal, then velar and uvular sounds, followed by true vowel

TABLE 3.5   The Experimenter: 7–12 Months

Age (Months)	Motor	Cognition	Socialization	Communication
7	Holds without palm; transfers object from hand to hand Cuts first tooth; has better chewing and jaw control; can eat some strained solids Pushes up on hands and knees; rocks	Visually searches briefly for toy that disappears Imitates a physical act if in repertoire	Resists Teases (beginning of humor)	Plays vocally Produces several sounds in one breath Listens to vocalization of others
8	Holds own bottle Uses thumb-finger apposition Manipulates objects to explore Pulls up to stand but needs help to get down Crawls	Can store color and form separately; recognizes object dimensions Prefers novel and relatively complex toys Explores shape, weight, texture, function, and properties (example: in/out)	Acts positively toward peers Is clearly attached to mother Shouts for attention	Listens selectively Recognizes some words Repeats emphasized syllable Imitates gestures and tonal quality of adult speech; echolalia
9	Stands alone briefly; gets down alone; cruises Sits unsupported; gets into and out of sitting position alone Explores with index finger Removes and replaces bottle	Recognizes object dimensions Uncovers object if observes act of hiding first Anticipates outcome of events and return of persons	Explores other babies "Performs" for family Imitates play Plays action games	Produces distinct intonational patterns Imitates coughs, hisses, tongue clicks, raspberries, etc. Uses social gestures Uses jargon

sounds and consonant-vowel babbling, has been found in infants from language environments other than English, such as Swedish (Landberg & Lundberg, 1989).

Hearing ability appears to be very important in this imitative play, for at this point the deaf child's vocalizations begin to decrease. In addition, the range of

TABLE 3.5 *continued*

Age (Months)	Motor	Cognition	Socialization	Communication
10	Crawls with bilateral leg-arm opposition Holds and drinks from cup Sits from a standing position	Points to body parts Attains a goal with trial-and-error approach Searches for hidden object but usually in a familiar place	Displays moods Helps dress and feed self	Imitates adult speech if sounds in repertoire Obeys some commands
11	Stands alone; gets up from all-fours position by pushing up Climbs up stairs Feeds self with spoon	Imitates increasingly Associates properties with objects	Seeks approval Anticipates mother's goal and tries to change it by protest or "persuasion"	Imitates inflections, rhythms, facial expressions, etc.
12	Stands alone; pushes to stand from squat Climbs up and down stairs Has complete thumb apposition; uses spoon, cup, and crayon; releases objects willfully Takes first steps with support	Can reach while looking away Uses common objects appropriately Searches in location where an object was last seen Imitates an absent model	Expresses people preferences Expresses many different emotions	Recognizes own name Follows simple motor instructions, especially if accompanied by a visual cue ("Bye-bye"); reacts to "no" intonation Speaks one or more words Practices words he knows and inflection; mixes words and jargon

consonants within babbling decreases for the deaf child, especially after 8 months (Stoel-Gammon & Otomo, 1986). Whereas the hearing child increasingly produces true consonants, the deaf child is limited increasingly to glottal stop (/h/) and glide (/l/, /r/) sequences (Oller, Eilers, Bull, & Carney, 1985). Although the deaf child may continue to babble until school age, without intervention the repertoire probably will not expand beyond that of the hearing infant (Locke, 1983).

Other differences in speech-sound production may appear earlier (Maskarinec, Cairns, Butterfield, & Weamer, 1981). Some hearing infants begin to produce more speechlike sounds as early as 6 weeks of age. Deaf children, however, do not show the same trend. The hearing child practices his speech sounds for long periods each day, seeming to enjoy his new ability. If his mother responds to his sounds, he is likely to repeat them. He may repeat "ma-ma" at his mother's urging, but he doesn't realize that this sound stands for or represents *mother*. The infant learns very quickly, however, that this behavior can be used to gain attention.

Initially, sound production passes through a period of marginal babbling before the infant achieves truly reduplicated babbling. Oller (1978) characterized marginal babbling as "sequences of fully resonant vowels alternating with closures of the vocal tract" (p. 535). At first the child's consonantal repertoire is restricted to labial and alveolar plosives such as /p/, /b/, /t/, and /d/; nasals; and the glide /j/ (Stark, 1979). (See Appendix A for an explanation of speech sound symbols and their classification.) The phonemes are not fully formed or matured and are produced slowly. In contrast, the resonant quality and timing of reduplicated babbling more closely approximate mature speech. Reduplicated babbling is characterized by consonant-vowel syllable repetitions in which the vowel duration is very brief. Initially, reduplicated babbling is self-stimulatory in nature and is not used when communicating with adults. Gradually, the child uses reduplicated babbling more in environmental contexts.

The 6-month-old has some limited knowledge of speech (Griffiths, 1986). First, speech predicts the presence of humans. Second, the effects of speech on others vary along a predictable continuum. Finally, speech can fill a turn in conversational interactions. Beginning from this base, the child must discover what speech means.

Infants attend auditorily to sound patterns and search their own repertoires for the closest match (Locke, 1986). In fact, regardless of the language modeled for the infant, his vocalizations and later first words have similar phonological patterns (Anderson & Smith, 1987; French, 1989; Locke, 1983; Stoel-Gammon & Dunn, 1985). For example, stops (/p, b, t, d, k, g/), nasals (/m, n, ŋ/), and glides (/w, j/) constitute approximately 80% of the consonants in infant vocalizations and the first 50 words of English-speaking children (Leonard, Newhoff, & Mesalam, 1980). While the percentages may differ, these sounds often predominate in other non-English-speaking toddlers, such as Spanish-speaking Puerto Rican children, as well (Anderson & Smith, 1987). The ratio of single consonants to consonant clusters — roughly 9:1 — is also similar in babbling and the first 50 words. Finally, the ratio of consonant-vowel to vowel-consonant syllables is also similar at roughly 3:1 in both English and Spanish (Anderson & Smith, 1987; Oller & Eilers, 1982).

Vowels used in reduplicated babbling may be treated somewhat differently. There is evidence that vowels reflect the parents' language in type and distribution (DeBoysson-Bardies, Hall, Sagart, & Durand, 1989).

In the second half of the first year, the infant responds more consistently to speech. By approximately 7 months, the infant will begin to look at objects that are named. Within another 3 months, he can recognize a familiar word within a larger speech unit, such as a short sentence (Ferguson, 1978).

At around 8 months, many changes occur in the infant's speech and inter-actional patterns. First, the infant begins to react more to the environment by transferring the imitation stimulus or model to a second person. This period, ranging from 8 to 12 months, has been called the *echolalic* stage. During this time the infant begins to imitate the communication of others, using echolalic speech. Echolalic speech, or **echolalia**, is speech that is an immediate imitation of some other speaker. Initially the infant imitates gestures and intonation, but by 8 months he exhibits the identifiable pitch and contour patterns of his parent language (DeBoysson-Bardies, Sagart, & Durand, 1984).

Soon he begins to imitate sounds, but at first only those he has produced spontaneously on his own. Within a few months the infant will begin to use imitation to expand and modify his repertoire of speech sounds. Babbled speech sounds that are not in his native language decrease in number. The infant will also imitate stressed syllables in certain often used words. For example, he may repeat "na-na" when his mother says "banana," though he may not be associating the sound with the actual referent or object.

Second, the infant begins using his own gestures, with or without vocaliza-tions, to communicate, though imitation is still very important. He begins to point, to show objects, to give objects, and to signal "no" or noncompliance. He also seems to enjoy just plain showing off for attention. He waves bye-bye, gives kisses, and (perhaps to his parents' chagrin) shakes his head from side to side for "no."

Third, the speech during this period is characterized by **variegated babbling** (Oller, 1978), in which adjacent and successive syllables are not identical. Sound sequences may also include VCV and CVC structures, although vowel and con-sonant sounds do not differ within these syllables (Stark, 1986). In addition, reduplicated babbling changes in function, becoming less self-stimulatory. It is used more in imitation games with adults. The vocalizations of 8-month-olds also change with location and with significant changes in experiences (Hilke, 1988). It should be noted that not all child language researchers have found reduplicated babbling followed by variegated babbling (Mitchell & Kent, 1990).

Between babbling and the appearance of words, there is a reduction in the number of long babbled strings and an increase in the number of transitional or more wordlike utterances (Menyuk, Menn, & Silber, 1986). In the second half of the first year, children begin to notice contrasts in pitch contours, in vowels, and in initial consonants in consonant-vowel syllables. Children selectively listen more frequently to word-length utterances than to connected speech. They begin to recognize recurring patterns of sounds within specific situations.

Fourth, the infant begins to experiment with **jargon**, long strings of unin-telligible sounds with adultlike prosodic and intonational patterns. Infants 7 to 10 months of age are sensitive to prosodic cues that help them segment speech into perceptual units corresponding to clauses (Hirsh-Pasek, Kemler Nelson, Jusczyk, Cassidy, Druss, & Kennedy, 1987). Mothers' speech to infants includes pauses at sentence boundaries, while mothers' speech to other adults does not. Thus, the child is given cues to the unit of speech that corresponds to the grammatical unit of language (Nelson, Hirsh-Pasek, Jusczyk, & Cassidy, 1989).

The child's babbling gradually comes to resemble the prosodic pattern of the language to which the child is exposed. Babbling patterns become shorter and phonetically more stable. These prosodic features will continue into speech. Words and utterances are acquired as a "whole tonal pattern" (Lenneberg, 1967, p. 279). The resultant jargon may sound like questions, commands, and statements. Many parents will swear at this point that their child is communicating in sentences, though the parents aren't exactly clear on what the child is saying. Apparently the paralinguistic aspects of language are easier for the child to reproduce than the linguistic aspects. Parental estimates of the infant's expressive abilities are frequently inflated. The amount of jargon produced and the number of months spent in this activity differ greatly across children (Stark, 1986).

Many speech sounds will develop sound-meaning relationships (Ferguson, 1978). Called **phonetically consistent forms (PCFs)** (Dore, Franklin, Miller, & Ramer, 1976), these sounds function as words for the infant, even though they are not based on adult words. The child may develop a dozen PCFs before he speaks his first words. PCFs tend to be of four varieties: (a) single or repeated vowels, (b) syllabic nasals, (c) syllabic fricatives, and (d) single or repeated consonant-vowel syllables (syllables consisting of one consonant and one vowel) in which the consonant is a nasal or stop (Halliday, 1975a, 1975b; Lewis, 1951). Although PCFs have relatively stable sound and syllable forms, the prosodic pattern is even more consistent than these patterns.

PCFs may be a link between babbling and adultlike speech in that they are more limited than babbling but not as structured as adult speech. In short, they are "babbling-like sounds used meaningfully" (Ferguson, 1978, p. 281). PCFs display the creative role of the child as a language learner. The child does not use PCFs just because the adult models are too difficult or unavailable. Rather, he gets the idea that there can be sound–meaning relationships. Thus the child demonstrates a recognition of linguistic regularities, though most PCFs are not found in adult speech.

By 9–13 months, children "understand" some words based on a combination of sound, nonlinguistic and paralinguistic cues, and context. In other words, children comprehend in a limited way some phonemic sequences in certain specific contexts. The words are probably not comprehended alone. The exception are the child's name and *no*, which children seem to recognize out of context. As a result of continued exposure to recurring sound patterns in context, the child learns to reproduce aspects of these patterns in these situations. These sound patterns are most likely learned as a whole rather than as specific individual sounds.

Acquisition of single phonemes alone cannot explain word production. Some aspects of vocal development are progressively coordinated and recombined into meaningful speech, while others are dropped. Sound production depends upon sound grouping and sound variation within individual words. Thus, the child adopts a problem-solving or trial-and-error approach to word production, gradually developing expressive strategies. Over time these strategies become more general, less word specific, and more automatic.

Finally, at around the first birthday, the child produces his first meaningful word. Although he has previously responded to and produced words, he now produces them in the presence of the referent. Most experts interpret this act to mean that the child associates the word with its meaning in some limited manner. Generally, first words name favorite toys or foods, family members, or pets. My own children began speaking with words such as *mama, dada, pepa* (the dog), *all gone*, and *bye-bye*. Single words are used for more than naming; the infant uses them to make requests, comments, and inquiries.

PCFs and first words are often function specific or used for a single function, such as *mama* to gain attention or *more* to request. Gradually, the child expands this system so that a single word can signal a variety of functions by altering its pitch contour or shape.

With the acquisition of words, the child's sound production becomes more constrained by the linguistic context. In short, "Emergence of the first words . . . is determined as much by the child's control of articulation as by his ability to associate labels with objects" (de Villiers and de Villiers, 1979, pp. 23–24).

Children's speech is a complex interaction of the ease of production and the ease of perception of the target syllable. The success of both processes is a function of the phonemes involved and of syllable stress and position within the target word (H. Klein, 1978).

Infants can be trained to identify speech sounds. Hillenbrand (1983) found that 6-month-old infants would respond when repeated speech sounds changed from plosives to nasals or the reverse, indicating that infants can organize speech sounds perceptually on the basis of auditory features. The order of appearance of the first sounds that children acquire—/m/, /w/, /b/, /p/—cannot be explained by the frequency of their appearance in English (Fourcin, 1978). The most frequently appearing English sounds are /t/, /n/, /d/, and /s/, but /b/, /m/, and /w/ are "the simplest consonants in production terms and their simplicity may well have a bearing on their early appearance in the young child's speech" (Fourcin, 1978, p. 60). The /p/ sound cannot be explained so easily because it is relatively more complex. Despite the complexities encountered in describing the parameters of /p/, ease of perception seems to be the key to early production.

After he acquires one word, the child will usually learn a few more within a short time and then plateau. More of his energy now goes into perfecting his walking ability and exploring.

The Explorer: Age 12–24 Months

With a beginning realization of self and a new (albeit shaky) method of locomotion, the infant begins the second year of life. During that year he will change from a dependent infant to a more independent toddler. His newly acquired walking skills and increased linguistic abilities give him mobility and tools to explore and expand his world (Table 3.6, pp. 96–97).

TABLE 3.6   The Explorer: 12–24 Months

Age (Months)	Motor	Cognition	Socialization	Communication
15	Enjoys unceasing activity; walks with rapid runlike gait Walks a few steps backwards and sideways Carries objects in both hands or waves while walking Throws ball with elbow extension Takes off shoes and socks Scribbles lines	Imitates small motor acts	Looks for adults when left alone Likes music and dancing Pushes toys Imitates housework Plays in solitary manner Begins make-believe play	Points to clothes, persons, toys, and animals named Uses jargon and words in conversation Has four-to six-word vocabulary
18	Walks up stairs with help Walks smoothly, runs stiffly Drinks unassisted Throws ball with whole arm Throws and catches without falling Jumps with both feet off floor Turns pages Scribbles in circles Has muscle control for potty training	Recognizes pictures Recognizes self in mirror Remembers places where objects are usually located Uses a stick as a toy Imitates adult object use	Explores reactions of others; tests others Enjoys solitary play; engages in increased cooperative play from here on Pretends to feed doll	Begins to use two-word utterances Has approximately 20-word vocabulary Identifies some body parts Refers to self by name "Sings" and hums spontaneously Plays question-answer with adults

TABLE 3.6 *continued*

Age (Months)	Motor	Cognition	Socialization	Communication
21	Walks up and down stairs with help of railing or hand Jumps, runs, throws, climbs; kicks large ball; squats to play Puts shoes on part way Unzips Fits things together, such as easy puzzle Responds rhythmically to music with whole body	Knows shapes Sits alone for short periods with book Notices little objects and small sounds	Hugs spontaneously Plays near but not with other kids Likes toy telephone, doll, and truck for play	Likes rhyming games Pulls person to show something Tries to "tell" experiences Understands some personal pronouns Uses *I* and *mine*
24	Walks smoothly, watching feet Runs rhythmically but unable to start or stop smoothly Walks up and down stairs alone without alternating feet Tiptoes for a few steps Pushes tricycle Eats with fork	Matches familiar objects Comprehends *one* and *many*	Can role play in limited manner Imagines toys have life qualities; engages in pretend play that is constrained by the objects Enjoys parallel play predominately Prefers action toys Cooperates with adults in simple household tasks Orders others around Communicates feelings, desires, and interests	Has 200–300-word vocabulary; names most common everyday objects Uses short, incomplete sentences Uses some prepositions (*in, on*) and pronouns (*I, me, you*) but not always correctly Uses some regular verb endings (*-s, -ed, -ing*) and plural *s*

Much of the second year is spent perfecting and varying walking skills. There is a deceleration in bodily growth rate, both in height and in weight. Brain growth also decelerates, and head size increases only slightly. By age 2 the brain is about 80% of its mature adult size. By 15 months the toddler is experimenting with different forms of walking, such as running and dawdling. Favorite games are hiding or being chased. The toddler learns to walk while carrying objects and to stoop and recover. One of my sons would stoop to pick up an object while forgetting the glass of juice clutched to his chest. After spilling the juice, he would turn to see what his parents would say, forget the puddle of juice, and inevitably sit in it.

By 18 months the toddler is able to walk backward and to stop smoothly, but he is not able to turn corners very well without assistance. He tries to climb out of his crib and to rearrange furniture. His walking is still not perfected, though he falls less often. He walks with his toes pointed out, his feet widely separated, and his body leaning forward. There is a rolling, "drunken sailor" quality to his movements. Within 6 months, he progresses to a stable walking rhythm. The 2-year-old is able to walk on tiptoes, stand on one foot with assistance, jump with both feet, and bend at the waist to retrieve an object on the floor.

Unlike the somewhat sedentary world of the 1-year-old, the toddler's environment becomes one of motion. He is always on the go. His new mobility, plus increasing control over his fine motor abilities, gives the toddler new freedom to explore. If allowed by his parents, the toddler will get into everything. "As soon as toddlers are really sure of themselves as walkers, they initiate an active and systematic exploration of their physical world" (Caplan & Caplan, 1977, p. 100). The toddler turns over wastebaskets and sorts through the uncovered "treasures"; he empties cabinets and drawers, and he hides objects. As a toddler, my brother went through the house dumping a liberal mound of baby powder into each opened drawer just after my mother had completed spring housecleaning.

Most of the toddler's play and exploration is solitary and nonsocial. As his pincer grasp becomes more coordinated, he demonstrates an interest in small objects, such as insects. By 15 months he explores by fingering everything. A favorite game is carrying objects and handing them to others. He can release objects at will and has a primitive whole arm throw. With his grasp, sticks become tools for retrieving and exploring. During the entire second year, the toddler tests objects' qualities by touching, pushing, pulling, and lifting. Mouthing decreases. Sensory exploration is still very important, however, and the toddler enjoys exploring new sights, sounds, and textures. Later he demonstrates definite likes and dislikes. As he nears 18 months, the toddler begins combining skills. He can carry one or several small objects in one hand and throw objects with the other. He begins to concentrate on fitting things together rather than separating them and on filling containers rather than emptying them. Increased fine motor skills and a longer attention span enable him to look at books. By 18 months he recognizes pictures of common objects. Six months later, he pretends to read books and has the fine motor skills to turn pages one at a time. He is also capable of holding a crayon and scribbling circles and vertical and horizontal lines.

The toddler's exploration changes his concepts of objects and people in the environment and, in turn, his concept of himself. Increased memory aids this realization process. "To understand that her ball or her doll exists independent of her, the child needs to be able to remember it" (Caplan & Caplan, 1977, p. 66). By 15 months the toddler demonstrates increased mental abilities at physical problem solving. He begins to plan new trial-and-error behaviors, without going through the actual physical events, by combining ideas from previous encounters. In addition, when moving objects disappear, he is able to anticipate their movement. By 18 months he uses objects increasingly for their intended function; he "combs" his hair with a comb, for example. In addition, toys are used increasingly in play. By 18 months the toddler plays appropriately with toy phones, dishes, and tools. He likes dress-up play. Dolls and stuffed animals become more important. My own children loved to pound pegs through a wooden toy workbench and to stack objects. The toddler often repeats daily routines with his toys and demonstrates short sequences of role playing at age 2. One of my sons loved to imitate his mother's morning ritual in the bathtub. All of this learning depends on better memory.

The toddler also enjoys routines and anticipates actions. From routines such as feeding, changing, and eating, the toddler develops a primitive sense of order and time. By 2 years of age, the toddler has gained a good grasp of the environment. He is able to predict routine behaviors and the location of familiar objects. With some confidence in the world and a better sense of himself, the toddler tries to influence the outcome of many routines and interactions.

Much of the social interaction of the second year involves the toddler's attempts to be in the spotlight. Having learned in the first year that he can influence others, the toddler will do almost anything for attention. He becomes an active imitator of adults and siblings. The 15-month-old gains attention by "dancing" to music. He turns, rocks his head, and swings his arms. He becomes more adept at imitating hand movements such as clapping and waving. At around 18 months he begins to imitate the family's housework, perhaps attempting to vacuum or sweep.

Increasing self-awareness and the ability to influence others are reflected in the toddler's growing noncompliance with the wishes of the family. At 16 months the toddler begins to assert some independence by ignoring or dawdling in response to parental commands or requests. By 21 months, this behavior has evolved into a very defiant "no." He frequently says "no" even when he really wants the help or advice being offered. Since the 2-year-old has many self-help skills, he expresses his desire not to be helped. For example, the 2-year-old can usually place food on his spoon and feed himself, undress himself except for shoelaces, wash himself, turn on simple appliances, open easy doors, and straighten his bed. When he needs help, he knows how to request it.

The toddler's growing sense of self is also reflected in his notion of possession. He becomes increasingly aware that objects have owners. At around 18 months the toddler becomes very possessive of his toys, using words such as *mine*. By 22 months the toddler may become more verbal in his defense of his possessions, though others may disagree as to just which objects are his. One of my sons insisted on sleeping with all of his toy cars in the bed. It was easy to tell how restless he was by the amount of clanking. The toddler's verbal defense of his possessions reflects his awareness that adults attend to him when he uses words.

Not all interactions are negative, however, and toddlers will play near other children. This play is usually parallel or side-by-side, with each child engaged in his own activity.

Language development also goes beyond the use of such single words as *no*, *mine*, and a few others. The second year is one of vocabulary growth and word combinations. Vocabulary growth is slow during the first few months, when the toddler is concentrating on gross motor refinement. Much of the toddler's speech consists of single words or jargon. These words are used to name objects or people, to gain attention, or to attain some object or information. Phrases frequently used by adults in the child's environment may be repeated as single words. For example, many children say "Wassat?" and "Go-bye." A favorite of the 18-month-old is the *name game*, in which the toddler touches an object, queries "Wassat?" and awaits a reply. Some words, such as *no*, *more*, and *gimme*, can be combined easily with others to form longer sentences. Other words represent common objects, food, pets, or household members. Each toddler has his own *lexicon*, or dictionary, with words that reflect, in part, the child's environment. In general, the toddler's definitions are not the same as those of the adults in the same environment. For example, the word *horse* might apply to all four-legged animals, regardless of size. The toddler must therefore rely upon extra linguistic cues to interpret adult speech accurately. This outcome is to be expected, since the child's experiences with the environment and with words are much more limited.

During the second half of the second year, the toddler begins to combine words and to increase his rate of vocabulary growth. The early word combinations appear to follow predictable patterns (Bloom, 1970), and the toddler is likely to produce phrases such as "More cookie," "Daddy eat," "No night-night," and so on. Within a few months, short-term memory has increased so that the child can attempt a few longer constructions, such as "Daddy eat cookie." At this time the toddler seems to be absorbed in speech and language play. He likes rhymes, songs, and stories, and much of his activity, such as playing and eating, is accompanied by speech. Vocabulary increases rapidly. At age 2 the toddler has an expressive vocabulary of about 150 to 300 words (Lipsitt, 1966; Wehrabian, 1970). Accompanying the increases in utterance length and vocabulary is a decrease in the use of jargon and babbling.

In summary, the 2-year-old is a relatively independent sort, though he is still very dependent upon adults for his protection and well-being. He has a good concept of his immediate environment and an expectation of daily routines. He has the social skills to attain and hold the attention of others and to express some emotions. His increased mobility enables him to explore the environment and to modify it. In addition, he has the linguistic skills to influence the behavior of others.

The Exhibitor: Age 3–5 Years

As the preschool child develops, he exhibits new independence (Table 3.7, pp. 102–3). He is very mobile and very curious about the world. During the preschool years, the child acquires many self-help skills, including dressing and feeding. Increased memory enables him to solve problems with less dependence on physical input, to understand temporal concepts, and to recall the past. Language skills develop rapidly during the preschool years. By age 5 the child has acquired about 80% of the syntactic structures he will use as an adult. Recall and increased language skills combine in the 5-year-old to produce a delightful storyteller and recounter. The 5-year-old, with his better-defined personality, is a more openly social being than he was at age 2.

Several studies have attempted to establish an order of phoneme acquisition by young children (Poole, 1934; Prather, Hedrick, & Kern, 1975; Templin, 1957; Wellman, Case, Mengert, & Bradbury, 1931). Templin (1957) gave children an articulation test. Each English speech sound was tested in the initial, medial, and final positions in words. The criterion for acquisition was correct production by 75% of the children at one age level. Sanders (1972) reanalyzed the data to reflect correct production by 50% and 90% of the children. In contrast, Olmsted (1971) collected data on spontaneous speech, considering a phoneme to be acquired when it was produced correctly by more than half of the children.

Comparing the results of all three studies (Figure 3.3), we can make the following statements:

1. As a group, vowels are acquired before consonants. English vowels are acquired by age 3.
2. As a group, the nasals are acquired first, followed by the glides, plosives, liquids, fricatives, and affricatives.
3. As a group, the glottals are acquired first, followed by the labials, velars, alveolars, dentals, and palatals.
4. Sounds are first acquired in the initial position in words.
5. Consonant clusters and blends are not acquired until age 7 or 8, though some clusters appear as early as age 4. These early clusters include /s/ + nasal, /s/ + liquid, /s/ + stop, and stop + liquid in the initial position and nasal + stop in the final position.
6. There are great individual differences, and the age of acquisition for some sounds may vary by as much as 3 years.

The 3-Year-Old

By age 3 the child has perfected walking on flat surfaces. He can run well, climb stairs without assistance, and balance on one foot. His newfound skill of tricycling expands his horizons beyond the immediate household. He is still very home oriented, however, and will remain so throughout the preschool period.

Fine motor abilities continue to develop slowly. The 3-year-old can dress himself except for shoe tying and can use a knife for spreading but not cutting. He continues to be interested in fine motor manipulation and explores by dismantling or dismembering household objects or favorite toys. Scribbling has developed into more representational drawing. Often a single "drawing" will represent many very different things. The representation is not constrained by the object or person portrayed. Most adults have experienced the rough-drawn circle with two lines below it that the child calls "mommy." Upon a second inquiry, the child announces that the same picture is now a doggie, next it's a tree, and so on. The circle is a symbol for some entity or entities.

The play of a 3-year-old is also less constrained by actual objects. He uses toys in imaginative ways and exhibits much make-believe play. Thus, one object

TABLE 3.7   The Exhibitor: 3–5 Years

Age (Years)	Motor	Cognition	Socialization	Communication
3	Walks up and down stairs without assistance; uses nonalternating step	Creates representational art: one shape represents several things	Plays in groups; talks while playing; selects with whom he'll play	Has 900–1,000-word vocabulary; creates 3–4 word sentences
	Walks without watching feet; marches to music; tiptoes 3 yards	Matches primary colors	Shares toys for short periods	Uses "sentences" with subject and verb, but simple sentence construction
	Balances momentarily on one foot	Can show two objects: understands concept of *two*	Takes turns	
	Rides tricycle	Enjoys make-believe play; is less constrained by objects		Plays with words and sounds
	Can spread with knife			Follows two-step commands
	Explores, dismantles, dismembers			Talks about the present
				"Swears"
4	Walks up and down stairs with alternating steps	Categorizes	Plays and cooperates with others	Has 1,500–1,600-word vocabulary
	Jumps over objects	Counts rotely to five; can show three objects; understands concept of *three*	Role plays	Asks many, many questions
	Hops on one foot			Uses increasingly more complex sentence forms
	Can copy block letters	Knows primary colors		Recounts stories and the recent past
		Labels some coins		Understands most questions about the immediate environment

may symbolize another. Such an event is called *symbolic play*. Unlike 2-year-olds, the child of 3 is likely to play in groups and to share toys and take turns. Play is often accompanied by sounds and words as he explains his actions, makes environmental noises, or takes various roles. Parents and teachers often hear themselves portrayed in the child's play—not always in flattering terms!

Speech and language are used in many other ways, and there is a tremendous relative growth in vocabulary. The 3-year-old uses an expressive vocabulary of 900 to 1,000 words and employs about 12,000 individual words per day (Lipsitt, 1966; Wehrabian, 1970). Most 3-year-olds have mastered the vowel sounds and

TABLE 3.7 *continued*

Age (Years)	Motor	Cognition	Socialization	Communication
4				Has some difficulty answering *how* and *why*
				Relies on word order for interpretation
5	Has gross motor control, good body awareness; plays complex games	Carries a rule through a series of activities	Plays simple games	Has vocabulary of 2,100–2,200 words
	Cuts own meat with a knife	Knows own right and left, but not those of others	Selects some playmates based on sex	Discusses feelings
	Draws well, colors in lines; creates more recognizable drawings	Counts to 13; can show four or five objects; understands concept of *greater than three*	Enjoys dramatic play	Understands *before* and *after*, regardless of word order
	Prints simple words	Accepts magic as an explanation	Shows interest in group activities	Follows three-step commands
	Dresses without assistance	Develops time concepts of today/tomorrow/yesterday, morning/afternoon/night, day/night	Plays purposefully and constructively	Has 90% grammar acquisition
	Still lacks eye coordination for sustained reading	Recognizes relationship of parts to whole		
	Has established hand preference			

FIGURE 3.3   Average Age of Acquisition of English Consonants
Compiled from Olmstead (1972) and Sanders (1972), representing the ages at
which 50% of English-speaking children can produce a sound correctly in all
positions in conversation and in formal testing.

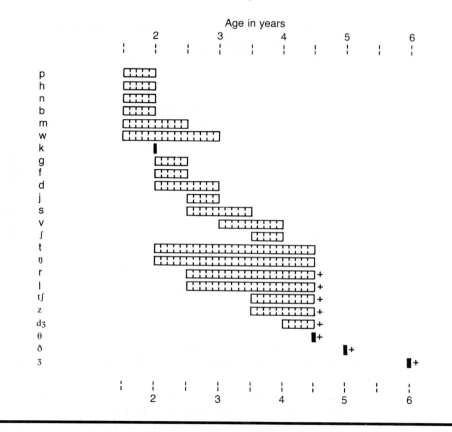

the consonants /p/, /m/, /h/, /n/, /w/, /b/, /k/, /g/, and /d/.* There is much individual
variation in speech sound development, however, and at least 50% of the 3-year-
olds are also proficient in their use of /t/, /ŋ/, /f/, /j/, /r/, /l/, and /s/ (Sanders, 1972)
(Figure 3.2).

The language of the 3-year-old consists of simple sentences that frequently
omit small, unstressed words. Most sentences follow a subject-verb-object format, though the child has begun to employ variations of adult negative, interrogative, and imperative forms. Negative words used are *no, not, can't, don't,* and
won't, usually employed interchangeably. The most frequent interrogatives are
what and *where; why* and *how* are used infrequently, and the 3-year-old cannot

_____
*Appendix A lists the phonetic symbols and words illustrating each one.

respond successfully to these types of questions. The 3-year-old uses some noun modifiers and articles, the plurals of high-frequency nouns, and possessive -'s. He also uses some pronouns and the prepositions *in*, *on*, and *under*. In addition, he has learned to use the *-ing* and *-ed* endings. Unfortunately, most 3-year-olds overgeneralize the *-ed* ending to irregular past tense verbs, such as *eat-eated*. The 3-year-old still has some difficulty with auxiliary verbs and the verb *to be*.

In short, the child's language is increasingly beginning to reflect his environment. This is not a passive imitative process, however. The child demonstrates his processing of language rules by using such constructions as *eated* and *goed*, though he does not hear those constructions used by adults around him. He is formulating language rules.

Two aspects of the linguistic environment more readily reflected in child speech of this age group are adult intonation and swearing. I recall eavesdropping on my 3-year-old daughter as she warned one of her dolls, "Now listen here, young lady!" Her intonation was flawless. I cringed to think from whom that had come. Swearing also causes parents to cower, and every family has at least one embarrassing story about the incident at Grandma's house or in a crowded shopping mall. Our most embarrassing tale involved an alphabet game in which children were telling words that began with certain sounds. One of our cherubs strayed from the traditional *apple, boy, cat* format. The preschool teacher ended the activity abruptly.

The 3-year-old exhibits good motor and language skills for his short period of experience. Much of his environment is reflected in his play and in his conversation.

The 4-Year-Old

The motor skills of the 4-year-old reflect his increased control of independent movements of his right and left sides. The child of 4 can hop on one foot for a short period and can ascend and descend steps with alternating foot movements. Hand preference is also more pronounced, and the child is able to copy simple block letters with the dominant hand.

Increased memory helps the child recount the past and remember short stories. This memory and recall are aided by the child's increased language skills. The child also demonstrates categorization skills that seem to indicate more advanced procedures for storage of learned information. The 4-year-old can name the primary colors and label some coins. Although he can count to 5 by rote, he has a notion of quantity only through 3.

Socially, most 4-year-olds play well in groups and cooperate well with others. Although there is still a lot of object play, role play becomes increasingly frequent.

The ability to carry a role through story play is reflected in the 4-year-old's language. He can tell simple stories of his own or others' authorship. His increased language skills enable him to form more complex sentences. His vocabulary has increased to 1,500 to 1,600 words, with approximately 15,000 used each day (Lipsitt, 1966; Wehrabian, 1970). Most 4-year-olds can correctly articulate the consonant sounds /p/, /m/, /h/, /n/, /w/, /b/, /k/, /g/, /d/, /t/, /ŋ/, /f/, and /j/. At least 50% of all 4-year-olds can produce /r/, /l/, /s/, /tʃ/, /ʃ/, and /z/ (Sanders, 1972) (Figure 3.2). Most sentences average four or five words, and the 4-year-old demonstrates good usage of declarative, negative, interrogative, and imperative forms. The 4-year-old child also joins sentences together to form longer units, using conjunctions such as *and, but*, and *if* and relative pronouns such as *who*. Frequently the child will begin sentences with *and* or use *and* to produce long run-on sentences that tell a story. Events are relayed in the order in which they occurred.

Four-year-olds also rely on word order for interpretation of temporal information. For example, the 4-year-old interprets the following sentences to mean the same thing:

> After you eat, go right home.
> Before you eat, go right home.

The child will ignore the words *before* and *after*. The order-of-mention strategy results in the interpretation "Eat, then go home."

Language becomes a real tool for exploration, and the 4-year-old is full of questions. He may ask several hundred in a single day, causing parents to wonder why they ever longed to hear their child speak. The child learns very quickly that he can exasperate Dad by continually asking "why?"

A subject is now used in all sentence forms except the imperative or command, in which it is not required. Usually one modifier or an article is used with the noun. Most regular and irregular past tense verbs are used correctly, as is the third person singular present tense *-s*, as in "Mommy *eats* at work." Thus 4-year-olds can be expected to say "ate," not "eat*ed*," and "Mommy eat*s*," not "Mommy eat." The specific verbs acquired and the speed of acquisition depend on many factors, including environmental input. Auxiliary verbs are also used in the interrogative and negative sentence forms that require their use.

In general, 4-year-olds are very social beings who have the linguistic skills and the short-term memory to be good, albeit limited, conversationalists. They are very curious and very anxious to exhibit their knowledge and abilities.

The 5-Year-Old

By his fifth birthday, the child has a good sense of the person he has become. He possesses a good awareness of his body and how to use it to accomplish complex tasks and games. The 5-year-old knows his own left and right but can't transfer them to others. Each hand can be employed independently for tasks such as dressing and cutting meat with a knife. Small muscle control enables him to draw recognizable pictures, to color within the lines, and to copy short words.

The child uses his body in play and enjoys group games. With increased memory skills, the child of 5 is able to play organized games with simple rules. He can concentrate on playing and still carry through certain rules of play.

The 5-year-old has a good temporal sense and understands words such as *yesterday, today*, and *tomorrow*. Temporal notions aid the child's understanding of explanations of cause and effect and comprehension of temporal terms such as *before* and *after*.

Although the 5-year-old has good physical reasoning abilities, he still believes in magic and sorcery as explanations for much that happens. When one of my sons turned 5, he asked for a magic kit. Mom and Dad complied. After opening it, he turned to us for a demonstration. My wife explained each trick and showed him how it was done. When she finished, my son said in a very disillusioned voice, "No, no, I wanted *real magic*."

Five-year-olds use very adultlike language, though many of the more subtle syntactic structures are missing. In addition, the child has not acquired some of the pragmatic skills needed to be a truly effective communicator. His expressive vocabulary has grown to about 2,200 words. Word definitions still lack the fullness of adult meanings, however, and this aspect continues to be refined throughout life. Most 5-year-olds can correctly articulate the /p/, /m/, /h/, /n/, /w/, /b/, /k/, /g/, /d/, /t/, /ŋ/, /f/, /j/, /r/, /l/, /s/, /tʃ/, /ʃ/, /z/, /dʒ/, and /v/ consonant sounds. At least 50% can produce the /ð/ correctly (Sanders, 1972) (Figure 3.2). Five-year-olds still have difficulty with a few consonant sounds and with consonant blends, as in "*street*" or "*clean*."

The child of 5 uses regular and irregular past tenses of common verbs correctly but still has difficulty with the past tense of the verb *to be* (*was* and *were*). The future tense modal *will* is also used correctly where required in context. Some of the other modal auxiliary verbs, such as *would*, *should*, *must*, and *might*, are used less frequently and often correctly. The 5-year-old child also has limited use of the comparative (*more . . . than* or *-est*); the possessive *-'s* and possessive pronouns (*his, her, your*); the conjunctions *and, but, if, because, when,* and *so*; relative pronouns for embedded clauses ("I know *who* lives next door"); gerunds ("We go *fishing*"); and infinitives ("I want *to eat* now"). These syntactic structures do not appear rapidly, and many children struggle with acquisition well into the school years. It frequently takes the child several years of practice to gain complete control of many linguistic structures. The child from a lower socioeconomic group or a stimulation-poor environment may take longer to acquire the structures mentioned. Many other, less obvious linguistic changes are also occurring.[†]

Although there are still many aspects of speech, language, and communication to be mastered, the 5-year-old has made spectacular progress in only a few short years. The child of 5 is able to use language to converse and to entertain. He can tell stories and has a budding sense of humor. In addition, he can tease and discuss emotions. Over the next few years, language development will slow and begin to stabilize, but it will be nonetheless significant.

The Expert: School-Age Years

In the first 6 years of school, the child develops cognitive and communicative skills that by age 12 almost equal those of the adult. Physical growth follows

---

[†]These changes will be discussed in greater detail in Chapters 8 and 9.

shortly as the 12-year-old begins adolescence. Increasingly the child becomes less home centered, as school and age peers become more important (Table 3.8).

Physically, the school-age child gains greater coordination of gross and fine motor movements. As the 6-year-old attains better coordination and balance, he learns to ride a bicycle and to throw and catch a ball well. It takes 6 months to a year of practice for him to become a proficient bicyclist. In ball handling, throwing skills precede catching skills by several months. Throughout the period, the child's physical coordination enables him to perform more motor acts at one time and therefore to enjoy sports and coordinated games. In addition, better fine motor abilities and eye–hand coordination enable the child to engage in hobbies and crafts. With more mature motor skills, he gains more self-help skills and increased independence.

Cognitive skills change markedly during the first 6 years of school. The brain is nearly adult in size by age 8, but development is not complete. Intracerebral association tracts must be better developed before the brain becomes mature. This internal growth is reflected in the relative weight of the brain to the whole body weight: by age 10 the child's brain is 1/15th of the total body weight, compared to 1/40th for the adult. Brain weight changes little; growth is internal. During the first 6 years of school, the child's mental abilities mature from concrete problem solving, requiring sensory input, to abstract thought. Drawing from Piaget, Flavell (1977) notes four major cognitive developments in the period from age 7 to 11: inferred reality, decentration, transformational thought, and reversible mental operations. *Inferred reality* is an inference about a physical problem based not only on perceived appearances but also on internal information. For example, a preschooler bases his judgment of a container's volume on its height alone. The school-age child bases his conclusion on all physical characteristics and on his knowledge of the volume of liquid poured into the container. The ability to maintain a notion of size or quantity regardless of the shape of the object or container is called *conservation*. *Decentration* is the ability to consider several aspects of a physical problem at once, rather than focusing on only a few. *Transformational thought* refers to the ability to view a physical problem as existing in time and to anticipate future consequences effectively. Finally, *reversible mental operations* enable the child to recognize that change can be undone or reversed.

In addition, the child's selective attention, both visual and auditory, improves, and he is able to filter out unnecessary information more effectively. Increased memory enables him to process and organize the remaining information for more efficient problem solving. Along with these increased abilities, the child gains a better understanding of his own mental processes.

The school-age child is also a very social being, and peers, especially same-sex peers, become very important. Thus, this period of social development is called the "gang age." The child may begin to use slang or peer group talk for added acceptance. This can be a trying period for parents, as children begin to establish an identity separate from their family. One afternoon one of my sons stormed into the house from his friend's house to demand to know "the truth."

TABLE 3.8   The Expert: The School-Age Child

Age (Years)	Motor	Cognition	Socialization	Communication
6	Has better gross motor coordination; rides bicycle Throws ball well Begins to get permanent teeth	Has longer attention span Is less distracted by additional information when problem solving Remembers and repeats three digits	Enjoys active games Is competitive Identifies with sex peers in groups Transforms ego-centric reality to more complex and relative reality view	Has expressive vocabulary of 2,600 words, receptive of 20,000–24,000 words; defines by function Has many well-formed sentences of a complex nature; uses all parts of speech to some degree
8	Has longer arms, larger hands Has better manipulative skills Has nearly mature-size brain Has more permanent teeth	Knows left and right of others Understands conservation Knows differences and similarities Reads spontaneously	Enjoys an audience Learns that others have different perspectives of a third person Has allegiance to gang, but also strong need for adult support	Talks a lot ✓ Boasts, brags ✓ Verbalizes ideas and problems readily Communicates thought Demonstrates little difficulty with comparative relationship
10	Has eyes of almost mature size Has almost mature lungs and digestive and circulatory systems	Plans future actions Solves problems with only minimal physical input	Enjoys games, sports, hobbies Discovers that he may be the object of someone else's perspective	Spends lots of time talking Has good comprehension
12	Experiences "rest" before adolescent growth (girls usually taller and heavier, may have entered puberty) Begins rapid muscle growth with puberty Can be on wide range of maturational levels	Engages in abstract thought	Has different interests than those of the opposite sex	Has 50,000-word receptive vocabulary Constructs adultlike definitions

"There's one thing you'll never tell me," he challenged. Fearing the worst, I suggested that he ask anyway. What a relief when he shot back, "Is there a real Easter Bunny?" With this peer socialization comes a less egocentric perspective. The child begins to realize that his reality is not the only one.

The child also realizes that he can manipulate and influence others, especially through the use of language. During the early school-age years, the child refines the conversational skills needed to be a truly effective communicator. He learns to introduce new topics and, once begun, to continue and to end conversation. While in a conversation, he makes relevant comments and adapts roles and moods to fit the situation. In addition, the school-age child learns to make certain assumptions about the level of knowledge of the listener and to adjust his conversation accordingly. This communication development reflects the child's growing appreciation for the perspective of others.

Toward more effective speech, the 6-year-old acquires most English speech sounds, adding the /θ/ and /ʒ/ sounds, as in *thin* and trea*su*re (Sanders, 1972). By age 8 he also acquires consonant clusters, such as *str*, *sl*, and *dr*.

In addition, the child's vocabulary continues to grow. The first grader has an expressive vocabulary of approximately 2,600 words but may understand as many as 20,000 to 24,000 English words. Aided by school, this receptive vocabulary expands to approximately 50,000 words by sixth grade and to 80,000 words by high school (Palermo & Molfese, 1972). Multiple word meanings are also acquired. In general, the child learns verbs that describe a simple action first, then verbs for complex actions or specific situations (Dunn, 1959). The age ranges for the following four verbs illustrate this trend:

Verb	Age Range of Understanding in Years-Months
hitting	4−3 to 5−5
balancing	7−6 to 9−5
directing	11−6 to 13−5
hoisting	13−6 to 15−5

Two aspects of school-age language development relative to vocabulary growth are divergent and convergent language abilities. **Divergent semantic production** is the process of producing a great variety of words, word associations, phrases, and sentences from a given topic. As such, divergent abilities add originality, flexibility, and creativity to language (Guilford, 1967). **Convergent semantic production** is the process of selecting a unique semantic unit given specific linguistic restrictions. For example, there are only a few words that can complete the sentence "The opposite of *up* is _____." Development of both abilities helps the school-age child become a more effective communicator.

In part, the school-age child's vocabulary growth reflects the systematic development of word formation rules. First grade is a period of stabilization of rules previously learned and addition of new rules (Menyuk, 1964). The major learning period for the rules of pluralization of nouns may be kindergarten through first grade (Koziol, 1973). By second grade the child uses regular plurals correctly. Irregular plurals and plurals of nouns ending in s blends, such as -sk and -st, are accurately produced by third grade. In second and third grades the child also attains accurate use of the rules for noun and adverb derivation (Berko, 1958; Carrow, 1973). For example, a verb can be changed to a noun by adding -er to the verb, producing *teacher* from *teach*. Some nouns require -man, -person, or -ist, as in *fisherman, chairperson,* or *cyclist*. Adverbs are derived by adding -ly to adjectives, producing *quickly* from *quick*.

The sentence structure of the school-age child becomes more elaborate as the child matures. Sentences of older children include increased embedding of subordinate clauses ("The man *who drives our bus* is crabby"). In addition, there are significant increases in the child's ability to comprehend comparative (*as big as . . .; bigger*), passive ("The girl is chased by the boy"), temporal or time (*before; after*), and spatial and familial relationships (Inhelder & Piaget, 1969; Piaget & Inhelder, 1969; Wiig & Semel, 1984). The school-age child begins to comprehend the sentence and its relationships as a whole and does not depend on word order for interpretation. Other relationships are more complex. Some words such as *promise* and *tell* can be used in the same position in a sentence but drastically alter our interpretation of who will perform the action that follows. For example, in "Jim promised Tom to run in the race," the runner will be different than in "Jim told Tom to run in the race." It takes a few years before the school-age child can accurately comprehend these contrasts (Chomsky, 1969).

The school-age child also learns to understand and use figurative language. *Figurative language* consists of idioms, metaphors, similes, and proverbs that represent abstract concepts not always stated in a literal interpretation. *Idioms* are expressions that often cannot be justified literally, such as "hit the roof" or "tied up." *Metaphors* and *similes* offer implied comparisons, such as "black as night" and "eats like a bird." *Proverbs* offer advice that differs from the concrete example used. For example, "look before you leap" concerns caution in decision making, not advice for long distance jumpers. Figurative relationships add richness to language but require higher language functions to interpret the deeper meaning. General usage of figurative language does not begin until the child attends school.

One of the greatest changes in language comes with the learning of reading and writing. Since these skills are formally taught, the acquisition pattern is quite different from that for language learning via the speech and auditory modes. Reading and writing training removes language from the conversational context and thus requires the child to consider language in the abstract. It is not surprising, therefore, that reading, writing, and metalinguistic skills seem to be related (Kemper, 1985).

In conclusion, by age 12 the child has many of the cognitive and linguistic skills of an adult. The rate of development in these areas decreases as the child prepares for the physical changes that will accompany adolescence.

CONCLUSION

Within 12 years the child develops from a dependent newborn to an adolescent approaching adulthood. Although physical growth is slightly behind cognitive and linguistic maturity, the overall rate of development is amazing. Language development is all the more remarkable in the first 5 years, when there is rapid development of most English syntactic structures—without formal instruction. In the succeeding chapters we will examine the language development process in detail. I hope you will return frequently to the tables in this chapter to remind yourself of the ongoing, multifaceted development of the child.

REFLECTIONS

1. The diverse development of children exhibits several patterns. What are these patterns, and what do they mean?
2. Explain briefly the four processes in speech production.
3. Some of the reflexive behaviors the newborn exhibits are related to oral movement. Describe these oral reflexes and when they disappear.
4. Babbling and vocal play differ considerably. Can you describe each form of behavior?
5. What are the major differences between 2-, 3-, 4-, and 5-year-olds?
6. What generalizations can we make about preschoolers' development of speech sounds?
7. Describe the overall changes that occur in the behavior of school-age children.
8. Explain these semantic skills: divergent and convergent production; figurative language.

4 Neurolinguistics

CHAPTER OBJECTIVES

The brain is the only primary organ in the body concerned with processing linguistic information. The study of the manner and location of this processing is called *neurolinguistics*. In this chapter you will learn about the structures and functions of the brain relative to language. When you have completed this chapter, you should understand

- Luria's basic brain functions.
- the major brain areas responsible for linguistic processing.
- the major theories of brain lateralization.
- the processes of language comprehension and production.
- the models that help explain linguistic processing.
- the following terms:

angular gyrus	information-processing theory
arcuate fasciculus	neurolinguistics
Broca's area	neuron
central nervous system (CNS)	peripheral nervous system
cerebrum	reticular formation
corpus callosum	sulci
cortex	supramarginal gyrus
fissures	synapse
gyri	thalamus
Heschl's gyrus	Wernicke's area

R ECENTLY I MET A preschool child with whom I'd been acquainted previously. After we exchanged greetings, he eyed me suspiciously for several seconds. When I inquired if anything was wrong, he asked, "Do I remember you?" In our study of language, we might ask our brains the same question regarding incoming and outgoing messages because memory is a large portion of linguistic processing. The study of the anatomy, physiology, and biochemistry responsible for language processing and formulation is called **neurolinguistics**.

In this chapter we will examine the main structures of the central nervous system, specifically those involved in processing language. We will also discuss the functioning of these structures and construct a model for language processing.

THE CENTRAL NERVOUS SYSTEM

The human nervous system consists of the brain, spinal cord, and all associated nerves and sense organs. The brain and spinal cord make up the **central nervous system (CNS)**. Any neural tissue that exists outside the CNS is part of the **peripheral nervous system**, which conducts impulses either toward or away from the

CNS. These two systems are responsible for monitoring the body's state, by conducting messages from the senses and organs, and responding to this information, by conducting messages to the organs and muscles. These messages are transmitted through nerves.

The **neuron** is the basic unit of the nervous system. There are approximately 12 billion neurons in the human nervous system. Each neuron consists of three parts: the cell body, a single long *axon* that transmits impulses away from the cell body, and several branchy *dendrites* that receive impulses from other cells and transmit them to the cell body. A nerve is a collection of neurons. Neurons do not actually touch each other but are close enough to enable chemical-electrical impulses to "jump" the miniscule space, or **synapse**, between the axon of one neuron and the dendrites of the next. In short, the electrical charge of one neuron is changed by the release of neurotransmitters at its axon, which in turn affects the release of other neurotransmitters at the dendrite end of the second neuron.

Most of the nervous system's neurons (approximately 85%) are concentrated in the CNS. At its lower end the CNS contains the spinal cord, which transmits impulses between the brain and the peripheral nervous system. At the top of the spinal cord is the brain stem, consisting of the medulla oblongata, the pons, the thalamus, and the midbrain. These structures regulate involuntary functions, such as breathing and heart rate. Within the brain stem is a compact unit of neurons called the **reticular formation**. This body acts as an integrator of incoming auditory, visual, tactile, and other sensory inputs and as a filter to inhibit or facilitate sensory transmission. The **thalamus** acts as a switching station that relays incoming sensory information (with the exception of smell) to the appropriate portion of the brain for analysis. Thus, the thalamus prepares the brain to receive certain select inputs (Lemme & Daves, 1982). To the rear of the brain stem is the cerebellum, which controls equilibrium (Figure 4.1).

Atop the brain stem and the cerebellum is the **cerebrum**. The cerebrum is divided into two halves, designated the left and right hemispheres. In general, sensory and motor functions of the cerebrum are *contralateral*, which means that each hemisphere is concerned with the body's opposite side. With a few exceptions, the nerves from each side of the body cross to the opposite hemisphere somewhere along their course. Two exceptions to this crossover are vision and hearing. In vision, nerves from the left visual field of each eye, rather than from the left eye, pass to the right hemisphere, and those from the right visual field pass to the left hemisphere. Hearing is predominantly contralateral but not exclusively. Thus, in the sensory and motor functions, the cerebral hemispheres are roughly symmetrical. For specialized functions such as language, however, the hemispheres are asymmetrical, and processing is the primary responsibility of one or the other hemisphere.

Each hemisphere consists of white fibrous connective tracts covered by a gray **cortex** of cell bodies approximately ¼th of an inch thick. The fiber tracts are of three types: association, projection, and transverse. Association fibers run between different areas within each hemisphere; projection fibers connect the

FIGURE 4.1   Schematic Lateral Surface of Cerebral Hemisphere

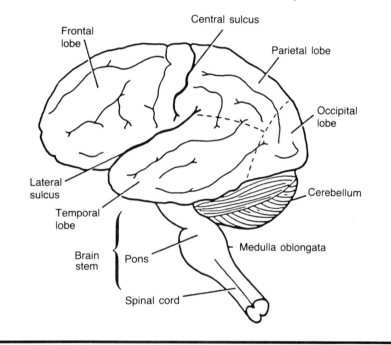

cortex to the brain stem and below; and transverse fibers, as the name implies, connect the two hemispheres. The largest transverse tract, containing approximately 200 million neurons, is the **corpus callosum**. The cortex has a wrinkled appearance caused by little hills called **gyri** and valleys called **fissures**, or **sulci**. Each hemisphere is divided into four lobes labeled frontal, parietal, occipital, and temporal (Figure 4.1).

The frontal and temporal lobes are separated by a deep lateral sulcus known as the *fissure of Sylvius*. The *fissure of Rolando*, or central sulcus, separates the frontal lobe from the parietal lobe. As in other mammals, large portions of the human cortex are designated for sensory and motor functions. Immediately in front of the central sulcus is the *primary motor cortex*, a 2-centimeter-wide strip that controls motor movements. Discrete sets of muscles are controlled from discrete areas of the motor cortex. In general, the finer the movement, the larger the cortical area designated for it. In other words, the fingers have a greater cortical area devoted to motor control than does the trunk (Figure 4.2). Behind and parallel to the motor cortex is the somatic sensory strip, which receives sensory input from the muscles, joints, bones, and skin. Other motor and sensory functions are found in specialized regions of the cortex. For example, the occipital lobe is primarily concerned with vision, and the temporal

FIGURE 4.2   Schematic of Motor Cortex
Parts of the body drawn to represent the portion of the motor cortex devoted
to each

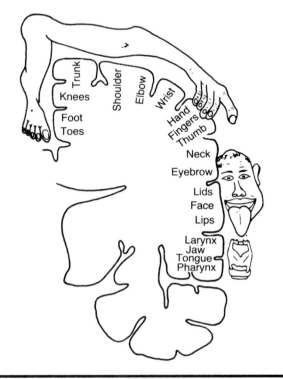

lobe processes auditory information. It is simplistic, however, to conceive of the brain as merely consisting of localized sensory and motor mechanisms because of the integration of sensory and motor information required for the body to respond. Rather, we must consider integrated processes.

Luria (1970) describes three basic brain functions: regulation, processing, and formulation. The regulation function is responsible for the energy level and for the overall tone of the cortex. By maintaining the brain at a basic level of awareness and responsivity, this process, located in the reticular formation of the brain stem, aids the performance of the other two functions.

The processing function, located in the rear of the cortex, controls information analysis, coding, and storage. Highly specialized regions are responsible for the processing of sensory stimuli, such as optic, acoustic, and olfactory stimuli. Within each region there is a hierarchical organization consisting of three zones (Figure 4.3). The primary zone sorts and records sensory information. This information is further organized and coded in the secondary zone. In the tertiary

FIGURE 4.3   Luria's (1970) Model of Brain Functioning with Emphasis on Linguistic Processing

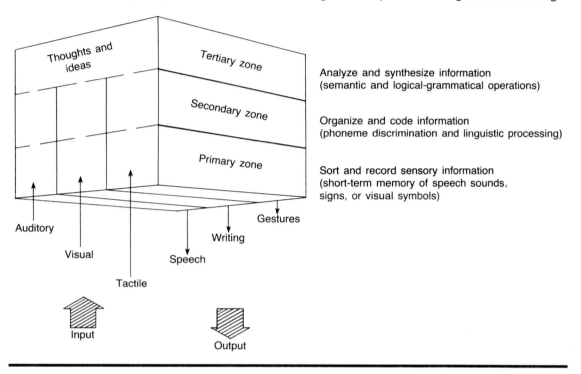

zone, data are combined with those from other sensory sources for analysis and synthesis.

Finally, the formulation process, located in the frontal lobe, is responsible for the formation of intentions and programs for behavior. This function serves primarily to activate the brain for regulation of attention and concentration. Motor behaviors may also be planned and coordinated, but not activated, within this function. Motor movements are sequentially organized based on the integrated information supplied by the tertiary zone from incoming sensory information. Movement is accomplished through a complex process of outgoing (efferent) signals to muscles and incoming (afferent) signals from muscles, joints, and bones.

Hemispheric Asymmetry

Although there is symmetry between the left and right hemispheres for many motor and sensory processes, there is a marked asymmetry for certain specific functions such as language. In other words, the distribution of specialized functions is different, usually lateralized to one hemisphere or the other. Although they may possess these separate functions, the two hemispheres are complementary, and information passes readily between them via the corpus callosum and other subcortical bodies. Overall, neither hemisphere is dominant, since each possesses specialized talents (Geschwind, 1979) and brings different skills to a given task. Neither hemisphere is competent to analyze data and program a response alone.

Specialization, or lateralization, of the brain is not unique to humans, although the human brain may be the most asymmetrical. It may be advantageous for an organism to be able to receive and process a greater variety of information through specialization than to duplicate such processing in both hemispheres (Geschwind & Galaburda, 1985).

The right hemisphere in humans is specialized for holistic processing through the simultaneous integration of information. When a specific ability is housed primarily in one hemisphere, we generally say that the hemisphere is *dominant* for that ability. In other words, the primary processing centers are located in that hemisphere. The right hemisphere, for example, is dominant in visuospatial processing such as depth and orientation in space and perception and recognition of faces, pictures, and photographs. In addition, the right hemisphere is capable of holistic or simultaneous recognition of printed words but has difficulty decoding information using grapheme–phoneme correspondence rules (Carman, Gordon, Bental, & Harness, 1977; Zaidel, 1977). (See the discussion of reading in Chapter 10.) Other language-related skills include comprehension and production of speech prosody and affect; metaphorical language and semantics; and comprehension of complex linguistic and ideational material and of environmental sounds, such as nonspeech sounds, music, melodies, tones, laughter, clicks, and buzzes (Gainotti, Caltagirone, Miceli, & Masullo, 1981; Millar & Whitaker, 1983; Ross, 1981; Shapiro & Danley, 1985). In general, these abilities seem limited to the receptive aspects of language.

In almost all humans the left hemisphere is specialized for language in all modalities (oral, visual, and written), temporal or linear order perception, arithmetic calculations, and logical reasoning. Whereas the right hemisphere engages in holistic interpretation, the left is best at step-by-step processing. As such, the left hemisphere is adept at perceiving rapidly changing sequential information, such as the acoustic characteristics of phonemes in speech (Mateer, 1983; J. Schwartz & Tallal, 1980; Yeni-Komshian & Rao, 1980). In other words, the left hemisphere specializes in the "separating and sorting of a complex of auditory parameters into phonological features" (Studdert-Kennedy & Shankweiler, 1970, p. 590). Processing these phonemes for meaning, however, involves representation in both hemispheres (V. Molfese, D. Molfese, & Parsons, 1983). The left hemisphere is also dominant for control of speech- and non-speech-related oral movements (Tognola & Vignolo, 1980).

Not all human brains are organized as described. In general, all right-handers are left hemisphere dominant for language. This condition might be expected, given the crossover of nerve fibers from one side of the body to the opposite hemisphere. But approximately 60% of left-handers are also left hemisphere dominant for language. The remainder of left-handers, approximately 2% of the human population, are right hemisphere dominant for language. A miniscule percentage of humans display bilateral linguistic performance, with no apparent dominant hemisphere. Thus, approximately 98% of humans are left dominant for language (Rasmussen & Milner, 1976). In actuality, lateralization may be a matter of degree rather than the all-or-nothing patterns suggested. Lateralization may, in fact, be a progressive pattern found in development (Lenneberg, 1967; Satz, 1975).

Brain Maturation

Language development is highly correlated with brain maturation and specialization. Whether this relationship is based upon maturation of specific structures or upon the development of particular cognitive abilities is unknown. (See Chapter 5 for a discussion of cognitive growth in the infant.)

One overall index of neural development is gross brain weight, which changes most rapidly during the first 2 years of life, with tripling of the original weight of the brain at birth. Average brain weights are presented in Table 4.1 on page 123. By age 12 the brain has usually reached its fully mature weight. Most of this increase is the result of myelination, or the sheathing of the nervous system, discussed in Chapter 3. In general, the myelinized areas are most fully developed. Myelination enhances the rapid transmission of neural information. Myelination is controlled, in part, by sex-related hormones, especially estrogen, which enhances the process (Geschwind & Galaburda, 1985). This fact may account for the more rapid development of girls.

Cell differentiation within the brain of the fetus begins during the 16th week of gestation. Subsequent brain maturation is differential and is reflected in the behavior of the infant at birth. For example, during prenatal existence, growth occurs rapidly in the brain stem and in the primary motor and somatic sensory cortices. After birth there is rapid growth in the cerebellum and in the cerebral hemispheres, especially in the visual receptor areas of the occipital lobe. The auditory receptor areas of the temporal lobes mature somewhat later than the visual receptor areas, possibly explaining the relatively early visual maturity of the infant compared to later-developing auditory maturity. The association tracts devoted to speech and language are not fully mature until the late preschool period or later (and some not until adulthood).

In the neonate, vocalization is controlled by the brain stem and pons. The emergence of reduplicated babbling may coincide with maturation of portions of the facial and laryngeal areas of the motor cortex of the brain. Maturation of the auditory association pathways, such as the arcuate fasciculus, that link auditory and cortical motor areas, is not achieved until early in the second year and may be essential for imitation of sounds and speech intonation (Stark, 1986).

The primary anatomical asymmetry in the brain is found in the left temporal lobe. This enlarged area, found even in the fetal brain, may account for the dominance of the left hemisphere in speech and language reception and production (Chi, Dooling, & Gilles, 1977). In addition, this area continues to grow

Much brain growth occurs in the first 2 years, enlarging the child's skull accordingly. Later maturation involves organization more than changes in brain size and weight.

TABLE 4.1   Gross Brain Weight of Child

Age	Weight (Grams)	Percentage of Adult Brain Weight
Birth	335	25
6 months	660	50
12 months	925	70
24 months	1065	80
5 years	1180	90
12 years	1320	100

Adapted from *Neurology for the Speech-Language Pathologist* by R. Love and W. Webb, 1986, Boston: Butterworths.

---

even larger in the mature brain and to myelinize at a slower rate than corresponding areas of the right hemisphere (Geschwind & Galaburda, 1985; Taylor, 1969). The white fiber tract beneath the temporal lobe, called the *planum temporal*, is larger in the left hemisphere of about two-thirds of the adult population.

The dominant view of lateralization of language in the left hemisphere is that it is progressive (J. Brown & Jaffe, 1975). This theory is based on brain measurement and on the *plasticity* of the CNS in young brain-injured children. In the infant brain, clear functional regions have not been delineated, so the brain is plastic, or capable of change. Early brain damage can result in shifts in cortical functional responsibilities to other areas of the cortex. Adjacent or surrounding areas may function in place of the damaged area. Possibly these areas share functional specialization with the damaged area. This specialization does not occur as long as the primary area is functioning normally (Geschwind, 1979). The plasticity of the cortex in the young child is taken as evidence that lateralization and specialization of functions are progressive, since the adult brain does not possess this degree of adaptability.

We should be careful, however, in drawing conclusions about healthy brain maturation from the plasticity of injured brains (Kinsbourne, 1978). We cannot assume that behavior and specialization represent a one-to-one relationship. A second and differing view holds that "language behavior is fully lateralized from the start" (Kinsbourne, 1978, p. 99). Electrophysiological studies of infants have supported the idea that lateralization occurs long before the development of specific abilities (Gardiner & Walter, 1976; Kinsbourne & Hiscock, 1977; Molfese, Freeman, & Palermo, 1975).

A third view assumes that much lateralization occurs during fetal development and that the environment contributes less to lateralization with age. Geschwind and Galaburda (1985) state that "the most powerful factors are variations in the chemical environment in fetal life and to a lesser extent in infancy and early childhood" (p. 431).

Whichever thesis we accept, there can be little disagreement on the left hemisphere dominance for most oral language processing in almost all adults. Therefore, let's explore the neural pathways and the processes involved.

LANGUAGE PROCESSING

Linking language processes with specific cortical locations is difficult because these processes are often "not localized in particular centers" (Luria, 1970, p. 66). The processes often overlap, and a particular region may be responsible for both incoming and outgoing information. In addition, language processing is extremely complex, requiring a broad range of functions. This situation often causes the lament among students that "everything is related to everything else" (G. Miller & Johnson-Laird, 1976, p. 2). And so it is. We will consider the parallel but opposite processes of comprehension and production, followed by a discussion of linguistic processing models.

Comprehension consists of linguistic auditory processing and language symbol decoding (Nation & Aram, 1977). Auditory processing is concerned with the nature of the incoming auditory signal, whereas symbol decoding considers representational meaning and underlying ideational concepts. Linguistic auditory processing begins with attending to incoming auditory stimuli. The reticular formation of the brain stem sets the tone for the brain and determines to which modality and stimuli the brain will attend. Undoubtedly, this focusing is directed by "orders from higher up." Since it has a limited capacity to process incoming data, the brain must allocate this capacity by focusing its attention on certain stimuli while ignoring or inhibiting others.

Auditory signals received in the brain stem by the thalamus are relayed to an area of each auditory cortex called **Heschl's gyrus** (Figure 4.4). Most of the nerve signal is received at Heschl's gyrus from the ear on the opposite side of the body. Heschl's gyrus and the surrounding auditory association areas separate the incoming information, differentiating significant linguistic information from nonsignificant background noise. This decision is made on the basis of stored linguistic knowledge. Linguistic information receives further processing. Coded linguistic input is sent to the left temporal lobe for processing, while paralinguistic input (intonation, stress, rhythm, rate) is directed to the right temporal lobe. Information is transmitted between the hemispheres via the transverse fibers of the corpus callosum.

Linguistic analysis is accomplished in **Wernicke's area**, located in the left temporal lobe (Figure 4.4). The **angular gyrus** and the **supramarginal gyrus** assist in this process. Called the "association area of association areas" (Geschwind, 1974), the angular and supramarginal gyri integrate visual, auditory, and tactile information and are responsible for linguistic representation. Damage to these areas disrupts the connection between oral and visual language and may necessitate the use of oral reading for comprehension. The importance of these gyri and of multimodality input may be signaled by the relatively late myelination of the association areas, occurring in adulthood, often after age 30. Although their

FIGURE 4.4   Receptive Linguistic Processing

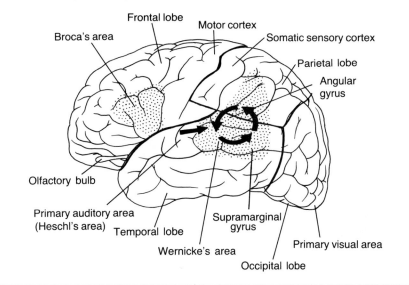

functioning is not totally understood, the angular gyrus aids in word recall and the supramarginal gyrus is involved in processing longer syntactic units, such as sentences. Wernicke's area and the two gyri function "by deriving representational meanings based on established linguistic rules" (Lemme & Daves, 1982, p. 355). Written input is received in the visual cortex and transferred to the angular gyrus, where it may be integrated with auditory input. This information is then transmitted to Wernicke's area for analysis.

Obviously, analysis for comprehension depends on memory storage of both words and concepts. The lexical store of word meanings required for semantic interpretation is diffusely located, centered primarily in the temporal lobe, although the exact location is unknown. Incoming information is transmitted to the *hippocampus* and related structures for consolidation prior to storage. Conceptual, experiential memory is stored throughout the cortex (Thatcher & John, 1977).

Production processes are located in the same general area of the brain as comprehension functions, many sharing the same structures. One difficulty in describing the process is that "oral language is highly redundant, only a portion of the signal being necessary for transmission of meaning" (Mateer, 1983, p. 146). The conceptual basis of a message to be produced forms in one of the many memory areas of the cortex. The underlying structure of the message is organized in Wernicke's area; the message is then transmitted through the **arcuate fasciculus**, a white fibrous tract underlying the angular gyrus, to **Broca's area**, in the frontal lobe (Figure 4.5). Broca's area is responsible for detailing and coordinating the programming for verbalizing the message. Signals are then passed to

FIGURE 4.5   Productive Linguistic Processing
Messages are transmitted from Wernicke's area to Broca's area via the white fibrous tract of the arcuate fasciculus.

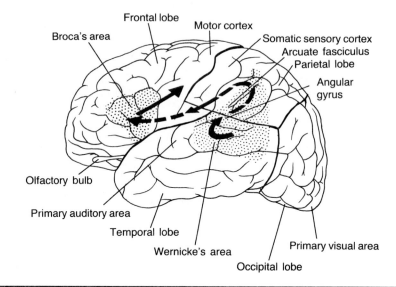

the regions of the motor cortex that activate the muscles responsible for respiration, phonation, resonation, and articulation. Damage to any of these areas results in disruption of linguistic production, but with different effects. Injury to Wernicke's area causes disruptions in both expressive and receptive language abilities. If damage occurs to the arcuate fasciculus, speech fluency and articulation are unaffected but the resultant speech doesn't make sense. Finally, damage to Broca's area results in speech difficulties, but writing and language comprehension may be relatively unaffected.

Geschwind (1974) characterizes the expressive process as one in which ideational or conceptual information is "fed forward" to the frontal regions. The message is conceived abstractly and given specific form as it passes from the posterior ideational areas to anterior motor execution areas. Writing follows a similar pathway, passing from Wernicke's area to the angular and supramarginal gyri. From here the message passes to *Exner's area* for activation of the muscles used for writing.

The actual processes are much more complex than our quick description suggests. Many areas have multiple or as yet unknown functions. Also, describing the location of a function does not explain how that function is performed. Several models of brain functioning have attempted to fill this need.

Models of Linguistic Processing

Several models help explain how language processing occurs. The model that actually applies varies, depending on the task and the individual language user (Lemme & Daves, 1982). First, we must distinguish between structures and control processes. Structures are the fixed anatomical and physiological features of the CNS. Structures and their functions are similar across the healthy brains of most individuals. How these structures respond to, organize, analyze, and synthesize incoming linguistic information varies with the individual and with the task involved. The way information is processed represents the voluntary problem-solving strategies of each person, called *information processing*.

Information Processing

The human brain can be described in terms of its structures and control processes. Structures of the CNS probably vary little from person to person. In contrast, processes or the manner of responding to, organizing, analyzing, and synthesizing incoming information are more individualized. Although the exact nature of these cognitive processes is unknown, there is a relationship between measured intelligence and the speed of information processing (Sperber & McCauley, 1984).

Information processing can be divided into the processes of *attention* and *discrimination, organization, memory,* and *transfer* (Figure 4.6). Basic anatomical structures are assumed to be similar for most individuals. Most researchers attribute observed qualitative differences to operational or processing differences. For example, there may be differences between the automatic and effortful processing abilities. Automatic processes are those that are unintentional or that have become routinized and thus require very little of the available cognitive capacity. Individual differences in automatic processing are minimized, and such processing neither interferes with other tasks nor becomes more efficient with practice (Hasher & Zacks, 1979). Effortful processing, on the other hand, requires concentration and attention by the brain. For some, effortful processing is slower to develop and requires greater effort.

Attention and Discrimination. Attention includes both awareness of a learning situation and active cognitive processing. The individual does not attend to all stimuli. Attending can be divided into orientation, reaction, and discrimination. *Orientation* is the ability to sustain attention over time. In part, this is related to the individual's ability to determine the uniqueness of the stimulus. *Reaction* refers to the amount of time required for an individual to respond to a stimulus. In part, reaction time is a function of the individual's ability to select the relevant dimensions of a task to which she is to respond. Discrimination is the ability to identify stimuli differing along some dimension. If an individual cannot identify the relevant characteristics, she will have difficulty comparing the new input with stored information.

FIGURE 4.6   Information Processing Model
Incoming information to which the brain attends is first subjected to discrimination to determine its relative novelty or familiarity. On the basis of this discrimination, information is organized for storage. The organization aids retrieval by making information readily available. This information can then be transferred to novel problems to aid in their solution.

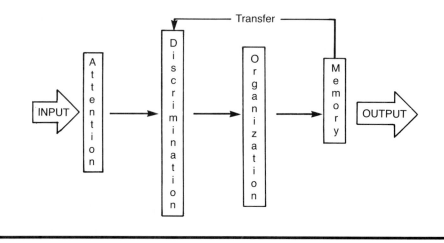

In general, less developmentally mature populations are less efficient at attention allocation and have a more limited attentional capacity (Nugent & Mosley, 1987). These processes are relatively automatic for more mature individuals and require only minimal allocation of the available resources of the brain. Thus, children must allocate more of the limited resources of the brain at this level, leaving fewer resources available for higher-level processes.

Organization.   The organization of incoming sensory information is important for later retrieval. Information is organized or "chunked" by category. Poor organization will quickly overload the storage capacity of the brain and hinder memory. It is theorized that memory capacity is fixed and, thus, that better memory results from better organization (Case, 1978). In other words, better organization results in more efficient use of the limited capacity. The lack of chunking hinders later recall, because it is more difficult to recall unrelated bits of information. Two organizational strategies seem to predominate, mediational and associative. In mediational strategies, a symbol forms a link to some information. For example, an image might facilitate recall of an event. In associative strategies, one symbol is linked to another, as in such common linkages as "men and _____" or "pins and _____."

Memory.   Recall or memory is the ability to recall information that has been learned previously. Short-term memory is very limited, and most adults can hold fewer than 10 items simultaneously. Information is retained in long-term memory by rehearsal or repetition and organization.

Every stimulus event has both a sensory impression or signal, which is inherent in the event, and an abstract or symbolic representation for that event (Dance, 1967; Whatmough, 1956). The signal is meaningful but nonlinguistic. For example, the sound of an engine may signal an automobile. In contrast, the abstract representation or word is linguistic in nature. In early presymbolic development, children seem to use sensory images in their cognitive processing. After the acquisition of language, these children have two available memory codes. In other words, the early meaning of *doggie* is based on the perceptual attributes of the examples of *dog* that are encountered. The symbol or word *doggie* is superimposed later. The ability to infer an entity from an auditory signal is part of the early linguistic knowledge base (Ervin-Tripp, 1973; Macnamara, 1972). *Echoic memory* is "the ability to hear a sound for some time after physical stimulation has ceased" (Watkins & Watkins, 1980, p. 252). In other words, echoic memory is the ability to remember what is heard when it is no longer present. It is a passive retention strategy related to immediate recall of linguistic stimuli, especially during the relatively rapid rates of presentation found in conversation (Hockey, 1973). This echo decays rapidly, requiring the signal to be processed quickly.

Transfer.   Transfer or generalization is the ability to apply previously learned material in solving similar but novel problems. The greater the similarity between the two, the greater the transfer. When the two are very similar, generalization is called *near transfer*. When very dissimilar, it is called *far transfer*.

Other Processing

The general nature of information processing theory makes it alone an inadequate explanation of purely linguistic processing. Several other types of processing have been proposed for linguistic information. These are *top-down/bottom-up*, *passive/active*, and *serial/parallel* processes.

Top-down/Bottom-up Processing.   Top-down and bottom-up processing differ with the level of information input. (See the discussion of reading in Chapter 10.) Top-down processing is *conceptually driven*, or affected by the expectations of the individual concerning incoming information. In a sense, the cortex prepares other areas of the brain to receive certain kinds of information. Hypotheses are thus formed regarding incoming data, enabling the individual to predict meaning. Knowledge, both cognitive and semantic, is used to cue lower-order functions to search for particular information. For example, when we hear "The cat caught a . . .," we predict the next word. In contrast, bottom-up processing is *data driven*. Analysis occurs at the levels of sound and syllable discrimination and proceeds upward to recognition and comprehension. For example, analysis of the word *mouse* would begin at the phoneme level with /m aʊ s/. The two processes may occur simultaneously or may be used for particular processing tasks.

Passive/Active Processing.   Passive and active processing are based on recognizing patterns of incoming information. In passive processing, incoming data are analyzed in fragments until enough information can be combined for the individual to recognize a pattern. This method is similar to bottom-up processing. The contrasting active process involves the use of a comparator strategy that matches input with either a previously stored or a generated pattern. In actual practice, both processes probably occur simultaneously.

Serial/Parallel Processing. Finally, serial and parallel or successive and simultaneous processing vary with the speed and volume of information flow (Das, Kirby, & Jarman, 1979). Serial, or successive, processes are temporal in nature and access information in a linear fashion as it comes in. Located in the left frontal and temporal lobes, successive processes analyze information at one level and then pass it on to the next level. For example, the incoming frequency, intensity, and duration of a signal are synthesized to determine the phonemic features. These features are bundled into phonemic characteristics, then syllables, words, and so on until the message is understood. Parallel, or simultaneous, processing accesses multiple levels of analysis at the same time. Located in the occipital and parietal association areas and possibly in the right hemisphere, simultaneous processing deals with underlying meaning and relationships. In practice, the two processes occur together, with overall comprehension dependent on the one that most efficiently processes incoming information or outgoing signals. Although successive processing is more precise, it necessarily takes more of the brain's processing potential and is relatively slow. It is therefore quickly overwhelmed, so simultaneous processing must carry the bulk of the responsibility for comprehension. When the incoming rate slows, successive processing again takes over.

Imagine that your brain is writing out each message that enters, in the way you do when taking notes. If the lecturer goes slowly over important points, you can write every word or process successively. Since this situation is rare, however, you usually scramble to summarize what the lecturer has said, recording the overall meaning of the information. This situation is similar to the two functions of successive and simultaneous processing.

An Overall Model of Linguistic Processing

The location in the brain and the exact neurological behaviors that result in functioning of the various processes are unknown. Also, it must be stressed that these four models are only attempts to explain brain processing of linguistic information; they may not represent actual neurological processing at all.

It may be helpful to conceptualize the processing of linguistic information as consisting of tiered peripheral and central systems (Whitaker, 1970) (Figure 4.7). Peripheral systems are concerned with the functioning of input and output modes, such as the actual reception of sound or production of speech. Central systems consist of tracking mechanisms in the cortex that serve as relay stations for the input and output information. These tracking mechanisms activate central language encoding and decoding.

Central systems include not only language processing and analysis but also attention and memory. The central system directs the brain, via the reticular system, to attend to certain stimuli. These stimuli are held in short-term memory

FIGURE 4.7   Schematic of Whitaker's Language System

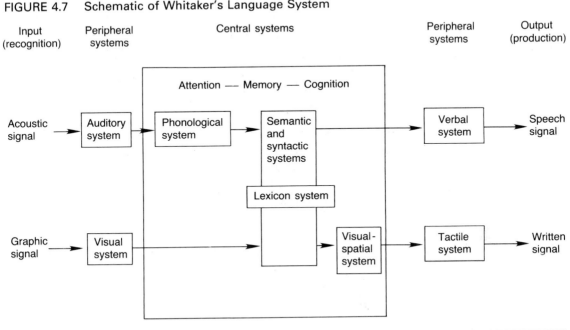

until they are perceptually decoded. Higher-order processing goes beyond perception and involves lexical and semantic-syntactic analysis. Written and oral communication pass through similar processing. Speech and writing are the reverse of audition and reading, respectively. Processing begins with semantic-syntactic formation and proceeds to the appropriate mode of production.

The lexical store is given a central location in the tiered model and is considered to be dispersed widely throughout the cortex. Comprehension and production rely on symbol recall and retrieval. This model prioritizes linguistic processes. The hierarchy may be helpful for conceptualizing these processes and their interactions.

CONCLUSION

Language processing, both expressive and receptive, is located primarily in the left hemisphere of the brain in most adults. Anatomical differences between the hemispheres have been noted in the fetus, but specialization for language develops later in the maturing child. Although most major language processing functions are generally situated anatomically within the brain, their exact location and function are not totally understood. The effects on these processes of past learning, problem-solving ability, memory, and language itself are also unclear. It is known, however, that cognition, or the ability to use the resources of the brain, is closely related to the overall language level of each individual.

REFLECTIONS

1. Luria (1970) described three basic brain functions: regulation, processing, and formulation. Explain how these functions, especially processing, relate to linguistic material.
2. In most humans the left hemisphere is dominant for linguistic processing. Can you name the major areas responsible for this processing?
3. Few theorists would argue with the notion of brain lateralization for language. Can you explain the major theories on how this lateralization occurs?
4. Explain briefly how language is processed relative to specific areas of the brain.
5. Describe information processing theory and the several models of language comprehension and production processes associated with it.

5 Cognitive and Perceptual Bases of Early Language

CHAPTER OBJECTIVES

The use of symbols requires a certain level of cognitive or mental skill, as well as certain perceptual abilities. In this chapter we shall explore both cognition and perception and relate them to the early development of symbols. When you have completed this chapter, you should understand

- the relationship of cognition to language.
- the basic principles of Piaget's theory of development.
- the developmental characteristics of the sensorimotor stage of development.
- the aspects of the sensorimotor stage that contribute to the ability to symbolize.
- the main aspects of information-processing theory.
- the contribution of perception to early learning.
- the following terms:

accommodation	linguistic determinism
adaptation	linguistic relativism
assimilation	organization
cognitive stimulation	perceptual stimulation
distancing	rehearsal
equilibrium	schemata
habituation	sign
index	signal
information processing	symbol
integrative rehearsal	

I N THE FIRST FOUR chapters, we looked at some cognitive developmental milestones and at the relationship of cognition to language. Many (though not all) theorists would agree that "the pacesetter in linguistic growth is the child's cognitive growth" (Slobin, 1973, p. 184).

The purpose of this chapter is not to reopen the cognition-first argument. Rather, it is to examine early cognitive development for clues to the child's ability to use symbols. In addition, this chapter will add substance and order to the cognitive development information provided in Chapter 3 and place these milestones in perspective. In this chapter I am assuming, as others have, that a certain level of cognitive functioning is required before a child uses expressive language (Bates, Camaioni, & Volterra, 1975; Bowerman, 1974; E. Clark, 1974b; Macnamara, 1972; Morehead & Morehead, 1974; Slobin, 1973). Further, I am assuming that certain perceptual abilities are also required for the child to learn language by hearing it, as most children do.

The infant is not a passive creature but is actively engaged in his environment, "building a vocabulary of . . . experiences and forming abilities on which later learning depends" (Caplan, 1973, p. 79). The infant organizes his experiences into general classes and larger concepts. Of particular importance for students of language development is the means by which the child learns to represent, or symbolize, these ideas and concepts. The importance of this representational ability cannot be overemphasized. "The ability to represent one thing with another can be regarded as one of the most fundamental cognitive prerequisites for language acquisition" (Bowerman, 1974, p. 192). For example, a child can use a piece of wood to represent a doll's chair. In a similar fashion, the word *chair* can also symbolize a chair.

In this chapter we will first explore the general question of the relationship of cognition and language. Next, we will examine two comprehensive theories of early cognitive development, Piaget's and information processing. After examining these theories, we will explore their relationship to language development. Finally, we will discuss early perceptual growth and its importance for language development.

WHICH CAME FIRST, COGNITION OR LANGUAGE?

In general, we can divide theories on the relationship of thought and language into four types (Figure 5.1). Piaget and others hypothesize a strong cognitive model, represented in Figure 5.1 by model A. According to this theory, cognition is responsible for language acquisition and cognitive knowledge is the basis for word meanings. (See the discussion of *cognitive determinism* in Chapter 2.) In

FIGURE 5.1   Models of the Cognition-Language Relationship

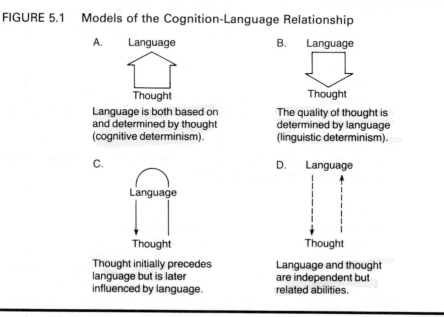

A.   Language

Thought

Language is both based on and determined by thought (cognitive determinism).

B.   Language

Thought

The quality of thought is determined by language (linguistic determinism).

C.

Language

Thought

Thought initially precedes language but is later influenced by language.

D.   Language

Thought

Language and thought are independent but related abilities.

contrast, others, such as Whorf, favor a model of language influencing thought called *linguistic determinism*, represented by model B. Whorf proposed that language strongly influences the very quality of thought. A more moderate position is that of Vygotsky, represented by model C, in which cognition precedes language but, in turn, is influenced by linguistic structures. Finally, in the independent theory of Chomsky, represented by model D, the two are considered to be relatively separate but related abilities, each having some limited influence upon the other.

Piaget proposed a model of cognitive functioning that clearly places language upon a cognitive base. According to Piaget, cognitive growth is responsible for language. In Piaget's words, "Language is not enough to explain thought, because the structures that characterize thought have their roots in action and in sensori-motor mechanisms that are deeper than linguistics" (1954b, p. 98). While cognition and language are interrelated, cognition is clearly the dominant member. Not all theoreticians and child development specialists agree; some conclude that "a perusal of Piagetian literature on language acquisition . . . provides scant evidence for the contention that language skills are a reflection of more general cognitive operations" (T. Moore and Harris, 1978, pp. 149–150).

Lev S. Vygotsky, a Soviet psychologist and linguist, formulated a theory of specific cognitive development that is somewhat different from Piaget's theory. His last work, *Thought and Language* (1962), was first published in 1934 after his premature death from tuberculosis at age 38. In this work, Vygotsky theorized that thought and language have different genetic origins and separate curves of development. At about 2 years of age, these curves join to initiate a new behavior. According to Vygotsky (1962), "Initially thought is nonverbal and speech nonintellectual" (p. 49), but at the point at which they come together, "thought becomes verbal and speech rational" (p. 44). He called this overlap of thought and language *verbal thought*.

In early development, Piaget's and Vygotsky's accounts are similar. Only later, when the child begins to speak, do the two theorists part company. Piaget's theory still concentrates on cognitive development, with language as a peripheral concern. Language is one of many symbolic processes used to represent reality. In other words, language is a symptom of the underlying cognitive development of the child. In contrast, Vygotsky viewed language as the force that drives cognitive development because language mediates the child's participation in his intellectual and social environments.

Vygotsky did not stress the symbolic development of early thought, as Piaget did. Rather, he claimed that first words are not symbols for objects but actual properties of those objects. Vygotsky (1962) stated, "At first he [the child] uses verbal forms and meanings without being conscious of them as separate. The word, to the child, is an integral part of the object it denotes" (p. 128).

According to Piaget, the child develops egocentric speech or self-talk to label his environment and then later participates in social interaction. While Piaget considered language to be relatively independent of its social-interactive context, Vygotsky considered the two to be intrinsically linked (Hickman, 1986).

Vygotsky claimed that language is, from the beginning, social but undifferentiated in function. In other words, initially, language merely accompanies ongoing actions in the context and serves as a means of social contact. Gradually language becomes differentiated and serves both a social and an internal function.

Thought can be represented by language, but language also enables humans to develop cognitively. According to Vygotsky, language leads to new forms of cognitive organization. The child develops cognitive skills through social interaction and then uses these skills in intrapersonal behavior. Thus, language is learned in interpersonal interaction and then used by the child in self-thought.

Counter to Piaget's cognition-first position, Vygotsky (1962) theorized that "the speech structures mastered by the child become the basic structures of his thinking. . . . Thought development is determined by language. . . . The child's intellectual growth is contingent on his mastering the social means of thought, that is, language" (p. 51). As a result, language is multifunctional, serving as a social-interactive tool and also as an abstract representation for internal logical reasoning.

Gradually, the regulative behavior of adults in interactions with the child is internalized by the child. Adults use language to guide the child's behavior in problem-solving tasks that the child cannot perform alone. The adults' communication patterns vary with the age and competence of the child and the nature of the problem-solving task. Thus, the language of the adult and, later, of the child is context related. Vygotsky was interested in these functions of language much more than in the structure of language, interested more in the process than in the product.

Benjamin Whorf (1956) also proposed an interdependent theory of thought and language (often referred to as the *Whorf hypothesis*) but emphasized the dependence of thought upon language. This position, called **linguistic determinism,** states that all higher thinking is dependent on language; language determines thought. The more lexical richness or breadth in a language, the more superior the resultant cognitive development. In addition, Whorf proposed a **linguistic relativism:** if language determines thought, Whorf reasoned, then the world must be experienced differently by speakers of different languages. In other words, experiences are interpreted relative to the linguistic base. One way in which language influences the interpretation of reality is by classifying it. For example, many arctic Indians and Eskimos have several different words to describe the quality of snow. We could hypothesize that these arctic dwellers have a different perception of reality than English speakers, who use only the word *snow.* This is a lexical classification. There are also grammatical classifications such as the particular manner used to describe an event. Some languages require gender markers; all nouns are either male or female. Others do not require articles or verb endings. Both of these classification systems influence thought.

The Whorf hypothesis is extremely difficult to prove because thought is influenced by so many additional factors. Furth (1966, 1971) found that deaf children performed as well as hearing children, who had much better oral and written language skills. Therefore, Furth concluded that language was not required for some forms of thought. Jerome Bruner viewed language as an instrument of thought. In his view, possession of language is not enough, for the child must learn to organize thinking and experience within the linguistic framework. Bruner wrote that lexical hierarchy, or organization, is more important than lexical richness, or breadth.

Finally, Noam Chomsky, with his psycholinguistic emphasis on innate structures, took issue with the experiential nature of Piaget's cognition-first notions. In a debate with Piaget, Chomsky (1980) summarized this point:

> It is a curiosity of our intellectual history that cognitive structures developed by the mind are generally regarded and studied very differently from physical structures developed by the body. . . . The expectation that constructions of sensorimotor intelligence determine the character of a mental organ such as language seems to me hardly more plausible than a proposal that the fundamental properties of the eye or the visual cortex or the heart develop on this basis. Furthermore, when we turn to specific properties of this mental organ, we find little justification for any such belief, so far as I can see. (p. 37)

Earlier, Chomsky (1968) had dismissed the cognition-first notion of language acquisition. "The child acquires language . . . at a time when he is not capable of complex intellectual achievement in many other domains. This achievement is relatively independent of intelligence or the particular course of experience" (p. 66).

The exact relationship of thought and language is unknown. For every example of thought influencing language, there is another of the opposite relationship. I. Schlesinger (1977) has proposed four hypotheses, any one of which may explain the relationship. First, cognitive attainment may explain some linguistic achievements, and linguistic attainment may explain others. Second, some children may use a sensorimotor approach to language acquisition, while others may use a linguistic approach. Third, both cognitive and linguistic factors may operate within the same child, but at different points in language acquisition. Therefore, cognitive and linguistic factors do not operate simultaneously. Fourth, cognitive and linguistic factors may operate simultaneously and be mutually supportive. It may be that thought and language are so closely aligned that it is difficult to separate them. Possibly the relationship changes at various stages of development or with the task involved. Jenkins (1969) posed the question as follows:

> What is the relationship between thought and language?
>
> 1. Thought is dependent on language.
> 2. Thought is language.
> 3. Language is dependent on thought. . . .
> 4. None of the above. Or perhaps, all of the above. (p. 212)

The correct answer, according to Jenkins, is "all of the above." Stated another way, as the child's "capacity to communicate symbolically develops, language and thought become so inextricably intermixed [that] it becomes almost impossible to separate [them]" (Lindsay & Norman, 1977, p. 437).

PIAGET'S THEORY OF COGNITIVE DEVELOPMENT

One of the foremost influences on modern cognitive development theory has been Jean Piaget, a Swiss biologist and scholar. In general, he viewed cognitive development not as a quantitative accumulation of ideas and facts but as qualitative changes in the process of thought. Piaget theorized that an organism organizes and stores material in differing ways as a result of its maturation. These changes occur through the organism's active involvement with the environment. The motivation for change or learning is internal as the organism attempts to reach a balance between new and previously known information.

Basic Theoretical Tenets

Through his early biological research, Piaget realized that all living organisms adapt to changes in the environment. He theorized that such adaptations were intellectual or cognitive as well as physical. In *The Origins of Intelligence in Children* (1952), Piaget declared that the basic principles of cognition and biological development are the same and that cognition cannot be separated from the organism's total functioning. Obviously, cognitive and biological functioning are not exactly the same, nor does cognitive development depend solely upon biological development. Therefore, Piaget repeatedly refers to intelligence as "a particular instance of biological adaptation" (1952, pp. 3–4), "a system of living and acting operations" (1950, p. 7).

As an organism develops, its conceptual system changes. In Piaget's theory, the conceptual system consists of organized patterns of reaction to stimuli he called *schemata*. **Schemata** are the cognitive structures of an individual that are used for processing incoming sensory information. As new stimuli are received, the organism (the person) tries to fit this information into existing schemata. An event is perceived in a certain way and organized or categorized according to common characteristics. This is an active process involving interpretation and classification. In addition, new information may require the reorganization of the cognitive structures. An individual's response to a given stimulus is based on his cognitive structures and his ability to respond. For example, successive viewings of different dogs may confirm the concept of *dog* as four-legged, fur-covered, and barking; they can therefore be organized within that general concept. *Elephant* does not fit into this concept, so the scheme for *dog* must be either disregarded or adapted to include the new concept. With experience, schemata change and become more refined. Thus, there is no one intelligence for humankind or for any one person; rather, there is a succession of "intelligences" as schemata evolve. An individual's response to stimuli at a given time reflects his concepts or schemata. This cognitive evolution, or development, is a result of organization and adaptation, two complementary processes.

Organization and adaptation are two basic functions found in all organisms (Figure 5.2). **Organization** is the tendency to systematize or organize processes (either physical or cognitive) into systems. For example, the body has several

FIGURE 5.2 Piaget's Cognitive Learning Process

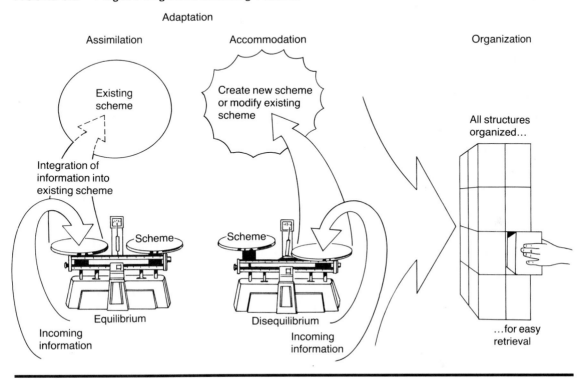

physical systems, including circulation and respiration. According to Piaget, behavioral and cognitive structures are also organized coherently. The organized cognitive structures are the schemata. **Adaptation** is the function or tendency of all organisms to change in response to the environment. Adaptation occurs as a result of two related processes, assimilation and accommodation.

Assimilation is the use of existing schemata or cognitive structures to incorporate external stimuli (Figure 5.2). In other words, assimilation is an attempt to deal with stimuli in terms of present cognitive structures. In this way, an organism continually integrates new perceptual matter into existing patterns. For example, an Irish setter is similar enough to be incorporated into the dog category along with collies and German shepherds. Obviously, these types of dogs are not identical, nor are they all examples of Irish setters, but the similarities are great enough to allow their assimilation into the same category. Without such categorization, we could make little sense of the environment. Thus, assimilation is the goal of all adaptation. However, not all stimuli fit into available schemata, and mental structures must be adapted to these stimuli.

Accommodation is a transformation of cognitive structures in response to external stimuli that do not fit into any available scheme and, therefore, cannot be assimilated (Figure 5.2). As such, an individual has the option of modifying an existing scheme or developing a new schema. The Irish setter could be included in the dog concept. An elephant, however, is sufficiently different to require a new category. The dog category is not elastic enough for both animals. Once the organism has accommodated its schemata to the external stimulus, the new information is assimilated, or incorporated, into the new or modified scheme. The new scheme does not replace the old one. They are both retained. Thus, the processes of assimilation and accommodation are complementary and mutually dependent. New or modified structures are created continually and then used to aid the organism's comprehension of the environment.

Each organism is more effective in interacting with the environment if that organism is in equilibrium with the environment. **Equilibrium** is a state of cognitive balance, or harmony, between incoming stimuli and the organism's cognitive structures. Obviously, equilibrium is only momentary for any given stimulus, but nonetheless it is the state toward which all organisms strive. Equilibrium is the "driving force" of cognitive and other biological changes. In *The Psychology of Intelligence* (1950), Piaget stated that intelligence "is the form of equilibrium towards which the successive adaptations and changes between the organism and his environment are directed" (p. 6). Thus, intelligence, or cognitive functioning, changes with each adaptation, or attempt to achieve equilibrium. The results of these changes are different cognitive structures that occur in fairly predictable patterns.

Cognitive Development

Qualitative changes in schemata are called *development*. Obviously, the operational schemata of the young child and the adult are very different. The adult's cognitive structures have adapted through experience. The child's schemata evolve through experience to become the schemata, or cognitive structures, of the adult. Thus, there is a slow evolution of gradual transformations. As an individual develops intellectually, he passes through stages characterized by recognizable cognitive structures and by distinct interactional patterns with the environment. The motivation behind this change is the intrinsic need of cognitive functioning "to master problematic situations, to be effective with respect to one's environment, to be competent . . . an important part of the cognitive system's power source" (Flavell, 1977, pp. 22–23).

"Piaget's general 'hypothesis' is simply that cognitive development is a coherent process of successive qualitative changes of cognitive structures (schemata), each structure and its concomitant change derived logically and inevitably from the preceding one" (Wadsworth, 1979, p. 27). For the purposes of explanation, Piaget divided intellectual development into stages, each characterized by qualitatively different cognitive structures.

Piaget's developmental stages are organized in a hierarchy. The order of the stages is invariant because each is necessary for movement to the next. Although each child must pass through each stage in the order given, the rate may vary due to heredity or experience. According to Piaget (1952), "The different stages do not succeed each other in a linear way . . . but in the manner of the layers of a pyramid . . ., the new behavior patterns simply being added to the old ones to complete, correct, or combine with them" (p. 329).

Piaget's four broad stages of cognitive development are *sensorimotor, preoperational, concrete operational,* and *formal operational.* Each represents progressively more complex cognitive operations. The characteristics of each period or stage are listed in Table 5.1. These characteristics merely highlight the most important distinctions and are not meant to imply that change is rapid or total. Within a given stage, there will be a great variety of cognitive behaviors between children. For example, a preoperational child of 2 years of age is, of course, very different from a child of 7. Of the four stages listed in Table 5.1, only the sensorimotor is germane to the topic of cognitive bases of language. The other stages will be mentioned in succeeding chapters.

TABLE 5.1   Piaget's Stages of Cognitive Development

Stage	Approximate Age (Years)	Characteristics
Sensorimotor	0–2	Reflexive to proactive behavior
		Ability to represent reality (symbolic function), to invent novel means to desired ends without trial-and-error methodology, to imitate when model not immediately present and to represent absent people and objects
		Symbolic play
Preoperational	2–7	Further development of symbolic function: language, physical problem solving, categorization
		Thinking characterized by centration, irreversibility, and egocentricity
Concrete operational	7–11	Thinking characterized by conservation, decentration, and reversibility
		Logical thought relative to concrete or physical operations
		Categorization into hierarchical and seriational categories
Formal operational	11 +	Capability of abstract thought, complex reasoning, flexibility
		Mental hypothesis testing

Sensorimotor Stage: Age Birth–2 Years

Officially, the sensorimotor stage or period of development begins at birth, but in fact, learning probably occurs in utero (Guerleu & Renard, 1981). In either case, the infant experiences tremendous cognitive growth during the 2 years following birth. It is within this period that the basic structures of intelligence begin to evolve. Whereas the newborn possesses only a few reflexive sensorimotor schemata, the 2-year-old child is capable of symbolic thought. By the end of the sensorimotor period, the child can solve many physical problems through thought and can communicate through the use of language. In addition, he can mentally invent means for reaching desired ends without the use of sensorimotor trial-and-error input.

It is possible, therefore, to speak of sensorimotor intelligence. As noted in Chapter 2, the infant is capable of many complex cognitive behaviors. Obviously, this functioning is not reflective in nature but is shown in organized patterns of actions that Piaget characterizes as prerepresentational. Sensorimotor intelligence is similar to the level of cognition used by adults for routine motor tasks, such as putting on socks. The sensorimotor child "thinks" to the extent that he interacts with familiar people and objects in predictable ways that demonstrate recognition. Thus, the child's cognitive structures, or schemata, represent action-oriented functioning. For example, rather than labeling or classifying an object, the sensorimotor child will behave toward that object in a way that indicates that he knows its function. His schemata are organized according to sensory input and motor responses. Flavell (1977) described a sensorimotor schema as follows:

> A scheme generally has to do with a specific, readily labelable class of sensory-motor action sequences that the infant repeatedly and habitually carries out, normally in response to particular classes of objects or situations. The scheme itself is generally thought of as referring to the inner, mental-structural basis for these overt action sequences; it is, in other words, the cognitive capacity that underlies and makes possible such organized behavior pattern. (p. 17)

Schemata may be coordinated or combined for more complex interactions.

Piaget has divided the sensorimotor period into six stages of progressively more complex cognitive structures. Each stage, according to Piaget (1964), is

> defined by the fact that the child becomes capable of certain behavior patterns of which he was up to then incapable; it is not the fact that he renounces the behavior patterns of the preceding stages, even if they are contrary to the new ones. (p. 299)

Again, the order of stages is invariant but the rate of progress varies with the individual. Cultural factors also influence rate, and there may be some variation between the Swiss children that Piaget studied several decades ago and modern American children. The major accomplishments of each stage are listed in Table 5.2. The behavioral changes accompanying each stage are observable in the play of children. Let's discuss the major observable changes in imitation, object concept, causality, and means-ends.

TABLE 5.2   Piaget's Sensorimotor Stages

Stage and Age (Months)	General	Imitation	Object Concept	Causality	Means–Ends
Stage 1 Birth–1	Reflexive Adaptive intelligence	Notion not present	No differentiation of self from objects	Egocentric	Notion not present
Stage 2 1–4	Primary circular reactions (self-repetitions) Coordination of sensory schema	Self-imitation of actions with unexpected results "Preimitation"	Object followed with eyes until out of view Change in perspective interpreted as change in object	No differentiation of self and moving objects	Notion not present Intentionality lacking
Stage 3 4–8	Secondary circular reactions Repetition of actions of others	Imitation of others' actions already in repertoire	Anticipation of position of moving objects; no manual search	Self as cause of all events	Repetition of events with unexpected outcomes; heightened interest in event outcome Intentionality follows initiation of behavior
Stage 4 8–12	Coordination of secondary schemata Known means applied to new problems	Imitation of behaviors different from those in repertoire Facial imitation	Manual search for object where last seen Object constancy	Some externalization of causality Realization that objects can cause action	Coordination and integration of schemata Establishment of goal prior to initiation of activity Anticipation of outcomes
Stage 5 12–18	Tertiary secondary schemata Experimentation	Imitation of behaviors markedly different from repertoire	Sequential displacements considered Awareness of object spatial relations	Realization that he is one of many objects in environment	New means through experimentation Tools used
Stage 6 18–24	New means through mental combination Representational thought	Deferred imitation	Representation of displacements Awareness of unseen movements	Representation of causality Able to predict cause–effect relationship	Language used to influence others Representation of outcome or end

Stage 1: Birth–1 Month

According to the theories of Piaget, the behavior of the stage 1 child is almost totally reflexive. The child makes no differentiation between stimuli and understands no causality beyond his own egocentric view of the environment. In the stage 1 child's view, he is a part of all objects and causes all events. Some reflexes, such as the gag reflex, remain unchanged throughout life and, therefore, are of little interest developmentally. Others, such as the sucking and rooting reflexes, undergo significant changes as a result of interaction with the environment. Piaget considered these latter behaviors to be the building blocks of cognitive development. This stage has been called one of *adaptive intelligence,* for the child continually adjusts his behavior to unfamiliar environmental conditions. In fact, by the end of stage 1, the child has already begun to differentiate his sucking response to accommodate to the environment. These small, yet significant, experience-based changes indicate cognitive growth.

Stage 2: 1–4 Months

In stage 2, reflexive behavior is further modified. As the infant reacts reflexively, he assimilates and accommodates to sensory information, thus producing the initial changes in his schemata. Continual practice of schemata, such as sucking, looking, and prehension or reaching, results in elaboration and refinements of these behaviors. Toward the end of stage 2, the sucking response begins to occur in anticipation of eating: the nipple becomes a sign for the event that will follow, and the child responds with sucking.

In addition to the continued change in sensorimotor schemata, there is a gradual coordination of these schemata. Increased coordination and integration are evidenced in eye–hand coordination, visual following of a moving object, localization to sound, and purposeful thumb sucking. Eye–hand coordination is particularly important for later exploration. Piaget has recorded several steps of eye–hand development of reaching. In the final step, the child is able to reach without watching his hand and the object simultaneously.

Localization of sound results from coordination of vision and audition. It represents an early object concept because of the association of the object with a specific sound. In general, the child is uninterested in an object that he cannot see but will follow an object's path briefly as it moves out of view. In addition to making object–sound associations, the child begins to associate people with their voices in stage 2.

Finally, thumb sucking, which begins prior to stage 2, becomes child directed or purposeful. This behavior was previously random or chance.

In general, however, the child lacks intentionality. He does not initiate behaviors with a desired end in mind. His behavior is reflexive for the most part, and goals are not identified until after he begins an action sequence. For example, the child will reach for an object in front of him but is incapable of uncovering or searching for an object that is not in view. "It is with the appearance of . . . deferred reactions," stated Piaget (1952), "that the purpose of the action, ceasing to be in some way directly perceived, presupposes a continuity in searching, and consequently a beginning of intention" (p. 143).

Imitation in stage 2 is primarily self-imitation, and it is for this reason that the stage has been called the stage of *primary circular reactions*. The child produces an action pattern, and the resultant feedback further elicits the behavior. For example, sucking produces the tactile pressure in the mouth to elicit more sucking. Piaget and others have also noted a behavior they label *preimitation*: the child will repeat a habitual behavior if someone imitates the behavior immediately after the child has performed it.

Stage 3: 4–8 Months

The third stage of cognitive development is characterized by *secondary circular reactions*, in which feedback is not solely proprioceptive, or from within the organism, but also results from the effect of moving some external object or from an event. The child will repeat his own actions in an attempt to sustain an event. This early goal-directed, or intentional, behavior has been called *reproductive assimilation* because the child continues to repeat a behavior for which he has a schema. As before, however, the goal of the behavior is established only after the activity begins.

Even though the child attempts to sustain an activity, it cannot be said that he has a concept of causality, or cause and effect, beyond himself. The stage 3 child remains egocentric, believing that he causes events to happen. Although he repeats an action for the pleasure desired, this is not true causality because the child makes little attempt to explore the effect of his behavior. Yet in stage 3 there is an increased interest in environmental effects beyond the preoccupation with his own actions seen in stages 1 and 2.

The child's increased interest in events beyond his body is also reflected in an increased orientation toward objects. The child reaches for familiar objects even if they are partially hidden from view. He grasps the object and manipulates it for inspection, thus exhibiting greater coordination between vision and prehension. Although the child is able to anticipate the future position through which a moving object will pass, he does not search for a hidden object. "Herein lies the essential limitation of stage 3," stated Flavell (1977). "The baby will exhibit brief and limited visual search for objects that have disappeared from sight, but he will show no manual search whatever" (p. 43). The lack of physical searching does not diminish the child's growing, albeit limited, concept of objects.

The stage 3 child applies his limited behavior repertoire rather indiscriminately to objects (Uzgiris, 1976). His primary behaviors include mouthing, banging, looking, and shaking. There appears to be little knowledge of, or concern for, the objects' properties. Near the end of stage 3, the child goes through a transition. He begins to combine or sequence schemata into an "examining" schema. In addition, he interacts more with responsive objects and people. Finally, the child begins to coordinate actions on different objects.

During stage 3 the child begins to imitate others when two conditions are met. First, he will only imitate behaviors he produced spontaneously on another occasion. Second, the child must see and hear himself as he produces the imitations. For example, the child can see his hands and hear the sound when he

The infant in sensorimotor stage 3 is increasingly interested in object play and object manipulation. He will inspect objects visually and can anticipate their location but will not search for hidden objects.

bangs an object on the table. If he has performed this motor act before on his own, then during stage 3 he is likely to imitate this action when it is performed by others.

Stage 4: 8–12 Months

According to Piaget, the stage 4 child exhibits the first clear evidence of thought. For example, the child displays true intentionality in the development of means–ends behaviors. To attain desired objectives, the child begins to integrate previous environmentally oriented schemata. Thus, this stage has been labeled *coordinated secondary schemata*. The stage 4 child is able to establish a goal and select a means to that end before he takes action. Often the means are coordinated for an end that is not immediately directly attainable. For example, the child may realize that he must put down one object in order to pick up another or that he can pull a string to obtain an object at the other end.

In part, this means–ends behavior reflects the child's developing ability to anticipate events independent of those currently in progress. The child is able to associate certain indices with actions that will follow, even though these signs may not be directly related. For example, the child may cry when his mother turns away but before she actually departs.

Stage 4 imitation is more flexible than that exhibited in stage 3. Physical imitation has now become a learning tool because the child can imitate behaviors that differ to some degree from those already in his repertoire. In addition, he can imitate motor behaviors that he cannot actually see on himself, such as facial expressions. That imitation requires a limited degree of short-term memory of motor behaviors.

The stage 4 child can also remember objects, and he realizes that they exist even when they are not seen. If an object is hidden, the child will manually search for it, usually in the location in which the object disappeared. However, unseen multiple displacements or multiple hidings cannot be solved in this stage. In addition to this early form of object permanence, the child shows evidence of concepts such as object constancy and causality. By stage 4 the child demonstrates that he is aware that an object has not changed when it appears to be smaller or when it is viewed from a different perspective. The child has learned that qualities such as shape and size do not change. He has also learned that objects can cause action. In this stage the child demonstrates what is called *differential saliency:* the recognition that some objects have more interesting or important features than others. Thus, the child plays longer and manipulates more complex toys more often. Object manipulation is characterized by differentiated actions. The child's action repertoire is applied more discriminately to objects. In stage 4, the child begins to externalize causality. He realizes that other people and objects may be the source of activity.

In summary, stage 4 is a very important stage in cognitive development. Several behaviors indicate an externalization of cognitive functioning. Through interaction with the environment, the child has become less egocentric in thought and action. In addition, the stage 4 child is able to interpret indices and thus anticipate actions. The use of indices is a step toward truly symbolic representation. Finally, the child demonstrates limited short-term motor memory. All of these behaviors will be significant for later symbol use.

Stage 5: 12–18 Months

Stage 5 is the last totally sensorimotor stage. It is filled with experimentation with objects and with exploration. Subtitled *tertiary secondary schemata*, this stage is characterized by the coordination of new schemes to solve problems. New means are established through trial-and-error experimentation. Thus, the stage 5 child is very adaptable to new situations. Piaget (1952) called this experimentation "empirical intelligence" and suggested that behavior becomes intelligent when a child acquires the ability to solve new problems. The child explores real properties of objects and experiments with object potentials. There appears to be an ongoing search for new methods of interaction. In addition, the child exhibits true experimentation as he waits to see the outcome of his behavior.

In addition, the stage 5 child is a skilled imitator. Within his motor limitations, the child is capable of imitating behaviors that are markedly different from those in his repertoire.

Finally, the concept of object permanence has developed to the point at which the child will manually search for an object through sequential or multiple displacements. This searching will be situationally oriented and not dependent on previous patterns of success.

Stage 6: 18–24 Months

Sensorimotor stage 6 is characterized by *new means through mental combination*. It is in this last sensorimotor stage that the child progresses from sensorimotor to representational intelligence. In this stage the child is able to represent objects internally and to solve problems through thought, demonstrating real symbolic functioning. Object representation is exhibited in the child's ability to solve *invisible displacements*. He searches for an object even though he did not see it hidden. Thus, he is freed from a reliance on immediate observational and perceptual information. This change is also noted in the child's problem-solving abilities. Experimentation is accomplished in thought, through symbolization of actions rather than through actions themselves. As Piaget (1952) explained:

> Before trying them, the child foresees which maneuvers will fail and which will succeed. . . . Moreover, the procedure conceived . . . is in itself new, that is to say, it results from an original mental combination and from a combination of movements actually executed at each stage of the operation. (pp. 340–341)

The child is able to solve problems in part because he can predict the cause–effect relationship.

The ability to use symbols is also exhibited in the child's ability to produce and comprehend words when the referents are not physically present. Most children produce their first words well before this stage, but only in the presence of the referent, or entity.

Deferred imitation, which appears in stage 6, is another example of representation. The stage 6 child can observe a behavior, store it, and retrieve it later for production. It is not unusual for the child to reproduce other children's behaviors, such as tantrums, at a later time.

Summary

The infant is born with certain reflexive sensorimotor schemata. These reflexes are gradually modified through interaction with the environment. During the sensorimotor period several developmental trends are evident. The child becomes less reflexive and less egocentric as he begins to act upon the environment. In addition, the child develops increased memory skills and increased ability to represent reality symbolically.

It is difficult to believe that the newborn is the same individual 2 years later. The overall cognitive changes are monumental. The child has moved from sensorimotor intelligence to truly symbolic thought. With this development, the child is freed from the slower process associated with motor actions and is less bound by actions or concrete objects. In addition, symbolic intelligence is a shared system that encourages communication with others. Symbols can be transmitted via speech to those who share the coding system.

Relation of Sensorimotor Period to Language

There is no Piagetian model of language development. According to Piaget, language is one of several symbolic functions. Sensorimotor intellectual development culminates with the development of symbolic or representational thought. In addition to language, other symbolic functions consist of all mental behavior that represents reality when it is not present, such as dreaming, drawing, and language.

Although there is no one-to-one relationship of cognition to language, the principles of cognitive organization apply to language. Piaget's sensorimotor cognitive development demonstrates a relational concept basis. Children learn object functions through manipulation and then use these functional characteristics to relate classes of objects. These common features may form the semantic basis for early words.

The sensorimotor development of language is a progression from signal to sign (Morehead & Morehead, 1974). Toward the end of sensorimotor stage 3, the child learns to respond to signals. A **signal** is "any indicator which elicits an action schema and in which there is no differentiation between the form of the action (signifier) and its content (significant)" (Morehead & Morehead, 1974, p. 161). For example, the bottle becomes a signal for *eat*. As you can see, many movements or vocalizations of the child and parent have the potential of becoming signals. Games such as peekaboo, for example, evoke a predictable child response; the actions of the game signal making a response.

In stage 4 the index replaces the signal as an early form of prerepresentation. The **index** is a shared property of some motor act of the child and others. The child uses similar or shared properties as a means of interpreting the actions of others. The action need not be part of its immediate context, as before. For example, when his mother puts on her coat, the child infers that the mother is leaving, though she is not actually in the process of going out the door. Each occasion of putting on her coat is similar enough to allow the child to generalize the meaning of this behavior. Before reaching stage 4, the child would respond to his mother's physical leave-taking as a signal but might not infer leave-taking from the isolated action of simply putting on a coat. In part, this change reflects the child's increased ability to anticipate behavior based on environmental cues.

The shared features of actions also aid the child's learning and are reflected in more mature motor imitation behaviors. In turn, the motor imitation is reflected in the child's beginning use of gestures and vocalizations. Children begin to imitate adult vocalizations at about 9 months of age. At about the same age, the child begins to shift from signals that represent response to an internal stimulus, such as crying, to intentional use of signals, such as gestures (Bates, Camaioni, & Volterra, 1975).

Symbols begin to appear along with first words in stage 5. A **symbol** is an entity used to represent another entity that has similar features (Morehead & Morehead, 1974). Just as a word can stand for *doggie* in the presence of a dog, a shoe may be used to represent a telephone receiver. This kind of representation presupposes an understanding of object use and properties.

Finally, in stage 6, the child begins to use signs. True **signs** denote thought about an entity or event. The sign, or word, represents cognitive structures, not the real entity or event. For example, when the stage 6 child discusses *doggie*, he is using a concept, not just the name of an entity before him. Thus the stage 6 child can talk about objects or events that are not present or are present in a novel context.

To understand the importance of cognitive development to language development, we will examine five specific aspects separately: imitation, object permanence, causality, means–ends, and play. The available research data are mostly correlational. Thus, though object permanence and language may be related, the exact nature of the relationship is unknown. Correlational results do not imply cause and effect.

Imitation

A number of studies have called early physical imitation a prerequisite to speech (Lewis, 1951; L. Snyder, 1978), to language (Bowerman, 1974; K. Moore & Meltzoff, 1978; Piaget, 1952), and to communication (K. Moore & Meltzoff, 1978; Rees, 1975). In general, imitation is important because of the developing ability to construct internal representations of the behavior of others and to duplicate them. To imitate physically, the child must be able to perform at least three tasks: turn taking, attending to the action, and replicating the action's salient features (Reichle & Yoder, 1979).

Bates and her colleagues (1979) found that vocal imitation and gestures are significantly correlated at about 9 months of age: an increase in one thus results in an increase in the other. Gestures are learned through imitation. Early gestures are *recognitory,* or functional, representing the use of objects. Appropriate use indicates that the child has a partial understanding of the object's properties. This behavior is an early form of labeling. Children "label a known object by carrying out an action typically associated with it" (Bates & Snyder, 1987). For example, using a spoon for its intended purpose signifies a knowledge of object function. In addition, the appearance of multiaction imitation schemata coincides with initial two-word utterances (McCall, Parke, & Kavanaugh, 1977).

Physical imitation is not, however, a necessary prerequisite for facial and vocal imitation, though there is a strong correlation. The speech sounds made during vocal play generally reflect environmental input. The tonal qualities of adult speech are also imitated very early. We can generalize that imitation is important for speech production.

The link of imitation to language is even less certain. Children begin to use words before stage 6 deferred imitation occurs. Although Bates and her colleagues (1979) found imitation to be significantly correlated with gestural development, this correlation occurred at 9 to 10 months of age, well before stage 6. On the basis of these studies, Bates and Snyder (1987) found a strong correlation between naming and the emergence of recognitory gestures and deferred imitation. Note, however, that Bates credited the child with deferred imitation prior to the first birthday, much earlier than Piaget's work would suggest.

In summary, imitation may aid early speech development and is correlated with symbolic representation. True symbol functioning is assumed to occur when deferred imitation is acquired because the model need not be present. This occurs beyond the first birthday when children are already using single words. The importance of imitation may be as a social behavior seen in child–parent interactions. Such early turn taking will be discussed in Chapter 6.

Object Permanence

Object permanence is "the cognitive basis for 'knowing' that an object which has been removed from . . . immediate perception still exists and thus can be made to recur" (McLean & Snyder-McLean, 1978, p. 23). One method of recurrence is through speech. By naming an entity, the speaker can cause the object to exist symbolically for himself and for the listener. Therefore, two people can discuss something, or someone, that is not present. Object permanence may be related to such early semantic functions as nonexistence, disappearance, and recurrence. If object permanence is a strong prerequisite for symbolic representation, the child must possesses this prerequisite prior to age 1, which is much earlier than Piaget suggested (K. Moore & Meltzoff, 1978).

Although there is some correlation between object permanence and language, other aspects of early cognitive development correlate more strongly with language acquisition (Siegel, 1979). In fact, the relationship of object permanence to language has been questioned by many professionals (T. Bower & Wishart, 1972; Cornell, 1978; M. Moore, 1973). Some have found no significant relationship between the two (Bates et al.,1979). At 9 to 10 months of age, the infant's development of imitation, play with toys, and means–ends seems to be most highly correlated with language development in the form of gestures. Object permanence is not related. Although stage 4 object permanence skills may be related to the child's ability to comprehend the names of persons present, at stage 6 invisible displacement does not correlate with comprehension of the names of absent individuals (J. Miller et al., 1980).

Although stage 6 object permanence may not be a necessary prerequisite for language, it does seem to be related to the large growth in vocabulary at the end of the second year. Some stage 6 behaviors are found among children at the single-word level, but vocabulary increase seems to occur when children exhibit all stage 6 object permanence schemata (Corrigan, 1978a; Ramsay, 1977).

Bates and Snyder (1987) concluded that stage 6 memory for absent objects is not a prerequisite for first words, although such memory may be related to developmental changes noted late in the second year of life. Stage 6 memory may indicate a stabilization of the ability to represent reality. Perhaps stage 4 object permanence is sufficient for development of single words (R. Brown, 1973). In stage 4 the child recognizes objects when they reappear. This may be sufficient to enable the child to refer to present objects. Stage 6 object permanence requires memory of absent objects. This skill is unnecessary for initial word use. Object use, or manipulation, may be more closely related to language than is object permanence.

Causality

Several authors have concluded that a sensorimotor notion of causality is a prerequisite for communication (Bates & Snyder, 1987; Greenwald & Leonard, 1979; L. Snyder, 1978) and for language (K. Moore & Meltzoff, 1978). Once the child realizes that he and others can be a source of action, then the means are available for language to become a vehicle of change. With the development of causality, the child can solve problems by representing them internally. This ability is a portion of the symbolic function of language. It should be obvious that recognition of self and others as sources of action is closely related to recognition of the means for solving problems. The latter is demonstrated in means–ends development.

Causal development in interactions with people and with objects seems to mature differently. Causality in social behavior may develop before the first birthday, whereas causality applied to objects may not occur until late in stage 4 (Sexton, 1980). Stage 5 causal understanding may be a necessary but not sufficient condition for communication development, as measured by expression of intentions (Harding & Golinkoff, 1978). There appears to be a strong relationship between causality and understanding of verbs and semantic relations (J. Miller et al., 1980).

Means-Ends

Sensorimotor means–ends schemata appear to be a critical feature in language development. Examples of means–ends behaviors are pulling a cord to get an attached toy or pulling the tablecloth to get an item on the table. Bates and her colleagues (1975, 1977, 1979) found means–ends skills to be significantly correlated with language development at 9 months of age, early in stage 4. This result is considered to be important because at 9 months the child begins to use gestures to communicate. Thus the development of stage 4 means–ends appears to be related to development of intentionality.

Bruner (1973) has described the action sequence that signals development of intention. Initially the child approaches the task with an anticipation of the outcome. He selects from among the appropriate means to attain the desired end. Once a means is selected, the child maintains that behavior. The action is terminated when the end is attained. Finally, if the end is not totally appropriate, the action taken to attain it is slightly modified.

Gestures have received considerable attention because they are an early communication form used to attain a desired end. Bates and her colleagues (1979) found that gestures and early words refer to the same content. Each begins in rigid, context-bound routines and gradually becomes more flexible. Sequences of gestures appear at about the same time as multiword utterances (Fenson & Ramsey, 1980; Nicolich, 1977).

Object retrieval and early tool use have generated particular attention. Attempts to retrieve an object help the child learn that one object can be used to attain another (Sund, 1976). Words can serve a similar function. Tool use may be related to symbolization in three ways (Bates et al., 1979). First, each requires analysis of the problem into part–whole relations. Second, the child must locate the missing part in order to solve the problem. Finally, a substitution must be found for the missing part. This process is analogous to using a word to represent, or substitute for, a referent.

Although means–ends abilities seem to be significantly correlated with communication and language development, there is little support for the notion that stage 6 is required for symbol use. Children use very low-level gestures at stage 4 means–ends (Bates et al., 1975; Greenwald & Leonard, 1979). At stage 5, children use words to communicate (M. Folger & Leonard, 1978). Stage 6 means–ends appears to be related to higher language functioning, such as the emergence of syntax (Zachary, 1978). The appearance of two-word utterances also correlates significantly with stage 6 means–ends.

Play

A number of studies have demonstrated the importance of play for language development (Bowerman, 1974; J. Miller, Chapman, Branston, & Reichle, 1980; L. Snyder, 1978). There is a significant correlation between object play and language at 10 to 13 months (Bates et al., 1979; James, 1980).

While play is an important learning strategy, symbolic play is of particular importance for development of the symbolic function. Symbolic play occurs when the child uses one object to represent another, such as a spoon for a telephone receiver. Words are used similarly to represent referents. This level of play does not occur until the middle of the second year of life. Children able and willing to drink from toy cars or to use a block as a spoon make significantly more progress in language than children who are symbolically less flexible (Bates, Bretherton, Snyder, Shore, & Volterra, 1980). The number of schemata that the children demonstrate during symbolic play and the number of symbolic schemata used in language have been found to be similar.

The level of play required for symbol use has been questioned. Early schemata with objects are a good indicator of later language growth (Bates et al., 1975; Greenwald & Leonard, 1979; Sugarman, 1978), but children use single words before they fully develop symbolic play.

Summary

Piaget theorized that stage 6 functioning is required for symbol use. The debate rages over the meaning of this hypothesis. If all spoken words fulfill a symbolic function, then Piaget's theory is not valid. There is no evidence that stage 6 behaviors are required for single-word production. Single-word language begins in late stage 4 or early stage 5 (Kelly & Dale, 1989). On the other hand, if true symbol use does not occur until the child is capable of representing absent referents, then the theory is more acceptable. In addition, stage 6 seems to be correlated closely with early multiword communication.

It may be that some of the confusion is related to Piaget's very notion of stages. J. Miller and his colleagues (1980) concluded that the notion of stages and their related behavior shifts is weak. In fact, the neo-Piagetian theories, such as those of Case (1978), abandon the stage notion in favor of development of specific skills. It would seem that a notion of object permanence develops early, as does causality relative to interactions with people. Other cognitive skills, such as means–ends, take longer to develop but are nonetheless significant. Finally, skills such as deferred imitation, invisible displacement, and symbolic play may be critical for vocabulary growth and early multiword combinations but unnecessary for single-word speech.

Neo-Piagetian Approaches

As we have seen, Piaget's theory of cognitive development has stimulated many research projects. These studies are responsible for uncovering evidence disproving some of Piaget's hypotheses, as well as for bringing about the reformulation of the original theory. For example, some researchers have proposed individual skill criteria rather than developmental stages (Case, 1978; Gopnik & Meltzoff, 1984, 1986). Case reanalyzed the sensorimotor stages in terms of the number of planning units or "chunks" that must be kept active in short-term memory in order to solve problems. This is an information-processing theory of development. Case hypothesized that since memory capacity is fixed, increased organization must account for more efficient processing. In the early stages of development, schemata are poorly organized and, therefore, less efficient. As a result, more memory capacity is used. Through experience, the schemata become better organized and leave more capacity for other schemata. Applied to language, Case's theory suggests that multiword utterances require greater efficiency and organization of individual lexical units.

Gopnik and Meltzofff found that certain semantic functions correlate well with cognitive development of specific skills rather than with stages of development. For example, the ability to solve complex object permanence problems correlates well with the first appearance of disappearance words and phrases, such as *all gone*. The ability to sort objects correlates with the appearance of naming or labeling. Meltzoff (1988) concluded that "particular semantic acquisitions occur concurrently with . . . particular cognitive achievements" (p. 57).

K. Moore and Meltzoff (1978) offered another revision of Piaget's theory. They did not find empirical support for the developmental correlations ascribed by Piaget to object permanence, imitation, and mental representation. According to their research, some representational abilities are present at birth. For example, they reported that 2- or 3-week-old infants are capable of facial imitation. At this age, the child reproduces actions that he "feels" himself producing. This proprioceptive imitation is quite different from later imitations, which serve a self-representative function. In those situations, which occur at around 9 to 10 months of age, the child imitates others with the realization that he now looks like the model. Nonetheless, claimed Moore and Meltzoff, the neonate is able to represent others by facial imitation. Therefore, the ability to represent the external world may not be the culmination of infant cognitive development but the beginning.

Throughout this period, the child learns to cope with changes in surface appearance by discovering underlying stability. This cognitive process relates to language acquisition in two ways. First, cognitive abilities allow the infant to understand the consistencies in the nonlinguistic context so that he and his communication partners share mutual meanings. Second, cognitive abilities help the infant learn how the speaker's words relate to these shared meanings. Most early shared meanings include object identity. It is this identity that enables the child to detect the relationship between adult speech and the nonlinguistic context of objects. According to Moore and Meltzoff (1978), the rules for object identity, not Piaget's action schemata, are the organizing principles of cognitive development. At about 5 months of age, the child uses the object identity rules to construct a notion of object invariance across transformations, or changes. Later the child learns words that name transformations or that do not vary across transformations or objects. This feature is reflected in children's first words. First words name actions, the sources of recipients of actions, and attributes. In language development, adult linguistic input also serves a greater function than Piaget theorized.

Conclusion

Piaget's theory of cognitive development has great appeal because of its broad-based approach. Further study has indicated, however, that Piaget's description of the sensorimotor stages and his representational prerequisites may not be totally accurate. In addition, "There are very few empirical studies that directly address language development within the context of Piagetian cognitive development" (T. Moore & Harris, 1978, p. 133). The most nagging difficulty is the theory's inability to describe the process by which the child associates words, or symbols, with their referents. In addition, it is one thing to use a piece of paper as a doll's blanket but quite another to use the word *blanket*. In fact, we do not know the child's deeper understanding of a concept such as *blanket*.

Recent studies have shown, however, that sensorimotor stage 6 is not a necessary prerequisite for language. Part of this conflict results from varying definitions of language. Most children begin to produce single-word utterances at the end of stage 4 but are limited to discussing objects and events that are present. In the second half of the second year, children begin to talk about entities that are absent or nonexistent. Although most of the sensorimotor studies are correlational in nature, it appears that only a subset of sensorimotor abilities correlates more closely with language development. In addition, advances in the methods of infant study have demonstrated that early theorists, such as Piaget, seriously underestimated infant capacities (Kessen, Haith, & Salapatek, 1970; Meltzoff & Moore, 1977; Trevarthen, 1979).

Piaget also deemphasized the influence of all external factors upon cognitive, and in turn linguistic, development and minimized the effect of environmental influences. Piaget assumed that the child is intrinsically motivated and that external environmental factors have little effect on cognitive development. Studies of infant learning, however, have shown that Piaget underestimated the power of external factors. Thus, many neo-Piagetians emphasize environmental influences, especially the social interactions between the child and the primary caregiver.

INFORMATION-PROCESSING MODEL

An alternative model of cognitive functioning and development, called **information processing,** is concerned more with processing information than with cognitive concepts or structures. Presented in Chapter 4, information processing is concerned with the steps involved in handling incoming and outgoing information. These include, but are not limited to, attention and discrimination, organization, memory or recall, and transfer. The major differences between the Piagetian and information-processing models are presented in Table 5.3. Of particular importance for learning are sensory information storage, short-term memory, and long-term memory (Lindsay & Norman, 1977). Long-term memory is

TABLE 5.3   Major Differences between Piagetian and Information Processing Theories

	Piagetian Approach	Information Processing Approach
Theoretical emphasis	Cognitive structures of thought	Cognitive processing of information
	Developmental stages of cognition	Mechanisms or processes of cognition
Learning	Reaching a state of equilibrium between internal schemes and incoming information through assimilation and accommodation	Integrating information into long-term memory through rehearsal; longitudinal changes reflect different processes or strategies for encoding information
Memory	Types of memory not delineated because memory is not a separate aspect of cognition	Interested in the component processes of sensory, short-term, and long-term memory
Storage	Within schema, either existing or newly created	Capacity fixed; increased quantity represents new strategies
Retrieval	Recall is a symbolic function that develops at about age one	Both recognition and recall are displayed by the infant

very important in this model. The limited time constraints of sensory memory and the limited capacity constraints of short-term memory enhance the importance of long-term memory for learning. Information is maintained by repetition, a process called **rehearsal**. Transferral to long-term memory requires a special type of rehearsal, **integrative rehearsal**. "The major task in the learning of new material is to integrate it properly within the structure of information already present within long-term memory" (Lindsay & Norman, 1977, p. 339). Memory is the transfer of information within the system. It includes acquisition, storage, and retrieval.

The major differences between process theory and Piagetian theory are as follows:

> Piaget posits that memory should not be regarded as a separate cognitive capacity, but rather, that it should be conceived of as integrally bound to intelligence; memory, like all cognitive functions . . . is assumed to depend on intelligence. Although most information-processing theorists would agree that memory is, in some sense, inseparable from cognitive functions, the emphasis is not comparable. Information processors generally analyze component processes of memory, and developmentalists with information-processing orientations attempt to relate age differences in memory performance to children's increasing repertoire and proficiency at memory skills. Piaget's principal focus, on the other hand, has been the study of development of intelligence, and this has led him to examine the ways in which changing cognitive structures affect children's remembrances. Whereas information processors study the mechanisms of memory, Piagetians concentrate on developmental changes in the content of memory. (Perlmutter & Lange, 1978, p. 246)

In information-processing theory, the structural components of memory do not change with age (Naus, Ornstein, & Hoving, 1978). Rather, substantial changes reflect changes in the control processes or strategies children use to encode information. Changes in memory performance are related to changes in long-term memory strategies. Children of different ages differ in the techniques they use to control information flow between parts of the system. Infants require more repeated rehearsals in order for information to be coded in long-term memory.

"A stimulus is first feature-analyzed, perceptually, then matched against stored abstractions, or pattern recognized, or meaning-associated; and then it may undergo further processing by enrichment or elaboration through association with past experiences" (N. Myers & Perlmutter, 1978, p. 192). Whereas Piaget stressed sensory learning within a wider cognitive function (intelligence), the information-processing model conceptualizes a general long-term storage system that affects sensory learning.

In general, infants learn best from repeated presentation of the stimulus. Only later are fewer physical stimuli needed for learning. "Perhaps as the child's cognitive capacity to generate his own memory cues develops, the necessity for strong external stimulus support is reduced" (N. Myers & Perlmutter, 1978,

p. 215). Deliberate strategic memory behaviors seem nonexistent, but they develop and increase with age as the child's cognitive demands become more extensive. The infant displays both recognition and recall in cognitive learning. In contrast, Piaget considered recall to be a symbolic function that develops at about 1 year of age.

EARLY PERCEPTUAL DEVELOPMENT

In addition to cognitive abilities, such as representation or symbol use, the infant must be able to discriminate between different sights and sounds within his environment. "Communication has as a prerequisite a relatively fine discrimination ability on the part of the communicating subject" (Moerk, 1977, p. 67). This ability to discriminate differences in incoming information is a portion of perception. "Perception ordinarily refers to any process by which we gain immediate awareness of what is happening outside ourselves" (T. Bower, 1977, p. 1). Of most interest for a study of linguistic development are the auditory perceptual skills related to voice and speech, but other perceptual skills are also important for the formation of early meanings based on the characteristics of various entities, such as the way they look or feel. Some of these perceptual abilities were mentioned in Chapter 3, so I will review them only briefly.

Perceptual development appears to have at least four aspects: growth, stimulation, habituation, and organization (T. Bower, 1977). Growth includes not only internal development of individual nerve cells but also development of the entire system, with an increased number of cells. Each cell becomes thicker, to carry more signals, and better insulated, to decrease close channel interference. Stimulation is environmental input. Several studies have demonstrated the importance of early stimulation for later development. **Habituation** is the result of schemata formed for frequently occurring stimuli. The child comes to expect certain stimuli that occur frequently. If that expectation or schema is fulfilled, then the stimulus does not elicit a significant response. Thus, habituation enables the infant to attend to new stimuli without competition from competing, but less novel, stimuli. Finally, organization enables the child to store information for later retrieval.

The newborn is capable of many auditory discriminations (Hirschman & Katkin, 1974; Kearsely, 1973). For example, he can discriminate between different sound durations (Clifton, Graham, & Hatton, 1968; K. Pratt, 1954) and different loudness levels (Bartoshuk, 1964; Steinschneider, Lipton, & Richmond, 1966). Newborns are also capable of discriminating different pitches or frequencies, especially in the human speech range (R. Eisenberg, 1976). In addition, the neonate responds to the human voice more often and with more vigor than to other environmental sounds (Freedman, 1971).

From birth, the infant is an active stimulus seeker who will even work to attain certain types of stimulation. In general, there are two types of stimulation, perceptual and cognitive (D. Stern, 1977). **Perceptual stimulation** (sometimes called *sensory stimulation*) refers to the recognition of the existence of a stimulus and of its parameters, such as loudness, pitch, or complexity. **Cognitive stimulation** involves the relationship between the incoming stimulus and a stored referent, and includes evaluation and comparison of a new stimulus with previously received information. In the neonate, most stimulation is solely perceptual. Cognitive stimulation develops later but still depends on perceptual modalities or channels and thus has a perceptual component.

The neonate is somewhat at the mercy of his perceptions, though he can shut out visual images by closing his eyes or averting his gaze. If the level of stimulation is too low, he loses interest quickly. His attention is captured more easily by moderate stimulation. At a moderate level of stimulus strength, the infant's attention is maintained longer and more frequently. As the stimulus strength increases, so does attention, until a point is attained at which stimulus strength reaches the infant's tolerance threshold. He will then avert his face, become restless, or cry for assistance.

Many of the infant's behavior-state changes reflect internal changes or intrinsic brain activities. During the first month of life, the infant is frequently asleep or drowsy. Even so, external stimuli can influence the duration of these states. The infant is most receptive to external stimuli when alert but not moving excessively. As can be seen, the ability to attend is influenced by the infant's internal state. Even so, "attentional capabilities," according to Moerk (1977), "are functioning on a high level of differentiation . . . during the neonatal period" (p. 66). Within a few months, the level of external stimulation is a greater determinant of attending than the infant's internal state. By this time the infant is capable of maintaining a rather stable internal condition.

By 2 months the infant exhibits selective attending skills. He is not stimulus bound and can remain unresponsive to background stimulus events. When presented with a stimulus repeatedly, the infant will react less strongly to each successive presentation. This habituation is exhibited in both vision (Kagan & Lewis, 1965) and audition, or hearing (Eimas et al., 1971).

At 1 month or less, the infant is able to discriminate different phonemes (Aslin & Pisoni, 1980). Initially these phonemes must be very different in order for the infant to discriminate between them. This ability is gradually refined. By 2 months the infant is also able to distinguish his mother's voice from those of others (Boyd, 1975; Culp & Boyd, 1975). The infant is also able to discriminate frequency changes by this age (Morse, 1972), or by 4 to 6 months at the latest (Berg, 1971; Moffitt, 1971). As intonational patterns are closely related to frequency shifts, we can expect to see discrimination of intonational patterns shortly after frequency shift discriminations; this occurs by 7 months.

These abilities demonstrate that at a very early age the infant engages in cognitive stimulation, evaluating and comparing stimuli. A face is not sufficient to hold the infant's attention for long periods. Rather, the infant focuses on the contrast between the face and the infant's schema of a face (D. Stern, 1977). Thus, stimulation is coming from both the stimulus and its relationship to the internal schema. These schemata provide the infant with an expectation of the properties of objects, events, and people in the environment.

At about 7 to 9 months, the infant begins to understand words. Not only does he perceive sequences of arbitrary phonemes, but he begins to associate these sound sequences with entities in the perceptual world. Each incoming acoustic stimulus is compared with stored sound traces and associated meaning and is thus analyzed.

Naturally, this analysis requires increased memory capacity. The first step in the memory process is organization and storage of perceptual information. Structuring or organizing incoming information is essential because "the organism has to continue to exchange information with the physical environment as long as it is alive" (Moerk, 1977, p. 60). This underlying organization can be inferred from the similar way in which infants interact with objects of similar perceptual attitudes. Although objects may have an infinite variety of characteristics, the infant has only a limited or finite quantity of motor responses. Therefore, the infant generalizes and classifies objects into general response classes. These generalized motor responses can be noted even in the newborn (Berlyne, 1965).

Storing sensory information "maintains a rather accurate and complete picture of the world as it is received by the sensory system" (Lindsay & Norman, 1977, p. 304), albeit for only a few tenths of a second. Memory may be short- or long-term. Short-term capacity is very limited and is not a complete image of events that have taken place. Only about five or six items can be retained at one time. In contrast, long-term storage has unlimited capacity, though retrieval may be problematic. The amount of information contained is so large that it would be difficult to find individual bits. Thus, the information must be highly organized. According to Lindsay and Norman (1977):

> The key to any large-scale memory system, then, is not its physical capacity for storing huge amounts of information. Rather, it lies in its ability to retrieve selected pieces of data on request, its ability to answer questions based on information stored. (p. 368)

Retrieval is the process of following organized pathways through the stored structure in order to find a particular bit of information.

Memory and retrieval can be seen in the infant's gradual differentiation of the sucking response. The early recognition of his mother's face and voice is also a good indicator. By 5 months the infant can remember geometric patterns for approximately 3 hours, but human faces for much longer (L. Cohen & Gelber, 1975; Fagan, 1973).

Distancing

Moerk (1977) has proposed that perceptual behavior may contain some clue to the development of representational skills. In particular, he is interested in the process of distancing. **Distancing** is a gradual increase in the perceptual distance of infants and the accompanying shift from the senses of touch, taste, and smell to vision and hearing. As the distance increases, the infant has less contact with the actual object and must rely on a longer-range visual or auditory image. For example, when the infant notices people at a distance, he recognizes them even though he cannot see all of their attributes. Moerk considers these long-range images to be symbols for the original perceptual attributes of the object. He concludes that "the infant has here his first encounter with 'representational' meaning" (p. 76). A gradual process of distancing seems to be part of the play activities of the child. Toys are one step removed from the real object, pictures even more so. Finally, according to Moerk, real or even imaginary objects are manipulated solely through language in stories. Symbolization is a more efficient way of manipulating objects because mental representation can be accomplished more quickly and with less effort than physical movement.

Summary

Perception of speech sounds is critical for later speech and language development in normal children. If some disability precludes normal use of these abilities, then extraordinary measures must be taken to ensure speech and language acquisition. Frequently an augmentative mode of communication, such as signing, must be employed.

For normal speech and language development, the child should be able to do the following:

1. Attend selectively to speech.
2. Discriminate "mother tongue" phonemes.
3. Hold a speech sound sequence in the correct order for processing.
4. Discriminate speech sound sequences.
5. Compare a sound sequence to a stored model.
6. Discriminate intonational patterns.

The loss of these abilities, even in a mature user of a language, usually results in speech and language deterioration unless some clinical intervention occurs.

At 1 year of age, the infant becomes master of the perceptual system. T. Bower (1977) has summarized this change:

> At this point [1 year] . . ., our infant begins to use his perceptual system, rather than being used by it. Internal memories and expectations control the baby's behavior, and he uses his perceptual system to realize these expectations. . . . There is a clear point in development when, it seems, the baby assumes a similar superior status in regard to the data provided by his senses. There is a developmental shift that results in babies, too, refusing to believe their eyes, when the visual evidence contradicts some internal knowledge about the world. . . . Distrust of the senses and reliance on other sources of knowledge grows during development. (pp. 50–51)

According to Piaget, shortly after this age the infant begins to represent reality internally through the use of symbols.

CONCLUSION

The strongest form of the cognitive hypothesis states that cognition precedes language development, that is, that the child expresses in his language only those relationships that he understands intellectually. Scholars continue to argue about this relationship. Without entering this battleground too far, it seems safe to assert that there are certain levels of cognitive functioning that must precede expressive language.

The child needs perceptual skills to discriminate the smallest units of speech and to process speech sound sequences. Both skills require good auditory memory. At a linguistic-processing level, these sound sequences are matched with the referents they represent. According to Piaget, these representational abilities develop in the infant during the first 2 years of life through adaptation to, and organization of, incoming sensory stimuli. Piaget has divided these first 2 years, the sensorimotor period, into six stages based on the changing abilities of the child. Recent studies have indicated that stage 5 representational abilities are adequate for expressive single-word utterances. Stage 6 appears to be more closely related to early multiword utterances. Those aspects of early cognitive development that are most highly correlated with language development are means–ends, imitation, causality, and symbolic play.

Unfortunately, there are still many unanswered questions about this early relationship of cognition, or thought, and language. As Moerk (1977) has concluded:

> It has to be admitted that there are too many unknown elements to assert confidently that all necessary prerequisites, as far as storage processes are concerned, are developed when the infant begins to learn his first language. On the other hand, much evidence for early and long-term learning exists. (p. 79)

In addition, the mental processes involved in word–referent association and in the use of true signs have not been adequately explained.

The cognitive basis of language is best illustrated in early semantic development. Much early expressive language development involves the child's learning how to express what he already knows (Macnamara, 1972). Stated somewhat differently, the child must develop a certain number of meanings before he can begin to confer information intentionally on his own environment. By interacting with objects and persons in the environment, the infant forms primitive definitions that are later paired with the word and the referent. This relationship will be discussed in more detail in Chapter 7.

In the final analysis, the cognitive and perceptual prerequisites for early language appear to be necessary for early language development but are not adequate for a full explanation of the process. This does not detract from the importance of early perceptual and cognitive development, but it begs for consideration of other factors. Language does not develop in a vacuum but, rather, within an environment of well-developed communication. This social and communicative basis of early language must also be examined, and we will do so in the next chapter.

REFLECTIONS

1. Explain briefly the several models of the cognition–language relationship that have been advanced.
2. According to Piaget, organisms learn and evolve through the processes of organization and adaptation. Explain how learning occurs and describe the effect of the environment on the child's schemata.
3. Describe the major developmental changes that occur in the sensorimotor stage.
4. Describe the sensorimotor aspects of imitation, object permanence, causality, means–ends, and play and the relative contribution of each to language.
5. Information-processing theory offers an alternative to Piagetian models. What are the differences between the two?
6. Perceptual development can be divided into four aspects: growth, stimulation, habituation, and organization. How does each one relate to early perceptual development?

6 The Social and Communicative Bases of Early Language

CHAPTER OBJECTIVES

Language is acquired within the context of early conversations between the caregiver and the child. In this chapter we will describe the early interactions of these individuals and the contributions of each to the conversational context. In addition, we will explore the child's development of both communication skills and the intention to communicate. When you have completed this chapter, you should understand

- the communication behaviors of the newborn.
- the importance of gaze coupling, ritualized behavior, and game playing.
- the development of gestures.
- the effects of baby talk, gaze, facial expression, facial presentation and head movement, and proxemics on the child's development.
- the importance of joint reference, joint action, and turn taking on the development of communication.
- the following terms:

communication functions	mutual gaze
deictic gaze	protoconversation
entrainment	referencing
indicating	social smile
marking	

T HE WORD INFANT is derived from the Latin *infans*, which means "not speaking." In fact, terms such as *prelinguistic* and *nonverbal* are frequently used to describe infants. All these terms indicate a subtle prejudice, which is reflected in the common assumption that it is the development of language that lets children become communicating beings. This supposition does not reflect the actual behavior of infants, who communicate before they have language. Actually, language is a communication tool whose development is dependent upon the prior development of communication.

In Chapter 5 we discussed the cognitive and perceptual bases of language. Before she can use symbols, the child is able to divide the world into classes and categories that are later reflected in her language (Anglin, 1977; R. Brown, 1977; Rosch, 1973). Thus, "based on encounters with objects, an individual perceives and remembers the constant features of an object class so that a similar object will be recognized in future encounters" (Bloom & Lahey, 1978, p. 7). Words and symbols have meaning only as they relate to these underlying cognitive representations. This process of association, however, does not occur in isolation. "The inanimate environment, in and of itself, provides the infant with only the most impoverished stimulus towards an understanding, in human terms, of the world in which he finds himself (Newson, 1979, p. 207). Though the child can, to some degree, understand the entities and relationships in her world by exploring with her own body, this knowledge can be expanded only by interacting within the social environment.

In addition, the social context in which language occurs helps the infant understand that language. Both the nature of communication situations and the process of communication exchanges aid linguistic development. In fact, the situational appropriateness of language is a necessary part of language understanding and learning (Lewis & Cherry, 1977). As we shall see, context is employed heavily by the mother, or other caregivers, to augment verbal communication. Caregivers talk about objects that are immediately present in the environment. In addition, infant–caregiver communication exchanges have a predictable quality that also facilitates comprehension and learning. The child's knowledge of give-and-take exchanges and nonlinguistic signaling equip her to interpret or "crack the code" used in such exchanges (Bruner (1974/1975). The routines of the caregiver enable the child to predict events. The caregiver's speech in these situations also becomes predictable and, therefore, more understandable; thus, the conclusion that "formal linguistic behavior has its origins in a general prelinguistic social communication system" (Freedle & Lewis, 1977, p. 164).

In short, language represents only a portion of a larger interactional pattern that reflects the way we socialize our children. "Human babies become human beings because they are treated as if they already were human beings" (Newson, 1979, p. 208). In the communication context, the caregiver assumes that the child is attempting to communicate meaningfully. Thus, in their early dialogues, the caregiver imparts the child's behaviors with social significance, thereby providing an opportunity for the child to take a conversational or pseudoconversational turn. Initially, any child response is treated as a meaningful turn. If the child gives no response, the caregiver proceeds with the next conversational turn. As the caregiver communicates with the child, the child learns that people can reciprocate feelings and meanings.

It is within this interaction of the infant and her caregiver, therefore, that we find the germ of language development. In this chapter we will discuss infant–caregiver interactions almost exclusively. In middle-class American culture, the mother tends to be the infant's primary caregiver and, therefore, the primary socializing agent. Certainly, in some homes the father or a sibling fulfills the "mothering" function, but nearly all infant interactive studies have focused on the female parent. You should keep in mind that we will be discussing a "generic" mother–child duo.

In lower socioeconomic groups, the mother's need to work, the family structure, and the neighborhood environment may result in older children becoming the primary caregivers. Studies indicate that these children behave much the same way as middle-class mothers in their communication adaptations. Even so, these older children or mothers from either lower socioeconomic groups or ethnic subcultures may interact differently with their children than middle-class mothers do. There are many different ways to learn language. In some African cultures, the mother and child have little face-to-face interaction. Instead, the mother spends the day reciting ritualized rhymes or songs. Through this process, the child learns that language is predictable. To assume a different interaction strategy does not imply a qualitative difference. "To understand the growth of language one must look at language as it is actually used, in naturalistic interactive sequences of . . . mother with child" (Freedle & Lewis, 1977, p. 152). That interaction provides the vocal and nonvocal components of a facilitative language-learning environment. Within the infant–caregiver exchange, the infant develops the essential skills for learning language. The dialogue is one of mutual participation. The infant's contribution is as important as that of the caregiver. "Never is one partner 'causing' the other to do something; they are mutually engaged in an activity" (Tronick, Als, & Adamson, 1979, p. 369). The caregiver integrates her behavior into the behavior system of the infant, and both seem to adjust their behaviors to maintain an optimal level of interaction.

Although the content and intonation of these dialogues can be characterized as "baby talk," the dialogue pattern is adult. Each partner takes a turn within the dialogue and signals shifts in topic, either nonverbally or verbally. From these dialogues the infant learns "the rudiments of initiation and termination of conversation, alternation and interruption, pacing, and interspersing of verbal and non-verbal elements" (Bateson, 1975, p. 110).

Naturally, the roles taken by the infant and mother are different. There are five basic differences in the infant–mother exchange (Kaye, 1979). First, the mother has superior flexibility of timing and anticipates the infant's rather rigid behavior schedule. Second, the mother has an intuitive curriculum. She has an agenda for the infant's development and leads the infant slightly. Third, she is able to monitor and code her changes of expression rapidly. The infant has less mature monitoring abilities and responds less rapidly. Fourth, the mother can alternate among different means to attain her desired ends. The infant does not have the cognitive ability to assess situations and determine alternative strategies to attain goals. Finally, the mother is more creative in introducing variations of her repetitions. Thus, she is able to hold the infant's attention by varying her vocalizations only slightly each time.

Communication is maintained because the mother is socially sensitive to the effect of her behavior on the infant (Newson, 1979). The mother displays this sensitivity and "drastically tailors her output at the start to the nature of the task and to the child's apparent competence" (Bruner, 1978a, p. 8). Mothers learn this skill in order to sustain the exchange and to hold attention. In addition, the mother assumes that the child is fully responsive and infers meaning from the child's behavior. For example, if the infant smiles, the mother assumes that she is happy. For the child, however, the smile may have a different meaning. The mother's attribution of meaning to the infant's behavior enables a dialogue to begin. The mother acts as if she has a competent communication partner.

Much of this early prelinguistic dialogue occurs in specific situations, or is situation dependent. Within these situations, the mother attempts to divide the incoming stimuli into more readily comprehensible segments to which the child can attach meaning. Daily routines also provide predictable patterns of behavior, which aid interpretation. As a result of her mother's behavior, the infant learns the conventions of conversation and a method for interpretation. It would be incorrect, however, to assume that the child does not influence the infant–caregiver interaction. Communication is not implanted in the child. Rather, mother and child engage as partners in a dialogue.

In summary, the child is capable of expressive communication long before she develops formal verbal language. The infant communicates prelinguistically for at least four purposes: relief from discomfort; attainment of desired ends; reestablishment of proximity; and initiation, maintenance, and termination of an interaction (McLean & Snyder-McLean, 1978). Gradually, these early intentions attain a linguistic form. Stated another way, "communication by 'other means' precedes linguistic communication and . . . fulfills some of the same functions that will be fulfilled by language proper later" (Bruner, 1976, p. 7).

In this chapter we will examine the behavior of both the caregiver and the infant in their early interactions. Of importance are the communication strategies that facilitate later speech and language development. Our discussion will be developmental in nature and will concern, specifically, interaction and communication development in newborns and during the first year. Later in the chapter, we will explore adult communication strategies and interactional behaviors such as joint reference and joint action, game playing, and turn taking.

DEVELOPMENT OF COMMUNICATION: A CHRONOLOGY

The infant's world is a world of people—people who do things for, to, and with the infant. Uniquely prepared for interacting with these individuals, the infant learns the conventions of communication into which she will eventually place linguistic elements. Every mother will verify the fact that her child began to communicate long before she developed language.

Before we examine specific communication situations and strategies, I would like to give an overview of communication development in the first year of life. Kaye (1979) has outlined the process as follows:

> The infant begins life with the capacity to elicit certain instructive kinds of behavior from adults. Somehow he gradually takes upon himself some of the aspects of the adult's role in interaction: imitation, adjustment of timing, etc. This in turn gives him even finer control over the adult's behavior, so that he gains further information and more and more models of motor skills, of communication, eventually of language. By the time his representational and phonemic systems are ready to begin learning language, he is already able to make his intentions understood most of the time, to orient himself in order to read and interpret others' responses, to elicit repetitions and variations. (p. 204)

The Newborn

Chapter 5 highlighted the newborn's perceptual and cognitive abilities. Taken together, these abilities might suggest that the neonate is "prewired" for communication. For example, vision attains best focus at 8 inches, where most infant–caregiver interactions occur. Within a few hours of birth, the infant can follow visually at this close range (Greenman, 1963). During feeding, the mother's eyes are at a distance of almost 8 inches exactly, and she gazes at the infant 70% of the time (Robson, 1967; D. Stern, 1977). The child is most likely, therefore, to look at and focus upon her mother's face, especially her mother's eyes. In addition, the neonate's optimal hearing range is within the frequency range of the human voice.

One example of the neonate's predisposition to speech is her movements in relation to speech patterns. Undoubtedly, the newborn has been exposed in utero to sounds, such as the mother's heartbeat and digestive sounds. She has also been hearing her mother's voice and experiencing the rhythmic movements that accompany her mother's speech. In response to speech, adults make discrete and continuous synchronous movements at the phoneme, syllable, phrase, and sentence levels (Condon, 1979). For example, when you listen to a speaker, you may nod in rhythm with his speech. This interactional synchronization, called **entrainment**, is also exhibited by the neonate within 20 minutes of birth (Condon & Sanders, 1974). Although she entrains, or moves, to patterns of connected speech almost as well as an adult listener, the neonate will not produce synchronous movements to disconnected vowel sounds or to tapping. Her body motion is parallel with the duration of a speech sound and changes when that sound pattern changes.

As noted in Chapter 5, the neonate is able to discriminate some parameters of voice and speech. In addition, she has definite auditory as well as visual preferences. Using the sucking response to maintain or change an auditory stimulus, newborns have registered a preference for the human voice over nonspeech sounds in several studies (R. Eisenberg, 1976; Jensen, Williams, & Bzoch, 1975). Infants also demonstrate a preference for male over female voices. Visual preference is for the human face or a face pattern (Fantz, 1963). Several studies have found no particular face configuration to be preferential. Rather, newborns prefer visual stimuli with angularity, light and shade, complexity, and curvature (Fantz, 1964; Freedman, 1964; Haaf & Bell, 1967). The infant is exposed frequently to the human face, and that face contains all the preferred parameters. "From the very beginning, then, the infant is 'designed' to find the human face fascinating; and the mother is led to attract as much interest as possible to her already 'interesting' face" (D. Stern, 1977, p. 37).

Typically, the newborn will search for the human voice and demonstrate pleasure or mild surprise when she finds the face that is the sound source. Upon sighting the face, the newborn's eyes widen, her face broadens, and she may tilt her head and lift her chin toward the source. Body tension increases, but the infant remains quietly inactive. Upon finding a nonhuman sound source, however, the infant does not demonstrate these recognition behaviors. "When the infant begins to register his preference for human stimuli, it is impossible for an adult interactant not to become 'hooked' to him" (Brazelton, 1979, p. 82).

The newborn's recognition of, and response to, the human voice have additional implications:

> A day-old child will stop crying to attend to his mother's voice. The mother, for her part, will stop doing almost anything, including sleeping, to attend to the voice of her child. Each is predisposed to attend to the sounds of the other. (Halliday, 1979, p. 171)

The selective attention of each partner predicts the later communication between the infant and caregiver.

The neonate also has a limited set of behaviors that will help her begin to communicate. In fact, she was communicating prior to birth, generally with kicks to express discomfort resulting from her mother's position. The newborn's facial expressions, for example, demonstrate the high degree of maturity of the facial neuromuscular system, resulting in neonatal expressions resembling displeasure, fear, sorrow, anger, joy, and disgust (Charlesworth & Kreutzer, 1973). No experts attribute these actual emotional states to the infant, but caregivers act as if these emotions are present. This process of "adultomorphizing" has even been noted among nurses in the hospital nursery (Bennett, 1971). Infant expressions have definite recognizable patterns. For example, displeasure, or the "cry face," begins mildly and progresses to a gasping for breath. Initially the face sobers; then the brows knit and a frown begins. The cheeks then become flushed, the lower lip quivers, and the eyes partially close. The lips pull back as the infant opens her mouth, then turns down the corners. Initial fussing is followed by catches of breath.

Eye gaze is another behavior in the neonate's repertoire. Almost from birth, the infant selectively attends to visual stimuli. Her visual preferences, mentioned previously, suggest that the angles at the corners of the eyes and the dark–light contrast of the eye itself and the eyebrow might be particularly attractive (D. Stern, 1977). The caregiver interprets eye contact as a sign of interest or attention.

Infant head movements also have high signal value for the caregiver. The face and head become important for communication very early because of the relatively advanced maturational level of these structures compared to the rest of the infant's body. The newborn will turn her head to view a human face. Initially the head and eyes move together, but not to the same degree. Three head positions, illustrated in Figure 6.1 (Stern, 1977), are important because the caregiver interprets them as communication signals.

The infant's state of wakefulness also influences adults' behaviors:

> His regulation of his states of consciousness becomes the behavioral basis on which a caregiving adult knows how to adjust her timing. The adult learns when it is appropriate to play with the neonate and when to leave him alone. And then within this basic communication system, she learns which signals . . . will elicit an altering response from the baby which says "Now we are in communication." The developing clarity of the baby's states and of his responses to his caregiver becomes a firmer reinforcer of further communica-

FIGURE 6.1   Head Positions of Newborn

Type	Description	Result for Infant and Maternal Interpretation
Central	Faces mother or turns away slightly to either side.	Infant: Can discern form Mother: Interprets as an approach or attending signal

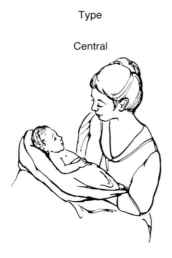

Type	Description	Result for Infant and Maternal Interpretation
Peripheral	Turns head 15 to 90 degrees	Infant: Cannot discern mother's facial features so form perception lost; motion, speed, and direction perception maintained, so can monitor mother's head Mother: Signal of infant aversion or flight

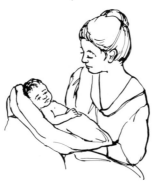

Type	Description	Result for Infant and Maternal Interpretation
Loss of visual contact	Turns head more than 90 degrees or lowers head	Infant: Loss of motion, speed, and direction perception Mother: Termination of interaction; head lowering interpreted as more temporary

Source: Drawn from D. Stern, *The First Relationship*. Cambridge: Harvard University Press, 1977.

tion and for the development of affective bonds between them. (Brazelton, 1979, p. 85)

Initially there is little synchrony between the newborn's sleep–awake cycle, or state of wakefulness, and caregiver behavior; but the synchrony increases as the newborn gets a few days older (Sander, Stechler, Burns, & Julia, 1970). The newborn establishes rhythmic patterns in utero, but these change rapidly at birth. Her states become regulated by bodily processes such as ingestion, elimination, respiration, and hunger. "The task of the caregiver over the first two or three weeks of postnatal life is to establish the new bases for temporal organization for both the infant and infant–caregiver system" (Chappell & Sander, 1979, p. 93). The sleep–awake patterns of the caregiver and child provide shared periods of wakefulness as a context for specific interactions. Under the caregiver's direction, the awake periods become specific action sequences. "The implication for the infant is that with each successive awakening his interaction with his environment becomes increasingly stable, thus predictable" (p. 106). This common context aids infant interpretation and becomes the forum for later introduction of new content.

The mother appears to maintain an optimal state of infant wakefulness by holding the child in close proximity and by speaking to her. Both of these behaviors become more frequent in the first 2 weeks of the infant's life. Manipulation by the mother is maximally effective at points of shift or change in the infant's state:

> During alert periods when the infant shifts to a more active state or into drowsiness, a posture change [by the mother] brings the infant back to alertness to conform to the phase-defined appropriate state. During the shift to sleep, when the infant becomes alert or active, a change in posture can facilitate the shift to sleep. (Chappell & Sander, 1979, p. 105)

Thus, the infant's state influences the mother's behavior, which in turn influences the infant's state.

Finally, the newborn has in her behavioral repertoire the ability to express her needs, albeit primitively. The expressive function of communication can be found, from birth, in reflexive crying, which expresses a general form of excitement (Moerk, 1977).

Socialization and Early Communication: Age Birth–6 Months

Shortly after birth, the infant becomes actively involved in the interactive process with the mother. By 1 month of age, the infant engages in participant exchanges, interactional sequences that began shortly after birth. When awake and in the appropriate position with the adult, the infant will gaze at the adult's face and vocalize (Bullowa, 1979a). In turn, the infant responds to the mother's vocalizations and movements.

As we have noted, the infant is especially responsive to the caregiver's voice and face. In fact, the young infant will attend to the human face to the exclusion of just about everything else. Within the first week of life, the infant begins to imitate gross hand gestures, tongue protrusions, and mouth opening (T. Bower, 1977; Meltzoff & Moore, 1977). Much of this "imitation" may be reflexive in nature, similar to a yawn. The caregiver treats the behavior, however, as if it is social in nature. She embellishes the infant behaviors with communicational intent in the context of these early dialogues. By 1 month of age, the infant may approximate imitations of the caregiver's pitch and duration of speech sounds (Trevarthen, 1979).

In addition, the infant responds differentially to the face and voice of her mother. By as early as 2 weeks, the infant is able to distinguish her mother from a stranger (T. Bower, 1977). Yet the infant is not afraid of strangers and displays a definite pattern of behavior in response to adult approach, speech, and touching. The infant will turn toward the adult and fix her gaze upon the adult's mouth or eyes. Her facial expression will be one of interest or mild surprise, followed by a smile (Trevarthen, 1979). At about 3 weeks of age, this smile of recognition is one of the first examples of a **social smile**, one not contingent upon the infant's internal physical state. During the first 2 weeks of life, smiling is exhibited in dreaming or rapid eye movement (REM) sleep (Wolff, 1966). At around 3 to 6 weeks of age, the infant begins to smile in response to external stimuli, such as the human face and eye gaze; to the human voice (especially if high-pitched); and to tickling. The caregiver, of course, responds in kind.

The young infant is so tuned to the human face that she will even smile at a very simplified outline of one (T. Bower, 1977; Fantz, 1963). Infants will respond to an outline with two large dots for eyes but will not respond to the outline or to the eyes separately. Researchers have suggested that infants find eyes to be the most attractive part of the human face (Carpenter, Tecce, Strechler, & Friedman, 1970; Lewis, 1969; Wolff, 1963, 1969). This preference for the human face, especially the eyes, increases even more during the second month of life (Caron, Caron, Caldwell, & Weiss, 1973; Maurer & Salapatek, 1976). Infant cooing also increases and is easily stimulated by attention and speech, and by toys moved before the baby (Trevarthen, 1979). The infant coos when she is not distressed, and the behavior develops parallel to social smiling (Ambrose, 1961; Wolff, 1963). By 2 months of age, the infant is stronger and her mouth movements are more distinct. Cooing often occurs in bursts or episodes accompanying other expressions.

By the third month the infant's cognitive abilities are such that the expressionless human face alone does not have the stimulus power to hold her attention. By 14 weeks the infant has a visual preference for complexity (Brennan, Ames, & Moore, 1966). According to D. Stern (1977), the 3-month-old has an internal schema of certain familiar objects, events, and persons. Therefore, the stimulus power of any one face resides in that face's similarity to, or difference from, the infant's internal schema, or what is expected. The degree of stimulation for the infant relates to the degree of stimulus–schema mismatch. If the mismatch is too great, however, the infant loses interest or gets upset.

To maintain attention, the caregiver must modify her behavior so that she provides the appropriate level of stimulation. She therefore exaggerates her facial expressions and voice, and she vocalizes more often. In turn, the infant responds to this new level of stimulation. "There is a progressive mutual modification in the child's and mother's behavior in that changes in the baby's development alter the mother's behavior and that this, in turn, affects the baby" (R. Schaffer, 1977, p. 53). In this developmental dance, first one partner leads and then the other. An example of this meshing of infant behavior and caregiver expectations is the infant's sleep–awake cycle. Initially the infant's sleep pattern is random: she sleeps about two-thirds of the time, both day and night. By week 16 she sleeps about 10 hours at night, with time out for a feeding or two, and about 5 hours during the day. The infant moves from an individual synchrony to an interpersonal one.

At any given moment, the caregiver must determine the appropriate amount of stimulation based upon the infant's level of attention. By 3 months the infant can maintain a fairly constant internal state, so she can be attentive for longer periods. The infant's level of excitation is positively related to her level of incoming stimulation. If her caregiver provides too much stimulation, the infant overloads and turns away or becomes overexcited.

The caregiver regulates not only the amount of stimulation but also the timing. Her behavior is not random but slots into the behavior of the child. By modifying her behavior, the caregiver maintains an interactional dialogue with the infant. There are six techniques that mothers use to create opportunities for their children to participate (R. Schaffer, 1977). These techniques—phasing, adaptive, facilitative, elaborative, initiating, and control—are listed in Table 6.1. The mother monitors the child's behavior continually and adapts her behavior accordingly. Her modifications enable the infant to enter the dialogue as a partner. These mutual dialogues seem to reach their greatest frequency at around an infant age of 3 or 4 months (S. Cohen & Beckwith, 1975).

Dialogues also become more important as handling decreases. By the third month, handling has decreased by 30% from that at birth, but dialogue has increased. The infant is a full partner in this dialogue, and her behavior is influenced by the communication behavior of her caregiver. The 12-week-old infant is twice as likely to revocalize if her caregiver responds verbally to her initial vocalization rather than responding with a touch, look, or smile (Lewis & Cherry, 1977). Similar revocalization patterns are also reported for 6-month-olds (Haugan & McIntire, 1972). There is a greater tendency for the infant's vocalizations to be followed by caregiver vocalizations, and those of the caregiver by the child's, than would be expected by chance (Bateson, 1975). Longer pauses after the caregiver's vocalizations may suggest that the caregiver perceives her role as that of "replier" to the infant's vocalizations (H. Schaffer, Collis, & Parsons, 1977).

This "conversational" turn taking by adults with 3-month-olds benefits the infants' babbling and turn taking (Bloom, 1988). Random responding by adults does not. In addition, this babbling may be more mature, containing syllables rather than individual sounds (Bloom, Russell, & Wassenberg, 1987).

There appears to be a shift in the infant–caregiver vocalization pattern beginning at about 12 weeks (Ginsburg & Kilbourne, 1988). Prior to this, the infant produces predominantly concurrent vocalizations that overlap with those of the mother. At 12 to 18 weeks, there is a sharp increase in the alternating vocalization pattern, although concurrent vocalizations still occur more frequently. Mothers are more likely to initiate and less likely to terminate their vocalizations if their infants are vocalizing (D. Stern, Jaffe, Beebe, & Bennett, 1975). For their

TABLE 6.1 Maternal Techniques for Infant's Participation

Techniques	Behaviors	Examples
Phasing	Monitors infant behavior to determine when to slot her behavior for most impact; must know when to intervene to attain predictable outcome	Mother attains infant's attention to an object before using it in some way. Mother monitors infant's gaze and follows it for clues to infant interest.
Adaptive	Exhibits behaviors that enable infant to assimilate information more rapidly; maintains infant's attention and provides highly ordered, predictable input	Mother uses slower arm movements than with adults. Mother has more emphatic gestures and more exaggerated facial expressions than with adults. Mother's speech is simpler and more repetitive than with adults.
Facilitative	Structures routine and environment to ensure infant success	Mother holds toy so child can explore. Mother assists infant physically. Mother supplies needed materials for task completion.
Elaborative	Allows child to indicate an interest, then elaborates upon it; talks following the infant's activities and interests closely	Mother demonstrates play with object of infant's interest. Mother talks about infant's behavior as she performs (parallel talking).
Initiating	Directs infant's attention to objects, events, and persons; follows sequence of gaining infant's attention, directing it, and looking back to ensure that the infant is attending	Mother points to direct attention. Mother brings object into child's view.
Control	Tells infant what she is to do; pauses after key words that are emphasized and makes extensive use of gestures	Mother insists that infant eat. Mother stresses what she wants the infant to do.

Source: Adapted from H. Schaffer, *Mothering.* Cambridge: Harvard University Press, 1977.

part, the infants are more likely to initiate vocalizations when their mothers are vocalizing. Turn taking is well adapted for auditory processing during the production of vocal output (Collis, 1979). Although vocal exchanges between mothers and infants are rather simple and contain little useful information, later more complex messages will necessitate a turn-taking pattern. In addition, both interactive partners make extensive use of smiles, head movements, and gestures. Mothers begin to imitate their infants' coughing at 2 months of age (Caplan, 1973). Initially this behavior is performed to attract attention, but eventually an exchange emerges. By 4 months the infant will initiate the exchange with a smile or a cough.

In order to share control in an interaction, the infant must have two skills (Trevarthen, 1979). First, she must exhibit *subjectivity*, or individual consciousness and intentionality. In other words, she must be aware of herself. Second, she must be able to mesh this self-awareness with an awareness of the other interactional partner. This process, called *intersubjectivity*, is displayed overtly by focusing attention, handling and exploring with attention to the consequences, and orienting or avoiding in anticipation of events. In addition, subjectivity is manifested in a distinctive interactional behavior toward others that is different from that toward objects. Subjectivity begins by 2 months of age and is well established by the time early mutual dialogues emerge a month or two later.

Eye gaze is also very important in these early dialogues. By 6 weeks of age, the infant is able to fix visually on her mother's eyes and hold the fixation, with eye widening and brightening (Wolff, 1963). The infant is more likely to begin and to continue looking if her caregiver is looking at her. In return, her caregiver's behavior becomes more social, and play interactions begin. At 3 months of age, the infant has a focal range that almost equals her mother's. Thus she becomes a true interactional partner in this modality.

Two types of gaze patterns have been identified, deictic and mutual. **Deictic gaze** is directed at objects. Mothers monitor their infants' gaze and follow its orientation (Collis, 1977; Collis & Schaffer, 1975). **Mutual gaze** may signal intensified attention (Bateson, 1979). At about 3 months, mutual gaze may be modified occasionally into gaze coupling, a turn-taking interaction resembling later gaze patterns observed in mature conversation (Jaffe, Stern, & Peery, 1973). Mutual eye gaze may be important for the formation of attachment or mutual bonding (Robson, 1967).

Infant–caregiver bonding is determined by the quality of their interactions. Several factors influence bonding and the infant's subsequent feelings of security. The levels of maternal playfulness, sensitivity, encouragement, and contingent pacing at 3 months have been found to be positively related to the security of attachment at 9 months (Blehar et al., 1977). Bonding is also strongly influenced by maternal responsiveness.

During the first 3 months, the caregiver's responding teaches the child the signal value of specific behaviors. The infant learns the stimulus–response sequence. If she signals, her mother will respond. When she cries, her mother answers her needs. Thus, she develops an expectation that she can change or control the environment. In addition, she learns that a relatively constant stimulus, or signal, results in a predictable response: the world has predictable outcomes. Possibly as high as 77% of infant crying episodes are followed by maternal responses, while only 6% are preceded by maternal contact (Moss & Robson, 1968). As a result of maternal responses, the cry becomes an infant's means of gaining contact with her mother.

The degree of parental responsiveness varies with the culture, as does the amount of infant crying (Devore & Konner, 1974; Mead & Newton, 1967). In general, more mobile societies, such as hunter-gatherer cultures, exhibit little child crying. Carried by the mother in a sling, the child is often attended to before crying begins.

Mothers not only respond to their infants' cries but can identify the type of cry produced. Mothers can reliably rate their 3- to 4-month-olds' cries along a continuum immediately following the infant's vocalization and even 3 weeks later on audiotape (Petrovich-Bartell, Cowan, & Morse, 1982). This is of interest when we consider that fewer nonacoustic and contextual cues are available after a delay.

By 3 to 4 months, two additional response patterns have emerged, rituals and game playing (Trevarthen & Hubley, 1978). These will be discussed in some detail later in this chapter. Rituals, such as feeding, provide the child with predictable patterns of behavior and speech. The child becomes upset if these rituals are changed or disrupted in any way (Schank & Abelson, 1977). Games, such as "peekaboo," "this little piggy," and "I'm gonna get you," have all the aspects of communication. There is an exchange of turns, rules for each turn, and particular slots for words and actions. Though the interaction reflects adult communication, it is constrained by the abilities of each partner. There are identifiable interactional phases in these sequences (Tronick, Als, & Adamson, 1979). Mothers and their 3-month-old infants exhibit initiation, mutual orientation, greeting, a play dialogue, and disengagement. However, any given exchange may not contain every phase. To initiate the exchange, the mother smiles and talks to her infant. For her part, the infant vocalizes and smiles at her mother when her mother has paused too long. When the partner responds with a neutral or bright face, the mutual orientation phase begins, and one partner speaks or vocalizes. The greeting consists of mutual smiles and eye gazes, with little body or hand movement. Turn taking is seen in the play-dialogue phase. The mother talks in a pattern of bursts interspersed with pauses, and the infant vocalizes during the pauses. Finally, disengagement occurs when one partner looks away. Within any phase, the behaviors of either partner may differ. These interactional exchanges have been called **protoconversations** (Bateson, 1975). Each contains the initial elements of emerging conversation.

Both partners are active participants in these exchanges. The infant moves her face, lips, tongue, arms, hands, and body toward the mother, whose behavior reflects that of her infant. In turn, the infant imitates her mother's movements. Frequently the behaviors of the mother and infant appear to be so simultaneous as to constitute a single act. The infant frequently leads by initiating the behavior

(Trevarthen, 1974). Her mother does not simply follow, however, but maintains a mutual exchange.

By 5 months the infant shows more deliberate imitation of movements and vocalizations (Uzgiris, 1972). Facial imitation is most frequent at 4 to 6 months of age (Pawlby, 1977). By 6 to 8 months, however, hand and nonspeech imitation become most frequent. The behaviors imitated are not new to the child but are "more a remodelling and integration of components already in spontaneous expression" (Trevarthen, 1979, p. 332).

By this time the child has a full repertoire of facial emotions. Between 3 and 6 months of age, the period of peak face-to-face play, the infant may be exposed to over 30,000 examples of facial emotions (Trotter, 1983). In interactions with her mother, the child mirrors her mother's expression and she, in turn, imitates the infant. The infant's repertoire of facial emotions is listed in Table 6.2.

The 5-month-old also vocalizes to accompany different attitudes, such as pleasure and displeasure, satisfaction and anger, and eagerness. She will vocalize to other people and to a mirror image, as well as to toys and objects.

As the infant approaches 6 months of age, this interest in toys and objects increases. Prior to this period, the infant is not greatly attracted to objects unless they are noise-producing or made mobile and lively by an adult. By 6 months, however, there is a small shift in interest away from people and toward objects. This change reflects, in part, the development of eye–hand coordination, which is exhibited in reaching, grasping, and manipulation (D. Stern, 1977). From this

TABLE 6.2   Infant Emotions

Emotion	Description	Emergence
Interest	Brows knit or raised, mouth rounded, lips pursed	Present at birth
Distress	Eyes closed tightly, mouth square and angular (as in anger)	Present at birth
Disgust	Nose wrinkled, upper lip elevated, tongue protruded	Present at birth
Social smile	Corners of mouth raised, cheeks lifted, eyes twinkle; neonatal "half smile" and early startle may be precursors	4–6 weeks
Anger	Brows together and drawn downward, eyes set, mouth square	3–4 months
Sadness	Inner corners of brows raised, mouth turns down in corners, pout	3–4 months
Surprise	Brows raised, eyes widened, oval-shaped mouth	3–4 months
Fear	Brows level but drawn in and up, eyes widened, mouth retracted	5–7 weeks

Source: Drawn from work of Carroll Izard as reported by R. Trotter in "Baby Face," *Psychology Today*, August 1983, *17*(8), pp. 14–20.

point on, interactions become more triadic; they include the infant, the caregiver, and some object.

Development of Intentionality: Age 7–12 Months

During the second 6 months of life, the infant begins to assert more control within the infant–caregiver interaction. She learns to communicate her intentions more clearly and effectively. Each success motivates her to communicate more and to learn to communicate better. "The experience the child has of being able to communicate his intention successfully may represent a powerful motive for the acquisition of language skills" (Moerk, 1977, p. 49). The primary modes for this expression are gestural and vocal.

Naturally, the infant–caregiver dyad continues to be important for communication development. By at least 7 months, the infant begins to respond differentially to her interactional partner (Ainsworth, 1963, 1964; H. Schaffer & Emerson, 1964). She stays close to her caregiver, follows her movements, and becomes distressed if she leaves. Even infant play with objects is influenced by maternal attending (Carr, Dabbs, & Carr, 1975). Infants play with toys as long as their mothers look on, but when their mothers turn away, infants leave their toys 50% of the time and attempt to retrieve the lost attention. This maternal attachment is related to the smoothness of the mother's movement in feeding interactions, in face-to-face interactions, and in responding to distress (Ainsworth & Bell, 1969; S. Bell & Ainsworth, 1972; Slayton & Ainsworth, 1973). The crucial factor may be the predictability of the mother's behavior.

In recognition of the infant's interest in objects and her increasing ability to follow conversational cues, the caregiver makes increasing reference to objects, events, and people outside of the infant–caregiver dyad. Increasingly, the infant demonstrates selective listening to familiar words and compliance with simple requests. The infant imitates simple motor behaviors; by 9 to 10 months she responds to requests to wave bye-bye. Infant response rates to maternal verbal and nonverbal requests increase with age (Liebergott, Ferrier, Chesnick, & Menyuk, 1981). At 9 months, infants respond to 39.5% of the maternal requests, compared to 52.0% at 11 months. Requests for action are answered 1 ½ times as frequently at both ages as requests for vocalization. By modifying her forms and frequencies of reply, the infant gains considerable control over the communicative exchange. Nine-month-olds can also follow maternal pointing and glancing or regard (Lempers, 1976). Following a line of regard depends upon the distance and spatial arrangement of the entity being noticed. The infant cues on a combination of head and eye orientation and on eye movement (Lempers, Flavell, & Flavell, 1977).

Visual orientation of both the infant and mother is usually accompanied by maternal naming (Collis, 1977). Bruner (1975) has interpreted this behavior as an attempt by the mother to use joint reference to establish the topic of a proto-conversation. The mother watches her infant's face more than the infant observes hers (H. Schaffer et al., 1977; D. Stern, 1977). She monitors the infant's glance and signs of interest. Newson (1979) reported that mothers of 8- to 14-month-olds look at their infants so frequently that the responsibility for maintaining eye contact really rests with the child. This monitoring by the mother decreases as the infant gets older.

Caregivers also monitor infant vocalizations. Parents of 8- to 12-month-olds can consistently recognize infant intonational messages that convey request, frustration, greeting, and pleasant surprise (Ricks, 1979).

Gaze and vocalization seem to be related. The infant's gaze is more likely to be initiated and maintained when the mother is vocalizing and/or gazing back, and in turn, the mother is more likely to initiate and maintain vocalization when the infant is looking at her (Collis, 1979). In addition, mothers and 1-year-olds exhibit very little vocal overlap (H. Schaffer et al., 1977). This turn taking contrasts to the co-occurring vocalizations of mothers and younger infants. Mothers and 1-year-olds depart from their turn-taking behaviors when they laugh or join in chorus or when the mother attempts to fill nonexistent pauses. The exchange is one of reciprocal actions, intonations, and gestures (Newson, 1979). The communication between infant and caregiver is closely related to the infant's resultant behavior state, and the child will show signs of distress when communication sequences end (Brazelton, Tronick, Adamson, Als, & Wise, 1975; Trevarthen, 1979). The infant will vocalize and gesture for attention, then exhibit sadness or grimace.

Communication Functions

At about 8 to 9 months, the infant begins to develop *intentionality*. Up to this point, the child has focused primarily on either objects or people. Even complex action sequences are really a series of discrete behaviors directed toward one category or the other. For example, the child might look at a person, smile, and touch. Intentionality is exhibited when the child demonstrates a coordinated person–object orientation (Sugarman, 1984). The child begins to encode her message for someone else. For the first time, she considers her audience. She may touch her mother, gain eye contact, then gesture toward an object. An explicit bid for attention is coupled with a signal behavior, although the order may vary. The child's uses of these signals are called **communication functions**, and they are expressed primarily through gestures. In other words, functions, such as requesting, interacting, and attracting attention, are first fulfilled by prelinguistic communicative means.

Bates and her colleagues (1975) have identified a three-stage sequence in the development of early communication functions: perlocutionary, illocutionary, and locutionary (Table 6.3). The perlocutionary stage begins at birth and continues into the second half-year of life. Throughout this stage the infant fails to signal specific intentions. Rather, she cries, coos, and uses her face and body nonspecifically. Crying indicates general pain, discomfort, or need but does not identify the cause of the problem. Her mother interprets her behavior as carrying intentions, however, and responds differentially. The infant's early behaviors do

TABLE 6.3   Development of Intentionality

Stage	Age (Months)	Characteristics
Perlocutionary	0–8 (approx.)	Intention inferred by adult
Substage 1		Shows self
Illocutionary	8–12	Emergence of intention to communicate
Substage 2		Shows objects
Substage 3		Displays full range of gestures
Locutionary	12 +	Words accompany or replace gesture to express communicative functions previously expressed in gestures alone or gestures plus vocalization

serve directive and referential functions (Moerk, 1977) in that her cry has a directive function for the mother, alerting her to some disorder, the cause of which she will investigate (Moss, 1973). As for the infant, only later does she recognize the means–ends potential of her communication. The referential function, in which an infant calls attention to the environment, is exemplified by infant scanning and searching. The mother follows her infant's visual line of regard and provides a label or comment.

Toward the end of the perlocutionary period, as the infant becomes more interested in manipulating objects, she begins to use recognitory gestures (Bates, Bretherton, Shore, & McNew, 1984). These gestures demonstrate an understanding of object purpose, or functional use, and include such behaviors as bringing a cup to the lips or a telephone receiver to the ear. As such, these gestures constitute a primitive form of naming and a categorization of an object, or referent, as belonging to a particular conceptual class. Thus, the infant demonstrates recognition that objects have stable characteristics and functions that necessitate specific behaviors. Occasionally the recognitory gestures are applied to objects that are related or look similar. These early gestures are usually brief and incomplete, often with some element missing. For example, the child may drink from an empty cup (the liquid being the missing element). In the early stages, sequences of events are also rare.

At this stage, the infant begins reaching for objects she desires. For objects that are beyond her grasp, the infant's reach becomes a pointing gesture. Later this whole-hand point becomes a finger point, following the physical law of minimal action (Moerk, 1977). In short, the infant makes only the minimal effort needed to convey her intention. Early pointing may be the first step toward definition (Olson, 1970).

The second, or illocutionary, stage of functional communication development begins at 8 to 9 months of age. Within this stage the infant uses conventional gestures or vocalizations to communicate her intentions. Several behaviors mark the emergence of intentional communication (Scoville, 1983).

- Gestures are accompanied by eye contact with the child's communication partner.
- The child uses consistent sound and intonation patterns of her own invention as signals for specific intentions. For example, the child might say "eh-eh" when she wants something.
- The child persists in attempting to communicate. If she is not understood, she may repeat her behavior or modify it for her communication partner.

In each behavior the child considers both the message and the partner's reception of it, thus exhibiting an intention to communicate.

There seem to be three sequential substages in the development of gestures (Bates et al., 1975). In the first substage, which begins prior to the illocutionary period, the infant exhibits or shows herself. She hides her face, acts coy, raises her arms to be picked up, or plays peekaboo. In the second substage the infant shows objects by extending them toward her caregiver but does not release them. Finally, in the last substage, fully within the illocutionary stage, the infant displays a full range of gestures, including conventional means of showing, giving, pointing, and requesting (Figure 6.2). Other nonconventional gestures, such as having tantrums and showing off, are also present. In general, each infant develops her own style with nonconventional gestures. Giving, unlike showing, includes a release of the object. Frequently giving follows a maternal request for the object. A favorite game becomes "the trade," in which the partners take turns passing an object between them. Pointing may include the whole hand or only a finger with the arm extended. Unlike requesting, pointing is not accompanied by movement of the upper trunk in the direction of the object. Requesting is a whole-hand grasping reach toward a desired object or a giving gesture accompanied by a call for assistance. In its most mature form, each gesture contains a visual check to ensure that the communication partner is attending. These initial gestures are used to signal two general communication functions (Bates et al., 1975). *Protoimperatives*, such as requests, signal an adult to attain an object. In contrast, giving, showing, and pointing, called *protodeclaratives*, use an object to attain adult attention.

Initially gestures appear without vocalizations, but the two are gradually paired. Consistent vocal patterns, dubbed *phonetically consistent forms (PCFs)*, accompany many gestures (Dore et al., 1976). PCFs occur between pauses, which clearly mark boundaries. In addition, PCFs occur repeatedly and are more phonetically stable than babbling but less so than words. For the child, PCFs do function as words. They are often imitations of environmental sounds, such as a dog's bark or a car's engine, or of the child's own or others' sounds (Reich, 1986). Finally, PCFs usually accompany events or actions in the environment. Once the infant begins to use PCFs, her mother will no longer accept other, less consistent

FIGURE 6.2   Infant Standardized Gestures
Infants develop a set of standardized gestures in addition to nonstandardized and functional gestures.

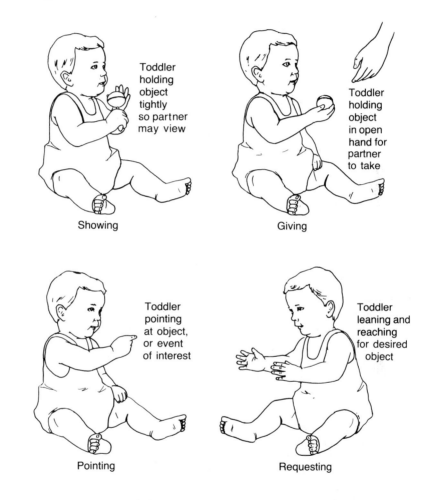

Toddler holding object tightly so partner may view

Showing

Toddler holding object in open hand for partner to take

Giving

Toddler pointing at object, or event of interest

Pointing

Toddler leaning and reaching for desired object

Requesting

vocalizations. PCFs are a transition to words in a highly creative developmental period when the child is also adept at employing gestures and intonation.

The appearance of intentional communication in the form of gestures requires a certain level of cognitive, as well as social, functioning. Children use very low-level gestures at stage 4 means–ends (Greenwald & Leonard, 1979). The infant must attain stage 5 means–ends behaviors, or at least object-to-object use, however, by the time she begins to use intentional speech (Bates et al., 1979; M. Folger & Leonard, 1978). Person–object sequences, such as requests, begin at 8 to 10 months, along with a shift to complex social interactions (Sugerman, 1978).

The final stage of functional communication development is the locutionary stage, which begins with the first meaningful word. Conventional verbalizations are used with or without gestures to accomplish the functions previously filled by gestures. Pointing develops within a shared attention context, then vocalization within pointing, and naming within vocalization. Words and gestures are used to refer to the same content (Bates et al., 1979). "New . . . forms most often enter to fulfill functions already served by older forms as if by a process of substitution" (Bruner, 1978a, p. 7). In other words, "what is content at one time becomes context later" (Bullowa, 1979b, p. 11). The gesture, which initially stands for the entire message, gradually becomes the context for more symbolic ways of communicating the message. Both gestures and words tend to be rigid and context bound but are gradually "decontextualized" and thus become more flexible in their use (Bates et al., 1979). True decontextualization occurs much later, when the child begins to read.

Summary

During the first 8 months of life, the infant learns the rituals and processes of communication from her caregiver (Table 6.4). The caregiver treats the infant as a full conversational partner and acts as if the infant communicates meaningfully. The infant also learns that her behavior can have an effect upon the environment. At first, her communication is general and unspecified. During the second 6 months she develops functional communication, first gesturally, then vocally. When the infant begins to use meaningful speech, she does so within this functional context of gestures and vocalizations.

MATERNAL COMMUNICATION BEHAVIORS

As we have noted, the infant and caregiver engage in mutual dialogue soon after birth. It is a complex interaction between infant character/temperament and maternal speech (Smolak, 1987). To some degree, both partners control this exchange. The infant sets the level of exchange because of her limited abilities. The initial infant responses are rather rigid and fixed. Only gradually does the infant expand this behavioral repertoire. In turn, the mother controls the exchange by providing the framework and adjusting her behaviors. The mother modifies "her displays to fit the infant's information processing limitations" (Tronick et al., 1979, p. 367). As a result, "many cognitively very important experiences of order in the care-taking environment occur because of the mother's willingness to learn from the infant and respond to his patterns—again, a matter of selectively intensified attention" (Bateson, 1979, p. 70). The mother's observation of the child's regular hunger rhythms, reflected in her readiness to nurse, instructs the infant on the nature of order. Within a given exchange, both partners adjust

TABLE 6.4   Infant Social and Communicative Development

Age	Behaviors
Newborn	Vision best at 8 inches; prefers light–dark contrasts, angularity, complexity, curvature
	Hearing best in frequency range of human voice; prefers human voice; exhibits entrainment
	Facial expressions
1 week	"Self-imitation"; reflexive actions but treated as meaningful by caregiver
2 weeks	Distinguishing of caregiver's voice and face
3 weeks	Social smile
1 month	Short visual exchanges with caregiver; prefers human face to all else
2 months	Cooing
3 months	Face alone not enough to hold infant's attention: in response, mother exaggerates her facial movements
	More frequent dialogues; decrease of handling by 30%
	Revocalization likely if caregiver's verbal response immediately follows child's first vocalization
	Vocal turn taking and concurrent vocalization
	Gaze coupling
	Rituals and games
	Face play
5 months	Purposeful facial imitation
	Vocalization to accompany attitude
6 months	Hand and nonspeech imitation
8 months	Gestures
9 months	Imitation of more complicated motor behaviors
	Following of maternal pointing
11 months	Response to about half of maternal verbal and nonverbal requests
12 months	Use of words to fill communicative functions established by gestures

their behavior continually to maintain an optimum level of stimulation. The mother maintains the infant's attention at a high level by her behavior. In response, the infant coos, smiles, and gazes alertly. Reinforced for her efforts, the mother tries even harder to maintain the infant's level of stimulation. The exchange is "a mutual feedback system" (D. Stern, 1977, p. 73), with each party responsive to the other. In addition, the mother helps expand the infant's abilities by deliberately "messing up" more consistently than expected. By exceeding the limits of the infant's behavior, she forces her to adjust to new stimuli.

Four caregiver behaviors form the background or foundation of infant–caregiver face-to-face exchanges: preparatory activities, state-setting activities, communication framework maintenance, and infantlike action modifications (Tronick et al., 1979). Table 6.5 describes and gives examples of each behavior category. Among the infantlike actions of mothers are exaggerated facial expressions, body movements, positioning, timing, touching, prolonged gaze, and baby talk. These modifications also occur in the behavior of other adults and children as they interact with infants. Preference for infant over adult faces seems to begin in girls of age 12 to 14 years and continues into adulthood (Fullard & Reiling, 1976). Boys began preferring infant faces (but less strongly) about 2 years later. Most children are able to perform infantlike actions by middle childhood. Prior experience with infants does not affect the behavior of either adults (Snow, 1972) or 4-year-olds (Shatz & Gelman, 1973), and prior

TABLE 6.5   Caregiver Behaviors that Form the Background for Face-to-Face Communication

Behavior	Description	Examples
Preparatory activities	Free infant from physiological state dominance	Reduce interference of hunger or fatigue
		Sooth or calm infant when upset
State-setting activities	Manipulate physical environment to optimize interaction	Move into infant's visual field
		Attain attention by modifying vocalizations
Maintenance of communication framework	Use of continuates by caregiver	Modulate speech, rhythmic tapping and patting, rhythmic body movements; provide infant with a focus of attention and action, a set of timing markers
Infantlike modifications of adult actions	Variation of caregiver activities in rate, intensity modulation, amplitude, and quality from those of adult–adult	Use baby talk—slowed and exaggerated
		Imitate baby movements—close, oriented straight ahead, parallel, and perpendicular to plane of infant

Source: Drawn from E. Tronick, H. Als, and L. Adamson. "Structure of early face-to-face communicative interactions." In M. Bullowa (Ed.), *Before Speech*. New York: Cambridge University Press, 1979.

learning seems to be unimportant (D. Stern, 1977). Three factors appear important in influencing the initial interactions of the infant and her mother: the medication used in delivery, the number of pregnancies, and the mother's socioeconomic and cultural backgrounds (Ramey, Farran, Campbell, & Finkelstein, 1978).

Most adults respond to the "babyness" (Lorenz, 1943) of the infant, particularly the face, which they find irresistible (Eibl-Eibesfeldt, 1971). The infant's head is large in proportion to her body, with large eyes and round cheeks. In brief, she looks cute. To this physical image, the infant adds smiles, gazes, mouth opening, and tongue thrust. Infants with a deviant look may elicit very different or negative responses.

Infant-Elicited Social Behavior

Infantlike caregiver responses can be characterized as "infant-elicited social behaviors" (D. Stern, 1977). They appear in response to infants but occur infrequently in adult-to-adult exchanges. Infant-elicited social behaviors have three characteristics. First, they are exaggerated in space, and the exaggeration may be maximal. Second, they are exaggerated in time, usually being slow or elongated. Finally, they form a select, limited repertoire that is performed frequently. The purpose of these modifications is to enhance recognition and discrimination of the behaviors by the child. The behaviors of one mother differ from those of another. "Each caregiver develops her own style . . ., fitted to who she is and who her baby is" (D. Stern, 1977, p. 10). Infant-elicited social behavior consists of maternal adaptations in speech and language (sometimes called *baby talk*), gaze, facial expression, facial presentation and head movement, and proxemics.

Baby Talk

The speech and language of adults and children to infants is systematically modified from that used in regular conversation. This adapted speech and language has been called *baby talk* or *motherese*. For our purposes, we shall use *baby talk* to signify the speech and language addressed to infants (Table 6.6). Use of this term does not imply that mothers use the diminutive or babyish forms, such as *horsie* or *ni-night*. Parents do not use such babyish forms until the child is old enough to understand them (Kaye, 1980). We will use the term *motherese* later to denote speech and language used with toddlers.

Baby talk is characterized by short utterance length and simple syntax. These qualities reflect, in part, the small core vocabulary used. Possibly to facilitate understanding or word–referent association by the infant, mothers paraphrase and repeat themselves. Topics are limited to the here and now. The mother's choice of content, type of information conveyed, and syntax appears to be heavily influenced by the context (D'Odorico & Franco, 1985). In addition, mothers use paralinguistic variations, such as intonation and pause, beyond those found in adult-to-adult speech. Employing more frequent facial expressions and gestures and an overall higher pitch, any one of us might engage in the following exchange:

TABLE 6.6   Characteristics of Baby Talk

Short utterance length (mean utterance length as few as 2.6 morphemes) and simple syntax

Small core vocabulary, usually object centered

Topics limited to here and now

Heightened use of facial expressions and gestures

Frequent questioning and greeting

Treating of infant behaviors as meaningful: mother awaits infant's turn and responds even to nonturns

Episodes of maternal utterances

Paralinguistic modifications of pitch and loudness

Frequent verbal rituals

> See the dog. (turn, look, pause)
> Big dog. (gesture, pause)
> Nice dog. (pause)
> Pet dog. (pet, pause)
> Can you pet dog? (pause)
> Nice dog. Do you like dog? (pause)
> Un-huh. Nice dog.

This little monologue contains most aspects of baby talk.

Short, simple utterances can be found in the baby talk of different languages (Ferguson, 1964). Maternal speech measured at 6, 13, and 23 weeks of infant age averages only 2.8 morphemes per utterance (Kaye, 1980). This average may increase to about 3.5 morphemes at 6 months (Lord, 1975). In part, this rise may reflect the increasingly complex communication of the mother and her infant, since there is a shift at 5 to 7 months to a more conversational mode with greater turn switching and more incorporation of objects (Snow, 1977a). After 1 year, average maternal utterance length is reported to be between 2.8 morphemes (Lord, 1975) and 3.5 morphemes (Phillips, 1973). The possible average of 3.5 morphemes at 6 months and 2.8 morphemes at 1 year may represent maternal modeling in anticipation of the infant's first words. Further research is needed to confirm this hypothesis. This issue aside, it is easy to see that an adult-to-infant average of 2.8 to 3.5 morphemes per utterance is well below the adult-to-adult average, which is around 8 morphemes. Researchers (Ferguson, 1964; Phillips, 1973) also disagree upon the degree of syntactic simplicity but concede that, here again, adult-to-infant speech is less complex structurally than adult-to-adult speech.

Mothers use a considerable number of questions and greetings with their infants (Snow, 1977a). These conversational devices may enable the mother to treat any infant response as a conversational turn, since both questions and greetings require a response. In turn, the mother responds to her infant's behavior as a meaningful response to her initial cue. Snow (1977a) reported that at 3 months "100% of both Ann's and Mary's burps, yawns, sneezes, coughs, coo-vocalizations, smiles and laughs were responded to by maternal vocalizations, suggesting that under conditions of reasonable proximity such responses were almost obligatory" (p. 12). Approximately 21% of maternal utterances are greetings such as *hi* and *bye-bye* or acknowledgments such as *sure, uh-huh,* and *yeah,* given in response to infant behaviors (Kaye, 1980). This maternal response pattern does not occur with nonstandard or nonsignaling infant behaviors, such as arm waving or bouncing.

For her part, the infant responds selectively. As mentioned previously, the 12-week-old infant is most likely to vocalize if her mother has just vocalized. Situational variations are also important: the infant is least likely to vocalize in activities such as being changed, fed, or rocked, or when her mother watches television or talks to another person (Freedle & Lewis, 1977). In contrast, some maternal nonvocal behaviors, such as touching, holding close, looking at, or smiling at the infant, increase the likelihood of infant vocalizations.

Maternal utterances often occur in episodes or strings of successive utterances referring to the same object, action, or event (Fogel, 1977; Kaye, 1977). Verbal episodes may facilitate understanding, because speech is less difficult to understand if recognizable strings of utterances are produced referring to the same object. "This would make it unnecessary to visually identify the referent of every new utterance and, more importantly, would help the child to understand the relationship between utterances so that information gained from preceding utterances could be used to assist the comprehension of the present one" (D. Messer, 1980, p. 30). Most episodes with infants begin with object manipulation and naming by the mother (D. Messer, 1980). At the beginning of the episode, pauses between utterances are twice as long as pauses within the episode itself. Young children receive help with object reference and episodic boundaries. Within each episode there is also a high proportion of naming. A typical episode might proceed as follows:

> (shake doll) Here's baby! (pause)
> Mommy has baby. (gesture, pause)
> Uh-huh, Betsy want baby? (gesture, pause)
> Here's baby! (pause)
> Oh, baby scare Betsy? (facial expression, pause)

High rates of redundancy also occur in the speech of mothers to their infants (Kaye, 1980). Maternal repetitions exceed the number expected by chance, and there is a great degree of semantic similarity between successive utterances. The high rate of syntactic and semantic redundancy increases the predictability and continuity of each episode. Mothers repeat one out of every six utterances immediately and exactly. These self-repetitions decrease as the child assumes increasing responsibility in the conversation. Of the remainder of maternal utterances, one-third are repeated partially within three utterances, although this value does not significantly exceed that found in the discourse of the mothers with other adults. Finally, the probability of a content word's appearing again within the next three utterances is high.

Early content tends to be object centered (Bruner, 1975) and concerned with the here and now (Phillips, 1973). For the mother, topics are generally limited to what her infant can see and hear. As the child's age approaches 6 months, her mother tends to use a more informational style. The mother's affective and contentless speech decreases, and she talks more about the environment and the infant's behavior (Penman, Cross, Milgrom-Friedman, & Meares, 1983).

Within an episode, the infant and her mother engage in a dialogue in which the infant's new communication functions can emerge (Ninio & Bruner, 1978). Certain elements appear over and over in the mother's speech. The mother presents "standard interactional routines" (Bruner, 1975) to give her infant the opportunity to predict and engage in the dialogue. These predictable maternal behaviors may aid the infant's comprehension (Macnamara, 1972). The mother "reduces degrees of freedom with which the child has to cope, concentrates his attention into a manageable domain, and provides models of the expected dialogue from which he can extract selectively what he needs for filling his role in discourse" (Bruner, 1976, p. 15). One of the most common sequences is that of joint, or shared, reference. **Referencing** is the differentiation and noting of a single object, action, or event and is signaled by indicating or marking. In **indicating**, the mother follows her infant's line of regard or visual attending and comments on the object of their joint attention (Collis & Schaffer, 1975). With **marking**, the mother shakes an object or exaggerates an action to attract her infant's attention.

In addition to linguistic modifications, mothers use paralinguistic variations. The manner of presentation may be more important than the form or content with young infants (D. Stern, 1977). Stated another way, "the prosodic feature or 'music' appears to be more important than the words or 'lyrics' " (D. Stern & Wasserman, 1979, p. 3). In fact, the infant will respond to intonation patterns before she comprehends language (Kaplan, 1969; Lewis, 1951). The mother uses a broad range of pitch and loudness, although overall, her pitch is higher than in adult-to-adult conversations (Sachs, 1985). This pitch contour has been found in a number of languages, although there is some variation (Bernstein Ratner & Pye, 1984). In general, 4-month-old infants seem to prefer a high, variable pitch (Fernald, 1981; Fernald & Kuhl, 1981). Conversational sequences may include instances of falsetto or bass voice and of whispers or yells. Content words or syllables receive additional emphasis. The mother also modifies her rhythm and timing. Vowel duration is longer than in adult-to-adult discourse. The mother uses longer pauses between utterances, though this delay may be a function of her infant's nonvocalization. After speaking, the mother waits approximately 0.6 second, the average adult turn-switching pause. Next, she waits for the duration of an imaginary infant response and another turn switch. Since many maternal utterances are questions, the duration of an infant response is relatively easy for the mother to estimate. Thus, the infant is exposed to a mature time frame in which later discourse skills will develop (D. Stern, 1977).

There are many similarities in prosody across parents from different languages, such as English, French, Italian, German, and Japanese (Fernald, Taeschner, Dunn, Papousek, deBoysson-Bardies & Fukui, 1989). Parents use a higher pitch, greater variability in pitch, shorter utterances, and longer pauses when talking to their preverbal infants than when talking to other adults. In general, mothers use a wider pitch range than fathers. Parents who speak American English seem to have more extreme modifications in their speech than do parents in other languages (Fernald et al., 1989; Shute & Wheldall, 1989).

In elicitation sequences with their infants, mothers use all of the baby talk behaviors mentioned above (Snow, DeBlauw, & Van Roosmalen, 1979). Unlike games, elicitation sequences continue even when the infant does not respond. In such situations, the mother redoubles her efforts with increasing use of baby talk.

Two events lead mothers to talk to their infants (Snow et al., 1979). First, selected infant behaviors are treated as meaningful communication turns and the mother responds. For the 3-month-old infant, these behaviors include smiling, burping, sneezing, coughing, vocalizing, looking intently, and gaze shifting. The second occasion occurs when the mother talks about what she is doing. She employs baby talk, asks her infant's permission, and gives reasons for her actions.

On other occasions, mothers talk to their infants for the fun of it. Three specific occurrences of "fun talking" are game playing, attempting to elicit infant vocalizations, and offering objects for play:

> All the talking-for-fun episodes were characterized by the fact that the baby was given the opportunity to do something contingent on the mother's behavior and on the content of her speech. . . . All these situations . . . create contexts within which communication can be "felt" to occur. (Snow et al., 1979, p. 286)

A prelinguistic infant can elicit baby talk if the mother is willing to treat the infant as a conversational participant (Snow, 1972).

Language development experts differ as to the purpose of baby talk (Fernald et al., 1989). Why do mothers and other adults and children use this style of talking with prelinguistic infants? Some experts suggest that these behaviors maintain the infant's attention; others believe that the goal is language teaching. Still another group attributes the maternal linguistic adaptations to conversational constraints.

First, a mother uses both repetition and variation to capture and maintain her infant's attention (Fernald et al., 1989). Maternal patterns of repetition are found in nonverbal as well as verbal behaviors (D. Messer, 1980; D. Stern, Beebe, Jaffe, & Bennett, 1977). There are also prosodic and intonational variations (Sachs, 1977), which reach a peak at 4 to 6 months, corresponding to a period of extensive face-to-face interaction (D. Stern, Spieker, Barnett, & Mackain, 1983). This variety helps keep the infant alert and interested. When "a mother (in fact, any adult playing with an infant) superimposes minor variations (novelty) upon repeated (familiar) movements . . . the mother is trying to make herself interesting to her infant" (Kaye, 1980, p. 491). As the infant gets older, her mother introduces more variety and rhythm declines (D. Stern & Wasserman, 1979).

The second rationale often advanced to justify maternal speech modification is that "simplified speech is admirably designed to aid children in learning language" (Snow, 1972, p. 564). For example, the ritualized structuring of the environment seems important for the learning of early meanings (Wells, 1974). The maternal modifications can be called a "perfect match" (Hunt, 1961) in that they differ only slightly from what the infant already knows (McLean & Snyder-McLean, 1978). Such stimuli provide an optimal level of training. During the infant's first year, when his verbal demands are minimal, "mothers seem to display a consistent verbal style that may well be a function of their knowledge about child development and their beliefs about what is important for development (Ramey et al., 1978, p. 423).

It seems improbable that maternal speech adaptations serve a specific language-learning function for very young infants. Although mothers' responses to 2-month-old infants are stimulating and inject meaning into infants' expressions, it seems doubtful at this stage that verbal meaning has any influence on the infant. " 'What' the mothers say does not tutor infants" (Trevarthen, 1979, p. 340).

A third reason for the maternal modifications may be to maintain the child's responsiveness at an optimal level (Fernald et al., 1989). However, explanations of the mother's speech modifications based purely on responsiveness to attention and comprehension from the child may be simplistic (Snow et al., 1979). The mother assumes that her infant is a communication partner. Thus, maternal speech modifications are an attempt to maintain the conversation despite the conversational limitations of the infant. With a 3-month-old infant, the mother structures the sequence so that any infant response can be treated as a reply.

A fourth, compromise rationale for maternal modifications is that mothers use baby talk "to communicate, to understand, to be understood, to keep two minds focused on the same topic" (R. Brown, 1977, p. 12). The mother's modifications are highly correlated with the level of performance of her infant. The main goal is to maintain a conversation in order to provide a context for teaching language use rather than form or content (Bruner, 1977b).

Specific goals aside, maternal speech adaptations fulfill three functions (Sachs, 1977). First, the mother's speech modifications gain and hold the infant's attention. Second, the modifications aid in the establishment of emotional bonds (Trevarthen, 1979). Third, maternal speech characteristics enable communication to occur at the earliest opportunity.

Gaze

The mother modifies her typical gaze pattern, as well as her speech, when she interacts with her infant. Mature adult gaze patterns, which rarely last more than a few seconds, can evoke strong feelings if extended. In a conversational exchange, the mature speaker looks away as she begins to speak and checks back only occasionally. When the mother gazes at her infant, however, they may remain in eye contact for more than 30 seconds (D. Stern, 1977). During play, gazing may occur up to 70% of the time. In addition, play is an activity in which gaze and vocalization can occur simultaneously.

The mother also monitors her infant's gaze. Infant gaze is a good predictor of the mother's conversational topic (Collis & Schaffer, 1975). In fact, the very young infant doesn't look where her mother points, even though she behaves as if she does. Actually, mothers "fit their own behavior into the infant's so that the infant's subsequent behavior will seem to be a contingent response" (Kaye, 1979, p. 202). Gradually, the infant's gaze behavior comes to follow her mother's pointing or naming, though she is still free to gaze where she chooses.

Maternal gaze modifications help maintain the infant's interest and focus attention on her mother's face. The mother's monitoring of the infant's gaze enables them to establish joint reference before they can establish a shared topic.

Facial Expression

The mother uses facial expression skillfully to complement her verbalizations. Facial expressions can fulfill a number of conversational functions, including initiation, maintenance and modulation of the exchange, termination, and avoidance of interaction (D. Stern, 1977). Mock surprise is frequently used to initiate, invite, or signal readiness. In this expression, the mother's eyes open wide and her eyebrows rise, her mouth opens, her head tilts, and she intones an "o-o-o" or "ah-h-h." Owing to the brevity of most episodes, the mother may express mock surprise every 10 to 15 seconds.

An episode can be maintained or modulated by a smile or an expression of concern. Similar to adult exchanges, a smile signals that communication is proceeding without difficulty. An expression of concern, characterized by open eyes but knitted brows and a partially opened mouth, signals communication distress and a willingness to refocus the exchange.

Termination is signaled by a frown, accompanying head aversion, and gaze breaking. A frown is characterized by low, knitted eyebrows, narrowed eyes, a downwardly curved or pursed mouth, and tense nostrils. Occasionally, the frown is accompanied by a vocalization with decreased volume and dropping pitch.

Finally, avoidance of a social interaction can also be signaled by head aversion, but with a neutral or expressionless face. There is little in the mother's face, therefore, to hold her infant's attention.

Naturally, the mother's repertoire includes a full range of affective facial expressions. Mothers use these expressions to maintain their infants' attention and to aid comprehension.

Facial Presentation and Head Movement

The mother uses a large repertoire of head movements to help transmit her messages, including nodding and wagging, averting, and cocking to one side. The sudden appearance of the face, as in "peekaboo," is used to capture and hold the child's attention. In a variation of this procedure, the mother lowers her face and then returns to a full face gaze accompanied by a vocalization. Many games, such as "I'm gonna get you" and "raspberries for your tummy," are accomplished by a full face presentation. Frequently, the mother also exhibits mock surprise.

Proxemics

Proxemics, or the communicative use of interpersonal space, is a powerful interactional tool. Each person has a psychological envelope of personal space that can be violated only in the most intimate situations. When communicating with her infant, however, the mother acts as if this space does not exist (D. Stern, 1977) and communicates from a very close distance.

Cultural, Socioeconomic, and Sexual Differences

The interactional patterns just described reflect the infant–caregiver behaviors found in the mainstream American culture. In other cultures, the caregiver does not provide the same types of linguistic input. Though mothers in other cultures may speak to their children less often in one way, they engage in other communication activities found less frequently in the American culture.

Differences in the interactions of mothers and infants may reflect cultural differences (Toda, Fogel, & Kawai, 1990). For example, mothers in the United States are more information oriented than mothers in Japan. U.S. mothers are more chatty and use more questions, especially of the yes/no type, as well as more grammatically correct utterances with their 3-month-olds. In contrast, Japanese mothers are more affect oriented and use more nonsense and onomatopoeic or environmental sounds, more baby talk, and more babies' names. These differences may reflect adult-to-adult styles of talking that are direct and emphasize individual expression in the United States, and are more intuitive and indirect and emphasize empathy and conformity in Japan.

Japanese mothers also vocalize less with their 3-month-old infants but offer, in turn, more physical contact than do mothers in the United States (Otaki, Durrett, Richards, Nyquist, & Pennebaker, 1986; Sengoku, 1983; Shand & Kosawa, 1985). This difference is also reflected in more frequent nonverbal responding by Japanese mothers and more frequent verbal responding by mothers in the United States (Fogel, Toda, & Kawai, 1988). The types of utterances to which mothers are most likely to respond also differ. U.S. mothers are more likely to respond to their 3-month-old's positive cooing and comfort sounds, while Japanese mothers are more likely to respond to discomfort or fussing sounds (Morikawa, Shand, & Kosawa, 1988). Japanese mothers try to soothe their infants with speech. These purposes may also differ across cultures, with U.S. mothers more likely to talk to maintain attention and Japanese mothers talking within vocal activities to elicit more vocalizations.

Mothers make use of pitch very early. In English, a rising contour is used to gain the infant's attention (Stern, Spicker, & MacKain, 1982). This pattern is not universal. For example, mothers speaking Thai to their infants use a falling pitch pattern (Tuaycharoen, 1978), and those using Quiche Mayan use a flat or falling contour (Pye & Ratner, 1984).

Within the American culture, race, education, and socioeconomic class each influence maternal behaviors toward the child. For example, black inner-city mothers reportedly engage in little vocal behavior (J. Brown, Bakeman, Snyder, Frederickson, Morgan, & Helper, 1975). This finding reflects, in part, the socioeconomic level of many inner-city dwellers. In general, lower-class mothers are less responsive to their infants' vocalizations (Lewis & Wilson, 1972). They exhibit fewer expansions and repetitions of their infants' vocal behavior (Snow, Arlmann-Rupp, Hassing, Jobse, Jootsen, & Vorster, 1976). Middle-class mothers ask more questions, while those from the lower socioeconomic classes use more imperatives or directives (Snow et al., 1976; Streissguth & Bee, 1972). Similarly, better-educated mothers are more verbal. Siblings and peers are more important in the infant socialization process within the homes of minority and lower socioeconomic class families.

As an infant gets older, her mother communicates more and more from a distance. The resultant decrease in touching is accompanied by increased eye contact (Lewis & Ban, 1971). In general, mothers tend to maintain closer proximity with their daughters than with their sons, at least until age 4 years (Lewis, 1972). This sexual difference is reflected in other ways. At 2 years of age, female infants receive more questions, male infants more directives. With female infants mothers are more repetitive, acknowledge more child answers, and take more turns. In short, more maternal utterances of a longer length are addressed to daughters than to sons. "The differential maternal behavior as a function of the child's sex is unrelated to the child's linguistic behavior, since in general there are no sex differences in children's [early] language performance" (Lewis & Cherry, 1977, pp. 239–240).

INTERACTIONS BETWEEN INFANT AND CAREGIVER

Some interactional behaviors are of particular interest for language development. These behaviors, which we will examine in detail, are joint reference, joint action (play), turn taking, and situational behaviors.

Joint Reference

As mentioned previously, *reference* is the ability to differentiate one entity from many and to note its presence. The term *joint reference* presupposes that two or more individuals share a common focus on one entity. Language develops as a means of regulating both joint reference and joint action (Bruner, 1975). "The deep question about reference is how one individual manages to get another to share, attend to, zero in upon a topic that is occupying him" (Bruner, 1978b, p. 69). Bruner (1977a) explained the issue in detail:

> Associative theories of naming or reference presuppose that a sound or a gesture emitted in the presence of a referent leads to automatic recognition by the child that the name stands for something at the focus of the child's attention. That is plainly not so. . . . *The objective of early reference, rather, is to indicate to another by some reliable means which among an alternative set of things or states or actions is relevant to the child's and mother's shared line of endeavor.* . . . "Efficiency of singling out" is the crucial objective. (p. 275)

In short, an essential communicative characteristic of any concept is that it can be shared with another human being.

Joint reference is particularly important for language development, because it is within this context that infants develop gestural, vocal, and verbal signals of notice. Many initial words serve a notice function. The child calls attention to an object, event, or action in the environment, thus conveying the focus of her attention to her mother.

Several researchers have noted that one of the first uses of language is naming (Atkinson, 1974; R. Brown, 1973; Greenfield & Smith, 1976; Nelson, 1973b; Werner & Kaplan, 1963). Approximately 65% of the first 50 words the child uses may be nominals, or nouns (Nelson, 1973b). This is not true of all children, and Horgan (1979) has suggested that children vary in their use of nouns and may be grouped into "noun lovers" and "noun leavers."

There appear to be three aspects of early referencing: indicating, deixis, and naming (Bruner, 1977a). *Indicating* can take a gestural, postural, or vocal form. At an early age the infant and her mother engage in a system to ensure joint selective attention. For example, the mother will shake an object before her infant to attract the infant's attention to it (Kaye, 1976). These routines are used to attain eye contact, the first step in establishing joint reference. As the infant matures, her indicating behaviors change. First, indicating behaviors become less dependent on specific situations for interpretation. Second, indicating becomes more economical, thus requiring less effort. As other forms develop, a gesture may carry less of the message content. In its turn, the gesture becomes the context for other content. A reaching gesture changes from an actual reach to a mere indication of a reach. Finally, indicating is gradually conventionalized. Idiosyncratic indicating methods become more standardized, more recognizable by others.

Deixis, the second aspect of referencing, is the use of spatial, temporal, and interpersonal features of the content to aid joint reference. Spatial cues relate the object to other aspects of the context, such as *next to* or *in front of*. Temporal cues fix the object in time, as in *after* or *before*. Interpersonal cues relate to role from the speaker's perspective, such as *you* or *me*. The listener must convert deictic aspects to her own perspective.

The third aspect of referencing is *naming*. Infants are able to associate names with their referents prior to developing the ability to produce names.

Development of Joint Reference

There appear to be four phases in the development of reference (Bruner & Sylva, in preparation). Phase I, lasting for the first 6 months of life, is characterized by mastery of joint attention. The goal is for the infant to look at objects and events in the environment in tandem with her mother. The infant must be able to maintain eye contact. The early presence of this behavior is well documented (Bruner, 1973; Stone, Smith, & Murphy, 1973; Wolff, 1963). Initially the mother interests her infant by using direct face-to-face techniques. She does not use objects until 4 to 6 weeks of infant age. At this point, the mother elects to bring the object into the infant's field of vision or to follow her line of regard. Both strategies are accompanied by shaking or moving of the object and talking, frequently using the infant's name or phrases such as "Oh, look." The mother's comments on the object of their joint attention become routine. As a result, interactional expectations are established for the infant. Initially these techniques may mean little to the infant. The infant's understanding develops slowly. By 8 weeks the infant is able to follow her mother's movements visually. At 3 months she can distinguish and attend to utterances addressed to her (Lewis & Freedle, 1973). The 4-month-old infant is able to follow her mother's line of regard (Scaife & Bruner, 1975). Within a short time, the infant's response quickens with her mother's directives, such as "Look!" Later the mother uses the object or event name to establish joint reference. By 6 months the mother's intonational pattern signals the infant to shift attention (Ryan, 1974). The mother assists in the shift by following her infant's gaze closely. In brief, by 6 months the mother and infant use a number of cues to regulate reference.

Phase II is characterized by the beginning of intentional communication. The infant's heightened interest in objects is accompanied by reaching. With the onset of reaching, face-to-face contact decreases from 80% to 15% of infant–mother contact time (Bruner, 1978b). Initially the infant's reach is solely a reach and is not intended to communicate any other meaning. The infant does not look toward her mother to see if she has received the message. Instead, she orients toward either the object or her mother. By 8 months the reach is less exigent, and the infant begins to look at her mother while reaching (Bruner, 1978b). At this point the infant has two reaches, a "reach-for-real" and a "reach-for-signal" (Bruner, 1978b). The infant is thus indicating that she expects maternal assistance. The infant's reach-for-signal becomes a stylized indicating behavior. The upper trunk is less clearly inclined toward the object, the arm is extended, and the hand is raised slightly at the wrist. The infant shifts her gaze from the object to her mother and back again. Her mother responds with the object or with encouragement of an even greater effort.

There are thematic changes in mothers' speech to their infants at 5 to 7 months (Snow, 1977; Trevarthen & Hubley, 1978). Mothers move from a social mode, in which they discuss feelings and states, to an activity mode, in which they discuss children's activities and events outside the immediate context. The concentration is on objects as children's focus of interest.

In phase III the infant begins to point and to vocalize. Gradually the full-hand reaching grasp becomes a finger point. The pointing behavior becomes separated from the intention to obtain an object. In response, the mother asks questions and incorporates the child's pointing and interests into the dialogue.

Finally, in phase IV the child masters naming and topicalizing. With this change in the child's behavior there is a corresponding increase in the mother's use of nominals, or nouns. Increasingly, exchanges involve objects. Initially the mother provides object and event labels. This strategy is modified when the child begins to talk. The mother attempts to get the child to look, to point, and to verbalize within the ongoing dialogue. She uses object-related questions to elicit these verbalizations. As the child assumes more control of the dialogue, the mother's questioning decreases.

Summary

The reference function, established months before meaningful language appears, is the vehicle for the development of naming and establishing a topic. More important, joint reference provides one of the earliest opportunities for the infant to engage in a truly communicative act of sharing information. Specific speech and language skills develop as more precise means to transmit the signal to a communication partner.

Joint Action

"What the child learns about communication before language helps him crack the linguistic code," stated Bruner (1977a, p. 274). He continued, "Communication is converted into speech through a series of procedural advances that are achieved in highly familiar, well learned contexts that have already undergone conventionalization at the hands of the infant and his mother (or other caretaker)" (p. 274). Throughout the first year of life, the caregiver and infant develop joint behaviors in contexts that support each participant. These routinized actions provide a structure within which language can be analyzed. Routinized activities have an aspect of convention that lets the child encounter rules within a pleasurable experience. From these same routines, the child learns turn-taking and conversational skills. Thus she learns to slot her behavior in the ongoing dialogue.

"These purely social interactions, sometimes called 'free play,' between mother and infant are among the most crucial experiences in the infant's first phase of learning and participating in human events" (D. Stern, 1977, p. 5). Within these joint action sequences, the infant begins to learn the conventions of human communication. For example, the infant's cry is gradually differentiated into recognizable signals by her mother's response.

There is a shift from the demand mode of crying to an anticipatory request mode (Bruner, 1974/1975). As the mother responds to the infant's demand cry, she establishes an expectation within her infant. The resultant request cry is less insistent. The infant pauses in anticipation of her mother's response. This shift is a forerunner of early dialogues in which a behavior or a vocalization is followed by a response. Early examples of these dialogues can be found in the anticipatory body games of infant and mother, such as "peekaboo" and "I'm gonna get you."

Gradually, the infant's and mother's contingent play evolves into an exchange mode in which the partners shift roles. For example, when passing an object back and forth, each partner plays the passer and the recipient in turn. Exchange, rather than possession, becomes the goal. Within these exchange games, the infant learns to shift roles, take turns, and coordinate signaling and acting (Bruner, 1978b). Role shifting and turn taking become so important that the infant will react with frustration, often accompanied by gestures and vocaliza-

Game playing is a joint action routine with many of the attributes of conversation.

tions, if her turn is delayed. She may even reach for an object being passed before her mother offers it. In coordinating her signals and actions, the infant learns to look at her mother's face in anticipation of the signals.

Finally, a reciprocal mode of interaction replaces the exchange mode. With the reciprocal mode, activities revolve around a joint task format, such as play with an object.

Game Playing

The infant and her caregiver(s) engage in play almost from birth. Each mother and infant develop a unique set of games of their own. As each mother becomes familiar with her infant's abilities and interests, she creates interpersonal games. These games, in turn, become ritual exchanges that comment upon or emotionally mark familiar patterns of interaction (Trevarthen, 1979).

The most striking feature is the consistency of each mother's behavior both within and between these play sequences, especially the repetitiveness of the mother's vocal and nonvocal behaviors (Kaye, 1979; D. Stern, 1975). Approximately one-third to two-thirds of maternal behavior directed toward the infant occurs in *runs*, or strings of behavior related to a single topic. This form of stimulation may be optimal for holding the infant's attention.

Early face-to-face play occurs in alternating cycles of arousal (Brazelton, Koslowski, & Main, 1974). The infant is less aroused by her own processes than by maternal stimulation (Thomas & Martin, 1976). Furthermore, there is a relationship between the modality of maternal stimulation and the infant's response. For example, if the mother stimulates vocally, the child is likely to respond vocally. A strong positive correlation exists between the frequency and quality of the mother's stimulation in a sensory modality and her infant's responses in that same modality (Osofsky & Danzger, 1974).

An infant as young as 6 weeks old can initiate games by modifying her internal state of alertness (Kaye, 1979). By 13 weeks she has adopted a true role in social games and thus signals her readiness to begin play. When the mother approaches with a still face, her infant initiates the interaction by performing her repertoire of facial expressions and body movements (Tronick, Adamson, Wise, & Brazelton, 1975). If the infant fails to get a response, she averts her gaze. This behavior is modified, in turn, to independent exploration play by 23 weeks. The mother adjusts gradually to these developmental changes and to changes in her infant's internal state in three dimensions: timing, infant arousal, and agenda (Kaye, 1979). First, the mother adjusts her timing to the infant's arousal and agenda to find the appropriate slot for her behavior. She is most likely to respond when the infant looks at her (Brazelton et al., 1974). By modifying her timing, the mother attempts to alter the interactional pattern, to prolong the interactions, or to elicit a response from the infant. Second, the mother buffers her infant's arousal state to maintain a moderate level of arousal. There is a continuum of maternal behaviors for fine-tuning adjustments in the infant's state. Thus, the infant maintains an optimal state for learning. In turn, the mother is reinforced by her infant's responsiveness. Finally, the mother maintains a balance between her agenda and her infant's behavior. For example, when the infant does not interact for a period of 5 to 10 seconds, the mother responds with her bag of tricks. She makes faces, smiles, protrudes her tongue, moves her limbs, or vocalizes. In so doing, she is careful to leave an opportunity or slot for the infant to respond.

One very popular infant–mother game is "copycat." "As soon as the infants join in communication the behavior of most mothers quickly becomes subdued and attentive to and dependent on what the infants do" (Trevarthen, 1979, p. 338). One characteristic of mothers' responses is that they are often imitative. Much of this imitation appears to be an unconscious following of the infant's most demonstrative behaviors. The importance of this particular game form cannot be overemphasized. "The whole process by which the infant comes to imitate his mother in a clearly intentional way is rooted in the initial readiness of the mother to imitate her infant" (Pawlby, 1977, pp. 219–220).

Maternal imitation is not an exact imitation, however, and the mother pulls her child in the direction of the mother's goals or agenda. Maternal imitation "is never a perfect match, always a variation, in the direction of an individual's personal style, a learner's incompetence or an instructor's agenda" (Kaye, 1979, p. 199). Three maternal modifications of the imitated behavior can be noted. The mother may maximize the imitation by exaggerating her infant's behavior and thus calling attention to it. On the other hand, she may minimize the imitation to a short, quick flash, used to draw the infant back to the mother's ongoing behavior. Finally, the mother may perform a modulating imitation such as responding with a mellowed version of the infant's behavior. For example, the mother may perform mellow crying in imitation of the child's wail. One inconsistency in maternal imitation is that mothers do not usually imitate prespeech or small hand movements such as pointing but do reply to these with baby talk (Trevarthen, 1979). Thus, infant behaviors that can be interpreted as having communicative intent receive a conversational response.

Early play consists primarily of social behaviors. During the first 6 months, the focus of play is social, and there are no specific game rules. Interpersonal rules are employed. For example, contingent social play is usually spontaneous and occurs frequently during routines. Once play begins, all other external tasks end.

In a typical social play period, play begins when the partners catch each other's glance (D. Stern, 1977). This initiation is followed by a moment of mutual gaze. If either partner breaks the gaze pattern, play ceases momentarily. Maintenance of the gaze signals readiness and is usually followed by a maternal face display. As in mock surprise, the mother raises her eyebrows, widens her eyes, opens her mouth, and repositions her head. Her infant responds with wide eyes, an open mouth, a smile, and head reorientation. The infant may wag her head or approach her mother's face, but the result is a full-face positioning. Play begins.

The initial exchange in actual play is a greeting. This exchange, which may last for only a second, accomplishes two things. First, all other activities stop; second, there is a reorientation to a face-to-face position, in which signals will be most visible. Often the infant is not prepared, and there are false starts.

Two subunits, or episodes, of the play sequence that may occur several times per minute are engagement and time-out (D. Stern, 1977). Episodes of engagement are variable-length sequences of social behaviors bounded by clearly marked pauses. Each sequence begins with a greeting that is less full than the initial greeting. Within each episode, the rate of caregiver verbal and nonverbal behaviors is relatively constant. These behaviors occur in discrete bursts within each episode. The mother keeps most of her behaviors under half a second in duration. This amount of time is a significant sensory unit for adults. If this unit is also significant for infants, then variations by the mother should attract the infant's attention. Tempo can be used to soothe or arouse the infant. For example, the mother increases her rate to exceed that of a fussy child, then gradually slows in order to soothe the infant. Although the rate of maternal behaviors within an episode is constant, the tempo between episodes may vary considerably. For example, the excitement caused by "I'm gonna get you" is due to changes in tempo. Generally, each episode has one major purpose—to establish attention, to maintain attention, or to enter into play. Within each episode, therefore, the mother's behavior is fairly predictable for her infant. These maternal consistencies, accompanied by slight variations, are ideal for gaining and maintaining the infant's attention.

Episodes of time-out, or periods of "relative behavioral silence" (Fogel, 1977), consist of rests used to readjust the interaction. Time-out episodes, usually lasting for 3 seconds or longer, occur when the infant signals, usually by fussing or averting her gaze, that she has exceeded her lower or upper boundary of excitement. Time-out provides an opportunity to retune the interaction. The mother changes the focus of the interaction by glancing away, or to some other infant body part, or by sitting quietly.

Maternal behaviors often occur in repetitive runs or in a repetitive series within each episode. The average run is three or more units in length (D. Stern, 1977). For example, the mother may introduce a topic and then vary it systematically, as in the following sequences:

> You're so big, aren't you?
> So big.
> Oh, so big.

> No, we can't do that.
> No, not that.
> Oh, no.

These repetitive maternal speech patterns have already been discussed (see p. 189). Between these repetitive runs, the mother may vary the tempo. Although these repetitions have enormous instructional potential, they may reflect more the mother's limited repertoire of behaviors. In short, she runs out of things to do. This is not meant to diminish the importance of these behaviors, however, because they expand the infant's range of experience and maintain her attention.

During the second 6 months of life, object play increases. Object play is almost nonexistent at 3 months of age. By 6 months, play often begins with the body but is repeated with a toy (Snow et al., 1979). Infant and mother participate in a ritualized give-and-take of objects that occurs frequently after 7 months of age. Infant possession time decreases steadily from 30 to 10 seconds during the period from 7 to 10 months (Bruner & Sylva, in preparation). By 11 months the child does not need coaxing before she releases an object. Another popular infant game is "retrieve," in which the child drops an object in anticipation that her mother will return it. Infants in all cultures seem to enjoy the shared "anticipation of some simple and predictable sequence of events under [their] own voluntary control" (Newson, 1979, p. 214). The importance of these games is in their "high level of shared meaningful communication at a completely non-verbal level." (p. 214). Throughout the first year, play demonstrates many of the characteristics of later conversation.

Summary

Although each infant–caregiver pair evolves different patterns of interaction, there are similarities that are important for later communication development. "What seems to be important is the 'process' of conventionalization, the mutual topic-comment, the modularization . . . of dyadic routines of 'some' kind, the learning to anticipate when and how a partner's behavior will change" (Kaye, 1979, p. 200). Play is particularly relevant to language acquisition (Ratner & Bruner, 1978). First, play usually occurs in a highly restricted and well-understood or conceptualized *semantic domain*. Games such as "peekaboo" and "I'm gonna get you" have a restricted format, limited semantic elements, and a highly constrained set of semantic relations. The mother is frequently the agent of some action upon an object. Second, play has a well-defined task structure. Although variation is permitted, an order of events enables the child to predict. The rules of language provide similar boundaries. Third, play has a demarcated role structure similar to that of conversation. The infant learns to recognize and to play various roles. In addition, she learns that roles have a property of reversibility.

Turn Taking

Most of the interactional behaviors discussed so far have contained an element of turn taking. The infant's development of this skill is essential for development of later conversational skills.

In very early feeding sessions, "the dialogue-like turn-taking . . . is a matter of the mother's fitting her behavior into the infant's natural rhythms" (Kaye, 1979, p. 196). Initially mothers jiggle the nipple to increase or to elicit feeding. The infants respond by decreasing their sucking behavior. Within 2 weeks mothers learn to cease their jiggling to elicit sucking. The resultant cycle becomes one in which an infant pause is followed by a jiggle. The jiggling soon stops. After a short delay, the infant begins to suck. The mother behaves as if a true dialogue has occurred. Thus, early feeding behaviors represent a pattern of turn taking found in later conversations.

Most infant and mother turns last for less than 1 second (Beebe, 1973); the interaction is not a series of stimulus–response matches, however. The pattern is more like a waltz in which "both partners know the steps and music by heart and can accordingly move precisely together" (D. Stern, 1977, p. 85). As a result, sequences of infant–mother behavior emerge. "The more they have danced together, the longer sequence of programmed patterns they can string together without requiring a lead stimulus and a following response" (p. 88).

Even body games, such as tickling, lifting, and bouncing, contain pauses for infant responses (Snow et al., 1979). The pauses are initially short, but they lengthen as the infant gains the ability to respond more fully. A lack of pauses can result in overstimulation and a less responsive infant. At 3 to 6 months of age, the infant responds or attends quietly. Gaze, facial expression, body movement, or vocalization can all fill a turn.

A set of conversational behaviors evolves from these infant turn-filling behaviors. Several child development specialists have noted the development of reciprocal and alternating patterns of vocalizations (Strain, 1974; Vietze & Strain, 1975), called *protoconversations* (Bateson, 1971). Gestures and, later, words will develop to fill the infant's turn in the conversation.

Situational Variations

Mothers use a variety of naturally occurring situations to facilitate language and communication development. Prelinguistic behaviors may be situationally bound, even at an early age (Freedle & Lewis, 1977). Certain infant–mother situations occur frequently. Lewis and Freedle (1973) found that eight interactional situations accounted for almost all locational activities of the 3-month-old infant. From most to least frequent, these situations are mother's lap, crib/bed, infant seat, table/tub, couch/sofa, playpen, floor, jumper/swing. The frequency of occurrence is less significant, however, than the frequency of vocalization within each situation. Although the vocalization frequency varies with the situational setting, it does not seem to bear any relationship to the frequency with which the situation occurs. It is not the location itself that is significant but the function associated with that location.

Within each situation certain infant–mother behaviors occur regularly. This regularity is the basis for the development of meaning, which emerges from nonrandom action sequences, especially vocalization sequences associated to different "situational" locations. "Just the arbitrary production of strings of non-random vocalization events, apart from their situational context, would not suffice to build up meaning" (Freedle & Lewis, 1977, p. 170). For example, the infant is usually placed in the crib to sleep. Therefore, the mother neither responds nor initiates vocalizations. On the other hand, at the table or in the tub, the infant is subjected to many vocalizations and nonrandom maternal behaviors. Situations provide a context within which the child can process the nonrandom content. Nonrandom behaviors form an early meaning base. These " 'naturalistically occurring situations' are . . . a basis for the development of formal language" (Freedle & Lewis, 1977, p. 168).

CONCLUSION

Symbolic communication in the form of spoken language develops within the context of a very early communication system that is integrated and nonspeech in nature. Only recently have professionals recognized and described the existence of this network. Bullowa (1979b) explained: "Until recently most scientifically minded people in our culture considered infants incapable of communication since they don't talk. Of course most mothers know otherwise but scientists and other 'experts' haven't always taken them seriously" (p. 1). It is now recognized, however, that "prespeech communication, which is a matter of changing patterns of interaction over the whole course of the first year, . . . enables the child to 'learn' language" (Kaye, 1979, p. 192). Over the first year, the infant's early behaviors acquire intentionality and serve several communication functions.

The child learns language by employing that language to communicate. Her initial behavior communicates little, if anything, beyond the immediate behavior itself. Infant behaviors are not as significant overall as the mother's response to these behaviors. Mothers perceive their infants as persons and "interpret baby behavior as not only intended to be communicative, but as verbal and meaning-ful" (Trevarthen, 1979, p. 340).

Humans are social animals who live generally within a social network. The infant is dependent upon others, especially her mother. The mother is controlled to a great extent by the infant's biological needs. In addition, the infant is adapt-able to the social world around her. The mother is very responsive to the infant's behavior and mindful of her current abilities. She accommodates quickly to in-fant behavior changes, but her own behavior always has a direction (Kaye, 1979). In general, the mother modifies her behavior by simplifying her speech, by in-creasing the amount and quality of her nonverbal communication, and by relying heavily on the context. She gives linguistic input while providing an opportunity or turn in which the infant can respond.

The input the infant receives contains sensory, motor, and affective ele-ments (D. Stern, 1977). Sensory elements include maternal vocalizations, facial expressions, and body movements. These behaviors are systematically modified by exaggerated performance, discrete packaging, slow formation, and repetitive runs. The infant's motor behaviors enable her to modify experiences and to affect her mother's behavior. Finally, the affective experience derives from the infant's and mother's joint regulation of the infant's states of attention, excitation, and emotion.

Both semantic structure and pragmatic functions are derived from social interaction. The child infers meaning from her mother's vocalizations and non-random behaviors in interactional situations. Case relationships are learned through joint action routines, such as games, in which the child takes a partic-ular semantic role within the interaction.

The reference function derives from joint attention. The mother and child attend jointly to a rather limited array of objects they share in common. These form the initial concepts that are then named, or referenced, by the child. In addition to reference, other communication functions, such as requesting and giving, are also expressed preverbally. "Well before speech can be said to have begun, a working arrangement of interactions between the infant and his care-givers, familiar to each, will have become established and will be accomplishing a great number of functions" (Chappell & Sander, 1979, p. 89). These functions develop as a result of the mother's responsiveness to her child's earliest inter-actional behaviors. As the infant learns that she can control the behavior of others, she begins to modify and conventionalize her signals in order to com-municate more specifically. The particular words that the infant later uses ex-pressively will be determined by pragmatic factors, such as functions, or the intentions these words express (Greenfield & Smith, 1976). The infant will use these words that are most accurate for expressing her intentions.

A structure-only approach to language development ignores the essential social nature of language used in communication. Social communication is found in mother–infant discourse over the first year of life. As a result, the "child has been prepared, by his prior interaction with primary caregivers, both to learn linguistic rules and to elicit instructive material under optimal circumstances for learning" (Kaye, 1979, p. 94). Communication skills develop within the infant–mother dyad and provide a basis for the infant's learning of the linguistic code.

REFLECTIONS

1. Discuss the abilities and behaviors of the newborn that suggest prewiring for communication.
2. Describe the aspects of conversation found in gaze coupling, ritualized behaviors, and game playing.
3. Why are gestures particularly important? Describe the sequence of gestural development.
4. What communicative behaviors does the infant elicit from the mother, and what is the effect of each on communication?
5. Explain why three interactions—joint reference, joint actions, and turn taking—are particularly important for the development of early communication and trace briefly the development of each.
6. What are phonetically consistent forms (PCFs)?

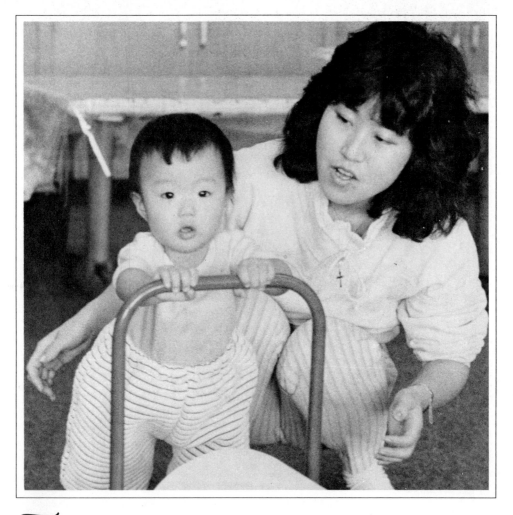

7 Language Learning

CHAPTER OBJECTIVES

It is difficult to explain language learning without discussing children's learning strategies and parents' teaching techniques. Though the relationship is not one of pupil and teacher, many of the elements of that relationship exist, although in a more subtle form.

Learning language is not just a process of accumulating language structures and content. The child uses certain strategies to comprehend the language he hears and to form hypotheses about the underlying language rules. The child's caregivers also aid his linguistic analysis by modifying the speech stream directed at him. When you have completed this chapter, you should understand

- the relationship between comprehension, production, and cognition.
- the role of imitation.
- the characteristics of motherese or parentese.
- the types of parental prompting.
- the effects of parental expansion, extension, and imitation.
- the effects of cultural variation on the language-learning process.
- universal language learning principles.
- the use of parental turnabouts.
- the importance of play.
- the following terms:

bootstrapping	hypothesis testing
contingent query	interrogative utterances
evocative utterances	motherese
expansion	selective imitation
extension	turnabout

I N CHAPTERS 5 AND 6 we discussed the prerequisites for language development. These prerequisites are inadequate, however, as an explanation of the extremely complicated process of language development. Language development is not haphazard. Rather, it occurs in an orderly, predictable fashion. The orderliness of development reflects underlying language-learning strategies, the linguistic complexity of the message, and cognitive-conceptual growth.

Even though adults do not attempt to teach language directly to normally developing children, we do adapt our language input to the child's level of attention and comprehension. In the process, we provide models of simplified language for the child. We also tend to react to the child's utterances in a way that increases the chance that the child will repeat the structures later. This reinforcement is not direct but instead includes such indirect behaviors as repeating and expanding the child's utterances. It is also important to remember the context of most language-learning exchanges. Children engage in conversations with their caregivers throughout the day while engaged in activities and routines that form the backdrop for communication.

In this chapter we will examine issues related to language learning. We'll begin by exploring the relationship between comprehension, production, and cognitive growth. Must the child comprehend language units before he produces them? If so, how much must he comprehend? In addition, child language-learning strategies and adult teaching strategies will be explored. Finally, we will discuss the conversational context in which the child's language develops and the maternal strategies for maintaining a conversation. Naturally, the strategies used by both the child and the adult differ with the language maturity of the child.

COMPREHENSION, PRODUCTION, AND COGNITIVE GROWTH

There is a strong link between comprehension, production, and cognition. Children "learn their language by first determining, independent of language, the meaning which a speaker intends to convey to them, and by then working out the relationship between the meaning and the language" (Macnamara, 1972, p. 1). This may be an overstatement, but it seems clear that access to meaning independent of language forms is critical. The child's cognitive conceptual development is his primary tool for comprehension of the language that he hears.

Cognitive skills and language abilities are associated, but not causally. A correlational relationship, in which they are strongly related because of underlying factors that pace the developmental paths of each, is more likely. Attainment of a skill may be evidenced first in either area (Gopnik & Meltzoff, 1986).

Piagetian stages of development are of little value in classifying corresponding cognitive and language development. Language skills seem to be more closely related to specific cognitive skills than to stages of cognitive development (Kelly & Dale, 1989). There seems to be a significant difference in the cognitive levels of play between children who use no words and those who use single words. Single-word users are more likely to engage in conventional play with "animate" objects. For example, children who do not produce words are more likely to play with toys such as blocks, while children who produce single words are more likely to play with dolls or action figures. Both imitation and play differ for single-word users and those who are beginning to combine words. The significant change in imitation is the ability of the child to imitate sounds not previously in his repertoire. The play of children beginning to combine words consists of combining two or more play sequences and/or performing the same action on a sequence of entities. Finally, early combiners and those using the semantic rules differ in means–ends abilities, with the rule users able to solve problems that require some level of foresight.

Cognitive growth may have a great influence upon early word combinations. Many of the principles of cognitive learning can also be applied to language learning. These might include the following (Peters, 1986):

- Pay attention to perceptually salient stimuli.
- Discriminate stimuli along salient dimensions.
- Remember stimuli.
- Classify stimuli according to the results of the discriminations.

These principles correspond to the steps taken in information processing presented in Chapter 4.

The child is an active learner, forming hypotheses based on patterns in the incoming language stream. Data are tested and incorporated into the system or used to reorganize the system. Once the mind stores a certain number of bits of information, it tries to organize them based on perceived relationships. Estimates of the number of bits or "things" that the brain can hold individually range from 15 to 40 (Peters, 1986). In language development, we see that at a vocabulary of around 40 to 50 individual words, children begin to form their first word combinations.

Organization of longer utterances requires better short-term memory and knowledge of syntactic patterns or frames and word classes. Hierarchical word-order organization develops, and individual words become "slot fillers" for various word classes.

Linguists continue to argue, however, over the relationship between language comprehension and production. Ingram (1974b) has stated flatly that "comprehension ahead of production is a linguistic universal of acquisition" (p. 313). This statement represents a commonly held though not universally supported view (Frazer, Bellugi, & Brown, 1963; Lovell & Dixon, 1967). In contrast, Bloom (1974) concluded that the relationship is one of mutual dependence; its exact nature is unknown. One difficulty is that the relationship is a dynamic one that changes with the child's developmental level and with each aspect of language. In other words, the relationship between comprehension and production changes because of different rates of development and different linguistic requirements made of the child.

In early phonological development, perception of speech sound differences greatly precedes expression. The child can perceive speech sounds very early. Intonational patterns are also discriminated early, at around 8 months of age (Nakazima, 1962).

First words pose a different problem. Obviously, the child does not fully comprehend the word before he produces it. Full comprehension would require a greater linguistic and experiential background than that of the year-old infant. The child's comprehension is aided by the nonlinguistic context because most speech addressed to the child is associated with the here and now. In fact, adults may overestimate a child's comprehension unless they analyze all the paralinguistic cues and situational redundancies (R. Clark, Hutcheson, & Van Buren, 1974). Estimates of production may also be inflated. The child may imitate others, either immediately or after some delay, and repeat stock phrases, songs, and rhymes. "Children come out with a lot of language which appears to indicate a more sophisticated level of language development than they have actually attained" (Elliot, 1981, p. 81). In comprehension the child uses both linguistic and conceptual input plus his memory (Bloom, 1974). In contrast, production also uses linguistic and conceptual input but relies on linguistic knowledge alone for encoding.

"The Original Word Game" (Brown, 1958b) demonstrates the relationship between comprehension and production. After the tutor labels an entity, the player forms hypotheses about its nature. In turn, the player tests these hypotheses by applying the label. The tutor monitors the player's output to check the accuracy of fit between his and the player's underlying concepts. The tutor improves the player's accuracy by providing evaluative feedback. Hence, the child's comprehension and production are fine-tuned essentially at the same time.

As mentioned previously, there are two types of knowing, nonlinguistic and linguistic. The meaning relationship between the two is not necessarily one-to-one. Even though the symbol signifies the particular referent, the meaning of the symbol goes beyond the referent. For example, the symbol or word *car* can be used to label a toy car or a limousine, but the meaning of *car* is quite different in each example. Therefore, "meaning is a mental event" (Pease & Berko Gleason, 1985, p. 105). The symbols used to convey that meaning are arbitrary, as discussed in Chapter 1.

Within the first 50 words, comprehension seems to precede production (Benedict, 1979). As a group, children may understand approximately 50 words before they are able to produce 10. The range of comprehended words varies greatly. The distribution of syntactic types also varies between comprehension and production. These values, presented in Table 7.1, may reflect the ages at which data were collected. As children mature, the distribution changes. While action words may account for 50% of the first 10 words understood, general naming words may account for only 14%. With increasing age, the percentage of action words drops and that of nominal words rises. The initial difference between the two word types is not reflected in production, where nominals outnumber actions by at least 2 to 1.

TABLE 7.1   Comprehension and Production of Single Words by Syntactic Category

	Comprehension (First 100 Words)	Production (First 50 Words)
Nominals		
Specific	17%	11%
General	39%	50%
Action	36%	19%
Modifiers	3%	10%
Personal-social	5%	10%

Source: Adapted from H. Benedict, "Early Lexical Development: Comprehension and Production," *Journal of Child Language*, 1979, *6*, 183–200.

During the second year of life, the child increases his vocabulary and begins to combine words within a single utterance. Gradually the child realizes that a word refers not to a single referent or type of referent but to a related group of referents (Oviatt, 1982). If comprehension precedes production, we would expect the child to understand word combinations before he uses his first multiword utterances. Here the nonlinguistic context is an essential comprehension aid (Bloom, 1974). In addition, comprehension of a sentence depends on recognition of highly meaningful words. The child need not know syntax if he knows the meanings of these words separately. The nonlinguistic context provides relational information. Yet, children seem to respond best to verbal commands that are slightly above their production level (Sachs & Truswell, 1978; Shipley, Smith, & Gleitman, 1969). In conclusion,

> understanding language does not simply involve responding to a familiar word or phrase, but determin[ing] the meaning of novel combinations of words. . . . In order to eventually discover the various syntactic devices used by his language, the child must first be able to integrate more than one word from an utterance. Only then can he discover that the order of elements, for example, makes a difference for the meaning of the message. The ability to make inferences based on more than one word from an utterance is a necessary bridge between one-word responses and syntax. (Sachs & Truswell, 1978, p. 23)

As the child approaches 2 years of age, the comprehension–production discrepancy seems to decrease. Nevertheless, production still lags behind comprehension, as it does throughout the "first language" period (Goldin-Meadows, Seligman, & Gelman, 1976).

Even though his production can be characterized as observing word-order rules of construction, the child does not appear to use word order as a primary tool for comprehension until about the third year, or when the average length of his utterances reaches 4.0 morphemes (Chapman & Miller, 1975; J. de Villiers & P. de Villiers, 1973).

Even children with MLUs of approximately 1.5 to 2.75 are more accurate in responding to adult linguistic forms than to child forms (Petretic & Tweney, 1977). These data suggest an early ability to comprehend adult forms. Although similar findings are reported with adult indirect requests, the child may be responding to a single action word within the request, not to the entire form (Shatz, 1978a). It is possible that the child has an action-oriented discourse rule that "Mother says; I do." In contrast, comprehension and production of directives seem to follow the same sequence (Roth & Spekman, 1981). The very young child who produces short directives would have difficulty processing long, complicated adult utterances. As expected, child responses increase in appropriateness with increased age (Tyack & Ingram, 1977).

Many grammatical constructions also reflect cognitive development. For example, the child's embedding of a phrase or clause within an utterance seems to follow the development of his ability to manipulate more than two objects

(Ingram, 1975; Piaget, 1926). The child must be able to perform the operation cognitively before he uses it linguistically. For example, truly functional use of *before* and *after* may require attainment of Piaget's preoperational skill of conservation (Ferreiro & Sinclair, 1971). Reversibility, or the ability to trace a process backward, is also strongly related to acquisition of *before* and *after*.

Interrogatives

Several linguists have investigated children's responses to questions in relation to production. The order is very similar. Early question forms include *what* and *where*, followed by *who*, and finally by *when*, *how*, and *why*. Most of the later forms involve concepts of cause, manner, or time. Their late appearance can be traced to the late development of these concepts (Piaget, 1926). In other words, the child must have a concept of time in order to comprehend *when* or to answer *when* questions. Occasionally, however, the child responds to or asks questions without fully understanding the underlying meaning. The child may be employing the following two answering strategies (Tyack & Ingram, 1977):

1. If you have already acquired a particular question word, answer with an appropriate subject (Ervin-Tripp, 1970).
2. If you have not acquired the word, answer on the basis of the semantic features of the verb.

Observing the first principle, the child would respond to "When are you going to eat?" with some temporal comment. Unaware of the meaning of *when*, the child might respond, on the basis of the verb, "A cookie!"

Semantic features of the verb are particularly important for certain types of responses. For example, the verb *touch* is more likely to elicit a response focusing on what was touched, where it was touched, and for what reason. Other verbs elicit different responses, with little regard for the *wh-* question form employed (Tyack & Ingram, 1977).

Recognition of the general type of information requested may precede the ability to give acceptable and accurate answers (Parnell, Patterson, & Harding, 1984). Even young school-age children have difficulty answering some forms of *wh-* questions.

Causal questions may be especially difficult for the child because of the reverse-order thinking required in the response. Piaget has demonstrated the difficulty the preoperational child experiences in reversing the order of sequential events. Yet it is this type of response that is required for the *why* interrogative. For example, "Why did you hit Randy?" requires a response explaining the events that preceded the fist fight. It is not unusual to hear a 3-year-old respond " 'Cause he hit me back," demonstrating an inability to reverse the order.

Temporal Relations

Temporal terms such as *when*, *before*, *since*, and *while* can convey information on the order of events, duration, and simultaneity. The order of acquisition of these terms is related to their use and to the concept each represents. In general, words of order, such as *after, before, since,* and *until,* precede words of duration, such as *since* and *until* used with the progressive verb form. These, in turn, precede terms of simultaneity, such as *while* (Feagans, 1980). This hierarchy reflects the sequence of cognitive development noted by Piaget (1966). Preschool children gain a sense of order before they have a sense of duration. Five-year-olds understand *before* and *after* better than simultaneous terms such as *at the same time* (Keller-Cohen, 1975). (See Table 7.2.)

Temporal terms are initially produced as prepositions and then as subordinating conjunctions (Coker, 1978). Thus the child will produce a sentence such as "You go *after* me" before he says "You can go home *after* we eat dinner." It is not uncommon for 6 ½-year-olds to have difficulty with some of the syntactic structures used with *before* and *after* to link clauses (Tibbits, 1980). When the meaning of a temporal term is unknown, the child tends to use two strategies of interpretation and ignore the temporal term. He will (1) rely on the order of mention and (2) interpret the main clause as the first event. The first strategy reflects the ease of interpretation of sequences that preserve the actual order of events (E. Clark, 1971; L. French & Brown, 1977; Hatch, 1971; H. Johnson, 1975). Employing this strategy, a 3-year-old will interpret the following sentences as having the same meaning:

> Before you go to school, stop at the store.
> Go to school before you stop at the store.
> After you go to school, stop at the store.
> Go to school after you stop at the store.

Note that the desired order of occurrence of events is the reverse of the word order stated in the first and last examples.

The second interpretive strategy reflects a syntactic approach. Difficulties of interpretation with *before* and *after* may reflect syntactic difficulties in process-

TABLE 7.2   Summary of Comprehension of Relationships

Age (months)	Relationships Understood
24	Locational prepositions *in* and *on*
36	Locational preposition *under*
40	Locational preposition *next to*
48 (approx.)	Locational prepositions *behind* and *in front of;* difficulty with *above, below,* and *at the bottom of;* kinship terms *mother, father, sister,* and *brother* (but the last two are nonreciprocating)
60	Temporal terms *before* and *after*
60 + (school-age)	Additional locational prepositions in temporal expressions, such as *in a week;* most major kinship terms by age 10; more precise locational directives reference the body (*left* and *right*)

ing subordinate clauses (Amidon & Carey, 1972). Thus the child adopts a strategy in which the main clause becomes the first event. For example, the sentence "After he arrived home, Tim bought a paper" would be interpreted as "Tim bought a paper, then he arrived home." The main clause precedes the subordinate in a temporal sequence.

When all else fails, the child relies on his knowledge of real-life sequences. This strategy of comprehension works as long as the utterance conforms to the child's experiential base.

Children 3½ to 5 years of age often omit one of the clauses when following directives (L. French & Brown, 1977). This behavior may be more common than order reversal and may reflect the cognitive-processing load. Preschoolers generally do not follow multiple directions well.

Relational Terms

Relational terms such as *thick/thin, fat/skinny, more/less,* and *same/different* are frequently difficult for preschool children to learn. In general, the child first learns that the terms are opposites, then the dimensions to which each term refers. The order of acquisition may be based on semantic–syntactic relations and the cognitive relations expressed (H. Clark & E. Clark, 1977). Terms such as *big* and *little* refer to general size on any dimension and would be acquired before more specific terms, such as *deep* and *shallow.* In other words, less specific terms are usually learned first. The positive member of each relational pair, such as *big* or *long,* represents the presence of the entity that it describes (size and length, respectively) and is learned first (Brewer & Stone, 1975; Donaldson & Wales, 1970; Eilers, Oller, & Ellington, 1974). There may be a conceptual basis for the prominence of the positive element (Klatsky, Clark, & Macken, 1973). For example, the presence of size is *big,* the positive term. The negative aspect or the absence of size is *little.* A general order of acquisition would be as follows:

> Big/little
> Large/small
> Tall/short, long/short
> High/low
> Thick/thin
> Wide/narrow
> Deep/shallow

The child seems to learn by accumulating individual examples of each term. Hence, understanding may be restricted to specific objects even if it appears to be more adultlike. General terms may also become more restricted as the child learns more specific ones (Maratsos, 1973, 1974).

Terms such as *more/less* and *same/different* pose a different problem for the preschool child. There may be an underlying concept for *more/less* in which the child interprets both terms to mean amount (H. Clark & E. Clark, 1977). When presented with a selection task, preschoolers tend to pick the larger grouping, whether cued with *more* or with *less* (Donaldson & McGarrigle, 1974; Siegel, 1977; Trehub & Abramovitch, 1978). In general, the child's concept of relative number appears to be based on varied criteria.

Conceptual development seems equally important for the acquisition of *same* and *different*. Elliot (1981) concluded:

> In the case of "same" and "different," it soon becomes particularly clear how difficult it is to separate information about semantic development from considerations of the development of cognitive skills, such as estimating quantity; from social skills, such as assessing the reasons behind the experimenter's questions; and from other features of language use, such as the use of determiners and anaphoric reference. (p. 136)

The ability to make same/different judgments seems to be related to development of conservation (Sinclair, 1967). Conservation, you will recall, is the ability to attend to more than one perceptual dimension without relying strictly on physical evidence.

Locational Prepositions

The child understands different spatial relations before he begins to speak about them. The exact nature of that comprehension is unknown, since a child as old as 3½ still relies on gestures to convey much of his meaning (Tfouni & Klatsky, 1983). As noted in Chapter 9, the first English prepositions appear at around 2 years of age. When a child does not comprehend a preposition, he seems to apply a few general interpretive strategies (E. Clark, 1973a):

Rule 1:   If B is a container, A belongs inside it.
Rule 2:   If B has a supporting surface, A belongs on it.

According to Clark, Rule 1 takes precedence since containers, whatever their orientation, always seem to be treated as containers. Thus, children often respond in relation to the objects mentioned rather than the prepositions used (Wilcox & Palermo, 1974/1975). This "probable event strategy" (Strohner & Nelson, 1974) predicts the responses of young children. Other possible interpretive cues may be the word order of adult utterances and the context (Macrae, 1978). Using these rules, children respond in predictable ways (H. Clark and E. Clark, 1977).

Children 18 months of age base their hypotheses about word meanings on Rules 1 and 2. As a result, they act as if they understand *in* all the time, *on* with surfaces but not containers, and *under* not at all. By age 3, most children have figured out the meanings of all three prepositions. When 3- and 4-year-olds are faced with more complex prepositions such as *above, below, in front of,* or *at the bottom of,* however, they tended to revert to strategies based on Rules 1 and 2.

Vertical alignment, however, does not result in the confusion found with other spatial relations (Macrae, 1976a). Terms such as *next to* or *in front of* offer special problems. For example, *next to* includes, but is not limited to, *in front of*, *behind*, and so on. In turn, these terms differ in relation to the locations to which they refer. With fronted objects, such as a chair or a television set, locational terms take their reference from the object. For example, *in front of the TV* means *in front of the screen*. With nonfronted objects, such as a saucer, the term takes its location from the speaker's perspective. Interpretation requires a certain level of social skill on the part of the listener. He must be able to adopt the perspective of the speaker. *Next to* is usually learned at about 40 months, followed by *behind* and *in front of* by about 49 months (Johnston, 1984) (see Table 7.2). Children seem to use fronting and the height of the object as cues for initial interpretation.

Movement between locations also seems to follow a locational rule. Several studies have found that a 3-year-old child interprets most prepositions of movement to mean *toward* (E. Clark & Garnica, 1974; Macrae, 1976b). This preference can be characterized as follows (H. Clark & E. Clark, 1977, p. 504):

Rule 3: If A and B are related to each other in space, they should be touching.

Hence, the child at first favors *to* over *from*, *into* over *out of*, and *onto* over *off*.

Applying these rules, we can predict that *in* is easier for the child than *on*, which in turn is easier than *under*. Terms that signal movement *toward* should be easier than their opposites. These predictions reflect the acquisitional order seen in young children.

Kinship Terms

The preschooler gains a very limited knowledge of kinship terms that refer to family members, such as *dad, sister*, and *brother* (see Table 7.2). At first the child treats the term as part of the person's name. For a short time, my sons called me "Daddy Bob." In this stage the child does not possess the components of the kinship term. Next, the child gains some features of the definition of the person but not of the relationship. For example, "A grandmother is someone who smells like flowers and wears funny underwear." The child gains a few of the less complex relationships first. After *mommy* and *daddy*, the child learns *brother* and *sister*. Roughly, the meanings are *brother = related boy* and *sister = related girl*. By age 4 the child may understand what a brother or sister is but doesn't realize that he can also be a brother to someone else. In other words, the term is not used reciprocally. Eventually the child will understand all features of the kinship terms and reciprocity (Haviland & Clark, 1974).

In general, kinship terms develop in the following three-group order:

Mother, father, sister, brother
Son, daughter, grandfather, grandmother, parent
Uncle, aunt, cousin, nephew, niece

Most of the major kinship terms are understood by age 10.

Summary

In the preschool years the relationship between comprehension, production, and cognition becomes very complex. In general, linguistic developments parallel much of the cognitive growth of the preschool child. This is not a one-to-one relationship. Such heterogeneity suggests that development is more complex than early stage theories suggest (Flavell, 1982). The relationship between the linguistic aspects of comprehension and production is less clearly defined, and it is no longer possible to make the blanket statement that comprehension precedes production. At the present time, we are not aware of all of the relationships between cognition, comprehension, and production. Further research is needed to understand these relationships more completely.

CHILD LEARNING STRATEGIES

Although there are many variations in the way in which children learn American English, there are ample similarities. These suggest underlying strategies used by most children to interpret and produce language. Naturally, these strategies differ with the language level of the child. In the following section, we shall consider the language-learning strategies most frequently associated with toddlers and preschoolers.

Toddler Language-Learning Strategies

To assume that toddlers merely produce what they comprehend is to oversimplify the acquisition of language. The child must use certain learning strategies to sort out relevant and irrelevant information. Speech and language in adult and sibling conversations are often poor. "Speech messages and language signals are deeply embedded in background noise; sound intensity levels are often inaudibly low or assaultively high; the speech stream flows with great rapidity; two or more people are often speaking at one time; and grammatical structures are often incomplete or very distorted" (Friedlander, 1970, pp. 26–27). As we already know, speech directed at the child is greatly modified from this description, but the child must decide which utterances are good examples of the language and must hypothesize about their underlying meanings and structures. Young children use four metalinguistic strategies to gain linguistic knowledge: *evocative utterances, hypothesis testing, interrogative utterances,* and *selective imitation* (Snyder-McLean & McLean, 1978).

Evocative utterances are statements by the child naming entities. After the child names, the adult gives evaluative feedback that confirms or negates the child's selection of exemplars. As a result, the child either maintains or modifies his hypothesis. As expected, there is a positive correlation between the quantity of verbal input at 20 months and vocabulary size and average utterance length at 24 months (Nelson, 1973a).

Hypothesis testing and interrogative utterances are more direct methods of acquiring linguistic knowledge. When seeking confirmation of a hypothesis, the child may say a word or word combination with rising intonation, such as "doggie" or "baby eat." A responding adult either confirms or denies the child's utterance. When unaware of an entity label, the child uses an interrogative utterance, such as "what?", "that?", or "wassat?" These requests for information can be found in the gestural-vocal behaviors that precede the appearance of the first word (Dore, 1975). *What* and its variants are found among the first words of many children, and at 24 months there is a positive correlation between the number of questions and vocabulary size (Nelson, 1973a).

The nature and significance of the final strategy, **selective imitation**, have generated much research. Most linguists would agree that imitation is selective. Children do not imitate indiscriminately. Given that a child may imitate an utterance in whole or in part, he is free to select any utterance from another speaker. Yet he will select short utterances for imitation (Lord, 1975). If imitation is a learning strategy, then surely the child is employing some criterion for selection. This criterion and the exact role of imitation in language acquisition have not been fully analyzed.

Role of Selective Imitation

Imitation has been reported as a device used in the acquisition of words, morphology, and syntactic–semantic structures (Bloom, Hood, & Lightbown, 1974; MacWhinney, 1976). In general, imitation is considered to be a whole or partial repetition of an utterance of another speaker within no more than three successive child utterances. It has been noted that much of what toddlers say—varying between 4 and 52% of their utterances—is an imitation of other speakers (Bloom et al., 1974; Rodd & Braine, 1971; Ryan, 1973; Slobin, 1968). Not all studies have shown such extensive use of imitation (McNeill, 1970). Widespread differences may reflect methodological or situational variations. The overall use of imitation as a learning strategy may also vary with individual children.

It has been argued that imitation is an inadequate explanation of development (McNeill, 1966). In fact, imitation may be too nonprogressive to be a source of linguistic change (Ervin, 1964). In addition, the spontaneous utterances of children are too creative to be imitations of adult speech (Brown & Bellugi, 1964). It has also been reported that there are no differences in the linguistic complexity of imitations and spontaneous speech (Ervin, 1964; Rodd & Braine, 1971). Yet Bloom and her colleagues (1974) reported that imitations are structurally just beyond the production capacities of children. That finding would seem to indicate the use of imitation as a learning strategy. At least "for some children, imitation plays a complex role as an aid in the acquisition of language" (Corrigan, 1978b, p. 240).

Much of the disparity in these results may relate to the populations studied. Individual children differ in their use of imitation. In addition, the overall amount of imitation decreases with age, especially after age 2 (Nelson, 1973b; Owens & MacDonald, 1982). It appears that imitation's usefulness as a language-learning strategy decreases as language becomes more complex. Interestingly, children with delayed development may maintain the strategy long after it has ceased to be a viable learning tool (Owens & MacDonald, 1982). Finally, a researcher's definition of imitation also influences the findings. Conflicting conclusions reflect individual and developmental differences and the definition used.

At the single-word level, imitation seems particularly important for lexical growth, although conceptual development seems to be central as well. Year-old infants are more likely to imitate adults than to imitate their own tape-recorded words, which in turn are more likely to be imitated than their own taped babbling. The presence of the referent also increases the likelihood of imitation. In other words, the child uses language to make some sense out of the world. In turn, his ability to imitate an utterance depends on his understanding of its meaning (Ricks, 1979). The best way for parents to teach a young child a new word is to provide the word and give a demonstration and explanation (Banigan & Mervis, 1988).

Many imitations and much early lexical growth take place within the context of daily routines of the caregiver and the child (Ferrier, 1978). Imitations may be immediate or may appear later in an altered form. Ferrier (1978) explained:

> Many of her [Ferrier's daughter's] early utterances were tied to repeated family routines . . ., in which my language was notably repetitious. But the very invariance of those routines and of my language within them allowed my daughter to hit on the productive strategem of utilizing the last word of my utterance by *transforming its function* [my emphasis] to that of a demand for goods or services. (p. 304)

It should be noted that even here the word is similar but is used for a different purpose.

The ends of utterances seem to have particular perceptual importance for children (Slobin, 1973). For example, when the child goes to the door, his mother says, "Do you want to go out?" When next the child goes to the door, he may say, "Out." The word is the same, but the illocutionary function has changed. In fact, the function of the mother's speech may have a great effect upon imitation. The amount of child imitation seems to reflect the amount of maternal imitation (J. Folger & Chapman, 1978). We will explore this relationship in greater detail in connection with parental teaching strategies.

Several studies have reported that multiword spontaneous productions may exceed imitative performance (Bloom, 1974; Slobin & Welsh, 1971). Other studies indicate that children imitate structures that are already in their spontaneous speech, usually forms that have appeared recently (Bellugi, 1971; Bloom et al., 1974; R. Brown & Fraser, 1964). As children become more proficient with a structure in spontaneous speech, their imitation of it decreases. Clearly, these studies confound the imitation issue. It is possible, however, that spontaneous utterances originate as an extract from an adult utterance or that a portion of the spontaneous child utterance originates as an imitation (R. Clark, 1977). For example, when the adult says, "I don't know where Billy is," the child may later ask, "Where Billy is?" In a second instance, the child may take a portion of an adult utterance and add to it or combine it with another.

It has also been suggested that imitation may serve as a discourse device, enabling the child to relate his utterances to those of more mature language users (Keenan, 1974). In the following exchange, note how the child uses imitation to tie his utterances to those of the adult.

PARENT: See Johnny ride his bike?
CHILD: Ride bike. Fall.
PARENT: No. He won't fall.
CHILD: Fall. Go boom.

As semantic–syntactic structures develop, so does discourse quality (Bates, 1976a, 1976b; Keenan & Schieffelin, 1976).

Development often proceeds from highly repetitive utterances to semantically diverse ones (Keenan, 1975). These diverse revisions by the child are an assimilative process in which he alters the preceding utterance in order to maintain discourse and semantic relations and to sustain the topic (Bates, 1976a, 1976b; Van Kleeck & Frankel, 1981). The child uses two strategies of revision: *focus operations* and *substitution operations*. Focus operations, which predominate until about age 3, require only minimal linguistic skills (Bloom, Rocissano, & Hood, 1976; Keenan, 1975). The child focuses on one or more lexical items of the preceding utterance and repeats them. For example, when the caregiver says, "Baby's going to sleep in her bed," the child might say, "Sleep bed." In a substitution operation, the child repeats only a portion of the utterance but replaces lexical items. For example, in response to "Baby's going to sleep in her bed," the child might say, "Sleep blanket." The topic is maintained, but the semantic-syntactic structure is changed. This behavior increases with age (Bloom et al., 1976). These child responses resemble the conversational replies found in more mature language use.

It is assumed that the child must store enough adult examples to allow him to abstract the relationship involved and to form a linguistic hypothesis (R. Clark, 1977). In this way, imitation and comprehension are related. Thus, Clark concluded, "it seems likely that imitation has a more positive role to play in the acquisition of syntax, by making adult forms available to a child, thus helping him to notice these forms more readily when adults use them, and enabling him to assimilate their function gradually through use." (p. 351) Although the exact role of imitation in language acquisition is unclear, it appears that children imitate most frequently items they are in the process of learning or that have recently appeared. As such, imitation may serve young children as a modeling and stabilizing process for new structures. Imitation would thus reflect the child's developmental level and the teaching strategies of the adults around him.

Preschool Language-Learning Strategies

Obviously, the usefulness of selective imitation is limited when the child begins to acquire structures of more than a few words. This accounts for the rapid decline of the use of imitation at around 30 months of age. Yet, development continues in a more or less orderly fashion. This suggests the use of other learning strategies.

In general, children use what they know about language to help them decipher what they don't know. For example, they may use semantics to decode syntax or semantics and context to figure out word meanings. This process is called **bootstrapping**. "To pull yourself up by your bootstraps" is to use the resources at hand to better yourself. This is what the child does when he uses knowledge in one area to enhance his performance in another.

According to the *semantic bootstrapping hypothesis* (Macnamara, 1982; Pinker, 1982, 1984), young language-learning children use semantic notions as evidence of grammatical entities. Persons and things form one category later indicated as nouns, actions indicate verbs, attributives indicate adjectives, and spatial relations and directions indicate adverbs and prepositions. Syntactic functions are formed similarly, with semantic agents indicating subjects, and so on (Matthei, 1987). While this early organization is limited—not all nouns are agents and objects, nor all verbs actions; and not all subjects are agents—it does provide a basis for the syntactic system.

In general, language rules are learned gradually. Initially, the rule may be unanalyzed and used in situation specific instances. Use will generally proceed sporadically until the rule is mastered by the child.

We can assume that children begin by learning the basic sentence type, which in English is subject-verb-object. This form is altered, however, in interrogatives and imperatives. Thus, the model presented to young language-learning children may have the basic sentence type only 40–60% of the time. It seems that children pick the most frequently modeled order to represent the basic sentence type. Additional intonational and situational cues may serve to differentiate those utterances that differ from the basic sentence type. For example, interrogatives usually end in a rising intonation and accompany certain activities or routines.

Most likely, children determine the syntactic rules by using cues provided by the meaning of the adult's utterance. Thus, the child figures out the meaning of the adult's utterance based on nonsyntactic information. Mothers aid in this process by talking primarily about the present context.

From a cross-linguistic perspective, the development of syntactic and morphological features seems to progress through three stages (Berman, 1986). In the first stage, use of the feature is context based and is dependent upon extralinguistic cues. The second stage is structure based or grammatical, in which the child relates meanings to forms. In the third stage, the child acquires mature language use of the feature based on internalized rules.

The first stage is a universal one prior to the development of language specific grammar. Regardless of the language being learned, children produce similar content or meanings and uses or functions. Thus, we find children using similar semantic and illocutionary categories that include words without morphological markers. These forms are the unmarked building blocks for later development.

Regardless of the language, certain semantic distinctions are learned before others. For example, *red, blue*, and *yellow* are learned before *green, brown*, and *orange*; *in* and *on* before *behind*. Similarly, one-time actions, such as *fall* and *break*, are likely to appear first in past tense, while ongoing durative actions, such as *eat* and *play*, appear in the present tense. Regardless of the language, changes in question form generally occur in yes/no questions prior to *wh-* questions. Within *wh-* questions, those that ask *what* and *where* appear first, while *why* and *when* questions appear later. This is true in languages as different as Korean, Tamil, and English (Clancy, 1989; Vaidyanathan, 1988).

Children in the initial stage of language development also talk about the same general types of things, using a restricted set of semantic categories. Sentence subjects are always animate agents and inanimate objects. Only later do children use inanimate subjects (*Ball* fall) and animate objects (Kiss *baby*).

It appears that initially the strategies for processing and acquiring language are similar across children learning different language. One is the *plausible event strategy* of comprehension (Berman, 1986). Basically, this strategy is one in which language is interpreted based on the most commonsense understanding in a particular context. Children use their knowledge of routines and contexts to decode the meaning of the language they hear. A second strategy is *rote learning* for production (Peters, 1983). Initially, the child learns to use certain words in certain contexts through imitation.

The second stage, which is grammatical, obviously differs with the language being learned. Even so, some operating principles seem universal. First, the child pays attention to how and where semantic distinctions are marked. For example, consonants and the inside of words are important in modern Hebrew, stems and word endings are important in Hungarian, and word and phrase relationships are important in English.

In addition to learning words and word meanings, the child learns the classes in which words belong. Language rules apply to word classes, not to individual words. Most likely the child hypothesizes that words are similar and thus belong together because of the way they are treated linguistically (Maratsos, 1988). For example, the child hears certain words receive *-ed* and *-ing* markers and begins to "chunk" these words together into what adults call *verbs*. Initially, words are learned individually and treated as if each is its own category. As the child discriminates similarities, words treated in the same manner are organized and stored together. New members are added as they meet the criteria for linguistic treatment. Although this explanation is somewhat simplified, it adequately describes an active process by the child that corresponds to our knowledge of information processing and hypothesis building by humans.

The second principle is to recognize words with the same consonants as related. Thus, *dog paddle* and *dog catcher* must have something in common. This strategy can backfire when older children encounter *dogma* and *dogwood*.

Third, word order is important. Initially, children rely on a few rigid formulas. In English, children become overdependent on the subject-verb-object sentence form. Later, they learn other forms and develop a flexible system that is adaptable to different discourse situations. The evolution from rigid to flexible systems has been reported in the development of English, Chinese, French, modern Hebrew, Hungarian, and Turkish (Aksu & Slobin, 1985; Berman, 1985; Erbaugh, 1980; Karmiloff-Smith, 1979; MacWhinney, 1985; Maratsos, 1983).

Universal Language Learning Principles

After studying 40 different languages, linguist Daniel Slobin (1978) noticed that there were patterns of development that suggested underlying universal learning strategies and operational principles (see table 7.3). Although we do not know the exact strategies children use, we can infer their presence from consistent language behaviors of young children. The following sections address each of Slobin's seven principles. It may be helpful when reading these principles to think of how you might proceed in attempting to decode an unfamiliar language. You would adopt certain strategies and look for familiar patterns.

Pay Attention to the Ends of Words.   Across languages, the same semantic notion, such as a verb tense or temporal relation, may be produced linguistically at very different ages. If we assume that the concept can be learned by all children at the same age, then differences in age of production must reflect differences in the rate of acquisition of linguistic markers for this concept. In general, children acquire linguistic markers that occur at the ends of words (-s, -er, -ed) before those that appear at the beginnings of words (un-, dis-, in-). Similarly, regular verb endings are acquired before auxiliary verb forms that precede the verb. A corollary could be stated as follows: For any given semantic notion, suffixes or postpositions will be acquired earlier than will prefixes or prepositions (Slobin, 1978). For example, the comparative -er and superlative -est endings are acquired before the alternative *more* and *most* markers. The child is thus more likely to learn *sweeter* than *more sweet.*

If, as Slobin suggests, the end of a word is a particularly important position, then this fact may account for more than acquisition of suffixes. As noted, many new or expanded grammatical structures, such as noun phrase elaboration and clausal embedding, initially occur in the object position in sentences. Initial noninversion of the auxiliary in children's questions may also reflect attention to

---

TABLE 7.3   Universal Language-Learning Principles

1. Pay attention to the ends of words.
2. Phonological forms of words can be systematically modified.
3. Pay attention to the order of words and morphemes.
4. Avoid interruption and rearrangement of linguistic units.
5. Underlying semantic relations should be marked overtly and clearly.
6. Avoid exceptions.
7. The use of grammatical markers should make semantic sense.

Source: Drawn from D. Slobin, "Cognitive Prerequisites for the Development of Grammar." In L. Bloom & M. Lahey (Eds.), *Readings in Language Development.* New York: John Wiley, 1978.

the ends of adult utterances. For example, after hearing his parent say, "I don't know where it is," the child may later produce the question form "Where it is?"

Phonological Forms Can Be Systematically Modified.   Through experimentation the child learns to vary pronunciation. Gradually the child recognizes that various sound changes can reflect underlying meaning changes.

Pay Attention to the Order of Words and Morphemes.   Word order is one of the earliest principles learned. The standard order of morphemes used in adult utterances is preserved in child speech. Slobin could find no reports of deviant order of bound morphemes. Thus the child produces "charm*ingly*," not "charm-*lying*." In English, general word order is maintained by preschoolers also, though there is some initial difficulty with negative and interrogative transformations. This ordering leads to a second developmental universal: word order in child speech reflects word order in adult forms of the language. This seems to be especially true in languages such as English, in which word order often reflects underlying meaning. In imitating tasks, the American child tends to retain word order (R. Brown, 1973; Frazer et al., 1963).

A third developmental universal states that in early stages of development, sentences that do not have standard word order will be interpreted using standard word order (Slobin, 1978). Two examples from English relate to interpretation of passive sentences and temporal ordering of conjoined sentences. The English-speaking preschooler interprets passive sentences as if they represent the more common subject-verb-object form (Frazer et al., 1963). Any noun-verb-noun sequence is interpreted as agent-action-object (Bever, 1970). The child will therefore interpret "The cat is chased by the dog" as "The cat chased the dog." In conjoined sentences the 3-year-old child will ignore the conjunctions *before* and *after*, interpreting the relationship of the clauses as an order of occurrence. In other words, clause 1 occurred first, then clause 2. This interpretation strategy and related cognitive growth will be discussed later.

Avoid Interruption and Rearrangement of Linguistic Units.   Interruption and rearrangement place a strain on the processing of the ongoing speech stream. Processing is most difficult with sentences that require the child to retain large amounts of information in order to complete the task (J. de Villiers, Tager-Flusberg, Hakuta, & Cohen, 1979).

A related developmental universal states that structures requiring rearrangement of elements will first appear in nonrearranged form (Slobin, 1978). In other words, a form that differs from the predominant subject-verb-object format will first appear in the subject-verb-object form. As we have noted, in the speech of some children the auxiliary verb in yes/no and in *wh-* questions appears originally in a noninverted form not found in adult queries (R. Brown et al., 1969; Klima & Bellugi, 1966). In addition, children have greater difficulty making subject-verb inversions for questions when there is a relative clause modifying the subject and thus separating the subject-verb-object elements of the sentence (Nakayama, 1987).

A second related universal states that discontinuous morphemes are reduced to, or replaced by, continuous morphemes whenever possible (Slobin, 1978). In English this universal is demonstrated in the progressive verb inflection *-ing*, which appears without the auxiliary.

There is a tendency, states a third universal, to preserve the structure of the sentence as a closed entity by initial sentence-external placement of new linguistic forms. In other words, new structures may be tacked on to the beginning or end of the sentence prior to moving within it. Early negatives are attached to the beginning, and occasionally to the end, of a sentence. Only later does the negative move next to the verb. Initial subordinate clauses and infinitive phrases also occur in the object position at the end of the sentence.

Finally, a fourth universal states that the greater the separation between related parts of a sentence, the more difficult it is for the child to process adequately. Several studies have shown that the difficulty of processing sentences is more closely related to the separation of elements than to the number of phrases or clauses embedded in it (Hakuta, de Villiers, & Tager-Flusberg, 1982; Menyuk, 1969; Slobin & Welsh, 1971; C. Smith, 1970). Thus, a sentence containing an embedded phrase or clause is more difficult to interpret if the embedded portion interrupts the subject-verb-object format. A sentence such as "I saw the man *who fell down*" is easier for preschoolers to interpret than "The man *who fell down* ran away" (Brogan, 1968).

Underlying Semantic Relations Should Be Marked Overtly and Clearly. As the child listens to and attempts to interpret speech, overt morphological markers may provide perceptually meaningful and consistent aids. With maturation, the child may be able to derive more and more semantic information from minimal cues. To some extent, children demonstrate the importance of these markers in their own speech. There is some evidence that small functor words (*the, of, and*) and other morphological markers may receive more emphasis in child speech than in adult speech.

Both the Tamil and Turkish morphological systems are learned early because of their regularity and clarity of marking (Raghavendra & Leonard, 1989). Each affix encodes only one feature, and by age 2, most children are using them correctly. Compare this to English, in which three phonological shapes (/s, z, Iz/) are used for plural, third person singular, and possessive marking.

A related universal states that a child will begin to mark a semantic notion earlier if its morphological structure is more obvious perceptually (Slobin, 1978). As evidence, Slobin noted the development of the passive in Indo-European languages such as English and in Egyptian Arabic. The concept of the passive form is not difficult for children to learn, but in English the linguistic marking is. Egyptian Arabic-speaking children learn the passive prefix *it-* rather early compared to the length of time required for English-speaking children (Omar, 1973). In English a passive sentence requires several changes in the basic subject-verb-object format.

A second universal states that there is a preference for marking even unmarked members of a semantic category (Slobin, 1978). This universal may ac-

count for some of the overextensions in English to unmarked words. For example, the clear *-ed* past tense marker may be used with irregular verbs that may
appear to the child to have no marking. Preference for marking may also be seen
with the plural. For example, the word *some* may mean a portion of one or a few
of many. The noun that follows may therefore be either singular or plural. It is not
uncommon to hear a child say "I want some cakes" when he really desires a
portion.

When a child first masters the full form of a linguistic entity that can be
contracted or deleted, contractions or deletions tend not to be used (Slobin,
1978). This universal has strong support in English. Young children will respond
with "I will" when asked to imitate "I'll" in a sentence (Bellugi, 1967). We have
already noted the early appearance of the uncontractible form of the copula and
auxiliary. In an imitation task, children may replace optionally deleted forms that
are not present in the model sentence (Slobin & Welsh, 1971).

Related to this finding is a final universal: it is easier to understand a complex sentence in which optionally deleted material is not deleted (Slobin, 1978).
This principle is demonstrated by the difficulty both children and adults experience with multiple embeddings and deletions (J. de Villiers et al., 1979; Fodor,
Garrett, & Bever, 1968).

Avoid Exceptions.   There is a tendency among children to overgeneralize linguistic rules and to avoid exceptions to these rules. The rules for a larger class,
such as past tense, are learned before those for a subclass, such as irregular past
tense. One developmental universal of this principle outlines the stages of linguistic marking of semantic notions (Slobin, 1978):

1. No marking.
2. Appropriate marking in limited cases.
3. Overgeneralization of marking (often accompanied by redundant marking).
4. Full adult system. (p. 425)

In support of the existence of this universal, Slobin cited the development of the
English past tense. Initially, there is no marking. Next, some irregular past tense
verbs are formed correctly, but the regular past is not used. Once learned, the
regular past is overextended to irregular verbs before full adult usage is acquired.

A second developmental universal states that rules for larger classes are
learned before rules for subdivisions, and general rules are learned before exceptions. Most plural nouns, for example, can use the word *many* to indicate
quantity, such as *many cookies* or *many blocks*. Children learn this rule quickly.
Mass nouns, a smaller class—identifying liquids or granular substances, such as
sand or *water*—require *much*. It takes children much longer to learn to use *much*
with the appropriate nouns. Other examples of this principle are the overgeneralization of the regular past tense *-ed*, as in *eated*, and the regular plural *-s*, as
in *mans*.

Grammatical Markers Should Make Semantic Sense.   Slobin (1978) noted that
overgeneralization of rules is always limited to the appropriate semantic cate-

gory. Inflectional markers and functor words are applied within grammatical classes. Thus, the *-ed* morphological marker is always applied to words in the verb class. Functor words, or smaller, less important words, are substituted for functors from the same class. For example, the child may use *in* incorrectly in place of *at*, but he will not substitute *the* for *at*. Semantically defined classes take precedence in selection. In contrast, purely arbitrary rules are very difficult to master.

One universal of this principle states that when selecting an appropriate marker from among a group performing the same semantic function, the child tends to rely on a single form (Slobin, 1978). For example, the selection of the /s/, /z/, or /Iz/ form of the plural is based on the ending consonant of the stem word. Initially the child relies on one form of the plural where possible.

A second universal indicates that the choice of the functor word is always within the given functor class and subcategory (Slobin, 1978). Although the child may confuse different words within a word class, such as prepositions, he rarely confuses words from different classes. Hence, an inappropriate preposition may be used, but it will not be confused with a pronoun. For example, a child may say "Kerry is going *at* school" when he means "*to* school." He is unlikely, however, to say "Kerry is going *when* school," since *when* is not a preposition.

Third, semantically consistent rules are acquired early and are relatively error free (Slobin, 1978). This universal was discussed earlier with reference to the progressive *-ing* ending. You will recall that for the action words a 2-year-old uses, there are no exceptions to the present progressive *-ing* rule.

Summary.   It must be stressed that Slobin's principles are theories that attempt to explain the order of acquisition. According to Slobin, the child has certain concepts, based on cognitive growth, that are expressed through the linguistic system. Using certain principles of acquisition, the child scans the language code to discover the means of comprehension and production.

Individual Differences

Children vary in the rate of language development but also in the route. Individual developmental differences are related to differences in intellect, personality and learning style, ethnicity and the language of the home, socioeconomic status, family structure, and birth order. In general, these relationships are very complex, not simply cause and effect. Some factors, such as intelligence, may be much stronger than others. Socioeconomic factors alone, for example, may have little overall effect on rate of language development (Wells, 1985). There may be more differences within socioeconomic classes than between them. In contrast, birth order or position in the family has a significant effect on early language development. Single children have a greater opportunity to communicate with adults than do children with several siblings and thus develop language more quickly.

The interactive or learning style of the child will affect language learning to some extent. In general, the active, outgoing child is more likely to learn language more rapidly than the placid, retiring child (Wells, 1985). The former is more inclined to join in and to communicate with whatever means is available, learning the language code as he does.

Comments on rate may be invalid without accompanying information on route. Certain children may exhibit advances in expressive language use, while others who seem somewhat delayed in this area exhibit superior comprehension skills.

ADULT CONVERSATIONAL TEACHING TECHNIQUES

Adults engage in very little direct language teaching, but they do facilitate language acquisition by their behaviors. Although very little time is spent in direct instruction, many caregiving and experiential activities relate to language acquisition. Obviously these parental techniques will vary with the language maturity of the child.

Adult Speech to Toddlers

Throughout the first 2 years of life, parents talk with the child, label objects and events, and respond to the child's communication. Within this context, parents engage in modeling, cueing, prompting, and consequating behaviors that affect the linguistic behaviors of their children.

Modeling: Motherese (Parentese)

Children's speech occurs in conversation and generally serves to maintain exchange (Cherry, 1976; Lieven, 1975; Shurger, 1975). As we noted previously, conversational behavior is well established by the time the child begins to speak. Almost from birth, he encounters a facilitative verbal environment that enables him to participate as a conversational partner.

As the child's communication behaviors develop, the mother modifies her own behaviors so that she requires more child participation (Moerk, 1975). "The mother's (often quite unconscious) approach is indeed exquisitely tuned" (Bruner, 1978a, p. 9). When the child follows her pointing, the mother immediately asks a question. Whether the child responds with a gesture or a smile, she will supply a label. Once the child is able to vocalize, the mother "ups the ante" and withholds the label or repeats the question until the child vocalizes. Then she gives the label. The mother may not accept babbled responses once her child begins to use vocables or single words (Ninio & Bruner, 1978). Instead, she responds to babbling with "What's that?"—a request for a restatement.

The mother provides object names, but within a short time she begins to request labels from the child. By the middle of the second year, she is labeling and requesting at approximately equal rates (Bruner & Sylva, in preparation) and dialogue is fully established. This dialogue becomes the framework for a new routine (Bruner, 1978b). The mother begins to shape the child's speech by distinguishing more sharply between acceptable and unacceptable responses. The child's verbalizations are not immediate imitations but responses that fill specific slots within the dialogue, usually following a question. Within the dialogue, the mother provides consistency that aids learning. These consistencies include the amount of time devoted to dialogue, the number of turns, the repetition rate, the rate of confirmation, and the probability of reciprocating (Bruner, 1978b).

In addition, the mother makes other speech modifications that, taken together, are called **motherese** (Newport, Gleitman, & Gleitman, 1977) or *parentese*. The characteristics of motherese are listed in Table 7.4. Compared to adult–adult speech, motherese exhibits (a) greater pitch range, especially at the higher end; (b) lexical simplification characterized by the diminutive ("doggie") and syllable reduplication (consonant-verb-consonant-verb); (c) shorter, less complex utterances; (d) less dysfluency; (e) more paraphrasing and repetition; (f) limited, con-

---

TABLE 7.4   Characteristics of Motherese Compared to Adult–Adult Speech

Paralinguistic

Slower speech with longer pauses between utterances and after content words

Higher overall pitch; greater pitch range

Exaggerated intonation and stress

More varied loudness pattern

Fewer dysfluencies (one dysfluency per 1,000 words versus 4.5 per 1,000 for adult–adult)

Fewer words per minute

Lexical

More restricted vocabulary

Three times as much paraphrasing

More concrete reference to here and now

Semantic

More limited range of semantic functions

More contextual support

Syntactic

Fewer broken or run-on sentences

Shorter, less complex sentences (approximately 50% are single words or short declaratives)

More well-formed and intelligible sentences

Fewer complex utterances

More imperatives and questions (approximately 60% of utterances)

Conversational

Fewer utterances per conversation

More repetitions (approximately 16% of utterances are repeated within three turns)

crete vocabulary and a restricted set of semantic relations; (g) more contextual support; and (h) more directives and questions.

Although mothers use a short conversational style with infants, they use even shorter, less adult utterances with toddlers. The lowering of the mother's MLU beginning in the second half of the child's first year is positively related to better receptive language skills by the child at age 1 ½ (Murray, Johnson, & Peters, 1990). There seems to be no measurable effect on expressive language. Mothers aid *bootstrapping*, mentioned previously, by maintaining this semantic–syntactic correspondence (Rondal & Cession, 1990). For example, in utterances addressed to children, mothers use agents as subjects almost exclusively. The mother's behavior makes it easier for the child to decipher the syntax of her utterances.

As the child's language matures, his mother's speech directed toward him likewise changes. In fact, several studies have shown that motherese seems well tuned to the child's language level (Gelman & Shatz, 1977; Newport, 1976; Newport et al., 1977). Not all elements differ with the language level of the child. For example, maternal use of copulas, tense markers, and verbs and nouns does not change (Smolak & Weinraub, 1983). Overall use of imperatives and initiations intended to elicit or provide information also remains consistent (Cross, 1978). Other elements, such as the amount of maternal speech produced, partial repetitions of the child, and initiated statements commenting on child activity or eliciting attention, vary with the child's overall language level. These dynamic elements appear to be strongly related to the child's subsequent development (Furrow, Nelson, & Benedict, 1979; Wells, 1980; Wells, Barnes, Gutfreund, & Satterly, 1983). Although language generally occurs in an action context, the dependence upon nonlinguistic contextual cues, such as gestures, decreases with an increase in the child's linguistic abilities (H. Schaffer, Hepburn, & Collis, 1983; Schnur & Shatz, 1984). Slow at first, the rate of change increases with age (Frazer & Roberts, 1975). The length and complexity of the mother's utterances change most between 20 and 27 months, when the child's language changes most rapidly, though at any given time the syntax is fairly consistent, at least among middle-class mothers (Bellinger, 1980; Wells et al., 1983). There seems to be little or no change in the structural complexity of motherese between 8 and 18 months (Phillips, 1973). During this period there is also little corresponding change in the complexity of child speech, the changes consisting primarily of the addition of single words.

Mothers fine tune their language input to the child based primarily on the child's comprehension level. Other factors that influence the level of the mother's language are the conversational situation, the content, and different conversational acts (Snow, 1986). Overall, adults will simplify their input if the child does not seem to comprehend.

Undoubtedly, the influence of the child's characteristics on the interaction and on motherese also has an influence on the language input to which the child is exposed (Yoder & Kaiser, 1989). The toys with which the child plays also influence the amount and types of language produced by the parent (O'Brien &

Nagle, 1987). In general, toys that encourage role play, such as dolls, elicit more language and a greater variety of language from parents.

If adults simplify their language in order to be understood, then these modifications must reflect cues coming from the child. Apparently, however, adults are not conscious of their modifications, nor are they attempting to teach language. Adult-to-child speech seems to be modified in response to the amount of child feedback and participation (Bohannon & Marquis, 1977; Glanzer & Dodd, 1975). Not only is much of the speech addressed to the child adapted for the child's linguistic level, but speech not adapted is simply ignored or not processed (Snow, 1986). In other words, children play an active role in selecting the utterances to which they will attend. A lack of response is important, for it informs the parent there has been a breakdown in communication that, in turn, necessitates linguistic changes by the parent. Although the exact nature of child feedback is unknown, the child seems to be the key to adult linguistic changes (Furrow & Nelson, 1984). "A child, by virtue of the way that she/he talks, may be influencing the way in which other people speak to her/him" (Lieven, 1978, p. 185). At least the pragmatic aspects of the mother's speech may be related to either the referential or the expressive style of the child. Mothers of referential children seem to use more descriptive words and fewer directives (Della Corte, Benedict, & Klein, 1983). In addition, these mothers use more utterances within a given situation than mothers of children with more expressive speech.

Nonlinguistic behaviors are also critical. Child linguistic behaviors alone are not sufficient to produce the adult changes (Cross, 1977; Snow, 1977b). It is necessary for the adult to see the child in order to gain some information (Rembold, 1980). In fact, maternal linguistic modifications are different when the child is absent (Snow, 1972). Thus children play some role in eliciting maternal speech modifications.

Since the child has already demonstrated some turn-taking ability, he is capable of engaging in some conversation with his caregiver. Despite his linguistic inadequacies, the child can participate effectively because of the mother's ability to maintain the conversation (Snow, 1977b). The steady, rhythmic flow of the dialogue depends on the structural similarity of the mother's and child's utterances and on the correspondence of the mother's speech to events in the environment (Prorok, 1980). She enables the child to participate through her use of turn-passing devices. She does not use turn-grabbing or turn-keeping behaviors, such as "well . . .," "but . . .," or pause fillers (Snow, 1977b). She maintains control, and the dialogue is much less symmetrical than it may appear. "We find the mother only slowly relinquishing her role as manager of both sides of the dialogue, over the course of the third year." (Kaye, 1980, p. 503). The mother maintains the interaction by (a) second-guessing the child's communication intentions, (b) compensating for the child's communication failures, and (c) providing feedback for those failures (L. Wilkinson & Rembold, 1982).

Within the interactional sequence, the mother analyzes, synthesizes, and abstracts language structures for her child (Moerk, 1985). Through modeling word equivalents, she aids the child's pattern learning. A sequence might be as follows:

CHILD: She's running.

MOTHER: She's running fast. Oh, she's tired. Now she's running slowly. She's stopping. She's jumping slowly. Now she's jumping quickly.

Thus, the child is not a lone linguist attempting to learn the language code. Moerk (1985) concludes that "most of the burden of analysis, synthesis, and abstraction [is] upon the mother, who is not only much further advanced in her information-processing skills but who also knows the language and its basic structure and therefore knows what content has to be transmitted" (p. 284).

Despite the name *motherese*, these speech modifications are not limited to mothers. Fathers and other caregivers modify their speech in very similar ways (Gleason, 1975; Hladik & Edwards, 1984; Kauffman, 1976; Rondal, 1980; A. Stern, 1973). In fact, fathers may provide even more examples of simplified adult speech than mothers (Hladik & Edwards, 1984).

The range of vocabulary used by fathers and mothers with their young language-learning children is similar, but fathers use more rare words and fewer common words (Ratner, 1988). In this way, fathers are more lexically demanding than mothers.

Although fathers make modifications similar to those of mothers, they are less successful in communicating with toddlers, as measured by the amount of communication breakdown (Tomasello, Conti-Ramsden, & Ewert, 1990). Fathers use more requests for clarification or *contingent queries* than mothers. In addition, the form of these requests is more nonspecific ("What?") than those of mothers ("You want what?"). Fathers also fail to acknowledge their children's utterances more frequently. In return, children tend to persist in conversation with their fathers less so than with their mothers following such nonacknowledgment by the parent. It is possible that fathers serve as a bridge for their children between communication with the mother and with less familiar adults.

Even children as young as 4 years of age make language and speech modifications when addressing younger language-learning children. Adult and peer language modifications differ somewhat. In general, peer speech to toddlers is less complex and shorter and contains more repetition than adult-to-toddler speech. Still, "peers may be less effective as models for language learning . . . and may be less effective teachers of language because they appear to elicit language responses significantly less often than parents" (Wilkinson, Hiebert, & Rembold, 1981, p. 387). On the other hand, peer interaction may provide a "proving ground" for trying new linguistic structures (Keenan, 1974; Lewis, Young, Brooks, & Michaelson, 1975).

Children enrolled in day-care centers also encounter a variety of motherese that varies with the size of the group and the age of the children (Scopesi & Pellegrino, 1990). In general, the larger the group of children, the less individual adaptation by the adult. Larger groups force teachers to concentrate on attention keeping and control.

The presence of older siblings may also influence the language a younger child hears and produces (Wellen, 1985). For example, an older child will usually respond to more of the parent's questions, thereby reducing the number of responses made by the younger child. The younger child will often respond by imitating his older sibling. In this situation, the mother uses fewer rephrased questions, fewer questions with hints and answers, and fewer questions as expansions or extensions when the older child is present. (Expansions and extensions will be explained in more detail in the section on consequating behaviors.) In addition, the mother uses more direct repetitions of questions.

The intentions of the mother can only be guessed. In general, parents who use a more conversational style with less instructing are more likely to have children who learn language more quickly (Wells, 1985). In other words, children benefit more from language input when parents are more concerned with their mutual understanding and participation and less so with direct instruction.

The exact effect of motherese on language acquisition is unknown. The modifications made by mothers may (a) aid in language acquisition, (b) bring maternal utterances into the "processing range" of the child, or (c) merely increase the mother's chances of getting a correct response from the child (Wilkinson & Rembold, 1982). Since we find similar modifications in many cultures, we can assume that, at least, they somehow facilitate communication between adults and children.

The modifications of motherese seem to be maximally effective with the 18- to 21-month-old child, although the acquisition of specific structures is not associated with its use (Gleitman, Newport, & Gleitman, 1984). Rather, the child attends selectively, focusing on the best examples of various structures. Thus, the greater the range of utterances—within limits—the more rapidly the child will discover the underlying rule system.

Prompting

Prompting includes any parental behaviors that require a child response (Moerk, 1972; A. Wilkinson, 1971). Three common types are fill-ins, elicited imitations, and questions. In fill-ins, the parent says "This is a _____ ." No response or an incorrect response from the child will usually result in additional prompts and recueing. In elicited imitations, the parent cues with "Say X." Young language-learning children respond to approximately 56% of the elicited imitations addressed to them (J. Folger & Chapman, 1978). Questions may be of the confirmational yes/no type, such as "Is this a ball?", or of the *wh-* constituent variety, such as "What's that?" or "Where's doggie?" Unanswered or incorrectly answered questions are usually reformulated (R. Brown, Cazden, & Bellugi, 1969). Approximately 20 to 50% of mothers' utterances to young language-learning children are questions (Broen, 1972; Moerk, 1972). The individual range varies greatly. Children's nonverbal replies to their mothers' questions seem to be significantly affected by the gestural information accompanying the questions. There appears to be a strong link between maternal gestures and children's action responses. Maternal gestures serve as attention getters or prompts for action. Gradually, over the course of the first year, the link between maternal gestures and the child's verbal responses increases (Allen & Shatz, 1983). In general, such language-teaching utterances have a shorter average length than the majority of the utterances addressed to the child (Lord, 1975). Maternal inverted yes/no interrogatives, such as "Are you going home?", appear to correlate with child language development gains in syntactic complexity, and intonational interrogatives, such as "You going home?", correlate with gains in the child's pragmatic ability. In contrast, maternal directives seem to correlate highly with child gains in utterance length and semantic–syntactic complexity (Wells et al., 1983).

One interesting technique that parents employ to give the child an opportunity to produce two related single-word utterances is called the *vertical strategy* (R. Schwartz, Chapman, Prelock, Terrell, & Rowan, 1985). After the child produces a single-word utterance, the parent uses questions to aid the child in producing other elements of a longer utterance. The parent concludes by repeating the whole utterance. The following exchange is an example of the vertical strategy:

CHILD: Daddy.
ADULT: Uh-huh. What's Daddy doing?
CHILD: Eat.
ADULT: Yeah, Daddy eat cookie.

Although prompting and cueing are effective teaching techniques, their exact effect on language development is unknown. Several studies have demonstrated the effectiveness of these training techniques with language-disordered children.

Consequating Behaviors

Parents do not directly reinforce the syntactic correctness of children's utterances verbally (R. Brown et al., 1969). In fact, less than 10% of children's utterances are followed by verbal approval (Nelson, 1973a; Schumaker, 1976). Generally, such reinforcement is given for truthfulness, not for the correctness of the syntax. Other consequating behaviors may serve a reinforcing function.

Several studies have demonstrated that approximately 30% of mothers' utterances to young children consist of expansions (R. Brown & Bellugi, 1964). An **expansion** is a more mature version that preserves the word order of a child's utterance. For example, if the child says "Mommy eat," his mother might respond with "*Mommy* is *eat*ing her lunch." By producing the expanded version, the mother assumes that the child intends to communicate a certain meaning. Approximately one-fifth of the 2-year-old's ill-formed utterances are expanded by the mother into a syntactically more correct version (Hirsh-Pasek, Treiman, & Schneiderman, 1984). As the child's average utterance length increases beyond two words, the rate of expansion decreases.

Children seem to perceive expansions as a cue to imitate (Scherer & Olswang, 1984). Nearly a third of adult expansions are in turn imitated by the child (J. Folger & Chapman, 1978). These imitations are more likely to be linguistically correct than the child's original utterance (Slobin, 1968). In general, spontaneous productions follow, and rules are generalized to conversational use. As spontaneous production of structures occurs, imitation of these structures decreases. Thus, many linguists conclude that expansions reinforce the child's speech and language and aid language development. As such, expansions may facilitate the learning of word classes and their combinations rather than the learning of specific lexical items (Scherer & Olswang, 1984). Expansion adds meaning to the child's utterance at a time when the child is attending to a topic he has established. In addition, expansion provides evaluative feedback. Although we don't fully understand the relationship between the mother's expansion and the child's imitation, expansions continue the topic of conversation and encourage the child to take his turn and, thus, to maintain the dialogue (Scherer & Olswang, 1984).

The type of expansion used by the mother may have an effect on the particular form being learned by the child (Farrar, 1990). For example, reformulating the child's previous utterance by adding, substituting, or moving a morpheme may aid learning of plurals and progressives but has less effect on the past tense or copula, which seem to benefit from removal of morphemes and restatement of correct forms with embellishment of other aspects of the utterance.

Extension, a semantically related comment or reply on a topic established by the child, may be even more helpful as a facilitative device (Cazden, 1965). For example, when the child says "Doggie eat," his partner replies, "Doggie is hungry." Thus, extension provides more semantic information. Its value lies in its conversational nature, which provides positive feedback, and in its *semantic and pragmatic contingency*. A semantically contingent utterance is one that retains the focus or topic of the previous utterance. A pragmatically contingent utterance concurs with the intent of the previous utterance, i.e., topics invite comments, questions invite answers, requests invite responses, and so on. In short, contingency maintains the flow, which is inherently rewarding to almost all children.

The order of acquisition of grammatical structures is more a reflection of adult free speech than of the form of expansion (R. Brown et al., 1969). Maternal extending utterances seem also to correlate significantly with changes in the length of the child's utterances (Barnes et al., 1983).

Finally, parents imitate their child's speech. Approximately 22% of adult repetitions are imitated, in turn, by the child (J. Folger & Chapman, 1978).

All three consequating behaviors—expansion, extension, and imitation—result in greater amounts of child imitation than adult topic initiation or nonimitative behaviors. Hence, expansion, extension, and imitation appear to be valuable language-teaching devices. Each consequates a child verbal behavior, and expansion and extension also provide models of more mature language. In addition, the adult utterance is semantically contingent upon the preceding child utterance. This characteristic decreases the linguistic processing load on the child because the adult utterance is close to the child's utterance in form and content. This " 'child-centered' interactive style is beneficial in language learning" (Lieven, 1984, p. 16). Parents do not consciously devise these teaching strategies; rather, they evolve within the conversation context of child–caregiver interactions.

Adult Conversations with Preschoolers

As noted in Chapter 6, caregivers alter their behavior to enable infants to engage in successful communication as early as possible. This process continues in the preschool years. Mothers provide opportunities for their children to make verbal contributions, draw them into conversations and provide a well-cued framework for the exchange, show the child when to speak, and thereby develop cohesiveness between the speaker and the listener. Mothers ask children to comment on objects and events within their experience, knowing that they can do this. They also expand information by talking about the same object or event in different ways or by adding new ideas and elaborating on them (Martlew, 1980). Moreover, these maternal modifications appear to be correlated with advances in the child's language abilities.

In general, the mother of a 3- to 4-year-old uses many techniques to encourage communication. Mothers use twice as many utterance prefixes, such as *well* and *now*, as their children do (Martlew, 1980). These signals, plus varied intonation, are used with responses and help the child understand by signaling that a response is coming. In addition, mothers use a high proportion of redundant utterances to acknowledge and reassure the child. The mother frequently acknowledges with "good" or "that's it," which add little additional information. The behavior fills a minimal turn, however, without being overly disruptive to the child's speech stream. Maternal repetition of the child's utterance seems to be for the purposes of emphasis and reassurance.

Mothers are not equally facilitative in all areas of language development. Even within pragmatics, mothers are not as facilitative with turn taking as they are with other pragmatic skills (Bedrosian, Wanska, Sykes, Smith, & Dalton, 1988). Here mothers seem more interested in control than with facilitation. Mothers are somewhat better at maintaining the topic through these interruptions.

Throughout the preschool years, mothers interrupt their children much more than their children interrupt them. When interrupting, mothers usually omit the politeness markers seen in adult–adult dialogue. The frequency of these interruptions decreases with the child's maturity level.

When interrupted, children usually cease talking and reintroduce the topic. In contrast, mothers usually continue to talk when interrupted by their children and do not reintroduce the topic as often.

Expansion is not as effective a teaching tool with the preschool child as it is with the toddler. Instead, a mother's "partial-plus expansion" of her own prior utterances may be more important (Hoff-Ginsberg, 1985). Partial-plus expansion is characterized by a maternal self-repetition followed by an expansion, such as

Want big cookie? Want big cookie? Does Tommy want a big cookie?

Thus the mother assists the child in finding the structural similarity by a comparison of adjacent utterances.

Mothers also continue to facilitate the structure and cohesiveness of discourse by maintaining or reintroducing the topic (Wanska & Bedrosian, 1985).

With increasing age and MLU, the child takes a greater number of turns on each topic, therefore being less discontinuous. The number of turns per topic is still low by adult standards and does not change radically until school age. Preschoolers also begin to use *shading*, or a change of topic focus, rather than a discrete transition to a new topic.

Compared to her preschool child's conversational behaviors, the mother makes more demands and suggestions. As the child gets older, the mother uses more imperatives. By 3 years, the child can approximate adult behavior in his interpretation of these direct requests for action (Reeder, 1980). The mother sustains her child's interest by the use of mild encouragement ("Oh, that's nice") and praise ("What a lovely picture") (Martlew, 1980).

Maternal speech to 30-month-olds benefits syntactic learning by providing language-advancing data and by eliciting conversation (Hoff-Ginsberg, 1990). From the mother's point of view, it seems more important to engage the child in conversation than to elicit advanced forms from the child. Generally, such elicitation and feedback on the quality of the child's productions does little to contribute to development (Pinker, 1989). In contrast, conversation keeps the child's attention on language input and motivates the child to participate.

The effects of conversation, however, appear to be structure specific. For example, questions help to keep the child's attention and to focus on the auxiliary verbs by placing them in a prominent position. As might be expected, questions contribute to the development of auxiliary verbs (Hoff-Ginsberg, 1986). Mothers use yes/no questions to reformulate their children's utterances.

The mother invites child utterances, primarily through the use of questions, often followed by self-responses. This form of "discourse modeling" (Berko Gleason, 1973) is an effective teaching tool. As with a younger child, the mother relies heavily on the questioning technique of elicitation. One variant of this technique has been called a *turnabout* (Kaye & Charney, 1981). A **turnabout** is an utterance that both responds to the previous utterance and, in turn, requires a response. Thus, a turnabout fills the mother's turn and then requires a turn by the child.

Turnabouts

The goals of adult–adult and adult–child conversations differ (Snow, 1977b). In adult–adult conversations the goal appears to be to attain a turn, whereas the adult goal in adult–child conversations is to get the child to take his turn. "The conventions respecting the exchange of speaking turns are well established by the third year of life" (Kaye & Charney, 1981, p. 47). By using turnabouts, the mother creates a series of successful turns that resemble conversational dialogue. Thus, the mother is "programming speech acts to build dialogue" (Ervin-Tripp, 1977b, p. 36).

With a child aged 2 to 2½, the mother is twice as likely to use a turnabout as the child (Kaye & Charney, 1981). Generally, a turnabout consists of some type of response to, or statement about, the child's utterance and a request for information, clarification, or confirmation that serves as a cue to the child. The use of maternal question cues is frequent and widespread (Ervin-Tripp, 1973a; Leach,

Caregivers continue to be important for the child's language development and to structure conversations to facilitate participation by the child. The goal of the caregiver is to encourage the child to take a conversational turn.

1972; Lombardino, 1978; Parker, 1976). The mother often initiates a topic or an exchange with a question, thus gaining control (Mishler, 1974). If asked a question, she regains control by responding with another question. Resultant dialogues consist of three successive utterances: the mother's first question, the child's response, and the mother's confirmation, which may include another question. Thus questions help connect dialogue. Chaining is a frequent form of questioning (Malzone & Parker, 1979). In chaining, the confirmation is contained within another question. For example, the mother might say "Can you tell me what this is?" and then respond to the child's answer with "Um-hum, and what does it do?" Thus the mother is now back in control. In contrast, there are few turnabouts in child speech; "children rarely caught the ball and threw it back" (Kaye & Charney, 1981, p. 36).

In addition, the child is less likely to respond to the mother unless she requests a response. "The child was far less likely to respond [,] . . . far less likely to continue unless the mother's turn was a turnabout" (Kaye & Charney, 1981, pp. 40–41).

There are several types of turnabouts, shown with examples in Table 7.5. One type, the **request for clarification** or **contingent query**, has received considerable study. The contingent query is a technique used by both adults and children to gain information that initially was not clearly transmitted or received. Its use requires that both the listener and the speaker attend to prior discourse in their production. Thus, its use may be related to the development of the ability to refer to what has come before. Children receive little negative feedback via

TABLE 7.5   Turnabouts

Type	Example
Tag	Child: *Baby's panties.* Mother:*It's the baby's diaper, isn't it?*
Clarification (contingent query)	*Huh?* *What?*
Specific request	*What's that?*
Confirmation	*Horse?* *Is that a hippopotamus?* (Hand object to partner and give quizzical glance)
Expansions Suggestions Corrections Behavior comment	 *I want one.* *No, it's a zebra!* (Expectant tone) *You can't sit on that.*
Expansive question for sustaining conversation	*What would the policeman do then?*

Source: Drawn from K. Kaye and R. Charney, "Conversational Asymmetry between Mothers and Children," *Journal of Child Language*, 1981, *8*, 35–49.

contingent queries when they have language errors (Morgan & Travis, 1989). Parental requests for clarification are just as likely to be attempts to clarify genuine misunderstandings and miscommunications as to correct production errors. The contingent query consists of four components: the original utterance, the query, the response, and the utterance for resumption of the speaker's turn (Gallagher, 1981). These four components are illustrated as follows:

Original utterance	CHILD:	We saw mahmees.
Query	ADULT:	What did you see?
Response	CHILD:	Monkeys.
Resumption	ADULT:	Oh, did they do funny things?

Children aged 3 to 5½ are able to produce and respond to contingent queries 80 to 85% effectively with their peers (Garvey, 1975, 1977), while children as young as 18 months are equally effective in responding to simple adult queries (Gallagher, 1977).

The 3-year-old is able to respond appropriately to neutral queries such as "What?" and "Huh?" The child's primary repair strategy, or way of ensuring understanding, is to repeat what was said previously. With a second query about the same utterance, the 3-year-old gets frustrated. In contrast, the 5-year-old responds to a second query but employs the same repetition strategy as the 3-year-old (Brinton, Fujiki, Loeb, & Winkler, 1986).

With 2- to 3-year-olds mothers employ yes/no questions in turnabouts most frequently (Gallagher, 1981). This form requires a confirmation and is easy for children as young as 18 months to process (Morgan, 1978; Steffensen, 1978). Recall that maternal yes/no questioning may be positively correlated with increased language abilities of the child (Furrow et al., 1979). If a child does not respond appropriately, the conversational expectations of his mother are not fulfilled, and his mother will ask fewer contingent queries. Noting this phenomenon, Garvey (1977) proposed the following hypothesis:

Y must satisfy X's needs before proceeding with any further talk and should do so in the manner that X's query has determined.

It is clear that the caregiver's conversational behaviors reflect the feedback she receives from the child.

THE IMPORTANCE OF PLAY

With so much terminology and scholarly research, it is easy to forget that much of the child's language develops within the context of play with an adult or with other children. Play can be an ideal vehicle for language acquisition for a number of reasons (Sachs, 1984):

- Since play is not goal oriented, it removes pressure and frustration from the interactive process. It's fun.

- Attention and the semantic domain are shared by the interactive partners, so topics are shared.
- Games have reciprocal role structure and variations in the order of elements, as do grammars.
- Games, like conversations, contain turn taking.

Initially both play and language are very concrete and depend on the here and now. As cognition develops, however, they both become less concrete (Bates et al., 1984). At about the time that children begin to combine symbols, they begin to play symbolically. One play object, such as a shoe, is used for another, such as a telephone. Children often attempt to involve their parents in this pretend play. As playmates, parents can show by example how to play. Often parents contribute running narratives of the play as it progresses and provide children with the basic problem–resolution narrative or story model. Even 2-year-olds can learn the basic problem–resolution format, as in "The baby cried; the mommy picked it up" (Sachs, 1972).

Role playing and accompanying linguistic style changes begin at around age 3. By age 4 the child is able to role-play a baby using a higher pitch, phonetic substitutions, shorter and simpler utterances, and more references to himself (Sachs & Devin, 1976). At about this time, the child begins to role play "Mom and Dad" differently (Andersen, 1977). In general, mothers are portrayed as more polite, using more indirect requests, with a higher pitch and longer utterances. Role-played fathers make more commands and give less explanation for their behavior. Prosodic and rhythmic devices are the first stylistic variations used by children, followed by appropriate content and then syntactic regularities.

Although the preschool child is too young for team games and is not cognitively ready to follow game rules, he does enjoy group activities. Language learning is enhanced by the songs, rhymes, and finger plays common among preschoolers. Within play, the child and his communication partner can participate in a dialogue free of the pressures of "real" communication. In addition, the child is free to experiment with different communication styles and roles.

CULTURAL AND SOCIAL DIFFERENCES

Obviously, not all children receive the sort of "idealized" language input reported in this chapter. In non-Western cultures, mothers use techniques other than conversation to gain and hold children's attention.

Middle-class American mothers talk *with* their children, not *at* them. Many maternal utterances consist of comments on topics established by the child through word or action. This tendency to follow the child's conversational lead is evidenced in maternal expansion and extension of the child's utterances. While these semantically related maternal utterances can enhance language acquisition, it has not been proven that they are crucial to the process. For example, not all cultures value verbal precosity in children or demonstrate the adult modifications seen in motherese. Among the Kipsigis of Kenya and rural African-

Americans in Louisiana, comprehension is more important than verbal production in young children, and many of the utterances directed to them consist of directives and explanations (Harkness, 1977; Ward, 1971). Kalui parents in New Guinea and Samoan parents rarely follow their children's conversational leads (Ochs & Schieffelin, 1984). Language acquisition does not seem to be slowed or delayed in any way.

These mothers use other strategies that seem equally effective. For example, Kaluli mothers in Papua, New Guinea, provide models of appropriate language for specific situations and direct their young children to imitate them. In situations with other adults, children are directed by their mothers in the appropriate responses. This recycling of appropriate utterances for recurring situations is presumably a language-learning device. Like semantically related adult utterances found in white middle-class American homes, these predictable situational responses may be highly comprehensible to the child without complete grammatical knowledge (Snow, 1986).

Parent-initiated communication with young U.S. girls and boys also differs in both play and nonplay situations. Adults tend to emphasize useful domestic activities with young girls, while they emphasize more free-ranging exploratory manipulation with young boys (Wells, 1986). It is unclear whether these preferences represent desires of the parent or the child.

Socioeconomic and cultural factors result in many different child–caregiver interactive patterns reflecting (1) the role of children, (2) the social organization of caregiving, and (3) folk beliefs about how children learn language (Schieffelin & Eisenberg, 1984). We must also be careful not to assume that the way middle-class mothers in the United States interact with their children is the only way or the most correct way. In general, interactive patterns between children and their caregivers have evolved to fulfill the special needs of the populations in which they occur.

In the middle-class American family, the child is held in relatively high regard. This is also true among the Kaluli people. In contrast, the relatively lower standing of children reported in western Samoa and among some rural Louisiana African-Americans results in an expectation that children are to speak only when invited to do so (Ochs, 1982). Within these same rural southern African-American communities, the child is not expected to initiate conversation but to respond to adult questions in the shortest possible form (Ward, 1971). The child is not expected to perform for adults, and most of his requests for information are ignored. What expansion exists is an expansion by adults of their own utterances, not those of the child.

The expectation of a quiet child does not always reflect a low status. Among the Apache Indians, it is a societal norm to value silence from all people (Basso, 1972). In general, the Japanese also encourage less talking by their children, although children are held in very high regard. Nonverbal behavior is more important in Japan than in the United States, and Japanese parents anticipate the child's needs more often, so he has fewer reasons to communicate.

The social organization of caregiving also varies widely, and reflects economic organization and kinship groupings. In some cultures, such as that of western Samoa, older siblings are more responsible for caregiving than in middle-class American homes. This arrangement is also characteristic of many inner-city households in the United States. There is no evidence, however, that children raised by older siblings learn language more slowly than those raised by adults.

Finally, folk "wisdom" on language acquisition varies widely and affects language addressed to the child. The Kipsigis of Kenya believe that the child will learn by himself. Thus, there is no baby talk or motherese. The child is encouraged to participate in conversation through imitation of the mother's model of adult speech. The Kaluli of New Guinea also require imitation from the child in certain social rituals, even though the child does not seem to understand what he is saying (Schieffelin, 1982). It should be noted that children can also learn language from speech that is not addressed to them (Oshima-Takane, 1988). This may be especially true of some pronouns, which may be best learned by observing their use in various contexts.

With all this variety, children from other cultures still learn their native languages at about the same rate as middle-class American children. In general, in the United States, most adults treat the child as a communication partner. The language-learning American child is raised primarily by his parent(s) or paid professionals or paraprofessionals who model and elicit language. Even within the United States, however, there is no definitive pattern. We'll discuss some of the American variations in Chapter 12.

Children are not limited to direct language input. They can also learn language by indirect means, such as conversational exchanges between other individuals (Schiff, 1979). Television can also provide some input with systematic viewing (Lemish & Rice, 1986). "As children acquire the system of language-based knowledge . . ., they draw upon the totality of their experiences" (Rice, 1984, p. 178).

CONCLUSION

Language learning is a complex process that involves linguistic processing and child and adult language-learning strategies. Different cultures exhibit different strategies.

Comprehension and imitation by the toddler seem to be particularly important. Both appear to be at the cutting edge of language development, though the exact relationship is unknown and seems to change with the child's functioning level.

Nor do we know the exact language-learning strategies used by young children. However, these strategies and their underlying cognitive abilities can be inferred from the child's behaviors. Consistency in the child's language suggests the presence of underlying rule systems. At present, linguists are unsure of the process of rule construction. Undoubtedly, though, comprehension and production are interrelated. This dynamic relationship changes with the level of development and with the structure being learned. The order of acquisition of structures for expressing complex relationships reflects the child's cognitive growth. The child must understand the concept of the relationship and the linguistic forms used to express that relationship before he can use this relationship in his own language.

Environmental influences strongly affect language development. Adult modeling and consequating behaviors are very important with toddlers. Adult–child language provides a simplified model. Certain consequating behaviors also reinforce the child's communication attempts.

Although a direct conditioning explanation of language development is inadequate, there is a strong indication that modeling, imitation, and reinforcement are central to the learning process. Those elements of maternal speech that change to reflect the child's overall language level seem to be most significant for later language development. The process is much more subtle than that employed in direct language training.

Although diminished, the role of significant caregivers is still critical with preschoolers. Caregivers continue to manipulate the conversational context to maximize language learning by the child. This context and play are important sources of language modeling and use for preschool children.

REFLECTIONS

1. Describe the complex relationship between comprehension and production as it relates to the young language-learning child.
2. Explain the relationship between language comprehension, production, and cognition, using examples from the development of interrogatives, temporal terms, relational terms, prepositions, and kinship terms.
3. Describe the role of imitation for toddlers and the development from repetitious utterances to semantically diverse ones.
4. Mothers and fathers talk very differently to their young child than they do to other adults. What are the characteristics of motherese or parentese?
5. List the various types of prompts parents use to encourage their children to speak.
6. Though parents may not directly reinforce their young language-learning children, they do expand, extend, and imitate. Describe the differences between these three behaviors and explain the effects of these behaviors on the child.
7. Children in the United States and in other cultures receive a variety of linguistic inputs and are expected to communicate in numerous ways.

What are the factors that affect parent–child interaction? What effects do these factors have on language development?

8. After noting similarities in children's structures in several languages, Slobin proposed a set of universal principles of language learning. State the main principles and give an example of each.

9. What is a turnabout, and how is it used by caregivers?

10. Describe the importance of play for language development.

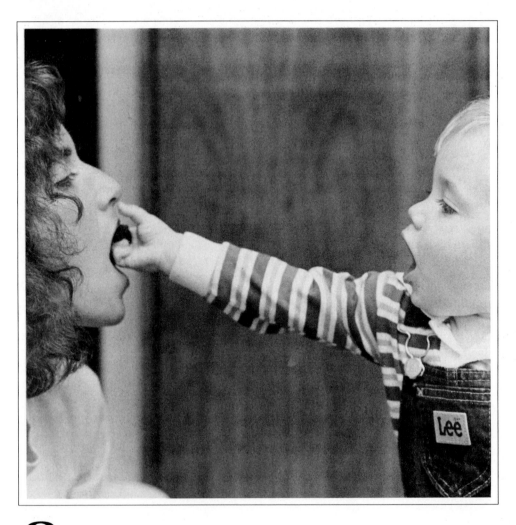

8 A First Language

CHAPTER OBJECTIVES

Children's initial language consists of more than the mere accumulation of single words. As with all language, children's initial attempts reflect rule-governed patterns of production. When you have completed this chapter, you should understand

- the most frequent categories and syllable constructions in first words.
- the intentions of early vocalizations/verbalizations.
- the bases for early concept development.
- the bases for extensions and overextensions.
- the two-word semantic rules of toddlers.
- the common phonological rules of toddlers.
- the following terms:

action relational words	possession relational words
agent	presupposition
associative complex hypothesis	prototypic complex hypothesis
attribution relational words	reduplication
consonant/cluster reduction	reflexive relational words
diminutive	relational words
functional-core hypothesis	semantic-feature hypothesis
location relational words	semantic–syntactic rules
object	substantive words
open syllable	underextension
overextension	

T HE POINT AT WHICH language is said to begin is arbitrary and depends upon your definition of *language*. For our purposes, we shall assume that language begins at around the first birthday with the appearance of the first word. Since the 6-month-old infant might say "dada," we will need to refine our definition a little. To be considered a true word, the child's utterance must have a phonetic relationship to some adult word. In addition, the child must use the word consistently to mark a particular situation or object. Consistent use in the presence of a referent implies an underlying concept or meaning. Therefore, a babbled "dada" would not qualify because there is no referent. Likewise, phonetically consistent forms would fail to meet the first criterion because they do not approximate recognizable adult words. (See Chapter 3 for a description of PCFs.)

Before you begin this chapter, take a few minutes to think about the 12- to 18-month-old child and what she knows. Soon she will begin talking about her world. Jot down a short list of words that she might say. Much of the pronunciation will not mirror her adult model's language. For that reason, you might write possible child pronunciations after applicable words. For example, *water* will probably be spoken as "wawa."

Once you have completed your list, imagine how these words might be used in conversation. Examine your list for patterns. You probably know more about language development than you realize. What types of words—nouns, verbs, and so on—predominate? What speech sounds are used most frequently? What syllabic constructions—CV, VC, CVCV-reduplicated, CVCV, CVC, and so on—are most frequent? It is also important to consider the contexts in which first words occur. The child's primary communication partner is her mother, sibling, or other caregiver. This person engages the child in *protoconversations* within familiar activities and routines. These events form the backdrop for communication and provide a script for what is said. The child's first words occur as requests for information, or for objects or aid, or as comments. The child's intentions, previously expressed through gestures and vocalizations, are now expressed through words. There is carryover of pragmatic functions from presymbolic to symbolic communication. As we progress through this chapter, you may be surprised by the accuracy of your responses.

SINGLE-WORD UTTERANCES

The first meaningful speech of the toddler consists of single-word utterances, such as "doggie," or single-word approximations of frequently used adult phrases, such as "thank you" ("anku") or "what's that?" ("wasat?"). At this point, "words" are phonetic approximations of adult words that the child consistently uses to refer to a particular situation or object. The meaning of the word may be very restricted at first and may apply only to one particular referent. For example, "doggie" (usually "goggie" or "doddie") may refer only to the family's pet but not to other dogs. Early meanings may have very little in common with those generally used by mature speakers. As a result of linguistic and nonlinguistic, or sensory, experience, the child will gradually modify her definition. At some point, the child's definition will approximate the generally shared notion of the word's meaning.

In general, the toddler talks about the world she knows. She will not comment on inflation, unemployment, politics, or nuclear holocaust. Instead, the toddler may request toys, call people, name pets, reject food, ask for help with clothing, and discuss familiar actions or routines.

Pragmatic Aspects of a First Language

In order to explain early child language fully, we must also consider the uses to which these utterances are put. As we noted in Chapter 6, communication is well established before the first word appears. The child develops the ability to communicate meanings before she acquires any language. Language "maps" or processes these early meanings within the established communication system. In many ways, the transition from presymbolism to symbolism can be best understood by considering this communication context.

Both the repetitiveness of certain daily verbal and nonverbal routines and the mother's willingness to assign meaningful intent to the child's speech aid language development (Ferrier, 1978; Ninio & Bruner, 1978). Parent responses also foster word–meaning associations by providing feedback to the child that her intended meaning was or was not comprehended in that way (Holzman, 1972).

In addition, the social functions of the child's early utterances are important in the actual words the child will select for her lexicon. Early words develop to fulfill the social functions originally conveyed by gestures.

There is a strong relationship between first words and the frequency of maternal input of these words (Harris, Barrett, Jones, & Brooks, 1988). Many of the words are used in the same context in which the mother used them previously, such as "Bye-bye" while waving and "choo-choo" while playing with a toy train. Not all words are used this way, however, and a significant number are also used to name or label entities.

Before we continue, return to the fictitious list of first words you generated at the beginning of this chapter. Pause for a moment and consider how these words might be used socially, that is, to attain information, fulfill needs, provide information, and so on.

Development

In Chapter 6 we examined the illocutionary functions or intentions of early gestures. Initially intentions are signaled by gestures only. To these the child adds vocalizations and then words. Many early words, however, can be interpreted only with consideration of the accompanying gesture (Braunwald, 1978). Gradually the child learns to express her intentions in more grammatically correct ways.

Gestures. Gestural development continues along with verbal growth. Not all gestures are of equal developmental importance. Pointing, for example, accompanies many early utterances with a variety of meanings. The early use of pointing by young children is a good predictor of early language performance (Bates, Benigni, Bretherton, Camaioni, & Volterra, 1979).

From age 12 to 18 months, there is a progression toward production of coordinated, dual-directional signals in which the child gestures and verbalizes while looking at her communication partner (Lempers, Flavell, & Flavell, 1977). Initially, the child merely gestures but may not look at her partner. The child then progresses to a gesture and verbalization plus divergent gaze, a gaze toward the communication partner rather than toward the object of the gesture. This dual directionality may be an important transition to the ability to consider two communication aspects—the topic and the listener—simultaneously (Masur, 1983). Finally, the child is able to look at her partner while performing two coordinated gestures in sequence or a gesture plus a conventional verbalization or word.

Primitive Speech Acts. There appear to be patterns in the vocalizations and gestures of young children that are used to express intentions (Dore, 1974). Since these behaviors frequently lack words or depend upon gestures to convey intent,

The young child develops her first words within the early intentions initially expressed by gestures. For example, pointing, originally used to direct attention, might accompany naming or questioning utterances.

we consider these patterns to be precursors to adultlike speech acts and label them *primitive speech acts (PSAs)* (Dore, 1974). A PSA is a single word or single vocal pattern that conveys intention. For example, when requesting an action, a child may use a word or a prosodic pattern and gestures while attending to the object followed by attending to the adult. The most common PSAs are presented in Table 8.1. Any given utterance is unifunctional; it carries only one social function. PSAs are similar to the intentions expressed in the speech of children in the second year of life (Owens, 1978; Wells, 1985). This continuity suggests differentiation with maturity. Not surprisingly, the range of early intentions seems to be universal (Roth & Davidge, 1985).

TABLE 8.1   Dore's Primitive Speech Acts

Primitive Speech Act	Child's Utterance	Child's Nonlinguistic Behavior	Adult Response	Relevant Contextual Features
Labeling	Word	Attends to object or event; does not address adult; does not await response	Most often none; occasional repetition of child's utterance	Salient feature focused on by child; no change in situation
Repeating	Word or prosodic pattern	Attends to adult utterance before his utterance; may not address adult; does not await response	Most often none; occasional repetition of child's utterance	Utterance focused on; no change in situation
Answering	Word	Attends to adult utterance before his utterance; addresses adult	Awaits child's response; after child's utterance, most often acknowledges response; may then perform action	Utterance focused on; no change in situation, unless child's response prompts adult reaction
Requesting (action)	Word or marked prosodic pattern	Attends to object or event; addresses adult; awaits response; most often performs signaling gesture	Performs action	Salient feature focused on by child and adult; change in condition of object or child
Requesting (answer)	Word	Addresses adult; awaits response; may make gesture regarding object	Utters a response	No change in situation
Calling	Word (with marked prosodic contour)	Addresses adult by uttering adult's name loudly; awaits response	Responds by attending to child or answering child	Before child's utterance adult is some distance away; adult's orientation typically changes
Greeting	Word	Attends to adult or object	Returns a greeting utterance	Speech event is initiated or ended
Protesting	Word or marked prosodic pattern	Attends to adult; addresses adult; resists or denies adult's action	Initiates speech event by performing an action the child does not like	Adult's action is completed or child prevents action
Practicing	Word or prosodic pattern	Attends to no specific object or event; does not address adult; does not await response	No response	No apparent aspect of context is relevant to utterance

Source: Adapted from J. Dore, "Holophrases, Speech Acts and Language Universals," *Journal of Child Language*, April 1975, *2*(1), p. 33. Reprinted by permission of the publisher, Cambridge University Press.

Intentions in Words.   First words fulfill the intentions previously expressed through gestures and vocalizations. Initially, different, often idiosyncratic verbal forms may develop to express different functions (Halliday, 1975b). This phase may last until about 16 months of age. At first, functions are isomorphic, that is, specific words or forms, such as PCFs, are used with each function. Just as different words appear gradually, functions fulfilled by words also emerge over time. As words and functions increase, words and utterances become more flexible and multifunctional. The disappearance of isomorphic forms usually occurs from 16 to 24 months, corresponding to the beginning of multiword combinations.

Wells (1985) identified six pragmatic categories that describe the general purposes of language: control, representational, expressive, social, tutorial, and procedural. Speakers use the control function to make demands and requests, to protest, and to direct others. The representational function is used to discuss entities and events and to ask for information. In contrast, the expressive function is not necessarily for an audience. The child may use language to accompany play or to exclaim. She may also express feelings and attitudes. The social function includes greetings, farewells, and talk routines. For young children, the tutorial function consists mostly of practice with language forms. Finally, the procedural function is used to maintain communication by directing attention or by requesting additional or misinterpreted information. Early toddler utterances fulfill aspects of all functions. The purpose or use of single words is marked by differing intonational patterns (Galligan, 1987). There is a continuity from PSAs to early verbal intentions. Table 8.2 illustrates the relationship of PSAs to later semantic categories and offers examples of early verbal illocutionary functions or intentions.

Along with the development of single words and word combinations, the child develops sound contrasts in a rather specific order (Halliday, 1975b; Menn, 1976) that appears to be true for both relatively nontonal languages, such as English, and tonal languages, such as Latvian, Thai, and Lao (Rūkė-Draviná, 1981; Tuaycharoen, 1978; Westermeyer & Westermeyer, 1977). These contrasts are used most often by 2-year-olds when talking to a conversational partner rather than in monologues, although these pitch patterns are not the same as those found in adult speech (Furrow, 1984).

Beginning with a falling contour only—similar to that used by adults for statements—children first develop a flat or level contour for naming or labeling, usually accompanied by variations, such as use of falsetto or variations in length or loudness. Between 13 and 15 months, children develop a rising contour to express requesting, attention getting and curiosity, and a high falling contour, which begins with a high pitch that drops to a lower one, to signal surprise, recognition, insistence, or greeting (Marcos, 1987). Next, children use a high rising and a high rising-falling contour to signal playful anticipation and emphatic stress respectively. Finally, at around 18 months, children use a falling-rising and a rising-falling contour for warnings and playfulness, respectively.

By 15 months, most children are naming or labeling favorite toys and foods and household pets, exclaiming, and calling to attract attention (Wells, 1985).

TABLE 8.2   Early Illocutionary Functions*

Broad Pragmatic Categories (Wells, 1985)	Primitive Speech Acts (PSAs) (Dore, 1974)	Early Verbal Intentions (Owens, 1978; Wells, 1985)	Examples
Control	Requesting action	Wanting demands	*Cookie* (Reach)
		Direct request/Commanding	*Help* (Hand object to or struggle)
	Protesting	Protesting	*No* (Push away or uncooperative)
Representational	Requesting answer	Content questioning	*Wassat?* (Point)
	Labeling	Naming/labeling	*Doggie* (Point)
		Statement/Declaring	*Eat* (Commenting on dog barking)
	Answering	Answering	*Horsie* (in response to question)
		Reply	*Eat* (in response to "The doggie's hungry."
Expressive		Exclaiming	Squeal when picked up
		Verbal accompaniment to action	*Uh-oh* (With spill)
		Expressing state or attitude	*Tired*
Social	Greetings	Greeting/Farewell	*Hi* *Bye-bye*
Tutorial	Repeating/practicing	Repeating/practicing	*Cookie, cookie, cookie*
Procedural	Calling	Calling	*Mommy*

*This table represents a combination of the work of several researchers and an attempt to remain true to the intended purposes of child speech.

Within another 3 months, the average child adds wanting demands ("I want . . ."). By 2 years of age, 50% or more of all children have added direct requesting or commanding; content questioning; unsolicited statements or declarations; verbal accompaniments to play ("Uh-oh"); and expressions of states and attitudes, most frequently "I'm tired" (Wells, 1985). Other early illocutionary functions include protesting ("no"), answering, greeting, and practice or repeating.

As children mature, the frequency of pragmatic functions changes (Wells, 1985). At 15 months, over 75% of all utterances are representational, expressive, and procedural, with the illocutionary functions of naming/labeling and calling predominating. By 21 months, control functions increase markedly, while expressive functions are reduced by nearly half. Throughout this period, social and tutorial functions occur infrequently. Some early illocutionary functions, such as wanting demands, naming/labeling, calling, and practice, decrease rapidly as a percentage of overall intentions from 24 to 36 months. Other relatively later-developing functions, such as direct requesting/commanding and statement/ declaration, gradually increase.

During the one-word stage, my own sons gave a striking exhibition of direct requesting. Both boys had stayed with their grandmother during their mother's hospitalization for our daughter's birth. While visiting with "Gran'ma," they learned to chase two particularly pesky stray tomcats with "Skat!" Later, when in a room alone with their newly arrived, sleeping sister, the two boys looked through the bars of her crib and ordered "Skat! Skat!" Fortunately, she didn't follow orders well even then.

Initially speech emerges to accompany action, not to convey information (Greenfield & Smith, 1976). Verbal language is manifested in requests to perform some "ritual" possibly as simple as *notice me*. The child's first words may accompany pointing and are used to display a wish or to express displeasure. The child may draw attention to herself first ("Mommy"), then make a request ("Up"). The child may use *look* for control or *there* to complete a task. As she matures, the child may attend to an object and the action associated with it. Thus, the child may use *eat* when referring to a cookie being eaten. Later, she notes object relations or comments on the event, such as asking for a repetition with *again*. Thus, the child is not just acquiring a stack of meanings. Rather, she is making her meanings known to a conversational partner by using them to build a communication system with that partner. A child's perceptual and cognitive abilities are a constraint on the meanings that are learned.

Two-word speech represents more complete speech acts because the content can be communicated completely without dependence on nonlinguistic channels (Chalkley, 1982). It is important to remember, however, that grammatical form is not the determiner of communication function (Searle, 1972). At the two-word level, "the child begins to use structure independent of function" (Woll, 1978, p. 325). A single illocutionary function can be realized in a variety of grammatical forms. A child can express a request with "gimme cookie," "want cookie," or "cookie please." Conversely, one form can serve a variety of functions. For example, an utterance such as "Daddy throw" can serve as a descriptor of an event, a request for action, or even a request for information (question).

At around age 2, the child begins to combine several language functions within a single utterance (Halliday, 1975a, 1975b). "The use of a lexicogrammatical system makes it possible to fulfill all necessary functions in a discourse virtually simultaneously" (Bruner, 1976, p. 8). For example, upon spying some fresh-baked cookies, the child might say, "Mommy, cookies hot?" Even though she is attempting to attain information, she also hopes to attain a cookie. Thus, we have a request for information and a request for an entity within the same utterance.

Conversational Abilities

Even at the single-word stage, the child has some knowledge of the information to be included in a conversation. For example, the child gives evidence of using **presupposition**, that is, the assumption that the listener knows or does not know certain information that the child must include or delete from the conversation. For example, as an adult, when you are asked, "How do you want your steak?" you might reply, "Medium rare." There is no need to repeat the redundant information, "I would like my steak. . . ." You omit the redundant information because you presuppose that your listener shares this information with you already. In contrast, you would call your listener's attention to new, different, or changing circumstances that may be unknown to the listener ("Did you know that . . .?" "Well, let me tell you about . . .").

Toddlers seem to follow certain rules for presupposition (Greenfield, 1978):

1. An object not in the child's possession is uncertain. The child's first utterance will label the object.
2. An object in the child's possession while undergoing change is relatively certain. The child's utterance will encode the action or change.
3. Once encoded, an object or action/state change becomes more certain and less informative. If the child continues, she will encode the other aspect that has not been stated.

The order of successive single-word utterances reflects the interplay of these rules. Therefore, the presuppositional rules may, in part, explain the variable order of successive single-word and early two-word utterances.

With the onset of two-word utterances, the child learns that a word-order rule overrides informational structure as a determinant of word order. For a few years, the child may lose the ability to use word order to signal the topic–comment distinction. Eventually, the child learns how to use certain syntactic devices involving variable word order to signal certain and uncertain aspects (Greenfield, 1978, p. 449). Since children often encode the here and now, it is relatively easy for adults to interpret the utterance in a manner similar to that of the child. This does not imply, however, that the child is able to adopt the listener's perspective. The significance of this common information extraction process "is that it can make verbal communication between child and adult possible long before the child has developed any such awareness of the listener's point of view" (Greenfield, 1978, p. 451). As noted earlier, the ability to establish joint reference develops prior to the appearance of first words.

Initial Lexicons

Initial individual vocabularies or *lexicons* may contain some of the words listed in Table 8.3. Although there are many variations in pronunciation, some of the common forms are included in parentheses. (See Appendix A for an explanation of the International Phonetic Alphabet.) How does this sample compare with the one you devised? As we note other patterns, check them against your list.

TABLE 8.3   Representative Early Words

juice (/dus/)	mama	all gone (/ɔdɔn/)
cookie (/tʊti/)	dada	more (/mɔ/)
baby (/bibi/)	doggie (/dɔdi/)	no
bye-bye	kitty (/tldi/)	up
ball (/bɔ/)	that (/da/)	eat
hi	dirty (/dɔti/)	go (/d oʊ/)
car (/tɔ/)	hot	do
water (/wʌwʌ/)	shoe (/su/)	milk (/mʌk/)
eye	hat	cap (/tʌp/)
nose (/n oʊ/)		

Most first words contain one or two syllables. Syllabic construction is usually VC (vowel-consonant), CV, CVCV-reduplicated, or CVCV. For example, in our list in Table 8.3 we find VC words, such as *eat* and *up*, CV words, such as *no* and *car* (*tɔ*), CVCV-reduplicated words, such as *mama, dada,* and *water (wʌwʌ)*, and CVCV words, such as *doggie (dɔdi)*. How does your list compare? There are very few CVC words, and many of these are modified in production. The final consonant may be omitted or followed by a vowellike sound, approximating a CVCV construction. For example, a word such as *hat* might be produced as *hat-a (hatʌ)*, approximating a CVCV construction. Front consonants, such as /p, b, d, t, m/, and /n/, predominate. No consonant clusters, such as /tr/, /sl/, or /str/, appear.

The child's first lexicon includes several categories of words. The most frequent words among the child's first 10 words generally name animals, foods, and toys (K. Nelson, 1973b). First words usually apply to a midlevel of generality (dog) and only much later to specific types (spaniel, boxer) and larger categories (animal) (Anglin, 1977). Even at this midlevel, however, the word is first used by the child to mark a specific object or event. Our list in Table 8.3 contains animals (*doggie* and *kitty*), foods (*juice* and *cookie*), and toys (*ball*).

Initial lexical growth is slow, and the child may appear to plateau for short periods. Some words are lost as the child's interests change and her production abilities improve (McLaughlin, 1978). In addition, the child continues to use a large number of vocalizations that are consistent but fail to meet the "word" criterion. At the center of the child's lexicon is a small core of high-usage words. The lexical growth rate continues to accelerate as she nears the 50-word mark. The second half of the second year is one of tremendous vocabulary expansion, although there is much individual variation (Stoel-Gammon & Cooper, 1984).

By 18 months of age, the toddler will have a lexicon of approximately 50 words. The most frequently produced categories of words and examples of each are listed in Table 8.4 (K. Nelson, 1973b). Noun or object words predominate (Benedict, 1979; Gleitman, Gleitman, & Shipley, 1972; Guillaume, 1970; Huttenlocher, 1974; McNeill, 1970). Most entries are persons and animals within the environment or objects the child can manipulate. Not all noun types are repre-

TABLE 8.4 Grammatical Classification of First 50 Words Produced

Grammatical Function	Percentage of Vocabulary		Examples
	Benedict (1979)	Nelson (1973b)	
Nominals			
General	50	51	milk, dog, car
Specific	11	14	mama, dada, pet names
Action words	19	14	give, do, bye-bye, up
Modifiers	10	9	mine, no, dirty
Personal-social	10	9	no, please
Functional	—	4	this, for

sented; individual objects and beings are most frequent. There are no collections, such as *forest*, or abstractions, such as *joy* (Gentner, 1982).

When the first 50 words are classified according to grammatical category and as a percentage of the child's vocabulary, the prominence of nouns is apparent (Table 8.4). Nouns account for 60 to 65% of the words the child produces (Benedict, 1979; K. Nelson, 1973b). In contrast, action words account for less than 20% of the total. In our list in Table 8.3, nouns account for approximately 60% of the total.

Several linguists have studied early lexicons, and most agree that the child initially produces referential nouns (Goldin-Meadow, Seligman, & Gelman, 1976; Huttenlocher, 1974; R. Schwartz & Leonard, 1984). This finding seems to be universal (Gentner, 1982), though there may be some minor differences across languages. These data generally reflect groups of toddlers rather than individuals. In fact, children exist along a continuum from those who use many nouns ("noun lovers") to others who use few ("noun leavers"), preferring interactional and functional words, such as *hi, bye-bye*, and *no* (Horgan, 1979). To some extent, this distinction appears to remain with children into the preschool years. Noun lovers tend to elaborate the noun portion or noun phrase of their sentences, whereas noun leavers prefer to elaborate the verb phrase (Horgan, 1979).

There are other differences relative to the proportion of nouns in the initial lexicon. Children with a high proportion of nouns—70% or more—exhibit a rapid increase in the number of words in their lexicons between 14 and 18 months of age. In contrast, children whose lexicons have more balance between nouns and other word types tend to have a more gradual increase in word acquisition. These differences may indicate two acquisition strategies: (1) naming "things" and (2) encoding a broad range of experiences (Goldfield & Reznick, 1990).

Modifiers and verblike words, such as *down*, appear soon after the first word. True verbs, such as *eat* and *play*, occur even later (Gentner, 1982; Greenfield & Smith, 1976).

Two theories have been offered to explain the early appearance of nouns. One theory contends that *nouns are conceptually simpler and perceptually/con-*

ceptually distinct. The "things" that nouns represent are more perceptually cohesive than events or actions, in which perceptual elements are scattered. Therefore the child can determine the referent more easily. The names for things are provided by the adult language that surrounds the child. Prelinguistic infants perceive objects as coherent and stable. "Words that refer to these concepts are easy to learn because the child has already formed object concepts, and need only match words and concepts" (Gentner, 1982, p. 328). The child names the object as a whole, not its constituent parts (Macnamara, 1972).

According to a second theory, it is the *linguistic predictability of nouns* that makes them easier to use. Nouns represent specific items and events, and thus relate to each other and to other words in specific, predictable ways.

Other theorists have proposed explanations such as frequency of adult use, adult word order, the limited morphological adaptations of nouns, and adult teaching patterns to account for the high proportion of nouns in children's first lexicons. None of these factors seems to affect children's production. The frequency of noun appearance in adult speech is low (N. French, Carter, & Koenig, 1930). In addition, several studies have found no relationship between the frequency of occurrence in adult speech and the child's later production (R. Brown, 1973; W. Miller, 1971). It may be that more frequently named items are learned in greater numbers but less quickly than those infrequently named (R. Schwartz & Terrell, 1981). Word order varies across languages, though nouns form a universal initial lexicon. Even in English, only certain nouns appear in the most salient, or final, position. In English, nouns have few morphological adaptations, only the addition of the plural *s.* Hence, the child hears the root word more often than with verbs, which are highly inflected. However, this distinction is not true for other languages, and initial lexicons are dominated by nouns in all cultures. Finally, noun teaching is also nonuniversal. In some cultures there is very little direct language teaching of any sort. Nouns still persist.

Verbs and other words serve a relational function; they bring together items or events. Thus, a child learning language is less able to guess their meanings.

Although parents engage in very little direct language training, as noted in Chapter 7, they do modify their speech with young children to emphasize content words such as nouns. It is possible, therefore, that nouns are learned before other categories of words because of perceptual salience, frequency of appearance in adult speech to toddlers, and conflationary patterning.

Meaning of Single-Word Utterances

The toddler initially uses her language to discuss objects, events, and relations that are present before her. She has spent a year or more organizing her world, making sense of, or giving meaning to her experiences, not deriving meaning from her experiences. "The meanings are not out there in the real world waiting to be discovered but rather they are in the person who encounters the real world and imposes a meaning upon it" (Palermo, 1982, p. 336). A word refers to a stored concept rather than to an actual entity. The child's exact word meaning—what she maps upon the word—is unknown. The child's early lexicon until about 18 months of age seems to follow a rule of incompatibility. Stated simply, *if the word means X, it can't mean Y or Z.*

In general, early words map previously existing nonlinguistic categories (Clark, 1983; K. Nelson, 1977; Roberts & Horowitz, 1986; Slobin, 1973). For example, at 10 months the child seems to be highly interested in objects (Husiam & Cohen, 1981; G. Ross, 1980). As a result, many first words are object nouns.

The child's communication partner generally interprets the child's utterance with reference to the ongoing activity and to the child's nonlinguistic behavior. Adults often paraphrase the child's utterance as a full sentence, thereby implying that the child encoded the full thought. This assumption is probably erroneous. The child is operating with several constraints of attention, memory, and knowledge. In particular, she has some difficulty with the organization of information for storage and retrieval (Ervin-Tripp, 1973b; G. Olson, 1973; Slobin, 1973). Language, as a behavior, "is the end point of an information processing sequence" (Mason, 1976, p. 284).

The child's comprehension or receptive vocabulary precedes her production or expressive vocabulary. Although there is wide individual variation, the receptive vocabulary may be four times the size of the expressive vocabulary between ages 12 to 18 months (Griffiths, 1986). Some meanings will be shared with adults, while others will be private or idiosyncratic. Private meanings have little effect on communication because no one understands them except the child.

More frequently, the child's meaning encompasses a small portion of the fuller adult definition. For example, the child might hear a mature speaker say "No touch—hot!" as the child approaches the stove. Subsequently, the child may use the phrase as a general prohibition. "One of the problems of child language, in its most basic formation, is how children first make sense of, and learn from, the presumably undifferentiated stream of language that envelops them" (Whitehurst, Kedesdy, & White, 1982, p. 398).

As we have seen in Chapter 7, however, the stream of language *is* differentiated. It is not one continuous "tape" that plays in the background. One differentiation is the "Original Word Game" (R. Brown, 1956), in which the tutor, a mature language user, names things for the player, a language-learning child, who then forms hypotheses about the categorical nature of the things named. The child tests her hypotheses by trying to name new things correctly. "The tutor compares the player's utterances with his own anticipations of such utterances and, in this way, checks the accuracy of fit between his own categories and those of the player . . . [and] improves the fit by correction" (R. Brown, 1956, p. 194). The child's sources of information are the tutor's naming in the presence of the referent and the feedback received for her own utterances. Thus, "language context represents the products of a child's processing of the sensory and social information gained through interactions within the environment" (McLean & Snyder-McLean, 1978, p. 44). "The fashionable assertion that language is learned but not taught . . . is nowhere less true than in the child's acquisition of a lexicon" (Ninio & Bruner, 1978, p. 2). New words are acquired more easily if the tutor presents the word and its referent simultaneously and exclusively, and if the referent is one for which the child has an expressed preference (Whitehurst et al., 1982). Unfortunately, this analysis explains very little of the child's underlying hypothesis construction and testing process.

Concept Formation

When a toddler uses the word *dog* for a horse but not for a poodle, it is difficult to determine the concept of *dog* that underlies the child's word. Naturally, adults might conclude that the child is using perceptual characteristics. This explanation is insufficient, however, for the meaning of words in other, nonnoun classes, such as *more* and *here*.

Several hypotheses have been proposed to explain concept formation and word learning. These include the semantic-feature hypothesis (E. Clark, 1973a, 1973b, 1975), the functional-core hypothesis (K. Nelson, 1974, 1977), and the associative (Vygotsky, 1962) and prototypic complex hypotheses (Bowerman, 1978). Each theoretical position assumes that the child organizes word concepts in a certain manner based on recognition of certain aspects of the referent.

Before we examine the concepts that underlie early words, we must state some seemingly obvious but easily forgotten points. As adults, we do not really know what a given word or statement means to a child. We can only infer the child's meaning from the linguistic and nonlinguistic contexts. When linguists perform this type of contextual analysis, it is called a *rich interpretation*. For example, a child might say "Open." Noting that she is struggling to get her shoe on and that she has responded to your query "What's the problem?", an adult concludes that the child wants help. The linguist interprets "Open" as a general request for aid.

Semantic-Feature Hypothesis. Eve Clark has proposed what is known as the semantic-feature hypothesis—that all referents can be defined by a universal set of semantic features, such as animate/inanimate or human/nonhuman. The child establishes meaning by combining features that are present and perceivable in the environment. These perceptual features are the attributes of the referent, such as shape, size, and movement. Clark has asserted that shape is the most salient of the perceptual features. Color does not appear to be particularly important to young children (Rice, 1978). Not all perceptual features are visible; children can also recognize entities by taste, smell, and hearing. For example, the child might shout "doggie" when she hears a dog bark.

The child's definition of *doggie*, therefore, may include features such as four legs, fur, barking, and tail. When she encounters a new example of the concept *doggie*, or one that is close, such as a bear, the child must apply the perceptual attribute criteria to determine the name of this new being. Since we occasionally encounter three-legged, hairless, nonbarking, or tailless dogs, the child may use a subset of the criteria, such as three out of four characteristics. As the child matures, she adds or deletes features, and the concept becomes more specific, thus more closely resembling the generally accepted meaning. Initially, the child may actually think that the label for the referent is a characteristic of that referent. In my own family, my children had always known me with a beard and called me "daddy." When I shaved off the beard, my daughter began to call me "Bob." As one of her toddler brothers explained, "You not daddy; now you bes Bob."

The major disadvantage of the feature approach is that it fails to explain the holistic nature of meaning or to discriminate between features to determine the most relevant ones (Palermo, 1982). In short, even a three-legged, hairless, non-barking, tailless dog is a dog, if a somewhat shopworn one. There is a totality to the definition that transcends the individual features of an object. The perception of the features alone is not the same as the concept. Even people who are unaware of the biological similarities of taxonomic categories use similar systems of classification for animals such as cats and dogs (Berlin, Breedlove, & Raven, 1973).

The feature hypothesis is also inadequate as an explanation of nonobject concepts, such as *more, all gone*, and *up*. "For many such words the governing concept or cross-situational invariance involves a certain kind of relationship between two objects or events or between two states of the same object or event across time" (Bowerman, 1978, p. 268). Frequently the objects involved have very few, if any, similar features.

Functional-Core Hypothesis.   After studying the early lexicons of 18 young children, Kathryn Nelson (1974) concluded that "the one outstanding general characteristic of the early words is their reference to objects and events that are perceived in dynamic relationship: that is, actions, sounds, transformations—in short, variation of all kinds" (p. 269). This dynamic base seems to result from learning principles of the child rather than being part of adult teaching strategies. Thus, in what Nelson calls the **functional-core hypothesis**, it is the motion features, rather than the static perceptual features, that are salient and from which the child derives meaning. Nelson has rejected the notion of class membership as determined by perceptual features. Concept formation begins with the formation of a functional-core meaning to which perceptual features may be added.

The child begins meaningful speech by naming objects that embody a high degree of movement or that she can manipulate. These are the entities to which young children attend (Kagan, 1970). The functional-core hypothesis is appealing because it relates to just such aspects of early child development. For example, Piaget observed that infants investigate object functions through manipulation and demonstrate early object knowledge by using an object for its intended purpose. A brush used in a certain accepted manner indicates that the infant has a notion or concept of "brushness." Thus early experience provides the basis for concept learning. In addition, functional concepts are relational in that they describe an entity's use in relation to other entities, such as the relationship of brush to hair. These relationships could explain the concepts underlying many early two-word utterances.

To some extent, the early spoken definitions of children lend support to an underlying functional concept. Stop for a moment and compose your own definition of *apple*. You would probably say that it is "a red, round fruit grown on trees in moderate climates" or something similar. In contrast, a child's definition might be "something you eat." A *dog* becomes "something that lives in your house and sleeps outside in a little house." Children's definitions have a strong element of function or action.

According to Nelson, the concept of static perceptual features is too analytical for very young children. Rather, concepts are defined in terms of logical relationships or logical acts. Concept acquisition is an "attempt to comprehend the exemplars of the concept with a functional or relational rule rather than through the specification of a set of critical attributes" (1974, p. 274).

Not everyone supports the functional-core hypothesis. Neither Bowerman (1978) nor E. Clark (1973b, 1975) could find extensive use of shared function in child utterances, and Nelson's own data (1973a) are not abundant. In contrast, Bowerman (1978) concluded, "Rather, the children often disregarded functional differences, i.e., gross disparities in the way objects act or can be acted upon, that were well known to them in the interests of classifying purely on the basis of perceptual similarities" (p. 265). For example, young Eva (in Bowerman's research) used the word *moon* for the moon, a half grapefruit, a lemon slice, a circular chrome dial, a ball of spinach on her plate, and so on. Although the action or use of these entities is very dissimilar, the shapes are all spherical or crescent. In addition, the word *moon* was uttered when the objects were static and at a distance.

Associative and Prototypic Complexes.   According to Melissa Bowerman (1978), "Theories built around only one basic class of similarities, whether perceptual or functional, are too restricted to account for the rich diversity of ways in which children can recognize constancies from one situation to the next" (pp. 268–269). Rather, Bowerman proposed, the child uses words "complexively," shifting from one feature to another with each use. This shifting might indicate the lack of some defining criteria or a loosely defined criterion for the concept. In fact, there seems to be little difference in the learning of labels whether the features are functionally or perceptually based (R. Schwartz & Leonard, 1984).

Vygotsky (1934), who was previously discussed in Chapter 5, theorized that successive instances of a word may not necessarily share anything with each other. According to his **associative complex hypothesis**, however, each instance shares some feature with a central instance or core concept. For example, Clark (1973a) described a child who produced the word *baby* in the presence of a younger infant, extended it to himself, to pictures of himself, to books with pictures, and finally to all books.

Bowerman and others have expanded this notion to propose a **prototypic complex hypothesis**, in which the child's underlying concept includes a central reference or prototype, usually the referent most frequently used with the adult speech model and the first referent for which the word was used. Thus the child has a highly specific, stored mental representation of the concept. A "best fit" criterion is used to decide if a new instance is an example of the concept (Palmer,

1978). In other words, the closer the new instance is to the prototype, the more it is likely to be called by that name. Bowerman reported that Eva originally produced the word *kick* when she propelled a ball with her foot. Subsequently, she used the word for a moth and for the "hitting of a bicycle with her kiddicar." The moth was similar in limb movement, and the kiddicar incident duplicated the striking of an object.

The prototypic complex hypothesis has much appeal. The nonlinguistic categories of 7- to 9-month-old children may be organized around prototypes as well, since exposure to prototypes facilitates category formation (Roberts & Horowitz, 1986). In addition, if children's meanings are based on a central referent, there appears to be a continuum from infancy to adulthood. Bowerman (1978) has noted that "a large number of adult semantic categories are characterized by this kind of structure" (p. 279). Some adult concepts are finite, while other concept boundaries, especially those of categorical terms, are fuzzy. Some instances are always included in the concept, others only in certain contexts. For example, the prototype for the concept *furniture* probably does not represent any one piece of furniture (Figure 8.1). In other words, there is no one best exemplar at the center of the concept. Some items, such as a table or a sofa, are good examples of the concept. Others, such as a footstool or a cot, are less so. A lamp, though considered to be furniture, is even further from the central concept (see Figure 8.1). A second example is the concept *bird*. Some examples, such as a robin and a sparrow, are prototypic. Others, such as a parrot, an ostrich, and a pelican, are not. The degree to which a particular instance is considered to be prototypic of the concept is related to the number of features the example has in common with other referents of the concept. The most prototypical examples share the most features. Obviously, some features are more central than others.

Older children and adults seem to analyze a concept into its essential features, which are used to determine the "goodness-of-fit" of new exemplars (Greenberg & Kuczaj, 1982). We are not sure of the process used by young children. They may use a holistic-based comparison (Anglin, 1975; Posner, 1973), "utilizing both perceptual and functional information" (Greenberg & Kuczaj, 1982, p. 298). It is possible that toddlers are capable of feature analysis for comparison purposes (Bowerman, 1978). Initially the child acquires a word with a prototypic referent. The mother aids the child's referential process by supplying superordinate or categorical names to the most typical examples of the concept. Typical dogs are labeled *doggie*. Atypical dogs are labeled by less frequently used breed names, such as *chihuahua* or *afghan* (Whitehurst et al., 1982). Larger categories, such as *animal*, have fewer perceptual or functional similarities (Horton & Markman, 1979). During this period the child makes a preliminary identification of the attributes and salient features that characterize the prototypic referent (Barrett, 1982). Therefore, meaning consists initially of the prototypic referent and a small group of features. These features can be recognized independently when they do not occur together. Hence, the child is able to extend the word to other exemplars. The child's meaning may lack some features critical to the adult concept but may

FIGURE 8.1   Possible Prototypic Concept of *Furniture* with Exemplars

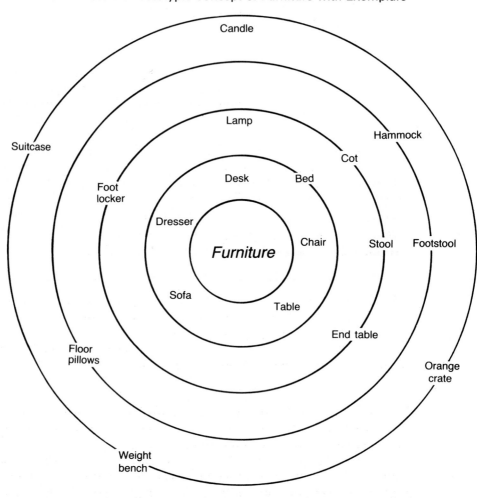

include other features that are not. It is important to note that it is the child who determines the related features; adults generally provide only the label.

The child now assigns the word to a particular semantic group based on the identified features (Barrett, 1982). The word's referent is grouped with other referents that have similar features. For example, the referent may be identified as a mover or causer of action and hence may be classed with other causative agents. Obviously, some features have more "definingness" for a semantic category than others (E. Smith, Shoben, & Rips, 1974).

The final step is to identify the features that distinguish the prototypic referent of this word from those of other words within the same semantic field.

For example, toys and foods are both receivers of action and fill a semantic function called *object*, discussed later in this chapter, but the two concepts are very different. Thus, meaning consists of the prototypic referent, a set of features that define the word's semantic field, and a set of features that differentiate the prototypic referent from the referents of other words in the same semantic field.

Initial prototypes will vary across children, reflecting different experiences. The concept prototypes change as well; concepts are modified as a result of experience. Concept formation and refinement is an ongoing process. Even among adults, subtle concept changes occur with experience and, as a result, meanings are refined.

Initial concept formation is based on holistic inclusion of prototypic exemplars. Decisions of relatedness, however, are determined by the similarities between the prototype and the new instance or example. According to Bowerman (1978), this analytic process is nonholistic in nature.

Extension: Under, Over, and Otherwise

In the process of refining meanings, the child forms hypotheses about underlying concepts and extends her current meanings to include new examples (R. Brown, 1965). Through this extension process, the child gains knowledge from exemplars and nonexemplars of the concept. Occasionally concepts are very restricted; others are widely extended. Overly restricted meanings that contain fewer exemplars than the adult meaning are called **underextensions**. Using "cup" for a "Tommy Tippee cup" is an example of underextension. In contrast, **overextensions** are meanings that are too broad, containing more exemplars than the adult meaning. Calling all men "Daddy" is an example of overextension. Note that these terms are used in reference to the adult meaning. As for the child, she is applying her hypothesized meaning, not the adult's meaning. It is also important to note that children usually do not overgeneralize or overextend in their comprehension of words (Fremgen & Fay, 1980). Children often comprehend the adult meaning but use their own meaning in expression.

The child receives implicit and explicit feedback about her concept extensions (Anglin, 1977). Implicit feedback can be found in the naming practices of others, to which the child attends. In contrast, explicit feedback includes direct correction or confirmation of the child's extensions by more mature language users. As the child extends her meaning of cup from her own "Tommy Tippee," she may include bowls and pots in addition to coffee mugs and tea cups. In the course of daily events, more mature speakers will call bowls and pots by their accepted names and correct the child's attempts more directly.

Much of the literature on early meanings is based on these meaning extensions. It may be incorrect to assume, however, that the criteria used for extension are those used in formation of the initial concept. Other factors, such as a lack of specific words in the child's lexicon, may account for behavior that appears to adults to be overextension. If the child could verbalize the situation, she might say, "I know that that thing is not a dog, but I don't know what else to call it, and it is like a dog, so I'll call it a dog" (L. Bloom, 1973, p. 79). It is possible for the child to underextend and overextend a word at the same time (Greenberg & Kuczaj, 1982). For example, the child may use the word *dog* to refer to a sheep but not a Newfoundland.

As the child gains experience, she uses fewer and fewer overextensions and underextensions. In addition, she broadens her categories to include more and more disparate but similar examples. Adult feedback to children can help them adjust their overextensions. An adult demonstration of the important attributes that make X an X is more helpful than providing the correct label or correcting the child's overextension error (Mervis & Mervis, 1988).

When we examine both extensions and overextensions of the first 75 words, perceptual similarity seems to account for nearly 60% of both (Rescorla, 1980). These results support a number of hypotheses on the bases of extension (Anglin, 1977; Barrett, 1978; Bowerman, 1976; E. Clark, 1973b; Thomson & Chapman, 1977). Most perceptual similarities seem to be visual. Action or functional similarity accounts for about 25% of children's extensions. Contextual association of an object with the event in which it is used seems to account for only about 12% of extensions. For example, a child may use the word *nap* when referring to a blanket. Finally, a very small number of extensions are based upon affective similarity. More than half of these extensions involve prohibitive or frightening words, such as *hot* or *bad*.

The majority of children seem to use words correctly (Rescorla, 1980). Most words are used for generalized referents rather than for a single referent. Within 1 month of acquisition, more than three-fourths of words are generalized to more than one referent. Of the remainder, most are names for specific entities, such as *mama*. Words acquired during initial lexical growth are more likely to be overgeneralized than words acquired later; however, the overgeneralization does not occur at once, but rather during the period of rapid vocabulary growth preceding early multiword utterances. Early words are also more likely to exhibit underextension and associative complexes. Thus, "it appears that there are a set of words present in many early vocabularies which are used multifunctionally as central or organizing concepts for articulation of much of the child's experience" (Rescorla, 1980, p. 330).

Approximately a third of the first 75 words seem to be overextended (Rescorla, 1980). Some categories, such as letters, vehicles, and clothing, are overextended at a greater rate than others. Many children may overextend words such as *car, truck, shoe, hat, dada, baby, apple, cheese, ball, dog*, and *hot*. "Words are not usually overextended to label objects for which the child already acquired more appropriate names" (Barrett, 1982, p. 325).

Underextensions are common in both receptive and expressive language. In contrast, overextension is usually limited to expressive language, although there is considerable individual variation (Rescorla, 1980; Thomson & Chapman, 1977). At this early stage of acquisition, toddlers comprehend many more words than they produce. The child who is able to point to a motorcycle, bike, truck, plane, and helicopter may label all of them *car* (Rescorla, 1976). When overextension does occur in comprehension, it is usually based on perceptual similarities

(Behrend, 1988). Overextensions tend to fall into three general types: categorical overinclusions, analogical overextensions, and predicate statements. Most overextensions are categorical overinclusions. Children frequently use a word to label a referent in a related category. For example, the child may use *baby* for all children, *hot* for cold, or *dada* for mother. The largest number of generalizations are within the people category.

Analogical overextensions include the use of a word to label a referent not related categorically. Rather, the inferred similarity is perceptual, functional, or affective. For example, children may use *ball* to refer to round objects or *comb* to label a centipede.

With predicate statements, children note the relationship between the object and some absent person, object, property, or state. For example, a child might say "doll" when seeing the empty bed or "door" when requesting adult assistance with opening or closing some object (Griffiths & Atkinson, 1978). Unlike the other two types, predicate statements are relational and therefore may represent presyntactic productions (Greenfield & Smith, 1976). Types of predicate overextensions are shown in Table 8.5.

In summary, it appears that extension and overextension are aspects of the same word-acquisition process. "In both cases, extension is generated in the same manner, is based on many of the same criteria of application, and takes place over the same period" (Rescorla, 1980, p. 334). Overextension seems to serve a dual function: as a device for expressing categorization and concept formation and as a presyntactic means to convey relationships. Overextension usually ends when the child begins to use the acceptable adult meaning, probably because of adult unwillingness to accept the child's overinclusiveness.

Semantic Class Distinctions

Several linguists have suggested that children organize their early words by semantic categories. (See the psycholinguistic-semantic/cognitive section of Chapter 2.) At the two-word stage, children follow simple word-order patterns of construction based on semantic distinctions. It has been assumed, therefore, that these distinctions are present prior to the appearance of two-word utterances. These distinctions suggest a continuity from single-word to multiword

---

TABLE 8.5   Predicate Overextensions

Statement type	Example
Former or unusual state	*Cookie* for empty plate
Anticipations	*Key* while before door
Elements	*Water* for turned-off hose
Specific activity	*Peepee* for toilet
Pretending	*Nap* while pretending to sleep

Source: Adapted from Thomson, J., & Chapman, R. Who is "Daddy" revisited: The status of two year olds' overextended words in use and comprehension. *Journal of Child Language*, 1977, 4, 359–375.

structures (Greenfield & Smith, 1976; Rodgon, Jankowski, & Alenskas, 1977; Starr, 1975). Some linguists have argued that different types of knowledge are required for the use of single-word and multiword utterances. Children at the single-word stage may refer to the total situation, both entities and dynamic states (Werner & Kaplan, 1963). For example, a child observes Daddy throwing a ball and says "ball" to describe the entire event. Behavior at the two-word stage indicates the cognitive ability to separate entities from dynamic states and relationships (Ingram, 1971; Macnamara, 1972). At this point, a child may say "Daddy throw" or "throw ball." Since the single-word utterance stage represents limitations in processing and production as well as in memory, we cannot be sure of the child's underlying referencing abilities. Children may be separating entities and dynamic states but may be unable to encode more than one element.

Substantive and Relational Categories.   Variation can be found in the semantic structure of early child utterances. In general, early single-word utterances can be classified as either of two large semantic categories, *substantive* or *relational*, depending on the words used and their intended meaning (L. Bloom & Lahey, 1978).

Substantive words refer to specific entities or classes of entities that have certain shared perceptual or functional features. Much of the early section of this chapter has been devoted to a discussion of this category of word. Examples include *mama, dada, doggie, cup,* and *hat.*

Early word combinations indicate that children classify substantive words on the basis of action. One class, **agents,** is the source of action; the other, **objects,** is the recipient of action. These noun-type words appear alone and in the singular, rather than plural, form.

Relational words refer to relations that an entity shares with itself or with other entities. In relation to itself, an entity can exist or not exist, disappear and reappear. For example, when an entity exists or is present, the child might point and say "that." In contrast, when it disappears, she might say "all gone." Other entities may share static states (possession and attribution), dynamic states (actions), or locations.

Relational words make reference across entities. As such, they express relational meanings that transcend the individual objects involved. For example, the utterance "all gone" can apply to an empty glass or bowl or to a vacant dog house. Use of relational words is evidence that the child is able to conceptualize and encode the dynamic state separately from the entity involved (Werner & Kaplan, 1963). This ability represents attainment of sensorimotor knowledge (Sinclair, 1970), including notions of object permanence, object constancy, and causality. The most common relational categories are reflexive, including existence, nonexistence, disappearance, and recurrence; action; location; possession; and attribution.

The most frequent relational words in early speech are reflexive in that they relate the object to itself (L. Bloom & Lahey, 1978). **Reflexive relational words** mark existence, nonexistence, disappearance, and recurrence (see Table 8.6). The re-

TABLE 8.6   Reflexive Relational Words in the Single-Word Utterances of Young Children

Type	Explanation	Examples
Existence	Child's attention gained by an entity, especially a novel one: notes that it exists	May point and say "this," "that," "here," or "what's that?"
Nonexistence	Child notes that an entity is not present though expected	"No" or "gone" or name of object with a rising intonation
Disappearance	Child notes that an entity that was present has disappeared	"Gone," "all gone," "away," "bye-bye" ("all gone" may be used as a request that an entity disappear or as a notice that it has moved)
Recurrence	Child notes that an object appears after an absence or that another object replaces an absent one	"More," "again," or "another" (may be used to request reappearance or to note additional entities)

lations are expressed by words such as *this, there, uh-oh, gone,* and *nuther.* For some children, these reflexive relational terms are the predominant forms found in their early lexicons (L. Bloom, 1973; Corrigan, 1976; Sinclair, 1970). Relational words conveying visual displacement, such as *bye* and *uh-oh,* occur in sensorimotor stage V, when these cognitive skills have been attained. Absent-relational terms, such as *all gone* and *more,* convey invisible displacement and occur later in stage VI (Tomasello & Farrar, 1984).

A second group consists of **action relational words**. The predominant concept in children's early speech is "the ways in which the different objects from the different concepts . . . relate to one another through movements or actions" (L. Bloom & Lahey, 1978, p. 134). Early meanings center on action. Although nominals dominate as a percentage of many children's vocabularies, they do not dominate in use even in languages as different as English and Japanese (L. Bloom, 1973; Tanouye, 1979). Even locatives initially signal a direction of movement rather than a location. Very few of the child's action words are true action verbs. Instead, the child uses words such as *in* to accompany putting one object into another or *off* to describe separation. These types of words, called *proto-verbs,* are the first action-type words to develop (Barrett, 1983; Clark, 1979). Although terms such as *in, out, off, up, down, no, on here, inside, there, get down, bye-bye,* and *ni-night* are not verbs, they are used by the child in verblike contexts (Barrett, 1983; Benedict, 1979; Clark, 1979). Children also use *here* and *there* to accompany action sequences (McCune-Nicolich, 1981). *Here* is often used to accompany exchange games. When a child passes an object to her partner, she may accompany that action with the word *here,* in imitation of her mother's behavior. *There* follows the completion of an action. A child may use both terms in this manner for several months before she uses them as location words (Carter, 1975b).

Following the development of protoverbs, several kinds of action-type words appear, including general-purpose, deictic, object-related action-specific, and intransitive action-specific (Clark, 1979; Huttenlocher, Smiley, & Charney, 1983). General-purpose action words, such as *do, put*, and *make*, do not refer to any specific action and must be interpreted from the context. Deictic action words, which must be interpreted from the perspective of the speaker, include words such as *lookit* and are used to direct the listener's attention. Object-related action-specific words, such as *push* and *drink*, refer to precise actions performed on objects. Finally, intransitive action-specific words represent precise non-object-related actions, such as *walk*.

Location relational words describe the directional or spatial relationship of two objects. Dynamic locative events are acquired before, and occur more frequently than, static spatial relationships (Bloom, Lightbown, & Hood, 1975). Thus, the child is more likely to comment on a knock at the door ("door") than on a shoe residing on a chair ("chair").

Finally, state relations include possession and attribution. **Possession relational words** recognize that an object is associated with a particular person. Initially possessives are used to mark alienable possessions, such as food, clothing, and toys, rather than body parts or relatives (R. Brown, 1973). The possessive relationship may be one of the few features of the object that the child knows. For example, the child may say "Juan" to note her brother's football gear but know little else about the equipment. In addition to names of other people, the child may use her own name or say "mine."

Attribution relational words mark the attributes, characteristics, or differences between similar objects, such as *big, little, dirty, hot, funny*, and *yukky*. Attributes seem to be used more as names than as properties of objects (L. Bloom & Lahey, 1978). As a class, attributes are rare in single-word and early multiword utterances.

One additional category may be *mismatch* (McCune-Nicolich, 1981), in which conditions conflict with the child's expectations, desires, or efforts. She may respond with a protesting "no" or with a startled "uh-oh" (Bloom, 1973; Carter, 1975a; Dore, 1974; Greenfield & Smith, 1976; Rodgon, 1976). Parents use both words in similar situations, the latter often accompanied by a high-low musical contour that may be learned before the actual phonetics.

Although substantive and relational words develop during the single-word period, the onset of relational words is "somewhat abrupt" (McCune-Nicolich, 1981). In contrast, use of substantive words has a more linear growth. Relational words are also less likely to occur as imitations, which lends support to the idea that the child has a sensorimotor knowledge base for the concepts she expresses. The supposedly universal nature of sensorimotor thought may account for the widespread appearance of these early semantic categories. Variation in the topics or substantives children "discuss" reflects the different experiential background of each child.

Order of Appearance. Several linguists have studied the order of acquisition of semantic categories or functions (Bloom et al., 1975; Leonard, 1976; Menyuk, 1974; Wells, 1985). For most children, initial words may be "pure performatives"; that is, the word itself performs the act named (such as *hi* and *bye-bye*) (Menyuk, 1974). These precede operations of reference (Leonard, 1976), including nomination of substantive words, existence, nonexistence, disappearance, recurrence, and negation. The action function develops next, coincident with the agent and object functions for substantive words. These are followed by the attribution, location, and possession functions. "Children seem to acquire words that encode concepts they have just developed or are in the process of developing" (Gopnik & Meltzoff, 1984, p. 495). The specific links between the acquisition of particular types of meanings and particular cognitive achievements are not known. Not all children will adhere to this order of appearance of semantic categories. The frequency of appearance of a semantic function may depend on the child's frequency of experience with the objects and events marked (Bloom, 1973). Later, the frequency of use probably reflects the communication value of the semantic functions for the child.

EARLY MULTIWORD COMBINATIONS

When children begin to combine words into longer utterances at about 18 months of age, they do so in predictable patterns that appear to be universal (R. Brown, 1973). With increasing memory and processing skills, the child is able to produce longer utterances by recombining these early patterns. Language learning in much of the latter half of the second year involves these combinations. It is important to keep in mind, however, that the child still produces a great many single-word utterances.

Transition: Early Word Combinations

Prior to the appearance of two-word utterances is a period in which the child produces sequences of words and sounds in seeming combination and in a variety of forms. One transitional form consists of a CV syllable preceding or following a word. The phonology of the extra syllable is inconsistent and has no referent (Dore, Franklin, Miller, & Ramer, 1976). For example, the child might say the following on several different occasions:

> ma baby
> te baby
> bu baby

Other forms may be more consistent but still have no referent. Empty forms include a word plus a preceding or following sound in which the word, rather than the nonreferential element, varies (Bloom, 1973). Examples of empty forms are as follows:

> beda cookie
> beda baby
> beda doggie

A third form consists of reduplications of a single utterance, such as "Doggie doggie" (Dore et al., 1976). Other seeming combinations may actually consist of two words learned as a single unit (Ingram, 1979). In general, the child uses the two words neither as single words nor in combination with others. Common examples of single-unit words include

> all gone
> go bye
> so big
> go potty

Finally, some children reportedly produce successive single-word utterances, although some child language experts question the occurrence of this behavior (Branigan, 1979). In these successive utterances, each word occurs with terminal falling pitch and relatively equal stress, and there is a pause between words (Dore, 1975; Rodgon, 1976; Scollon, 1974). To understand the terminal falling pitch contour, try a little experiment. Say "mommy" in a matter-of-fact manner. Note that you drop your pitch at the end of the word.

> Mommy. ↓

Now say "laugh." Again, there should have been a drop in pitch.

> Laugh. ↓

The next part is more difficult. Say the two words in succession, with a momentary pause between them. Since "mommy" + "laugh" approximates a mature sentence form, it may be difficult to drop your pitch after each word. It may help if you reverse the order.

> Mommy ↓   Laugh ↓   or   Laugh ↓   Mommy ↓

Compare this pitch contour to the utterance "Mommy laugh." In the two-word combination, the drop in pitch occurs only at the end of the utterance.

> Mommy laugh ↓

Bloom and others noted these pitch contour differences between successive single-word and early two-word utterances. In addition, the word order of single-word utterances is variable, unlike that of two-word combinations.

Not all linguists agree, however, on the existence of successive single-word utterances. It is possible that both successive single-word and two-word patterns are present at the same time. Initial successive single-word utterances may exhibit a terminal falling pitch with each word. The child soon modifies pitch contours to resemble those of short adult utterances, though she still uses a somewhat longer pause. Such a progression might be expected, given the well-documented ability of young children to adopt adult intonational patterns. Finally, at about 18 months of age, the pitch, pause, and word-order characteristics approximate those of the adult. At this point, most child specialists credit the child with multiword utterances.

Two-Word Combinations

Children seem to comprehend two-word utterances before they produce them. This statement is not absolute, however, because children may key into certain words or to context rather than to word order for interpretation (Bloom, 1974; R. Clark, Hutcheson, & van Buren, 1974; Wetstone & Friedlander, 1973).

In the initial period of word combination, the child may experiment with a variety of rules. Individual differences in the actual words chosen and in the combination forms used are great (Goldfield & Snow, 1985) and may reflect individual strategies for rule acquisition. Some children seem to focus on individual words and their combinations, whereas others focus on small groups of words classed according to meaning (B. Brown & Leonard, 1986). By 24 months, however, the average child is using two-word utterances frequently in her speech (Wells, 1985).

Some words are used without any positional consistency. In this *groping pattern* (B. Brown & Leonard, 1986) the child uses a word regardless of semantic class. For example, the child might say "Eat cookie" or "Cookie eat" without regard for word order or position. A second form, the *positional associative pattern* (Braine, 1976), is characterized by consistent word order but reflects patterns heard in adult speech, such as "Stop that" and "Come here," and does not appear to be a creative rule system. Finally, a third strategy, the *positional productive pattern* (Braine, 1976), is characterized by consistent word order and creative combinations. Following a rule such as action + object (Table 8.7), the child might create "Eat cookie," "Throw ball," "Up me," "Drink juice," and so on.

The child's earliest two-word combinations probably reflect rules that she has constructed for each of the words involved. Before long, these rules proliferate and become cumbersome. There appears to be a developmental order in the child's acquisition of two-word phrases. Words used in positional productive patterns (consistent word order as heard in adult speech) are acquired before those used in the other two patterns, groping and associative (B. Brown & Leonard, 1986), possibly because the child has had more time to become familiar with the semantic aspects of these earlier words.

Simple word-order rules relative to the child's semantic categories provide an adequate system for elaborating upon her meanings and for interpreting adult utterances beyond the information contained in the words themselves. "By arranging words in orders agreed upon by the language community, the child can go beyond the words alone to express the relationships holding between them" (J. de Villiers and P. de Villiers, 1979, p. 46). In fact, in languages such as English in which word order is important, the earliest rules used relate to ordering (R. Brown, 1973).

TABLE 8.7   Two-Word Semantic Rules*

Semantic-Syntactic Rule (L. Bloom, 1973; R. Brown, 1973; Schlesinger, 1971)	Examples
Modifier + head	
Attributive + entity	*Big doggie*
Possessor + possession	*Daddy shoe*
Recurrent + X	*Nuther cookie* *More up*
Negative + X	
Nonexistence or disappearance	*No juice* *Allgone (ba)nana*
Rejection (of proposal)	*No bed* (when told it's bedtime)
Denial (of statement)	*No baby* (when referred to as such)
Demonstrative + entity	*This cup*
X + locative	*Doggie bed* *Throw me*
X + dative	*Give mommy* *Cookie mommy*
Agent + action	*Daddy eat* *Mommy throw*
Action + object	*Eat cookie* *Throw ball*
Agent + object	*Daddy cookie* *Mommy ball*

*This table represents a combination of the work of several researchers and an attempt to remain true to the meanings of early child utterances.

The early combination rules can be described as **semantic–syntactic**—semantic because the bases for combination are meaning relations and syntactic because word-order rules and relationships pertain (L. Bloom & Lahey, 1978). Thus, "children launch their syntactic careers by learning simple order rules for combining words which perform semantic functions" (Bowerman, 1973b, p. 213). Initially word order varies, but it stabilizes shortly before the child begins to use grammatical markers, such as possessive *s* (Chi-Minh's toy) and past tense *ed* (walk*ed*). Use of these markers would seem to indicate that the grammatical functions they serve are present earlier but marked by other means, such as word order.

Semantic Rules

One of the results of the Semantic Revolution of the early 1970s was that linguists attempted to describe the two-word linear or word-order rules of young children. The motivation was to describe the rules for word combination that children seemed to be following and to find similarities in the language of young children that might suggest universal meaning categories (R. Brown, 1973). The resultant rules, combined in Table 8.7, may account for as much as 70% of the multiword utterances of English-speaking children. Not all researchers have found so large a percentage (Arlman-Rupp, van Niekerk de Haan, & van de Sandt-Koenderman, 1976).

Reflexive two-word semantic expansions, such as "More milk" or "Allgone juice," represent a combined meaning of little more than the individual words. Neither word's meaning changes as a result of the combination. The linear order of combination is relatively constant, and initial two-word utterances usually are of this type (L. Bloom, 1973; Wells, 1985). Other expansions, such as those involving a verb, do not have a constant word order. The word order depends on the semantic relationship of the words involved. The relationship is not simply linear but represents the relationship of verbs to different types of nouns. Some types of nouns precede the verb; others follow it. Action expansions, possessives, and locatives develop after the reflexive expansions (L. Bloom, 1973; Wells, 1985).

The reflexive functions, "the three basic operations of reference" (R. Brown, 1973, p. 193), include nomination (*this/that* + *nominative*), recurrence (*recurrent* + *head*), and nonexistence (*negative* + *X*). A two-word nomination consists of the demonstrative or introducer word (*this, that*) plus some entity, as in "That ball." If the child initiates the utterance, she accompanies it with a pointing gesture. In contrast, she usually does not point when responding to a question.

Recurrence is used initially as a request, such as "Nuther (another) cookie" or "More jump." Later, such forms will also be used to comment on a situation. Although children seem to make little distinction between *more* and *another*, they usually do not use *another* with verbs (R. Brown, 1973).

Nonexistence/disappearance is the predominant type of negative. It is often used with the expectation of return. As with recurrence, nonexistence/disappearance may be used to comment or request. Negative forms can also be used for rejection, as when the child pushes away a bowl of strained peas with a "No" or "No peas." A third form of negative is denial, often found in the word games of parents and children. To the parent's question "Is this a book?", asked while holding a cup, the child responds "No book."

Nearly all children are using reflexive semantic functions before 15 months of age (Wells, 1985). This category dominates in children's utterances, accounting for approximately 70%, until almost 2 years of age. By 36 months, reflexive functions may account for as little as 10% of children's utterances (Wells, 1985).

The primary "relational types" (R. Brown, 1973) consist of *X* + *locative*, in which *X* may be almost any word, *possessor* + *head* (possession), *attributive* + *entity*, *agent* + *action*, *action* + *object*, and *agent* + *object*. Usually, the locative function is signaled in two ways: *entity* + *locative*, which develops first, and *action* + *locative*. *Entity* + *locative* constructions include a stationary entity and its location or an entity moving or being moved plus the direction of movement (*up*) or the location. In general, the static entity develops prior to the moving one

(Wells, 1985). In the *action + locative* type, the child names the action and direction of movement in relation to some location (*up*) (L. Bloom, Miller, & Hood, 1975). By 21 months, the average child is using locative functions (Wells, 1985).

Two-word locative utterances (*X + locative*) and possessive (*possessive + head*) begin to appear at about the same time as the object-related utterances but take longer for most children to learn (Wells, 1985). By age 2, 90% of children are using these constructions. The use of agents or objects in the *X* position of locatives precedes the use of action words. This is expected because children encode static locations and possessions before directional movement or changing possession.

Generally, the *possessor + possession* construction is used for alienable possessions, such as clothes or toys, as in the single-word phase. Inalienable entities, such as body parts, do not appear with possessor words initially because the owner is obvious. Very few possessive pronouns are used, except *my*.

Attributive (*attributive + head*) and *agent + action* and *action + object* two-word utterances are used by some children at around 1 ½ years but take even longer than the other categories for most children to learn (Wells, 1985). They are not used by 90% of children until 30 months. Initially attributive words describe physical characteristics, such as "big." In English the *attributive + head* construction may vary in word order. English-speaking adults may say "blue book" or "the book is blue." At this stage, however, the attribute generally precedes. By 24 months, the average child is using this construction.

The action categories initially take the two-word forms *agent + want* and *want + object*. Some studies have found very few true action words in early constructions (Wells, 1985). Action words appear later in two-word utterances, initially as unspecific actions or protoverbs, such as "do," or as particles of verbs, such as *off*, *on*, and *away*.

The child's initial notion of agent words is probably restricted to animate entities (J. de Villiers & P. de Villiers, 1978). Nonagentive words usually do not appear in this position in child utterances, although these can fulfill the subject function in adult sentences. The child probably does not have the abstract notion of subject (Bowerman, 1973b). While agents cause action, objects are the recipients of the action. The *agent + object* construction has a very low incidence and is not found universally (R. Brown, 1973).

Stress Patterns and Meaning. At the two-word level, a child's meaning is often difficult to interpret. Small functor words, such as articles and prepositions, are omitted. In general, more mature language users employ a rich interpretation using the linguistic and nonlinguistic contexts to determine meaning. The child's word order is a clue to her meaning, but it may be ambiguous. Suppose that the child says "doggie bed." Is she commenting on the dog's new cushion (*possessor + possession*) or warning that Fido still prefers to sleep on Mommy's bed (*entity + locative*)? The child may aid this interpretive process.

Children use stress, or emphasis, to indicate meaning (W. Miller & Ervin-Tripp, 1964). As shown in the hierarchy of stress (Figure 8.2), a child could be

---

FIGURE 8.2   Hierarchy of Stress in Child Speech

Increasing stress	↑	New information
		Locative
		Possessor
		Noun object
		Action
		Pronoun object
Decreasing stress	↓	Agent

---

expected to stress the action term in an *agent + action* utterance and the object in an *action + object*. New information receives the most stress, as we might expect, since it is novel to the conversation. The newness criterion is seen throughout the hierarchy. We can assume, for instance, that a pronoun object is old information, since pronouns are used to refer to previously identified entities. In contrast, noun objects would represent newer information. Applying the hierarchy to "doggie bed," interpretation becomes easier. A comment on the dog's new bed would be "*doggie* bed," while a warning of the dog's location would be "doggie *bed*."

The child's meaning thus may be interpreted from a number of indicators. The ongoing events and the preceding utterances establish the nonlinguistic and linguistic contexts. Word order and stress help us interpret the semantic categories produced.

Longer Utterances

When approximately half of the child's utterances contain two words, she begins to use three-word combinations. The most common three-word utterances are *agent + action + object*, such as "Mommy eat cookie," and *agent + action + location*, such as "Mommy throw me" (to me) or "Mommy sleep chair." These and other three-word utterances consist of two types, recombinations and expansions (R. Brown, 1973). Action relations, such as *agent + action* and *action + object*, recombine and the redundant term is deleted.

> [agent + action] + [action + object] = agent + action + object
> Daddy   throw   Throw   ball   Daddy   throw   ball

This process is also seen in the locative functions.

> [entity (agent) + locative] + [action + locative] = agent + action + locative
> Mommy   chair   Sit   chair   Mommy   sit   chair

In contrast, other semantic relations expand from within to express attribution, possession, or recurrence. The noun term is expanded. For example, within the recurrent "more cookie," the noun portion could be expanded to "big cookie," resulting in "more big cookie." Other examples are as follows:

action + object → action + (attributive + entity)
Eat   cookie   Eat   big   cookie

action + locative → action + (possessor + possession)
Sit   chair   Sit   baby   chair

Four-word or four-term utterances are expanded in the same way. No new relations are learned while the child develops a skill with longer word combinations. The average child is producing some four-word utterances by age 2.

PHONOLOGICAL PATTERNS

During the first 2 years, children learn that sound sequences can carry distinct meanings. These sequences and meanings are stored together in the brain. Categorization and storage are based initially on the entire phonological pattern or auditory image of the word rather than on the individual phonemes involved.

With her first words, the child shifts to greater control of articulation. Babbling requires less constrained production, but when the child adds meaning to sound, she needs some phonological consistency to transmit her messages. After the onset of meaningful speech, there is much individual variation in the pattern and rate of vocabulary growth, the use of invented words, and the syllable structure of the words acquired.

Single-Word Utterances

As noted previously, nearly all of the initial words are monosyllabic CV or VC units or CVCV constructions (Ferguson, 1978; Ingram, 1976; Lewis, 1951). Labial and dental consonants, mostly plosives, predominate but there are occasional fricatives and nasals (no, mama) (Lewis, 1951; Waterson, 1978). Vowel production varies widely among children and within each child, but the basic triangle of /a/, /i/, and /u/ is probably established early (Ingram, 1976). Within a given word, the consonants tend to be the same or noncontrasting, such as baby, mama, daddy, dawdie (doggie). It is the vowels that initially vary. Consonant contrasts occur more frequently in CVC constructions, such as cup (Waterson, 1978).

The child begins to construct her own production capacity with the words that she selects to produce. Some words are actively avoided, even though the child recognizes and understands them. Two possible selection patterns for initial words are (a) the size and complexity of the syllable structure and (b) the sound types included (Ferguson, 1978). The child may choose to produce words that contain only certain sounds (Farwell, 1976). Theoretically, she could attempt words with any speech sound. "The baby talk lexicon of the child's speech community provides a reservoir of phonologically simplified models from which the child can draw for his early words" (Ferguson, 1978, p. 286).

Different children exhibit different "favorite sounds" and use these in selecting the first words that they will produce (Ferguson & Farwell, 1975; Shibamoto & Olmstead, 1978). Thus, vocabulary expansion occurs at the expense of phonological differentiation. Although there is a wide range of individual differences (Grunwell, 1981), certain language-based phonetic tendencies are seen in most children, including a preference for monosyllables over longer strings and stops (/p, b, t, d, k, g/) over all other types of consonant production (Locke, 1983). Preferences for particular speech sounds at age 1 year do not correspond to mastery of these speech sounds at age 3 years (Vihman & Greenlee, 1987). Relationships are more subtle. In general, the greater the proportion of true consonants in babbling and true words at age 1, the more advanced the phonological development of the child at age 3 (Vihman & Greenlee, 1987).

Phonological organization may exist along a continuum from those who are very cautious or systematic to those who are exploratory (Ferguson, 1979). Children classified as systematic operate with strong phonetic and structural constraints that are relaxed in a gradual, orderly manner. In contrast, exploratory speakers have a loose, variable phonological organization and attempt words well beyond their capabilities. This variability at age 1 tends to become inconsistent production of sounds at age 3 (Vihman & Greenlee, 1987).

Phonological rules or processes are systematic procedures for making adult words pronounceable. The patterns and systemicity enable children to produce an approximation of an adult model. In other words, phonological processes are a way of getting from an auditory model to speech production by the child. As such, phonological processes don't exist in and of themselves. Rather, they are a method of achieving a goal of production.

During the period from 12 to 18 months of age, children exhibit no phonological rules. These evolve slowly as each child's lexicon grows and each child attempts to say more words. Instead, children follow two rather broad strategies of sound production: selection and modification (Menyuk, Menn, & Silber, 1986). Following a selection strategy, a child decides to avoid certain words and to exploit or favor others based on the sounds contained in those words. Thus, the child's lexicon is shaped, in part, by the presence of certain phonemes. There are no rules as such other than those used with each word. In other words, rules are word specific. Modification is the slow expansion and change of the child's phonological rule system as new rules are created and new words are modified to fit the child's existing sound patterns. In this process, two or more similar words may initially exist separately but may then be collapsed into one sound pattern.

Phonological patterns are not easy to encode. Initial attempts at word production involve trial and error and may be very unstable.

In addition to being complex, phonological processes exhibit tremendous individual variation for several reasons (Ingram, 1986). First, the entire system of each child is constantly changing. Initially the child may have one phonemic form for several adult words or several forms for the same word. Thus, *baba* may be used for *baby, bottle,* and *rabbit,* or *doddie* and *goggie* may be used for *doggie.* Gradually, the child develops processes that enable her to distinguish between similar adult words. Word production strategies may even precede the development of selection patterns. For example, a child with the rule CV = /dV/ may produce *no*, which becomes *do* (/d oʊ/), and *key*, which becomes *dee* (/di/) (Braine, 1971).

Second, some words are produced consistently, while others vary greatly. "The acquisition of specific patterns and sounds may be greatly influenced by the words in which they occur" (Ingram, 1976, p. 19). Within a given word, there may be "trade-offs": the acquisition of one part of a word may, in turn, distort another part, which the child produced correctly in the past (M. Edwards & Garnica, 1973).

Third, most toddlers use differing, although similar, phonological production patterns or processes, such as reduplication, diminutives, open syllables, and consonant cluster reductions (Table 8.8). *Reduplication* occurs when the child attempts a polysyllabic word (*daddy*) but is unable to produce the second syllable correctly (Ferguson, Peizer, & Weeks, 1973; Menn, 1971). She compensates by repeating the first syllable (*dada*). In contrast, the *diminutive* is an /i/ added to the end of a word, frequently a CVC (*dog*), to produce a CVCV (*doggie*). "Reduplication and diminutive do not have morphological value but are attempts to represent syllabic noise" (Ingram, 1974a, p. 54). Multisyllabic words or words with final consonants are frequently produced in a CV multisyllable form (Waterson, 1978). For example, *teddybear* becomes /tedibɛ/ (CVCVCV). *Open syllables*— those that end in a vowel—predominate in multisyllabic words. Thus, *dirty* may become /dɔti/ and *blanket* may become /bæki/. Closed syllables—those that end in a consonant—occur only at the ends of early words. In addition, *consonant cluster reduction* results in single-consonant production, as in *poon* for *spoon*. Other phonological rules of preschool children are found in Chapter 9. The child produces those parts of words that are perceptually most salient (Waterson, 1978). Auditory saliency is related to relatively low pitch or frequency, high in-

---

TABLE 8.8   Common Phonological Rules of Toddlers

Type	Examples
Reduplication (CVCV)	
Same syllable	*Water* becomes *wawa* (/wawa/)
	Mommy becomes *mama* (/mama/)
	Baby becomes *bebie* (/bibi/)
Same consonant	*Doggie* becomes *goggie* (/gɔgi/) (diminutive)
	Candy becomes *cacie* (/kæki/)
CVCV construction	*Horse* becomes *hawsie* (/hɔsi/)
	Duck becomes *ducky* (/dʌki/)
Open syllables	*Blanket* becomes *bakie* (/bæki/)
	Bottle becomes *baba* (/baba/)
Cluster reduction	*Stop* becomes *top* (/tap/)
	Tree becomes *tee* (/ti/)

tensity, and long duration. Intensity or force is perceived as loudness. For similar reasons, children often delete weak syllables, resulting in *nana* for *banana*.

Fourth, children may exhibit multiple processes within the same word. The result may only vaguely resemble the target word. For example, *tee* may be used for *treat*. In this example, the child has deleted the final consonant and simplified the consonant cluster. In similar fashion, suppose that the child has one rule that says that clusters reduce to a front consonant, a second that all initial sounds are voiced, and a third that words with a closed-syllable ending receive a final vowel. If the target word is *treat*, it might change as follows:

Target	Treat
Apply rule 1 (cluster = front C)	Peat
Apply rule 2 (initial C = voiced)	Beat
Apply rule 3 (CVC = CVCV)	Beatie (/biti/)

Of course, this is neither a conscious nor a step-by-step process for the child. The child may even use a similar process to produce the same form for two different words. She may interpret adult words as having identifiable and unidentifiable portions to which different rules apply (Ingram, 1974a). For example, suppose that the child produces both "spoon" and "pudding" as "poo" (/pu/). Consonant clusters, such as *sp*, may be reduced to the plosive—in this case—and final consonants, such as *n*, are omitted. Thus, *spoon* becomes *poo*. If the child also omits unfamiliar sounds, such as *-ing*, "pudding" would become *pud*, which in turn, with omission of the final consonant, might be reduced to *pu* (also /pu/). The child reduces the complexity of the adult model to a form she can produce.

Finally, each child may have phonological preferences as well. Such preferences might involve different articulatory patterns, classes of sounds, syllable structures, and location in words. Particular words may conform to the child's production patterns. As the child learns different phonological patterns, she applies them to the production of words.

The most frequent phonological process found in children below 30 months of age is consonant cluster reduction, although there is a dramatic drop in the use of this process after 26 months (Preisser, Hodson, & Paden, 1988). Overall, phonological processes decrease rapidly just prior to the second birthday. Liquids (/l, r/) seem to be the most difficult sounds to acquire, and substitution processes are frequently used.

Multiword Utterances

When the child begins to combine words, she still uses many phonological patterns to produce single words. Familiar words appear in succession just as syllables appeared in CVCV words. Words and sentences with repeated elements are used frequently as a particular structure is being assimilated into the child's phonological system. With maturity, the number of repetitive elements gradually decreases and differentiation increases (Waterson, 1978). It appears that at least some of the multiword constructions produced may have a phonological as well as a semantic–syntactic base.

Learning Units and Extension

Most likely, individual speech sounds are not the units of development. Rather, "the total word seems to function as a phonetic unit, i.e., the child remembers and recognizes the phonetic shapes of whole words and articulates in terms of phonetic word shapes" (Ferguson, 1978, p. 287). Only later does the child become aware of speech sound contrasts. The child's spoken "word" is a representation of its adult model called a *phonological idiom* (A. Moskowitz, 1973). The primacy of words may be reflected in (a) the wide variation in pronunciation of individual words, (b) the difficulty of establishing phonemic contrasts within the wide range of word pronunciations, and (c) movement of sounds or prosodic interchange within but not between words (Ferguson, 1978).

The child's earliest words are very limited in the number and type of syllables and in the phoneme types. These restraints are gradually relaxed, resulting in greater structural complexity and phonetic diversity. In this progression, the child frequently generalizes from one word to another. Thus, "the phonological development of the child at the early stages proceeds by changes in the pronunciation of individual words" (Ferguson, 1978, p. 289). Some changes result in improved identification of structures and sounds, others in new skills of production, and still others in the application of new phonological rules governing production.

While constructing her own phonological system, the child will extend segments or rule hypotheses to other words. As a result, some child "words" will change to versions that are closer to the adult pronunciation, and others will become more unlike the model. In these cases, the rules or segments have been overextended. These changes reflect the acquisition of underlying phonological rules rather than word-by-word or sound-by-sound development (Kiparsky & Menn, 1977).

It appears, then, that the child's first language is governed by phonological rules in addition to those for pragmatics, semantics, and syntax. The child invents and applies a succession of phonological rules reflecting increasing phonological organization via a problem-solving, hypothesis-forming process (Ferguson, 1978).

CONCLUSION

First language acquisition offers an informative look into the organizational world of the child. In order to understand this world, adults have categorized and subdivided the child's language in adult terms. But there is some danger in doing this. As adults, we may assume that children must be expressing one of the meanings that an adult can express. This implies that children conceptualize the world and language as an adult does, and that children's motivation or communicative intent to use language is also adultlike. "One does not know what meanings the child is capable of conceptualizing, or for what purposes the child might use language" (Rodgon, 1977, p. 111). We cannot assume that the salient features of an event that we might encode also have meaning for the child. In fact, as adults, we may be describing merely the products of the child's rule system and not analyzing the actual rules the child uses. For example, "the 'boy' in the utterance 'boy push truck' may be simply the first element in a perceived physical event" (McLean & Snyder-McLean, 1978, p. 37), not an agent.

The child's utterances are the result of a complex process that begins with the referents involved. In single-word utterances, the child's selection of lexical items seems to be strongly influenced by the pragmatic aspects of the communication context and by the concepts she can encode. Many of her words represent a very limited repertoire of phonetic elements. In addition, longer utterances follow simple ordering rules that express meaning. This rule system is independent of pragmatic rules and illocutionary functions but is strongly influenced by both in actual use.

Although the child's language is different from the adult's, it is nonetheless a valid symbolic system for the child. It works for her within her world. "Indeed he often need say only a word or two or nothing at all in order to be understood" (R. Brown, 1973, p. 242). This statement in no way detracts from the accomplishments of the child. First language acquisition is an important initial step in language development. Many of the relations the child has learned to express via a combination of gestures, vocalizations, single words, and word order are now ready for more adultlike linguistic forms.

REFLECTIONS

1. First words follow predictable patterns. List the most frequent categories of first words and give some explanation for the things children talk about. Describe the syllable structure of first words.
2. Describe the various intentions toddlers express in their early vocalizations and verbalizations.
3. Compare the three hypotheses that have been advanced as explanations of early concept formation: semantic-feature, functional-core, and prototypic complex.
4. Children extend early words to novel examples. Describe the bases for most over- and underextensions and explain the possible uses of extensions by children.
5. List the linear word-order rules, based on semantic categories, that children follow when they begin to combine words, and give examples of each.
6. Three common phonological rules of toddlers are reduplication, open syllables, and consonant cluster reduction. Explain each and give an example.
7. Define the terms *agent* and *object*.

9 Preschool Language Development

CHAPTER OBJECTIVES

The preschool years are a time of tremendous growth in all aspects of language, especially syntax. From two- and three-word utterances, the child progresses to sentences that approximate adult language in their complexity. When you have completed this chapter, you should understand

- narrative development.
- the conversational abilities of the preschool child.
- how to compute the mean length of utterance.
- the major characteristics of the stages of syntactic development.
- preschool morphological development.
- pronoun acquisition order.
- the acquisition order for negative and interrogative sentences.
- the differences between embedding and conjoining and their acquisitional order.
- the major phonological processes observed in preschool children.
- the following terms:

anaphoric reference	mean length of utterance (MLU)
aspect	modal auxiliary
backward reduction	narrative level
centering	object noun phrase complement
chaining	phrasal coordination
clause	phrase
complex sentence	relative clause
compound sentence	sentential coordination
copula	sibilant
ellipsis	simple sentence
epenthesis	subordinate clause
fast mapping	tense
forward reduction	topic
main clause	

T̲ʜᴇ sᴘᴇᴇᴅ ᴀɴᴅ ᴅɪᴠᴇʀsɪᴛʏ of language development during the preschool years are exciting. Within a few short years, the child moves from using simple multiword utterances to sentences that approach adultlike form. This development is multidimensional and reflects the child's cognitive and socioemotional growth. In general, the child observes the regularized patterns of language use in his environment and forms hypotheses about the underlying rules. These hypotheses are then tested in production. Over time, the rules change to reflect the child's greater sophistication in producing and using the linguistic code in conversation. The term *acquisition* suggests an instantaneous event. This is unfortunate because many months or years may be required before the child has complete control of a linguistic element in all contexts. In addition, it is an inappropriate way in which to describe the learning process.

Although we will not attempt to explain every detail of preschool language development, we can highlight the major achievements within each aspect of language. First, we'll examine the social context of language development and the use of language within that context. Special attention will be given to conversational abilities and narrative development. Then we'll explore morphological and syntactic development. These changes will be related to cognitive development. Finally, we'll examine preschool phonological growth.

PRAGMATIC DEVELOPMENT

In general, children learn language within a conversational context. For most children, the chief conversational partner is an adult. During the preschool years the child acquires many conversational skills. Still, much of the child's conversation concerns the here and now, and he has much to learn about the conventional routines of conversation. Even though he has learned to take turns, his conversations are short and the number of turns is very limited. These skills will be refined during the school years.

In general, the 2-year-old is able to respond to his conversational partner and to engage in short dialogues of a few turns on a given topic. He can also introduce or change the topic of discussion. His language is used in imaginative ways and in expression of feeling. He considers his conversational partner only in small measure by providing descriptive details to aid comprehension. He uses pronouns, however, without previously identifying the entity to which they refer.

By age 3 he can engage in longer dialogues beyond a few turns. Yet spontaneous speech is still easier than contingent speech for the child (Bloom, Rocissano, & Hood, 1976). Contingent speech is influenced by, and dependent upon, the preceding utterance of the partner. As the 3-year-old becomes more aware of the social aspects of discourse, he acknowledges his partner's turn with fillers, such as *yeah* and *uh-huh*. Soon the child demonstrates a form of motherese when he addresses very young children. This code-switching behavior is evidence of a growing awareness of conversational roles.

Finally, by kindergarten age, the child is able to cloak his intentions more skillfully and to use indirect requests. He is able to use deictic terms, such as *here* and *there* or *this* and *that*, correctly. These concepts develop only gradually due to their shifting reference and boundaries.

Much of the child's conversation still occurs within the mother–child dialogue. "This linguistic environment . . . must be considered a significant contributor to all aspects of the language learning process" (Furrow, Nelson, & Benedict, 1979, p. 435). Even though the child is becoming a fuller conversational participant, his mother is still very much in control. "Mothers continue their leadership role in creating and maintaining a semblance of true dialogue" (Kaye & Charney, 1981). This conversational asymmetry continues throughout the preschool period.

In addition to conversation, the child engages in monologues, self-conversations with no desire to involve others. Monologues can serve many purposes for preschoolers, such as self-guidance. The presleep monologues of many children are rich with songs, sounds, nonsense words, bits of chitchat, verbal fantasies, and expressions of feelings. Much of this verbal play involves buildup and breakdown of the child's utterance. Some children engage in presleep self-dialogue in which the child takes both parts. Gradually the child's monologues become more social. First, the child engages in them when others are nearby; then he shares a topic. In general, throughout the preschool years, audible monologue behavior declines with age, but inaudible mumbling increases (W. Klein, 1963; Kohlberg, Yaeger, & Hjertholm, 1968). Inaudible self-talk decreases after age 10 but doesn't disappear. As adults, most of us talk to ourselves.

In this section, we shall explore the conversational context of preschool language development and discuss a few aspects of the child's conversational abilities.

The Conversational Context

The young language-learning child is limited in the topics he can discuss. In addition, he has limited skills in a conversational mode, although he learned turn taking as an infant. Within mother–child conversations, the child begins to learn to maintain a conversational flow and to take his listener's perspective. He is aided by the facilitative behaviors of his mother. In general, mother and child each engage in roughly 30% opening and 60% responding behaviors (Martlew, 1980). Initiating behaviors include introductions of a new topic, referrals to a previous one for the purpose of shifting the topic, and deliberate invitations for the partner to respond. Responding behaviors include acknowledgments (*I see, uh-huh*), yes/no responses, answers, repetitions, sustaining or reformulated responses, and extensions. Mothers appear to be in control, however, and maneuver the conversation by inviting verbal responses (Martlew, 1980).

Child Conversational Skills

The young child is very good at introducing new topics in which he's interested but has difficulty sustaining that topic beyond one or two turns. Taking his turn or building a bridge for the next speaker's turn is especially difficult. With increased age the child gains the ability to maintain a topic, which in turn results in fewer new topics being introduced within a given conversation. Nearly 50% of 5-year-olds can sustain certain topics through about a dozen turns (Garvey & Hogan, 1973).

There is a large increase in the amount of verbal responding between ages 24 and 30 months (Mueller, Bleier, Krakow, Hegedus, & Cournoyer, 1977). The 30-month-old is, in addition, very successful at engaging the listener's attention and responding to listener feedback (H. Wellman & Lempers, 1977). There is an increase in overall talkativeness at around 36 months of age (Wells, 1985). The largest proportion of the speech is socially directed.

Between ages 3 and 4, the child seems to gain a better awareness of the social aspects of conversation. In general, utterances addressed to conversational partners are clear, well formed, and well adapted for the listener (Mueller, 1972). Becoming more aware of his listener's shared assumptions or presuppositions, the child uses more elliptical responses than previously. He need not repeat shared knowledge contained in his partner's questions. If his mother asks, "What are you doing?" the child responds, "Playing," the *I am* being redundant information. By age 4 the child uses twice as many affective utterances as the child of 3, discussing feelings and emotions (Martlew, 1980). There is also a related shift in verb usage. By age 5 the child uses *be* and *do* predominantly, in place of *go* and *do* (Bennett-Kaster, 1986). This change indicates that the child is speaking more about state, attitude, or feeling and less about action. My children constantly amazed me with their affective responses. Once, my 4-year-old son Todd comforted an elderly neighbor at Christmas by stating, "I hope our lights will make you happy."

The preschool child appears to be aware of the conventions of turn taking but does not use as many turnabout behaviors as adults. Conversational turn taking between mothers and their 2- to 2 ½-year-old children is very smooth (Kaye & Charney, 1981). Less than 5% of the turns of either participant are interrupted by the other partner.

Throughout the preschool period, about 60% of the child–partner exchanges are characterized by the child's attempts to control the behavior of the partner or to relay information. The exchange of information gains in importance and by age 4 is clearly the most important function, accounting for approximately 37% of these exchanges (Wells, 1985). Other exchanges serve functions such as establishing and maintaining social relations, teaching, managing and correcting communication, expressing feelings, and talking to self.

Contingent Queries

Young children use questions and **contingent queries**, or requests for clarification ("What?," "Huh?," "I don't understand"), to initiate or continue an exchange, but not to the extent that adults do when addressing young children. Approximately one-fourth of the contingent queries of 2-year-olds are nonverbal, such as showing a confused expression (Gale, Liebergott, & Griffin, 1981). This percentage decreases as the primary means of communicating confusion when dealing with older children.

Although 2 ½-year-olds are able to respond to requests for clarification, they do not respond consistently and do not resolve the breakdown at least 36% of the time when they do (Shatz & O'Reilly, 1990). Young preschoolers are more likely to respond, and with more success, to requests for clarification that follow their own requests for action rather than to those that follow their assertions or declarations.

In general, these children are more motivated to have something happen than to be understood. They probably understand little about communication breakdown, but they recognize the need to maintain the conversational flow (Shatz, 1987). Conversational turn-taking skills are learned very early.

The types of clarification preschoolers seek appear to be nearly equally divided between general or nonspecific ("What?," "Huh?"), specific, and metalinguistic misunderstanding. The child may lack the ability to state what is desired, however, in part because he has difficulty determining what he doesn't understand. It is not until mid-elementary school that the child develops the ability to make specific requests for clarification (Ironsmith & Whitehurst, 1978).

The preschooler is not always successful in getting his message across. He has difficulty detecting ambiguity (Bearison & Levey, 1977). The preschooler is unable to reformulate his message in response to a facial expression of noncomprehension and must be specifically requested to clarify. The most common clarification strategy among preschoolers is a simple repetition, especially if the request is nonspecific, such as "Huh?" or "What?" The abilities to clarify and to organize information more systematically also do not develop until mid-elementary school (Pratt, Scribner, & Cole, 1977).

Topic Introduction, Maintenance, and Closure

A **topic** can be defined as the content about which we speak. Topics are identified by name as they are introduced. You might say, "I had escargots last night," in an attempt to establish the topic of eating snails. I might reply, "Oh, did you like them?" We are sharing a topic. My reply was an agreement to accept the topic. Not all topics are as direct, and the listener may have to identify the topic by noting the central focus or central concern of the utterance. For example, the utterance "Well, what did you think of the rally last night?" might be used to establish several different topics, depending upon the manner in which it is stated.

In a larger sense, a topic is also the cohesion in the conversation. Through skillful manipulation, we can make the conversation successful or unsuccessful (Maynard, 1980). For example, the topic of professional sports will work in conversation with many adult males; needlepoint, French cuisine, and American folk art may not. There are conversational partners, however, who could converse on any of these topics for hours.

Once introduced by identification, the topic is maintained by each conversational partner's commenting on the topic with additional information; altering the focus of the topic, called *shading*; or requesting more information (Goodenough & Weiner, 1978; Keenan & Schieffelin, 1976; Schegloff & Sacks, 1973). The topic is changed by introducing a new one, reintroducing a previous one, or ending the conversation. Obviously, "Topic development is . . . an aspect of language development that evolves in the context of face-to-face communication" (Foster, 1986, p. 247).

At first, the infant attracts attention to himself as the topic. By age 1, the child is highly skilled at initiating a topic by a combination of glances, gestures, vocalizations, and verbalizations, although he is limited to topics about items that are physically present. Typically, topics are maintained for only one or two turns at this age. Only about half of the utterances of children below age 2 are on the established topic (Bloom et al., 1976). Child utterances on the topic usually consist of imitations of the adult or of new related information. Extended topic maintenance beyond a turn or two seems to be possible only within well-established routines. These routines, such as bathing or dressing, provide a structure for the discourse, thus relieving the young child of the (for now) nearly impossible task of conversational planning (Andersen & Kekelis, 1983).

By age 2, the child is capable of maintaining a topic in *adjacency pairs* or *fixed form* utterances. These utterances follow a pattern, such as question/answer. The mature language partner usually offers the toddler choices, as in "Do you like candy or ice cream best?"; asks questions; or makes commands or offers (Ervin-Tripp, 1979). In this way, the mature partner interprets events for the child and scaffolds or structures the conversation for coherence (Foster, 1981; Kaye & Charney, 1981).

Between ages 2 and 3, the child gains a limited ability to maintain coherent topics (Foster, 1986). By age 3 ½ years, about three-fourths of the child's utterances are on the established topic (Bloom et al., 1976). Four-year-olds can maintain most topics for only a few turns. Topics may last through more turns when children are enacting familiar scenarios or engaged in sociodramatic play, describing a physically present object or an ongoing event, and problem solving (Schober-Peterson & Johnson, 1989). Shorter topics may occur when capturing someone's attention, establishing a play situation, and ensuring cooperation when assigning toys or roles.

Repetition is one tactic used by preschoolers to remain on a topic. Even 5-year-olds continue to use frequent repetition to acknowledge, provide cohesion, and fill turns. Still, topics change quickly, and 5-year-olds may discuss an average of 50 different topics within 15 minutes (Brinton & Fujiki, 1984).

Presuppositional Skills: Adaptation to the Listener's Knowledge

Presupposition, as we mentioned earlier, is the process whereby the speaker makes background assumptions about the listener's knowledge. This occurs on several levels. The speaker needs to be aware of the listener's word meanings, as well as his knowledge of the social context and the conversational topic. You and I can't have a meaningful conversation if you don't understand either the words I'm using or the topic. Every one of us has had to stop a speaker—usually someone close to us—at some time and say, "I don't have any idea what you're talking about." We didn't understand the topic.

In general, the preschool child becomes increasingly adept at knowing what information to include, how to arrange it, and which particular lexical items and linguistic forms to use. This ability "emerges gradually . . . on a usage-by-usage basis" rather than as a single linguistic form (DeHart & Maratsos, 1984). Nonetheless, some linguistic forms are used as presuppositional tools. These include articles, demonstratives, pronouns, proper nouns, some verbs, *wh-* questions, and forms of address. The definite article (*the*), pronouns, demonstratives (*this, that, these, those*), and proper names refer to specific entities that, it is presupposed, both the speaker and the listener can identify. In addition, pronouns and demonstratives must be interpreted from the position of the speaker. For example, *I* always refers to the speaker and *you* to the listener(s). The process of interpreting words with reference to the speaker is called *deixis* and will be discussed later. The speaker must presuppose that his listener understands this process.

Some verbs, such as *know* and *remember*, when used before a *that + clause* construction, presuppose the truthfulness of the clause that follows. In the following sentences, the speaker is conveying his belief in the truthfulness of the ending clause:

> I know that you have a red dress.
> I remember that the cat was asleep in this chair.

In like fashion, *wh-* questions are used to gain more information about a presupposed fact stated in the clause. In the example "What are you eating?" it is presupposed that the listener is eating. In "Where is the party?" the speaker presupposes that there is one and that the listener knows its location. Finally, the form of address used is based on presuppositions relative to the social situation. As speakers, we address only certain people as *dear* or *honey* or by their nicknames. These forms are not used with strangers or with people in positions of authority over us. In addition, the choice of topic itself is based on an assumption of participant knowledge or at least interest. Once the topic is introduced, each participant generally presupposes that the other knows what the topic is, so there is no need to keep restating it. New topics or information are generally introduced in the last position or near the end of a sentence. As we have already noted, new information is also emphasized in order to signal the listener. In addition, through a process called **ellipsis,** the speaker omits redundant information that has been previously stated. For example, in response to "Who is baking cookies?" the speaker says "I am," leaving out the redundant information "baking cookies." Acquiring presuppositional skills requires learning to use all of these linguistic devices. Thus, the acquisition process extends well into school age.

Prior to age 3, most children do not understand the effect of not providing enough information for their listener. By age 3, however, the child is generally able to determine the amount of information the listener needs (Bretherton & Beeghly, 1982; Shatz, Wellman, & Silber, 1983). Children usually mention the most informative items first. Three-year-olds are able to adjust their answers based on decisions of what the listener knows and does not know (Parner & Leekam, 1976). Thus, the more knowledgeable listener receives even more information and more elaborate descriptions while receiving less redundant information (Menig-Peterson, 1975).

Most 3-year-olds also can distinguish between definite and indefinite articles. At this age they use the articles with approximately 85% accuracy (Maratsos, 1976). If the preschooler makes errors in usage, it is usually because he has assumed erroneously that the listener shares the referent. For example, the child might say, "I liked *the* popsicle," without ever having mentioned it before. Thus the definite article is often used without first identifying the referent. This same error of assuming a shared referent is also evident in the use of pronouns. Even older preschool children will point to the referent rather than identify it verbally (VanHekken, Vergeer, & Harris, 1980). The referent may be even more ambiguous if it is not present.

Verbs such as *know, think, forget,* and *remember* are used correctly as presuppositional tools by age 4. Not all verbs presuppose the truth of the following clause, such as in the case of "I think. . . ." In this instance, the speaker is not as certain as when he says, "I know. . . ." By age 5 or 6 the child understands the use of these verbs and others, such as *wish* and *pretend.* These verbs presuppose that the following clause is false. Thus, when I say "I wish I had a pony," it is assumed that I do not. Verbs such as *say, whisper,* and *believe* are not comprehended until age 7 (Abbeduto & Rosenberg, 1985; DeHart & Maratsos, 1984).

The presuppositions that accompany *wh-* questions seem to be learned with each *wh-* word. Children seem to be able to respond to specific *wh-* words even though these words may be used only infrequently in their own speech (Gallagher, 1981).

Finally, the use of other devices, such as word order, stress, and ellipsis, also changes with age. At the two-word level, children initially place new information first, as in "Doggie eat," establishing *doggie* as the topic. This practice declines with longer, more adultlike utterances in favor of the more widely used last position, as in "Wasn't that a great picnic?", establishing *picnic* as the topic (MacWhinney & Bates, 1978). Children use stress at the two-word stage to mark new information for the listener. With age the child becomes even more reliable in his use of this device (MacWhinney & Bates, 1978). In general, ellipsis is used more selectively and with greater sophistication as the child's language and conversations become more complex throughout the preschool years.

Directives and Requests

One area of child language that has received considerable study is the use of directives and requests. The purpose of these instrumental or goal-fulfilling forms is to get others to do things for the speaker. Examples include

> Stop that! (direct)
> Could you get the phone? (indirect, conventional)
> Phew, it's hot in here. (indirect, nonconventional)

In the first example, the goal is clearly stated or direct. In the second, the form appears to be a question, although the speaker is not really interested in whether the listener has the ability to perform the task; the ability is assumed. Finally, in the third, an indirect nonconventional form, the goal is not mentioned and cannot be identified by strict syntactic interpretation.

By 2 years of age, the child is able to use some attention-getting words with gestures and rising intonation; however, he is usually unsuccessful at gaining attention (Ervin-Tripp, O'Connor, Rosenberg, O'Barr, 1984). He tends to rely on less specific attention-getting forms, such as "Hey," and to be ignored by adults. Request words such as *more, want,* and *mine,* problem statements such as *I'm tired* and *I'm hungry,* and verbal routines are common (Newcombe & Zaslow, 1981). Two early directive types are the need statement ("I want/need a . . .") and the imperative ("Give me a . . .") (Ervin-Tripp, 1977b). Few, if any, indirect forms are used. The child refers to the desired action or object. These requests become clearer with age, and the child identifies all elements of the request, not just what is desired.

Two- to 3-year-olds make politeness distinctions based on the age or size, familiarity, role, territory, and rights of the listener. Often young children will use *please* in a request, especially if the listener is older or bigger, less familiar, in a dominant role, or possessor of an object or privilege desired (Ervin-Tripp & Gordon, 1986).

Action requests addressed to the child are likely to be answered with the action even when information is sought (Shatz, 1975, 1978a). Thus, when Grandma says, "Can you sing?" and is seeking a simple "yes" response, she may get a tuneful rendition that she didn't really want. Interpretation seems to be based on past experience and on the child's knowledge of object uses and locations, activity structures, and roles.

At age 3 the child begins to use some modals in indirect requests ("Could you give me a . . .?"), permissive directives ("Can/may I have a . . .?"), and question directives ("Do you have a . . .?"). These forms reflect syntactic developments and the child's increasing skill at modifying his language to reflect the social situation. These changes, especially the use of auxiliary verbs within interrogatives, enhance the child's skill at politeness and the use of requests.

The 4-year-old is more skilled with indirect forms, although he is still unsuccessful more than half of the time at getting someone else's attention (Ervin-Tripp et al., in press). Only about 6% of all the requests by 42- to 52-month-olds are indirect in nature. There is a sharp increase in the use of this form at around age 4½ (Garvey, 1975; James & Seebach, 1982; L. Wilkinson, Calculator, & Dollaghan, 1982). Examples include "Why don't you . . ." and "Don't forget to. . . ." The child also offers more explanations and justifications for his requests. At around age 4, the child becomes more aware of his partner's point of view and role, and of the appropriate form of request and politeness required (D. Gordon & Ervin-Tripp, 1984). The 4-year-old is able to respond correctly to forms such as "You should . . .," "Please . . .," and "I'll be happy if you . . ." (Carrell, 1981).

A desired goal may be totally masked in the directive of the 5-year-old. The form of his request may be very different from the child's actual intention. For example, desiring a glass of juice, the child might say, "Now, you be the mommy and make breakfast." Such inferred requests or other nonconventional forms are very infrequent, however, even in the language of 5-year-olds. In general, the child relies on conventional, ritualized forms and the use of markers such as *please* (Ervin-Tripp & Gordon, 1986). The 5-year-old continues to increase his use of explanations and justifications, especially when there is a chance of noncompliance by the listener. Often the justifications are self-contained statements, such as "I need it" or "I want it," but they may refer to rights, reasons, causes, or norms. Justifications are initially found in children's attempts to stop an activity. My daughter gained neighborhood notoriety for her very precise "Stop it, because I do not like it!"

Although he has made tremendous gains, the preschooler is still rather ineffectual in making requests or in giving directives. He needs to become more efficient at gaining his potential listener's attention, more effective in stating his goal, more aware of social role, more persuasive, and more creative in forming requests. The increased complexity of the school-age child's social interactions and the new demands of the school environment require greater facility with directive and request forms.

Deixis

Deixis is an ancient Greek word meaning indicating or pointing. This is only one aspect of deixis. Deictic terms may be used to direct attention, to make spatial contrasts, and to denote times or participants in a conversation from the speaker's point of view (E. Clark, 1974a). Thus correct use of these terms indicates pragmatic and cognitive growth by the child. It is not easy for young children to adopt the perspective of another conversational participant. Therefore several linguists have studied deixis in an attempt to understand this development. In this section, we will discuss the development of *here/there, this/that*, and personal pronouns. As many as 30% of 7-year-olds may have difficulty comprehending some deictic contrasts, even those used in their own speech production.

The development of *this, that, here*, and *there* illustrates the difficulties inherent in learning these terms (Wales, 1986). Mothers use *that* and *there* more frequently than the other two, although children use all four more equally. The most frequent use of these terms by mothers is in directing the child's attention. *There* is also used to note completion. It is not surprising, then, that children first use *that* and *there* for directing attention.

Later, children use *this* and *here* for the same purpose but make little differentiation based on the location of the object of interest. The child's comprehension is aided by the gestures used by adults.

Gradually, children begin to realize that these terms denote a contrast in location relative to the speaker. Adult gestures are not depended on for interpretation. Children still experience difficulty with the actual size of the area covered by terms such as *here*. This is made more difficult by the fact that these terms can be used for a variety of references, from "Come *here*," meaning this very spot, to "We have an environmental problem *here*," meaning on the entire earth.

There are three problems in the acquisition of deictic terms: point of reference, shifting reference, and shifting boundaries (E. Clark & Sengul, 1978). The point of reference is generally the speaker. Hence, when you use the term *here*, you are speaking of a proximal or near area. The child must learn two principles in order to understand the point of reference (E. Clark & Sengul, 1978). These principles, the speaker principle and the distance principle, also relate to the second and third problem areas. First, the speaker principle states that the speaker is the point of reference. This introduces a potential problem, since the reference point will shift with each new speaker: each new speaker creates a new *I*. Terms that shift most frequently seem to be the hardest to learn (E. Clark, 1978a). The *I* shifts to each new speaker, the *you* to any other conversational partner(s), and the *he* or *she* to any third party. This hierarchy describes the developmental sequence *I* before *you*, followed by *he* and *she*. Even the initial use of *he* and *she* may be based more on gender than on the deictic role fulfilled (Brener, 1983). Adverbs such as *here* and *this* are proximal to the speaker, while *there* and *that* may be anywhere else. The proximal terms should thus be easier to learn.

The second, or distance, principle states that pairs such as *this/that* and *here/there* contrast distance dimensions. The boundaries of these dimensions shift with the context and are not generally stated by the speaker. For example, the term *here* has very different boundaries in the following two sentences:

> Put your money here, please.
> We have a democratic form of government here.

At least one deictic term—*here, there, this*, or *that*—is usually present in the first-50-word lexicon of most children (Nelson, 1973b).

Some pronoun contrasts develop prior to spatial deictic terms. As mentioned previously, *I/you* and *my/your* develop relatively early. These terms refer to the speaker and listener regardless of the number of other persons in the context. The 2 ½-year-old can comprehend and produce *I*, *you*, and *he* (Tanz, 1980). These terms may be easier to learn than spatial contrasts because of the relatively distinct boundaries. The pronoun meaning is integral to the concept of person (Tanz, 1980). Words such as *come/go* and *give/take* have meaning independent of the person involved.

There appear to be three phases of acquisition of deictic terms (E. Clark & Sengul, 1978). In the initial phase there is no contrast between the different dimensions. As previously discussed, terms such as *here* and *there* are used for directing attention or for referencing (Lyons, 1975). In other words, deictic terms are used nondeictically (Carter, 1975a; Griffiths, 1974). Among 2 ½-year-olds, deictic words seem to be used indiscriminately, with a gesture to indicate meaning (A. Snyder, 1914). Because there are no definitive boundaries between terms such as *here* and *there*, it is difficult to determine the child's concept. Huxley (1970) could find no difference between the use of *this* and *that* as late as age 4 and concluded,

"It was difficult to be certain of any distinction such as 'proximal' or 'non-proximal' " (p. 158). In the no-contrast phase, children tend to employ one of four possible strategies of comprehension (E. Clark & Sengul, 1978). All deictic terms are interpreted as being (a) near the speaker, (b) far from the speaker, (c) near the child, or (d) far from the child. Children seem to prefer to use themselves or a near point as reference (Tanz, 1976; Webb & Abrahamson, 1976).

The second phase is characterized by a partial contrast. The child frequently uses the proximal term (*this*, *here*) correctly but overuses it for the nonproximal (*that*, *there*). An alternative pattern is characterized by correct child use only in reference to himself or to some inconsistent point (Charney, 1979).

In the final phase, the child masters the full deictic contrast. The age of mastery differs for the various contrasts, and many children continue to produce deictic errors beyond age 4. In general, mastery of *here/there* precedes mastery of *this/that*, possibly because the concept of *here/there* is an integral part of the latter pair (J. Thorne, 1972). Exact ages of comprehension and production mastery differ widely among studies, and results seem to be dependent upon the study design (Charney, 1979; Webb & Abrahamson, 1976). Even a large number of 7-year-olds have difficulty comprehending some deictic contrasts, although they use them in their speech (Wales, 1979). In contrast, terms such as *in front of* and *in back of* are mastered by age 4 (Kuczaj & Maratsos, 1975; Tanz, 1980). Less precise terms, such as *beside* and *behind*, develop later (Bangs, 1975). Mastery of the adult system of deixis requires several years.

Intentions

As might be expected from the preceding sections, the child's language intentions are increasing in number and diversity. By about 30 months, the relative frequency of the six large pragmatic categories noted by Wells (1985)—control, representational, expressive, procedural, social, and tutorial—stabilizes throughout the rest of the preschool period. The control and representational functions account for 70% of all child utterances. Table 9.1 lists the major functions mastered by preschoolers.

Within the control function, there is great diversity. The *wanting* function that dominated in toddler language decreases rapidly after 24 months of age. In contrast, *direct requesting* continues a slow increase until around 39 months, when its frequency levels off at 25% of all control utterances and remains the dominant control function throughout the preschool years. Other control intentions or illocutionary functions used by at least 90% of 5-year-olds include *prohibition* ("Don't do that"), *intention* ("I'm going to put it in"), *request permission* ("Can I have one?"), *suggestion* ("Should we have ice cream?"), *physical justification* ("I can't 'cause the dollie's there"), *offer* ("Do you want this one?"), and *indirect request* ("Will you pour the juice?") (Wells, 1985).

The representational category is dominated by the *statement* function, which gradually increases to 50% of all representational utterances and roughly 20% of all utterances by age 5. The earlier dominance of *naming* in toddler language no longer exists, and these utterances, as might be expected, account

TABLE 9.1   Intentions Exhibited by 90% of Children

Intention	Age at Which 90% of Children Use Intention (in months)
Exclamation and Call	18
Ostention (naming)	21
Wanting, Direct request, and Statement	24
Content question	30
Prohibition, Intention, Content response, Expressive state, and elicited repetition	33
Yes/no question, Verbal accompaniment, and Contingent query	36
Request permission	45
Suggestion	48
Physical justification	54
Offer and Indirect request	57

(handwritten annotation: "Don't Do that" with arrow pointing to Prohibition row)

Source: Adapted from Wells (1985).

for very few representational utterances by age 5. Other representational functions used by at least 90% of 5-year-olds include *content questions* ("What . . .?", "Where . . .?"), *content response*, and *yes/no questions* (Wells, 1985).

Expressive functions used by at least 90% of 5-year-olds include *exclamation, expressive state*, and *verbal accompaniment*, all noted previously in toddler language. Procedural functions used by at least 90% of 5-year-olds include *call, contingent query*, and *elicited repetition*, in which the child repeats the speaker's utterance with a rising intonation. Finally, the *social* and *tutorial* functions together account for less than 4% of the child's utterances at age 5.

Narratives

Oral narratives are an uninterrupted stream of language modified by the speaker to capture and hold the listener's interest. Unlike a conversation, the narrator maintains a social monologue throughout, producing language relevant to the overall narrative while presupposing the information needed by the listener. Narratives include self-generated stories, telling of familiar tales, retelling of movies or television shows, and recounting of personal experiences. Most conversations include narratives of this latter type, often beginning with "You'll never believe what happened to me on the way to work."

Although conversation and narratives share many elements, such as a sense of purpose, relevant information, clear and orderly exchange of information, repair, and the ability to assume the perspective of the listener, they differ in very significant ways. Conversations are dialogues, while narratives are essentially decontextualized monologues. *Decontextualization* means that the language does not center on some shared experience within the immediate context but rather communicates some experience not directly shared.

Narratives contain organizational patterns not found in conversation. In order to share the experience, the speaker must present an explicit, topic-centered discussion that clearly states the relationships between events. Thus, events are linked to one another in a predictable temporal or causal manner.

Narratives usually have an agentive focus, which means that they concern people, animals, or imaginary characters engaged in events (Longacre, 1983). Conversations usually involve activities in the immediate context.

Other differences include the narrative use of extended units of text; introductory and organizing sequences that lead to a narrative conclusion; and the relatively passive role of the listener, who provides only minimal informational support (Roth, 1986). The narrative speaker is responsible for organizing and providing all of the information in an organized whole (Roth & Spekman, 1985). It is not surprising, therefore, that narratives are found more frequently in the communication of more mature speakers.

Development of Narratives

Before the appearance of first words, children have some understanding of familiar events and of the positions of some actions at the beginning, middle, and end of sequences (Bruner, 1975; DeLemos, 1981; Ninio & Bruner, 1978; Ratner & Bruner, 1978). Although 2-year-olds possess basic patterns for familiar events and sequences, called *scripts*, they are not able to describe sequences of events accurately until about age 4 (Karmiloff-Smith, 1981; Nelson & Gruendel, 1977; Peterson & McCabe, 1983; Slobin, 1973). Nonetheless, children as young as age 2 to 3 ½ can tell narratives about things that have happened to them. These early *protonarratives* have five times as much evaluative information as their regular conversation. Between ages 2 and 2 ½, the number of these protonarratives doubles, and children begin to sequence events with very little help from others (Miller & Sperry, 1988).

The overall organization of a narrative is called the **narrative level**. In general, children use two strategies for organization: *centering* and *chaining* (Applebee, 1978). **Centering** is the linking of entities to form a story nucleus. Although causal links are not present, sequential ones may be. Links may be based on similarity or complementarity of features. *Similarity* links are formed using observable attributes, such as actions, characteristics, scenes, or situations. *Complementary* links consist of conceptual bonds based on abstract, logical attributes, such as members of a class or events linked by cause-and-effect bonds. **Chaining** consists of a sequence of events that share attributes and lead directly from one to another.

Children begin to tell self-generated, fictional narratives between 2 and 3 years of age (Sutton-Smith, 1986). Most of the stories of 2-year-olds are organized by centering. By this age, children have a burgeoning notion of time and of the temporal relationship of events. The child's stories usually center on certain highlights in the child's life and may have a vague plot. Considering the listener only minimally, the child demonstrates little need to introduce, to explore with, or to orient his audience. Thus, these stories often lack easily identifiable beginnings, middles, and ends. The theme is usually some disquieting event in the child's life. Frequently children tell of events that they find disruptive or extraordinary (Ames, 1966). By age 3, however, nearly half of the children use both centering and chaining. This percentage increases, and by age 5, nearly three-fourths of the children use both strategies.

Initially, identification of the participants, time, and location may be nonexistent or minimal. Although these elements improve with maturity, even children of 3 ½ may not identify all participants (Peterson, 1990). In part this may result from the fact that most stories involve individuals well known to the child and to most listeners. A sense of time frame is also vague or nonexistent initially but improves with the use of terms such as *yesterday* or *last year*, even though these terms may be used inaccurately. Location is more commonly identified, especially when the narrative events occurred in the home. With maturity, children become better able to identify out-of-home locations.

The organizational strategies of 2-year-olds represent *heaps* or sets of unrelated statements about a central stimulus. These additive chains consist of one sentence added to another. The statements provide additional information or identify aspects of the stimulus. Although there is no overall organizational pattern, there may be a similarity in the grammatical structure of the sentences:

> The doggie go "woof." The cow go "moo." The man ride tractor—Bpt-bpt-bpt.

There is no central focus, no story line, no sequencing, and no cause and effect. The sentences may be moved anywhere in the text without changing the overall meaning. Additive chains may also be used to describe a scene.

Somewhat later, children begin to tell narratives characterized as *sequences*. These include events linked on the basis of similar attributes or events that create a simple but meaningful focus for a story. The organization is additive, not temporal, and sentences may be moved without altering the narrative:

> I ate a hamburger (Mimes eating). Mommy threw the ball. Daddy took me swimming (Moves hand, acts silly). I had two sodas.

In these early stories, there is a dominance of performance and textual qualities over text or verbal information (Sutton-Smith, 1986). In other words, the child uses sound production and prosody to move the story along (Scollon & Scollon, 1981). Gradually, between ages 3 and 7 years, children's narratives increase in the use of prose and plots (Sutton-Smith, 1986).

Temporal or time-based event sequences emerge between ages 3 and 5 years. Events follow a logical sequence. *Primitive temporal narratives* are organized around a center with complementary events:

> We went to the parade. There was a big elephant. And tanks (Moves arm like turret). The drum was loud. There was a clown in a little car (Hand gestures "little"). And I got a balloon. And we went home.

Although there is sequencing, there is no plot and no cause and effect or causality.

Event description, such as explaining how to make cookies, involves more than describing single events in a sequential order (Comrie, 1976; Halliday & Hasan, 1976). To describe sets of event sequences called *event structures*, the speaker must be able to describe single events and event combinations and relationships and to indicate the significance of each event within the overall event structure.

Event structures or descriptions of entire events are based on a framework of scripts. Scripts based upon actual events form an individual's expectations about sequences and impose order upon event information (Johnston, 1982). These familiar activity sequences or scripts consist of ordered events within routine or high-frequency, regularized activities. These scripts influence interpretation and telling of events and narratives. By age 3, children are able to describe chains of events within familiar activities, such as a birthday party (Nelson, 1981b).

The speaker must have knowledge of both single events and connected event sequences, the linguistic knowledge of the method for describing events, and the linguistic skill to consider the listener's perspective (Duchan, 1986). Linguistic devices that speakers use include marking of event beginnings and endings, marking of perfective and imperfective aspect, and modal verbs. Beginnings can be marked by words or phrases such as *once upon a time*, *guess what happened to me*, *let's start at the beginning*, and so on. Endings include *the end*, *all done*, and *and that's how it happened*.

The elements of event knowledge are seen in the narratives of 4-year-olds. Underlying every story is an *event chain* or chronology of events. Events include actions, physical states such as possession and attribution, and mental states such as emotions, dispositions, thoughts, and intentions that are causally linked as motivations, enablements, initiations, and resultants in the chain. Causal explanations contain many of these features.

Narratives characterized as *unfocused temporal chains* lead directly from one event to another while other attributes—characters, settings, and actions—shift. This is the first level of chaining, and the links are concrete. As a result of the shifting focus, unfocused chains have no centers:

> The man got in the boat. He rowed. A big storm knocked over the trees—whish-sh, boom. The doggie had to swim. Fishies jumped out of the water. He had warm milk. And then he went to bed.

Temporal chains frequently include third-person pronouns; past tense verbs; temporal conjunctions such as *and, then*, and *and then*; and a definite beginning and ending.

Focused temporal or causal chains generally center on a main character who goes through a series of perceptually linked, concrete events:

There is this horsie. He eats—munch, munch—hay for breakfast. He runs out of the barn. Then he plays in the sun. He rolls in the warm grass. He comes in for dinner. He sleeps in a bed (Mimes sleep).

Causal chains are infrequent until age 5–7 years.

By the time children begin school, most have acquired the basic elements of narratives and can recount sequentially familiar or significant events. These narratives form much of the content of the conversations later encountered in older children and adults.

Summary

Although there is a considerable difference among families in the overall amount of talking, there are certain patterns. The amount of talking is a function of the energy level of the child and his conversational partners. Therefore, the largest proportion of talking occurs in the morning shortly after breakfast (Wells, 1985). The amount of talking is also related to the activity in progress. Most speech accompanies solitary play or play with others or occurs within activities devoted primarily to conversation. The amount of talking within these latter activities increases throughhout the preschool years. In contrast, very little talking occurs while either game or role playing, looking at books or television, or doing chores (Wells, 1985). In general, preschool boys play more alone, talking to themselves and calling bystanders to notice this play. In contrast, girls engage more in household activities and are drawn into talk while organizing the task at hand (Wells, 1985). The conversational context is dynamic, influencing what is said and, in turn, being influenced by it.

Throughout the preschool years the child learns to become a truer conversational partner, using a greater variety of forms to attain his ends. In addition, the child expands his suppositional skills and is better able to take the perspective of the other participant. Although he takes his conversational turn without being prompted with a question, the child still tends to make more coherent contributions to the conversation if he is discussing an ongoing activity in which he is engaged at the time. He is more aware of social roles at age 5 than at age 2 and can adjust his speech for younger children (Shatz & Gelman, 1973) or for role playing (Gearhart, 1978; Sachs & Devin, 1976), but he lacks many of the subtleties of older children and adults. As he begins to attend school, he will be under increasing pressure by both teachers and peers to use his language even more effectively.

STAGES OF SYNTACTIC AND MORPHOLOGICAL DEVELOPMENT

It may be helpful to our understanding if we divide the preschool period into stages of syntactic and morphological development. Several researchers have suggested just such a framework (R. Brown, 1973; Wells, 1985). After considering these frameworks, I have decided to organize this discussion on the model of Roger Brown because of its ease of understanding. Other significant studies, especially the exhaustive work of Wells (1985), will be highlighted throughout. Naturally, any discussion of language form requires the use of syntactic terms (parts of speech). These are defined as introduced in the chapter and also in the Glossary.

After completing a longitudinal study of child language, Brown noted that there are certain characteristic periods of language development that correspond to increases in the child's average utterance length, measured in morphemes. This value, the **mean length of utterance (MLU)**, is a moderately reliable predictor of the complexity of the language of English-speaking young children. Some researchers have found that for English-speaking preschoolers, MLU relates well to age, is reliable, and is a good predictor of language development (Rondal, Ghiotto, Bredart & Bachelet, 1987). Up to an MLU of 4.0, increases in MLU correspond to increases in utterance complexity. Above an MLU of 4.0, complexity of utterances relates more to the context, and utterance length is not necessarily increased (D'Odorico & Franco, 1985).

At best, MLU is a crude measure that is sensitive to only those language developments that increase utterance length. For example, the movement of elements within the utterance may result in more mature utterances but will not increase the MLU. Although there is a positive correlation between MLU and age, MLU may vary widely for children with the same chronological age (J. Miller, 1981; J. Miller & Chapman, 1981; Wells, 1985). It is also important to note that although MLU is a rough estimate of language complexity for English-speaking preschoolers, it is not so for users of other languages such as modern Hebrew, in which complexity does not necessarily result in longer utterances (Dromi & Berman, 1982).

From age 1 ½ to 5 years, MLU may increase by approximately 1.2 morphemes per year, although there is some indication of a decreased rate after 42 months (Scarborough, Wyckoff, & Davidson, 1986). MLU is a simplistic predictor of language development, a gross developmental index that itself provides no information on specific structural complexity or grammatical competence, even among children with the same MLU (Cazden, 1968; Klee & Fitzgerald, 1985). We use it here because of its conceptual simplicity for discussion.

Computing MLU

In general, 50 or 100 utterances are considered a sufficient sample from which to generalize about a speaker's overall production. An utterance may be a sentence or a shorter unit of language that is separated from other utterances by a drop in the voice, a pause, and/or a breath that signals a new thought. Once transcribed, each utterance is analyzed by morphemes; the total sample is then averaged to determine the speaker's MLU.

When analyzing the language of young children, several assumptions about preschool language must be made. Let's use the past tense as an example. The regular past tense includes the verb stem plus -ed, as in *walked* or *opened*. Hence, the regular past equals two morphemes. In contrast, the irregular past is signaled by a different word, as in *eat/ate* and *sit/sat*. As adults, we realize that *eat* plus a past tense marker equals *ate*. It could thus be argued that *ate* should also be counted as two morphemes. It seems, however, that young children learn separate words for the present and the irregular past, and are not necessarily aware of the relationship between the two (R. Brown, 1973). Therefore, the irregular past counts as one morpheme for young children. A similar logic exists for words such as *gonna* and *wanna*. As adults, we can subdivide these words into their components: *going to* and *want to*. Young children, however, cannot perform such analyses. Therefore, *gonna* counts as one morpheme for the child, not as the three represented by *going to*.

Although we may not agree with this rationale, we must adopt it if we are to discuss language development within Brown's framework. Guidelines for counting morphemes are presented in Table 9.2. Applying these rules, we would reach the following values:

> *Daddy bring me choo-choo s.* = 5 morphemes
> *Mommy eat-ed a-a-a sandwich.* = 5 morphemes
> *Doggie-'s bed broke baboom.* = 5 morphemes
> *Smokie Bear go-ing night-night.* = 4 morphemes
> *He hafta.* = 2 morphemes

TABLE 9.2   Brown's Rules for Counting Morphemes

Rule	Example
Count as one morpheme:	
Reoccurrences of a word for emphasis	*No! No! No!* (3 morphemes)
Compound words (two or more free morphemes)	*Railroad, birthday*
Proper names	*Billy Sue*
Ritualized reduplications	*Night-night, choo-choo*
Irregular past tense verbs	*Went, ate, got, came*
Diminutives	*Daddie, doggie*
Auxiliary verbs and catenatives	*Is, have, do; gonna, hafta*
Irregular plurals	*Men, feet*
Count as two morphemes (inflected verbs and nouns):	
Possessive nouns	*Tom's, daddie's*
Plural nouns	*Doggies, kitties*
Third person singular present tense verbs	*Walks, eats*
Regular past tense verbs	*Walked, jumped*
Present progressive verbs	*Walking, eating*
Do not count:	
Dysfluencies, except for most complete form	*C-c-c-candy, bab-baby*
Fillers	*Um-m, ah-h, oh*

Source: Adapted from R.Brown, *A First Language: The Early Stages*. Cambridge: Harvard University Press, 1973.

Once the morphemes for each utterance are counted, they are totaled and then divided by the total number of utterances. The formula is very simple:

$$\text{MLU} = \frac{\text{Total number of morphemes}}{\text{Total number of utterances}}$$

Thus, if the total number of morphemes for a 100-utterance sample is 221, the MLU will equal 2.21 morphemes per utterance. Remember that this is an average value and does not identify the length of the child's longest utterance. In other words, an MLU of 2.0 does *not* mean that the child uses only two-word utterances. The shortest and longest utterances are also important when considering the child's overall performance.

MLU and Stage of Development

The thrust of development changes with increased MLU. Major developments occur that can characterize certain MLU phases or stages. These stages are as follows (R. Brown, 1973):

Stage	MLU	Approximate Age (months)	Characteristics
I	1.0–2.0	12–26	Linear semantic rules
II	2.0–2.5	27–30	Morphological development
III	2.5–3.0	31–34	Sentence form development
IV	3.0–3.75	35–40	Embedding of sentence elements
V	3.75–4.5	41–46	Joining of clauses
V+	4.5+	47+	

Stage I is characterized by single-word utterances and by the word-order rules of early multiword combinations. Chapter 8 described this stage in some detail. Stage II is characterized by the appearance of grammatical morphemes, which mark many of the relations expressed previously by the child with word order in stage I. By stage III the child exhibits simple sentence forms, and he begins to modify these forms to mirror more adultlike forms for different sentence modalities, such as yes/no questions, *wh-* questions, negatives, and imperatives. Stage IV is marked by the beginning of embedding of phrases and clauses within another sentence. For example, the clause *who laughed* can be embedded in the clause *the boy is funny* to produce "The boy *who laughed* is funny." Finally, stage V is characterized by conjoining or by compound sentences. For example, the clauses *Mary washed* and *John dried* can be combined to form "Mary washed and John dried." Although each stage has some characteristic linguistic modifications, it should be noted that other, less obvious changes are also occurring.

MORPHOLOGICAL DEVELOPMENT

Several morphological developments begin in stage II but continue well into the school-age years. "Overt grammar or morpheme-combining begins really as soon as the MLU rises above 1.00" (R. Brown, 1973, p. 65), although the period of greatest acquisition is from 4 to 7 years. Since many morphemes are redundant or have alternative forms of expression, it is difficult to determine their age of acquisition. Even as adults, we are not aware of many morphological differences, such as the difference between *data* and *datum* or between *uninterested* and *disinterested*. (In court, however, we would clearly prefer a disinterested judge over an uninterested one.) Only the most commonly used morphemes will be discussed in the following section.

Stage II: Brown's 14 Morphemes

Stage II can be described by the appearance of morphemes that signify the semantic relations specified in stage I through word order. R. Brown (1973) isolated 14 morphemes for study. Selection was based on obligatory use. If use is obligatory rather than optional, then absence of the morpheme would indicate nonacquisition, not choice.

The 14 selected morphemes, presented in Table 9.3, have the following characteristics:

1. They are phonetically minimal forms. In general, they include simple phonemic additions or changes, such as the addition of an *s*.
2. They receive only light vocal emphasis.
3. They belong to a limited class of constructions, as opposed to the larger number of nouns and verbs.
4. They possess multiple phonological forms and can vary with the grammatical and phonetic properties of the words to which they are attached. For example, the *s* in *cats* is pronounced /s/, whereas the *s* in *dogs* is pronounced /z/.
5. Their development is slow.

Each morpheme emerges in stage II, but most morphemes are not fully mastered (used correctly 90% of the time) until later. The order presented in Table 9.3 reflects the order of mastery, not of appearance.

Present Progressive

The present progressive verb tense is used in English to indicate an activity that is currently in progress and is of temporary duration, such as *I am swimming*. The form consists of the auxiliary or helping verb *to be* (*am, is, are, was, were*), the main verb, and the *-ing* verb ending. Children initially express this verb tense with only the *-ing* ending. For example, a child might say "Swimming" or "Mommy eating." The present progressive verb tense without the auxiliary is the earliest verb inflection acquired in English and is mastered within stage II for most verbs used by young children (R. Brown, 1973; Kuczaj, 1978; J. Miller, 1981).

The present progressive can be used with action verbs in English but not with verbs of state, such as *need, know,* and *like*. Young children learn this distinction early, and few overgeneralization errors result (R. Brown et al., 1969).

TABLE 9.3   Brown's 14 Morphemes

Morpheme	Example	Age of Mastery* (in months)
Present progressive -ing (no auxiliary verb)	Mommy driving.	19–28
In	Ball in cup.	27–30
On	Doggie on sofa.	27–30
Regular plural -s	Kitties eat my ice cream. Forms: /s/, /z/, and /ɪz/ Cats (/kæts/) Dogs (/dɔgz/) Classes (/klæsɪz/), wishes (/wɪʃɪz/)	24–33
Irregular past	Came, fell, broke, sat, went	25–46
Possessive 's	Mommy's balloon broke. Forms: /s/, /z/, and /ɪz/ as in regular plural	26–40
Uncontractible copula (verb to be as main verb)	He is. (response to "Who's sick?")	27–39
Articles	I see a kitty. I throw the ball to daddy.	28–46
Regular past -ed	Mommy pulled the wagon. Forms: /d/, /t/, /ɪd/ Pulled (/pʊld/) Walked (/wɔkt/) Glided (/g l aɪ d ɪ d/)	26–48
Regular third person -s	Kathy hits. Forms: /s/, /z/, and /ɪz/ as in regular plural	26–46
Irregular third person	Does, has	28–50
Uncontractible auxiliary	He is. (response to "Who's wearing your hat?")	29–48
Contractible copula	Man's big. Man is big.	29–49
Contractible auxiliary	Daddy's drinking juice. Daddy is drinking juice.	30–50

* Used correctly 90% of the time in obligatory contexts. Adapted from Bellugi (1964), R. Brown (1973), and Miller (1981).

The child probably learns the rule one-verb-at-a-time by applying it to individual verbs to determine whether they are "-ingable" (R. Brown, 1973). Later the child abandons this strategy as being too cumbersome.

The child is capable of making a semantic distinction between action and state verbs and applying the rule for the present progressive appropriately. State verbs are not capable of expressing the present progressive meaning of temporary duration. When a child says "I eating," it is assumed that he'll stop soon. The action is temporary. On the other hand, adults don't say "I am knowing," because with *know* it is assumed that this state is of some duration. Thus a child learns some general rule of application that enables him to generalize the progressive form while not overgeneralizing to inappropriate verbs. Early learning may also reflect the difference between the progressive and many other morphological inflections (Kuczaj, 1978). There are no irregular progressive forms, resulting in less confusion for the child. Forms that are overgeneralized by children, such as the regular past tense *-ed*, have both regular and irregular forms. For example, *walked* and *ran* both express "past-ness," though only *walk* employs the regular past tense form *-ed*.

Prepositions

In and *on* are the only two prepositions to occur frequently enough for Brown to have declared that they are acquired within stage II (R. Brown, 1973; J. Miller, 1981). Often the child relates the preposition to the object itself. For example, you can put something *in* a cup but rarely *on* it. Other early prepositions include *away, out, over*, and *under* (W. Miller & Ervin-Tripp, 1964). Simple topographic or locational relations, such as *in, on*, and *under*, appear to be easier for the child to comprehend than dimensional spatial relations, such as *behind, beside, between*, and *in front of* (Washington & Naremore, 1978). Spatial relations describe a position relative to some object. In turn, these spatial relations are easier for the child if applied to an object with a recognizable side, such as the front of the television, rather than to an object such as a stool that does not have distinct sides. In the latter case, spatial directions relate to the perspective of the speaker and therefore require greater cognitive and pragmatic skill development, as noted in Chapter 7.

Plural

In English there is no morpheme to indicate the singular form of a noun; thus a singular noun is called *uninflected* or *unmarked*. The regular form of the plural, marked in writing by *-s*, is acquired within stage II (R. Brown, 1973; J. Miller, 1981). Learning of irregular forms takes considerably longer and largely depends upon how frequently these forms are used in the preschooler's environment.

The regular plural appears in short phrases first, then in short sentences, and finally in longer sentences. In addition, there appear to be four phases of development (W. Miller & Ervin-Tripp, 1964). Initially there is no difference between the singular and plural, and a number or the word *more* may be used to mark the plural. In other words, the child might say "Puppy" for one or more than one, or he might say "Two puppy" or "More puppy" to indicate plural. Next, the plural marker will be used for selected instances, probably on plural words that are used frequently. In the third phase, the plural generalizes to many instances, some of which are inappropriate. Thus, we get such delightful forms as *foots* and *mouses*. Finally, the regular and irregular plural are differentiated.

Acquiring the English plural involves phonological learning as well. Three different speech sounds are used with the plural: /s/, /z/, and /Iz/. If a word ends in a voiced consonant, the voiced plural marker /z/ is used, as in *beds* (/bɛdz/). In contrast, voiceless consonants are followed by the voiceless /s/, as in *bets* (/bɛts/). These rules do not apply if the final consonant is similar to the /s/ and /z/. The /s/,

Preschool children's language becomes more complex as the utterances increase in length.

/z/, /ʃ/, /ʒ/, /tʃ/, and /dʒ/ are called *sibilant sounds*, or **sibilants.** If a word ends in a sibilant, the plural marker is /Iz/ or /əz/, as in *bridges* (/brIdʒIz/). The /s/ and /z/ rules are learned first, followed by the rule for /Iz/. The child may be in stage V or beyond before these phonological rules are acquired. This distinction is especially difficult for deaf children because of the relatively high frequency or pitch and the complexity of sibilant sounds.

Irregular Past

Irregular past tense verbs, those that do not use the *-ed* ending, are a small but very frequently used class of words in English. A small subset of these verbs appears in single-word utterances and is acquired in stage II, probably learned individually by rote. These include *came, fell, broke, sat,* and *went.* Although the child acquires these forms early, he may later use the regular *-ed* marker to produce *goed/wented* or *falled/felled.* The irregular past of common verbs is once again produced correctly by stage V. Many irregular verbs are not learned until school age. Even some adults have difficulty with irregular verbs such as *drink, lie,* and *lay.* I avoid writing or saying the last two whenever possible. Like adults, children may generalize from a known form to one being learned. Thus, knowledge of *sing/sang* may yield *bring/brang*. Likewise, knowledge of *drink, drank, drunk* may result in *think, thank, thunk*.

Possessive

The possessive is originally marked with word order and stress; the use of the possessive marker (*'s*) appears relatively late. Initially, the possessive is attached only to single animate nouns, such as *Mommy* or *doggie*, to form *Mommy's* or *doggie's*. The earliest entities capable of being "possessed" are alienable objects, such as clothing, rather than inalienable entities, such as body parts. The morphological form is mastered by stage III. Phonological mastery takes much longer, however, as in the case of the plurals /s/, /z/, and /Iz/.

Uncontractible Copula

The verb *to be* (*am, is, are, was, were*) may serve as a main verb or as an auxiliary, or helping, verb. As a main verb it is called the **copula** and is followed by a noun, an adjective, or some adverbs or prepositional phrases. For example, in the sentences "He *is* a teacher," "I *am* sick," and "They *are* late," the verb *to be* is the only verb, and hence the main verb. All of these sentences contain the copula. In one sentence the copula is followed by a noun, *teacher*; in the second, by an adjective, *sick*; and in the third, by an adverb, *late*.

The copula appears initially in an uncontractible or full form (R. Brown, 1973). The notion of uncontractibility is based on those adult uses of the copula in which it is not permissible to form a contraction. In the sentence "She *is* angry," we can contract the copula to form "She's angry." Thus, the copula is contractible. It is not permissible to contract the copula when the answer to a question omits known or redundant information, leaving only the verb *to be*. For example, in response to the question "Who is hungry?", it is acceptable only to say "I *am*," not "I'm." In addition, the copula may not be contracted when it is the first or last word in a question ("*Is* he ill?" or "Do you know where she *is*?") or appears in negative sentences in which *not* is contracted (*n't*), as in "He *isn't* a lawyer." It would be incorrect to say "He'sn't a lawyer." The copula may be contracted, however, if the negative is in its full form, as in "He's not a lawyer." Finally, the copula may not be contracted in the past tense, as in "She *was* here." "She's here" is clearly present tense and would thus be incorrect because it changes the tense of the sentence.

In general, the copula, both uncontractible and contractible, is not fully mastered until stage V (J. Miller, 1981). It takes some time before the child sorts through all the copular variations for person and number (*am, is, are*) and tense (*was, were, will be, been*).

Articles

The articles *the* and *a* appear in stage II but take some time to be mastered. Initial use of *a* and *the* is probably undifferentiated, and it is sometimes difficult to ascertain from the child's pronunciation which article is being used. For adults, the indefinite article *a* is used for nonspecific reference and the definite *the* denotes specific reference. In addition, pragmatic considerations of informativeness influence article use. New information is generally marked with *a*, whereas old information is signaled by *the*. For example, you might introduce a new topic with "I need *a* new car." The subject of an automobile is new information, and the specific vehicle has not been identified. In your next sentence you might say, "*The* red one I saw last night was beautiful." Since *car* has already been mentioned, it is old information, and you have now identified a specific automobile. For both reasons, *the* is appropriate.

Distinctions in article use do not appear early. In general, articles are first acquired in a nominative, or naming, function. For example, the child might point to an object and say, "See the puppy." Initially the indefinite article tends to predominate, as in expressions such as "That's *a* kitty." As the child begins to use articles for reference, he uses the definite article predominantly, as in "*The* kitty go meow" when he's describing the behavior of cats in general. Use of the indefinite article in referencing expressions is acquired later (Emslie & Stevenson, 1981).

The age of article acquisition varies widely among children. Three-year-olds generally observe the indefinite–definite distinction, although they tend to overuse the definite article (Warden, 1976). This overuse, discussed under presuppositional skills, may reflect the child's egocentric assumption that more is known by his listener than adult speakers would assume. By age 4, the child is more capable of making complicated inferences about the listener's needs (Emslie & Stevenson, 1981; J. Miller, 1981). In addition, the 4-year-old knows that he must use *some* and *any* rather than *a* and *the* with mass nouns, such as *sand* and *salt* (Gordon, 1982). It has been noted that some children as old as 9 years, however, continue to overuse the definite article (Warden, 1976).

Regular Past

As we mentioned earlier, the regular past tense *-ed* marker is acquired after the child has demonstrated the use of a limited number of irregular past verbs. Few regular past inflected verbs appear at the single-word level (Trantham & Pedersen, 1976). Once the child acquires the regular past tense rule, he overgeneralizes it to irregular past tense verbs, producing forms such as *comed, eated,* and *falled*. Like other morphemes, the regular past has several phonological variations. The voiced /d/ follows voiced consonants, as in *begged* (/bɛgd/), and the unvoiced /t/ follows unvoiced consonants, as in *walked* (/wɔkt/). The third variation, /ɪd/ or /əd/, follows words ending in /t/ or /d/, such as *sighted* (/saɪtɪd/). The /ɪd/ form is acquired later than the voiced–voiceless /d–t/ distinction, which may explain why the regular past ending only occasionally overgeneralizes to irregular verbs ending in /t/ or /d/, such as *heard, told,* and *hurt* (Slobin, 1971).

Third Person Singular Marker: Regular and Irregular

The person marker on the verb is governed by the person (I, you, he/she) and number (he/she, they) of the subject of the sentence. In English the only present tense marker is an *s* on the third person singular verb, as in "That dog barks too much" or "She runs quickly." All other forms are uninflected, as in *I run, you dance, we sit,* and *they laugh*. The third person singular marker is redundant in most instances, since the subject generally expresses person and number. Only a few English verbs, such as *do* and *have*, are irregular. Although the regular and irregular forms appear in stage II, they are not mastered until stage V, and there is a long period of inconsistent use (Trantham & Pedersen, 1976).

Uncontractible Auxiliary

In general, the auxiliary or helping verb *to be* develops more slowly than the copula. Brown did not report on other helping verbs, such as *do* and *have*. Unlike the copula, the auxiliary is followed by a verb, as in "She *is* singing," which is a present progressive form. The uncontractible auxiliary is most frequent in the past tense, in which contraction of "He *was* eating" to "He's eating" would change the meaning. Like the copula, the uncontractible auxiliary *to be* is also used when it is the first or last word in a sentence, when the negative is contracted, or when redundant information is omitted, as in "He *is*" in response to the question "Who's painting?" The uncontractible auxiliary is mastered by stage V (J. Miller, 1981).

Contractible Copula

The contractible copula is mastered in late stage V or afterward (J. Miller, 1981). The copula is contractible if it can be contracted, whether or not it is actually contracted. Therefore, "Mommy *is* tall" and "Mommy's tall" are both examples of the contractible copula. The form does not alter the meaning of the sentence.

    The copula may take many forms to reflect person and number. In general, the *is* and *are* forms develop before *am* (Trantham & Pedersen, 1976). The *is* form tends to be overused, contributing to singular–plural confusion, such as "He *is* fast" and "They *is* big" or "We *is* hungry." The overlearning of contractions, such as *'s* and *'re*, also seems to add to the confusion. Contracted forms are short, often unemphasized, and therefore easily undetected when used incorrectly.

    There is considerable variation with *it's*. Initially, young children use *it's* and *it* interchangeably (Bellugi-Klima, 1969; R. Brown, 1973). In addition, the copula that appears on *it's* generalizes only very gradually.

Contractible Auxiliary

The development of the auxiliary is similar to that of the copula in the contractible form. The auxiliary *is* and *are* forms precede the *am* form, as in the copula. The contractible auxiliary is mastered after stage V.

Determinants of Acquisition Order

The cognitive relationship between the semantic and syntactic complexity of these morphemes is the key to developmental order, not the frequency of use in adult speech (R. Brown, 1973). Syntactic and semantic complexity become more evident when we note the order of acquisition in other languages. For example, the concept underlying plural—one and more than one—is quite simple and is learned early. Plural marking is very complex in Egyptian Arabic, however, and there are many exceptions to the plural rule. In contrast to English-speaking preschoolers, many Egyptian teenagers still have difficulty with the plural (Omar, 1973). Distinctions of gender can also be difficult. In English, as in French, there are only two genders, male and female, although most English words are not marked for gender. Fulani, a Niger-Congo language, contains about a dozen genders. These forms are semantically and syntactically complex, so children learn them more slowly and over a longer period of time than children learning English gender markers.

Initial morphological development of verb markers may be related to the underlying semantic aspects of the verb (Bloom, Lifter, & Hafitz, 1980). The child begins by developing a few protoform verbs that are general and nonspecific, such as *do, go,* and *make.* Once these general forms are developed, the verb markers appear quickly. This finding suggests that initial morphological learning may be on a word-by-word basis. In contrast, more specific verbs employ only one marker. The underlying temporal concept of the verb seems to be a factor. For example, the present progressive *-ing* first appears on verbs that display a discrete end, such as *drive,* but not on verbs that describe a discrete event, such as *hit* or *drop.* In contrast, the past tense marker is more likely to appear on verbs that describe a discrete event. Thus, initially the child is more likely to say "Daddy is *driving* the car" and "I *dropped* my cup." Initial morphological use is limited.

Morphological learning requires that the child correctly segment words into morphemes and correctly categorize words into semantic classes. If the child undersegments, he won't break the word or phrase into enough morphemes. The result is a creation such as "He *throw-uped* at the party" or "I like *jump-roping.*" Most of us learned the alphabet as ". . . J, K, *Elemeno,* P, Q, . . .," another good example of undersegmenting. In oversegmenting, the child uses too many morphemes, as in "Daddy, you're *interring-upt* me!" (Hockett, 1967). One of my sons referred to grown-ups as *dolts,* having oversegmented *adult* into the article *a* and *dolt.* Judging from some of the adults I know, maybe my son was more observant than we gave him credit for being!

Morphemes are not treated the same way by all language-learning children. In polymorphemic languages such as Mohawk, a northern New York and southern Quebec Native Indian language, in which words consist of many morphemes, children initially divide words by syllables rather than morphemes (Mithum, 1989). Children are more likely to note and produce stressed syllables rather than morphemes. In English, however, morphological development is more important.

Morphological rules apply to classes of words. Hence, *-ing* is used only with action verbs. If the child miscategorizes a word, errors may result. He may use inappropriate morphological prefixes and suffixes, as in the following:

> I'm *jellying* my bread. (using a noun as a verb, although we do say "buttering my bread")
> I got *manys.* (using a pronoun as a noun)
> He runs *fastly.* (using an adjective as an adverb)

Often these errors reflect the child's limited descriptive vocabulary. Undercategorization occurs when the child applies a category rule to subcategories, such as the regular past *-ed* on irregular verbs. Other examples include the following:

I saw too many *polices*. (using the plural *s* inappropriately on a mass noun)

I am *hating* her. (using the present progressive *-ing* inappropriately on a state verb)

Finally, in overcategorization the child applies a limited morpheme to other words, as in *unsad* and *unbig*. Many of the humorous utterances that young children produce reflect errors in segmentation or categorization.

Other Early Morphemes

Other morphemes appear and develop within Brown's stages but were not studied in detail by Brown. As a consequence, less is known about their acquisition.

Pronouns: Interdependence of Form, Content, and Use

Learning the English pronominal system is a very complex process. Although a pronoun is a simple device that enables one word to be the equivalent of one or several other words, the listener must understand these constituent equivalences. Speakers use **anaphoric reference**, or referral to what has come before. We can thus decipher *his* and *it* in the sentence "The boy was watching *his* television when *it* caught fire."

Some pronouns appear in stage II, whereas others emerge much later. (See Table 9.4 for the general order of pronoun acquisition.) The actual order is variable with each child. Initially children use labels or pronouns that can signal notice, such as *that*, as in "*That* a doggie" (Bellugi, 1971). As a group, subjective pronouns, such as *he, she,* and *they,* are acquired before objective pronouns, such as *him, her,* and *them.* These are followed by possessive pronouns, such as *his, her,* and *their,* and finally by reflexive pronouns, such as *himself, herself,* and *themselves.*

Not all linguists agree that there is a clear-cut order of pronoun acquisition, although most agree that the child begins with *I* and *it* and then adds *you* (Chiat, 1986). From there, children exhibit great individual diversity. Initial use tends to

TABLE 9.4   Development of Pronouns

Brown's Stages	Pronouns
I	*I, it* (subjective and objective)
II	*My, me, mine, you*
III	*Your, she, he, yours, we*
IV	*They, us, hers, his, them, her*
V	*Its, our, him, myself, yourself, ours, their, theirs*
V+	*Herself, himself, itself, ourselves, yourselves, themselves*

Source: Adapted from Haas & Owens (1985); Huxley (1970); Morehead & Ingram (1973); Waterman & Schatz (1982); and Wells (1985).

be sporadic and stereotypic. For example, *it* first appears in unanalyzed phrases, such as *stop it* and *look it.*

Children's production of nouns and pronouns suggests a number of use strategies (Haas & Owens, 1985):

- When in doubt, use a noun.
- Look for regularity. After learning the *her* (objective)/*hers* (possessive) relationship, the child may produce *him/hims.* Similarly, *her/herself* may generalize to *his/hisself.*
- Simplify complex pronominal forms. Reflexives may be reduced to objective case. For example, the child might say, "You looked in the mirror and saw *you*," rather than *yourself.* Plural pronouns may also be broken into their singular components. For instance, *they* may become *he* and *she*, and *we* may become *you* and *me.*
- Use previously learned pronominal forms to aid in the production of unlearned forms. Thus, children may use subjective forms for objective, objective forms for possessive, and possessive forms for reflexive. The following examples illustrate these substitutions:

  "I gave it to *he*." (subjective for objective)
  "It's *hims*" or "It *them* toy." (objective for possessive)
  "He sees *his* self." (possessive for reflexive)

By 36 months, children have mastered nearly all subjective and objective pronouns and the two demonstrative pronouns *this* and *that* (Wells, 1985). By age 5 nearly all children have mastered the subjective, objective, and possessive pronouns. They still must learn reflexive pronouns and the plural demonstrative pronouns *these* and *those.*

Pronouns offer a special situation in which it is easy to see the complex relationship between form, content, and use. In part, the lengthy acquisition period for pronouns reflects this complex interaction. Pronouns fill syntactic and semantic roles; make semantic distinctions based on gender, person, and number; and act as cohesive discourse devices. In short, the preschooler's usage may reflect learning of only one component of the pronoun's complex definition (Baron & Kaiser, 1975). Children seem to acquire one feature of the definition at a time. In general, the distinction of conversational role (*I/you*) is acquired before the gender distinction (*he/she*), which is followed by the distinction of participant/nonparticipant (*I, you/he, she*) (Brener, 1983; Charney, 1980; Sharpless, 1974).

The appearance of the first person singular pronoun *I* is quickly followed by the use of *you.* The child learns early to make the distinction between the speaker and the listener. Although children make errors within type, such as *I* for *me*, most children do not make errors between types, such as *I* for *you* (Waryas, 1973). *You* is first used in the imperative form, as in the command "*You* shut door" (Trantham & Pedersen, 1976).

The child follows a general strategy in which *I* is used if it is the first word in the sentence and *me* if it is not. This strategy very gradually evolves into a subjective/objective (*I/me*) case distinction (Bellugi-Klima, 1969). Not all children progress through the often-reported stages of referring to themselves by name, then by *me*, and finally by *I* (Trantham & Pedersen, 1976). In general, parents of toddlers avoid pronouns and refer to the child by name or as "Baby."

Other pronouns also cause some subjective/objective confusion. *He* and *she* are often confused with the possessive pronouns *his* and *her* (Trantham & Pedersen, 1976). The child's developing phonological system no doubt contributes to the overlapping use of *he, his*, and *him*. Similar errors are seen with *she, her*, and *hers*. The possessive pronouns *my* and *your* do not appear to be overextended to other pronominal cases and are usually mastered by late stage II or early III.

Morphological distinctions related to possession may also pose a problem for the child. Inconsistent use of the possessive marker (*'s*), present in "Mommy's hat" but not in "her hat," may result in confusion. It is not uncommon to hear utterances such as "This is *hers* hat," in which the child adds the possessive marker to subject and object pronouns.

As a conversational device, pronouns provide cohesion between old and new information. As we discussed earlier, new information is first identified by name. Then, once identified, it becomes old information and can be referred to by a pronoun. The pronoun refers to what came before or makes anaphoric reference to it. When there is possible confusion, preschool children often use pronominal apposition, as in "My mother, she . . ." (Cotton, 1978). Unless it is a dialectal device, pronominal apposition begins to disappear by school age.

In general, the deictic function of pronouns is acquired before the anaphoric one. In other words, children use pronouns initially to mark the spatial relationship of persons and things to the speaker (*I, me* vs. *you* vs. *it*), and only later to mark nouns previously identified (*Mary* becomes *she*) (Wales, 1986).

It is easy to see why pronouns are so difficult for some children to learn. The pronoun system is very complex and combines elements of all aspects of language. Confusion between pronouns is rare (Chiat, 1986). Although children may overuse nouns in place of pronouns, the reverse is almost nonexistent.

Other Auxiliary Verbs

Auxiliary, or helping, verbs in English can be classified as primary, such as *be, have*, and *do*, or as secondary or modal, such as *will, shall, can, may*, and *must* (F. Palmer, 1965). In general, auxiliary verbs are the only verbs that can be inverted with the subject to form questions or that can have negative forms attached. Examples of auxiliary forms include the following:

> *Are* you running in the race?
> What *have* you done?
> I *can*'t help you.
> I *may* not be able to go.

The copula (*to be*) is an exception to this rule, since it can also be inverted and made into a negative form, as in *Is she sick?* or *This isn't funny.*

TABLE 9.5   Auxiliary Verb Use by 50% of Children

Auxiliary Verb	Age (in months)
Do	27
Have + V-en	27
Can	30
Be + V-ing	30
Will	30
Be going to	33
Have got to	36
Shall	39
Could	42

Source: Adapted from G. Wells, "Learning and Using the Auxiliary Verb in English." In V. Lee (Ed.), *Language Development*. New York: Wiley, 1979, p. 258.

In addition, auxiliary verbs are used to avoid repetition in elliptical responses that omit redundant information and for emphasis (F. Palmer, 1965). For example, when asked "Who can go with me?" a respondent avoids repetition by the elliptical reply "I *can*." To affirm a statement emphatically, a speaker might say, "I *do* like to dance."

There is wide variation in the acquisition of auxiliary verbs (Wells, 1979). Table 9.5 presents the ages by which 50% of the children studied had begun to use selected auxiliary verbs. The auxiliaries *do*, *have*, and *will* are used by most children by 42 months.

Noun and Adjective Suffixes

During the preschool years the child masters a few additional suffixes for nouns and adjectives. These include the adjectival comparative *-er* and the superlative *-est*. By adding these to descriptive adjectives, the child can create forms such as *smaller* or *biggest*. The superlative is understood by about 3 ½ years of age; the comparative somewhat later, at age 5 (Carrow, 1973). Correct production follows shortly. Specific forms, such as *better* or *best*, which are exceptions to the rule, usually take longer to master.

The derivational noun suffix *-er*, added to a verb to form the name of the person who performs the action, is also understood by age 5 and mastered in production within a short time. For example, the person who *teaches* is a *teacher*; the one who *hits is a hitter*, and so on. One reason for the late appearance of this marker may be its ambiguous nature. The *-er* is used for the comparative (*bigger*) and for noun derivation (teacher). In addition, several other derivational noun suffixes, such as *-man*, *-person*, and *-ist*, can also be used. Two-year-olds tend to rely on the *-man* suffix, often emphasizing it, as in *fisherman*, which contains both the *-er* and the *-man*. Other more creative examples are *busman*, *storewomen*, and *dancerman*.

Cognitive Learning and Morphological Rules

Morphological rule learning reflects phonological and semantic rule learning as well. Morphological rules are learned at an early age and may be a continuum from rules that apply to specific words through sound sequence rules (Derwing & Baker, 1977). Initial learning, as with the plural marker, may occur on a case-by-case basis. Higher-order rules require more complex integrative learning. Lexical generalizations relate concepts to "vocal symbols." In so doing, the child learns that a concept may have more than one form or that forms that he originally construed to be morphologically distinct, such as *big* and *bigger*, are actually alternatives of the same concept. At the next level, morphophonemic rules are required to account for commonalities. For example, the /f/ turns to /v/ preceding a plural, as in *knife/knives* and *wolf/wolves*. This rule is not true for all words ending in /f/, though, such as *cough* or *laugh*. The child recognizes regularity but must sort out the exceptions. Each of us has heard a small child say a word such as *knifes* (/n aI fs/) during this phase. At the highest level, such phonotactic or sound sequence rules may cross several morphological variations to govern sound sequences. The plural, possessive, and third person markers all follow the same "both voiced or voiceless" rule discussed earlier.

In fact, phonological variations may influence early morphological use. The child may not recognize the common morpheme beneath these variations. For example, the child may not realize that the ending sound on *cats*, *dogs*, and *bridges* signals the same morphological change, pluralization. In other words, morphemic inflections may have no psychological reality for the child. Morpheme recognition is easier if the semantic and phonological variations are minimal, as with *teach–teacher* rather than *good–better–best*.

In addition to phonological considerations, the underlying semantic concept may influence morphological development. For example, cognitive and semantic distinctions may be reflected in the order of acquisition of auxiliary verbs (Wells, 1979). Initially the child learns auxiliary verbs concerned with the agent in actual events (*do, have, will*), then with the agent as potential doer (*can, have got to, have to, must, should, had better*), then with a likelihood of events (*might, may*), and finally with inferences about events not experienced (*could*). Thus the child progresses from a more concrete action orientation to an abstract reference. Early morphological development focuses on more concrete relationships, such as plural and possession. Abstract relationships such as person and number markers on the verb tend to take longer to master. The progression from concrete to abstract is also reflected in the developing child's cognitive processing.

SENTENCE FORM DEVELOPMENT

By the time the child enters stage III, at around 30 months, he has mastered the basic subject-verb-object and subject-copula-complement forms of the English sentence (Wells, 1985). Shortly thereafter, the subject also becomes obligatory. Recall that the most basic of Chomsky's phrase structure rules is that a sentence consists of a noun phrase and a verb phrase. The only required syntactic elements are the noun (subject) and the verb (predicate). Therefore the child has acquired both elements of simple adult declarative sentences by late stage II to early III. Once these are acquired or in the process of being acquired, the child begins to experiment with and to modify the basic pattern. Thus, development occurs at two levels: within sentence elements and at the sentence level. The result is the internal development of noun and verb phrases and the development of declarative, interrogative, and imperative sentence types and the negative forms of each.

Sentence Elements

Before we look at different sentence forms, we should examine internal sentence development. Of interest are development of noun and verb phrases.

Noun Phrase Development

Singular nouns form the largest syntactic class represented in the first 50 words of children. Although combined with other words in stage I, nouns are generally elaborated only when they occur alone. Initially elaboration includes the addition of the indefinite article (*a*) or the demonstrative *that* to the noun or *head* word. The average child is forming these combinations by 21 months (Wells, 1985). Thus, the child is likely to say such phrases as "a kitty" or "that candy." Later noun phrase expansions include the addition of possessive nouns (*Daddy's* shoe), quantifiers (*some* cookie), and physical attributes (*big* doggie) to the head. Multiple modifiers are rare in stage I; the child is not yet likely to say "my big doggie." The list of early modifiers is generally small and only gradually expands.

In stage II, both objective case nouns and nouns that appear alone in a phrase are modified. For example, the child might say "Daddy throw *big ball*" (objective case) but rarely "*Big doggie* go 'ruff' " (subjective case). In addition, the child uses a limited set of pronouns in the head function, including *I*, *it*, and *that*. The 2-year-old child is thus capable of achieving contextual coherence by using noun phrases (Bennett-Kaster, 1983). He is able to introduce new noun phrases and to reflect the noun phrase's given or old status later.

Children seem to acquire a general rule that adjectives precede nouns very early. In addition, they learn that adjectives do not precede pronouns and proper nouns (P. Bloom, 1990). For example, it is not acceptable for mature English speakers to say *little he* or *old Charles*. Two-year-olds rarely use this form. Possibly they make a semantic distinction between nouns, which can take descriptors, and pronouns and proper nouns, which in full noun phrases do not.

Elaboration occurs in both the subjective and the objective case by stage III, with both articles and modifiers preceding the noun (R. Brown & Bellugi, 1964; Wells, 1985). Both singular and plural nouns are elaborated. Demonstratives and articles may include *this, that, these*, or *those* and *a* or *the*, respectively. Modifiers include quantifiers, such as *some, a lot*, and *two*; possessives, such as *my* and *your*; and adjectives.

By stage IV, the child demonstrates by his production that he knows that a noun or pronoun subject is obligatory or required for a sentence (Ingram, 1971). Nouns dominate in the head function until 33 months, when they decrease as pronouns increase sharply. At 39 months, nouns level off in 30% and pronouns increase in more than 40% of all noun phrase head functions (Wells, 1985). Modifiers may include *some, something, other, more,* and *another.* The most frequent noun phrase elaborations still involve only one element preceding the noun, such as "*A* girl eated *my* cookie." Only gradually does the child learn the different noun phrase elements and the rules for sequential ordering. For example, as mature language users, you and I intuitively know that the words in the phrase *my big red candy apple* are in the correct order but that those in *red big candy my apple* are not. The ordering of elements of the noun phrase is illustrated in Table 9.6.

TABLE 9.6   Elements of the Noun Phrase

Initiator	+	Determiner	+	Adjective	+	Noun	+	Postnoun Modifier
Only, a few of, just, at least, less than, nearly, especially, partially, even, merely, almost		Quantifier: *All, both, half, no, one-tenth, some, any, either, each, every, twice, triple* Article: *The, a, an* Possessive: *My, your, his, her, its, our, your, their* Demonstratives: *This, that, these, those* Numerical Term: *One, two, thirty, one thousand*		Possessive Nouns: *Mommy's, children's* Ordinal: *First, next, next to last, last, final, second* Adjective: *Blue, big, little, fat, old, fast, circular, challenging* Descriptor: *Shopping,* (center), *Baseball,* (game), *hot dog,* (stand)		Pronoun: *I, you, he, she, it, we, you, they, mine, yours, his, hers, its, ours, theirs* Noun: *Boys, dog, feet, sheep, men and women, city of New York, Port of Chicago, leap of faith, matter of conscience*		Prepositional Phrase: *On the car, in the box, in the gray flannel suit* Adjectival: *Next door, pictured by Renoir, eaten by Martians, loved by her friends* Adverb: *Here, there,* Embedded clause: *Who went with you, that you saw*
Examples: *Nearly*		*all the one hundred*		*old college*		*alumni*		*attending the event*
Almost all of		. . . *her thirty*		*former brother's*		. . . . . *clients*		
Nearly		*half of your*		*old baseball*		*uniforms*		*in the closet*

The first postnoun modification appears in early stage IV with short phrases, such as in "That *there*" and "The one *with the collar*." By the end of stage IV, nouns appear with both prenoun determiners and postnoun phrases (Wells, 1985).

With the appearance of relative clauses—subordinate or dependent clauses that modify nouns, such as *who lives next door*—the child begins in stage V to use *clausal postnoun modifiers* as well, such as in "The dog *who lives next door* is big." Neither phrasal nor clausal postnoun embedding is widely used by children until school age.

Between ages 4 and 5, the child makes dramatic changes in his ability to use several noun phrases in succession (Bennett-Kaster, 1983). Thus his stories become denser and longer. Five-year-olds can introduce noun phrases throughout a narrative and weave events relevant to these noun phrases. The result is that younger children tell stories about a relatively limited number of characters and events, while older children spin episode after episode with "mini" narrative for nearly all noun phrases within the larger narrative (Bennett-Kaster, 1983).

Verb Phrase Development

Verb phrases may be of three types: *transitive, intransitive,* and *stative* (Table 9.7). In mature language, transitive verbs take a direct object and include words such as *love, hate, make, give, build, send, owe,* and *show*. With few exceptions—verbs such as *have, lack,* or *resemble*—transitive verbs can be changed from active to passive voice by exchanging the positions of the two noun phrases.

Active Voice	*Passive Voice*
Mary sent a letter.	A letter was sent by Mary.
Sue loves Fran.	Fran is loved by Sue.

In contrast, intransitive sentences do not have a passive form, nor do they take direct objects. Examples include *swim, fall, look, seem,* and *weigh*. Although we say "She swam the river," it is awkward to say "The river was swum by her." Some verbs may be both transitive and intransitive:

I *opened* the door slowly. (transitive: *door* is direct object)
The door *opened* slowly. (intransitive: no direct object)

Overall, transitive verb phrases are more common in English than in other languages.

Stative verbs, such as the copula *to be*, are followed by a *complement*, an element that sets up an equality with the subject. In *She is a doctor*, *doctor* complements or describes what *she* is.

Many verbs appear in the single-word phase of development. At this time, both *transitive* and *intransitive* verbs are produced, but the child does not observe the adult rules for each. Obviously, the child using solely single-word action or *want* utterances will be using verbs without direct objects.

In stage II the child begins to use the morphological modifications we discussed previously. The present progressive tense *-ing* marker is mastered within this stage. In addition, the child begins to use semi-infinitive forms such

TABLE 9.7   Elements of the Verb Phrase

Modal Auxiliary	+	Perfective Auxiliary	+	Verb to be	+	Negative*	+	Passive	+	Verb	+	Prepositional Phrase, Noun Phrase, Noun Complement, Adverbial Phrase
May, can, shall, will, must, might, should, would, could		Have, has, had		Am, is, are, was, were, be, been		Not		Been, being		Run, walk, eat, throw, see, write		On the floor, the ball, our old friend, a doctor, on time, late

Examples:
Transitive (may have direct object)

May . . . . . . have . . . . wanted . . . . a cookie
Should . . . . not . . . . throw . . . . . the ball in the house

Intransitive (does not take direct object)

Might . . . . . have . . . . . . been . . . . walking . . . . to the inn
Could . . . . not . . . . talk . . . . with you

Equative (verb to be as main verb)

. . . . is . . . . not . . . . a doctor
. . . . was . . . . late
. . . . were . . . . on the sofa
May . . . . be ill

*When modal auxiliaries are used, the negative is placed between the modal and other auxiliary forms, for example, might not have been going.

as gonna, wanna, and hafta (J. Miller, 1981). *Infinitives* consist of *to verb*, as in *to go*. When we say "I'm gonna go" we include the infinitive in our meaning "I'm going *to go*." These forms may be used with a main verb, as in "I gonna eat," or alone, as in a response such as "I hafta." *Auxiliary* or helping **verbs**, such as *can, do*, and *will/would*, first appear in their negative form in later stage II. Every parent can attest to the appearance of forms such as *can't, don't*, and *won't*.

True auxiliary verbs appear in late stage III, including *can, do*, and *will*. As noted in our previous discussion, the verb *be*, used as an auxiliary, may not correctly reflect the verb tense or the number and person of the subject. This inappropriate marking is also evident in the copula. Thus the child may produce "He *am*," "You *is*," and so on, although initially he may overuse *is*. In addition, the stage III child will usually begin to overextend the regular past *-ed* marker to irregular verbs, thus producing *eated, goed*, and so on.

The variety but not the frequency of maternal verb usage appears to be a strong predictor of the child's development of verbs (J. de Villiers, 1985). The child seems to learn verbs as individual items rather than as categories of words. As the child acquires each new verb, he observes similarities of syntactic use across items and uses these similarities to predict novel combinations. "For children, rules may first apply to particular lexical items, then to semantically . . . coherent subclasses, then finally to the category appropriate in adult grammar" (J. de Villiers, 1985, p. 588).

By stage IV the modal auxiliaries *could, would, should, must*, and *might* appear in negatives and interrogatives or questions (Chapman, 1978; J. de Villiers & P. de Villiers, 1973). Semantically, **modal auxiliaries** are used to express moods or attitudes such as ability (*can*), permission (*may*), intent (*will*), possibility (*might*), and obligation (*must*).

The child still overextends the regular past in stage IV. A sentence may be doubly marked for the past, producing sentences such as "I *didn't* throw*ed* it." In this example, the child applies the past tense marker to the main verb even though the auxiliary verb assumes the tense marker.

By stage V the child has mastered both the regular and the irregular past tense in most contexts, as well as other morphemic inflections, such as the third person singular and the contractible copula (J. Miller, 1981). Auxiliary verbs and sentence subjects are inverted appropriately in questions ("What *is she* doing?"), and *do* is inserted when no auxiliary is present ("What *do* you want for your birthday?"). For example, the statement "Mother is eating a cookie" forms a question when the subject and the auxiliary verb are inverted, resulting in "Is mother eating a cookie?" When no auxiliary is present, as in "Joey wants a cookie," a *do*, called the *dummy do*, is inserted before the subject to form "*Does* Joey want a cookie?"

Many verb forms are still to be mastered after stage V. These include many of the forms of the verb *be*, past tense modals and auxiliaries, and the passive voice.

Time and Reference.   In English, time and reference to that time are marked by both verb *tense* and *aspect*. **Tense**, such as past or future, relates the speech time, which is in the present, to the event time, or the time when the event occurs. **Aspect** concerns the dynamics of the event relative to its completion, repetition, or continuing duration. The development of tense and aspect reflects both cognitive development and linguistic differences. Not all languages use tense and aspect. For example, Mandarin Chinese uses only aspect, and modern Hebrew uses only tense. The appearance of the linguistic markers for tense and aspect depends on the relative difficulty of acquiring these markers in each language. In English, tense and aspect, which are intertwined, are acquired later than in Japanese, in which there are distinct suffixes for each (Weist, 1986).

Children's sense of time and reference to it go through phases of development during the preschool years. These are noted in Table 9.8 (Weist, 1986). Initially, the child is limited to the here and now. The event time is the same as

---

TABLE 9.8   Development of a Sense of Time and Reference

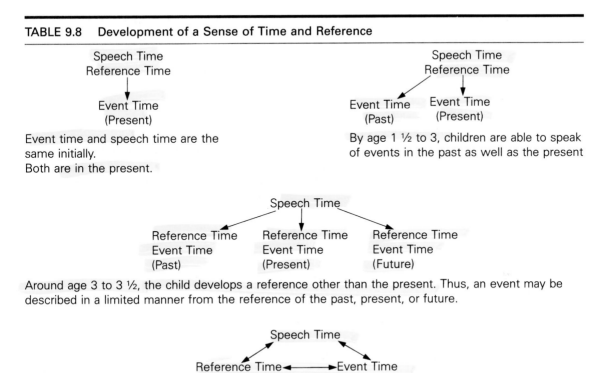

Speech Time
Reference Time

↓
Event Time
(Present)

Event time and speech time are the
same initially.
Both are in the present.

Speech Time
Reference Time

Event Time   Event Time
(Past)   (Present)

By age 1 ½ to 3, children are able to speak
of events in the past as well as the present

Speech Time

Reference Time   Reference Time   Reference Time
Event Time   Event Time   Event Time
(Past)   (Present)   (Future)

Around age 3 to 3 ½, the child develops a reference other than the present. Thus, an event may be
described in a limited manner from the reference of the past, present, or future.

Speech Time

Reference Time ◄────────► Event Time

By age 3 ½ to 4, the child develops a flexible system that enables the child to describe events in the
past, present, or future from the perspective of all three times.

Source: Adapted from Weist (1986).

---

the speech time. In other words, the child talks about things that are occurring
now. There is no tense or aspect marking, although verbs have various pragmatic
functions (Wells, 1985). In languages as different as English, Polish, Hebrew, Japanese, and Mandarin Chinese, children use the imperative form for requests
("Want juice") and the indicative form to comment ("Doggie run")(Berman, 1985;
Clancy, 1985; Erbaugh, 1982; Zarebina, 1965).

Between age 1 ½ and 3, children speak about the past or present, although
the reference point is always in the present. Although children are capable of
distinguishing aspect, these markers are not combined with tense. In languages
as different as English, French, Turkish, Japanese, Polish, Spanish, and Brazilian
Portuguese, children can distinguish past from nonpast, complete from noncom-
plete, continuative from noncontinuative, and future from nonfuture (Aksu &
Slobin, 1985; Clancy, 1985; Clark, 1985; DeLemos, 1981; Eisenberg, 1982).

Around age 3 to 3 ½, the child gains a sense of reference other than the
present. This occurs at about the same age in languages as different as English,
Italian, French, Mandarin Chinese, German, Turkish, and Polish (Clancy, Jacob-

sen & Silva, 1976; Clark, 1985; Weist, 1986). The notion of referent points can be explained with the following two examples:

Kim drove yesterday.
We had hoped to go yesterday.

In the first, the action was completed in the past but we are describing it from the reference point of the present. In the second, the event is clearly in the past but the reference is some time even earlier, prior to yesterday. Initially, children use adverbs of time such as *yesterday* and *tomorrow*. Only later do they use terms such as *before* and *after*.

Finally, between age 3 ½ and 4, the child acquires a flexible reference system. This development allows free reference to different points in time. For example, the child might say, "Yesterday, Gran'ma asked, 'Would you like to go to the zoo next week?' " A flexible reference system evolves at about the same time that the child acquires the cognitive skills to arrange things in a series and to reverse this sequential order.

Sentence Types

Within stage III the child begins to use more adult sentence types to express basic relationships, such as *declarative*, *interrogative*, and *imperative* and the *negative* forms of each (Table 9.9). Initial development of each appears early, but the emergence of adult forms takes some time. The majority of children, however, possess the basic sentence types in English by age 5 (Wells, 1985).

In general, preschool sentence development can be gauged by an increase in the number of sentence elements and in the diversity of sentence forms. Description of this process becomes increasingly difficult, as complexity reflects internal movement of elements and diversity results in many forms, each occurring only infrequently. Increases in the number of elements usually occur in declaratives before occurring in other sentence types, probably because of the extra processing demands required for interrogatives and negative (Wells, 1985). Likewise, changes in verbs occur later in the copula than in other verbs.

Declarative Sentence Form

Declarative sentences or statements gradually increase in complexity and in number of elements or constituents throughout the preschool years. Beginning with the *agent* + *action* and *action* + *object* semantic relationships, the child develops the basic *subject* + *verb* + *object* sentence format by about 30 months. Additionally, acquired lexical items enable the child to form transitive, intransitive, and stative clauses.

By stage III, the child has added the auxiliary verb forms *do, have, can, be,* and *will*. The *subject* + *auxiliary* + *verb* + *object* form ("Mommy *is* eating ice cream"; "*I'll* drive that") appears before the *subject* + *auxiliary* + *copula* + *complement* form ("Daddy *will* be here"), which occurs in late stage III or early stage IV (Wells, 1985). Declaratives with double auxiliaries, as in "You *will have* to do it" (Wells, 1985), appear in late stage IV.

TABLE 9.9 Acquisition of Sentence Forms within Brown's Stages of Development*

Stage	Age (in months)	Declarative	Negative	Interrogative	Embedding	Conjoining
Early I (MLU: 1–1.5)	12–22	Agent + action; Action + object	Single word – *no, all gone, gone;* negative + X	*Yes/no* asked with rising intonation on a single word; *what* and *where*		Serial naming without *and*
Late I (MLU: 1.5–2.0)	22–26	Subj + verb + obj appears	*No* and *not* used interchangeably	*That + X; what +* noun phrase + *(doing)? Where* + noun phrase + *(going)?*	Prepositions *in* and *on* appear	*And* appears
Early II (MLU: 2.0–2.25)	27–28	Subj + copula + compl appears				
Late II (MLU: 2.25–2.5)	28–29	Basic subject-verb-object used by most children	*No, not, don't,* and *can't* used interchangeably; negative element placed between subject and predicate	*What* or *where* + subj + pred; Earliest inversion appears with copula in *What/where* + copula + subj	*Gonna, wanna, gotta,* etc. appear	
Early III (MLU: 2.5–2.75)	31–32	Subj + aux + verb + obj appears; auxiliary verb forms *can, do, have, will* and *be* appear	*Won't* appears;			*But, so, or,* and *if* appear
Late III (MLU 2.75–3.0)	33–34	Auxiliary verb appears with copula in subj + aux + copula + X		Auxiliary verbs *do, can,* and *will* begin to appear in questions; inversion of subject and auxiliary verb appears in yes/no questions		

(handwritten note: mean length (morphemes) utterances)

TABLE 9.9 Continued

Stage	Age (in months)	Declarative	Negative	Interrogative	Embedding	Conjoining
Early IV (MLU: 3.0–3.5)	35–37		Negative appears with auxiliary verbs (subj + aux + neg + verb)	Inversion of auxiliary verb and subject in wh- questions	Object noun phrase complements appear with verbs such as *think, guess,* and *show;* embedded *wh-* questions	Clausal conjoining with *and* appears (most children cannot produce this form until late stage V); *because* appears
Late IV (MLU: 3.5–3.75)	38–40	Double auxiliary verbs appear in subj + aux + aux + verb + X	Adds *isn't, aren't, doesn't,* and *didn't*	Inversion of copula and subject in yes/no questions; adds *when* and *how*	Infinitive phrases appear at the ends of sentences	
Stage V (MLU: 3.75–4.5)	41–46	Indirect object appears in subj + aux + verb + ind obj. + obj	Adds *wasn't, wouldn't, couldn't,* and *shouldn't;* negative appears with copula in subj + copula + neg.	Adds modals; stabilizes inverted auxiliary; some adultlike tag questions appear	Relative clauses appear in object position; multiple embeddings appear by late stage V; infinitive phrases with same subject as the main verb	Clausal conjoining with *if* appears; three-clause declaratives appear
Post-V (MLU: 4.5+)	47+		Adds indefinite forms *nobody, no one, none,* and *nothing;* has difficulty with double negatives	Questions other than one-word *why* questions appear; negative interrogatives beyond age 5	Gerunds appear; relative clauses attached to the subject; embedding and conjoining appear within same sentence above an MLU of 5.0	Clausal conjoining with *because* appears with *when, but,* and *so* beyond an MLU of 5.0; embedding and conjoining appear within the same sentence above an MLU of 5.0

*Based on approximately 50% of children using a structure.

Finally, in stage V, the child acquires indirect objects. The *subject + verb + indirect object + object* form ("He gave *me* the ball") appears prior to the *subject + verb + object + to + indirect object* form ("He gave the ball to me") (Wells, 1985). Other later developments include embedding, conjoining, and the internal development of the noun phrase.

Interrogative Sentence Form

Through the use of intonation, children learn to ask questions very early. By age 4 the child, according to many parents, seems to do nothing else. Questioning is a unique example of using language to gain information about language and about the world in general. I recall my own sense of loss when I replied "I used to" to my daughter's query "Do you ever talk to the trees?"

There are three general forms of questions: those that assume a yes/no response, those that begin with a wh- word and assume a more complex answer, and those that are a statement to which agreement is sought by adding a tag, such as ". . . isn't he?" Yes/no questions seek confirmation or nonconfirmation and are typically formed by adding rising intonation to the end of a statement, as in "You're eating snails?" ↑ ; by moving the auxiliary verb, as in "Are you eating snails?"; or by adding an auxiliary verb to a position in front of the subject, as in "Do you like snails?" Typical *wh-* or constituent questions use words such as *what, where,* and *who.* The verb is inverted, as in yes/no questions, and the *wh-* word appears before the subject unless it is the subject, as in *who* questions. In tag questions, a proposition is made, such as "He loves sweets," then negated in the tag: "He loves sweets, doesn't he?" A reverse order might produce "He doesn't love sweets, does he?"

Questions are very prevalent in the speech adults address to children (Remick, 1976; Snow, 1978). Though the amount of questioning doesn't change much in the first 18 months for each parent–child pair, the types of questions and the topics do. At first, questions are used to comment on the child's gaze or to direct the child's attention to the mother's activity. By 18 months the questions are mostly tutorial or genuine requests for information.

Children begin to ask questions at the one-word level through the use of rising intonation ("Doggie?" ↑), through some variation of *what* ("Wha?", "Tha?", or "Wassat?"), or through a PCF. There appear to be three phases of question development in young children (Table 9.9) (Klima & Bellugi, 1966). The first phase, which corresponds to an MLU of 1.75 to 2.25, is characterized by the following three types of question form:

Nucleus + intonation	That horsie?
What + noun phrase + (*doing*)	What that?
	What doggie (doing)?
Where + noun phrase + (*going*)	Where ball?
	Where man (go)?

These questions are confined to a few routines in which the child requests the names of objects, actions, or locations. The child neither comprehends nor asks other *wh-* questions appropriately, although *why* may be used as a turn filler to keep the conversation going. *What* and *where* may appear early because they relate to the child's immediate environment (Tyack & Ingram, 1977). *What* is used to gain labels; *where*, to locate lost objects. In addition, both are heavily used by parents to encourage the child's performance, and are related to the semantic categories of nomination and location.

During the next phase, which corresponds to late stage II and early stage III, the child continues to ask *what* and *where* questions but uses both a subject and a predicate. Examples include "What doggie eat?" and "Where Johnnie is?" Other questions, such as the yes/no type, are still identified by rising intonation alone, as in "Daddy go work?" ↑ .

The first subject-verb inversion occurs at the end of this phase in *wh-* interrogatives with the copula (*wh-* + *copula* + *subject*) (Wells, 1985). Inversion may occur in this form first because of its simplicity. As might be expected, the first *wh-* words in this construction are *what* and *where*.

In the third phase, the child begins to use the auxiliary forms required in adult question form (Klima & Bellugi, 1966). This phase corresponds to late stage III and stage IV (MLU, 2.75 to 3.5). It is during this stage that the child is developing the auxiliary verb in other sentence types, and there is carryover to interrogatives. Although rising intonation continues to be an alternative form for asking yes/no questions, the auxiliary begins to be inverted, as in the adult form. Shortly after the child inverts the auxiliary in yes/no questions appropriately, he begins to invert within *wh-* and yes/no copular interrogative constructions (Bellugi, 1971; Wells, 1985), although for some children there may be no lag between auxiliary inversion in yes/no and constituent questions (Ingram & Tyack, 1979). Some children may begin to use auxiliaries in the properly inverted form (Klee, 1985). In *wh-* questions, the type of *wh-* word used may influence whether or not the auxiliary is inverted (Kuczaj & Brannick, 1979). In general, the earlier the *wh-* word is acquired, the more likely the verb is to be inverted. Hence, the child would be more likely to invert the verb in what questions than in why questions. Inverted forms, whether in yes/no or *wh-* questions, are not mastered for some time. These forms require the child to learn the following three rules:

1. The auxiliary verb is inverted to precede the subject.

   She can play house. *Can* she play house?
   Tom is eating candy. What *is* Tom eating?

2. The copula is inverted to precede the subject.

   They are funny? *Are* they funny?
   Mary is in school. Where *is* Mary?

3. The dummy do is inserted before the subject if no copula or auxiliary exists.

   Carol loves Tony. *Does* Carol love Tony?
   Mike drank a soda. What *did* Mike drink?

By the end of stage IV, the child has attained the basic adult question form. Additional constituent forms, such as *who, when,* and *how,* also appear, though the child still has some difficulty with the temporal aspects of the last two (Kuczaj & Maratsos, 1975). This difficulty has been discussed in relation to cognitive growth in Chapter 7.

The general order of acquisition of *wh-* question types may also relate to the elements in the sentence that each *wh-* word replaces (Wootten, Merkin, Hood, & Bloom, 1979). Words such as *what, where,* and *who* are pronoun forms for the sentence elements they replace. For example, in the sentence "Mother is eating ice cream," we can substitute *what* for *ice cream.* The resultant question is "What is mother eating?" In contrast, words such as *how,* and *when* are used to ask for semantic relations within the sentence. These semantic relations are more difficult than simple noun substitutions; they develop later and cannot usually be replaced by a single word. The late development of *why* interrogatives can be explained in similar fashion. Unlike the other *wh-* types, *why* interrogatives affect the entire clause rather than sentence elements or relationships.

The ability to respond to *wh-* questions is also related to semantics and to the immediate context (Parnell, Patterson, & Harding, 1984). In general, preschool children are more successful in giving appropriate and accurate responses when the question refers to objects, persons, and events in the immediate setting. Recognition of the type of information sought, such as an object or a location, seems to precede the ability to respond with the specific information requested, such as the name of the object or location.

As in negation, stage V interrogative development is mainly concerned with tensing and modals. In addition, the child stabilizes the use of the inverted auxiliary. The adult tag question form doesn't appear until stage V because of its relative complexity and its infrequent usage in American English (Klee, 1985). Less complex forms—using tags such as *okay, huh,* and *eh,* as in "I do this, okay?"—develop earlier. These forms are more commonly used among English-speaking populations of Canada and Australia in sentences such as "Nice day, eh?"

There are three phases in the development of tag questions (Reich, 1986). At first, one tag form, such as *okay,* is used for all tag questions. Truer tags are added later, but with no negation of the proposition. For example, the child might ask, "You like cookies, *do* you?" Finally, the full adult tag, as in "You like cookies, *don't you?*" or "You don't like cookies, *do you?*", is acquired during early school age. American English-speaking children acquire the adult form later than do British and Australian children because of its infrequent use in American English. Canadian children may also be somewhat late in mastering the full adult form because of the colloquial use of *eh* or *aye,* as in "You bought a new suit, *eh?* Just right for this weather, *eh?*" (Dennis et al., 1982). I usually tease my Canadian students that it is impossible for them to make a declaration because they always attach *eh* to the end of every sentence.

Negative interrogatives appear after age 5. In general, negative interrogatives, such as "Aren't you going?", are first acquired almost exclusively in the uninverted form, as in "You aren't going?" (Erreich, 1984).

Imperative Sentence Form

Adult imperative sentences appear in stage III. In the imperative form the speaker requests, demands, asks, insists, commands, and so on that the listener perform some act. The verb is uninflected and the subject, *you*, is understood. Examples include the following:

> Gimmee a cookie, please.
> Throw the ball to me.
> Pass the peas, please.

It is somewhat difficult to recognize the imperative in English because there are no morphological markers. In addition, stage I children will produce early forms that mirror imperative sentence form, such as "Eat cookie." These are not true imperatives, however, because young children often omit the subject from sentences clearly intended to be declarative (R. Brown, 1973). Omission reflects processing limitations. There is no unequivocal marking of younger children's imperative forms. This is not meant to imply that toddlers cannot demand of or command others. Even at a prelinguistic level, infants are very adept at expressing their needs.

Negative Sentence Form

There are five adult forms of the negative: (1) *not* and *-n't* attached to the verb; (2) negative words, such as *nobody* and *nothing*; (3) the determiner *no* used before nouns or nounlike words, as in "*No* cookies for you"; (4) negative adverbs, such as *never* and *nowhere*; and (5) negative prefixes, such as *un-*, *dis-*, and *non-* (Klima & Bellugi, 1973). Rejection of, or opposition to, a proposition is the first type of negation to emerge, possibly because the child is expressing attitudes toward events and entities that are within his sensorimotor knowledge. The side-to-side head shake to indicate negation appears at 10–14 months (Pea, 1979). The child uses this gesture to express rejection of an event, object, or activity that is being proposed or to reprimand himself for attempting some prohibited activity. The earliest symbolic negative to appear is the single-word form *no*, which is frequently found within the first 50 words (K. Bloom, 1970; Bowerman, 1973a; Nelson, 1974). This appearance suggests that the very young child develops the negative concept and uses it nonsyntactically. The order of emergence of negative types is not the same for nonverbal and verbal modes (J. de Villiers, 1984). In contrast to the nonverbal use of negative initially as rejection, in the verbal mode the child expresses nonexistence first, then rejection, and finally denial (Clancy, 1985).

Syntactic negation appears in two-word utterances, generally as "negative + *X*," though the reversal may also be seen (Bellugi, 1967; Klima & Bellugi, 1966). In this period, *no* and *not* are used interchangeably. The *X* is usually less complex than an entire sentence (K. Bloom, 1970). For example, the child might say "Baby eat ice cream," but when negating would produce "No eat ice cream" rather than "No Baby eat ice cream." Thus, the negative element appears prior to the verb, as in adult negation, and utterances such as "No Daddy go bye-bye" appear rarely.

In general, the full *negative + sentence nucleus* form is usually seen in rejection of a proposed or current course of action (J. de Villiers & P. de Villiers, 1979). For example, if the father were in the process of leaving and the child objected, he might state, "No Daddy go bye-bye." Other negative utterances use the *negative + verb* format, such as "No go bye-bye" when describing Daddy's return from putting something in the car or "No eat ice cream," mentioned previously. The specific negative element(s) the child uses seems to reflect parental use with the child. Some parents prefer to control behavior with *no*; others employ *don't*. In general, children prefer to use certain forms to fulfill specific functions. Since this is an individual preference, there is great variety (J. de Villiers & P. de Villiers, 1979).

Within stage II the child may also use the negative in nonsyntactic statements such as "No Daddy." These can be explained only as a conversational or discourse device (Bellugi, 1967). The child may produce "*No/not* + an affirmative statement" in response to a previous utterance. For example, if the mother says "Mommy pick you up," the child may respond with "No Daddy." While the surface interpretation appears to negate any help from her father, the child may mean "*No,* Mommy, *Daddy* will do it."

There seem to be three periods of syntactic development of negation (Table 9.9), which do not correspond exactly to Brown's stages (Bellugi, 1967). The first period, discussed earlier, occurs in stage I and early stage II up to an MLU of 2.25. In the second period, which corresponds to late stage II and early III, the child uses the contractions *can't* and *don't* interchangeably with *no* and *not*. The child does not differentiate these forms, and their positive elements, *can* and *do*, appear only later (R. Brown et al., 1969). Hence, the sentences "I don't eat it" and "I can't eat it" may mean the same thing. *Won't* appears in late stage III and may also be used interchangeably with *no, not, don't,* and *can't*. Within a sentence, the negative structure is placed between the subject and the predicate or main verb.

In the final period, an MLU of 2.75 to 3.5, the child develops other auxiliary forms. This period corresponds roughly to Brown's stage IV. The child develops the positive elements *can, do, does, did, will,* and *be,* which may be used with *not* followed by a verb, as in "She *can not* go." Contracted forms also continue to occur. It will be some time, however, before the child correctly uses all the morphological markers for person, number, and tense with auxiliary verbs. Because use of auxiliaries is a relatively new behavior, the child may continue to make errors, such as double tense markers, as in "I didn't did it." By late stage IV the child's negative contractions include *isn't, aren't, doesn't,* and *didn't* (J. Miller, 1981). This development of negative forms continues in stage V with the addition of the past tense of *be* (*wasn't*) and modals such as *wouldn't, couldn't,* and *shouldn't.* These forms appear infrequently at first. In addition, the *copula + negative* form, as in "She *is not (isn't)* happy," appears in stage V (Wells, 1985).

The period of most note for negation is around stage III, when the child begins to vary the negative in form and to insert it between the subject and predicate. Thus, negative utterances move from the *negative + X* form to a *subject + negative + predicate* form. These changes are obvious adaptations toward the structure used by adults to express negation. Hence, the development of negation appears to be one of the significant aspects of stage III (R. Brown, 1973).

It would be incorrect to assume, however, that children master the negative within the preschool period. Negative interrogatives do not appear until after age 5. In addition, indefinite forms, such as *nobody, no one, none*, and *nothing*, prove troublesome even for some adults. It is not uncommon to hear

> I don't want none.
> Nobody don't like me.
> I ain't scared of nothing.
> I didn't get no cookies.

Some of these double negatives occur so frequently in the speech of children and some adults that they almost seem acceptable.

EMBEDDING AND CONJOINING

Sentences are strings of related words or larger units containing a noun subject and a verb or predicate. For example, the sentence "She ate cookies" is a string of words related in a certain way. *She* has acted upon *cookies*. Other strings can be in a series, one following another. We have all heard a child's sentence similar in form to this one:

> I ate popcorn, cotton candy, hot dogs, soda, ice cream, pretzels, and threw up.

Here the subject acts upon several serial objects.

The units within sentences are composed of clauses, phrases, and words. A **phrase** is a group of related words that does not include a subject and a predicate and is used as a noun substitute or as a noun or verb modifier. For example, the phrase *to fish* can take the place of a noun. In the sentence "I love candy," *to fish* can be substituted for *candy*, a noun, to form "I love to fish." Other phrases modify nouns, as in "The man *in the blue suit*," or verbs, as in "He fought *with a vengeance*." The phrase is said to be embedded within a sentence.

In contrast to a phrase, a **clause** is a group of words that contains both a subject and a predicate. A clause that can stand alone as grammatically complete is a **simple sentence**. Thus, "Jesus wept" is a simple sentence. Occasionally a sentence may contain more than one clause. When a sentence is combined with another sentence, they each become **main clauses**. A **compound sentence** is made up of two or more main clauses joined as equals, as in "*Mary drove to work, and she had an accident*." Both "Mary drove to work" and "She had an accident" are simple sentences serving in the larger compound sentence as main clauses. Main clauses may be joined by conjunctions, such as *and, but, because, if,* and so on. This process is called *conjoining* or coordinating.

Some clauses, such as *whom we met last week*, cannot stand alone even though they contain a subject and a predicate. In this example, *we* is the subject and *met* is the predicate, or main verb. Such clauses, called **subordinate clauses**, function as nouns, adjectives, or adverbs in support of the main clause. For example, *she is the girl*, a simple sentence, or main clause, can be joined with the subordinate clause above to form "She is the girl whom we met last week." A sentence such as this, made up of a main clause and at least one subordinate clause, is called a **complex sentence.** The subordinate clause is said to be embedded within the main clause. In general, subordinate clauses are introduced by subordinating conjunctions, such as *after, although, before, until, while*, and *when,* or by relative pronouns, such as *who, which,* and *that.* For example, the sentence "He doesn't know when it began to rain" contains the subordinate clause *when it began to rain*, which serves as the object of the verb *know.* In "The man who lives here hates children," *who lives here* is a subordinate clause modifying *man.*

In the following sections, we shall discuss the development of both embedding within a sentence and conjoining. As you can imagine, multiple embeddings may result in very complicated sentences.

R. Brown (1973) found embedding to be one of the primary characteristics of stage IV. Most children use some form of embedding within this stage (J. Miller, 1981). Conjoining characterizes stage V, though early conjoining may begin in stage IV. In embedding, a phrase or sentence becomes a grammatical constituent of another sentence, such as acting as an adverb or postnoun modifier. Though conjoining also combines simple sentences, these sentences are not assigned constituent roles within another sentence because each is a main clause.

Phrasal Embedding

Phrases can be formed in four ways: (1) with a preposition, (2) with a participle, (3) with a gerund, and (4) with an infinitive. A prepositional phrase contains a preposition, such as *in, on, under, at,* or *into*, and its object, along with possible articles and modifiers, as in *on the roof* or *at the school dance*. These forms have developed throughout stages II through V, beginning with the appearance of *in* and *on.* Development continues throughout the school-age years. Children begin adding prepositional phrases to the ends of sentences at around age 3.

A participial phrase contains a participle (a verb-derived word ending in *-ing, -ed, -t, -en*, or a few irregular forms) and serves as an adjective. Examples of participles include the *setting sun, a lost cause, a broken promise*, and *a fallen warrior.* In the sentence "The boy riding the bicycle is athletic," *riding the bicycle* is a participial phrase describing or modifying *boy.*

In contrast, a gerund, which also ends in *-ing*, functions as a noun. Gerunds may be used as a subject ("*Skiing* is fun"), as an object ("I enjoy *skiing*"), or in any other sentence function that may be filled by a noun.

Finally, an infinitive phrase may function as a noun but also as an adjective or adverb. An infinitive consists of *to* plus a verb, as in "He wanted *to open* his present." The entire phrase *to open his present* is an infinitive phrase serving as the object of the sentence. The *to* may be omitted after certain verbs, as in "He helped *clean up the mess*" or "He dared not *speak aloud.*"

Infinitive Embeddings

At around age 2 ½ the child develops semiauxiliaries such as *gonna* and *wanna*. Occasionally these forms are followed by a verb, as in "I want (or *wanna*) eat cookie," but they may be used alone, as in "I wanna" (Wells, 1985). The word *to* is first used at about this time, but as a preposition indicating "direction toward," as in "I walked *to* the store" (Bloom, Tackeff, & Lahey, 1984). By stage IV, forms such as *gonna, wanna, gotta, hafta,* and *sposta* are being used regularly with verbs to form infinitive phrases, usually in the object position. Examples include "I gotta go home" and "I wanna play." The semiauxiliary and the verb share the same subject.

More complex infinitives also begin to appear, usually at the ends of sentences. For example, the child develops *wh-* infinitives, such as "I know *how to do it*" and "Show me *where to put it*." The child also begins to use unmarked infinitive phrases following verbs such as *help, make,* and *watch,* as in "She can help me *pick up these*." This form is more difficult for the child because the infinitive is not clearly marked.

In stage V the child begins to use infinitives with nouns other than the subject. For example, the child may say "This is the right way *to do it*" or "I got this *to give to you*."

Most post–stage V children (MLU of 4.5 to 5.0) use simple but true infinitives with the same subject as the main verb (J. Miller, 1981). Infinitives are initially learned and used with a small set of verbs, such as *see, look, know, think, say,* and *tell,* as in "I want *to see it*" or "I don't have *to tell you*" (Bloom et al., 1984).

Gerund Embeddings

In general, gerund development follows that of infinitives (Table 9.9). Gerunds appear after stage V. They first appear in the object position at the end of the sentence. Gerunds are one of the first forms of derivational suffixes acquired, using *-ing* to change a verb to a noun. Occasionally the results are amusing. One of my kids declared "I hate nightmaring."

Subordinate Clause Embedding

Embedding of subordinate clauses appears at about the same time as true infinitives (Table 9.9). In general, we find three types of embedding: (1) object noun phrase complements, (2) indirect or embedded *wh-* questions, and (3) relative clauses. Although object noun complements and embedded *wh-* questions appear first, they are quickly replaced by more elaborate forms. As a result, by age 4 ½ to 5, these types of subordination account for less than 15% of all two-clause utterances (Tyack & Gottsleben, 1986).

Object noun phrase complements consist of a subordinate clause that serves as the object of the main clause. For example, we could say "I know *X* (something)" in which *X* is the object. We could also replace *X* with a subordinate clause, such as *(that) I hate it* to form "I know *(that) I hate it.*" An early form such as "I want *that*" may initially appear in stage III (Wells, 1985). The fuller clausal object noun phrase complements first appear in stage IV (R. Brown, 1973; Limber, 1973; Tyack & Gottsleben, 1986). These subordinate clauses generally have the form of simple sentences, as in

> I know *that you can do it.*
> I think *that I like stew.*

By late state V, the child may omit the conjunction *that*. In general, the subordinate clause fills an object role for transitive verbs, such as *think, guess, wish, know, hope, like, let, remember, forget, look,* and *show*. The verb in the main clause is most often *think*. By stages IV and V, these types of embedding account for over 85% of all two-clause utterances (Tyack & Gottsleben, 1986) A similar construction following the copula, as in "That is what I know," develops after stage V (Wells, 1985).

 Indirect or **embedded** *wh-* **questions** may fill a role similar to that of the object of the sentence. In the following sentences, the *wh-* subordinate clause fills the object function, as in "I know *X*":

> I know *who did it.*
> She saw *where the kitty went.*

Initial subordinating words include *wh-* words such as *what, where,* and *when,* with *what* being used most frequently (Scott, 1988). Since this form appears at about the same time that the child begins to acquire the adult interrogative form, the child may show some confusion. Resultant forms may include

> I know *what is that.*
> Tell me *where does the smoke go.*

 Relative clauses are subordinate clauses that follow and modify nouns. Rather than take the place of a noun, these clauses are attached to a noun with relative pronouns, such as *who, which,* and *that*. The earliest relative pronouns are *that, what* and *where* (Scott, 1988; Wells, 1985). At first, these clauses modify empty or nonspecific nouns—*one, kind, thing*—or abstract adverbs—*place, way*—to form sentences such as "This is the one *(that) I want*" or "This is the way *(that) I do it*" (Wells, 1985). In these examples, the object of the sentence is *one* or *way,* and the subordinate clause specifies *which one* or *which way*. Later relative clauses are used to modify common nouns.

 Relative clauses appear in late stage V, close to the fourth birthday, and develop only gradually, accounting for less than 15% of the two-clause utterances of 4 ½- to 5-year-olds. (R. Brown, 1973; Limber, 1973; J. Miller, 1981; Wells, 1985). As with other types of embedding, expansion begins at the end of the sentence, as in the following:

> This is the kind *what I like.*
> This is the toy *that I want.*

In these examples, the relative clause is attached to and modifies the object of the sentence. Some examples of relative clauses attached to the subject include

> The one *that you have* is big.
> The boy *who lives in that house* is a brat.

Relative clauses attached to the subject do not develop until after 5 years of age (Menyuk, 1977; Wells, 1985). These forms are still rare by age 7.

Many connective words used to join clauses are first learned in nonconnective contexts. For example, *what* and *where* appear in interrogatives prior to their use as relative pronouns. The connective *when* is an exception (Wootten et al., 1979). *When* is used as a connector to mark temporal relations before the *when* question form develops. Thus, children are likely to produce "I don't know *when* he went" before "*When* did he leave?"

Mature English speakers can omit some relative pronouns, such as *that*, without changing the meaning of the sentence. At first, the child needs these pronouns in order to interpret the sentence. By stage V, however, he can comprehend a sentence that omits the subordinate conjunction. The child begins to omit some relative pronouns in his own production in late stage V, though this form is rare in the speech of preschool children (Menyuk, 1977):

> This is the candy *that* I like. (relative pronoun present)
> This is the candy I like. (relative pronoun omitted)

By late stage V, most children can produce multiple embeddings within a single sentence, although such forms are rare even throughout the early school years (J. Miller, 1981). For example, a child may combine a subordinate clause (italicized) with an infinitive (underlined) to produce

> I think *we gotta go home now*.

Later forms also include conjoined clauses and embedding in the same sentence.

Clausal Conjoining

In stage I the child may produce two-word or three-word utterances that consist of a series of objects, such as "Coat hat" or "Cookie juice." No relation seems apparent other than a naming sequence. The child may omit the conjunction *and*, which is, however, the first conjunction to appear, usually by late stage I. Once *and* is acquired, it becomes an all-purpose conjunction used in place of the others, even though the child acquires *but, so, or*, and *if* in stage III. Most children have appropriate production of *and* between 25 and 27 months of age (Bloom, Lahey, Hood, Lifter, & Fiess, 1980; Lust & Mervis, 1980). Characteristically, the child lists entities or produces compound objects, such as "You got *this and this*." Such listing reflects cognitive growth. Cognitively, children are able to form collections of things before they can form an ordered series (Inhelder & Piaget, 1969). Individual sentences within a series may begin with *and*, as in the following:

> And I petted the dog. And he barked. And I runned home.

In this example, *and* fills an temporal function meaning *and then*.

In stage IV the conjunction *because* appears, either alone or attached to a single clause, as in the following examples:

ADULT: Scott, why did you do that?
CHILD: Because.
ADULT: Scott, why did you do that?
CHILD: Because Roger did.

Utterances with *because* are particularly interesting. Since the 3- or 4-year-old child has difficulty recounting events nonsequentially, he will respond to event queries with a result response rather than a causal one (see the discussion of 4-year-olds in Chapter 3). In response to "Why did you fall off your bicycle?" he is likely to respond " 'Cause I hurted my leg"—a result, not a cause.

The first clausal conjoining occurs with the conjunction *and* in stage IV (Table 9.9). For example, the child might say "I went to the party *and* Jimmie hit me." It is not until late stage V, however, that most children can use this form (Lust & Mervis, 1980; J. Miller, 1981). In general, *and* is used as the all-purpose conjunction, marking most conjunctive semantic relations (Bloom, Lahey, Hood, Lifter, & Fiess, 1980; Scott, 1988). For example, *and*, which is additive, will be used for temporal, causal, and adversative functions in place of *when*, *then*, *because*, and so on, as in the following:

We left *and* mommy called. (meaning *when*)
We had a party *and* we saw a movie. (meaning *then*)
She went home *and* they had a fight. (meaning *because*)

Depending on the child, *and* may be used 5–20 times as frequently as the next most common conjunction in the child's repertoire (Scott, 1988). Even in the narratives of 5-year-olds and school-age children, *and* is the predominant connector of clauses (Bennett-Kaster, 1986; Scott, 1987).

Clausal conjoining with *if* appears in late stage V, *because* in post-stage V, and *when*, *but*, and *so* even later, beyond an MLU of 5.0 morphemes. Most children are capable of conjoining clauses with *if* during this latter period (J. Miller, 1981). These are not usually complicated sentences; they are more likely to be of the "I can *if* I want to" form. Initially, the causal relationship may be signaled by *that's why*, as in "They're running; that's why they broke the window" (Wells, 1985). The order of conjunction acquisition reported for American English seems to be true for other languages as well and may reflect the underlying cognitive relationship (Clancy, Jacobson, & Silva, 1976).

The conjunctions *because* and *so* are initially used to mark psychological causality or statements of people's intentions (H. Johnson & Chapman, 1980). For example, use of *because* might explain "He hit me *because he's mean*" rather than "The bridge fell *because the truck was too heavy*." If the child were to discuss the bridge falling, he might state, "The bridge fell *because it was tired*," using feeling or intention to explain the event. Young children tend to talk about the present or the future, although there is a trend toward recounting the past as children get older and, as noted, narratives become more causally related (McCabe &

Peterson, 1985). With this recounting, there is a greater necessity to discuss the intentions preceding behaviors.

At around age 4, the child may begin to exhibit conjoining and embedding within the same sentence. Most children are using this type of structure, although rarely, by age 5. Such multiple embedding might result in the following:

Sally wants to stay on the sand and *Carrie is scared of crabs.*

Three-clause sentences, both embedded and conjoined, appear at about the same age. The child might join three main clauses, as in the following:

Johnny flew his kite, I ate a hot dog, and *daddy took a nap.*

Another variation might include the embedding and conjoining of three clauses, as in the following:

I saw Bambi, and *Billy saw the one that had the Ninja turtles.*

Although both multiple embedding and three-clause sentences are rare in the speech of the typical kindergartener, they do occur occasionally. By age 4 ½ to 5, multiple embeddings and three-clause sentences may account for about 11% of all child utterances.

Conjoining may include whole clauses or clauses with deleted common elements, called **phrasal coordination**, as in "Mary ran and fell." In full clausal or **sentential coordination**, such as "Mary ran and Mary fell," *Mary* is redundant and may be deleted, as in the first example. Obviously, sentential coordination, such as "Mary ran and John fell," does not lend itself to such shortening. Conjoining is relatively independent of the length of the two units to be conjoined, although, obviously, the very young child is not capable of producing long utterances (Bloom, Miller, & Hood, 1975; Lust & Mervis, 1980). Initially sentential coordination seems to be used for events that occur at different times in different locations, while phrasal coordination is used for simultaneous or near-simultaneous events in the same location (Jeremy, 1978).

In phrasal coordination, forward reductions are more common and appear earlier than backward reductions (Lust & Mervis, 1980). In **forward reductions** the full clause is stated first, followed by a conjunction, plus the nonredundant information. "Robbie made the cookies by himself and ate them before dinner" is an example of forward reduction. *Robbie* is redundant in the second clause. Conversely, in **backward reductions** the full clause follows the conjunction, as in "Robbie and Carolyn baked cookies together." Ease of processing may be more closely related to the amount of information the child is required to hold than to the direction of reduction (Hakuta, de Villiers, & Tager-Flusberg, 1982). Preschool children have great difficulty with a sentence such as "The sheep patted the kangaroo and the pig the giraffe" because of the amount of information that must be held in short-term memory while deciphering this sentence.

Pragmatic and semantic factors seem to affect conjoining as well. Clausal conjoining occurs where two referents must be clearly distinguished. The child encodes only what he presupposes the listener needs to interpret the sentence

(P. de Villiers, 1982). The complexity of semantic relations expressed by conjoining is also a factor (Bloom, Lahey, Hood, Lifter, & Fiess, 1980). These might be additive, causal, or contrastive. Initial clausal conjoining is additive; no relationship is expressed, as in "Tom went on the hike and Bob was at Grandma's." Then conjoining is used to express either simultaneous or sequential events, as in "I went to school and I went shopping after dinner." Causal relationships with *and* appear next, as in "*X and* [led to] *Y.*" Later *because* is used for causality. Finally, the child expresses adversity or a contrasting relationship, usually with the use of *but*. The late appearance of the conjunction *but* in clausal conjoining is probably related to the complex nature of such propositions. The expectation that is set up in the first clause is not confirmed in the second (R. Brown, 1973), as in "I went to the zoo, but I didn't see any tapirs." Although the forms of these compound sentences are all *clause + conjunction + clause*, the relations between the clauses, as expressed in the conjunction, form a hierarchy that affects the order of acquisition.

Summary

The syntactic development of the preschool child is rapid and very complex. The interrelatedness of both syntactic structure and syntactic development makes it difficult to describe patterns of development. In general, the preschool child tries to discover and employ syntactic regularity. He uses the predominant subject-verb-object sentence structure and depends on order of mention for sequencing. Newly acquired structures, such as the negative and embedded phrases and clauses, are initially attached to either end of the sentence and only later integrated into it. These and other language-learning principles were discussed in detail in Chapter 7.

SEMANTIC DEVELOPMENT

The preschool period is one of rapid lexical and relational concept acquisition. It is estimated that the child adds approximately five words to his lexicon every day between age 1 ½ and 6 years (Carey, 1978).

It is possible that the preschool child employs a **fast mapping** strategy that enables him to infer a connection between a word and its referent after only one exposure (Pinker, 1982). Fast mapping may be the first in a two-step process of lexical acquisition (Carey & Bartlett, 1978). First, the child roughs out a tentative definition connecting the word and available information. This step may be followed by an extended phase in which he gradually refines the definition with new information acquired on subsequent encounters. How much the child stores through fast mapping is unknown, but initial acquisition may be receptive rather than expressive in nature (Dollaghan, 1985; Holdgrafer & Sorenson, 1984).

Most likely, young children learn single words as unique units, each with its own meaning, probably unrelated to other word meanings. Although these word meanings lack relationship, the system is simple and easy to use.

Children may use two operating principles to establish meanings: *contrast* and *conventionality* (Clark, 1990; Gathercole, 1989). Contrast is the assumption that every form—morpheme, word, syntactic structure—contrasts to every other in meaning. A speaker chooses a form because it means something other than what some other expression means. In other words, it contrasts to other options. Conventionality is the expectation that certain forms will be used to convey certain meanings.

Taken together, the two principles predict that, whenever possible, speakers will use established forms with conventional meanings that contrast clearly to other forms. Difficulty occurs when a well-established form has a meaning similar to that of a newly learned form. Thus, it may be easier for children to have unrelated unique meanings initially.

New word meanings come from both the linguistic and nonlinguistic contexts (Au, 1990) and from the surrounding syntactic structure (Naigles, 1990). Let's assume that a child hears the following sentence: "Bring me the *chromium* tray, not the red one" (Gathercole, 1989, p. 694). He might proceed through the following steps to differentiate the meaning:

1. Assume that Mommy is trying to communicate with me.
2. Unknown word used in reference to trays as descriptor.
3. Only observable difference between the trays is color.
4. Chromium must be a color.
5. One tray is red.
6. Must not have wanted red tray or would have asked for it.
7. Therefore, must want other than red tray, which is chromium in color.

The acquisition of relational terms, such as those for location and time, is a complex process. In general, the order of acquisition is influenced by the syntactic complexity, the amount of adult usage in the child's environment, and the underlying cognitive concept. This development was examined in Chapter 7 in relation to cognitive growth.

PHONOLOGICAL DEVELOPMENT

Many of the morphological and syntactic changes noted in the preschool years are related to phonological development and reflect the child's underlying phonological rule system. In addition to developing the phonetic inventory described in Appendix A, the preschool child is also developing phonological rules that govern sound distribution and sequencing. Distributional rules govern the positions of sound in words. For example, in English /ŋ/ and /ʒ/ cannot appear at the beginning of words, and /h/ cannot appear at the end. Sequential rules, usually related to the distributional rules, state which sounds may appear together. In English, for example, words cannot begin with /bn/ or /tl/, but these sequences may appear in other positions, as in *abnormal* and *sweetly*. (Note, however, that the adjacent consonants are in different syllables.)

As with other aspects of language, the child's phonological development progresses through a long period of language decoding and hypothesis building. The child uses many rule forms that he will discard or modify later. Several linguists have attempted to determine children's phonological rule systems from their performance (Ingram, 1976; Oller, 1974). Many of the rules are listed in Table 9.6. These rules reflect "natural processes" (Oller, 1974) that act to simplify adult forms of speech for young children. Much of the child's morphological production will depend upon his ability to perceive and produce phonological units. During the preschool years, the child not only acquires a phonetic inventory and a phonological system; he also "develops the ability to determine which speech sounds are used to signal differences in meaning" (Ingram, 1976, p. 22).

Some sounds and rules are more difficult to perceive and produce. This is evidenced by the long acquisitional process, which continues into early elementary school. It appears that perception of speech sounds precedes production but that the two aspects are not parallel (M. Edwards, 1974; Garnica, 1973). Some sound contrasts are very difficult for the child to perceive and produce.

Phonological Processes

We will discuss the phonological processes of the preschool child, summarized in Table 9.10, in some detail. Additional descriptive information and examples will also be presented. Most of these processes are discarded or modified by age 4.

Syllable Structure Processes

Once the child begins babbling, the basic speech unit he uses is the CV syllable. During the preschool years, the child frequently attempts to simplify production by reducing words to this form or to the CVCV structure.

The most basic form of this process affects the final consonant (Ingram, 1976; Oller, 1974; Templin, 1957). The final consonant may be deleted, thus producing a CV structure for a CVC—*ba* (/bɔ/) for *ball*—or followed by a vowel to produce a CVCV structure—*cake-a* (/k eI kə/) for *cake*. This process of vowel insertion is termed epenthesis. The child may also lengthen the vowel that precedes the final consonant or may substitute a glottal stop or plosive (/h/) for the consonant. These three behaviors—addition of a final vowel, lengthening of the preceding vowel, and glottal stop substitution—are usually the first steps in the acquisition of final consonants. Nasal sounds are some of the first to appear as final consonants. These final consonant processes usually disappear by age 3 (Grunwell, 1981).

In addition, the child may delete unstressed syllables to produce, for example, *way* for *away* (Oller, 1974). Initially any unstressed syllable may be eliminated, though the child gradually adopts a pattern of deleting only initial unstressed syllables. This deletion process continues until age 4.

Reduplication, or syllable assimilation, is a third process for simplifying syllable structure in which one syllable becomes similar to another in the word, resulting in the reduplicated structure, as in *wawa* for *water* (Oller, 1974). It

TABLE 9.10   Phonological Processes of Preschool Children

Processes	Examples
Syllable structure	
Deletion of final consonants	*cu* (/kʌ/) for *cup*
Deletion of unstressed syllables	*nana* for *banana*
Reduplication	*mama, dada, wawa* (water)
Reduction of clusters	/s/ + consonant (*stop*) = delete /s/ (*top*)
Assimilation	
Contiguous	
Between consonants	*beds* (/bɛdz/), *bets* (/bɛts/)
Regressive VC (vowel alters toward some feature of C)	nasalization of vowels: *can*
Noncontiguous	
Back assimilation	*dog* becomes *gog*
	dark becomes *gawk*
Substitution	
Obstruants (plosives, fricatives, and affricatives)	
Stopping: replace sound with a plosive	*this* becomes *dis*
Fronting: replace palatals and velars (/k/ and /g/) with alveolars (/t/ and /d/)	*Kenny* becomes *Tenny*
	go becomes *do*
Nasals	
Fronting (/ŋ/ becomes /n/)	*something* becomes *somethin*
Liquids: replaced by	
Plosive	*yellow* becomes *yedow*
Glide	*rabbit* becomes *wabbit*
Another liquid	*girl* becomes *gaul* (/gɔl/)
Vowels	
Neutralization: vowels reduced to /ə/ or /a/	*want to* becomes *wanna*
Deletion of sounds	*balloon* becomes *ba-oon*

Source: Drawn from D. Ingram, *Phonological Disability in Children.* London: Edward Arnold, 1976.

appears that reduplication is a step in the acquisition of final consonants; thus, it should not surprise us that this process disappears for most children before 30 months of age (Grunwell, 1981).

There are several factors influencing reduplication processes in polysyllabic words (H. Klein, 1981). An interaction of syllable stress and order seems to be most significant. The final syllable is usually deleted or changed, as in *wawa*. Otherwise, the clearly stressed syllable is most often reproduced, while gradations of stress result in a less clear reproduction pattern (Clumeck, 1977; Priestley, 1977). The final position is not particularly important unless it is preceded by an *unstressed* syllable, as in *elephant* or *ambulance* (H. Klein, 1981). The reduplication of stressed final syllables may reflect (a) the increased duration of the final syllable when it follows an unstressed syllable or (b) the reduced vowel quality of the unstressed syllable (Oller, 1973; B. Smith, 1978). Reduced quality occurs when the vowel is a middle or neutral vowel, such as /ə/. This occurs in the second syllable of *elephant* (/ɛləfɪnt/). In this case, the final syllable receives more emphasis, and the child is likely to produce something such as "ehfafa" (/ɛfafa/), reduplicating this syllable.

Finally, preschoolers reduce or simplify consonant clusters, usually by deleting one consonant. In the next phase, the child will substitute another consonant for the previously deleted one (Greenlee, 1974). In general, we can predict which member will be deleted from a cluster (Oller, 1974; N. Smith, 1973).

Cluster	*Deletion*	*Example*
/s/ + plosive	/s/	*stop* becomes *top*
plosive or fricative + liquid or glide	liquid or glide	*bring* becomes *bing* *swim* becomes *sim*

Nasal clusters are more complex. If a nasal plus a plosive or fricative is reduced, younger children will delete the nasal. Thus, *bump* becomes *bup*. Older preschoolers will delete the plosive if it is voiced. Employing this rule, the child reduces *mend* to *men* (N. Smith, 1973). The child may also exhibit epenthesis, producing both consonants with a vowel between them. Thus, *tree* becomes *teree*. This vowel insertion process is infrequent (Olmsted, 1971). The specific strategy used and the speed of consonant cluster development vary with the sounds involved (Grunwell, 1981; Vihman & Greenlee, 1987). Most children stop using the cluster reduction process by age 4.

Assimilation Processes

Assimilation processes simplify production by producing different sounds in the same way. In general, one sound becomes similar to another in the same word. Assimilation processes may be contiguous or noncontiguous and progressive or regressive. Contiguous assimilation occurs when the two elements are next to each other; noncontiguous assimilation, when apart. Progressive assimilation occurs when the affected element follows the element that influences it; regressive assimilation, when the affected element precedes. For example, children generally produce two varieties of *doggie*. One, *doddie*, exemplifies progressive assimilation, while the other, *goggie*, is regressive.

Regressive contiguous assimilation is exhibited in both CV and VC syllables. The consonant in CV structures may be affected by the voicing of the vowel, as when the voiceless *t* in *top* becomes the voiced *d* in *dop*. In regressive VC assimilation the vowel alters toward some feature of the consonant, as in the nasalized vowels in *can* and *ham*. Progressive contiguous assimilation is much less common.

The most common type of noncontiguous assimilation is back assimilation, in which one consonant is modified toward another that is produced farther back in the oral cavity. The *d* in *dark*, for example, may become a *g* to produce *gawk* (/gɔk/) (Ingram, 1976).

Substitution Processes

Many preschoolers substitute sounds in their speech. These substitutions are not random. Specific substitutions are usually in one direction. The /w/ is often substituted for /r/, for example, but only rarely does the opposite occur. In addition, when the child masters a phoneme, it does not overgeneralize to words in which the substituted sound is the correct sound. For example, the child may say *wabbit* and *wooster* until he masters /r/. At that point he can produce *rabbit* and *rooster*, but the /r/ does not overgeneralize to the /w/ in *what* and *wanna*, in which /w/ is correct.

In general, the types of substitutions can be described according to the manner of production of the target sound. Obstruant sounds, which include plosives, fricatives, and affricatives, may experience *stopping*, in which a plosive is substituted. Stopping is most common in the initial position in words (Oller, 1974), as in *dat* for *that* or *dis* for *this*. This process decreases gradually as the child masters fricatives and affricatives, although stopping with *th* sounds (/θ,ð/) may persist until early school age (Grunwell, 1981; Ingram, 1975). Another process, mentioned previously, is *fronting*, a tendency to replace palatals and velars with alveolar sounds. Thus, /t/ and /d/ are substituted for /k/ and /g/, producing *tan* for *can* and *dun* for *gun*. As many as 23% of 3-year-olds demonstrate fronting. This percentage decreases rapidly, so that by age 4 ½ only about 3.5% of children still exhibit this behavior (Lowe, Knutson, & Monson, 1985). Fronting is also evident in nasal sounds. The /n/ may be substituted for /ŋ/, as in *sinin* for *singing*. Early production of nasal sounds may also be accompanied by stopping. This denasalization, similar to "head cold" speech, substitutes a plosive from the similar position in the oral cavity for a nasal (*Sam* becomes *Sab*).

Liquids, /l/ and /r/, may also experience stopping initially but are generally replaced by a glide or another liquid. *Gliding*, in which /j/ or /w/ replaces /l/ or /r/, evolves only slowly and may last for several years (Oller, 1974). I recall one example of gliding that occurred after I had broken my leg in a bicycling accident. Out of concern, one of my children inquired, "How your yid?" (leg). Not only does this demonstrate gliding on the /l/; the /g/ is fronted as well.

Syllabic nasals and liquids may also be replaced. Frequently a vowel is substituted for the syllabic unit. For example, *flower* becomes *fawa* (Ingram, 1976). In contrast, glides and vowels are not difficult for most children. There is a tendency, however, for vowels to be neutralized or reduced to /ə/ and /a/.

Multiple Processes

In actual practice, it may be difficult to decipher the phonological rules a young child is using. Often several processes will be functioning at once. For instance, my children all called our family dog "Peepa" (/pipə/). Her real name was Prisca (/prɪskə/), which is Hungarian for Priscilla. In child production, we see reduction of the *pr* cluster (in a *stop + liquid* cluster, the liquid is deleted). The second cluster, *sc*, may also experience reduction; but even more importantly, it demonstrates progressive noncontiguous assimilation. Finally, the first vowel, /ɪ/, is replaced by /i/, which may be the result of the vowel's altering toward some feature of /p/, another assimilation effect.

Perception and Production

Although several infant studies have demonstrated that very young children can discriminate phonemes, all this research was accomplished in a nonlinguistic context. Sounds were presented individually or in isolated short words with no meaning attached.

Several studies suggest that the more symbolic perceptual skills develop relatively late. Although 3- and 4-year-olds can be taught to separate the sounds in words, these skills are very limited (Zhurova, 1973). Much of the evidence for early perceptual development is based on spontaneous production. These same children do not perform well when asked to make judgments of the appropriateness of sounds. For instance, when K.C., the child of a friend, was in kindergarten, he drew a painting with streaks of bright color and put a big *W* on it. His mother was delighted. "Is that 'W' for 'Whalen'?" (his last name). He looked at her with scorn. "No silly-wainbow!" A number of studies suggest that preschool children do not perceive spoken language as containing phoneme-size units (Downing & Oliver, 1973/74; Fox & Routh, 1976; Hakes, 1980; Liberman, Shankweiler, Fischer, & Carter, 1974). Yet they seem able to make different speech sounds. Children may "know that words are different and are similar in sound considerably earlier than they know the basis of those differences and similarities" (Hakes, 1982, p. 190). Through slow evolution from relatively pure sound play, speech sounds gradually change into more deliberate productions that focus on phonological segments and their relationships.

Summary

The preschool child follows a set of phonological rules that provide for consistent speech performance. Gradually these rules change and evolve as the child develops better production skills. "The child acquires the adult system by creating its own structures and then changing these as the adult system becomes better known" (Ingram, 1976, p. 49). The child's perception does not just mirror that of the adult; therefore, initial production also differs.

Not all theorists agree with Ingram's interpretation of perceptual development. According to Kuczaj (1983), the child has two representations, or models, of production: the adult model and his own. The child considers the adult model to be the correct one. He monitors both productions for comparison.

During the preschool years the child also acquires much of his phonetic inventory. He does not master all English speech sounds until about age 7. In addition, there are many phonological rules related to morphological acquisition that are not mastered until school age (Atkinson-King, 1973; Berko, 1958; A. Moskowitz, 1973).

Even at age 3, however, there are wide differences in rate of development, phonological processes used, and phonological organization. The processes of assimilation, and of consonant and syllable deletion, are very common. Cluster reduction is determined, at least in part, by the sounds involved.

CONCLUSION

Within a conversational context, the preschool child has progressed from two-, three-, and four-word sentences to longer utterances that reflect adultlike form and content rules. Caregivers continue to treat the child as a conversational partner, and his contribution increases in meaningfulness in addition to skill of formation. The child can sustain a conversation on limited topics and is able to relate action narratives of past and imagined events.

Forms that will be mastered within the school years and adulthood have already begun to appear. The order of acquisition of language forms reflects patterns of underlying cognitive and social growth, as well as learning strategies. Resultant forms often reflect the use environment and the child's attempt to simplify complex forms.

By age 5 the child uses most of the major varieties of the English sentence. Dale (1976) reported that a free sample of 5- and 6-year-old speech is not significantly different from that of adults, although there are important syntactic advances to be made during the school-age years (Palermo & Molfese, 1972). Muma (1978) characterized the school years as a period of coordination of messages and situations. Knowledge of language use increases, and use begins to influence form more decisively. Having acquired much of the *what* of language form during the preschool years, the child turns to the *how* of language use.

REFLECTIONS

1. Describe the development of preschool narratives.
2. Describe the many pragmatic skills of the preschool child.
3. MLU, the average length of the child's utterances, is a good predictor of the child's functioning level. How does one compute the MLU?
4. Roger Brown described five stages of language development based on the MLU. What are they, and what are the main characteristics of each?
5. Stage II is characterized by morphological changes. List the 14 morphemes that Brown studied, and explain each briefly.
6. Explain the order of pronoun acquisition based on the unique semantic, syntactic, and pragmatic aspects of each one.
7. Describe the acquisition order of negative and interrogative sentences.
8. Stages IV and V are characterized by embedding and conjoining. Describe each of these processes and briefly explain their order of acquisition.
9. Language is a rule-governed behavior. Preschool children follow rules for sound placement and production. What are the phonological processes observed in the language of preschool children?

10 School-Age and Adult Language Development

CHAPTER OBJECTIVES

The school-age and adult years are a very creative period for language development. Emphasis shifts from language form to content and use. The adult speaker is versatile and able to express a wide range of intentions. In addition, during this period the child learns to use the visual modes of writing and reading. When you have completed this chapter, you should understand

- the conversational abilities of school-age children.
- gender differences between men and women.
- story grammar development.
- the developmental sequence for passive sentences.
- additional development of embedding and conjoining.
- the syntagmatic-paradigmatic shift.
- the development of figurative language.
- morphophonemic development.
- metalinguistic abilities.
- reading processing models.
- the development of reading.
- the following terms:

account	nonegocentrism
critical period	recount
demonstrative	story
eventcast	story grammar
metaphoric	syntagmatic-paradigmatic
transparency	shift

U NTIL RECENTLY, MANY LINGUISTS assumed that a child's language development was nearly complete by the time she entered school (McNeill, 1970). The main thrust of school-age and adult development was believed to consist of lexical expansion. In addition, the child tried to tidy or fine-tune the syntactic structures she had acquired earlier. We now realize not only that language development continues into adulthood but that the school years are much more important than was previously recognized. Throughout this period there is an increase in the size and complexity of the child's linguistic repertoire and in the use of that repertoire within the context of conversation and narration.

The preschool years have been viewed as the **critical period** for language learning. Most of the data for this claim are based on studies of people learning a second language or with brain injury. It is assumed that, by school age, the brain has lost much of the organic plasticity found in young children. Thus, with age, the brain becomes "fixated" and the various functions cannot be assumed as easily by other, related segments of the brain. In children as young as 4 years, there is evidence that the hemispheres of the brain process symbolic communication differently, with left hemisphere dominance in speech and language (D. Molfese, 1972; Nayafuchi, 1970). In adults this functional location phenomenon is even more pronounced. Older adults are less able to recover functions lost through brain injury than are children. In addition, studies of second-language learning have demonstrated the limitations inherent in later language acquisition. It is reasoned that if the brain becomes less flexible with age, and if learning a second language beyond the early school years is limited, then the optimum or critical period for language growth must be the early years of childhood. But although the early years do appear to be very important, there is little empirical support for the critical period notion.

In fact, the early school-age period is one of tremendous linguistic creativity filled with rhymes, songs, word games, and those special oaths and incantations passed along on the "underground" from child to child. Each small gang of children attempts to adopt its own special secret language. Children learn to pun and to find humor in word play: "All the royalty were there: counts, countesses, no-counts, and people who couldn't count at all. . . ." Special terms are invented, such as *bad*, which means "really good," and *dweeb* or *geek* to note those to be excluded. There are also rules children consider as binding as any adult legal code:

> Finders keepers.
> Cross your heart.
> Dibs *or* Call it.
> No call backs.
> Pinky swear.

For those who break the rules or who, for some other reason, earn a child's enmity, there is that special area of school-age cruelty, the taunt or tease:

> Fatty, fatty, two-by-four . . .
> Hey, metal mouth.
> Liar, liar, pants on fire.

The list of taunts, which are often based on physical characteristics, can go on for longer than any of us care to recall. In its literary forms, the creative language of school-age children can be heard in camp songs, nursery rhymes, jump-rope rhymes, and jokes or read in autograph book inscriptions and graffiti. Those of us who grew up in inner-city areas experienced an especially rich heritage of urban rhymes and rumors, not to mention graffiti, such as my favorite paraphrase of Descartes:

> I think, therefore, I am . . .
>   . . . a figment of my own imagination.

Such creativity is mirrored in overall language development.

The school-age, and to a lesser degree the adult, years are characterized by growth in all aspects of language, although the development of semantics and pragmatics seems to be the most prevalent (Table 10.1). In addition to mastering new forms, the child learns to use these and existing structures to communicate more effectively. "What is crucial is not so much a better understanding of how language is structured, but a better understanding of how language is used, not so much what language is, as what language is for" (Hymes, 1972, p. xii). One of the main differences between children and adults may be in the development of narration and of special styles of communicating found only in adulthood (Obler, 1985).

Much of the development in the school years is intrasentential, at the noun and verb phrase level. Other development involves the refinement of features learned earlier, such as determiners, pronouns, and embedding. The child continues to operate from her own mini-theories about language, which are correct for some situations but not all (Karmiloff-Smith, 1986). These theories become broadened and more flexible as they blend with the language use skills that the child continues to acquire.

The most significant development after preschool is the development of narratives, long spans of organized utterances. Prior to age 5, narratives are a collection of utterances rather than a single structured unit. In mature narratives, each utterance becomes constrained by the manner in which it advances the overall theme and purpose of the narrative. By age 8 or 9, children are using many cohesive markers, such as pronouns, anaphoric reference, and deixis.

Other areas of development include metaphors, jokes, and riddles (Fowles & Glanz, 1977), presupposition in complex sentences (Hopmann & Maratsos, 1978), and intonational refinement (Cruttenden, 1974). The primary manner of joining clauses shifts gradually from coordination to subordination or embedding. While many rules are learned during the preschool years, many exceptions are discovered during the school years. Finally, with a more flexible language system at hand, the child learns to be more economical in its use and to avoid redundancy such as the double negative.

Metalinguistic ability, the awareness that enables a language user to think about and reflect upon language, also becomes well developed during the school-age period. The ability to think about language in the abstract is reflected in the development of writing and reading skills.

Reading and writing, plus the demands of the classroom, require major changes in the way a child uses language. Very different rules for talking apply in the classroom than in conversation. The child must negotiate her turn by seeking recognition from the teacher and responding in a highly specific manner to questions, which may represent over half the teacher's utterances (Bellack, Kliebard, Hyman, & Smith, 1966; Mehan, 1978). "Text-related" or ideational language (Olson & Nickerson, 1978) becomes relatively more important than social, interpersonal language. The child is held highly accountable for her responses and is required to use precise word meanings. The minority child, as we will see in the next chapter, may come to school with different language skills and expectations and may suffer as a consequence.

Language development continues, albeit at a slower pace, throughout the life span. Although lexical recognition and comprehension seem unaffected by

TABLE 10.1   Summary of School-age Child's Language Development

Age (Years)	Syntax/ Morphology	Semantics	Phonology	Pragmatics*
5	Produces short passives (*lost, left, broken*)			Uses mostly direct requests Repeats for repair Begins to use gender topics
6	Comprehends parallel embedding, imperative commands, *-man* suffix (*-er* by 6.5) Uses *many* with plural nouns		Identifies syllables Acquires rule for plural (/s/, /z/, /ɪz/)	Responds to indirect hints Repeats with elaboration for repair Uses adverbial conjuncts *now, then, so, though*
7	Comprehends *because* Follows adult ordering of adjectives	Uses *left/right* and *front/back*	Is able to manipulate sound units to rhyme or produce stems Recognizes unacceptable sound sequences	Uses and understands most deictic terms
8	Uses full passives (80% of children)		Is able to produce all English sounds	Sustains concrete topics Begins considering others' intentions
9	Comprehends and uses *tell* and *promise*	Has generally undergone complete syntagmatic-paradigmatic shift Begins to interpret psychological states described with physical terms (*cold, blue*) but misinterprets		Sustains topics through several terms Addresses perceived source of breakdown in repair

TABLE 10.1   *continued*

Age (Years)	Syntax/ Morphology	Semantics	Phonology	Pragmatics*
10	Comprehends and uses *ask*	Comprehends *in* and *on* used for temporal relations Comprehends most familial terms		
11	Comprehends *if* and *though* Creates *much* with mass nouns	Creates abstract definitions Uses conventional form definitions Understands psychological states described with physical terms		Sustains abstract topics
12			Uses stress contrasts	Uses adverbial conjuncts *otherwise, anyway, therefore,* and *however;* disjuncts *really* and *probably*
13–15 (junior high)	Comprehends *unless* Comprehends embedding of all types	Comprehends proverbs Comprehends *at* used for temporal relations		
16–18 (high school)			Uses vowel-shifting rules (*divine–divinity*)	Uses sarcasm and double meanings Makes deliberate use of metaphors Knows partner's perspective and knowledge differ from his own

* Throughout the school-age years there is an increase in the use of indirect forms, in the appropriate uses of politeness, and in the abilities to code switch and to maintain a topic.

aging (Bayles, Tomoeda, & Boone, 1985; Bowles & Poon, 1985; Howard, 1983), longer units of language may alter subtly. Syntactic comprehension accuracy declines after age 60, although semantic comprehension remains unchanged. By the seventies the distance between syntactic components of a sentence affects syntactic comprehension, indicating that age may influence the interaction between sentence components (Davis & Ball, 1989).

PRAGMATIC DEVELOPMENT

The area of most important linguistic growth during the school-age and adult years is language use, or pragmatics (Table 10.1). A preschool child does not have the skill of a masterful adult storyteller or even of a junior high student who wants something. No adult is fooled by the compliment, "Gee, Mom, those are the best-looking cookies you've ever made." But both parties understand the request, however indirect it may be.

Throughout the school years, the cognitive processes of nonegocentrism and decentration increase and combine to enable the child to become a more effective communicator. **Nonegocentrism** is the ability to take the perspective of another person. In general, as the communication task becomes more complex or difficult, the child is less able to take the speaker's perspective. Thus, as the child gains greater facility with language structure, she can concentrate more on her audience. Not even adults can be totally nonegocentric, but being able to shift perspective enables the speaker and listener to use deictic terms and lets the speaker consider what the listener knows when constructing a conversation. You will recall that deictic terms are those that must be interpreted from the perspective of the speaker, such as *here* and *there*. Preschool children frequently begin a conversation assuming that *here* for them is *here* for everyone or without announcing the topic. Once, in imaginative play, my preschool daughter shifted characters on me with no announcement. As the daddy, I was being told to go to my room! When I balked, she informed me that now I was a child—an abrupt demotion. It had not occurred to her to prepare me for the shift in conversation.

Decentration is the process of moving from rigid, one-dimensional descriptions of objects and events to coordinated, multiattributional ones, allowing both speaker and listener to recognize that there are many dimensions and perspectives to any given topic. Five- to 6-year-olds are less able to communicate information than older children (Krauss & Glucksberg, 1967). In general, younger children's descriptions are more personal and do not consider the information available to the listener. Accuracy depends on what is being conveyed, with abstract information being communicated least accurately by children (Glucksberg, Krauss, & Weisberg, 1966).

Narratives

Five- and 6-year-olds produce many different types of narratives. Anecdotal narratives of a personal or vicarious nature predominate, possibly accounting for as many as 70% of all narratives (Preece, 1987). In contrast, fantasy stories are relatively rare.

Children learn about narratives within their homes and their language communities. The emerging narratives reflect different sociocultural groups and learning situations (Heath, 1986b). Although every society allows children to hear and produce at least four basic narrative types, the distribution, frequency, and degree of elaboration of these types vary greatly. The four genres include three factual types, called *recounts, eventcasts,* and *accounts,* and fictionalized *stories* (Stein, 1982).

The **recount,** common in school performance, tells about past experiences in which the child participated or observed or about which the child read. Usually, an adult who has shared this experience asks the child to speak.

The **eventcast** is an explanation of some current or anticipated event. Eventcasts may be used by children to direct others in imaginative play sequences, as in the following:

> You're the daddy. And you pretend to get dressed. You're going to take the baby to the zoo.

Eventcasts enable the child to consider and analyze the effect of language on others.

Accounts are spontaneous narratives in which children share their experiences ("You know what?"). Unlike recount narratives, the listener usually does not share the accounted experience. Children initiate this narrative form, rather than reporting information requested by adults. This gives accounts their highly individualized form.

In contrast, **stories,** though fictionalized and with seemingly endless content variation, have a known and anticipated pattern or structure. Language is used to create the story form, and the listener plays a necessary interpretive function. The usual pattern is one in which the main character must overcome some problem or challenge.

In middle- and upper-class school-oriented families in the United States, the earliest narratives are eventcasts that occur during nurturing activities, play, and reading with children. Within these activities, caregivers share many accounts and stories. By age 3, children are expected to appreciate and use all forms of narration. Parents invite children to give recounts. These invitations decrease as the child gets older.

By the time most children begin school, they are usually familiar with all four forms of narration. In the classroom, children are expected to use these forms. This expectation may be unrealistic given the experiences of some minority or bidialectal children. For example, Chinese-American children are encouraged to give accounts within their families, but not outside the immediate household (Cheung, forthcoming).

In some white working-class Southern communities, recounts are tightly controlled by the interrogator and seem to be the predominant form during the preschool years. Accounts do not begin until children attend school. Children and young adults also tell few stories, a form predominantly used by older, higher-status adults (Heath, 1983).

In contrast, Southern African-American working-class children produce mostly accounts or eventcasts and have minimal experience with recounts. This may relate to the general difficulty children in this environment have gaining adult attention. Societal expectations for children are different from those found in the majority culture.

When these minority or bidialectal children go to school, they may be at a disadvantage for narration (Heath, 1986a). The expectations of educational institutions are usually those of the majority culture. Children are expected to be familiar with all narrative types. By enabling children to perform, narratives help children maintain a positive self-image and a group identification within their families and communities.

Development of Narratives

Most 6-year-olds can convey a simple story or recount a movie or television show. These narrations may be long, rambling accounts of sequential events both real and fictional. During the school-age period, these narratives undergo several changes, primarily in their internal structure.

As noted in Chapter 9, children gradually learn to link events in linear fashion, and only later with causal connectives (Hood & Bloom, 1979). Generally, by age 6, children's narratives become causally coherent (Kemper, 1984). These narratives require the child to manipulate content, plot, and causal structure. Causality involves descriptions of intentions, emotions, and thoughts and the use of connectives, such as *because, as a result of,* and *since,* to name a few. To some degree, use of causality requires the speaker to be able to go forward and backward in time. While 2- and 3-year-olds can sequence in a forward direction, they have great difficulty with the reverse. The stories of these preschoolers consist predominantly of actions, with few initiations or causes of events and few motivations for characters' actions. Even so, the conjunction *and* continues to be used as frequently in the narratives of 9-year-olds as it did in those of preschoolers (Peterson & McCabe, 1987). The purpose seems to be cohesion (*And then . . . And then . . .*) rather than coordination (clause + *and* + clause).

Although 2- and 3-year-olds have mastered some causal expressions, they are unable to construct coherent causal narratives (Kemper & Edwards, 1986). Causality can be seen, however, in 2- and 3-year-olds' use of plans, scripts, and descriptions of their own behavior and thoughts (Kemper & Edwards, 1986). A *plan* is a means or series of actions intended to accomplish a specified end. Thus, a plan is an intention or a model of causality. Many of the first words of children refer to intentions and consequences, such as *all gone, there, uh-oh,* and *oh dear. Scripts* are dialogues that accompany familiar routines in the child's everyday environment. Children incorporate these into their narratives. By age 2 ½, the child has acquired the words to describe perceptions (*see, hear*), physical states (*tired, hungry*), emotions (*love, hate*), needs, thoughts (*know*), and judgments (*naughty*) (Bretherton & Beeghly, 1982).

Between ages 2 and 10, the child's stories begin to contain more mental states and more initiations and motivations as causal links (Kemper & Edwards, 1986). Initially, psychological causality, such as motives, is more frequently used than physical causality or the connection between events (McCabe & Peterson, 1985). At around age 4, children's stories begin to contain more explicit physical and mental states. Purposeful actions or natural or social processes influence characters' thoughts and emotions. By age 6, children's stories describe motives for actions.

In mature narratives, the center develops as the story progresses. Each incident complements the center, follows from previous incidents, forms a chain, and adds some new aspect to the theme. Causal relationships move toward the ending of the initial situation, called the *climax:*

> There was a girl named Ann. And she got lost in the city. She was scared. She looked and looked but couldn't find her mommy and daddy. She slept in a cardboard box by the corner. And one day the box got blowed over and a police lady found her sleeping. She took her home to her mommy and daddy.

Mature narratives may consist of a single episode, as above, or of several episodes. An episode contains a statement of the problem or challenge, and all elements of the plot are directed toward its solution.

Although 4- and 5-year-olds have many elements of narration in their conversation, such as plans and scripts, they lack the linguistic skill to weave a coherent narrative. Between ages 5 and 7, plots emerge consisting of a problem and some type of resolution. Gradually, these simple plots are elaborated into a series of problems and solutions or are embellished from within.

Both adults and children prefer stories directed toward a goal, such as the overcoming of an obstacle or problem (Stein & Policastro, 1984). Narratives of the 7-year-old typically involve a beginning, a problem, a plan to overcome the problem, and a resolution.

The development of causal chains within episodes is a very gradual process. Initially the narrative may be truncated so that the problem is solved, but it is unclear how this happened. This occurs in the following:

> And there was this bad guy with a— "k-k-k-k"—death ray. And he was gonna blow up the city. So, the Ninja Turtles snuck in to his house and stopped him. The end.

In another early form, the problem is resolved without the intervention of the characters in the story. A common device is to have the main character awaken from a dream, resulting in the disappearance of the problem:

> . . . He was in the middle of all these hungry lions. And he lost his gun. He couldn't get away. And then he woke up. Wasn't that funny?

By second grade, the child uses beginning and ending markers (*once upon a time, lived happily ever after, the end*) and evaluative markers (*that was a good one*). Story length increases and becomes more complex with the aid of syntactic devices such as conjunctions (*and, then*), locatives (*in, on, under, next to, in front of*), dialogue, comparatives (*bigger than, almost as big as, littlest*), adjectives, and causal statements. Although disquieting events are still central to the theme, characters tend to remain constant throughout the narrative, and distinct but similar episodes have been replaced by a multiepisodic chronology. The plot is still not fully developed.

The sense of plot in fictional narratives is increasingly clear after age 8 (Labov, 1972; Peterson & McCabe, 1983; Sutton-Smith, 1981, 1986). Now there is definite character-generated resolution of the central problem. The narrative presentation relies largely on language rather than on the child's use of actions and vocalizations. Like a good storyteller, the child manipulates the text and the audience to maintain attention.

In general, the narratives of older children are characterized by the following (Johnston, 1982):

1. Fewer unresolved problems and unprepared resolutions.
2. Less extraneous detail.
3. More overt marking of changes in time and place.
4. More introduction, including setting and character information.
5. Greater concern for motivation and internal reactions.
6. More complex episode structure.
7. Closer adherence to the story grammar model.

These changes represent the child's growing awareness of story structure and increasing understanding of the needs of the audience. The internal organization can be described by *story grammar*.

Story Grammar Development. Narratives are organized in predictable, rule-governed ways. The structure of the narrative consists of various components and the rules underlying the relationships of these components (Mandler & Johnson, 1977; Rummelhart, 1975; Stein & Glenn, 1979; Thorndyke, 1977). These components and rules, collectively called a **story grammar**, form a narrative framework. As such, story grammars are content-free story outlines that describe the internal structure of a story.

Story grammars provide an organizational pattern that can aid information and narrative processing, as well as narrative interpretation and memory (Christie & Schumacher, 1975; Johnston, 1982; Mandler & Johnson, 1977; Rummelhart, 1978; Snyder & Downey, 1983; Stein & Glenn, 1979; Whaley, 1981). Components may help the listener anticipate content (Baggett, 1979). The competent storyteller constructs the story and the flow of information to maximize comprehension.

The typical story involves an animate or inanimate protagonist in a particular setting who faces some challenge to which she responds. The character makes one or more attempts to meet the challenge and, as a consequence, succeeds or fails. The story usually ends with the character's emotional response to the outcome. This outline contains the main components of a story grammar.

A story grammar consists of the setting plus the episode structure (*Story grammar = Setting + Episode structure*)(Johnston, 1982). Each story begins with an introduction contained in the setting, as in "A long, long time ago, in a far off galaxy . . ." or "You'll never guess what happened on the way to work this morning; I was crossing Main Street. . . ." An episode consists of an initiating event, an internal response, a plan, an attempt, a consequence and a reaction (Stein & Glenn, 1979). Each component is described in Table 10.2. Episodes may be linked additively, temporally, causally, or in a mixed fashion. A story may consist of one or more interrelated episodes.

There appears to be a sequence of stages in the development of story grammars (Glenn & Stein, 1980). Certain structural patterns appear early and persist, while others are rather late in developing. The resultant narratives can be described as *descriptive sequences, action sequences, reaction sequences, abbreviated episodes, complete episodes, complex episodes,* and *interactive episodes.* The structural qualities of each type of story grammar are listed in Table 10.3.

TABLE 10.2 Story Grammar Components

Component	Description	Example
Setting statement	Introduce the characters; describe their habitual actions and the social, physical, and/or temporal contexts; introduce the protagonist.	There was this boy and
Initiating event	Event that induces the character(s) to act through some natural act, such as an earthquake; a notion to seek something, such as treasure; or the action of one of the characters, such as arresting someone.	. . . he got kidnapped by these pirates.
Internal response	Characters' reactions, such as emotional responses, thoughts, or intentions, to the initiating events. Internal responses provide some motivation for the characters.	He missed his dog.
Internal plan	Indicates the characters' strategies for attaining their goal(s). Young children rarely include this element.	So he decided to escape.
Attempt	Overt action(s) of the characters to bring about some consequence, such as to attain their goal(s).	When they were all eating, he cut the ropes and
Direct consequence	Characters' success or failure at attaining their goal(s) as a result of the attempt.	. . . he got away.
Reaction	Characters' emotional response, thought, or actions to the outcome or preceding chain of events.	And he lived on an island with his dog. And they played in the sand every day.

TABLE 10.3   Structural Properties of Narratives

Structural Pattern	Structural Properties
Descriptive sequence	Setting statements (S) (S) (S)
Action sequence	Setting statement (S) Attempts (A) (A) (A)
Reaction sequence	Setting statement (S) Initiating event (IE) Attempts (A) (A) (A)
Abbreviated episode	Setting statement (S) Initiating event (IE) or Internal response (IR) Direct consequence (DC)

Complete episode	Setting statement (S)
	Two of the following:
	    Initiating event (IE)
	    Internal response (IR)
	    Attempt (A)
	Direct consequence (DC)

Complex episode	Multiple episodes
	    Setting statement (S)
	    Two of the following:
	        Initiating event (IE_1)
	        Internal response (IR_1)
	        Attempt (A_1)
	    Direct consequence (DC_1)
	    Two of the following:
	        Initiating event (IE_2)
	        Internal response (IR_2)
	        Attempt (A_2)
	    Direct consequence (DC_2)
	Expanded complete episode
	    Setting statement (S)
	    Initiating event (IE)
	    Internal response (IR)
	    Internal plan (IP)
	    Attempt (A)
	    Direct consequence (DC)
	    Reaction (R)

Interactive episode	Two separate but parallel episodes that influence each other

Descriptive sequences consist of descriptions of characters, surroundings, and habitual actions. There are no causal or temporal links. The entire story consists of setting statements:

> There was this magician. He had a big hat like this. He turned elephants into mice. And he had birds in his coat. The end.

This type of structure is characteristic of the initial narratives of preschool children, described as *heaps*.

Action sequences have a chronological order for actions but no causal relations. The story consists of a setting statement and various action attempts:

> We got up early on Christmas morning. We light the tree. We opened gifts. Mommy made cinnamon buns. Then we played with the toys.

This type of story grammar is the type seen in early sequential and temporal chain narratives of preschool children.

Reaction sequences consist of a series of events in which changes cause other changes with no goal-directed behaviors. The sequence consists of a setting, an initiating event, and action attempts:

> There was a little puppy. He smelled a kittie. The kittie scratched the puppy. The puppy ran away. He smelled a girl. The girl took the puppy home and gave the pu . . . him milk. And that's the end.

In contrast, *abbreviated episodes* contain an implicit or explicit goal. At this level, the story may contain either an event statement and a consequence or an internal response and a consequence:

> This girl hated spinach. And she had a big plate of it. And she fed the spinach to the dog under the table. After her plate was all clean, she got a big dessert. That's all.

Although the character's behavior is purposeful, it is usually not premeditated or planned. Reaction sequences and abbreviated episodes are characteristic of the narratives of young school-age children.

Complete episodes contain an entire goal-oriented behavioral sequence consisting of a consequence statement and two of the following: initiating event, internal response, and attempt:

> Once this man went hunting. He waked up a big bear. The bear chased him up a tree and climbed up. To get away, the man waved at a helicopter. The helicopter gave the man a rope. He climbed up and got away from the bear. The end.

Complex episodes are expansions of the complete episode or contain multiple episodes:

> Spiderman saw a bank robber. He jumped down and captured one of them with a punch. And he called the police. One bank robber got

away in his truck. Spiderman ran after the truck. He threw his net over the truck and got the bank robber. And that was the end of the bank robbers.

Finally, *interactive episodes* contain two characters who have separate goals and actions that influence the behavior of each other:

> Mary decided to build a doghouse. She bought all the wood she needed. Her cat got jealous. Mary cut all the wood and hammered it. The cat rubbed her leg and meowed. Mary was too busy to stop and she painted it. The cat meowed more. When Mary was all done, she let the dog go to sleep. And then she hugged the kitty too.

Complete, complex, and interactive story grammars are seen in the narratives of mid- and late-elementary school children, adolescents, and adults. Most children produce all the elements of story grammar by age 9.

Language Uses

Almost from the time the child begins to speak, she is able to provide information and to discuss topics briefly. By age 3 she can request permission, invoke social rules, express feelings, and make judgments (Dore, 1976, 1977). In addition, she begins to use language for fantasies, jokes, and teasing. These three responses reflect the ability to separate literal meaning from function. For example, fantasies ignore the fact that what is said is not true.

During the school years, the child gains the ability to clarify messages and to be more subtle in the use of language. To clarify messages, she must monitor and evaluate communication and cues regarding the success or failure of the communication effort. The young school-age child displays the following communication abilities or "talents" (White, 1975):

1. To gain and hold adult attention in a socially acceptable manner.
2. To use others, when appropriate, as resources for assistance or information.
3. To express affection, or hostility and anger, appropriately.
4. To direct and follow peers.
5. To compete with peers in storytelling and boasts.
6. To express pride in herself and in her accomplishments.
7. To role-play.

By late adolescence, the child is aware that a communication partner's perspective and knowledge may differ from her own and that it is important to consider these differences. The high schooler also uses language creatively in sarcasm, jokes, and double meanings (Shultz, 1974). These begin to develop in the early school years. It can be a memorable event when a child devises her first joke. I remember my daughter's first one very well. We were discussing groupings of animals, such as *herds* of cattle, *flocks* of chickens, *packs* of wolves, and so on when someone asked about bees. One son ventured *hive*, another *school*. At this point my daughter, age 7, chimed in with "If bees went to school, they'd have to ride the school *buzz*!" Even if she heard it elsewhere, she gets some credit for good timing. High schoolers also make deliberate use of metaphor (H. Gardner, Kircher, Winner, & Perkins, 1975) and can explain complex behavior and natural phenomena (Elkind, 1970). These changes reflect overall development within all five aspects of language.

The communication experiences and needs of adults result in a language system characterized by many special *registers*, or styles of speech, not found in childhood. For example, most adults have jobs that require specific language skills—talking on the phone, writing, giving directives—or terminology, called *jargon*. Also, special communication rules reflect the power structure of the workplace. Special styles exist for those with whom the adult is intimate, such as pet names (*poobear, wissycat, lovems*) or terms of endearment (*honey, dear*), that are distinct from those reserved for strangers or business associates. Many adults also belong to ethnic, racial, or sexual-orientation minorities or to social groups that require still other styles. These act as a bond for these groups, whether they are African-American teenage males, Jewish elders, lesbians, avid CB or shortwave radio enthusiasts, or art patrons. Adults also engage in diverse social functions, such as funerals, public speaking, sports, or even card playing, that require special lexicons and manners of speaking. It is even possible to detect political orientation from the adult's choice of terms. For example, in the present political climate, the contrasts *women's lib–women's movement, Negroes—African–Americans*, and *pro-life–antiabortion* signal conservatism by the first term, liberalism by the second. Most adults use several different registers as they are needed. Exposure and need are the determining factors in acquisition, and registers disappear from a person's repertoire with infrequent use.

The conversational abilities of adults should continue to diversify and to become more elaborate with age if health is maintained (Obler, 1985). Except for the small percentage of older adults who have suffered some brain injury or disease, most continue to be effective communicators throughout their lives.

Indirect Requests

One verbal strategy adults use widely is the indirect request, an unmarked statement that does not refer directly to what the speaker wants. For example, in the proper context, the statement "The sun sure is a scorcher today" may be an indirect nonconventional request for a drink. Development of indirect requests is particularly noteworthy because such requests represent a growing awareness of the importance of both socially appropriate requests and the communication context.

Indirect requests are first produced in the preschool years. The proportion of indirect to direct requests increases between ages 3 and 5 (Garvey, 1975). This proportion does not change markedly between ages 5 and 6, though the internal structure of requests develops (Levin & Rubin, 1982). In general, the 5-year-old is successful at directly asking, commanding, and forbidding. By age 7 she has acquired greater facility with indirect forms (Garvey, 1975; Grimm, 1975). Flexibility in indirect request forms increases with age. For example, the proportion of hints—"That's a beautiful jacket, and it would go so well with my tan"—increases from childhood through adulthood (Ervin-Tripp, 1980).

The school-age child is more effective than the preschooler at recognizing the need to attract attention and at doing so. With an enhanced awareness of the needs of the listener, the child uses increasingly nonconventional requests. She seems to be following two rules: be brief and be devious (or avoid being demanding) (Ervin-Tripp & Gordon, 1986). The school-age child is more creative and more aware of social roles than the preschooler. The 8-year-old can be more polite to adults and to those perceived as uncooperative than she is to her peers (Corsaro, 1979; Parsons, 1980). She is also aware that overpoliteness is inappropriate.

After age 8 a change occurs in the child's awareness of others, and she increasingly takes their intentions into consideration (Ervin-Tripp & Gordon, 1986). While the younger child acts as if she expects compliance, the 8-year-old may signify the possibility of something else. She may more tentatively inquire, "Do you have a _____ that I could possibly borrow?" In general, the 8-year-old is more polite when she is not from the listener's peer group, when she interrupts the listener's activities, and when the task requested is difficult (Mitchell-Kernan & Kernan, 1977). Although the child's use of requests is similar to that of adults, she still has some difficulty with nonconventional requests and may interpret them literally. It's not until adolescence that the child approaches adult proficiency.

The preschool child has difficulty understanding many forms of indirect request (Ervin-Tripp, 1977a,b). She needs more explicit goal statements. In contrast, the young school-age child does not require identification of what is desired. The 6-year-old is even able to respond to such indirect hints as loud sighs (Cherry-Wilkinson & Dollaghan, 1979). Although 6-year-olds generally respond to literal meanings, 8-year-olds and adults recognize nonliteral requests for action as well (Ackerman, 1978). For example, the 6-year-old who is asked "Can you pass the cup?" may respond "Yes" but not follow through. More mature language users consider the context more fully and deduce that these questions are indirect requests for action.

There seems to be a general developmental pattern to the comprehension of indirect requests by 4- to 7-year-olds (Carrell, 1981). As a child matures, her comprehension of most types of indirect request increases. Interrogative forms, such as *shouldn't you?* and *should you?*, are more difficult than declarative forms, such as *you shouldn't* and *you should*. Interrogatives may be perceptually more difficult because of the word order, or their meaning may be more difficult to deduce. Negative forms, such as *please don't* and *you shouldn't*, are more difficult for 4- to 7-year-olds than positive forms, such as *please do* and *you should*. Here the surface polarity is a strong factor, especially when it differs from the literal meaning. *Shouldn't you?*, for example, is in a negative form but is a prod for positive action, as in "Shouldn't you leave?". *Must you?*, though positive in form, conveys caution or cessation, as in "Must you stop now?". These levels of relative difficulty change little from childhood to adulthood and reflect the same comprehension difficulties experienced by adults (H. Clark & Chase, 1972). In part, development of comprehension also reflects the words used. Four- and 5-year-olds understand most simple indirect requests containing *can* and *will* but have difficulty with others, such as *must* and *should* (Leonard, Wilcox, Fulmer, & Davis, 1978).

Conversational Repair

More mindful of her listener's needs, the school-age child attempts to clarify the conversation through a variety of strategies (Konefal & Fokes, 1984). Rather than merely repeating herself, as most 3- to 5-year-olds do, the 6-year-old may elaborate some elements in her repetition, thus providing more information. Until age 9, however, the predominant repair strategy is repetition. The 9-year-old clearly provides additional input for her listener. Though not as proficient as adults, 9-year-olds are capable of addressing the perceived source of a breakdown in communication by defining their terms, providing more background context, and talking about the process of conversational repair (Brinton, Fujiki, Loeb, & Winkler, 1986).

Deictic Terms

By school age, most children can produce deictic terms (*here, there*) correctly. By about age 7, a child should be able to produce and comprehend both singular and plural **demonstratives** (*this, that, these, those*) or words that indicate to which object or event the speaker is referring. Children under age 7 do not incorporate all semantic features of demonstratives (Webb & Abrahamson, 1976). First, the child must understand that *this* and *that* are demonstrative pronouns when used alone, as in "See *that*," and demonstrative articles when followed by a noun, as in "*That* one's big." Second, the child must comprehend the feature of more or less far, that is, of distance. Third, the child must realize that the speaker is the referent, the deictic aspect of demonstratives. The last two features overlap with those of *here* and *there*.

An initial strategy for the acquisition of deictic verbs, such as *bring* and *take*, is to use them with locational terms for directionality, as in *bring it here* or *bring it there*. The causal meaning of the verb—it causes something to happen—is acquired first. Later, the child learns the deictic meaning of the verb and depends less upon the locational terms (Abkarian, 1988).

Conversational Constraints

The school-age child is able to introduce a topic into the conversation, sustain it through several turns, and close or switch the topic. These skills develop only gradually throughout elementary school and contrast sharply to preschool performance. The 3-year-old, for example, sustains the topic only 20% of the time if her partner's preceding utterance was a topic-sharing response to one of the child's prior utterances (Bloom, Rocissano, & Hood, 1976). In other words, topics change rapidly. Four-year-olds can remain on topic when explaining how a toy works but still cannot sustain dialogue (Gelman & Shatz, 1977). In general, the proportion of introduced topics maintained in subsequent turns increases with age, with the most change occurring from late elementary school to adulthood (Brinton & Fujiki, 1984). A related decrease in the number of different topics introduced or reintroduced occurs during this same period. Thus, there is a growing adherence to the concept of relevance in a conversation. Adults effectively use *shading*, or modifying the focus of the topic, as a means of gradually moving from one topic to another while maintaining some continuity in the conversation. The topic-shading utterance includes some aspect of the preceding utterance but shifts the central focus of concern. The 8-year-old can sustain a topic, but her topics tend to be concrete. Sustained abstract discussions emerge around age 11.

In conversation, the child is slowly learning to link sentences with adverbial discourse devices that are peripheral to the clause (Scott, 1984a). By bridging utterance, these devices provide continuity within discourse. The devices consist of *adverbial conjuncts*, which signal a logical relation between sentences, such as *still*, *as a result of*, and *to conclude*; and *adverbial disjuncts*, which comment on or convey the speaker's attitude toward the content of the connected sentence, such as *frankly*, *to be honest*, *perhaps*, *however*, *yet*, and *to my surprise*. In the following example, the conjunct *as a result of* signals the relationship of the two sentences:

> We were up all night. *As a result of* our effort, our group won the competition.

The following are examples of adverbial disjuncts used in conversation:

> *Honestly*, I don't know why you bought that car.
> *In my opinion*, it was a bargain.
> Well, *to be honest*, I think it's a lemon.

By age 6 the child uses the adverbial conjuncts *now*, *then*, *so*, and *though*, although disjuncts are rare. By age 12 she has added *otherwise*, *anyway*, *therefore*, and *however*, plus the disjuncts *really* and *probably*. This development continues well into the adult years, with adults using 12 conjuncts per 100 utterances compared to the 12-year-old's 4 (Scott, 1988).

Adults still exercise control over much of the conversation of the young school-age child by asking questions. Role, power, and control relationships are evident in children's responses. In general, responses to adult queries by first graders are brief, simple, and appropriate, with little elaboration. In contrast, responses to peer questions are more complex and more varied (Mishler, 1976).

In peer interaction among young school-age children, approximately 60% of the utterances are effective. Effectiveness is measured by the clarity and structural completeness of the utterance sent, the clarity of reference and relevance to the situation, the form of the utterance, the requirement for and maintenance of attention, and approximately 4 feet of communication distance (Mueller, 1972). When they talk to their peers, 8-year-olds speak differently than when addressing infants or adults (Berko Gleason, 1973). The code-switching behavior reported for

4-year-olds (Shatz & Gelman, 1973) is even more pronounced by age 8. When speaking with peers, the child makes more nonlinguistic noises and exact repetitions and engages in more ritualized play. With adults, the child uses different codes for her parents and for those outside the family. In general, parents are the recipients of more demands and whining, and of shorter, less conversational narratives.

Gender Differences

In the early elementary school years, the language of boys and girls begins to reflect the gender differences of older children and adults (Haas, 1979). These differences can be noted in vocabulary use and conversational style. Although the changing status of women in our society may lessen these differences, they nonetheless exist currently.

Vocabulary Use

The lexical differences between men and women are generally in frequency of usage rather than in form (B. Thorne, Kramerae, & Henley, 1983). In general, women avoid swearing and coarse language in conversation and tend to use more polite words, such as *please, thank you*, and *good-bye* (Greif & Berko Gleason, 1980). Other descriptive words, such as *adorable, charming, sweet, lovely*, and *divine*, are also associated with women (R. Lakoff, 1973). In addition, women use a fuller range of color terms.

Considerable differences can be found in emphatic or emotional expressions. Women tend to use expressions such as *oh dear, goodness*, and *gracious me*, while men tend to use expletives like *damn it* (Farb, 1973; R. Lakoff, 1973). Even first graders are reasonably accurate at selecting the gender of a speaker who says "Damn it, you broke the TV" or "My goodness, you broke the TV" (Edelsky, 1977). These expressions may reflect the perceived role or status of women within our society. In emergency situations in which an active, assertive response is needed, however, "feminine" interjections, such as *oh dear*, are rare.

Conversational Style

Although American English-speaking men and women may possess the same language, they use and understand it in very different ways (Tannen, 1990). While women tend to be more indirect, to seek consensus, and to listen carefully, men tend to lecture and may seem inattentive to women. These styles can be characterized as *rapport talk* and *report talk*, respectively. Women see their role as conversation facilitators, while men see theirs as information providers. Thus, women face their conversational partners, giving vocal or verbal feedback and often finishing the listener's thought. Men often do not face their partners, looking around the room and giving only fleeting eye contact.

The cartoon of the wife and husband at the breakfast table, she talking while he reads the newspaper, has its basis in the conversational styles of adults. In short, men talk more in public and less at home. Wives lament, "My husband just doesn't listen (or talk) to me." In fact, the most frequent reason for divorce given by women in the United States is lack of communication.

Much of this difference stems from the different expectations of men and women in conversation. Men see conversations as an opportunity for debate or competition, and thus act combative. When listening, they are silent, giving little vocal feedback, which they may consider to be interruptive. For men, conversations are ritual combat in which talk maintains status and independence. The goal, therefore, becomes "scoring" on one's opponent and protecting oneself from put-downs. To score, a man may dismiss the topic and, by association, the conversational partner as trivial or unimportant.

The combatant cannot allow anyone to get too close or to know him too intimately. Therefore, topics are changed often and rarely involve personal issues or feelings. One unfortunate result is the lack of intimacy experienced by many men throughout adulthood. It is difficult to build meaningful relationships based on talk of sports, work, and politics.

In contrast, women see conversations as a way to create intimacy. For women, intimacy is built through talking. The topics discussed are not as important as closeness and the sharing of feelings and emotions. Topics are often shared at length and explored thoroughly.

As good conversationalists, women see their role as an agreeable and supportive one. They make more "listener noise" to let the speaker know that they are attending. Women tend to face each other directly and to look into each others' faces.

It is not surprising, therefore, to find that men and women differ in the amount of talking, in nonlinguistic devices, and in turn-taking behaviors. In general, men tend to be more verbose than women (Swacher, 1975). In a conversational context, the longest speaking time occurs when men speak with other men. Contrary to contemporary "wisdom," women's conversations with men or with other women are shorter.

During a conversation, women's nonlinguistic behaviors suggest a less dominant role. Women maintain more eye contact and smile more often than men.

Within a conversation, men and women use different turn-taking styles. In general, adult listeners of either sex are more likely to interrupt a female speaker than a male (Parlee, 1979; Willis & Williams, 1976). Men usually interrupt to suggest alternative views or to argue.

Women relinquish their conversational turns more readily than men. A frequently used device is a question, compliment, or request. Women ask more questions, thus indirectly introducing topics into the conversation. Only about 36% of these topics become the focus of conversation. In contrast, 96% of male-introduced topics are sustained (Ehrenreich, 1981; Parlee, 1979).

Given these characteristics and the societal roles of men and women, men may feel no need to talk at home because there are no other men with whom they must prove themselves. In contrast, women may feel secure within the home and feel that they are free to talk without offending or being seen as combative.

Development

Parental speech to children of different sexes varies. As early as 2 years of age, daughters are imitated more by their mothers and talked to longer than are sons (Cherry & Lewis, 1976). Fathers use more imperatives and more insulting terms, such as *ding-a-ling* and *nutcake*, with their sons (Berko Gleason & Greif, 1983) and address their daughters as *honey* and *sweetie*. These terms may reflect the combatant nature of adult male conversations. Fathers use the diminutive form (adding a suffix to denote smallness or affection) more frequently, and interrupt daughters more often than sons (Warren-Leubecker, 1982). The overall effects of these parental behaviors are not yet known.

Preschool boys seem more aware of the differences between male and female adults than girls do (Garcia-Zamor, 1973). As early as kindergarten, boys' topics tend to be space, quantity, physical movement, self, and value judgments. In contrast, kindergarten girls talk more about "traditional" female roles (Sause, 1976). Boys begin to talk about sports and girls about school possibly as early as age 4 (Haas, 1979; Staley, 1982).

From early childhood, boys' relationships are based less on talking and more on doing. Boys' groups tend to be larger and more hierarchical than those of girls. Actions and talking are used in the struggle to avoid subordination. The listener role is seen as one of passivity and submissiveness, while the talker role is assertive.

In contrast to boys, girls usually play in pairs, sharing the play, talking, and telling "secrets." Personal problems and concerns are shared, with agreement and understanding by the participants.

Summary

The communication behaviors of men and women may reflect the traditional status of women within our society. Women demonstrate nonlinguistic behaviors, such as increased eye contact, which suggest that they hold a less dominant position within conversations. The freedom to interrupt and the sustaining of male-introduced topics reflect a higher relative status for males. In addition, women's use of "feminine" exclamations such as *oh goodness* suggests a lack of power or a lack of conviction in the importance of the message.

The actual basis for these gender differences has not been determined. It will be interesting to see the effects of the equal rights movement on the communication behavior of both sexes.

Summary

As the child gains greater facility with the form and content aspects of language, she is able to concentrate more on language use in narratives and in conversational give-and-take. Some aspects of communication, especially the message itself, are more central than others, such as style. As the child develops, she requires less and less of her limited-capacity system for planning and encoding the message. More capacity is therefore available for adapting messages to specific audiences and situations. Gradually the child is able to reallocate her limited resources and so to increase the effectiveness of the system.

SEMANTIC DEVELOPMENT AND COGNITIVE PROCESSING

During the school-age period and the adult years, the individual increases the size of her vocabulary and the specificity of definition. Gradually she acquires an abstract knowledge of meaning that is independent of particular contexts or individual interpretations. In the process, the individual reorganizes the semantic aspects of her language (Francis, 1972) (Table 10.1). The new organization is reflected in the way she uses words. One outgrowth is the creative or figurative use of language for effect. This entire process of semantic growth beginning in the early school years may be related to an overall change in cognitive processing.

Throughout life, the average healthy person will continue to add new words to her lexicon. Other than for reasons of poor health, language growth should continue, albeit at a slower rate. Although the ability to access or recall words rapidly may decline some after age 70, lexical items are not lost (Obler, 1985). Older adults are as able as younger language users to define words appropriately (Bostwinick, West, & Storandt, 1975). In some ways, the language performance of older adults may seem to others to be deteriorating. For example, seniors generally do not hear as well as the young. They may therefore miss critical pieces of information. Senior citizens also tend to use older terminology, which makes them appear to be less adept at using language. Newer terms may be more difficult for them to recall. Thus, the older adult might use the terms *braces*, *dungarees*, and *tennis shoes* in place of *suspenders*, *jeans*, and *sneakers*. The popular image of the incoherent, rambling older adult with poor word memory is untrue and unfair to most seniors.

Vocabulary Growth

School-age and adult years are a period of continued growth in the understanding of words and relationships. New words are added to the child's lexicon. For example, 75 to 90% of children at varying ages understood the following words (Dunn, 1959):

	Portion of Age Group	
Word Understood	75%	90%
harvesting	11.6	13.5
dwelling	15.6	17.5
confining	17.6+	

Added lexical items are only a portion of the change. Vocabulary growth is not the same as semantic sophistication or depth of understanding—the overall development of the child's semantic system (Pease & Berko Gleason, 1985). While new words may increase the size of the child's lexicon, they may not cause any changes in the interrelated semantic concepts that underlie the system. For example, a word belongs to certain semantic classes and has synonyms, homonyms, and antonyms. These are all part of a child's understanding of a word.

During school-age and adult years, there are two types of increases in word meanings: horizontal and vertical (McNeill, 1970). In horizontal increases, the child adds features to her definition that are common to the adult definition. Vertical increases involve bringing together all the definitions that can fit a single word. The multiple meanings of school-age children and the less flexible semantic systems of younger children are illustrated in the following closing retort of an argument between my two nieces, Michelle and Katie:

> MICHELLE: Well, when I have children, I hope they don't get any of your genes.
>
> KATIE (after a short pause): No, and they won't get any of my sneakers, either.

Between the ages of 7 and 11, there are significant increases in comprehension of spatial, temporal, familial, disjunctive, and logical relationships. The child acquires many dictionarylike and multiple meanings during this period (Menyuk, 1971). In non-English languages, children also continue to acquire more informative and complete definitions throughout the school years (Benelli, Arcuri, & Marchesini, 1988). The rate of growth slows and stabilizes during the teen years.

Semantic constraints may delay full mature use of even seemingly simple words such as *in*, *on*, and *at* (Arlin, 1983). Many prepositions can mark both locative and temporal relationships. For example, prepositions such as *in* and *on* represent periodicity of duration, whereas *at* represents a moment in time. The temporal concept of periodicity develops much later than the locative—not until about age 10. A child is into her teenage years before she can explain the periodicity/moment distinction. In general, *in* and *on* are used for periods of time, such as days (*on Monday*) or parts of days (*in the morning*), or for months (*in May*). In contrast, *at* is used for specific times (*at midnight, at 9:15*).

These new relations require new, more complex syntactic structures because they presuppose sequential relations. For example, words such as *first* and *last* can be applied to single words, but newly acquired terms such as *before* and *after* are clausal or phrasal connectives requiring a more complex structure.

In the process of defining new lexical items or redefining old ones, the child initially forms a hypothesis of their meanings. This hypothesis is reshaped or confirmed through use. For example, kindergarten children seem to assign an exclusively vertical dimension to their definition of *big* (Maratsos, 1973). Thus, they misinterpret *big* more frequently than younger children do. Obviously, this is a semantic rather than a perceptual problem and represents a more restricted definition than that used previously.

In the early years of elementary school, a change also occurs in the use of spatial relational terms. There is a decrease in the use of nonspecific and general terms and a corresponding increase in the use of specific spatial terms from ages 4 to 7 (Cox, 1985; Durkin, 1978). Usage shifts gradually from nonspecific deictic terms, based on the speaker's perspective (*here, there*), through environmental-based terms (*away from the window, toward the door*), to correct spatial terms (*top, up, left*) (Cox & Richardson, 1985). From age 3 on, the child gains increasing knowledge of horizontal-frontal (*front/back*) and horizontal-lateral (*left/right*) relationships. After age 7, the child uses more appropriate lateral terms and more varied frontal terms. Increasing precision of use continues into adulthood.

As discussed in Chapter 8, words refer to categories that are defined by prototypes or best exemplars. As she matures, the child acquires more features of the exemplar. Some instances are more typical than others and are easier for children to learn. In general, the child has a less definitive exemplar than the adult and relies more on perceptual knowledge (M. Bernstein, 1983). In contrast, adult definitions reflect both perceptual attributes and functions.

The child's ability to define words may progress in two ways during the early school years (Litowitz, 1977). First, the child progresses conceptually from definitions based on individual experience to more socially shared meaning. Second, she moves syntactically from single-word action definitions to sentences expressing complex relationships. This shift in form occurs at around second grade (Wehren, DeLisi, & Arnold, 1981). Similar shifts in definition content occur throughout grade school. In general, adult definitions are abstract or represent a concept of function modified by perceptual attributes. They tend to be descriptive, with concrete terms or references to specific instances used to modify the concept. In addition, adult definitions include synonyms, explanations, and categorizations of the word defined (Al-Issa, 1969; Litowitz, 1977). Unlike child meanings, adult definitions are exclusionary and also specify what an entity is not (Wehren et al., 1981). Adult definitions reflect an individual's personal biases and experiences, in addition to the constraints of the situation (D. Johnson, Toms-Bronowski, & Pittelman, 1982).

Children's performance in giving definitions is most strongly affected by previous opportunities to do so (Snow, 1990). Frequent conversational exchanges with adults or siblings in which children are challenged to explain what they mean provide such opportunities.

Vocabulary knowledge is highly correlated with general linguistic competence. It has been hypothesized that there is a relationship between stored word knowledge and comprehension of discourse (Anderson & Freebody, 1979). Throughout the school years, the child becomes better at deducing word meaning from context. While the 5-year-old defines a word narrowly in terms of sentence meaning, the 11-year-old abstracts and synthesizes meaning to form a definition.

Syntagmatic-Paradigmatic Shift

Several linguists have noted that, around age 7, the child begins to associate words in a different way than previously (R. Brown & Berko, 1960; Deese, 1965; Ervin, 1961, 1963; Jenkins & Palermo, 1964; McNeill, 1966). Young children's word associations are primarily heterogeneous, in contrast to the homogeneous associations of adults (R. Brown & Berko, 1960). Ervin (1961) has called this change from one system of association to the other the **syntagmatic-paradigmatic shift**. A syntagmatic association is based upon a syntactic relationship. For example, the stimulus word *girl* might elicit a child response *run*. In contrast, a paradigmatic association is based upon semantic class and occurs as a result of pairing of semantic attributes. In this case, the word *girl* might elicit *boy* or *woman*. The shift may represent a refinement and organization of semantic features (McNeill, 1966) or a change in general cognitive-processing strategies (Emerson & Gekoski, 1976).

It is likely that the shift is more gradual than researchers first suggested, beginning at age 5 and continuing into adulthood (Muma & Zwycewicz-Emory, 1979). The period of most rapid change occurs between 5 and 9 years. It is not until the adult years, however, that paradigmatic associations become consistent and fully integrated. In addition, adults also use conceptual categorization, especially with abstract relations (Anglin, 1970). For example, words from a sensory domain, such as *hot* and *cold*, may be associated with psychological states in order to form sentences such as "She is a *cold* person." These associations may be related to the more figurative uses of languages, which will be discussed later.

Some of this shift in cognitive organization is reflected in children's definitions. In addition to becoming more elaborate, definitions of the school-age child contain more superordinate categories, such as *furniture* and *clothing*. Some superordinate categories—*animal*, for example—are established as early as age 3. As the school-age child's definitions gradually become more literate or dictionarylike, they share certain characteristics. The definitions become more explicit, conventional representations of the implicit word meanings found in conversation. The linguistic form becomes more constrained with age until around age 11, when the child has acquired all the elements of the conventional adult definition. The developmental sequence of required elements for definitions is as follows:

Elements Required	*Example*
Noun phrase$_1$ . . .	*Dogs* have yukky breath.
NP$_1$ is . . .	*Dogs are* always barking and breathing.
NP$_1$ is NP$_2$ . . .	*Dogs are things* with four legs, a tail, bad breath, and barking.
NP$_1$ is NP$_2$ (superordinate category)	*Dogs are animals* that usually live in people's houses.

The preschooler's individual, experientially based definition thus shifts to a more conventional, socially shared one.

Related Cognitive Processing

During the school years, there appears to be a change in cognitive processing, storage, and retrieval that reflects a shift from a nonlinguistic visual-perceptual mode to linguistic categorization. The initial change occurs in elementary school, with a shift from concrete to abstract during adolescence. The latter shift corresponds to Piaget's formal operational period (Palermo & Molfese, 1972), in which the child begins to use abstract thought. The increasing reliance upon linguistic categorization allows the child to process greater amounts of linguistic information.

Several factors affect vocabulary acquisition (D. Johnson et al., 1982). First, both children and adults use a strategy of "clustering" or "chunking" semantically related information into categories for remembering (G. Bower, Lesgold, & Tieman, 1969). Children begin to exhibit improved recall of "semantically well integrated" units. Seventh graders rely more on grouping or chunking for recall than do first graders (Vanevery & Rosenberg, 1970). Second, the use of semantic relations resolves word ambiguities (Perfetti & Goodman, 1970). For example, *there, their,* and *they're* sound very similar and could be confused, except for the very different semantic relations they represent. Third, categorical structures are stored hierarchically or organized (Collins & Loftus, 1975). Fourth, facilitative neural networks connect related word concept structures (Collins & Loftus, 1975; Kintsch, 1977). Thus new vocabulary acquisitions are associated with previous knowledge.

Two complementary information processing models have been proposed for vocabulary use (Collins & Quillian, 1969, 1970). According to the *subway map model,* the neural signal takes the path of least resistance until enough word concepts are connected. Closely related categories are also activated via the *spreading activation model,* in which one concept triggers a related one. This process is best illustrated by daydreaming, in which one thought calls up another one, and so on. This model functions as an additional path to complement the main path activation of the subway map model. For example, suppose that I ask you to visualize *ocean.* Cognitively, you might go straight to the concept *ocean.* You might even be able to imagine it. At the same time, you might begin to imagine sand, warm sunshine, and your favorite beach. These concepts represent the spreading activation model.

Some linguists have suggested that individuals may use several levels of linguistic processing simultaneously (Kosslyn & Bower, 1974; Strohner & Nelson, 1974):

- Surface—syntactic rules and phonetic strings
- Deep—semantic categories and relations
- Contextual—situation or image

The mode or modes of processing relied upon reflect the properties of the sentence and the maturation of the processor (Danks & Sorce, 1973).

Children show a shift in linguistic processing from reliance on surface to deep structure strategies during early school years (Mehler, 1971). This shift may reflect decreasing cognitive reliance on visual input for memory and recall, a gradual change from visual encoding by preschoolers to overt naming as the dominant memory process of school-age children (Conrad, 1972). Kindergarteners also employ a naming strategy to enhance recall, though vocalization seems to interfere with recall of a set of similar-sounding words. Dependence on visual input for recall does not appear to lessen greatly until approximately age 9.

The shift may be more complex than merely one from visual to linguistic processing. Certainly, this change is significant and can be seen in the better recall by young children of sentences that produce similar imagery (Kosslyn & Bower, 1974). Adults have better recall when there is conceptual similarity. The processing shift may also reflect the child's increasing ability to integrate situational nonlinguistic information with linguistic information (Paris & Mahoney, 1974). These abilities are needed for effective daily communication. An example is the use of stress or emphasis in sentence decoding. There is a progression in the ability to use stress cues throughout elementary school and into the teenage years (F. Myers & R. Myers, 1983).

Adults may use the following sequence of processing strategies (Bever, 1970):

1. Segment the message into the underlying sentences.
2. Mark the relations between the underlying sentences.
3. Determine the semantic relations of the lexical items.
4. Determine the semantic probabilities of co-occurrence.
5. Label the functions and properties of specific lexical items.

Children may begin to employ these strategies as early as age 5 (Menyuk, 1977).

The evolution of processing strategies may be reflected in the shifting recall patterns that occur with age changes. The free recall of linguistic material with increased complexity decreases with age (Craik, 1977). These changes in cognitive operations may be more quantitative than qualitative (Spilich, 1983). The elderly have more difficulty with linguistic processing that requires greater organization in order to recall. In general, the elderly are more sensitive to theme or underlying meaning but are less able than young adults to recall syntax.

Figurative Language

The school-age child also develops figurative language, which lets her use language in a truly creative way. Figurative language uses words in an imaginative sense, rather than a literal one, to create an imaginative or emotional impression. The primary types include idioms, metaphors, similes, and proverbs. Idioms are short expressions that have evolved through years of use and cannot be analyzed grammatically. The following is a list of some American English idioms:

Strike a bargain	Jump the gun
Superior *to* (Better *than*)	Hit the road
Break a date	In search *of* (Search *for*)
Take a cab	Hop a plane
Throw a party	Robbed blind

These colorful terms are not learned as part of a rule system and cannot be interpreted literally. They are acquired through continual use, and their meanings are inferred from context. For example, *hit the road* does not mean to strike a sharp blow to the asphalt but rather to leave.

Metaphors and similes are figures of speech that compare actual entities with a descriptive image. In a metaphor a resemblance or comparison is implied, such as "She kept a *hawk-eyed* surveillance." In contrast, a simile is an explicit comparison, usually introduced by *like* or *as*, such as "He ran *like a frightened rabbit*." To form a metaphor or a simile, the speaker must perceive a resemblance between two separate elements. The basis of the similarity is not literally true. The two disparate entities may not be joined meaningfully.

Preschool children produce many inventive figures of speech. H. Gardner and Winner (1979) have offered the following examples:

- A bald man is described as having a "barefoot" head.
- A stop sign is described as a "candy cane."
- A folded potato chip is described as a "cowboy hat."

I recall my daughter's description of the Lincoln Memorial, with its many columns, as "Lincoln's crib." One of my students reported her daughter crying because she had hurt her "foot thumb" or big toe. The same child requested "ear gloves" or earmuffs for her cold ears. These early figures of speech are usually based on physical resemblance or on similarities of use or function. They appear to be an extension of, or an accompaniment to, symbolic play (H. Gardner, 1974; Gentner, 1977). In these expressions, *pretend* is often suggested (Billow, 1979). The young child's creative descriptions, however, do not imply that she can use figurative language (Hakes, 1982). "The linguistic creativity of younger children results from their not knowing enough not to be creative" (Hakes, 1982, p. 196). Metaphors become less frequent in spontaneous speech after age 6. Two possible reasons for this decline are, first, that the child now has a basic vocabulary and is therefore less pressured to stretch her vocabulary to express new meanings; and, second, that the rule-guided linguistic training of school leaves little room for creativity (H. Gardner & Winner, 1979).

The remaining figures of speech, though less numerous, are more adultlike. The school-age child is able to make metaphoric matches across several sensory domains (H. Gardner, 1974). For example, colors can be used to describe psychological states, as in "I feel *blue*." Child explanations for the matches change markedly with age. Usually the quantity of metaphors in creative writing increases in later elementary school. The decline in what children produce spontaneously, however, does not reflect a decline in what they are capable of producing (Hakes, 1982). Rather, the decline is evidence of the elementary school child's orientation toward the real and the literal. Thus, Piaget characterized this period as one of concrete operational thought.

While the spontaneous generation of figures of speech declines with age, comprehension improves. The 5- to 7-year-old avoids crossing from physical into psychological domains and prefers to associate two terms rather than equating them. Child interpretation thus alters the relationship. For example, "She is a cold person" may be interpreted as "She lives at the North Pole." In contrast, the 8- to 9-year-old is beginning to appreciate the psychological process (H. Gardner

& Winner, 1979). She still misinterprets the metaphor, however, because she does not fully understand the psychological dimension.

Proverbs, the last type of figurative speech, are short, popular sayings that embody a generally accepted truth, useful thought, or advice. Often quite picturesque, proverbs are very difficult for young school-age children to comprehend. Examples of proverbs are:

> Don't put the cart before the horse.
> A new broom sweeps clean.
> You can't have your cake and eat it, too.
> Look before you leap.

The 6-, 7-, or 8-year-old child interprets proverbs quite literally. Development of comprehension continues throughout adolescence and adulthood.

Accuracy in interpreting idioms and proverbs slowly increases throughout late childhood and adolescence (Gibbs, 1987; Nippold & Martin, 1989; Nippold, Martin, & Erskine, 1988). Although 5-year-olds interpret most figurative expressions literally, even they can interpret some idioms in context. Figurative understanding begins gradually and is not complete even by age 18 (Gibbs, 1987; Nippold & Martin, 1989; Prinz, 1983; Thorum, 1980). Of course, development of individual figurative expressions varies widely and depends, among other things, on the learning context and on metaphoric transparency (Gibbs, 1987).

Figurative expressions are easier for adolescents to comprehend in context than in isolation, possibly because figurative language is learned in context (Strand & Fraser, 1979). A figurative expression may be learned and stored as a large single lexical item—just as a word is learned and stored—rather than as individual words within the expression. As with single words, the meanings of figurative expressions are inferred from repeated exposure to these expressions in different contexts. For example, after the election, Grandpa says of the side with the poor showing, "They better *throw in the towel*." After working hard at her job, Mom sighs exhaustedly and says, "I'm *throwing in the towel*." Soon the child infers that the expression means something akin to *admitting defeat*. This task is an analytical one in which the child must actively think about the meaning of the expression in context and perceive the metaphoric comparisons.

Metaphoric transparency, or the extent of the literal–figurative relationship, directly affects ease of interpretation. Idioms such as *hold your tongue* have closely related literal and figurative meanings, or are metaphorically transparent, because the meanings relate to speaking and to the tongue. In contrast, *beat around the bush* and *kick the bucket* do not have closely related meanings and are therefore metaphorically opaque. Metaphorically transparent idioms are easier for children to interpret than metaphorically opaque ones (Gibbs, 1987).

The ability to comprehend proverbs is strongly correlated with perceptual analogical reasoning ability (Nippold et al., 1988). Analogical reasoning problems follow the format *A is to B as C is to D*. In similar fashion, the child attempting to comprehend a proverb must understand the underlying relationships between the proverb and the context. Both figurative language comprehension and analogical reasoning are strongly related to receptive vocabulary development, underscoring the semantic link between these skills (Nippold & Sullivan, 1987).

The figurative and literal interpretations of figurative language may be retrieved in parallel (Glass, 1983; Swinney & Cutler, 1979). The figurative meaning is stored in the child's lexicon along with single words. The sequencing of the retrieval process is unknown. Interpretation may occur at the idiomatic and literal levels simultaneously (Fraser, 1974; Heringer, 1976) or with the idiomatic preceding the literal (Schweigert, 1986).

Summary

With increased age, the individual sharpens word definitions and relationships, resulting in more accurate communication. At the same time, she learns to use language figuratively to create nonliteral relationships. As a result of both processes, communication is both more precise and more creative.

SYNTACTIC AND MORPHOLOGICAL DEVELOPMENT

Language development in the school-age period consists of simultaneous expansion of existing syntactic forms and acquisition of new forms (Table 10.1). The child continues with internal sentence expansion by elaborating the noun and verb phrases. Conjoining and embedding functions also expand. Additional structures include the passive form.

Although the child has achieved basic sentence competence by age 5 (McNeill, 1970), fewer than 50% of first graders can produce correct pronouns, "cause" clauses, and nominalizations or gerunds (Menyuk, 1969). Fewer than 20% can produce *if* and *so* clauses and participle complements, which are somewhat similar to gerunds. You will recall that gerunds are verbs to which *-ing* has been added to produce a form that fulfills a noun function. For example, *to fish* and *to run* become

> He enjoys *fishing*.
> *Running* is his favorite exercise.

In participle complements, the same form fills an adjectival role, as in

> We bought *fishing* equipment.
> Do you like your new *running* shoes?

Learning to use a morphological rule begins with the hypothesis that a small set of words are treated in a certain way grammatically. The first uses of a morphological marker are probably the result of rote memorization. This is followed by morphological "schemas" or loose generalizations about phonological marking (/d, t/) and meaning (past tense) (Bybee & Slobin, 1982). Finally, the child forms a rule. It is a complex process that begins in preschool but continues throughout adolescence. The -*y* marker used to form adjectives such as *sticky* and *fluffy* is not acquired until age 11, and the -*ly* marker used to form adverbs such as *quickly* is learned in adolescence.

Some morphological learning, such as the use of the -*er* marker, is even more complex and requires semantic word class knowledge. The -*er* suffix is initially acquired in the agentive sense to mark the initiator of some action, such as paint*er* for the person who paints and teach*er* for the person who teaches. Although this suffix may appear in late preschool with some specific words, children are not able to use it generatively until age 8 (Derwing & Baker, 1986).

The instrumental -*er*, which marks the instrument used to accomplish some action, is acquired even later, around age 11 (Clark & Hecht, 1982). Examples of the instrumental -*er* include lighting a cigarette with a light*er* or erasing with an eras*er*. In part, the late development of the instrumental -*er* can be explained by the child's use of other words in place of the "verb + *er*" form. Thus, the child uses stove for cook*er* and shovel for dig*ger*. While *stove* and *shovel* are perfectly correct and more mature than *cooker* and *digger*, their use does not help the child learn the instrumental -*er* rule.

Noun and Verb Phrase Development

Children of 5 to 7 years use most elements of noun and verb phrases but frequently omit these elements even when they are required. Even at age 7, they omit some elements but expand others redundantly. The rhythm of a sentence seems to be more salient, and children often miss small, unstressed functor words when counting words heard in a sentence (Holden & MacGinitie, 1972). In addition, school-age children still have difficulty with some prepositions, verb tensing and modality, and plurals (Menyuk, 1965). Unique instances or rule exceptions are particularly difficult.

Modality is a semantic notion of possibility, obligation, permission, intention, validity, truth, and functionality. It is expressed in modal auxiliary verbs and in different sentence types. School-age children and adults also express modality in adverbs (*possibly, maybe*), adjectives (*possible, likely*), nouns (*possibility, likelihood*), verbs (*believe, doubt*), and suffixes (-*able*). Obviously, not all forms of modality develop simultaneously. In general, the possibility, obligation, permission, and intention forms develop before the validity, truth, and functionality forms (Stephany, 1986). Adverbs of likelihood, such as *definitely, probably*, and *possibly*, can pose a problem even for school-age children. In general, preschoolers don't understand the distinction between the terms. By fourth grade, however, most children know the difference. The terms are not learned at the same time, but *definitely* is learned first and understood best by most children (Hoffner, Cantor, & Badzinski, 1990). Even within a form, such as *will*, different functions develop at different rates. Cognitively, *will-do* (I will go) seems to develop before *will-happen* (It will take some effort)(Pea & Mawby, 1981). This is true in languages as different as English, Greek, and Turkish (Goossens, 1981; Slobin & Aksu, 1982; Stephany, 1986). Even 12-year-olds do not have an adult sense of modality (Coates, 1988).

Verbs appear to offer greater difficulty for school-age children than nouns. These difficulties may be related to varied syntactic marking of semantic relationships (Gentner, 1982). For example, verb action can be reversed in three ways:

1. Use of the prefix *un-*: "She is tying her shoe. She is *untying* her shoe."
2. Use of a particle following the verb: "Pull *on* your boots. Pull *off* your boots."
3. Use of separate lexical items: "She *opened* the door. She *closed* the door."

Certain forms may be used only with specific verbs. The child's resultant confusion produces sentences such as these (Bowerman, 1981):

> I had to untake the sewing. (take out the stitches)
> I'll get it after it's plugged out. (unplugged)

The difficulty of learning how to state underlying verb relationships may account for the greater amount of time needed for acquisition of verbs compared to common nouns.

Within the noun phrase, pronoun and adjective development continues. The child learns to differentiate better between subject pronouns, such as *I*, *he*, *she*, *we*, and *they*, and object pronouns, such as *me*, *him*, *her*, *us*, and *them*, and to use reflexives, such as *myself*, *himself*, *herself*, and *ourselves*. In addition, she learns to carry pronouns across sentences and to analyze a sentence to determine to which noun a pronoun refers. For example, the child must perform some complex analysis in order to interpret the following sentences:

> Mary's mother was very sick. Mary knew that *she* must obtain a doctor for *her*.

The child may be able to hold more than one dimension of the noun phrase or of an entire clause and to comprehend or use a pronoun in its place. This procedure is demonstrated in the following sentences:

> The earth began to tremble shortly before rush hour, reaching full force 40 minutes later. *It* was devastating.

Adjective ordering also becomes evident within the noun phrase. In English, multiple properties are generally described by a string of sequentially ordered adjectives, each referring to a different attribute. Different semantic classes of adjectives have definite positions based on a complex rule system (Whorf, 1956). For example, it is acceptable to say "the *large red moving van*" but very awkward to say "the *moving red large van.*"

Three-year-olds display the same ordering preference as adults for the first adjective in a sequence (Richards, 1980). Adjectives of size, shape, and length are consistently chosen for this position. But the child does not show positional preferences that approximate adult ordering for the other adjectives until school age. Earlier ordering preferences may reflect an imitative or holistic strategy rather than an analytical approach to the separate adjectives. The period from age 5 to 7 marks a phase of improved cognitive ability to discriminate perceptual attributes and their relationships (Day, 1975).

The distinction between mass and count nouns and their quantifiers is acquired only slowly throughout the school years (Gathercole, 1985; P. Gordon, 1988). Mass nouns refer to homogeneous, nonindividual substances, such as *water, sand*, and *sugar*. Count nouns refer to heterogeneous, individual objects, such as *cup, bicycle*, and *house*. Mass nouns take quantifying modifiers, such as *much* and *little*, while count nouns take quantifiers, such as *many* and *few*. Although children as young as age 2 can make a distinction between count and mass nouns, it is not until much later that they learn the rule for use of the determiner with count nouns and not with mass nouns (P. Gordon, 1988). By early elementary school the child has learned most of the correct noun forms, so that words like *monies* and *mens* are rare. *Many* then appears with plural count nouns, as in "many houses." *Much* is usually learned by late elementary school, although the adolescent still makes errors. Early on, the child discovers a way around the quantifier question by using *lots of* with both types of nouns.

Sentence Types

In general, comprehension of linguistic relationships expressed in sentences improves throughout the school years (Inhelder & Piaget, 1969; Piaget & Inhelder, 1969) (Table 10.1). The comparative relationship is the easiest one for first to third graders to interpret. Comparative sentences contain phrases such as "*as* big *as*," "smaller *than*," and "*more* fun *than*." The cognitive skills needed for comparative relationships develop during the preschool years but must await linguistic development. Other sentential relations, such as passive, temporal, spatial, and familial, are more difficult for school-age children to interpret.

Passive Sentences

Passive sentences are troublesome, both receptively and expressively, for English-speaking children. The passive form is acquired earlier in non-Indo-European languages, such as Sesotho (Demuth, 1989, 1990), a west African language; Zulu (Suzman, 1987); and Quiche Mayan (Pye, 1988), a native Mexican language. The form of passive sentences varies from the predominant, though not universal (Hakuta, 1979), subject-verb-object arrangement used by English-speaking children. Thus, the passive form requires a change in sentence-processing strategy. Five-year-olds have difficulty interpreting any sentence that omits the subject, verb, or object element (C. Chomsky, 1969). Adults use the passive form infrequently (R. Brown, 1973). As you might imagine, then, 5-year-old children rarely produce full passive sentences (Harwood, 1959).

Children do not truly comprehend passive sentences until about age 5 ½. Prior to this age, children use extralinguistic strategies, such as contextual support, to interpret sentences (Bridges, 1980). Children may also rely on action verbs for interpretation (Maratsos, Kuczaj, Fox, & Chalkley, 1979). True comprehension skill is related to the ability to view an event from another person's perspective and to alternate or shift perspective (Sinclair & Ferreiro, 1970). This less egocentric behavior occurs late in Piaget's preoperational period, at around age 6 or 7. Another skill, conservation, appears at about the same time and is strongly correlated with the comprehension and production of passives (Beilin, 1975).

An additional clue for passive interpretation may be the presence of a preposition (Maratsos & Abramovitch, 1975; Shorr & Dale, 1981). In general, young school-age children interpret a sentence as passive when *from* or *by* is present and as active when *to* is used. Thus "The picture was painted *by* Mary" is passive, and "The picture was given *to* John" is active.

Production of passives begins in the late preschool years with short sentences containing noun + *be/get* + verb(-*en/-ed*), such as "It got broken" or "It was crushed." In these early passives the noun is almost always inanimate. These forms may be based on the predicate adjective form seen with the copula, such as "He was sad" (Bowey, 1982). Verbs of state, such as *lost*, *left*, and *broken*, tend to predominate in these short passives (Horgan, 1978). Later the child uses action verbs, such as *killed*, *hit*, and *crashed*, in both short and long or full passives.

Approximately 80% of 7 ½- to 8-year-olds produce full passive sentences (Baldie, 1976). In general, a full passive contains some form of *be* or *got*, a past tense marker, and a preposition followed by a noun phrase that is agentive or instrumentive. Some passive forms do not appear until 11 years of age (Horgan, 1978).

Passives may be of three general types: *reversible, instrumental nonreversible*, and *agentive nonreversible* (Horgan, 1978). In the reversible type, either noun could be the actor or the object: "The dog was chased by the cat" could be reversed to read "The cat was chased by the dog." In the nonreversible type, the nouns cannot be reversed. The two nonreversible passives include one in which the subject is an instrument, such as *ball*, and another in which the subject is an agent, such as *boy*. An example of the instrumental type is "The window was broken by the ball." In the agentive type, "The window was broken by the boy." Both are nonreversible since we could not say "The ball/boy was broken by the window." These semantic distinctions appear to be important for development of the passive form.

As a group, children use about an equal number of reversible and nonreversible passives. Prior to age 4, children produce more reversible passives, although their use suggests word order confusion (Baldie, 1976; Horgan, 1978). Children say "The boy is chased by the girl" when in fact the boy is in pursuit. This confusion is reflected in sentence interpretation as well. Only about 50% of 5-year-olds can correctly interpret reversible passives (Bridges, 1980).

A marked increase in nonreversible passive production occurs just prior to age 8 (Baldie, 1976). The type of nonreversible passive that is most prominent changes with age. Agentive nonreversibles appear at age 9. Instrumental nonreversible passives are the most frequent nonreversibles for 11- to 13-year-olds. For this age group, semantic distinctions are also signaled by preposition use. Reversible passives use *by*, whereas nonreversibles use *with*. Adults may use either *by* or *with* in the instrumental nonreversible type. Both children and adults use *by* with the agentive nonreversible passive. Children's passives thus seem to be semantically different from those of adults.

Embedding and Conjoining

The child's repertoire of embedded and conjoined forms increases throughout the school years. Syntactic rules for both forms are observed more frequently. Clausal conjoining expands with the use of the following conjunctions (Menyuk, 1969):

Type	Examples
Causal	*because, so, therefore*
Conditional	*if*
Disjunctive	*but, or, although*
Temporal	*when, before, after, then*

The conjunction of choice for narration, however, remains *and*. Between 50 and 80% of the narrative sentences of school-age children begin with *and* (Scott, 1987). This percentage decreases as the children mature. By 11–14 years of age, only approximately 20% of narrative sentences begin with *and*. This percentage decreases to 5% under the somewhat more formal constraints of writing (Scott, 1987).

Other conjunctions are more frequently used for clausal conjoining. Up to age 12, *because* and *when* predominate, with *if* and *in order to* also used frequently (Loban, 1976; Scott, 1987).

Even though *if*, *so*, and *because* are produced relatively early in the school years, full understanding does not develop until much later (Bates, 1976a; Hood & Bloom, 1979). Semantic concepts of time and pragmatic aspects of propositional truth may affect comprehension.

Learning to understand and use *because* is not an easy task. To understand a sentence with *because*, the child must comprehend not only the relationship between two events but also their temporal sequence. This sequence is not necessarily the same as the order presented in the sentence. In "I went because I was asked," the speaker was invited before she actually left, though the linguistic ordering is the reverse. At first, the child tends to confuse *because* with *and* and *then*, using them all in a similar fashion (Corrigan, 1975). Thus the preschool child may say "I fell off my bike 'cause I hurted myself." In both comprehension and production, the preschool child appears to follow an order-of-mention strategy. Although the causal relationship appears to be understood prior to age 7, knowledge of the ordering role of *because* seems to be weak. Comprehension of *because* does not seem to develop until age 7 (Corrigan, 1975; Kuhn & Phelps, 1976). Consistently correct comprehension may not occur until around age 10 or 11 (Emerson, 1979).

Pragmatic factors may also affect the development of conjunctions. Children are more accurate at judging the speaker's meaning if the speaker expresses belief in the truthfulness of her utterance and if the two clauses are related positively. The conjunction *because* expresses both strong belief and a positive relationship. Other conjunctions express different relations. For example, both *because* and *although* presuppose that the speaker believes the two expressed propositions to be true:

> It is a block because it is cubical.
> It is a block, although it is made of metal.

In contrast, *unless* and *if* presuppose speaker uncertainty about at least one of the propositions:

> It is a block unless it is round.
> It is a block if it is wooden.

Similarly, *because* and *if* express a positive relationship between the two clauses, while *although* and *unless* express a negative relationship. *Although* expresses an exception or an illogical relationship. *Unless* requires that the truth of one proposition be denied in order for the relationship to be logical. Figure 10.1 expresses these concepts. In general, the more positive the belief expressed or the more positive the relationship, the easier it is to comprehend the conjunction. Thus *because* is learned before *if* and *although*, which in turn are followed by *unless*. Even fifth graders may have difficulty understanding *unless* (Wing & Scholnick, 1981). Younger children do not understand the appropriate pragmatic cues for disbelief and uncertainty. Therefore, they rely on syntactic cues.

Syntactic strategies are also important in the production and interpretation of embedding. The percentage of embedded sentences increases steadily to 20–30% in children's narratives throughout the school years (Scott, 1984b). Relative pronoun use is expanded with the addition of *whose, whom,* and *in which* (Scott, 1988). Multiple embeddings also increase with maturity and are one of the most significant differences between the narrative syntactic structure of 6- to 8-year olds and 10- to 12-year olds.

FIGURE 10.1   Concepts Expressed by Conjunctions

Relationship	Belief about Propositional Truth	
	Belief	Disbelief or Uncertainty
Positive	*Because*	*If*
Negative	*Although*	*Unless*

Source: Adapted from Wing, C., & Scholnick, E. Children's comprehension of pragmatic concepts expressed in "because," "although," "if," and "unless." *Journal of Child Language*, 1981, *8*, 347–365.

Although school-age clausal embeddings include relative pronoun deletions and center or subject relative clause embedding, these forms are rarely produced prior to age 7 (Menyuk, 1971). Examples of each of these forms include the following:

I'm engaged to someone [*whom*] you know. (relative pronoun deletion)
The book *that Reggie read* was exciting. (center or subject relative clause embedding)

Center embedding is particularly difficult in that it disrupts the subject-verb-object format found in so many preschool sentences.

For children, semantic role is also an important factor in interpretation (Maratsos, 1974). If the object of a center embedding is inanimate, it is less likely to be misinterpreted than an animate object is. In the following sentences, *window* cannot *run*, so there is no confusion, but the second sentence may be misinterpreted by a child:

The boy, who broke the window, ran away. (interpreted correctly)
The boy, who hit the girl, ran away. (could be interpreted to mean that the girl ran away)

Faced with confusion, the child resorts to a subject-verb-object interpretation strategy.

Comprehension of embedded sentences also seems to be based on the place and manner of the embedding. Embeddings may occur at the end of a sentence or in the center. The two clauses may be parallel, in which both share the same subject or object, or nonparallel, in which they do not:

The *boy who* lives next door gave me a present. (parallel central embedding: the same subject—*boy*—serves both clauses)

He gave me a *present that* I didn't like. (parallel ending embedding: the same object—*present*—serves both clauses)

He gave me the *present that* is on the table. (nonparallel ending embedding: the object of one—*present*—is the subject of the other)

He hit the *girl who* lives next door. (nonparallel ending embedding in both sentences: the object of the main clause—*present/girl*—is the subject of the embedded clause)

The *dog that* was chased by the boy is angry. (nonparallel central embedding: the subject of the main clause—*dog*—is the object of the embedded clause)

This order is the general developmental sequence from easiest to most difficult (Abrahamsen & Rigrodsky, 1984; J. de Villiers et al., 1979; Lahey, 1974; Sheldon, 1974; Sinclair, 1976). First graders rely heavily on word order for interpretation and are confused by semantic class reversals between subject and object class. By seventh grade, the child has little difficulty interpreting these sentences and relies primarily on grammatical cues (Abrahamsen & Rigrodsky, 1984). This change probably reflects the child's underlying cognitive development.

The Special Case of Ask, Tell, and Promise

The grammatical relations expressed by *ask, tell*, and *promise* are not explicit in the surface structure (C. Chomsky, 1969). Using the *minimal distance principle*, the child initially interprets the noun closest to the verb as the subject. In the sentence "Bob tells Foster to do a somersault," Foster is correctly identified as the one who will perform. If "Bob promises Foster to do a somersault," however, the minimal distance strategy will yield an incorrect interpretation. In the second sentence, Bob will perform the somersault. Since *tell* follows the principle consistently, it is relatively easy to learn. Likewise, *promise*, which consistently violates the principle, is also relatively easy to learn. The contrast is acquired receptively by age 9 (C. Chomsky, 1969). But *ask*, which is inconsistent, is more difficult to learn and is not comprehended completely until age 10.

The ability to comprehend and generate *ask/tell/promise* utterances increases until seventh grade and then changes little. Some forms are still incorrectly used, however, by some adults.

While even preschoolers are able to commit themselves to action (*I will . . .*), it is not until age 11 that children fully understand and are able to *promise* to do something (Astington, 1988a). In part, comprehension of *promise* is confused with the actual completion of the act. Even 13-year-olds are unsure if a promise is a promise when the promiser doesn't deliver (Astington, 1988b).

Summary

During the school-age years, the child adds new morphological and syntactic structures and expands and refines existing forms. These developments enable her to express increasingly complex relationships and to use language more creatively. Underlying semantic concepts are often the key to this complex learning.

PHONOLOGICAL DEVELOPMENT

During the early school years, the child completes her phonetic inventory (Table 10.1). By age 8 she can produce all English speech sounds competently (McCarthy, 1954). Sounds in longer words or blends may still be difficult. The acquisition of sounds, however, is only one aspect of a child's phonological competence.

By age 6 the child can identify phoneme segments in syllables (Hakes, 1980). Very few 4-year-olds are able to identify these units (Liberman et al., 1974). Words and phonemes may not be real entities for preschool children (Elliot, 1981). Not until later in the school years does the child recognize that spoken language is composed of phoneme-sized units (Downing & Oliver, 1973/74; Fox & Routh, 1975, 1976; Holden & MacGinitie, 1972).

Phonemic competence is evident in the child's rhyming ability. Children become sensitive to phonetic patterns in the preschool years and often rhyme words by substituting one sound or syllable for another, producing *cat, bat, rat, fat, hat,* and so on. This process is spontaneous, automatic word play; a more deliberate, controlled process evolves later. Although the result may be similar in sound, it is not until the school years that the child understands the basis of the sound similarity (Jusczyk, 1977). In other words, the fact that the young child knows that *bat* and *cat* are different words does not mean that she also knows, as adults do, that they differ only in their initial sound (Hakes, 1982). From kindergarten to third grade, the child is increasingly able to discriminate words that rhyme from those with other similarities (Knafle, 1973, 1974). For example, *hug* and *rug* rhyme, but *rug* and *rig,* though similar, do not.

By age 7 the child is able to produce a resultant word after one sound is removed from a word (Bruce, 1964). For example, removing /s/ from *sink* produces *ink.* Younger children can repeat a stem (*ink* in *sink*) better if the stem forms a meaningful word. Removing /s/ from *soap,* for example, produces *oap,* a meaningless word, and hence a more difficult stem to repeat. Thus, the child may rely more on semantic than on structural rules (Calfee, Chapman, & Venesky, 1972).

The 4-year-old child is able to decide if a sound sequence conforms to the phonological rules of English (Morehead, 1971). She will repeat words that contain possible sequences even when the words are not real, but she will modify impermissible sequences when she repeats them in order to produce sequences more like English (S. Messer, 1967). A 7-year-old tends to replace the impermissible or permissible but meaningless words with actual words. These changes most likely reflect the increasing metalinguistic skills of the child, which will be discussed later.

Morphophonemic Development

Morphophonemic changes are phonological or sound modifications that result when morphemes are placed together. For example, *electric* changes to *electricity* (Ingram, 1974a). Several rules for morphophonemic change are learned gradually throughout elementary school.

One rule, usually learned by first grade, pertains to the regular plural *-s* mentioned in Chapter 9 (Berko, 1958; Menyuk, 1964). The 5- to 6-year-old has learned the rule for /s/ and /z/ but not for /Iz/ or / z/ (Berko, 1958). You will recall that /s/ is used with voiceless and /z/ with voiced ending consonants. In contrast, /Iz/ is used with words that end with a sibilant sound, such as /s/, /z/, /ʃ/, and /ʒ/. Nouns ending in *-sk* and *-st* clusters may be difficult for some students to pluralize, even in third grade (Koziol, 1973). Is the plural of *desk* /desks/ or /deskIz/?

During the school years the child also learns the rules for vowel shifting. For example, the /aI/ sound in *div<u>i</u>ne* changes to an /I/ in *div<u>i</u>nity.* Other examples are as follows:

/aɪ/—/ɪ/	/eɪ/—/æ/	/i/—/ɛ/
divine—divinity	explain—explanation	serene—serenity
collide—collision	sane—sanity	obscene—obscenity

Knowledge of vowel shifting is gained only gradually. The 5-year-old child does not understand the rules (A. Moskowitz, 1973). It is not until age 17 that most children learn to apply all the rules (Myerson, 1975).

Stress, or emphasis, is also learned during the school years. The stress placed on certain syllables or words reflects the grammatical function of that unit. In English, stress varies with the relationship between two words and with the word's use as a noun or verb. For example, two words may form a phrase, such as *green house*, or a compound word, such as *greenhouse*. If you repeat the two, you will find that you stress *house* in the phrase and *green* in the compound word. Here are some other examples:

Phrase	*Compound Word*
red *head*	*red*head
black *board*	*black*board
high *chair*	*high*chair

Noun–verb pairs also differ. In the noun *record*, emphasis is on the first syllable, whereas the verb *record* is pronounced with stress on the last. Other examples are:

Noun	*Verb*
*pre*sent	pre*sent*
*con*duct	con*duct*

Pitch contours are initially acquired on isolated words. These are gradually integrated into larger units. The period from age 3 to 5 seems to be particularly important in several languages for the acquisition of stress patterns (Allen, 1983). It is not until age 12, however, that the full adult stress and accent system is acquired (Atkinson-King, 1973; Ingram, 1986).

Summary

It is not enough for the child to acquire the sounds of her native language. These are only the building blocks. Throughout the school years the child learns rules for permissible combinations and for the use of stress, which is related to syntactic and semantic growth as well. Thus the child is again forming rule systems that bring order to her linguistic world. She is not just mirroring the speech she hears around her.

METALINGUISTIC ABILITIES

Metalinguistic abilities enable the language user to think about language independently of her comprehension and production abilities. The child focuses on and reflects on language as a decontextualized object (Van Kleek, 1982). It is these "linguistic intuitions" that let us make decisions about the grammatical accept-ability of an utterance. Thus, the child treats language as an object of analysis and observation, using language to describe language (Cazden, 1974). Adults are able to make these decisions, but this ability develops only gradually throughout the school years (Downey & Hakes, 1968; Gleitman & Gleitman, 1970). In general, these abilities are not used in conversation because most adult utterances, how-ever fragmented, are acceptable in context (Labov, 1978).

In adults, comprehension and production are almost automatic, and pro-cessing occurs at the rate of communication. There is no inordinate burden on either the speaker or the listener (Foulke & Sticht, 1969). Even children's com-prehension strategies seem to be unconscious (Chapman & Kohn, 1977). Con-trolled conscious processes tend to be minimal, since comprehension includes the total linguistic and nonlinguistic contexts. "Conversations between familiars tend to be inexplicit and elliptical, and the listener's prior knowledge and the context minimize the speaker's need to find exactly the right word or syntactic structure" (Hakes, 1982, p. 176).

Metalinguistic abilities appear in the preschool years, but "full awareness is found only in the 7 to 8 year old who can repeatedly demonstrate awareness of many linguistic activities" (Saywitz & Cherry-Wilkinson, 1982, p. 247). Prior to this age, children view language primarily as a means of communication, rather than focusing on the manner in which it is conveyed (Van Kleek, 1982). After age 7–8, the development of decentration enables the child to develop the ability to con-centrate on and process simultaneously two aspects of language: message mean-ing and linguistic correctness. Preschool children tend to make judgments of utterance acceptability based on the content rather than on the grammatical structure. Thus, a 4-year-old might judge "Daddy painted the fence" as unac-ceptable since, in her realm of experience, "Daddies don't paint fences, they paint walls" (Hakes, 1980). By kindergarten the child is just beginning to separate what is said from how it is said, to separate referents from words, and to notice structure. Even so, school-age children may still judge correctness more on semantic intent or meaning than on grammatical form (Sutter & Johnson, 1990). The ability to detect syntactic errors develops first. The school-age child dem-onstrates an increasing ability to judge grammatical acceptability and to correct unacceptable sentences (Bowey, 1986). The metalinguistic skills to correct regular and irregular nouns and verbs appear at about age 6 (Cox, 1989). This change reflects a growing knowledge of language structure. "The more one knows about the rules, the fewer ways there are of putting words together acceptably" (Hakes, 1982, p. 181).

Metalinguistic abilities usually emerge after the child has mastered a lin-guistic form. For example, it is some time after the child both comprehends and produces passives that she can judge passive and active sentences as synony-mous (Beilen & Spontak, 1969). Therefore, it is possible that the young school-age child becomes aware at a metalinguistic level of language forms and content unconsciously used in the preschool years (Cazden, 1974). Some metalinguistic abilities are an almost unconscious or implicit aspect of feedback, whereas others are extremely explicit and conscious. An order of development based on this continuum is presented in Table 10.4 (E. Clark, 1978b).

Like emerging pragmatic skills, metalinguistic abilities depend on development of the other four aspects of language. With increased structural and semantic skills, the child is freed from the immediate linguistic context and can attend to how a message is communicated (A. Brown, 1978; Flavell, 1977; Flavell & Wellman, 1977). In addition, metalinguistic skill development is related to

TABLE 10.4   Development of Metalinguistic Skills and Awareness

Abilities	Approximate Age

1. Monitor one's own on-going utterances
  a. Repair spontaneously
  b. Practice sounds, words, and sentences
  c. Adjust one's speech to different listeners
	1½–2 yrs.

2. Check the result of one's utterance
  a. Check whether the listener has understood; if not, repair or try again
  b. Comment explicitly on own utterances and those of others
  c. Correct others
3. Test for reality
  a. Decide whether a word or sentence "works" in furthering listener understanding
4. Attempt to learn language deliberately
  a. Practice new sounds, words, and sentences
  b. Practice speech styles of different roles
	3–4 yrs.

5. Predict the consequences of using particular forms (inflections, words, phrases, sentences)
  a. Apply appropriate inflections to "new" words
  b. Judge utterances as appropriate for a specific listener or setting
  c. Correct word order and wording in sentences judged as "wrong"
6. Reflect on the product of an utterance (structure independent of use)
  a. Identify specific linguistic units (sounds, syllables, words, sentences)
  b. Provide definitions of words
  c. Construct puns, riddles, or other forms of humor
  d. Explain why some sentences are possible and how to interpret them
	School age

Source: Adapted from E. Clark, "Awareness of Language: Some Evidence from What Children Say and Do." In A. Sinclair, R. Jarvella, and W. Levelt (Eds.), *The Child's Conception of Language.* New York: Springer-Verlag, 1978.

cognitive development, reading ability, academic achievement, IQ, environmental stimulation, and play (Saywitz & Cherry-Wilkinson, 1982).

Metalinguistic abilities are similar to metacognition and metamemory in the cognitive domains. Metacognition is an individual's knowledge of her cognitive processes, and metamemory is knowledge of the variables that influence memory (Cavanaugh & Perlmutter, 1982). As in language use, one aspect of cognition and memory is knowledge of the process. The individual recognizes her need to employ certain strategies, her own limitations and abilities, and the demands of the task (Flavell, 1981). Metalinguistic skills require similar considerations.

READING AND WRITING: A NEW MODE

With entry into school, the child is required to learn a new mode of communication through the visual channel. Although there is only moderate overlap between the processes of oral and visual communication, among the best indicators of a child's potential for success with reading and writing are her oral language and metalinguistic skills (R. Katz, Shankweiler, & Liberman, 1981; Kemper, 1985; Mann, Shankweiler, & Smith, 1984; Shankweiler, Liberman, Mark, Fowler, & Fischer, 1979). "Since written language is regarded as being more abstract and less natural than spoken language . . ., the act of reading would appear to require deliberate control and manipulation of various language characteristics; i.e., metalinguistic sophistication" (Kemper, 1985, p. 15). Metalinguistic skills enable the child to decontextualize and segment linguistic material. A strong relationship exists between early segmentation skills and reading and spelling. About half of kindergartners and 90% of first graders are able to segment words into syllables. By the end of first grade, with some formal instruction, approximately 70% of the children can segment by phoneme (Liberman et al., 1974). Awareness of the sound system is also very important. The abilities to recognize and create rhymes and to create words that begin with certain sounds in kindergarten correlate highly with reading success later on (Calfee, Chapman, & Venezky, 1972; Jusczyk, 1977; Knafle, 1974). In short, the child is gaining the ability to make judgments with language about language.

Children with a history of preschool speech and language problems frequently have difficulty with reading (Maxwell & Wallach, 1984; P. Weiner, 1985). There are strong indications that speech/audition and writing/reading share, at least in part, a common linguistic base, although they differ in other ways.

Both reading and writing are complex processes that are not totally understood by development and education professionals. It is understood, though, that reading is the synthesis of a complex network of perceptual and cognitive acts along a continuum from word recognition and decoding skills to comprehension and integration. Beyond the printed page, the skilled reader draws conclusions and inferences from what she reads. Of all the factors involved in early reading success, early exposure to reading by parents and a literate atmosphere at home seem to be most important (Goldfield & Snow, 1985; Snow, 1983).

The Process of Reading

Reading requires the processing of language that is decontextualized from any ongoing event. Decontextualized language is characterized by the fact that the speaker and listener do not directly share the experience being communicated. The speaker must create the context by her language, as in narration. It is not surprising, therefore, that poor readers also exhibit poor narrative skills (Norris & Bruning, 1988). In general, poor readers have more difficulty with the use of linguistic cohesion in narratives. The narratives of poor readers tend to be shorter and less well developed than those of better readers.

Familiarity with nursery rhymes is also correlated with better reading skills (Bryant, Bradley, MacLean & Crossland, 1989). In addition to helping the child become sensitive to rhyming and to phonemes, nursery rhymes provide experience with language play, a building block for metalinguistic skills.

Two major theoretical positions attempt to explain the processes involved in reading. Dubbed the *bottom-up* and *top-down* approaches, they describe the extremes of a theoretical continuum. Most professionals would subscribe to an interactive processing model somewhere between the two.

In school, children learn a new means of transmitting the language code that they have acquired.

The bottom-up theory succinctly concludes that *"Reading is the trar* *of written elements into language"* (italics in the original) (Perfetti, 1984, p. 41). Hence, bottom-up theories emphasize lower-level perceptual and phonemic processes and their influence on higher cognitive functioning. Knowledge of both perceptual features in letters and grapheme–phoneme correspondence, as well as lexical retrieval, aid word recognition and decoding. The overall process of reading is the same as the processing of oral language except for breaking the grapheme code. In contrast, the top-down, or problem-solving, theory emphasizes the cognitive task of deriving meaning. Higher cognitive functions, such as concepts, inferences, and levels of meaning, influence the processing of lower-order information. The reader generates hypotheses about the written material based on her knowledge, the content, and the syntactic structures used. Sampling of the reading confirms or does not confirm these hypotheses. The relationship between these two theories is illustrated in Figure 10.2.

The bottom-up theory assumes that the child must learn to decode print into language. In English, the input for the child is *orthography*, or a written alphabetic system containing 26 letters. The child must be able to segment, or divide, each word into phonemic elements and learn the alphabetic code that corresponds (Juel, 1984). Only when this process is automatic can the child give sufficient attention to the meaning of what she is reading. The progression may

FIGURE 10.2   Bottom-up and Top-down Theories of Reading Processing

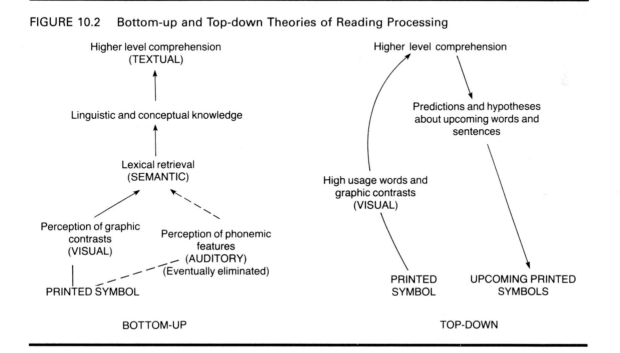

be one in which the child gains increasing automaticity at each stage as she develops and as the process becomes less conscious (LeBerge & Samuels, 1974). Thus, the child first gains automatic processing at the visual and auditory levels; the other stages are still processed consciously (Figure 10.2). Information processing theory (Chapters 4 and 5) may help to explain how automaticity develops (Morton & Long, 1976). According to this theory, each word has a switchboard that activates the visual, auditory, and semantic features of that word. If the reader has enough information from these features, the information is automatically presented to the other parts of the system for processing. It takes a child approximately 0.5 second to recognize a familiar short word; adults average 0.25 second for word recognition of all types. It has been proposed that there are limited facilities for processing; thus, poor or early readers, who spend relatively more capacity on lower-level decoding, have less available for higher-level, comprehension-type tasks (Perfetti, Finger, & Hogoboam, 1978; Wolf, Bally, & Morris, 1984).

The most basic difference between oral and visual language is the input. At the level of word recognition, the two inputs share the same cognitive processes. Auditory and visual features from perceptual analysis are used to enter the reader's mental dictionary, or lexicon (Baron, 1977). Initially a child performs oral reading; therefore, both inputs are available. Eventually the more indirect auditory route is deleted. The child goes directly from visual analysis to word recognition. The route used depends on the sophistication of the reader (Barron, 1981; Frith, 1985). Higher processing involves linguistic and conceptual knowledge (Kintsch & Kosminsky, 1977). Reading information is stored temporarily in a speech-sound code for processing, regardless of the input mode.

Initial slow reading learning in English, according to the bottom-up theory, is caused by the lack of correspondence between English speech sounds and letters. The 26 letters of the English alphabet are used to form approximately 24 consonants and 21 vowels or diphthongs, plus consonant clusters (*str, cl*) and vowel doubling. Most of you have probably seen the example of *ghoti*, which for the uninitiated is pronounced "fish." The analysis is as follows:

$$(enou)gh + (w)o(men) + (na)ti(on) = ghoti$$
$$/f/ \qquad /\text{I}/ \qquad /\text{ʃ}/ \qquad /\text{fɪʃ}/$$

The letters used in English writing and reading are abstractions that can only be mastered by continual exposure to phonemic patterns.

The bottom-up theory may explain some of the initial difficulties children have with reading, but it cannot account for the entire reading process. It does not explain sentence comprehension, the effects of context on comprehension, or the use of hypothesis testing with unfamiliar or upcoming words in the text.

The top-down, or problem-solving, model of reading addresses these inadequacies by viewing reading as a "psycholinguistic guessing game" (K. Goodman, 1976) in which the reader uses language and her conceptual knowledge to aid her in recognizing words sequentially (Bransford & Johnson, 1972; F. Smith, 1971). As she reads, the child makes predictions from syntactic and semantic cues about upcoming words and sentences. The text acts as her confirmation. At first, a child will learn high-usage words, such as *the* and *is*, on sight; she will then use them plus the overall text to form hypotheses regarding unknown words. In other words, the child uses her knowledge of language to help her figure out the word. The mature silent reader doesn't even read whole words. Rather, she samples enough of a word to confirm her hypothesis and recognizes others quickly by sight. In this manner, she can read rapidly for overall meaning.

Since neither theory fully explains the reading process or its development, a third, interactive model has been proposed that incorporates portions of each (Rumelhart, 1977; Stanovich, 1980). According to this theory, reading consists of parallel processes, both top-down and bottom-up, that provide information simultaneously at various levels of analysis. This information is then synthesized. The processes are interactive, and relative reliance on each varies with the material being read and the skill of the reader. By third or fourth grade, children employ both a bottom-up strategy when reading isolated words and a top-down strategy when reading text. Thus, faster top-down processes are used with textual material and slower bottom-up when such support is lacking.

A variation on this theory incorporates the simultaneous and successive processing noted in Chapter 4 (Das, 1984). In simultaneous processing of linguistic material, large chunks of the message are surveyed all at once. In contrast, successive processing is temporal in nature, so the message is processed in a linear fashion. Both processes are necessary for beginning reading (Cummins & Das, 1977). The order of appearance of printed material is important initially for comprehension. The poor reader has difficulty with both processes, but especially with successive processing, in both visual and auditory tasks (Das, Snart, & Mulcahy, 1982). The better reader relies more on simultaneous processing for comprehension.

The complex process of reading is closely related to linguistic processing. In addition to the initial use of two input modes, the reader processes material on at least two levels: bit by bit and holistically. The relative reliance of the reader on each level varies with reading competence.

Reading Development

Like speech, prereading may be acquired through social interaction rather than formal instruction (Ferreiro, 1984; Pflaum, 1986; Snow, 1983). Reading together is a highly social activity in which both parents and children participate. The adult uses many of the conversational techniques described in Chapter 7 for oral language development, including focusing attention, asking questions, and reinforcing the child's attempts at reading (Ninio & Bruner, 1978; Teale, 1984).

Many parents introduce books to their children prior to age 1, using a naming activity in which the child identifies pictures (Snow & Ninio, 1986). Parents sometimes provide a narrative, thus indirectly teaching the child about story structure. Actual text reading by parents usually begins late in the second year or in the third year.

Parent–child reading is not the only way of developing a concept of literacy (Teale, 1984). Television shows, such as *Sesame Street* or *Electric Company,* and parental activities, such as the use of cookbooks and TV schedules or bill paying, are also important (Anderson & Stokes, 1984; Brice Heath, 1983). The child learns that books and writing or print convey information.

There are several phases of reading development (Chall, 1983). In the prereading phase, which occurs prior to age 6, the child learns letter and number discrimination, recognition, and scanning. Most children are able to recognize their names in print and a few memorized words. Usually learned within an environmental context, such as signs, these words gradually become decontextualized until they are recognized in print alone. Approximately 60% of 3-year-olds and 80% of 4- and 5-year-olds recognize the word *stop* (Y. Goodman, 1986).

In phase 1, up to approximately second grade, the child concentrates on decoding single words in simple stories. In order to read, the child needs to know what reading is, what it does, and the principles of the writing system; she also needs to exploit this knowledge to achieve an increasingly automatic, fluent, error-free performance (P. Smith, 1986). Undoubtedly, the most difficult part of this learning involves the metalinguistic skills needed in order to integrate the sound and writing systems. In English, the phoneme, as represented by a grapheme or letter, is the basis for the orthographic system. Among such systems, only Korean (Taylor, 1980) has phonemic features such as place and manner of sound production included in the written symbols. Other languages, such as Japanese, use an orthography system based on the syllable or word as the basic unit.

Unfortunately, knowing that a phoneme roughly corresponds to a grapheme is not enough. As discussed previously, the correspondence is not one-to-one. In addition, English orthography sometimes favors morphological stability over phonemic difference, as in using *-ed* for the past tense marker, even though it may be pronounced as /t/, /d/, or /Id/.

Second, syllable knowledge is needed in order to decode and pronounce written words. Along with syllable knowledge is a knowledge of syllable stress. The noun "*entrance*" differs from the verb "en*trance*" only in the stress placed on each syllable. By age 7, the child has a rigid stress rule that is the same for all words. This is gradually modified into a more flexible system as the child matures.

Finally, the child must be aware of word boundaries. The child must begin to realize that *jumping rope* is two words and that forms such as *jump-roping* are incorrect.

By age 7 or 8, most children have acquired the graphemic, syllabic, and word knowledge they need to become competent readers. Much of this knowledge is acquired in school in most countries. Among the Vai, a Liberian population, however, knowledge of written syllabic symbols is learned informally within the family (Scribner & Cole, 1981).

Once the child gains some control over letter discrimination and syllable and word boundaries, she becomes a more efficient attender, and some higher comprehension skills become evident. Meaningful words in context are read faster than random words (Doehring, 1976). At this stage the child begins by relying heavily on visual configuration for word recognition (Torrey, 1979). She pays particular attention to the first letter and to word length, ignoring letter order and other features (Marsh, Friedman, Welch, & Desberg, 1981). She is aware of the importance of the letters but is unable to use them in analyzing the word (Allington, 1984). Next, the child learns sound–spelling correspondence rules and is able, using this phonetic approach, to sound out novel words (Frith, 1985). Thus, segmental detail, or the arrangement of sound and letter sequences, becomes more important (Barron, 1981). In addition, the child learns that the text, not the reader, is the bearer of the message and that the text does more than just describe the pictures (Ferreiro & Teberosky, 1982). Successful first-grade oral readers are able to use the text to analyze unknown words. Thus, incorrectly substituted words make sense in the context. Poor readers tend to guess wildly (Biemiller, 1970).

By phase 2, roughly the third and fourth grades, the child is able to analyze unknown words using orthographic patterns and contextual inferences. Phase 3, from grades 4 to 8, seems to be a major watershed in which the emphasis in reading shifts from decoding skills to comprehension. Thus, the scanning rate continues to increase steadily. By secondary school, firmly within phase 4, the adolescent uses higher-level skills such as inference and recognition of viewpoint to aid comprehension. Lower-level skills are already firmly established. Finally, at phase 5, the college level and beyond, the adult is able to integrate what she reads into her current knowledge base and make critical judgments about the material.

From age 7 or 8 through adulthood, reading becomes more automatic, with direct access to both phonological-orthographic and semantic coding. Adjustments in reading strategy that depend on one more than the other are based on text difficulty. The differences between the 7-year-old and the adult reader are primarily quantitative, not qualitative, although there are some obvious differences (P. Smith, 1986). Adults have a larger, more diverse vocabulary and a more flexible pronunciation system, and they are able to comprehend larger units than elementary schoolchildren (Harris, Kruithof, Terwogt, & Visser, 1981).

Not all children follow the same progression. Children have different cognitive styles that influence the manner in which they approach tasks. In addition, which language is being read and whether it is the reader's first or second language will influence the processes emphasized (Hakes, 1980).

The Process of Writing

Written language is not just transcription of oral language. Therefore, children must learn to use constructions other than those they use in speech. Initially the structures in both are very close, but they display less maturity in the written form. This is probably because the physical process is so laborious. Once writing becomes automatic, however, the grammar in writing becomes more advanced than that in speech.

There may be four phases in the development of writing (Kroll, 1981): preparation, consolidation, differentiation, and integration. In the preparation phase, the child learns the physical aspects of handwriting by copying words written by adults.

At around age 7, the child enters the consolidation phase (Harpin, 1976; Wilkinson, Barnsley, Hanna, & Swan, 1979). In this phase, the child can write independently using structures from speech in the same proportion as they appear in speech.

In the differentiation phase, the child's writing begins to take on its own grammatical characteristics. Speech and writing become differentiated. This occurs at about age 10.

Finally, a minority of mature writers enter the integration phase. In this phase, writing has become sufficiently differentiated and integrated that the personality of the writer can come through when desired and appropriate. Change is not smooth but appears to occur in a series of spurts at ages 9, 13, and 17, followed by periods of consolidation (Harpin, 1976; Loban, 1976; O'Donnell, Griffin, & Norris, 1967).

Grammatical development can be described for writing, as we have done for speech (Perera, 1986). For example, the types of sentences change. There is a threefold increase in the number of written passive sentences between ages 8 and 13 (O'Donnell et al., 1967).

At the sentence level, clause length increases in writing, as it does in speech (Hunt, 1970). The mean length of the written clause is 6.5 words for the 8-year-old writer, 7.7 for the 13-year-old, 8.6 for the 17-year-old, and 11.5 for the adult. As in speech, there is also an increase in embedded subordinate clauses and a decrease in coordination or compound sentences. Relative clauses double in frequency between ages 7 and 17 and continue to increase into adulthood (Harpin, 1976; Hunt, 1965; O'Donnell et al., 1967). Adverbial clauses, especially those signifying time (when . . .), also increase and diversify.

At the phrase level, there is an increase in pre- and postnoun modifiers. By adolescence, writers are modifying nouns with adverbs as well as adjectives and are often using four or more modifiers with a noun (Hunt, 1965; O'Donnell et al., 1967). Verb phrases are expanded by increasing use of modality, tense, and aspect.

Some structures are common to speech but occur rarely, if at all, in writing. Other structures are more typical of writing than of speech. Structures found almost exclusively in speech include dysfluencies, fillers (well, you know), vague expletives (. . . and all, . . . and everything), this and these used for old information (And there was this man . . .), and pronoun apposition (My dog, he got a bath) (Perera, 1986). Dysfluencies, such as false starts, reformulations, redundant repetitions, and ungrammatical strings of words, are nine times as frequent in the speech of 10-year-olds as in their writing (O'Donnell et al., 1967). No doubt this reflects the additional time that writers have to plan, reflect upon, and modify their message.

Studies of older elementary children who speak standard dialects indicate that dialectal structures also do not occur in written communication. These studies have not included younger or nonstandard dialectal speakers.

In general, writing is more formal and more complex, and the structures found more frequently in writing reflect this quality. By ages 11 to 13, the syntax used in writing far exceeds that used in speech (O'Donnell et al., 1967). This is a gradual process. For example, postnoun modifiers become more common in writing at about age 8 and embedded clauses at about age 10.

While complex subjects are rare in speech, they are found more frequently in the writing of 9-year-olds than in the speech of adults (Crystal, 1980; Quirk, Greenbaum, Leech, & Svartvik, 1972). This reflects the use of embedded phrases and clauses, some of which, such as *whose, whom, on which,* and *in which,* occur almost exclusively in writing (Handscombe, 1967). In addition, written sentences include more prepositional and adverbial phrases (*Opposite the drug counter . . ., About 5 miles down the beach . . .*).

In general, by age 9 or 10, writing is free of many of the features of speech. At about this time, writing becomes more mature than speech, reflecting linguistic performance that is closer to linguistic knowledge.

Writing Development

There is only a moderate amount of overlap between writing and reading. In general, better writers are better readers, and vice versa. The process of writing is close to drawing in that both represent an underlying symbolization (Dyson, 1983; Gourley, McClellan, Bennett, & Gundersheim, 1983). The two systems are different, however, and become differentiated around age 3 (Gibson & Levin, 1975).

Children go through a hierarchy from drawing through scribbling to creating forms that resemble letters. Figure 10.3 is an example of the drawing of a 4-year-old. Well-learned words appear next, followed by inventive spelling and, finally, conventional spelling (Sulzby, 1986). At first, the child may pretend to write, even though she doesn't know letter names or that print represents words (Sulzby, 1981). Well-learned words, such as *stop* or the child's name, help the child learn that different letters represent different sounds.

With inventive spelling, the child tries to impose some regularity on her writing system by matching sounds and letters (Read, 1981). The sounds in the letter name are matched to the sounds the child hears. Initially the first letter represents the entire word, with little attention given to the other letters. For example, *MBRS* or *MTC* might represent *Mommy.* This is similar to the initial stage of reading, in which the child pays attention to the first letter only. Next, the child represents syllables, without some vowels and some spacing. For example, *grass* might be written as *GRS* or *game* as *GM.* Several of the following characteristics of inventive spelling are important because they let us know the salient features of words for children (Pflaum, 1986; Read, 1971):

FIGURE 10.3 With drawings such as this (entitled *Me*), children begin to communicate information graphically prior to the development of writing.

- Use vowel names if the vowel is long:

    DA = day   LIK = like

- But do not use vowel names if the vowel is short:

    FES - fish   LAFFT = left

- Spell the word the way it's pronounced:

    BEDR = better   WOODR = water   PREDE = pretty

- Spell according to placement of the tongue (Temple, Nathan, & Burris, 1982; Chomsky, 1979). (Note that different vowels are used for *a* and that medial *n* is often omitted.):

    PLAT = plant   WOTED = wanted

- Do not use vowels with medial and final nasals (/m/, /n/) or liquids (/r/, /l/):

    GRDN = garden   LITL = little

- Write past and plural endings generally as they are heard. (*T* is used first, then both *T* and *D*.):

STOPT = stopped   DAZ = days   FESEZ = fishes   PLATS = plants

In the final phase of inventive spelling, called *phonemic spelling*, the child is aware of the alphabet and the correspondence of sound and symbol. The following is a short story (Temple, Nathan, & Burris, 1982):

> HE HAD A BLUE CLTH. IT TRD IN TO A BRD.
> (He had a blue cloth. It turned into a bird.)

With school instruction the child develops a more conventional system.

Initially spelling seems to be very phonologically based, although word recognition seems to be more visually based (Bryant & Bradley, 1980). Many spelling errors resemble phonological processes in preschool children, such as weak syllable deletion, cluster reduction, and sound substitution based on phonological similarity rather than visual resemblance (Hoffman & Norris, 1989). If this is true, then simplification strategies for words in spelling and in early pronunciation are similar.

Writing, of course, involves more than spelling. Young writers, like preschool speakers, are often oblivious of the needs of the reader. (See the discussion of presuppositional skills in Chapter 9.) The 6-year-old pays very little attention to format, spacing, spelling, and punctuation. Often other aspects of writing will deteriorate when one aspect is stressed. For example, spelling and sentence structure deteriorate when the child changes from printing to script. Writing on a difficult topic may also result in spelling, handwriting, or text deterioration. Despite these deficiencies, the stories of young children are often direct and beautiful in their simplicity, as evidenced by the short story that follows. Created especially for this book by my friend Christina, aged 6, the story concerns two frogs (*Tow forg*).

> Tow forg
> Tow forg on a TV. Where anr tow forgs? I will go to The TV. This is My
> Tow forgs. My forgs are fun. I Love forgs. I Love forgs To.
>
> by Christina

By the middle school years, the length and diversity of children's productions increase. Along with the longer writing required in school come increasing cognitive demands on the child for coherence of ideas. First using drawings to highlight important portions and to help organize the text, the child moves on to order of recall, usually the order of occurrence. Text forms, such as letter format, are used later to help organize material.

Around third or fourth grade, there is a shift in the child's writing from an egocentric focus to a concern for reader reaction. Writers begin to revise and to proofread their work (Bartlett, 1982; Graves, 1979). This is influenced by the writer's syntactic knowledge. In general, the school years bring a decrease in incomplete oral and written sentences and in dependence on the subject-verb-object format, and an accompanying increase in complex clauses and phrases and in sentence format variety (J. de Villiers & P. de Villiers, 1978; Loban, 1976). Near the end of elementary school, the complexity of written language surpasses that of spoken language (Gundloch, 1981). Organizational changes continue also, and in high school adolescents are able to organize arguments logically and to produce persuasive writing (Nold, 1981).

The last writing style to develop is expository writing. Essays contain a logical, very condensed organization with complex syntactic structures. Each sentence is linked to the topic, and the overall organization is coherent and unambiguous.

Summary

Once children have gained a working knowledge of spoken language, most adapt to the new mode of written language with relative ease. Initial difficulties with symbol relationships slow the first stages. The underlying linguistic relationships between spoken and written language, however, make eventual success possible and help explain the process. In addition to the child's linguistic knowledge, emerging metalinguistic skills enable her to decontextualize language and thus use her knowledge to understand language in another form or mode.

CONCLUSION

By kindergarten age, the child has acquired much of the structure of the mature oral language user (L. Bloom, 1975; Palermo & Molfese, 1972). Development continues, however, as the child adds new forms and gains new skills in transmitting messages. The process continues throughout life, especially in the semantic aspects of language.

Through formal instruction the child learns a new mode of language transmission. Reading and writing open new avenues of exploration and learning for the child and are essential skills in the modern literate society.

Older children and adults have the linguistic skills to enable them to select, from among several available communication strategies, the one best suited to a specific situation. Mature language is efficient and appropriate (Muma, 1978). It is efficient because words are more specifically defined and because forms do not need repetition or paraphrasing in order to be understood. It is appropriate because utterances are selected for the psychosocial dynamics of the communication situation. Less mature language users are less able to select the appropriate code because they have a limited repertoire of language forms.

REFLECTIONS

1. Explain the different types of passive sentences and briefly sketch their developmental sequence.
2. Embedding and conjoining, begun in preschool, continue to develop during the school years. Explain this development briefly and give possible reasons for the sequence of conjunction development.
3. Between the ages of 5 and 9, the child undergoes the syntagmatic-paradigmatic shift in her concept formation. What is this shift? What is its effect on the child's definitions?
4. Figurative language cannot be taken literally; the child must use other cues to interpret. What are the major types of figurative language? Explain the development of this form of language.
5. Morphophonemic development is the major phonological change present in the school years. Describe the morphophonemic changes and provide an example.
6. The conversational abilities of the school-age child increase dramatically. Describe these pragmatic abilities.
7. Describe the differences between the speech of men and women and suggest possible related factors.
8. Explain metalinguistic abilities.
9. Reading may be either symbol generated or the result of predictive hypotheses. Describe briefly the bottom-up and top-down theories of reading processing.
10. As in oral language, the child goes through a developmental sequence in written language. Describe the development of reading and writing.

11 Language Research and Analysis

CHAPTER OBJECTIVES

Our knowledge of child language development is only as good as the research data that we possess. In turn, these data reflect the questions that researchers ask and the studies they design to answer these questions. This chapter explores these questions and presents actual language samples and a description of each. When you have completed this chapter, you should understand

- the effect of the method of data collection on the resultant data.
- the effect of the sample size and variability on the resultant data.
- the issues of naturalness and representativeness.
- collection and analysis procedures.
- the value of cross-language studies.

T HROUGHOUT THIS TEXT, we have been discussing child language development information that has been gathered from studies of child language. These data are difficult to collect and often require extraordinary procedures in order to ensure valid, reliable, and objective reporting.

In general, there are four goals of child language research (Bennett-Kastor, 1988):

1. To confirm general linguistic principles.
2. To discover principles of language development.
3. To clarify the relationship of language to developments in other areas, such as cognition.
4. To provide a more or less theoretical description of language development.

The purpose and the researcher's theoretical predisposition will influence the type of data collection procedure used. The behavioral, linguistic, cognitive, or eclectic theories of the researcher will influence the specific language features studied and the overall study design. Research is usually based on a model of language or language development that may not reflect the actual language hypotheses of the child. Thus, the results might describe the child's fit or lack of fit to a model rather than the child's actual operating principles, hypotheses, or linguistic performance.

Just as there are different methods of collection, there are many considerations that influence the data gathered by these procedures. In this chapter, we will briefly explore issues related to child language study, such as the method of study, the population and language sample size and variability, the naturalness and representativeness of the language sample, data collection, and data analysis. I shall refer frequently to two studies that we have discussed previously, those of R. Brown (1973) and Wells (1985). Other studies will be mentioned as appropriate without burdening the discussion with specific details of each. Cross-linguistic studies and data will also be discussed. Finally, we shall examine portions of actual language samples, and note differences and similarities between children.

ISSUES IN THE STUDY OF CHILD LANGUAGE

While the notion of collecting and analyzing child language data may seem simple, in fact it is very complex. Several decisions must be made prior to data collection. The methods and procedures used can influence the resultant data and may unintentionally color the conclusions drawn from these data.

Method of Data Collection

Language development data are usually collected in two ways: spontaneous conversational sampling or natural observation and structured testing or experimental manipulation. Each method raises issues of appropriateness for the language feature being studied. Either one alone may be insufficient to describe the child's linguistic competence, that is, what he knows about language. Data yielded in one context may not appear in another. For example, in a study of pronouns in which I participated, children produced a wider variety in conversation and produced more advanced forms in more formal testing (Haas & Owens, 1985). Ideally, the linguist would employ both approaches, using the structured procedures to obtain more in-depth information on the data collected by the more broad-based naturalistic procedures (Wells, 1985).

Some researchers prefer testing or experimental manipulation in order to control for some of the variables inherent in more naturalistic collection. Within a test or experimental procedure, various linguistic elements may be elicited using verbal and nonverbal stimuli in a structured presentation. Such control of the context, however, may result in rather narrow sampling.

Formal procedures also enable researchers to gather data that may not be readily available using conversational or observational techniques. For example, it is difficult to assess children's comprehension or their metalinguistic skills without direct testing. Many hypotheses cannot be tested directly for ethical reasons, however, so researchers must test indirectly or observe some features of language development.

Unfortunately, testing and experimental tasks do not necessarily reflect the child's performance in everyday use. For example, in an experimental task, the child may rely on on-the-spot problem-solving techniques rather than on his own everyday operating theories and hypotheses (Karmiloff-Smith, 1986). In addition, noncompliance with testing or experimental procedures may not mean noncomprehension or lack of knowledge. Especially with preschoolers, incorrect responding may indicate a lack of attention or interest.

The results of testing can be especially suspect unless they are analyzed thoroughly. Test scores alone tell researchers nothing about performance on individual items. Two children may have the same score and very different responses. Scoring of individual items may be limited to a wrong-or-right dichotomy, with little analysis of the types of incorrect responses and the underlying processes that these answers may reflect. Testing contexts may provide more or fewer stimuli than are found in the real world, thus modifying the difficulty of the task for the child.

In short, testing and experimental data may be very accurate but very limited. The results must be examined within the context of the specific tasks designed to elicit certain behaviors. A better measure is the consistency of use of a language feature across tasks (Bennett-Kastor, 1988; Derwing & Baker, 1986).

Sampling spontaneous conversation is more naturalistic and, ideally, ensures analysis of real-life behaviors. Such collection is not without its problems. For example, the data collected may be affected by several variables, such as the amount of language, the intelligibility of the child, and the context. To date, linguists have not identified all the possible variables that can affect performance or the extent of their influence. As a result, certain linguistic elements may not be exhibited even when they are present in the child's repertoire. Some linguistic elements occur infrequently, such as passive voice sentences, and others are optional, such as the use of pronouns. Usually, only one conversational sample is inadequate to demonstrate the full range of a child's communication abilities. It is difficult to estimate the child's competence or ability based on actual behavior. In addition, information on the child's production provides only a general estimate of comprehension.

Any given naturalistic situation may be insufficient for eliciting the child's systematic knowledge of language (Ingram, 1969). Nor is there certainty that a given test situation will represent the naturally occurring communication of the child. Thus, it is best to have data from a combination of collection procedures. In either case, the linguist is sampling the child's performance. The child's linguistic competence—what he knows about language—must be inferred from this performance.

Sample Size and Variability

The researcher must be concerned about two samples, the sample or group of children from whom data are collected and the sample of language data. In both samples, the researcher must be concerned with size and variability. Too small a sample will restrict the conclusions that can be drawn about all children, and two large a sample may be unwieldy. The two samples, subjects and language, also interact, one influencing the other.

The number of children or subjects should be large enough to allow for individual differences and to enable group conclusions to be drawn. The overall design of the study will influence the number of subjects considered adequate. For example, it may be appropriate to follow a few children for a period of time, called a *longitudinal study* (Trantham & Pedersen, 1976), but inappropriate to administer a one-time-only test to the same limited number of children. Other considerations will also influence the number of children studied. In a longitudinal study, for example, as many as 30% of the children may be lost because of family mobility, illness, or unwillingness to continue over a 4- or 5-year period. It might be better, therefore, to adopt an overlapping longitudinal design with two different age samples, each being observed for half the length of time that would have been needed in a longitudinal study (Wells, 1985).

Wells (1985) sampled 128 children for 2 years each, using such an overlapping longitudinal model. R. Brown (1973) studied three children intensively for 10 to 16 months. Wells recorded each child for analysis for 27 minutes at 3-month intervals throughout the study, collecting an average of 120 utterances on each occasion. In contrast, Brown averaged 2 hours of sampling each month.

The sample of children should accurately reflect the diversity of the larger population from which they were drawn. In other words, the children sampled should represent all socioeconomic, racial and ethnic, and dialectal variations found in the total population, and in the same proportions found there. Other variables that may be important include size of family, birth order, presence of one or both parents in the home, presence of natural parents in the home, and amount of schooling. Some variables, such as socioeconomic status, may be difficult to determine, although parental education and employment seem to be important contributing factors. Mixed-race children may force the researcher to make decisions about racial self-identity that are not appropriate. Other variables, such as birth order, may be more important than more traditional variables, such as gender (Bennett-Kastor, 1988).

Characteristics of the tester, experimenter, or conversational partner are also important. In general, preschool children will perform better with a familiar adult. There is also some indication that minority children may perform better with adults from the same minority group.

Some children found in the general population may be excluded when the study attempts to determine normal development. These may include children with known handicaps; bilingual children; twins, triplets, and other multiple births; and children in institutional care or full-time nursery school. Children may also be excluded who are likely to move during the course of the study or whose parents were deemed uncooperative or unreliable (Wells, 1985). For example, children with parents in the military are likely to move frequently, possibly prior to the completion of a longitudinal study. With each exclusion, the "normal" group becomes more restricted and, thus, less representative.

In order to draw group conclusions, subjects must be matched in some way. Although the most common way to group children is by age, such matching of subjects in language development studies may be "fundamentally inappropriate" (Pine & Lieven, 1990). Many language differences reflect developmental changes in other areas. Therefore, reliable age-independent measures of development, such as level of cognitive development, may be a better gauge of real developmental differences and may allow more appropriate comparisons of children's language development.

The problem of the appropriate amount of the child's language to sample becomes especially critical with low-incidence elements. Usually at least 100 utterances are needed in order to have an adequate sample, although the sample size depends on the purpose for which it is collected. Elements that occur less than once in 100 utterances may not occur within the typical sample of that length. In addition, a single occurrence is very weak evidence upon which to base an assumption that the child has this linguistic element within his repertoire. This assumption is strengthened, however, if a large proportion of the individuals being studied exhibit this linguistic element (Wells, 1985).

As mentioned, the amount of language collected will vary with the language feature being studied. Pragmatic aspects of language, which vary with the context, may require the inclusion of several contexts to provide an adequately varied sample. Such language uses as conversational openings, which occur only once in each conversation, would require varied contexts in order to allow the researcher to reach even tentative conclusions.

In general, the larger the sample of children and/or speech, the fewer data it is possible to analyze. Conversely, the more detailed the analysis, the fewer children or the smaller the amount of speech it is possible to sample. Resources such as personnel, time, and money are always limited. The linguist must decide on an appropriate sample size and an adequate level of analysis.

Naturalness and Representativeness of the Data

Any sample should fulfill the twin requirements of naturalness and representativeness. Even testing should attempt to use familiar situations with the child. The conversational sample will be more natural if the participants are free to move about and are uninhibited by the process of sample collection. A representative sample should include as many of the child's everyday experiences as possible. Unfortunately, little is known about the range and frequency of children's activities. To address this issue, Wells (1985) sampled randomly throughout the day for short periods. While the specific details of his study are not important for this discussion, they do provide a model of the extraordinary procedures that may be required in order to get a representative sample.

Wells collected daily 24 randomly scheduled samples of 90 seconds' duration each. Samples were scheduled so that four occurred within each of six equal time periods throughout the day. Eighteen of the 24 samples, totaling 27 minutes of recording, were needed for analysis. This allowed a possible 25% of the samples to be blank as a result of having been recorded while the child and microphone were beyond the range of the microphone's transmission. Two samples from each of the six time blocks were randomly chosen for transcription. After these had been transcribed, the process continued randomly with the remaining six samples until 120 intelligible utterances had been amassed. The remaining utterances were not transcribed for analysis. This procedure was followed once every 3 months for 2 years for each child.

As you can see, it is not always easy to obtain natural and representative language data. At least three potential factors may be problems (Wells, 1985). One problem is that of the "observer paradox" (Labov, 1972). Stated briefly, it is that the absence of an observer may result in uninterpretable data, but the presence of an observer may influence the language obtained, so that it lacks spontaneity and naturalness.

The presence of an observer can also affect the sample being collected. The behavior of the child and the conversational partner may be influenced by the presence of another person. For this reason, Wells (1985) collected his samples on a tape recorder, with no observer present. The recorder was programmed to begin taping at randomly assigned times throughout the day. In contrast, R. Brown (1973) included two observers: one to keep a written transcript of the linguistic and nonlinguistic behaviors of the parent and child, and the other to tend the tape recorder and to be a playmate for the child.

The absence of an observer may also complicate the process of determining the exact context of the language sample. At the end of each recording day, parents might be asked to identify contexts by the activity and participants present, although the reliability of such recalled information is doubtful (Wells, 1985). In addition, the immediate nonlinguistic context of each utterance cannot be reconstructed from audiotape alone.

A second problem is the child's physical and emotional state at the time the information is collected. Usually the child's caregiver is asked to comment on the typicalness of the child's performance.

A third problem relates to the context in which the sample is collected. Occasionally, information is collected in experimental or test-type situations. The rationale for collecting this type of data is that through manipulation of the context, the linguist can obtain language features from the child that may not be elicited in conversation. Unfortunately, the language obtained is likely to be divorced from meaningful contexts in the child's experience and, thus, does not represent the child's use of language to communicate with familiar conversational partners in everyday contexts. Theoretically, the most representative sample should be elicited in the home for preschoolers and in the home or classroom for older children, with a parent, sibling, or teacher as the conversational partner.

Language samples should be representative in two ways discussed previously. First, the population sample from which the language is collected should be representative of all aspects of the total population. Second, each child's language sample should be representative of his typical language performance. This is best ensured if the sample is collected in a variety of typical settings in which the child is engaged in everyday activities with his usual conversational partners.

Collection Procedures

Questions relative to collection of the language sample must of necessity concern the presence or absence of a researcher and the actual recording method. Wells

(1985) attempted to minimize observer influences by having the child wear a microphone that transmitted to a tape recorder preprogrammed to record at frequent but irregular intervals throughout the day. Of course, there are problems with this process, such as the compactness and sensitivity of the microphone transmitter. In contrast, Brown (1973) used two researchers in the setting while data were recorded on tape recorder.

Electronic means of collection seem essential. Videotaping, while more intrusive, is better than audiotaping alone, because it enables the researcher to observe the nonlinguistic elements of the situation in addition to the linguistic elements. Written transcription within the collection setting is the least desirable method for several reasons. First, it is easy to miss short utterances. Second, it is nearly impossible to transcribe the language of both the child and the conversational partner because of the large number of utterances within a short period of time. Third, transcription within the conversational setting does not enable the researcher to return to the child's speech for missed or misinterpreted utterances.

The language sample should be transcribed as soon after it is collected as possible. Caregivers familiar with the child's language should be consulted to determine if the sample is an example of the child's typical performance.

Analysis Procedures

Transcription may also be difficult. The result will vary with the playback unit used. Transcribers can check each other's work, but they must be careful not to be influenced by the initial transcript. It is best if two independent transcriptions are prepared and compared for discrepancies. The life experiences of each transcriber will affect his expectations for various conversational samples and, thus, modify what each believes he hears.

Because transcription offers many opportunities for error, studies should ensure intratranscriber reliability. This is not always easy to accomplish. Many published studies either do not establish intratranscriber reliability or do not report it. Several factors contribute to transcription errors, including the type of speech sampled, the intelligibility of the child, the number of transcribers, the level of transcription comparison, and the experience of the transcriber(s) (Pye, Wilcox, & Siren, 1988). In general, the more defined the speech sampled, the better the intelligibility, the greater the number of transcribers, the larger the unit of comparison, and the more experienced the transcriber, the better the chance of having an accurate transcript. The type of speech sample may range from individual words to whole conversations. Larger units are more difficult to transcribe accurately. The use of more than one transcriber reduces the possibility of errors if the transcribers compare their transcriptions and resolve their differences in a consistent manner. Finally, lower levels of comparison, such as phonemes, increase the likelihood of error because of the precise nature of such units.

Actual analysis may be even more ticklish, especially when trying to determine the bases for that analysis. For example, MLU is still the most common measure of language growth, although its value is questionable. Numerical scores

Child language researchers must make several theoretical and methodological decisions prior to and during data collection and analysis.

and measures, such as MLU, are inadequate for describing language development in detail.

It is also difficult to determine when a child or group of children actually knows or has mastered a language feature. The criteria for establishing that a child knows a word or a feature have not been preestablished (Nelson, 1973b). For example, with word knowledge, the researcher must have clear evidence that a child comprehends the word. In contrast, production criteria would probably be based on spontaneous use and consistent semantic intent. With young children, the researcher would also note consistent phonetic form and semantic intent, with decisions of knowledge not necessarily based on whether the form and meaning are related to an adult word.

Usually mastery is based on children using a feature in 90% of the obligatory locations or on 90% of the children using the feature consistently, but these percentages vary with the researcher. Some researchers consider the average age for acquisition to be that at which 50% of children use a language feature consistently. Of course, such measures are complicated by the complex nature of most language features and the extended period of time often needed for mastery. As we have seen, forms such as passive voice and language uses may take several years from first appearance to full mature use.

An example of one real-life analysis difficulty may be illustrative. In a study of preschool pronoun development (Haas & Owens, 1985), a colleague and I were very surprised to find no errors in pronoun use in conversations among children even as young as age 2. The children had adopted the rule *when in doubt, use a noun*. Thus, analysis that focused on pronouns yielded no errors. When analysis expanded beyond pronouns, however, we found overuse of nouns.

CROSS-LANGUAGE STUDIES

Cross-linguistic studies are usually undertaken in order to investigate universality, linguistic specificity, relative difficulty, or acquisitional principles (Berman, 1986). Studies of universality attempt to determine which aspects of language, such as nouns and verbs, appear in all languages.

In contrast, studies of linguistic specificity attempt to determine whether development is the result of universal cognitive developments or unique linguistic knowledge. The development of temporal terms, for example, seems to be based on cognitive temporal knowledge but also on specific linguistic forms used to mark that knowledge.

Relative difficulty studies look for language development differences that may be explained by the relative difficulty of learning structures and forms in different languages. For example, the passive sentence form is very difficult in English and is mastered much later than the relatively easier form in Egyptian Arabic.

Finally, studies that investigate acquisitional principles try to find underlying language-learning strategies that children apply regardless of the language being acquired. The learning principles described by Slobin in Chapter 7 are the result of this type of study.

There are two basic methods of collecting cross-linguistic data. The first is to gather a range of studies completed in different languages, although these studies may differ in their aims and methods (Braine, 1976; Levy, 1983; MacWhinney, 1978; Peters, 1983; Slobin, 1985). While this method may be quicker, because the studies have already been completed, it may not be easy to draw conclusions from such a diverse collection. The second method is to use a similar design across subjects from different language groups (Bates, MacWhinney, Caselli, Devescove, Natale, & Vanza, 1984; Clark & Berman, 1984; Clark &

Hecht, 1982; Mulford, 1983; Slobin, 1982). This method yields much more definitive data, with fewer complicating variables, but takes much more time and effort to organize, coordinate, and collect. This type of cross-linguistic study can be extremely difficult.

EXAMPLES OF CHILD LANGUAGE DATA

It might be helpful to examine a few child language samples and to comment upon the language demonstrated in each. In this section, we shall examine the language of three children from monolingual English-speaking homes. I have not included the entire sample, but rather one contiguous segment that is somewhat illustrative. Surface differences will be obvious.

The first segment (Table 11.1) was collected in the home and is a conversation between a 22-month-old child and her mother. The overall MLU of the child, T., is approximately 1.9, placing her in the upper end of Brown's stage I. It should be noted that this MLU was calculated from two different situations. Although it has not been calculated, the mother's MLU is also low. The mother makes extensive use of imitation, expansion, and extension.

At first reading, it is obvious that the conversation is very concrete and concerned with the task of coloring. There is no great variety in the words used, and the child repeats these words frequently. The child engages in turn taking and is very responsive. Many of the child's utterances, such as 9 and 14, are whole or partial imitations. The child has a wide range of illocutionary functions in the entire sample. Within this segment, she answers (1, 2, 3, 5, 8, 12) and asks questions (7), replies to her mother's utterances (4, 6, 13, 16), makes declarations (10, 18), gives directions to her mother (11, 17, 21), and makes demands (15, 19, 20).

The second segment (Table 11.2) was also collected in the home and is also a conversation between a child and her mother. The two are engaged in role play with a child's sink, table, and dishes. The mother's speech is complicated by her taking two roles: that of the baby, Michelle, and that of another person in the situation. The child, J., plays herself as the mother of Michelle. She uses turn-abouts to a greater extent than the mother in the first segment. Expansion is very limited and occurs only after child utterance 24.

The child is 32 months old, and her MLU from the larger sample is approximately 3.3. In general, the child is very responsive. As might be expected, her greater output of language compared to T. also demonstrates many more language features. Like T., J. has much variety in of her language, and she initiates and responds to conversation.

Noun and verb phrases are present or understood in many utterances, and have expanded with the use of articles, adjectives, and pronouns and auxiliary verbs, respectively. When expanded, noun phrases usually contain only one additional element, such as an article or adjective (*some*), but not both. The child demonstrates some of her own rule application in utterances 12 and 14, in which she uses the rule of adding *y* to a noun to produce an adjective (*coldy*), and in 23, in which she places *-ed* on an irregular verb (*eated*). She also has some difficulty

---

TABLE 11.1   Toddler Language Sample

What do you see?

1. Birthday cake Kelly house.
   A birthday cake at Kelly's house? What else was at Kelly's house?

2. Birthday cake mommy.
   Mommy had a birthday cake. What else did you have?

3. Kelly house.
   Kelly's house. Oh, look.

4. Color on the table.
   The man colored on the table. Well, that's all right. What are you making?

5. Doggie.
   Are you making a doggie?

6. Okay.
   All right. Oh, that's nice, T.

7. Where more doggie there?
   Is there another doggie underneath?

8. Yeah.
   Where can you find the picture? Is that what you're looking for, the picture of the doggie? Where's the doggie?

9. A doggie.

10. Color a doggie.
    Okay, you color the doggie.

11. Mommy color crayon.
    Mommy has crayons. Mommy's coloring. What's mommy making?

12. Doggie.
    A doggie?

13. Okay.
    All right, I'll make a doggie. Is this the doggie's tail?

14. The doggie's tail.
    Doggie's tail.

15. More.
    More doggie?

16. Okay.
    Can T. color? Hum?

17. More doggie there.

18. More doggie daddy.
    More doggie daddy?

19. Wants a more doggie.

20. More doggie.

21. Put more doggie there.
    Okay, you color doggie on this.

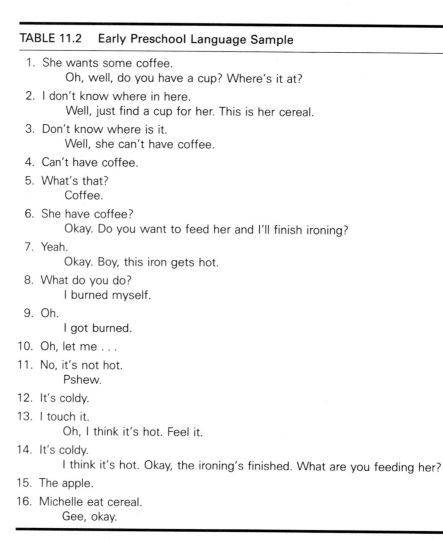

TABLE 11.2   Early Preschool Language Sample

1. She wants some coffee.
    Oh, well, do you have a cup? Where's it at?
2. I don't know where in here.
    Well, just find a cup for her. This is her cereal.
3. Don't know where is it.
    Well, she can't have coffee.
4. Can't have coffee.
5. What's that?
    Coffee.
6. She have coffee?
    Okay. Do you want to feed her and I'll finish ironing?
7. Yeah.
    Okay. Boy, this iron gets hot.
8. What do you do?
    I burned myself.
9. Oh.
    I got burned.
10. Oh, let me . . .
11. No, it's not hot.
    Pshew.
12. It's coldy.
13. I touch it.
    Oh, I think it's hot. Feel it.
14. It's coldy.
    I think it's hot. Okay, the ironing's finished. What are you feeding her?
15. The apple.
16. Michelle eat cereal.
    Gee, okay.

with the irregular verb *have* in 6, but not in 24. Auxiliary verbs are omitted in 13, 16, and 29. In addition, the third person singular -*s* is used inconsistently (1, 17, 27, 31). As might be expected at this level of development, the child demonstrates some embedding of infinitive phrases in 24 (*to go*) but has not mastered this form, as noted in the same utterance [*(to) sleep*]. Her only embedded clauses are of the early object noun phrase complement type seen in 27 (*that's good*) and 3 (*where is it*). Number 3 demonstrates confusion with the *wh-* question form and the *wh-* embedded clause form. The child has some difficulty with the interrogative form (6, 18) and with the comprehension of tag questions (20).

The third segment (Table 11.3) is a conversation between two preschool children, M. and E., both 48 months of age. They are role-playing in an area of a

---

TABLE 11.2   Continued

---

17. She wants some, some, some coffee.
    Oops.
18. That's her coffee.
    Okay, I'll pour some more. Oh, my goodness.
19. It's hot.
    I better put this back on the stove, don't you think?
20. Yeah, don't think.
    Where's the milk?
21. In the refrigerator.
    Okay, let me get some milk. There, got her bottle ready for you.
22. All right.
    Okay.
23. She eated it alldone.
24. She has to go sleep.
    She has to go to sleep. Well well, you better wipe her face.
25. Oh.
    Gee, J., you don't know what you're doing, do you?
26. Yeah.
    Oh, come here, Michelle. Oh, she's still hungry. Can you feed her some more?
27. She wants one that's good.
    Oh.
28. I fix.
    What are you fixing now?
29. I fixing her cereal.
    Oh, the poor little baby's so hungry. Don't you ever feed her?
30. Yeah.
    I think you need to buy her . . .
31. She want some bottle.

---

preschool in which there is a child kitchen. We shall concentrate on M., whose MLU is approximately 5.1. The longer utterances, the imaginative use of language, and the frequent interruption of speakers are very evident. It's an enjoyable sample to read. The conversational behaviors of two preschool partners are not as organized as those of a preschooler and an adult.

The noun phrases of M. have been expanded to include a noun and an adjective in utterances 1 (*the other*) and 25 (*a real*), and M. has a much better command of auxiliary verbs than J., although she omits the auxiliary in 18 [*(are) just kidding*]. Most singular and plural nouns are used correctly, although an irregular, such as *leaf, leaves,* still offers some difficulty (25). Conjunctions appear, alone (19), at the beginning of utterances (9, 31), and in joining clauses (21). Several

---

TABLE 11.3   Late Preschool Language Sample

---

1. Oh, this almost looks like the other one.
2. See?
   > But it has the same hat.
3. Hey, I'm gonna put the sticker right here, okay?
4. Put your stickers right here.
   > So we can pretend these are the TV's.
5. Okay.
   > I'm making dinner.
6. Oh, onions.
   > Oh.
7. Oh, let me toast it.
   > No way.
8. I'm gonna cook, okay?
9. While you do your stuff, okay?
   > I'm toasting. I'm making a piece of bread.
10. I'm eating this bread.
11. Good bread.
12. I think I'm gonna go to work soon.
13. Get this orange out of here.
    > Honey . . .
14. What?
15. Let's get married now.
16. Just a place to get married . . . under the table.
    > We have to have our toast under. . . . You be married too. Don't touch me.
17. Mine.
    > No, you can touch me, you can touch me. I just kidding. . . .

---

infinitive phrases are present, usually of the *gonna X* variety (3, 8, 12), but there are other forms as well (21). Prepositional phrase embedding is also evident in 16 (*under the table*), as well as clausal embedding, again of the object noun phrase complement type, in 18 [*(that) you (are) just kidding*] and 26 [*(that) they're real leaves*]. This last utterance is very complex in that the statement would be *You know that they're real leaves* and must be changed considerably to form the question seen in 26.

     These three samples offer great variety and demonstrate the differences in child language as children develop. It is much easier to comment upon the behaviors demonstrated by a few children than it is to collect samples from a number of children in the hope of analyzing them definitively and extrapolating data about the language development of all children.

TABLE 11.3 *continued*

---

18. I know you just kidding.
    Why'd you say "bye"?
19. Because.
20. I said "bye". . . .
    Here have a piece of bread.
21. I said "bye" just because . . . I said "bye" 'cause I had to go to work and you won't let me.
22. That's why.
    Go to work, honey.
23. Mmmm.
24. It got real leaves.
25. This is a real leaves.
26. They're real leaves, you know?
27. See?
    What? 'Cause they come off?
28. Uh-huh.
29. Wanna see?
    Don't do it. You'll break their toys.
30. Mmmm, bye, I'm going to work.
    Bye-bye. Pretend you came back with that hat on from work and I made you a piece of bread and put a piece of bread.
31. And I won't eat it.
    Okay. When you came back from work, I'll give you a piece of bread.
32. Okay, then I won't eat it.
33. Bye.
    Bye-bye, hon.

CONCLUSION

Complex topics such as language and language development require a great amount of study and research. If the data that result from such research are to be of value beyond the children from whom they were collected, researchers must consider a great variety of questions relative to the language features studied, the children selected, the amount of data, and the collection and analysis procedures. Describing child language development accurately is a difficult and time-consuming job.

REFLECTIONS

1. Explain the two primary methods of data collection and the types of data generated by each.
2. Explain the way in which language sample and population sample size and variability affect the data collected.
3. Why are natural and representative language samples desired, and what are the potential problems that can interfere with collecting these types of samples?
4. How can the method of collection affect the language sample collected?
5. Discuss the issues related to analysis that may affect the results of language studies.
6. Discuss the primary areas of investigation undertaken in cross-language studies.

12 Language Differences: Bidialectism and Bilingualism

CHAPTER OBJECTIVES

In actual usage, a language is a collection of dialects, or rule-governed variations, of a nonexistent standard language. Dialects represent a difference, not a disorder. Some dialects are the result of learning English as a second language. Differences in the way children learn two languages depend on which languages are being learned and the age of the child. When you have completed this chapter, you should understand

- a definition of a dialect and its relation to its parent language.
- the major factors that cause dialects to develop.
- the major characteristics of Black English.
- the major characteristics of Hispanic English.
- the major characteristics of Asian English.
- the differences between simultaneous and successive second-language acquisition.
- the educational problems encountered by dialectal and second-language children.
- the following terms:

archiform	free alternation
bilingual	register
code-switch	style shifting
deficit approach	vernacular
dialect	

THE UNITED STATES is becoming an increasingly pluralistic society. The notion of the melting pot is giving way to one of a *stew* in which cultural and ethno-racial groups contribute to the whole but retain their essential character. One characteristic of these groups may be either language or dialect. Most minority groups continue to embrace their culture and, where non-English, their language.

It is conservatively projected that the minority population in the United States will increase to 45 million by the year 2000 and to 63 million by 2030 (Spencer, 1984). At the same time, the majority white population will increase at a slower rate and will thus become a smaller proportion of the entire U.S. population. If current trends continue, white non-Hispanics will be the largest *minority* by the year 2080 (Bouvier & Gardner, 1986).

At present, in the United States approximately one in four Americans identifies with a minority group. In the state of California, a score of cities, and several counties, minorities represent more than 50% of the population. This situation reflects traditional demographics and a population shift that is the result of recent immigration, internal migration, and natural increase.

Within the last 20 years, 80% of the legal immigrants to the United States have come from Asia and Latin America (Robey, 1985; Russell, 1983). Approximately 40% of all recent legal immigrants are Asian. As a result, there are over 5 million Asians and Asian-Americans residing in the United States. Although this number represents only about 2% of the total U.S. population, it does not indicate the impact of Asians and Asian-Americans on the country. Asians and Asian-Americans tend to settle in coastal states, especially in the West, where they form large segments of the population. In addition, Asians and Asian-Americans represent the fastest-growing segment of the U.S. population. Approximately three-fourths of the legal Asian immigrants come from the five countries of Vietnam, the Philippines, Korea, China, and India. They represent several languages and dialects of those languages.

There are approximately 19 million Hispanics in the United States. In addition, there are several million more Spanish-surnamed individuals who identify with Hispanic culture to a lesser degree. Approximately 40% of all recent legal immigrants are Hispanic. These immigrants come primarily from Mexico and Central America, Puerto Rico and Cuba, and South America, and speak various dialects of Spanish.

In addition, there are approximately 80,000 legal black immigrants per year from the Caribbean, South and Central America, and Africa. It is estimated that this group will represent slightly less than 1% of the U.S. population by the year 2000. This minority represents a number of languages, as is evident from the many geographic areas of origin.

The exact number of illegal immigrants is unknown. Estimates range from 5 to 10 million, with a growth of approximately 500,000 per year (Bouvier & Gardner, 1986; Robey, 1987; Slater, 1986). These also increase the numbers of various minorities.

The largest internal migration is and has been that of African-Americans who number 30 million, or 12% of the U.S. population. Reversing the trend of the early-to-mid twentieth century, African-Americans began returning to the South in the early 1970s (Robinson, 1986; Russell, 1982). Many of these individuals speak regional and/or ethno-racial dialects, such as Black English.

To a smaller extent, Native Americans, totaling 1.6 million, or 0.7% of the population, have also experienced internal migration. At present, just over 30% of Native Americans live on reservations or historic trust properties compared to 90% in 1940 (U.S Department of Health and Human Services, 1985, 1986). Their language may reflect their native language or the specific dialect of American English that they learned.

Birth rates differ across groups and also contribute to the changing demographics of the U.S. population. The majority white birth rate is 1.7, inadequate to maintain the relative proportion of whites in the United States (Hodgkinson, 1986). Birth rates for minority populations are higher, for example, 2.4 for African-Americans, 2.5 for Hispanic-Americans, and 1.8 for Vietnamese (Gardner, Robey, & Smith, 1985; National Center for Health Statistics, 1983, 1985).

We cannot discuss language development adequately without considering dialectal variations, such as Black English, and what we shall call Hispanic English and Asian English, and their effect on the learning of American English and on the learner. In addition, recent immigrations raise issues of bilingualism, second-language learning, and language use within the majority language. Many of the issues discussed will also apply to dialectal differences in British and Canadian English and to bilingual countries such as Canada.

DIALECTS

In the musical comedy *My Fair Lady* (Lerner & Loewe, 1956), Professor Higgins laments:

> Why can't the English teach their children how to speak?
> This verbal class distinction by now should be antique. . . .
> An Englishman's way of speaking absolutely classifies him.
> The moment he talks he makes some other Englishman despise him. . . .
> But use proper English, you're regarded as a freak.
> Why can't the English learn to speak?

His anxiety relates to the various dialects of British English. His contention, and that of Shaw, the author of *Pygmalion* (1916) (upon which *My Fair Lady* is based), is that language is related to the way others view us and make judgments about us. Inherent in his argument is the notion that there is one correct English language and that all variations are substandard. This **deficit approach** seems unfounded in light of recent research on dialectal differences.

Not all speakers of a language use the same language rules. Variations that characterize the language of a particular group are collectively called a *dialect*. A **dialect** is a language rule system used by an identifiable group of people that varies in some way from an ideal language standard. Dialects usually differ in the frequency of use of certain structures rather than in the presence or absence of these structures. The ideal standard is rarely used except in formal writing, and the concept of a standard spoken language is practically a myth (Foss & Hake, 1978). Each dialect shares a common set of grammatical rules with the standard language. Thus, dialects of a language are theoretically mutually intelligible to all speakers of that language. No dialect is better than any other, nor should a dialect be considered a deviant or inferior form of a language. "To devalue his language or to presume Standard English is a 'better system' is to devalue the child and his culture and to reveal a naiveté concerning language" (Baratz, 1968, p. 145). Each dialect is a systematic rule system that should be viewed within its social context. Sociolinguists assume that a dialect is adequate to meet the demands of the speech community in which it is found. Like languages, dialects evolve over time to meet the needs of the communities in which they are used.

Despite the validity of all dialects, society places relative values on each one. The standard dialect becomes the "official" criterion. Speakers of the language determine what is acceptable, often assuming that their own dialect is the most appropriate. In a stratified society, such as that of the United States, some dialects are accorded higher status than others. But, in fact, the relative value of a dialect is not intrinsic; it represents only the listener's bias. Dialects are merely differences within a language.

Dialects, which may reflect regional, ethnic, or other differences, are valid, role-based language codes that vary from some theoretically ideal language standard.

FIGURE 12.1   The Relationship of the Idealized Standard Language and
Its Dialects

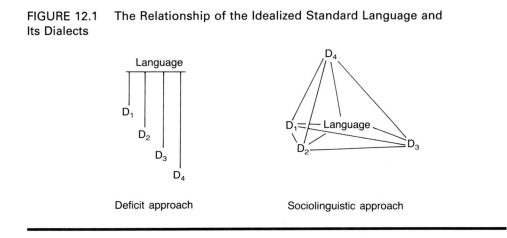

The two ways of classifying dialects are illustrated in Figure 12.1. Under the deficit approach, each dialect has a different relative status. The sociolinguistic approach views each dialect as an equally valid rule system. Each dialect is related to the others and to the ideal standard language. In the diagram, those that are closer to each other in the frequency of rule use are separated by less distance.

Related Factors

Several factors are related to dialectal differences. These include (a) geography, (b) socioeconomic level, (c) race and ethnicity, (d) situation or context, (e) peer group influences, and (f) first- or second-language learning. A child born and raised in Boston will not sound like a child from Charleston, South Carolina. In turn, a poor child and a wealthy preparatory school child from Charleston will not speak the same way. These differences are called *dialectal differences*. In general, the language of these children reflects the environmental influences of the language spoken around them. No children learn dialect-free English. From birth, each child hears English spoken with some dialectal variation. The study of these dialectal influences is an integral part of sociolinguistics.

The United States was established by settlers who spoke many different languages and several dialects of British English. Members of various ethnic groups chose to settle in specific geographic areas. Other individuals remained isolated by choice or by natural boundaries. In an age of less mobility, before there were national media, American English was free to evolve in several separate ways. A New York City dialect is very different from an Ozark dialect. Yet both are close enough to Standard American English (SAE) to be identified as variants of SAE. As a child matures, she learns the dialect of her region, and she learns to distinguish it from other dialects. Each region has lexical items and grammatical structures that differ slightly. What are *sack* and *pop* to the Midwestern American are *bag* and *soda* to the Middle Atlantic speaker. The Italian sandwich changes to *submarine, torpedo, hero, wedge,* and *hoagie* as it moves about the United States. Within each region there is no confusion. Order a milkshake in Massachusetts and that's what you get—flavored milk that's been shaken. If you want ice cream in it, you need to ask for a *frappe.*

Some regions of the United States seem to be more prone to word invention or to novel use than others. In the southern Appalachian region, for example, you might encounter the following (J. Miller, 1985):

A man might raise enough corn to *bread* his family over the winter.
To do something without considering the consequences is to do it *unthoughtedly.*
Something totally destroyed would be torn to *flinderation.*
Long-lasting things are *lasty.*

Note that the form of each word follows generally accepted morphological marking rules, such as the *-ly* in *unthoughtedly.*

One of my sons was given a vivid example of regional dialectal differences while conversing with a child from the Southern United States. Although she was white, the child's older half brother was the product of a racially mixed marriage. Trying to figure out this situation, my son ventured the opinion, "Your brother is really *tan.*" He was corrected quickly with "No he ain't; he's *eleven.*"

A second factor in dialectal differences is socioeconomic level. This factor relates to social class (B. Bernstein, 1971; A. Edwards, 1976), educational and occupational level (Hollingshead, 1965), home environment (Anastasiow & Hanes, 1976), and family interactional styles, including maternal teaching (Snow, Arlmann-Rupp, Hassing, Jobse, Jootsen, & Vorster, 1976) and child-rearing patterns. In general, people from lower socioeconomic groups use more restricted linguistic systems. Their word definitions often relate to one particular aspect of the underlying concept. Those from higher socioeconomic levels generally have more education and are more mobile. These factors generally contribute to the use of a more standard dialect.

Racial and ethnic differences are a third factor that contributes to dialect development. By choice or as a result of de facto segregation, racial and ethnic minorities may become isolated and a particular dialectal variation may evolve. It has been argued that the distinctive Brooklyn dialect reflects the strong influence of the Irish upon American English. Yiddish influences have also affected the New York City dialect. The largest racial group in the United States with a characteristic dialect is African-American. Their dialect, called *Black English,* is spoken by working-class African-Americans, primarily in large industrial areas. Thus, not all African-Americans speak Black English.[*]

Fifth, dialect is influenced by situational and contextual factors. These variations may be structural, stylistic, or pragmatic. With a single speaker, the par-

_____
[*]The specific characteristics of Black English will be discussed later.

ticular situation may result in the use of different dialects. All speakers alter their language in response to situational variables. These situationally influenced language variations are called **registers**. Motherese, the special form of adult language addressed to language-learning children, is an example of a register. The selection of a register depends on the speaker's perception of the situation and the participants, her attitude toward or knowledge of the topic, and her intention or purpose. A casual, informal, or intimate register is called a **vernacular** variation. For example, informal American English uses more contractions and particles than formal American English. Thus, there is greater reliance on *can't* and *don't* and on phrases such as *get up* instead of *rise* and *go away* instead of *leave*. The variation from formal to informal styles or the reverse is called **style shifting** (Labov, 1970a) and is practiced by all speakers. Regardless of the socioeconomic status of the speaker, style shifts seem to be in the same direction for similar situations (Labov, 1970a). For example, in formal reading there is greater use of *-ing* (/ŋ/), while informal conversation is characterized by an increase in the use of *-in* (/n/). Most shifts are made unconsciously. Thus, we might read aloud "I am writing" but say in conversation "I'm writin'."

A fifth influence on language is the peer group. In the United States, teenagers frequently use a variant of language that the elderly do not understand. From a safe distance, we can look back at the teens of the 1950s who were *cool*, longed to be *beats*, and began every sentence with *Like*. Peer influence is particularly important during adolescence (Wolfram & Fasold, 1974). Generally the teen dialect is used only with the peer group. Within our society, other groups, such as gays, have their own lexicons and idioms that are not understood by the society as a whole.

Finally, a dialect may reflect the primacy of another language. Speakers with a different native language often retain vestiges of that language. These people typically **code-switch** from one language to the other (R. Bell, 1976; McCormack & Wurm, 1976). In this process, one language may interfere with the other. The area where the two languages conflict is called an *interference point*. The speaker's age and education and the social situation influence the efficacy of code switching.

American English Dialects

Standard American English (SAE) is an idealized version of American English that occurs rarely in conversation, though many Americans can be classified as users. It is the form of American English that is used in textbooks and on network newscasts. Even though most speakers vary from SAE, there are limits in the amount of variation that is acceptable.

There are at least 10 regional dialects in the United States (presented in Figure 12.2): Eastern New England, New York City, Western Pennsylvania, Middle Atlantic, Appalachian, Southern, Central Midland, North Central, Southwest, and Northwest (Nist, 1966). In general, the variations are greatest on the East Coast and decrease to the West. Each geographic region has a dialect marked by distinct sound patterns, words and idioms, and syntactic and prosodic systems.

FIGURE 12.2   Major American English Speech Varieties

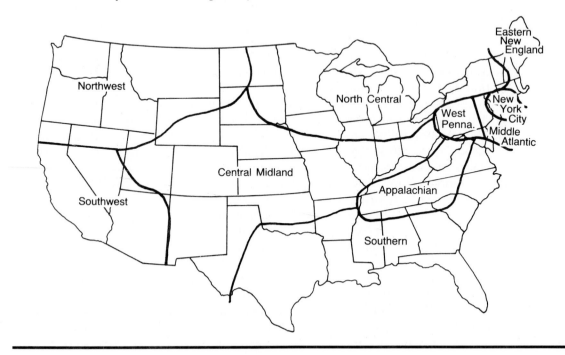

The major racial and ethnic dialects in the United States are Black English, Spanish-influenced or Hispanic English, and "Asian English." In part, these dialects are influenced by geographic region and by socioeconomic factors. Spanish influences also differ depending upon the country of Spanish origin. "Asian English" differs with the country of origin and the native language.

Black English

For the purposes of description, we shall consider Black English (BE) to be the relatively uniform dialect used by African-Americans in the inner cities of most large urban areas and in the rural South when they are speaking casually. In short, it is the linguistic system used by working-class African-American people within their speech community. As such, BE shares many of the characteristics of Southern and working-class dialects. Obviously, not all African-Americans speak the dialect. Conversely, white speakers who live or work with speakers of BE may use some of its features. It is also important to remember that there are variations of BE that its speakers use for certain situations. As with other dialects, there is a formal–informal continuum.

BE is a systematic language rule system of its own, not a deviant or improper form of English. Its linguistic variations from SAE are not errors. The linguistic differences between BE and SAE are minimal. Most of the grammatical rules and underlying concepts are similar. Variations are the result of a different and equally complex rule system (R. Brown, 1973). Many aspects of BE are shared with other dialects. There is considerable overlap between BE and both Southern English and Southern white nonstandard English. Some aspects, however—such as the use of *be* in the habitual sense, as in "She *be* working there since 1985," and the triple negative, as in "Nobody don't got none"—are primarily characteristic of BE. Much of the sense of the dialect can also be found in its intonational patterns, speaking rate, and distinctive lexicon.

The major characteristics of BE are listed in Tables 12.1 and 12.2, and 12.3. It is unlikely that any given individual who speaks BE will exhibit all of these characteristics. The frequency of appearance of each feature will change with situational variations and over time. There is decreasing use of some features of BE in favor of more SAE as children advance through elementary school (Light, 1971).

We shall discuss some of the more outstanding differences between SAE and BE. The phonemic differences, especially the weakening of final consonants, relate to some of the more evident structural contrasts. Many morphological endings are omitted or not pronounced. Other words tend to sound similar because of omission, weakening, or substitution. The following are a few examples (Labov, 1972):

SAE	*BE*	*SAE*	*BE*	*SAE*	*BE*
guard	god	Carol	Cal	past	pass
sore	saw	fault	fought	boot	boo
court	caught	toll	toe	death	deaf
called	call	hits	hit	feed	feet

Sociolinguists have yet to determine if the *called–call* contrast reflects consonant cluster simplification or a syntactic rule relating to the fact that the regular past tense marker is nonobligatory, since past tense can be inferred from the context.

The speech of young African-American children does not reflect the phonological contrasts presented in Table 12.1 (Seymour & Seymour, 1981). Four- and 5-year-old African-American children have not mastered the adult BE phonological system. Their phonological rules reflect their developmental level. "Consonantal features that contrast between black English and standard English [are] undifferentiated from developmental errors typical of white children" (Seymour & Seymour, 1981, p. 279).

Many BE structural rules reflect a recognition of the redundant nature of many SAE constructions. For example, the possessive *'s* is unnecessary when the relationship is expressed by word order. Similar arguments can be made for certain cases of the plural *-s*, the third person *-s*, and verb tense markers. If a numerical quantifier such as *five* or *dozen* appears before a noun, the listener knows that the noun is plural and that the plural *-s* is thus redundant. Likewise, the use of *he*, *she*, or a singular noun subject marks the third person, negating the need for the third person *-s*. In addition, context often signals the verb tense. Similar arguments about redundancy have been advanced by linguists to explain

TABLE 12.1 Phonemic Contrasts between BE and SAE

SAE Phonemes	Position in Word		
	Initial	Medial	Final*
/p/		Unaspirated /p/	Unaspirated /p/
/n/			Reliance on preceding nasalized vowel
/w/	Omitted in specific words (*I'as, too!*)		
/b/		Unreleased /b/	Unreleased /b/
/g/		Unreleased /g/	Unreleased /g/
/k/		Unaspirated /k/	Unaspirated /k/
/d/	Omitted in specific words (*I'on't know*)	Unreleased /d/	Unreleased /d/
/ŋ/		/n/	/n/
/t/		Unaspirated /t/	Unaspirated /t/
/l/		Omitted before labial consonants (*help–hep*)	"uh" following a vowel (*Bill–Biuh*)
/r/		Omitted or /ə/	Omitted or prolonged vowel or glide
/θ/	Unaspirated /t/ or /f/	Unaspirated /t/ or /f/ between vowels	Unaspirated /t/ or /f/ (*bath–baf*)
/v/	Sometimes /b/	/b/ before /m/ and /n/	Sometimes /b/
/ð/	/d/	/d/ or /v/ between vowels	/d/, /v/, /f/
/z/		Omitted or replaced by /d/ before nasal sound (*wasn't–wud'n*)	

Blends

/str/ becomes /skr/

/ʃr/ becomes /str/

/θr/ becomes /θ/

/pr/ becomes /p/

/br/ becomes /b/

/kr/ becomes /k/

/gr/ becomes /g/

Final Consonant Clusters (second consonant omitted when these clusters occur at the end of a word)

/sk/	/nd/	/sp/
/ft/	/ld/	/dʒ d/
/st/	/sd/	/nt/

*Note weakening of final consonants.

Sources: Data drawn from Fasold and Wolfram (1970); Labov (1972); F. Weiner and Lewnau (1979); R. Williams and Wolfram (1977).

TABLE 12.2   Grammatical Constrasts between BE and SAE

BE Grammatical Structure	SAE Grammatical Structure
Possessive -'s	
Nonobligatory where word position expresses possession	Obligatory regardless of position
Get *mother* coat.	Get *mother's* coat.
It *be* mother's.	It's *mother's.*
Plural -s	
Nonobligatory with numerical quantifier	Obligatory regardless of numerical quantifier
He got ten *dollar.*	He has ten *dollars.*
Look at the *cats.*	Look at the *cats.*
Regular past -ed	
Nonobligatory, reduced as consonant cluster	Obligatory
Yesterday, I *walk* to school.	Yesterday, I walk*ed* to school.
Irregular past	
Case by case, some verbs inflected, others not	All irregular verbs inflected
I *see* him last week.	I *saw* him last week.
Regular present tense third person singular -s	
Nonobligatory	Obligatory
She *eat* too much.	She *eats* too much.
Irregular present tense third person singular -s	
Nonobligatory	Obligatory
He *do* my job.	He *does* my job.
Indefinite an	
Use of indefinite *a.*	Use of *an* before nouns beginning with a vowel
He ride in *a* airplane.	He rode in *an* airplane.
Pronouns	
Pronominal apposition: pronoun immediately follows noun	Pronoun used elsewhere in sentence or in other sentence; not in apposition
Momma *she* mad. She . . .	Momma *is* mad. She . . .
Future tense	
More frequent use of *be going to* (gonna)	More frequent use of *will*
I *be going to* dance tonight.	I *will* dance tonight.
I *gonna* dance tonight.	I *am going to* dance tonight.
Omit *will* preceding *be*	Obligatory use of *will*
I *be* home later.	I *will* (I'll) *be* home later.
Negation	
Triple negative	Absence of triple negative
Nobody don't never like me.	*No* one ever likes me.
Use of *ain't*	*Ain't* is unacceptable form
I *ain't* going.	I'm *not* going.

TABLE 12.2 *continued*

BE Grammatical Structure	SAE Grammatical Structure
Modals	
Double modals for such forms as *might, could,* and *should*	Single modal use
I *might could* go.	I *might be able to* go.
Questions	
Same form for direct and indirect	Different forms for direct and indirect
What *it is?*	What *is it?*
Do you know what *it is?*	Do you know what *it is?*
Relative pronouns	
Nonobligatory in most cases	Nonobligatory with *that* only
He the one stole it.	He's the one *who* stole it.
It the one you like.	It's the one (*that*) you like.
Conditional *if*	
Use of *do* for conditional *if*	Use of *if*
I ask *did* she go.	I asked *if* she went.
Perfect construction	
Been used for action in the distant past	*Been* not used
He *been* gone.	He left a long time ago.
Copula	
Nonobligatory when contractible	Obligatory in contractible and uncontractible forms
He sick.	He's sick.
Habitual or general state	
Marked with uninflected *be*	Nonuse of *be;* verb inflected
She *be* workin'.	She's *working* now.

Sources: Data drawn from Baratz (1969), Fasold and Wolfram, (1970), Williams and Wolfram (1977).

the development of some syntactic structures. Other BE forms introduce redundancy. These include double and triple negatives, pronominal apposition, and certain double modal forms.

The verb *to be* offers a special case. The verb may be nonobligatory in BE as a contractible copula or as a contractible auxiliary in the present progressive. Some linguists have used these omissions as evidence that the verb *to be* does not exist at a deep structural or conceptual level. On the other hand, the verb *to be* is used to mark the future, a habitual state, or the distant past (Labov, 1970b). The verb *to be* is also present in all uncontractible positions. Thus, it appears that the SAE rule for contractibility is similar to the BE rule for nonobligatory use. The rules of the verb *to be* represent not the presence or absence of a structure but dif-

TABLE 12.3   Pragmatic and nonlinguistic contrasts between BE and SAE

BE	SAE
Touching of one's hair by another person is often considered offensive.	Touching of one's hair by another person is a sign of affection.
Preference for indirect eye contact during listening, direct eye contact during speaking as signs of attentiveness and respect.	Preference for direct eye contact during listening and indirect eye contact during speaking as signs of attention and respect.
Public behavior may be emotionally intense, dynamic, and demonstrative.	Public behavior is expected to be modest and emotionally restrained. Emotional displays are seen as irresponsible or in bad taste.
Clear distinction between "argument" and "fight." Verbal abuse is not necessarily a precursor to violence.	Heated arguments are viewed as suggesting that violence is imminent.
Asking "personal questions" of someone one has met for the first time is seen as improper and intrusive.	Inquiring about jobs, family, and so forth of someone one has met for the first time is seen as friendly.
Use of direct questions is sometimes seen as harassment, e.g., asking when something will be finished is seen as rushing that person to finish.	Use of direct questions for personal information is permissible.
Interruption during conversation is usually tolerated. Access to the floor is granted to the person who is most assertive.	Rules of turn-taking in conversation dictate that one person has the floor at a time until all his points are made.
Conversations are regarded as private between the recognized participants. "Butting in" is seen as eavesdropping and is not tolerated.	Adding points of information or insights to a conversation in which one is not engaged is seen as being helpful.
Use of expression "you people" is seen as pejorative and racist.	Use of expression "you people" tolerated.
Accusations or allegations are general rather than categorical, and are not intended to be all-inclusive. Refutation is the responsibility of the accused.	Stereotypical accusations or allegations are all-inclusive. Refutation or making exception is the responsibility of the person making the accusation.
Silence denotes refutation of accusation. To state that you feel accused is regarded as an admission of guilt.	Silence denotes acceptance of an accusation. Guilt is verbally denied.

Source: Taylor, O. (in press). Clinical practice as a social occasion. In L. Cole & V. Deal (Eds.), *Communication disorders in multicultural populations.* Rockville, MD: American Speech-Language-Hearing Association. Reprinted with permission.

ferences in use. Question inversion rules offer a similar example when compared to indirect questions and to the use of the conditional *if*.

In addition to the phonological and structural differences between SAE and BE, there are also vocabulary differences. In any dialect, words may take on broadened definitions or, conversely, either more restricted meanings or new definitions. BE words and phrases often influence and change SAE. Many slang expressions used in SAE originated in BE. These include *rock 'n' roll, cool, rap, and jivin'*. Other terms, such as *chitlins* or *cracker*, a derisive term for whites, are used almost exclusively in BE.

Language use also differs. There is a strong oral tradition in some black communities, and superior verbal skills are highly regarded (Burling, 1973; Labov, Cohen, Robins, & Lewis, 1968). In inner-city groups, youths with good verbal skills are usually in high positions within the group power structure. Long, spontaneous lyric poems, called *raps*, now popularized in modern music, are used to boast or to put down, or humiliate, an opponent.

Other nonlinguistic differences may be found between some speakers of BE and other dialects (Taylor, in press). For example, touching someone's hair may be considered an offense to some BE speakers but a sign of affection by users of dialects closer to SAE. Similarly, indirect eye contact, the use of personal questions, and interrupting are acceptable conversational conduct in some African-American communities but would be considered rude in those closer to SAE. Conversational silence may signal opposite messages, refutation for BE speakers and acceptance or agreement for SAE. Finally, emotional or demonstrative, even abusive, outbursts may be tolerated in BE but not in SAE.

BE and the Wider Society

For an individual child, the main effects of using BE are social and educational. To the extent that BE is stigmatized within our multidialectal society, the child may also be stigmatized. Unfortunately, many people attach relative values to certain dialects and to the speakers of those dialects. Individuals tend to respond to dialects in terms of stereotypes (Naremore, 1971; F. Williams, Hewitt, Miller, Naremore, & Whitehead, 1976). This generalized or stereotypic response may, in turn, affect other judgments. Employment and educational opportunities may be denied because of dialectal differences. In general, BE speakers are granted shorter employment interviews, offered fewer positions, and offered lower-paying positions (Terrell & Terrell, 1983) than speakers of more standard English dialects. Apparently, this discrimination does not significantly affect the self-concept of BE speakers. Research has indicated that black children who speak BE seem to have a higher self-concept than those who do not (Lefley, 1975).

It has been found that some educators exhibit a bias in favor of SAE or a regional dialect. Teachers may use any of the following reasons for assuming that minority students are inferior to white children speaking dialects closer to SAE (Labov, 1970b):

1. Minority students demonstrate a lack of verbal capacity in formal or threatening situations.

2. Poor school performance is a result of this verbal deficit.
3. Middle-class speech habits are necessary for learning, as evidenced by the better school achievement of middle-class children.
4. Dialectal differences reflect differences in the capacity for logical analysis.
5. Logical thinking can be fostered by teaching children to mimic the formal speech patterns of their teachers.
6. Children who adopt these formal patterns think logically and thus do better in reading and arithmetic.

Unfortunately, scores on norm-referenced tests, usually based on standard language skill usage, can be, and often are, used to bolster this position (Labov, 1970b).

Throughout this book we have concentrated on the "generic" child, most typically white and middle class. Some studies have shown, however, that lower-class African-American children do not acquire language within a similar social context. Urban African-American children may pass through three stages of language acquisition. First, they learn the basics of language at home; then, from ages 5 to 15, they learn a local vernacular dialect from their peers; and finally, they develop the more standard BE dialect (Labov, 1971). Ward (1971) has reported that Southern, rural, lower-class African-American children are not encouraged to communicate conversationally or to ask questions. In a southeastern Appalachian working-class town, dubbed "Trackton," Brice Heath (1983) reported that children are not addressed directly, nor are they expected to provide information. Children are exposed to a wide variety of language, however, through extended families and neighbors who tease and verbally challenge toddlers. The children often begin to speak by imitating the ending phrases of these speakers. Children who try to interrupt adult conversation may be scolded for their speech inaccuracies or for their use of baby talk. Within other regions, language stimulation may appear in other forms, such as rhymes, songs, or stories. In general, the mothers of these children do not feel obligated to teach language. The "children's linguistic development differs mostly in the demands for communication that are placed upon them" (F. Williams & Naremore, 1969, p. 100). Therefore, children differ in their expectations of appropriate communication behavior.

If children are discouraged from talking with adults, it seems logical that they would respond poorly in the adult-centered question-answer format of the classroom. In this situation, lower-class children tend to give only minimal responses (F. Williams & Naremore, 1969). Teachers may assume that these minimal responses reflect a lack of knowledge or of understanding. Yet the classroom give-and-take may be a situation in which the child feels "at risk" (Labov, 1970a). She may be afraid that she will be punished for her responses.

Classroom teachers, faced with dialectal differences and an unresponsive child, may assume that the differences signify inferior abilities. Language-based testing encourages such thinking. Teachers may assume that students who speak BE do not understand SAE. But this does not appear to be the case. African-American children's comprehension seems to be as good for SAE as for BE (Frentz, 1971). In fact, African-American students perform better at sentence completion when cued in SAE (Copple & Suci, 1974). Finally, there is no difference between African-American lower-class and white middle-class children in imitation of SAE sentences (Anastasiow & Hanes, 1976). Apparently, the ability of African-American children to comprehend BE and SAE continues into adulthood. African-American adults find child speakers of both dialects equally intelligible, whereas adult SAE speakers find child SAE speakers significantly more intelligible than BE speakers (Nober & Seymour, 1979).

Speakers of BE may have difficulty with reading and spelling. In general, children read orally in accordance with their dialects. The resultant differences are not errors in word recognition (Burke, Pflaum, & Knafle, 1982). Phonemic differences may make it difficult, however, for the teacher to interpret the child's oral reading. Surface phonemic differences may also account for the child's spelling errors (O'Neal & Trabasso, 1976). In addition, BE speakers may not recognize the significance of the grammatical markers that they omit. This suggests that the BE-speaking child may not hear a difference or may not understand its significance. It is easy to see how this difficulty could be transferred to other academic areas.

Hispanic English

Within the United States, the largest ethnic population is Hispanic. Not all people with Spanish surnames speak Spanish; some do exclusively, and still others are **bilingual**, speaking both Spanish and English. The form of English spoken depends on the amount and type of Spanish spoken. The two largest Hispanic groups in the United States are of Puerto Rican–Caribbean and Mexican–Central American origin. Although both groups speak Spanish, their Spanish dialectal differences influence their comprehension and production of American English. The dialect of American English spoken in the surrounding community also has an effect. As a result, the interference points may be very different for individual speakers. We will discuss the general characteristics of these speakers and refer to their dialect as *Hispanic English (HE)*. Tables 12.4, 12.5, and 12.6 (p. 446) summarize the major differences found between HE and SAE.

As expected, there are phonological differences between Spanish and English. Some English speech sounds, such as /θ/, /ð/, /z/, /ʒ/, /ʃ/, /ʌ/, /æ/, and /ʌ/, do not exist in Spanish. As a result, these sounds are frequently distorted or replaced with other sounds by speakers of HE. In addition, all final plosives are voiceless in Spanish, and initial voiceless plosives are not aspirated.[†] In HE, sounds may be altered from their English articulation. Finally, Spanish does not distinguish between /b/ and /v/, and the Spanish /r/ and /l/ are produced differently from their English equivalents. As expected, speakers of HE use /b/ and /v/ interchangeably, while they use Spanish /r/ and /l/ in place of their English equivalents.

Spanish vowels are a special consideration. There are five vowels and four diphthongs in Spanish. In contrast, English has many more. In addition, Spanish vowels have the same quality or length, whether in a stressed or an unstressed

---

[†]Aspiration results when a small puff of air is released with the sound.

TABLE 12.4   Phonemic Contrasts between HE and SAE

SAE Phonemes	Position in Word		
	Initial	Medial	Final*
/p/	Unaspirated /p/		Omitted or weakened
/m/			Omitted
/w/	/hu/		Omitted
/b/			Omitted, distorted, or /p/
/g/			Omitted, distorted, or /k/
/k/	Unaspirated or /g/		Omitted, distorted, or /g/
/f/			Omitted
/d/		Dentalized	Omitted, distorted, or /t/
/ŋ/	/n/	/d/	/n/ (*sing–sin*)
/j/	/dʒ/		
/t/			Omitted
/ʃ/	/tʃ/	/s/, /tʃ/	/tʃ/ (*wish–which*)
/tʃ/	/ʃ/ (*chair–share*)	/ʃ/	/ʃ/ (*watch–wash*)
/r/	Distorted	Distorted	Distorted
/dʒ/	/d/	/j/	/ʃ/
/θ/	/t/, /s/ (*thin–tin, sin*)	Omitted	/ʃ/, /t/, /s/
/v/	/b/ (*vat–bat*)	/b/	Distorted
/z/	/s/ (*zip–sip*)	/s/ (*razor–racer*)	/s/
/ð/	/d/ (*then–den*)	/d/, /θ/, /v/ (*lather–ladder*)	/d/

Blends

/skw/ becomes /eskw/*

/sl/ becomes /esl/*

/st/ becomes /est/*

Vowels

/I/ becomes /i/ (*bit–beet*)

*Separates cluster into two syllables.

Sources: Data drawn from Sawyer (1973); F. Weiner and Lewnau (1979); F. Williams, Cairns, and Cairns (1971).

syllable. English vowels vary with stressing. As a result, English vowels can present a special problem in perception and production.

Structural contrasts between HE and SAE also reflect interference points between Spanish and English. Many redundant SAE markers are nonobligatory, as they are in BE. Other markers, such as the postnoun possessive, reflect Span-

TABLE 12.5   Grammatical Contrasts between HE and SAE

HE Grammatical Structure	SAE Grammatical Structure
Possessive -'s	
Use postnoun modifier	Postnoun modifier used rarely
This is the homework of *my brother.*	This is my brother's homework.
Article used with body parts	Possessive pronoun used with body parts
I cut *the finger.*	I cut *my* finger.
Plural -s	
Nonobligatory	Obligatory, excluding exceptions
The *girl* are playing.	The *girls* are playing.
The *sheep* are playing.	The *sheep* are playing.
Regular past -ed	
Nonobligatory, especially when understood	Obligatory
I *talk* to her yesterday.	I *talked* to her yesterday.
Regular third person singular present tense -s	
Nonobligatory	Obligatory
She *eat* too much.	She *eats* too much.
Articles	
Often omitted	Usually obligatory
I am going to store.	I am going to *the* store.
I am going to school.	I am going to school.
Subject pronouns	
Omitted when subject has been identified in the previous sentence	Obligatory
Father is happy. Bought a new car.	Father is happy. *He* bought a new car.

ish constructions. A similar example can be found in the placement of adjectives following the noun in Spanish and in HE. In addition, the speaker of HE may scatter her speech with many vocabulary words of Spanish origin.

Nonlinguistic differences also persist between HE and SAE (Taylor, in press). In general, a closer or smaller relative distance is tolerated among many HE speakers, as is a greater incidence of touching between conversational partners. Other differences, such as avoidance of direct eye contact, may signal attentiveness and respect for HE speakers while signaling the opposite for speakers of more standard American English dialects.

Asian English

Although we shall use the term *Asian English* (AE), it is clearly a misnomer because no such entity exists. It is merely a term that enables us to discuss the various dialects of Asian-Americans as a group.

The most widely used languages in Asia are Chinese, Filipino, Japanese, Khmer, Korean, Laotian, and Vietnamese. Of these, Chinese has had the most

TABLE 12.5   Continued

HE Grammatical Structure	SAE Grammatical Structure

Future tense
Use *go + to*
  I *go to* dance.
	Use *be + going to*
	  I *am going to* the dance.

Negation
Use *no* before the verb
 	
  She *no* eat candy.
	Use *not* (preceded by auxiliary verb where appropriate)
	  She does *not* eat candy.

Question
Intonation; no noun–verb inversion
  Maria is going?
	Noun–verb inversion usually
	  Is Maria going?

Copula
Occasional use of *have*
  I *have* ten years.
	Use of *be*
	  I *am* ten years old.

Negative imperatives *No* used for *don't* *No* throw stones.	*Don't* used *Don't* throw stones.

***Do* insertion**
Nonobligatory in questions
  You like ice cream?
	Obligatory when no auxiliary verb
	  Do you like ice cream?

Comparatives
More frequent use of longer form (*more*)
  He is *more* tall.
	More frequent use of shorter *-er*
	  He is tall*er*.

Sources: Data drawn from Davis (1972), Taylor (1986).

pervasive influence upon the evolution of the others. Other cultures, such as Indian and colonial European, have also influenced these languages. Each language has various dialects and features that distinguish one from the other. Thus, there is, in reality, no Asian English as a cohesive unit.

Nonetheless, the English of Asian language speakers has certain characteristics in common. These are listed in Tables 12.7 (p. 447) and 12.8 (p. 448). The omission of final consonants, for example, is prevalent in AE. In contrast to English, most Asian languages have open or vowel-final syllables.

BILINGUALISM

We cannot really discuss HE or AE without addressing the issue of bilingualism. Spanish, the various Asian languages, and English are separate languages with their own lexicons and rule systems, and children from other than English-speaking families are encouraged to become speakers of English in the public schools. HE and AE reflect the effects of Spanish and the various Asian languages

TABLE 12.6   Pragmatic and nonlinguistic contrasts between HE and SAE

HE	SAE
Hissing to gain attention is acceptable.	Hissing is considered impolite and indicates contempt.
Touching is often observed between two people in conversation.	Touching is usually unacceptable and usually carries sexual overtone.
Avoidance of direct eye contact is sometimes a sign of attentiveness and respect; sustained direct eye contact may be interpreted as a challenge to authority.	Direct eye contact is a sign of attentiveness and respect.
Relative distance between two speakers in conversation is close.	Relative distance between two speakers in conversation is farther apart.
Official or business conversations are preceded by lengthy greetings, pleasantries, and other talk unrelated to the point of business.	Getting to the point quickly is valued.

Source: Taylor, O. (in press). Clinical practice as a social occasion. In L. Cole & V. Deal (Eds.), *Communication disorders in multicultural populations.* Rockville, MD: American Speech-Language-Hearing Association. Reprinted with permission.

upon English. Neither HE nor Spanish is spoken by all Hispanic Americans. Similarly, not all Asian-Americans speak some variety of AE or an Asian language. Those individuals who speak both Spanish and English are said to be *bilingual.*

There is a subtle prejudice against other languages in the general American culture. Again, the users of dialects closer to the standard tend to respond to these languages or to AE or HE stereotypically. Unfortunately, this prejudice can even be seen in the speech of bilingual adults. For example, when speaking with an Anglo, Hispanic adults tend to Americanize Spanish words, but they do not do so with a Hispanic audience (Sawyer, 1973).

The non-English-speaking or bilingual child faces some danger in the schools, including educational placement. In at least one case of which I know, a non-English-speaking child has been classified as mentally retarded based on an English receptive vocabulary test. It can only be hoped that this case is a rarity.

The prevalence of bilingualism reflects the cultural mixing within a nation. In an isolated country, such as Iceland, the rather homogeneous nature of the culture is reflected in the scarcity of bilingualism. In the United States, approximately 17% of the population is bilingual, mostly Spanish and English (Kloss & McConnell, 1978). Canada, which fosters more cultural diversity than its neighbor to the south and has two official languages, has a bilingual population of 24% (deVries & Vallee, 1980). Other countries may have large bilingual populations because of a large, influential neighbor with a different language or because the official language differs from the indigenous one.

TABLE 12.7   Phonemic Contrasts between AE and SAE

SAE Phonemes	Position in Word		
	Initial	Medial	Final
/p/	/b/[§]	/b/[§]	Omission
/s/	Distortion*	Distortion*	Omission
/z/	/s/[†]	/s/[†]	Omission
/t/	Distortion*	Distortion*	Omission
/tʃ /	/ʃ /[§]	/ʃ /[§]	Omission
/ʃ /	/s/[†]	/s/[†]	Omission
/r/, /l/	Confusion[‡]	Confusion[‡]	Omission
/θ/	/s/	/s/	Omission
/dz/	/d/ or /z/[§]	/d/ or /z/[§]	Omission
/v/	/f/[‡]	/f/[‡]	Omission
	/w/[†]	/w/[†]	Omission
/ð/	/z/*	/z/*	Omission
	/d/[§]	/d/[§]	Omission

Blends

Addition of /ə/ between consonants[‡]

Omission of final consonant clusters[§]

Vowels

Shortening or lengthening of vowels (*seat–sit, it–eat**)

Difficulty with /ɪ/, /ɔ/, and /æ/, and substitution of /e/ for /æ/[†]

Difficulty with /ɪ/, /æ/, /U/, and /ə/[§]

*Mandarin dialect of Chinese only.
†Cantonese dialect of Chinese only.
‡Mandarin, Cantonese, and Japanese.
§Vietnamese only.
Source: Adapted from Cheng, L. (June, 1987). Cross-cultural and linguistic considerations in working with Asian populations. *Asha, 29*(6), 33–38.

Effects of Bilingualism on Language Learning

It has long been assumed that bilingual children are at a disadvantage when learning language and that their progress in one or both languages is delayed. This premise has not been wholly borne out in the recent research. The effects of bilingualism differ with the age of the individual and the manner of language acquisition. It is important to make a distinction between simultaneous and sequential acquisition.

TABLE 12.8   Grammatical Contrasts between AE and SAE

AE Grammatical Structure	SAE Grammatical Structure
Plural -s	
Not used with numerical adjective: *three* cat	Used regardless of numerical adjective: *three cats*
Used with irregular plural: *three sheeps*	Not used with irregular plural: *three sheep*
Auxiliaries to be and to do	
Omission: *I going home. She not want eat.*	Obligatory and inflected in the present progressive form: *I am going home. She does not want to eat.*
Uninflected: *I is going. She do not want eat.*	
Verb have	
Omission	Obligatory and inflected: *You have been here. He has one.*
You been here.	
Uninflected	
He have one.	
Past tense -ed	
Omission: *He talk yesterday.*	Obligatory, nonovergeneralization, and single marking: *He talked yesterday. I ate yesterday. She didn't eat.*
Overgeneralization: *I eated yesterday.*	
Double marking: *She didn't ate.*	
Interrogative	
Nonreversal: *You are late?*	Reversal and obligatory auxiliary: *Are you late? Do you like ice cream?*
Omitted auxiliary: *You like ice cream?*	
Perfect marker	
Omission: *I have write letter.*	Obligatory: *I have written a letter.*
Verb–noun agreement	
Nonagreement: *He go to school. You goes to school.*	Agreement: *He goes to school. You go to school.*

Simultaneous Acquisition

Simultaneous acquisition is the development of two languages prior to age 3 (McLaughlin, 1978). Simultaneous bilingual acquisition can be characterized as follows (Grosjean, 1982):

1. Initial language mixing, followed by a slow separation and increasing awareness of the differences.
2. Influence of one on the other when one is favored by the environment.
3. Avoidance of difficult words and constructions in the weaker language.
4. Rapid shifts in the dominance of either language with environmental shifts.
5. Final separation of the phonological and grammatical systems but enduring influence of the dominant system in vocabulary and idioms.

TABLE 12.8   Continued

AE Grammatical Structure	SAE Grammatical Structure
Article Omission: *Please give gift.* Overgeneralization: *She go the school.*	Obligatory with certain nouns: *Please give the gift. She went to school.*
Preposition Misuse: *I am in home.* Omission: *He go bus.*	Obligatory specific use: *I am at home. He goes by bus.*
Pronoun Subjective/objective confusion: *Him go quickly.* Possessive confusion: *It him book.*	Subjective/objective distinction *He gave it to her.* Possessive distinction: *It's his book.*
Demonstrative Confusion: *I like those horse.*	Singular/plural distinction: *I like that horse.*
Conjunction Omission: *You I go together.*	Obligatory use between last two items in a series: *You and I are going together. Mary, John, and Carol went.*
Negation Double marking: *I didn't see nobody.* Simplified form: *He no come.*	Single obligatory marking: *I didn't see anybody. He didn't come.*
Word order Adjective following noun (Vietnamese): *clothes new.* Possessive following noun (Vietnamese): *dress her.* Omission of object with transitive verb: *I want.*	Most noun modifiers precede noun: *new clothes.* Possessive precedes noun: *her dress.* Use of direct object with most transitive verbs: *I want it.*

Source: Adapted from Cheng, L. (June, 1987). Cross-cultural and linguistic considerations in working with Asian populations. *Asha, 29*(6), 33–38.

The rate and manner of development appear to be the same whether the child is monolingual or bilingual (Doyle, Champagne, & Segalowitz, 1978; Padilla & Lindholm, 1976). "In all essential respects early simultaneous bilingualism does not differ from the acquisition of a single language" (Dulay, Hernández-Chávez, & Burt, 1978, p. 277). In spite of the bilingual linguistic load, the child acquires both languages at a rate comparable to that of monolingual children (Padilla & Liebman, 1975). The degree of dissimilarity between the two languages does not appear to affect the rate of acquisition. The key to development is the consistent use of the two languages within their primary use environments.

There seem to be three stages in the simultaneous acquisition of two languages in young children (Volterra & Taeschner, 1978). During the first stage, the child has two separate lexical systems (Padilla & Liebman, 1975; Swain, 1972;

Vihman, 1985). Vocabulary words rarely overlap (Prinz & Prinz, 1979). The child learns one word from either language for each referent. When there is an overlap, the child does not treat the words as equals. Some words are treated as corresponding, though they are not considered so by adults. This is similar to the early meaning differences found between adult words and words of the monolingual child. Initially words from both languages are combined indiscriminately (Vihman, 1985).

It has been argued that in the initial stage of simultaneous bilingual development, children actually have two different language systems that they are able to use in different contexts or in functionally different ways (Genesee, 1989). Thus, the child may use one system with adults of one language and one with adults of the other. Rather than signifying a mixing of the two languages, such things as the use of words from both languages may be an example of overextension. The child uses whatever vocabulary she has available. Mixing of grammatical elements may reflect lack of development of structures in one of the languages, possibly because these structures are too difficult at present.

Mixing may also reflect mixed input. Children who hear "Spanglish" (Spanish + English) in the southwestern United States or "Franglais" (Français or French + Anglais or English) in parts of Quebec province can be expected to have more mixing in their own language (Redlinger & Park, 1980).

Phonological differentiation is also occurring (Albert & Obler, 1978). The earliest phonology is usually a combination of the two different inputs into a single system, although the least interference seems to occur in this aspect of language. Differentiation of the phonological systems begins at around 24 to 30 months (Burling, 1959; Dulay et al., 1978; Major, 1976; Vogel, 1975). "By age 2, children have acquired a conception of their native phonology that specifies certain contrasts as relevant and others . . . as irrelevant to the language's meaning system" (Oller & Eilers, 1983, p. 53). Thus, in tasks involving identification of meaning, the child may ignore contrasts that do not pertain.

In the second stage, the child has two distinct lexicons but applies the same syntactic rules to both. This lexical generalization process is difficult and occurs slowly. The child must separate a word from its specific context and identify it with the corresponding word in the other language. Each word tends to remain tied to the particular context in which it was learned, and corresponding words are not usually learned simultaneously. The child is able to move between the two lexicons and to translate words freely. Unfortunately, this flexibility is not found at the syntactic level. The nonparallel sequence of syntactic learning reflects the difference in linguistic difficulty of particular syntactic structures within the two languages (Slobin, 1973). In general, the child learns structures common to both languages first, the simpler constructions before the more complex. Thus, if a construction is more complex in one language, it will be learned first in the other language in its simpler form.

Finally, in the third stage, the child correctly produces lexical and syntactic structures from each language. Although there is still a great deal of interference, it is mostly confined to the syntactic level. As few as 2% of bilingual preschoolers' utterances may contain some mixing (Lindholm & Padilla, 1978). In general, mixes are used when the child lacks an appropriate word in one language or when the mixed entry is a more salient word to the child. Mixing by the child seems to result from a mixed adult input. For Spanish-speaking children in the United States, mixing consists primarily of inserting English nouns into Spanish utterances. The structural consistency of the utterance is maintained.

To decrease interference, the child may try to keep the two languages as separate as possible, associating each with a particular person (Redlinger & Park, 1980). "The act of labelling a person with one of the two languages makes the choice of the words and rules a kind of automatic process" (Volterra & Taeschner, 1978, p. 324). As the child becomes more familiar with the syntactic differences, the tendency to label people with a certain language decreases. The child becomes truly bilingual and can manage two separate languages at about age 7 (Albert & Obler, 1978).

The truly bilingual person possesses a dual processing system. For example, "the bilingual has a knowledge of two sets of phonotactic constraints and . . . both . . . are simultaneously available . . . during processing" (Altenberg & Cairns, 1983, p. 174). In addition, semantic input may be processed in each language regardless of the language of input (Preston & Lambert, 1969). Most information is processed at the semantic level because the interpretation of surface syntax requires much greater proficiency (Heras & Nelson, 1972; Macnamara, 1970).

Successive Acquisition

Most bilingual children develop one language, such as Spanish, at home and a second, such as American English, with peers or in school, usually after age 3. The learning of a second language, such as French or Spanish, as an academic subject in high school is beyond the scope of this chapter. Suffice it to say that by the late teens it is difficult for a speaker to acquire native speaker pronunciation characteristics in a second language (Oyama, 1976, 1978; Snow & Hoefnagel-Hohle, 1978).

"There exists a long-standing myth that the earlier a language is acquired, the more fluent a person will be in it" (Grosjean, 1982, p. 192). Except for the late-teenage disclaimer made above, the notion of the importance of age of acquisition is not supported in actual practice (Genesee, 1978; Krashen, 1973; Seliger, 1978). Success in nonsimultaneous language acquisition is more closely related to the learner's attitude toward, and identity with, the users of the language being acquired. Need is another strong motivating factor. Most children acquire a second language rapidly, though the strategies used differ with age, the child's linguistic knowledge, and the nature of the two languages.

Successive acquisition of a second language may occur in three stages (L. Fillmore, 1976). In the first stage, the child establishes social relations with speakers of the second language. The interaction is more important than information exchange, and the child relies on "fixed verbal formulas." These fixed formulas are learned as single units, such as *lookit, okay, ya know,* and *wait a minute.* During this stage, the child assumes that what is being said is relevant to the situation or to what the speaker is experiencing. The child scans the formulas for recurring linguistic patterns. Her social strategy is to join the group and act as if she knows what is being communicated. She tries to use the few phrases and words that she knows to give the impression that she can speak the second language.

In the first phase of nonsimultaneous language development, speakers seem to adopt one of two strategies: other-directed or inner-directed. Those choosing the other-directed strategy approach the language-learning task as an interpersonal one. The goal is to get the message across in any way possible. In contrast, those who choose an inner-directed strategy approach the task as an intrapersonal one. Focus is less on communication and more on breaking the language code. Inner-directed individuals may appear to be rather quiet and withdrawn. Actually, they are engaging in "private" speech in which they repeat the utterances of others, recall and practice phrases, create new utterances, modify and expand existing utterances, and rehearse for future social performance (Saville-Troike, 1988).

In the second stage, communication becomes the goal. The child's strategies include using to the utmost the linguistic units she understands and working on overall communication while saving the details for later. She begins talking with whatever units she can produce and comprehend.

Finally, in the third stage, the child concentrates on correct language forms. She is more mature than the typical simultaneous bilingual learner, and she can apply her general knowledge of language to an analysis of this particular language (Keller-Cohen, 1980). From her previous learning, the child recognizes that language is organized sequentially and that order is important. In addition, she recognizes that, though language units may have multiple meanings or functions, meaning is often related to the immediate context. The child scans the speech of others, paying attention to order and sequences. In her production, she attempts not to interrupt or rearrange these sequences and to present her message as simply as possible.

Since the child already has one linguistic system, she has an acoustic-perceptual system, an articulatory repertoire, and a cognitive-semantic base from which to begin acquiring a second language. Therefore her errors, though similar, are more limited than in her first language acquisition (Dulay et al., 1978). Errors cannot be predicted based on the linguistic form of the two languages (Gillis & Weber, 1976; Hernández-Chávez, 1972, 1977b; Ravem, 1974). The effects of either language upon the other vary with each child, and interference appears to be minimal. Children do not use their knowledge of the first language to formulate utterances in the second. "Rather, they seem to treat the new language as an independent system, which they gradually reconstruct from the L[anguage]2 speech data they hear" (Dulay et al., 1978, p. 266). Usually the first language continues to develop to adult norms, while the second achieves somewhat lower "bilingual norms" (Haugen, 1956). This isn't always the case, however, and the first language may be forgotten unless it is maintained at home. In actual practice, use determines which language will become dominant.

In general, second-language learning by young children mirrors first-language learning (Dulay et al., 1978). At first, the child begins with single words or common short phrases, and then moves to short sentences and morphological markers. Semantic relations are expressed first by order and then with morphological markers (Hernández-Chávez, 1977a, 1977b). Sentence alterations, such as negation and interrogation, follow acquisition patterns similar to those found in first-language learning (Dulay & Burt, 1974; Hernández-Chávez, 1972). The errors made by the child learning English as a second language are also similar to those made by English first-language learners. Common errors noted in HE (Table 12.4) include omission and overextension of morphological inflections (Venable, 1974), double marking, misordering of sentence constituents, and the use of archiforms and free alternation (Dulay et al., 1978). An **archiform** is one member of a word class used exclusively, such as *that* for all demonstratives. As more members of a class are acquired, perhaps *this*, *these*, and *those*, the child may vary her usage among the members without concern for the different meanings; this is called **free alternation.**

Phonological development also follows a similar pattern in first and second languages. The phonological system from the first language forms a foundation for the second. Gradually the two phonological systems become differentiated.

Code Switching and Development

Bilingual speakers often exhibit code switching, especially when both languages are used in the environment, as in the Southwestern United States, in Quebec, or in sections of many major U.S. cities. The behavior is not random, nor does it reflect an underlying language deficit. Rather, code switching is the result of functional and grammatical principles (McClure, 1981). Code switching is confined almost exclusively to free morphemes, most frequently nouns, and tends to occur where the surface structures are similar (Poplack, 1981). Children begin by code-switching single words from one language to another. In contrast, adults tend to substitute whole sentences (Huerta-Macias, 1981). Certain words and phrases tend to be switched predictably across different conversations by the same speaker.

Rather than representing the integration of both grammars into a third, new grammar, code-switching rules demonstrate the continuing separation of the two languages (Lederberg & Morales, 1985). Two of these rules are as follows:

1. Code switching occurs only when code-switched words are positioned in accordance with the rules for the language from which the word is selected.
2. Code switching cannot occur within word boundaries.

Whereas the first rule is observed by bilinguals of all ages, the second is frequently violated by children under 10.

For children, systematic code switching appears to be a function of the participants in a conversation (McClure, 1981). Three characteristics of the participants are important: their perceived language proficiency, their language preference, and their social identity. In general, children below age 5 combine proficiency and preference decisions. A listener either knows a language or she does not. Older children make finer distinctions and may therefore consider their speaker more often. Their behavior reflects the developing presuppositional skills seen in school-age children. Children also identify certain people with certain languages. If unsure, they try to use physical characteristics as a guide. For example, in the Southwestern United States, Anglo teachers may be addressed in English even though they are proficient in Spanish (McClure, 1981).

Other functional variables also influence code switching (McClure, 1981). Although physical setting alone has little influence, the type of discourse is a factor. Interviews and narratives contain few switches, instead remaining in one language or the other. Conversations, in contrast, are characterized by frequent switches. In addition, code switching can be a stylistic device used for direct quotes, emphasis, clarification or repetition, elaboration, focus on a particular portion of a message, attention getting and maintenance, and personal interjections or asides. Topics alone do not usually influence switching, though within the bilingual home the language of a specific group may be used when discussing that group. In the Southwestern United States, for example, Spanish-speaking families may use English when discussing the Anglos (Huerta-Macias, 1981).

The exact developmental function of code switching is unknown. It has been suggested that "code switching may be one approach to the acquisition of bilingualism [and] . . . a very viable means of maintaining a language" (Huerta-Macias, 1981, p. 168). Thus, the function may be twofold. First, it may be an aid for retention of the first language while a second is learned. Once the two languages are learned, code switching may ensure that both are used.

Bilingualism and Brain Organization

Second-language learning may involve right hemisphere mechanisms not involved in single-language learning. "Bilinguals demonstrate not only the left hemispheric role in language but also a major right hemispheric contribution" (Albert & Obler, 1978, p. 243). Further, if a second language is learned before puberty, there is symmetrical representation within the two hemispheres. Later language learning results in more complex, less symmetrical lateralization. In short, learning a second language may result in modified brain organization. The resultant pattern depends on a number of factors, including the age at second-language acquisition, the manner of learning, the patterns of usage, and the similarity of characteristics of the languages. "There is no special reason to assume . . . that the second language sits in the brain of a bilingual in exactly the same manner as does the first and only language in the brain of a monolingual" (Albert & Obler, 1978, p. 12).

Not all researchers agree with the lateralization model. In contrast to what was stated above, there may be more right hemisphere involvement the later the second language is acquired relative to the first and the more informal the exposure to the second (Vaid, 1983), especially if the second language was learned after age 6 (Sussman, Franklin, & Simon, 1982). In addition, the right hemisphere is more likely to be involved if the languages differ greatly. The more advanced the second language, however, the greater the left hemispheric involvement. Obviously, the resultant hemispheric pattern will reflect an interaction of these variables. Overall, the reported differences between monolinguals and bilinguals may reflect different processing strategies rather than distinctive organizational and functional differences (Vaid, 1983).

Cultural Diversity

It is easy for many middle-class, English-speaking, white Americans to assume that the manner in which they function is the only way or the right way. Just as there are dialectal differences within American English, there are child-nurturing and language-teaching differences as well. Not all cultures within the United States place the same emphasis on verbal communication. Among some Latinos, silence is associated with aloofness and self-restraint, certainly admirable qualities. Children are expected to be silent and thoughtful, to listen, and to hesitate before speaking (Coles, 1977; Murillo, 1976). Apache Indians value silence. Individuals developing within these cultures will have different communication standards.

Neither the model of mother-as-communication-partner nor the use of motherese is universal. For example, among Mexican-Americans, mothers may act as a language assistant or coach, helping the child imitate, and thus maintain an interaction with, a third party (A. Eisenberg, 1982). By the later preschool years, the child is very adept in conversations involving multiple participants and is able to perform before an audience. Inner-city Puerto Rican and African-American children, on the other hand, are generally raised in an environment in which much of the socialization is accomplished through peers (Iglesias, 1986).

The prospective teacher or speech-language pathologist should be aware that her expectations and the communication abilities of minority children may differ. For example, middle-class children come to school with the basics of the literary strategy. Their narratives are topic oriented and sequentially organized. Children from Hispanic and some Native American cultures may be more visually oriented. Stories may be descriptive rather than narrative or may deviate from the middle-class story pattern (Iglesias, 1986). In general, the stories the child encounters in reading texts and those she is expected to write follow the literary pattern of the narrative.

In each of the cases discussed, the minority culture or individual is not wrong, just different. Even if the methods of middle-class American mothers and their children had been proven to be the most efficient way to learn language — which they haven't — these methods would not necessarily be so in cultures in which other conditions exist.

CONCLUSION

Dialectal differences and bilingualism can pose special problems for the language-learning child, especially when the child enters school. Yet children who speak with a dialect of American English seem to understand SAE. These young children, if motivated, follow a developmental sequence and learn a second language or dialect relatively easily. They already have a language rule system that enables them to understand other dialects and learn other languages. Although different from SAE, other dialectal systems are not deviant. The U.S. district court for eastern Michigan, in a ruling known as the *Ann Arbor decision* (1979), has ruled that BE is a rule-governed linguistic system. Furthermore, educators must develop methods for teaching SAE to dialectal speakers.

Bilingual children appear to learn both languages with a minimum of delay. The key to development seems to be the pattern of use within the language community. Even young monolingual children can learn a second language easily. This second-language development seems to mirror the sequence found in the initial language.

REFLECTIONS

1. How do dialects relate to each other and to the parent language?
2. What factors contribute to the development of dialects? Relate these to the dialects found in the United States.
3. List the major differences between BE and SAE.
4. List the major differences between HE and SAE.
5. List the major differences between AE and SAE.
6. Explain the differences between simultaneous and successive second-language acquisition.
7. What are some of the special problems encountered in the educational system by children who speak BE or HE or who are bilingual?

13 Disorders and Development

CHAPTER OBJECTIVES

When you have completed this chapter, you should be able to discuss the applicability of your knowledge of speech and language development to language disorders.

N OT ALL CHILDREN develop speech and language as outlined in the preceding chapters. Approximately 5% of the total population, including about 10% of the children in elementary school, have communication disorders of various types and severity. These range from the common /w/-for-/r/ articulation substitution—as in *wun* (/wʌn/) for *run*—to the lack of language use of severely autistic children.

In addition to their disorder, affected individuals must also bear the stigma of difference. According to Love (1981):

> Even speech disorders considered minor and easily remediable . . . are apparently viewed as stigmatizing by large groups of listeners in the general public. . . . Speech, language, and hearing disorders which greatly reduce intelligibility of conversation and therefore limit the communicative exchange of thoughts and feelings are often met with outright public rejection and result in obvious social isolation. (p. 486)

Communication disorders have traditionally been classified as organic, nonorganic, or combined in origin. Organic disorders have some physical origin, such as brain damage or hearing loss. Nonorganic causes include such things as faulty learning or environmental deprivation. In actual practice, most communication disorders have both organic and nonorganic origins. For example, cerebral palsy results from brain injury, an organic etiology, but may have nonorganic correlates. Suppose that a child with cerebral palsy has been allowed to communicate with grunts and gestures even though he is capable of short, spoken (albeit difficult-to-understand) phrases. His use of grunts and gestures reflects a combined origin.

Even seemingly obvious causes, such as various syndromes that result in mental retardation, usually do not produce strictly organic language disorders. Several factors, such as residence at home or in an institution and the type of language intervention, usually influence the rate and form of language development.

Some children may be language delayed for various nonspecific or unknown reasons. Language-delayed children often show severe, broad impairments in all aspects of language. As these children mature, their deficits may become milder and more narrow. By 60 months, most of these children seem to have overcome their earlier delay. Lingering problems may be seen in many of these children when they begin to learn to read (Scarborough & Dobrich, 1990). Other children, such as those with retardation or learning disabilities, may have serious language problems that persist in both breadth and severity. At present, the speech and language of many autistic individuals may remain extremely impaired throughout their lives. Finally, adults who are deaf, even those with a good education, may have language skills in English well below those expected for their chronological age.

Similar behaviors may also result from very different origins. For example, hypernasal or overly nasal speech may result from cleft palate or poor learning, to name just two of the many possible causes. Immature or delayed language acquisition may also result from causes as diverse as mental retardation and environmental deprivation. This situation is further complicated when we consider the higher incidence of mild mental retardation among lower socioeconomic groups than among the general population. The poor are also more likely to experience environmental deprivation, so the two causes may become combined.

Language disorders may be based on organic, nonorganic, or a combination of causes that can affect the rate or direction of development.

Children with language disorders are the special charge of the speech-language pathologist and, to a lesser extent, of the special education and resource teacher. These professionals often employ a developmental approach in remediation.

THE DEVELOPMENTAL APPROACH

Although not all communication disorders lend themselves to a developmental intervention strategy, a developmental approach seems most justifiable in the area of language disorder or delay. The speech-language pathologist should base "programming strategies and targets on an intimate knowledge of normal language." (Schiefelbusch, 1978a, p. 9) For severely delayed or low-functioning individuals, training may begin at a prelinguistic level, targeting the early social, communicative, cognitive, and perceptual skills outlined in Chapters 5 and 6 (Owens, 1982). It seems especially important to establish an early communication base for the delayed or disordered child (Reichle, 1990). With a knowledge of language development and its prerequisites, professionals do not need to wait until a child starts to speak before beginning intervention. Intervention should begin as soon as there is any indication of possible language delay or disorder (Kent, 1979). Infants with syndromes associated with delay or disorder, such as Down's syndrome, should begin training shortly after birth in infant stimulation programs in order to achieve their potential in language skill development.

Early intervention is especially important for deaf children and should emphasize language input. The hearing infant is exposed to thousands of brief verbal interactions before he produces his first meaningful word. In contrast, the deaf child misses much of this prelinguistic interaction that is so important for later language development. Early use of signs, gestures, and speech could help establish a communication base for the deaf child.

With autistic and retarded children, an environmental approach to communication training that includes the child's conversational partners and contexts seems justified (Horstmeier & MacDonald, 1978; Nietupski, Scheutz, & Ockwood, 1980; Owens, 1982, 1991). An isolated therapy model is not sufficient. All those who interact with the child are potential language trainers. In addition, conversational approaches may result in avoidance of the stereotypic responsive behavior observed with many autistic children (Prizant, 1982). Unfortunately, many "language training programs appear to take for granted that spontaneous, initiated communication will naturally emerge out of receptive and expressive respondent training" (Prizant, 1982, p. 534). Language training should occur within a communication framework.

Once a child begins to use language expressively, the knowledgeable clinician can select training targets based on normal language development. In addition to first words, semantic and illocutionary functions of early language may be targeted (Guess, Sailor, & Baer, 1978; MacDonald, 1978; J. Miller & Yoder, 1974; Owens, 1982, 1991). Prutting (1979) has suggested a stage approach to training that follows the guidelines of normal development. The child progresses from one developmental stage to the next.

Not all professionals support a developmental intervention strategy, especially stage proposals such as Prutting's (1979). While pronouncing the developmental intervention model "basically sound," Winitz (1983) has contended that it is "generally used incorrectly" (p. 26). According to Winitz, the basic premises of the developmental approach are that intervention should begin at the lowest level of functioning and should continue within that level and succeeding ones until the client demonstrates expertise in all aspects of language associated with that level. He has contended that testing measures achievement rather than underlying rule systems. Therefore, programming reflects "age points at which mastery has been achieved, but does not indicate successive points in a learning sequence" (p. 32). Language learning is not a linear process. Winitz concluded:

> Developmental language profiles should . . . serve as a guide for the "emphasis" of certain structures and, perhaps, the avoidance of others. However, these profiles should not be used as a fixed set of sequences from which the clinician cannot deviate. (p. 33)

It would be a gross misuse of the developmental model to assume that children will all follow in the same lockstep sequence. "Language intervention is an individualizing process" (Schiefelbusch, 1978a, p. 8). Each language-disordered or -delayed child must be considered in terms of his own communicative context and needs (Keogh & Kopp, 1978).

Age-related developmental data, such as those supplied within this text, can supplement the intervention data from the language-impaired child (Chapman & Miller, 1980). Behavioral descriptions from different stages can be used to aid intervention planning. This information can provide a rationale for individual programming decisions.

In short, normal development is a guide for language remediation and assessment. Language benchmarks can alert parents and professionals to expected behaviors and to the approximate point in development when a behavior usually appears. In addition, normal development can provide direction for training those children who are not developing normally.

Normal development is not the only intervention guide, but it is one of the most useful. A teacher or speech-language pathologist must rely on many sources of information and, according to Schiefelbusch (1978b), "should be a behaviorist, a pragmatist, a cognitivist, a linguist, a developmentalist, and an optimist in order to put together an effective means of teaching language to children" (p. 461). I hope this text has provided a basis for your own development of some of these skills.

Appendix
American English Speech Sounds

The smallest unit of speech is the phoneme. It consists of a family of sounds that are close enough in perceptual qualities to be distinguished from other phonemes. Thus, though phonemes are meaningless, they make semantic difference in actual use. For example, the final sounds in *kiss* and *kick* are perceptually different enough to alert the listener to differences in meaning. Recognition of this distinction could be crucial, especially on a first date. Phonemes are written between slashes (as in /s/) to distinguish them from the alphabet. The International Phonetic Alphabet (IPA) is used rather than the English alphabet for two reasons. First, a sound may be spelled several ways, as in *go, row, hoe,* and *though.* In contrast, some letters, such as *c,* can be pronounced more than one way (as *s* or *k*). Similarly, the *o* in *comb* differs from the one in *come.* Second, the pronunciation of the English alphabet cannot be applied to other languages. Although French uses an identical alphabet, the pronunciation of the individual letters is quite different.

The actual sound produced by a speaker at a given time is called a **phone**, and no two phones are alike. Phones may be grouped perceptually as **allophones**, but even allophones may differ slightly. For example, the /p/ in *stop* may or may not be accompanied by a puff of air, or aspiration. The /p/ sound in *spot* is not aspirated. These two allophones are similar enough, however, to be classified as the phoneme /p/. A phoneme is thus made up of a group of allophones. As speakers of English, we have no difficulty recognizing the phonemic variations in *pop, pot, top,* and *tot.* Many English words differ by only one consonant or vowel. Consider *bet, get, let, met, net, pet, set, vet,* and *wet* or *bat, bet, bit,* and *but.* Perception of the different phonemes is extremely important for interpretation.

Each spoken language employs particular phonemes. In English, these sounds are classified as vowels or consonants. The distinction is based mainly on sound production characteristics. Vowels are produced with a relatively unrestricted air flow in the vocal tract. Consonants require a closed or narrowly constricted passage that results in friction and air turbulence. The number of

463

phonemes attributed to American English differs with the classification system used and the dialect of the speaker. In this text we discuss 45 phonemes—21 vowels and 24 consonants.

Phonemes can be described as being voiced or voiceless. **Voiced phonemes** are produced by phonation, or vibration, at the vocal folds of the larynx; **voiceless phonemes** are produced without vibration. All vowels in English are voiced; consonants may be either voiced or voiceless.

Two classification systems are currently used for English phonemes. The more traditional approach emphasizes the phoneme and classifies each according to place or manner of articulation. In contrast, the second, called the *distinctive feature approach*, emphasizes the characteristics or constituents of each phoneme.

TRADITIONAL PHONEMIC CLASSIFICATION

Traditional classification of English phonemes is based on the locus or place of articulation, usually the position of the tongue; and additionally, for consonants, on the manner of articulation, usually the type of release of air. Vowels are classified by the highest arched portion of the tongue and by the presence or absence of lip rounding. Consonants can be described by the site of articulation, by the manner of articulation, and by the presence or absence of voicing.

Vowels

Vowels can be described in terms of tongue height and front-to-back positioning (Schane, 1973). Heights can be characterized as high, mid, or low, depending on the position of the highest portion of the tongue. The location of this high point within the mouth can be described as front, central, or back. For example, a vowel can be described as high front, or low back, or any position in between. The English vowels are displayed graphically by position in Figure A.1. Words using each sound are printed next to each phoneme.

Lip rounding is an additional descriptive term used in vowel classification. During lip rounding, the lips protrude slightly, forming an O shape. Rounding is characteristic of some, but not all, back vowels, such as the last sound in *construe*. In contrast, there is no lip rounding in *construct*.

One group of vowellike sounds is more complex than the single-vowel phonemes. These sounds are called *diphthongs*. A **diphthong** is a blend of two vowels within the same syllable. In other words, the sound begins with one vowel and glides smoothly toward another position. When the word *my* is repeated slowly, the speaker can feel and hear the shift from one vowel to another.

Consonants

Consonant sounds are somewhat more complex than vowel sounds. They are described by their manner of articulation, place of articulation, and voicing (Table A.1). *Manner* refers to the type of production, generally with respect to the release of air. The six generally recognized categories of manner are:

FIGURE A.1   Classification of English Vowels by Tongue Position

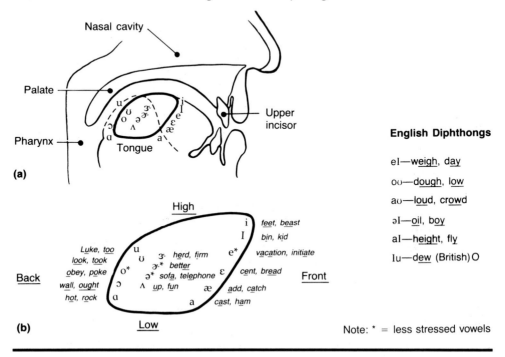

(a)

English Diphthongs

eɪ—weigh, day

oʊ—dough, low

aʊ—loud, crowd

ɔɪ—oil, boy

aɪ—height, fly

ɪu—dew (British) O

(b)

Note: * = less stressed vowels

- Plosive (/p/, /b/, /t/, /d/, /k/, /g/)—Complete obstruction of the airstream, with quick release accompanied by an audible escape of air; similiar to an explosion.
- Fricative (/f/, /v/, /θ/, /ð/, /s/, /z/, /ʃ/, /ʒ/, /h/)—Narrow constriction through which the air must pass, creating a hissing noise.
- Affricative (/tʃ/, /dʒ/)—A combination that begins with a plosive followed by a fricative, as the IPA symbols suggest.
- Liquid (/l/, /r/)—Consonants with the vowellike quality of little air turbulence. The /l/ is produced by raising the midline of the tongue and allowing air to pass around the sides. The /r/ has no closure and is produced by raising either the tip or back of the tongue.
- Glide (/w/, /j/)—Produced while gliding from one vowel position to another; vowellike.
- Nasal (/m/, /n/, /ŋ/)—Oral cavity closed to exiting air but velum lowered to allow breath to exit via the nasal cavity. Variations result from constriction within the oral cavity.

The *locus* or place of articulation varies across the six manner categories and describes the position where the maximum constriction occurs. Constriction may be partial or complete. The seven locations are:

TABLE A.1   Traditional Classification of English Consonants

Place of Constriction	Plosives U	Plosives V	Fricatives U	Fricatives V	Affricatives U	Affricatives V	Semivowels† V	Nasals† V
Bilabial	p (pig)	b (big)					w (watt)	m (sum)
Labiodental			f (face)	v (vase)				
Lingua-dental			θ (thigh, thin)	ð (thy, this)				
Lingua-alveolar	t (tot)	d (dot)	s (seal)	z (zeal)			l,r* (lot) (rot)	n (sun)
Lingua-palatal			ʃ (shoe, mission)	ʒ (visual, measure)	tʃ (choke, nature)	dʒ (joke, gentle)	j (yacht)	
Lingua-velar	k (coat)	g (goat)						ŋ (sung)
Glottal			h (happy)					

U = unvoiced; V = voiced.

* In production of /l/, air goes around the sides of the tongue. In contrast, air goes through a small aperture between the tongue and palate for production of /r/.
† All voiced.

- Bilabial (/p/, /b/, /w/, /m/)—Lips together.
- Labiodental (/f/, /v/)—Lower lip to upper incisors.
- Lingua-dental (/θ/, /ð/)—Tongue tip to upper incisors.
- Lingua-alveolar (/t/, /d/, /s/, /z/, /l/, /r/, /n/)—Front of tongue to upper alveolar (gum) ridge.
- Lingua-palatal (/ʃ/, /ʒ/, /tʃ/, /dʒ/, /j/)—Tongue to hard palate.
- Lingua-velar (/k/, /g/, /ŋ/)—Back of tongue to soft palate or velum.
- Glottal (/h/)—Restriction at glottis or opening to larynx.

Many pairs of English consonant sounds differ only in voicing. When two phonemes have the same manner and place of articulation but differ in voicing, they are called **cognates**. For examples, the /f/ and /v/ phonemes are cognates. If you repeat the words *face* and *vase*, you can feel the difference at the level of the larynx. The place and manner of articulation do not differ. All English plosives, affricatives, and fricatives, except /h/, are organized in voiced and voiceless pairs. The English liquids and glides are all voiced, adding to their vowellike quality. Finally, all English nasals are also voiced.

You should be aware that the voicing distinction is indefinite. This problem can be explained by **voice onset time (VOT)**, which is the interval between the burst of a plosive and the commencement of phonation. In other words, no English plosives are truly voiceless; rather, thay have a delayed VOT. The VOT is usually less than 30 milliseconds for voiceless plosives. The mean delay is 58 milliseconds for /p/ and 70 milliseconds for /t/ (Lisker & Abramson, 1965).

Theoretically, speech sounds could be produced in almost any tongue position and in all configurations of manner, placing, and voicing. Other languages use some of the phonemes of English, plus additional speech sounds, even some with other production characteristics. Some English distinctions are not present in other languages. In Spanish there is no distinction between /s/ and /z/; they are not separate phonemes. Other languages make finer distinctions. In Zulu, meaning is often differentiated by the degree of aspiration, or breathiness, of a sound. Thus, there are different varieties of /t/, /k/, and /p/ that are not relevant to speakers of English (and are difficult for us to distinguish).

DISTINCTIVE FEATURE CLASSIFICATION

The distinctive feature approach to the study of speech sounds is an attempt to break phonemes into smaller analytic units. A phoneme's **distinctive features** are the significant acoustic or articulatory characteristics that distinguish it from other phonemes. There are several theoretical classification systems based on acoustic (Jakobson, Fant, & Halle, 1951), articulatory (N. Chomsky & Halle, 1968), and perceptual characteristics (Singh, Woods, & Becker, 1972). Some systems are binary, noting merely the presence or absence of a feature, while others are scaled, noting the strength of the feature on a continuum.

In general, the greater the agreement on distinctive features between two phonemes, the more alike the phonemes. Thus, common features describe the relationship between two phonemes. Table A.2 displays the Chomsky and Halle (1968) classification system. Note the similarity between sounds such as /t/ and /d/ and between /s/ and /z/. In contrast, /n/ and /l/ are very dissimilar.

Though helpful in analysis, distinctive feature classification systems are abstractions. There is little indication that the features noted have any psychological reality for children, nor do these features tend to spread rapidly to all affected phonemes.

SOUNDS IN SPEECH

Although we can describe English speech sounds in isolation, they rarely occur alone in actual use. Plosives cannot be produced in isolation but must be combined with some other phoneme. Speech is a dynamic process in which individual sounds are seldom treated as discrete units. Movement patterns for more than one sound may occur simultaneously, their features overlapping (Mac-Neilage, 1970). This co-occurrence of production characteristics of two or more phonemes is called *coarticulation*. **Coarticulation** is the result of the motor commands from the brain and the mechanical response of the speech muscles. As a

TABLE A.2 English Consonants Including the Glottal Stop by Chomsky-Halle Extended Features

Features	k	q	t	d	p	b	f	v	θ	ð	s	z	ʃ	ʒ	tʃ	dʒ	m	n	ŋ	l	r	h	w	j	ʔ
Vocalic	−	−	−	−	−	−	−	−	−	−	−	−	−	−	−	−	−	−	−	+	+	−	−	−	−
Consonantal	+	+	+	+	+	+	+	+	+	+	+	+	+	+	+	+	+	+	+	+	+	−	−	−	−
High	+	+	−	−	−	−	−	−	−	−	−	−	+	+	+	+	−	−	+	−	−	−	+	+	−
Back	+	+	−	−	−	−	−	−	−	−	−	−	−	−	−	−	−	−	+	−	−	−	+	−	−
Low	−	−	−	−	−	−	−	−	−	−	−	−	−	−	−	−	−	−	−	−	−	+	−	−	+
Anterior	−	−	+	+	+	+	+	+	+	+	+	+	−	−	−	−	+	+	−	+	−	−	−	−	−
Coronal	−	−	+	+	−	−	−	−	+	+	+	+	+	+	+	+	−	+	+	+	+	−	−	−	−
Round																							+	−	−
Tense																							−	−	
Voice	−	+	−	+	−	+	−	+	−	+	−	+	−	+	−	+	+	+	+	+	+	−	+	+	−
Continuant	−	−	−	−	−	−	+	+	+	+	+	+	+	+	−	−	−	−	−	+	+	+	+	+	+
Nasal	−	−	−	−	−	−	−	−	−	−	−	−	−	−	−	−	+	+	+	−	−	−	−	−	−
Strident	−	−	−	−	−	−	+	+	−	−	+	+	+	+	+	+	−	−	−	−	−	−	−	−	−

Blank ± not relevant.
− = binary feature not present.
+ = binary feature present.

- *Vocalic*—Constriction in the oral cavity is not greater than required for the high vowels /i, u/.
- *Consonantal*—The sound is made with a radical constriction in the midsagittal region of the oral cavity.
- *High*—The body of the tongue is elevated above the neutral position.
- *Back*—The body of the tongue retracts from the neutral position.
- *Low*—The body of the tongue is lowered below the neutral position.
- *Anterior*—The sound is produced further forward in the mouth than /ʃ/.
- *Coronal*—The sound is produced with the blade of the tongue raised from the neutral position.
- *Round*—The lip orifice is narrowed.
- *Tense*—The sound is produced deliberately, accurately, and distinctly.
- *Voice*—During the production of the sound, the larynx vibrates periodically.
- *Continuant*—The vocal tract is partially constricted during the production of the sound.
- *Nasal*—The velopharyngeal valve is sufficiently open during the production of the sound to permit the air-sound stream to be directed through the nose.
- *Strident*—The air stream is directed over a rough surface in such a way as to produce an audible noise.

Source: R. Owens, Jr., ''Communication, Language, and Speech,'' in G. Shames & E. Wiig, *Human Communication Disorders: An Introduction*, Columbus, Ohio: Merrill Publishing Co., 1986 p. 41. Reprinted with permission. 2nd ed.

good organizer, the brain sends movement and position commands in advance of the actual occurrence in an utterance. Through high speed X-ray studies, we can demonstrate that movement may occur several phonemes prior to the appearance of the phoneme associated with this movement (Daniloff & Moll, 1968). For example, in the word *construe*, lip rounding begins well before the /u/ sound. You can see this movement with the aid of a mirror. These anticipatory movements are a clear indication that the brain is not functioning on a phoneme level but rather with larger organizational units. The type of coarticulation demonstrated by anticipatory movements is called *anticipatory, or forward, coarticulation.*

In any mechanical system, including the speech mechanism, there is also some built-in inertia, or drag. Muscle movements lag behind brain commands and continue after the commands have ceased. The result is that the production characteristics of one phoneme may persist during production of a following phoneme. The nasalization of the /z/ in *runs* (/rʌnz/) is caused by the insufficient time available for the velum to return to its upward position after /n/ (Daniloff 1973). This type of coarticulation is called *carryover, or backward, coarticulation.*

References

Abbeduto, L., & Rosenberg, S. (1985). Children's knowledge of the presuppositions of *know* and other cognitive verbs. *Journal of Child Language, 12*, 621–641.

Abkarian, G. (1988). Acquiring lexical contrast: The case of *bring-take* learning. *Journal of Speech and Hearing Research, 31*, 317–326.

Abrahamsen, E., & Rigrodsky, S. (1984). Comprehension of complex sentences in children at three levels of cognitive development. *Journal of Psycholinguistic Research, 13*, 333–350.

Ackerman, B. (1978). Children's understanding of speech acts in unconventional directive frames. *Child Development, 49*, 311–318.

Ainsworth, M. (1963). The development of infant-mother interaction among the Ganda. In B. Foss (Ed.), *Determinants of infant behavior* (Vol. 2). London: Methuen.

Ainsworth, M. (1964). Patterns of attachment behavior shown by the infant in interaction with his mother. *Merrill-Palmer Quarterly, 10*, 51–58.

Ainsworth, M., & Bell, S. (1969). Some contemporary patterns of mother-infant interaction in the feeding situation. In J. Ambrose (Ed.), *Stimulation in early infancy*. New York: Academic Press.

Ainsworth, M., Bell, S., & Slayton, D. (1974). Infant-mother attachment and social development: "Socialization" as a product of reciprocal responsiveness to signals. In M. Richards (Ed.), *The integration of a child into a social world*. New York: Cambridge University Press.

Aksu, A., & Slobin, D. (1985). Acquisition of Turkish. In D. Slobin (Ed.), *The crosslinguistic study of language acquisition*. Hillsdale, NJ: Erlbaum.

Al-Issa, I. (1969). The development of word definitions in children. *Journal of Genetic Psychology, 114*, 25–28.

Albert, M., & Obler, L. (1978). *The bilingual brain*. New York: Academic Press.

Allen, G. (1983). Linguistic experience modifies lexical stress perception. *Journal of Child Language, 10*, 535–549.

Allen, R., & Shatz, M. (1983). "What says meow?" The role of context and linguistic experience in very young children's responses to what questions. *Journal of Child Language, 10*, 321–335.

Allington, R. (1984). Oral reading. In P. Pearson, R. Barr, M. Kamil, & P. Mosenthal (Eds.), *Handbook of reading research*. New York: Longman.

Altenberg, E., & Cairns, H. (1983). The effects of phonotactic constraints on lexical processing in bilingual and monolingual subjects. *Journal of Verbal Learning and Verbal Behavior, 22*, 174–188.

Ambrose, A. (1961). The development of the smiling response in early infancy. In B. Foss (Ed.), *Determinants of infant behavior*, Vol. 1. London: Methuen.

Ames, L. (1966). Children's stories. *Genetic Psychological Monographs, 73,* 307–311.

Amidon, A., & Carey, P. (1972). Why five-year-olds cannot understand *before* and *after. Journal of Verbal Learning and Verbal Behavior, 11,* 417–423.

Anastasiow, N., & Hanes, M. (1976). *Language patterns of poverty children.* Springfield, IL: Charles C Thomas.

Andersen, E. (1977). *Learning to speak with style.* Unpublished doctoral dissertation. Stanford University.

Andersen, E., & Kekelis, L. (1983). *The role of children in determining the nature of their linguistic input.* Paper presented at the Eighth Annual Conference on Language Development, Boston University.

Anderson, A., & Stokes, S. (1984). Social and institutional influences on the development and practice of literacy. In H. Goelman, A. Oberg, & F. Smith (Eds.), *Awakening to literacy.* Exeter, NH: Heinemann.

Anderson, R., & Freebody, P. (1979). *Vocabulary knowledge and reading.* Urbana-Champaign, IL: Center for the Study of Reading.

Anderson, R., & Smith, B. (1987). Phonological development of two-year-old monolingual Puerto Rican Spanish-speaking children. *Journal of Child Language, 14,* 57–78.

Anglin, J. (1970). *The growth of meaning.* Cambridge: MIT Press.

Anglin, J. (1975, July). The child's first terms of reference. In S. Elrich & E. Tulving (Eds.), *Bulletin de psychologie.*

Anglin, J. (1977). *Word, object, and conceptual development.* New York: W. W. Norton.

Applebee, A. (1978). *The child's concept of story.* Chicago: University of Chicago Press.

Appleton, T., Clifton, R., & Goldberg, S. (1975). The development of behavioral competence in infancy. In F. Horowitz (Ed.), *Review of child development research.* Chicago: University of Chicago Press.

Arlin, M. (1983). Children's comprehension of semantic constraints on temporal prepositions. *Journal of Psycholinguistic Research, 12,* 1–15.

Arlman-Rupp, A., van Niekerk de Haan, D., & van de Sandt-Koenderman, M. (1976). Brown's early stages: Some evidence from Dutch. *Journal of Child Language, 3,* 267–274.

Aslin, R., & Pisoni, D. (1980). Some developmental processes in speech perception. In G. Yeni-Komshian, J. Kavanaugh, & C. Ferguson (Eds.), *Child phonology: Vol. 2, Perception.* New York: Academic Press.

Astington, J. (1988a). Children's production of commissive speech acts. *Journal of Child Language, 15,* 411–423.

Astington, J. (1988b). Children's understanding of the speech act of promising. *Journal of Child Language, 15,* 157–173.

Atkinson, R. (1974). *Prerequisites for reference.* Paper presented to B.A.A.L. Seminar on Applications of Linguistics to Language Development.

Atkinson, R., & Shiffrin, R. (1968). Human memory: A proposed system and its control processes. In K. Spence & J. Spence (Eds.), *The psychology of learning and motivation: Advances in research and theory* (Vol. 2). New York: Academic Press.

Atkinson-King, K. (1973). Children's acquisition of phonological stress contrasts. *UCLA Working Papers in Phonetics,* No. 25.

Au, K. (1990). Children's use of information in word learning. *Journal of Child Language, 17,* 393–416.

Austin, J. (1962). *How to do things with words.* London: Oxford University Press.

Baggett, P. (1979). Structurally equivalent stories in movies and text and the effect of medium on recall. *Journal of Verbal Learning and Verbal Behavior, 18,* 333–356.

Baldie, B. (1976). The acquisition of the passive voice. *Journal of Child Language, 3,* 331–348.

Bangs, T. (1975). *Vocabulary Comprehension Scale.* Boston: Teaching Resources.

Banigan, R., & Mervis, C. (1988). Role of adult input in young children's category evolution: II. An experimental study. *Journal of Child Language, 15,* 493–504.

Baratz, J. (1968). Language in the economically disadvantaged child: A perspective. *ASHA, 10,* 145–146.

Baratz, J. (1969). Language and cognitive assessments of Negro children: Assumptions and research needs. *ASHA, 11,* 87–92.

Barnes, S., Gutfreund, M., Satterly, D., & Wells, G. (1983). Characteristics of adult speech which predict children's language development. *Journal of Child Language, 10,* 65–84.

Baron, J. (1977). Mechanics for pronouncing printed words: Use and application. In D. LaBerge & S. Samuels (Eds.), *Basic processes in reading: Perception and comprehension.* Hillsdale, NJ: Erlbaum.

Baron, J., & Kaiser, A. (1975). Semantic components in children's errors with pronouns. *Journal of Child Language, 4,* 303–317.

Barrett, M. (1978). Lexical development and overextension in child language. *Journal of Child Language, 5,* 205–219.

Barrett, M. (1982). Distinguishing between prototypes: The early acquisition of meaning of object names. In S. Kuczaj (Ed.), *Language development: Vol. 1. Syntax and semantics.* Hillsdale, NJ: Erlbaum.

Barrett, M. (1983). *Scripts, prototypes, and the early acquisition of word meaning.* Paper presented at the annual conference of the British Psychological Society.

Barron, R. (1981). Development of visual word recognition: A review. In G. Mackinnon & T. Waller (Eds.), *Reading research: Advances in theory and practice.* New York: Academic Press.

Bartlett, C. (1982). Learning to write: Some cognitive and linguistic components. In R. Shuy (Ed.), *Linguistics and literacy series,* No. 2. Washington, D.C.: Center of Applied Linguistics.

Bartoshuk, A. (1964). Human neonatal cardiac responses to sound: A power function. *Psychonomic Science, 1,* 151–152.

Basso, K. (1972). To give up on words: Silence in western Apache culture. In P. Giglioli (Ed.), *Language and social context.* New York: Penguin Books.

Bates, E. (1976a). *Language and context: The acquisition of pragmatics.* New York: Academic Press.

Bates, E. (1976b). Pragmatics and sociolinguistics in child language. In D. Morehead & A. Morehead (Eds.), *Normal and deficient child language.* Baltimore: University Park Press.

Bates, E., Benigni, L., Bretherton, I., Camaioni, L., & Volterra, V. (1977). From gesture to the first word: On cognitive and social prerequisites. In M. Lewis & L. Rosenblum (Eds.), *Interaction, conversation, and the development of language.* New York: John Wiley.

Bates, E., Benigni, L., Bretherton, I., Camaioni, L., & Volterra, V. (1979). *The emergence of symbols: Cognition and communication in infancy.* New York: Academic Press.

Bates, E., Bretherton, I., Shore, C., & McNew, S. (1983). Names, gestures and objects: The role of context in the emergence of symbols. In K. Nelson (Ed.), *Children's language,* Vol. 4, Hillsdale, NJ: Erlbaum.

Bates, E., Bretherton, I., Snyder, L., Shore, C., & Volterra, V. (1980). Vocal and gestural symbols at 13 months. *Merrill-Palmer Quarterly, 26,* 407–423.

Bates, E., Camaioni, L., & Volterra, V. (1975). The acquisition of performatives prior to speech. *Merrill-Palmer Quarterly, 21,* 205–216.

Bates, E., MacWhinney, B., Caselli, C., Devescove, S., Natale, F., & Vanza, V. (1984). Cross-linguistic study of the development of sentence interpretation strategies. *Child Development, 55,* 341–354.

Bates, E., & Snyder, L. (1987). The cognitive hypothesis in language development. In I. Uzgiris & J. Hunt (Eds.), *Infant performance and experience: New findings with the ordinal scales.* Urbana: University of Illinois Press.

Bateson, M. (1971). The interpersonal context of infant vocalizations. *Quarterly Progress Report, Research Laboratory of Electronics, MIT, 100,* 170–176.

Bateson, M. (1975). Mother-infant exchanges: The epigenesis of conversational interaction. In D. Aaronson & R. Rieber (Eds.), *Developmental psycholinguistics and communication disorders.* New York: New York Academy of Sciences.

Bateson, M. (1979). The epigenesis of conversational interaction: A personal account of research development. In M. Bullow (Ed.), *Before speech.* New York: Cambridge University Press.

Bayles, K., Tomoeda, C., & Boone, D. (1985). A view of age-related changes in language function. *Developmental Neuropsychology, 1,* 231–264.

Bearison, D., & Levey, L. (1977). Children's comprehension of referential communication: Decoding ambiguous messages. *Child Development, 48*, 716–720.

Bedrosian, J., Wanska, S., Sykes, K., Smith, A., & Dalton, B. (1988). Conversational turn-taking violations in mother–child interactions. *Journal of Speech and Hearing Research, 31*, 81–86.

Beebe, B. (1973). *Ontogeny of positive affect in the third and fourth months of the life of one infant.* Doctoral dissertation, Columbia University.

Behrend, D. (1988). Overextensions in early language comprehension: Evidence from a signal detection approach. *Journal of Child Language, 15*, 63–75.

Beilin, H. (1975). *Studies in the cognitive basis of language development.* New York: Academic Press.

Beilin, H., & Spontak, G. (1969). *Active-passive transformations and operational reversibility.* Paper presented at a meeting of the Society for Research in Child Development.

Bell, K. (1968). A reinterpretation of the direction of effects in studies of socialization. *Psychological Review, 75*, 81–95.

Bell, R. (1976). *Sociolinguistics: Goals, approaches and problems.* London: Batsford.

Bell, S., & Ainsworth, M. (1972). Infant crying and maternal responsiveness. *Child Development, 43*, 1171–1190.

Bellack, A., Kliebard, P., Hyman, R., & Smith, F. (1966). *The language of the classroom.* New York: Teacher's College Press.

Bellinger, D. (1980). Consistency in the pattern of change in mothers' speech: Some discriminant analyses. *Journal of Child Language, 7*, 469–487.

Bellugi, U. (1967). *The acquisition of negation.* Unpublished doctoral dissertation. Harvard University.

Bellugi, U. (1971). Simplification in children's language. In R. Huxley & E. Ingram (Eds.), *Language acquisition: Models and methods.* New York: Academic Press.

Bellugi, U., & Brown, R. (1964). The acquisition of language. *Monographs of the Society for Research in Child Development, 29*, (No. 92).

Bellugi-Klima, U. (1969). *Language acquisition.* Paper presented at a symposium on cognitive studies and artificial intelligence research, University of Chicago.

Benedict, H. (1979). Early lexical development: Comprehension and production. *Journal of Child Language, 6*, 183–200.

Benelli, B., Arcuri, L., & Marchesini, G. (1988). Cognitive and linguistic factors in the development of word definitions. *Journal of Child Language, 15*, 619–635.

Bennett, S. (1971). Infant-caregiver interactions. *Journal of the American Academy of Child Psychiatry, 10*, 321–335.

Bennett-Kaster, T. (1983). Noun phrases and coherence in child narratives. *Journal of Child Language, 10*, 135–149.

Bennett-Kaster, T. (1986). Cohesion and predication in child narrative. *Journal of Child Language, 13*, 353–370.

Bennett-Kaster, T. (1988). *Analyzing children's language.* Oxford: Blackwell.

Berg, W. (1971). *Habituation and dishabituation of cardiac responses in awake four months old infants.* Unpublished doctoral dissertation. University of Wisconsin.

Berko, J. (1958). The child's learning of English morphology. *Word, 14*, 150–177.

Berko Gleason, J. (1973). Code switching in children's language. In T. Moore (Ed.), *Cognitive development and the acquisition of language.* New York: Academic Press.

Berko Gleason, J. (1985). Studying language development. In J. Berko Gleason (Ed.), *The development of language.* Columbus, OH: Merrill.

Berko Gleason, J., & Greif, E. (1983). Men's speech to young children. In B. Thorne, C. Kramerae, & N. Henley (Eds.), *Language, gender, and society.* Rowley, MA: Newbury House.

Berlin, B., Breedlove, D., & Raven, R. (1973). General principles of classification and nomenclature in folk biology. *American Anthropologist, 75*, 214–242.

Berlyne, D. (1965). *Structure and direction in thinking.* New York: Wiley.

Berman. R. (1985). Acquisition of Hebrew. In D. Slobin (Ed.), *The crosslinguistic study of language acquisition.* Hillsdale, NJ: Erlbaum.

Berman, R. (1986). A crosslinguistic perspective: Morphology and syntax. In P. Fletcher & M. Garman (Eds.), *Language acquisition* (2nd ed.). New York: Cambridge University Press.

Bernstein, B. (1971). Socialization: With some reference to educability. In B. Bernstein (Ed.), *Class, codes, and control: Theoretical studies towards a sociology of language*. London: Routledge & Kegan Paul.

Bernstein, M. (1983). Formation of internal structure in a lexical category. *Journal of Child Language, 10,* 381–399.

Bernstein Ratner, N., & Pye, C. (1984). Higher pitch in BT is not universal: Acoustic evidence from Quiche Mayan. *Journal of Child Language, 11,* 515–522.

Bever, T. (1970). The cognitive basis for linguistic structures. In J. Hayes (Ed.), *Cognition and the development of language*. New York: Wiley.

Biemiller, A. (1970). The development of the use of graphic and contextual information as children learn to read. *Reading Research Quarterly, 6,* 75–96.

Billow, R. (1979). *Observing spontaneous metaphor in children*. Paper presented at the annual meeting of the American Psychological Association.

Blehar, M., Lieberman, A., & Ainsworth, M. (1977). Early face-to-face interaction and its relation to later mother-infant attachment. *Child Development, 48,* 182–194.

Block, E., & Kessel, F. (1980). Determinants of the acquisition order of grammatical morphemes: A re-analysis and re-interpretation. *Journal of Child Language, 7,* 181–188.

Bloom, K. (1988). Quality of adult vocalizations affects the quality of infant vocalizations. *Journal of Child Language, 15,* 469–480.

Bloom, K., Russell, A., & Wassenberg, K. (1987). Turntaking affects the quality of infant vocalizations. *Journal of Child Language, 14,* 221–227.

Bloom, L. (1970). *Language development: Form and function of emerging grammars*. Cambridge: MIT Press.

Bloom, L. (1973). *One word at a time: The use of single-word utterances before syntax*. The Hague: Mouton.

Bloom, L. (1974). Talking, understanding, and thinking. In R. Schiefelbusch & L. Lloyd (Eds.), *Language perspectives: Acquisition, retardation and intervention*. Baltimore: University Park Press.

Bloom, L. (1975). Language development. In F. Horowitz (Ed.), *Review of child development research* (No. 4). Chicago: University of Chicago Press.

Bloom, L. (1983). Of continuity, nature, and magic. In R. Golinkoff (Ed.), *The transition from preverbal to verbal communication*. Hillsdale, NJ: Erlbaum.

Bloom, L., Hood, L., & Lightbown, P. (1974). Imitation in language development: If, when and why. *Cognitive Psychology, 6,* 380–420.

Bloom, L., & Lahey, M. (1978). *Language development and language disorders*. New York: Wiley.

Bloom, L., Lahey, P., Hood, L., Lifter, K., & Fiess, K. (1980). Complex sentences: Acquisition of syntactic connectors and the semantic relations they encode. *Journal of Child Language, 7,* 235–262.

Bloom, L., Lifter, K., & Hafitz, J. (1980). Semantics of verbs and the development of verb inflection in child language. *Language, 56,* 386–412.

Bloom, L., Lightbown, P., & Hood, L. (1975). Structure and variation in child language. *Monographs of the Society for Research in Child Development, 40.*

Bloom, L., Miller, P., & Hood, L. (1975). Variation and reduction as aspects of competence in language development. In A. Pick (Ed.), *Minnesota Symposia on Child Psychology* (Vol. 9). Minneapolis: University of Minnesota Press.

Bloom, L., Rocissano, L., & Hood, L. (1976). Adult-child discourse: Developmental interaction between information processing and linguistic interaction. *Cognitive Psychology, 8,* 521–552.

Bloom, L., Tackeff, J., & Lahey, M. (1984). Learning *to* in complement constructions. *Journal of Child Language, 11,* 391–406.

Bloom, P. (1990). Syntactic distinctions in child language. *Journal of Child Language, 17,* 343–355.

Bock, J., & Hornsby, M. (1981). The development of directives: How children ask and tell. *Journal of Child Language, 8,* 151–164.

Bohannon, J., & Marquis, A. (1977). Children's control of adult speech. *Child Development, 48,* 1002–1008.

Bolinger, D. (1975). *Aspects of language.* New York: Harcourt Brace Jovanovich.

Bosma, J. (1975). Anatomic and physiological development of the speech apparatus. In D. Tower (Ed.), *Human communication and its disorders* (Vol. III). New York: Raven.

Bostwinick, J., West, R., & Storandt, M. (1975). Qualitative vocabulary response and age. *Journal of Gerontology, 30,* 574–577.

Bouvier, L., & Gardner, R. (1986). *Immigration to the U.S.: The unfinished story.* Washington, DC: Population Reference Bureau.

Bower, G., Lesgold, A., & Tieman, D. (1969). Grouping operations in free recall. *Journal of Verbal Learning and Verbal Behavior, 8,* 481–493.

Bower, T. (1977). *The perceptual world of the child.* Cambridge: Harvard University Press.

Bower, T., & Wishart, J. (1972). The effects of motor skill on object permanence. *Cognition, 1,* 165–172.

Bowerman, M. (1973a). *Learning to talk: A cross-linguistic comparison of early syntactic development with special reference to Finnish.* London: Cambridge University Press.

Bowerman, M. (1973b). Structural relationships in children's utterances: Syntactic or semantic? In T. Moore (Ed.), *Cognitive development and the acquisition of language.* New York: Academic Press.

Bowerman, M. (1974). Discussion summary— Development of concepts underlying language. In R. Schiefelbusch & L. Lloyd (Eds.), *Language perspectives—Acquisition, retardation, and intervention.* Baltimore: University Park Press.

Bowerman, M. (1976). Semantic factors in the acquisition of rules for word use and sentence construction. In D. Morehead & A. Morehead (Eds.), *Normal and deficient child language.* Baltimore: University Park Press.

Bowerman, M. (1978). The acquisition of word meaning: An investigation in some current conflicts. In N. Waterson & C. Snow (Eds.), *The development of communication.* New York: Wiley.

Bowerman, M. (1981). *The child's expression of meaning: Expanding relationships among lexicon, syntax and morphology.* Paper presented at the New York Academy of Science Conference on Native Language and Foreign Language Acquisition.

Bowey, J. (1982). The structural processing of the truncated passive in children and adults. *Journal of Psycholinguistic Research, 11,* 417–436.

Bowey, J. (1986). Syntactic awareness and verbal performance from preschool to fifth grade. *Journal of Psycholinguistic Research, 15,* 285–308.

Bowles, N., & Poon, L. (1985). Aging and retrieval of words in semantic memory. *Journal of Gerontology, 40,* 71–77.

Boyd, E. (1975). Visual fixation and voice discrimination in 2-month-old infants. In F. Horowitz (Ed.), *Visual attention, auditory stimulation, and language discrimination in young infants. Monographs of the Society for Research in Child Development, 39.*

Braga, L., & Braga, J. (1975). *Learning & growing: A guide to child development.* Englewood Cliffs, NJ: Prentice-Hall.

Braine, M. (1971). The acquisition of language in infant and child. In C. Reed (Ed.), *The learning of language.* New York: Appleton-Century-Crofts.

Braine, M. (1976). Children's first word combinations. *Monographs of the Society for Research in Child Development, 41* (Serial No. 164).

Branigan, G. (1979). Some reasons why successive single word utterances are not. *Journal of Child Language, 6,* 411–421.

Bransford, J., & Johnson, M. (1972). Contextual prerequisites for understanding: Some investigations of comprehension and recall. *Journal of Verbal Learning and Verbal Behavior, 11,* 717–726.

Braunwald, S. (1978). Context, word and meaning: Towards a communicational analysis of lexical acquisition. In A. Lock (Ed.), *Action, gesture and symbol: The emergence of language.* New York: Academic Press.

Brazelton, T. (1979). Evidence of communication during neonatal behavioral assessment. In

M. Bullowa (Ed.), *Before speech.* New York: Cambridge University Press.

Brazelton, T., Koslowski, B., & Main, M. (1974). The origins of reciprocity: The early mother-infant interaction. In M. Lewis & L. Rosenblum (Eds.), *The effect of the infant on its caregiver.* New York: Wiley.

Brazelton, T., Tronick, E., Adamson, L., Als, H., & Wise, S. (1975). Early mother-infant reciprocity. In *Parent-infant interaction.* Ciba Foundation Symposium. Amsterdam: Elsevier.

Brener, R. (1983). Learning the deictic meaning of third person pronouns. *Journal of Psycholinguistics Research, 12,* 235–262.

Brennan, W., Ames, E., & Moore, R. (1966). Age differences in infants' attention to patterns of different complexities. *Science, 151,* 354–356.

Bretherton, I., & Beeghly, M. (1982). Talking about internal states: The acquisition of an explicit theory of mind. *Developmental Psychology, 18,* 906–921.

Bretherton, I., McNew, S., Snyder, L., & Bates, E. (1983). Individual differences at 20 months: Analytic and holistic strategies in language acquisition. *Journal of Child Language, 10,* 293–320.

Brewer, W., & Stone, J. (1975). Acquisition of spatial antonym pairs. *Journal of Experimental Child Psychology, 19,* 299–307.

Brice Heath, S. (1983). *Ways with words: Language, life, and work in communities and classrooms.* Cambridge: Cambridge University Press.

Bridges, A. (1980). SVD comprehension strategies reconsidered: The evidence of individual patterns of response. *Journal of Child Language, 7,* 89–104.

Brinton, B., & Fujiki, M. (1984). Development of topic manipulation skills in discourse. *Journal of Speech and Hearing Research, 27,* 350–358.

Brinton, B., Fujiki, M., Loeb, D., & Winkler, E. (1986). Development of conversational repair strategies in response to requests for clarification. *Journal of Speech and Hearing Research, 29,* 75–81.

Broen, R. (1972). The verbal environment of the language-learning child. *Monograph of the American Speech and Hearing Association, 17.*

Brogan, P. (1968). The nesting constraint in child language. Unpublished paper in the series *Language, society, and the child.* University of California, Berkeley: Language-Behavior Research Lab.

Brown, A. (1978). Knowing when, where, and how to remember: A problem in metacognition. In R. Glaser (Ed.), *Advances in instructional psychology.* Hillsdale, NJ: Erlbaum.

Brown, B., & Leonard, L. (1986). Lexical influences on children's early positional patterns. *Journal of Child Language, 13,* 219–229.

Brown, J., Bakeman, R., Snyder, P., Frederickson, W., Morgan, S., & Helper, R. (1975). Interactions of black inner-city mothers with their newborn infants. *Child Development, 46,* 677–686.

Brown, J., & Jaffe, J. (1975). Hypothesis on cerebral dominance. *Neuropsychologia, 13,* 107–110.

Brown, R. (1956). Language and categories. Appendix in J. Bruner, J. Goodner, & G. Austin, *A study of thinking.* New York: Wiley.

Brown, R. (1958a). How shall a thing be called? *Psychological Review, 65,* 18–21.

Brown, R. (1958b). *Words and things.* New York: Free Press.

Brown, R. (1965). *Social psychology.* New York: Free Press.

Brown, R. (1973). *A first language: The early stages.* Cambridge: Harvard University Press.

Brown, R. (1977). Preface. In C. Snow & C. Ferguson (Eds.), *Talking to children: Language input and acquisition.* New York: Cambridge University Press.

Brown, R., & Bellugi, U. (1964). Three processes in the child's acquisition of syntax. *Harvard Educational Review, 34,* 133–151.

Brown, R., & Berko, J. (1960). Word association and the acquisition of grammars. *Child Development, 31,* 1–14.

Brown, R., Cazden, C., & Bellugi, U. (1969). The child's grammar from I to III. In J. Hill (Ed.), *Minnesota Symposia on Child Psychology* (Vol. 2). Minneapolis: University of Minnesota Press.

Brown, R., & Fraser, C. (1964). The acquisition of syntax. In U. Bellugi & R. Brown, *The acquisition of language. Monographs of the Society for Research in Child Development, 92.*

Brown, R., & Hanlon, C. (1970). Derivational complexity and order of acquisition. In J. Hayes (Ed.), *Cognition and the development of language*. New York: Wiley.

Bruce, D. (1964). Analysis of word sounds by young children. *British Journal of Educational Psychology, 34,* 158–169.

Bruner, J. (1969). Eye, hand, and mind. In D. Elkind & J. Flavell (Eds.), *Studies in cognitive development: Essays in honor of Jean Piaget.* New York: Oxford University Press.

Bruner, J. (1973). Volition, skill and tools. In L. Stone, H. Smith, & L. Murphy (Eds.), *The competent infant: Research and commentary.* New York: Basic Books.

Bruner, J. (1974/75). From communication to language—A psychological perspective. *Cognition, 3,* 255–287.

Bruner, J. (1975). The ontogenesis of speech acts. *Journal of Child Language, 2,* 1–19.

Bruner, J. (1976). *On prelinguistic prerequisites of speech.* Paper presented to the Stirling Conference on Psychology of Language.

Bruner, J. (1977a). Early social interaction and language acquisition. In R. Schaffer (Ed.), *Studies in mother-infant interaction.* New York: Academic Press.

Bruner, J. (1977b). *The role of dialogue in language acquisition.* Paper presented at Child's Conception of Language Conference, Max-Planck Institute Project Group in Linguistics.

Bruner, J. (1978a). *Acquiring the uses of language.* Paper presented as Berlyne Memorial Lecture, University of Toronto.

Bruner, J. (1978b). Learning how to do things with words. In J. Bruner & A. Gurton (Eds.), *Wolfson College Lectures 1976: Human Growth and Development.* Oxford: Oxford University Press.

Bruner, J., & Sylva, K. *Acquiring the uses of language.* Manuscript in preparation.

Bryant, P., & Bradley, L. (1980). Why children sometimes write words which they do not read. In U. Firth (Ed.), *Cognitive processes in spelling.* New York: Academic Press.

Bryant, P., Bradley, L., MacLean, M., & Crossland, J. (1989). Nursery rhymes, phonological skills and reading. *Journal of Child Language, 16,* 407–428.

Bullowa, M. (1979a). Infants as conversational partners. In T. Myers (Ed.), *The development of conversation and discourse.* Edinburgh: Edinburgh University Press.

Bullowa, M. (1979b). Introduction: Prelinguistic communication: A field for scientific research. In M. Bullowa (Ed.), *Before speech.* New York: Cambridge University Press.

Burke, S., Pflaum, S., & Knafle, J. (1982, January). The influence of black English on diagnosis of reading in learning disabled and normal readers. *Journal of Learning Disabilities, 15,* 19–22.

Burling, R. (1959). Language development of a Garo- and English-speaking child. *Word, 15,* 45–68.

Burling, R. (1973). *English in Black and White.* New York: Holt, Rinehart & Winston.

Bybee, J., & Slobin, D. (1982). Rules and schemas in the development and use of the English past. *Language, 58,* 265–289.

Calfee, R., Chapman, R., & Venesky, R. (1972). How a child needs to think to learn to read. In L. Gregg (Ed.), *Cognition in learning and memory.* New York: Wiley.

Caplan, F. (1973). *The first twelve months of life.* New York: Grosset & Dunlap.

Caplan, F., & Caplan, T. (1977). *The second twelve months of life.* New York: Bantam Books.

Carey, S. (1978). The child as word learner. In M. Halle, J. Bresnan, & G. Miller (Eds.), *Linguistic theory and psychological reality.* Cambridge: MIT Press.

Carey, S., & Bartlett, E. (1978). Acquiring a single new word. *Papers and Reports on Child Language Development, 15,* 17–29.

Carman, A., Gordon, H., Bental, E., & Harness, B. (1977). Retraining in literal alexia: Substitution of a right hemisphere perceptual strategy for impaired left hemisphere processing. *Bulletin of the Los Angeles Neurological Societies, 42,* 41–50.

Caron, A., Caron, R., Caldwell, R., & Weiss, S. (1973). Infant perception of the structural properties of the face. *Developmental Psychology, 9,* 385–399.

Caron, R., Caron, A., & Meyers, R. (1982). Abstraction of invariant facial expressions in infancy. *Child Development, 53,* 1008–1015.

Carpenter, G., Tecce, J., Strechler, G., & Friedman, S. (1970). Differential visual behavior to human and humanoid faces in early infancy. *Merrill-Palmer Quarterly, 16,* 91–108.

Carr, S., Dabbs, J., & Carr, T. (1975). Mother-infant attachment: The importance of the mother's visual field. *Child Development, 46,* 331–338.

Carrell, P. (1981). Children's understanding of indirect requests: Comparing child and adult comprehension. *Journal of Child Language, 8,* 329–345.

Carrow, E. (1973). *Test of auditory comprehension of language.* Austin, TX: Urban Research Group.

Carter, A. (1975a). The transformation of sensorimotor morphemes into words: A case study of the development of "here" and "there." *Papers and Reports on Child Language Development, 10,* 31–48.

Carter, A. (1975b). The transformation of sensorimotor morphemes into words: A case study of the development of "more" and "mine." *Journal of Child Language, 2,* 233–250.

Case, R. (1978). Intellectual development from birth to adulthood: A neo-Piagetian interpretation. In R. Siegler (Ed.), *Children's thinking: What develops?* Hillsdale, NJ: Erlbaum.

Cavanaugh, J., & Perlmutter, M. (1982). Metamemory: A critical examination. *Child Development, 53,* 11–28.

Cazden, C. (1965). *Environmental assistance to the child's acquisition of grammar.* Unpublished doctoral dissertation, Harvard University.

Cazden, C. (1968). The acquisition of noun and verb inflections. *Child Development, 39,* 433–438.

Cazden, C. (1974). Play and metalinguistic awareness: One dimension of language experience. *The Urban Review, 7,* 28–39.

Chafe, W. (1970). *Meaning and the structure of language.* Chicago: University of Chicago Press.

Chalkley, M. (1982). The emergence of language as a social skill. In S. Kuczaj (Ed.), *Language development: Vol. 2, Language, thought and culture.* Hillsdale, NJ: Erlbaum.

Chall, J. (1983). *Stages of reading development.* New York: McGraw-Hill.

Chapman, R. (1978). Comprehension strategies in children. In J. Kavanaugh & W. Strange (Eds.), *Speech and language in the laboratory school and clinic.* Cambridge: MIT Press.

Chapman, R., & Kohn, L. (1977). Comprehension strategies in two- and three-year-olds: Animate agents or probable events? *Papers and Reports on Child Language Development, 13,* 22–29.

Chapman, R., & Miller, J. (1975). Word order in early two-and three-word utterances: Does production precede comprehension? *Journal of Speech and Hearing Research, 18,* 355–371.

Chapman, R., & Miller, J. (1980). Analyzing language and communication in the child. In R. Schiefelbusch (Ed.), *Nonspeech language and communication.* Baltimore: University Park Press.

Chappell, P., & Sander, L. (1979). Mutual regulation of the neonatal-maternal interactive process: Context for the origins of communication. In M. Bullowa (Ed.), *Before speech.* New York: Cambridge University Press.

Charlesworth, W., & Kreutzer, M. (1973). Facial expressions of infants and children. In P. Ekman (Ed.), *Darwin and facial expression.* New York: Academic Press.

Charney, R. (1979). The comprehension of "here" and "there." *Journal of Child Language, 6,* 69–80.

Charney, R. (1980). Speech roles and the development of personal pronouns. *Journal of Child Language, 7,* 509–528.

Cheng, L. (1987a). *Assessing Asian language performance.* Rockville, MD: Aspen.

Cheng, L. (1987b, June). Cross-cultural and linguistic considerations in working with Asian populations. *Asha, 29,* 33–38.

Cherry, L., (1976). *Interactive strategies in language development: A model of social cognition.* Paper presented to the Conference on Language, Children, and Society.

Cherry, L. & Lewis, M. (1976). Mothers and two-year-olds: A study of sex-differentiated aspects of verbal interaction. *Developmental Psychology, 12,* 278–282.

Cherry-Wilkinson, L., & Dollaghan, C. (1979). Peer communication in first grade reading groups. *Theory Into Practice, 18,* 267–274.

Cheung, D. (_____) *The Tao of learning: Socialization of Chinese American children.* Unpublished doctoral dissertation, Stanford University.

Chi, J., Dooling, E., & Gilles, F. (1977). Left-right asymmetries of the temporal speech areas of the human fetus. *Archives of Neurology, 34,* 346–348.

Chiat, S. (1986). Personal pronouns. In P. Fletcher & M. Garman (Eds.), *Language acquisition* (2nd ed.). New York: Cambridge University Press.

Chomsky, C. (1969). *The acquisition of syntax in children from 5 to 10.* Cambridge: MIT Press.

Chomsky, N. (1957). *Syntactic structures.* The Hague: Mouton.

Chomsky, N. (1959). A review of Skinner's *Verbal Behavior. Language, 35,* 26–58.

Chomsky, N. (1964). Current issues in linguistic theory. In J. Fodor & J. Katz (Eds.), *The structure of language.* Englewood Cliffs, NJ: Prentice-Hall.

Chomsky, N. (1965). *Aspects of the theory of syntax.* Cambridge: MIT Press.

Chomsky, N. (1968). *Language and mind.* New York: Harcourt, Brace & World.

Chomsky, N. (1969). *Deep structure, surface structure, and semantic interpretation.* Bloomington: Indiana University Linguistics Club.

Chomsky, N. (1980). On cognitive structures and their development: A reply to Piaget. In M. Piattelli-Palmarini (Ed.), *Language and learning: The debate between Jean Piaget and Noam Chomsky.* Cambridge: Harvard University Press.

Chomsky, N. (1981). *Lectures on government and binding.* Dordrecht, Holland: Foris.

Chomsky, N., & Halle, M. (1968). *The sound pattern of English.* New York: Harper & Row.

Christie, D., & Schumacher, G. (1975). Developmental trends in the abstraction and recall of relevant vs. irrelevant thematic information from connected verbal material. *Child Development, 46,* 598–602.

Clancy, P. (1985). Acquisition of Japanese. In D. Slobin (Ed.), *The cross-linguistic study of language acquisition.* Hillsdale, NJ: Erlbaum.

Clancy, P. (1989). Form and function in the acquisition of Korean wh- questions. *Journal of Child Language, 16,* 323–347.

Clancy, P., Jacobson, T., & Silva, M. (1976). The acquisition of conjunction: A cross-linguistic study. *Papers and Reports on Child Language Development, 12,* 71–80.

Clark, E. (1971). On the acquisition of the meaning of "before" and "after." *Journal of Verbal Learning and Verbal Behavior, 10,* 266–275.

Clark, E. (1973a). Non-linguistic strategies and the acquisition of word meanings. *Cognition, 2,* 161–182.

Clark, E. (1973b). What's in a word? On the child's acquisition of semantics in his first language. In T. Moore (Ed.), *Cognitive development and the acquisition of language.* New York: Academic Press.

Clark, E. (1974a). Normal states and evaluative viewpoints. *Language, 50,* 316–322.

Clark, E. (1974b). Some aspects of the conceptual basis for first language acquisition. In R. Schiefelbusch & L. Lloyd (Eds.), *Language perspectives—Acquisition, retardation, and intervention.* Baltimore: University Park Press.

Clark, E. (1975). Knowledge, context and strategy in the acquisition of meaning. In D. Dato (Ed.), *Developmental psycholinguistics: Theory and application.* Washington, DC: Georgetown University Press.

Clark, E. (1978a). From gesture to word: On the natural history of deixis in language acquisition. In J. Bruner & A. Garton (Eds.), *Human growth and development.* Oxford: Oxford University Press.

Clark, E. (1978b). Awareness of language: Some evidence from what children say and do. In A. Sinclair, R. Jarvella, & W. Levelt (Eds.), *The child's conception of language.* New York: Springer-Verlag.

Clark, E. (1979). Building a vocabulary: Words for objects, actions, and relations. In P. Fletcher & M. Garman (Eds.), *Language acquisition.* Cambridge: Cambridge University Press.

Clark, E. (1983). Meaning and concepts. In P. Mussen (Ed.), *Handbook of child psychology* (Vol 3). New York: Wiley.

Clark, E. (1985). Acquisition of Romance, with special reference to French. In D. Slobin (Ed.),

The crosslinguistic study of language acquisition. Hillsdale, NJ: Erlbaum.

Clark, E. (1990). On the pragmatics of contrast. *Journal of Child Language, 17,* 417–431.

Clark, E., & Berman, R. (1984). Structure and use in the acquisition of word formation. *Language, 60,* 542–594.

Clark, E., & Garnica, O. (1974). Is he coming or going? On the acquisition of deictic verbs. *Journal of Verbal Learning and Verbal Behavior, 13,* 559–572.

Clark, E., & Hecht, B. (1982). Learning to coin agent and instrument nouns. *Cognition, 12,* 1–24.

Clark, E., & Sengul, C. (1978). Strategies in the acquisition of deixis. *Journal of Child Language, 5,* 457–475.

Clark, H., & Chase, W. (1972). On the process of comparing sentences against pictures. *Cognitive Psychology, 3,* 472–517.

Clark, H., & Clark, E. (1977). *Psychology and language: An introduction to psycholinguistics.* New York: Harcourt Brace Jovanovich.

Clark, R. (1977). What's the use of imitation? *Journal of Child Language, 4,* 341–358.

Clark, R., Hutcheson, S., & van Buren, P. (1974). Comprehension and production in language acquisition. *Journal of Linguistics, 10,* 39–54.

Clifton, R., Graham, F., & Hatton, H. (1968). Newborn heart-rate response and response habituation as a function of stimulus duration. *Journal of Experimental Child Psychology, 6,* 265–278.

Clumeck, H. (1977). Topics in the acquisition of phonology: A case study. *Papers and Reports in Child Language Development, 14,* 37–73.

Coates, J. (1988). The acquisition of the meaning of modality in children aged eight and twelve. *Journal of Child Language, 15,* 425–434.

Cohen, L., & Gelber, E. (1975). Infant visual memory. In L. Cohen & S. Salapatek (Eds.), *Infant perception: From sensation to cognition* (Vol 1). New York: Academic Press.

Cohen, S., & Beckwith, L. (1975). *Maternal language input in infancy.* Paper presented to American Psychological Association.

Coker, P. (1978). Syntactic and semantic factors in the acquisition of "before" and "after." *Journal of Child Language, 5,* 261–277.

Coles, R. (1977). Growing up Chicano. In R. Coles (Ed.), *Eskimos, Chicanos, Indians.* Boston: Little, Brown.

Collins, A., & Loftus, E. (1975). A spreading-activation theory of semantic processing. *Psychological Review, 82,* 407–428.

Collins, A., & Quillian, M. (1969). Retrieval time from semantic memory. *Journal of Verbal Learning and Verbal Behavior, 8,* 240–247.

Collins, A., & Quillian, M. (1970). Does category size affect categorization time? *Journal of Verbal Learning and Verbal Behavior, 9,* 432–438.

Collis, G. (1977). Visual co-orientation and maternal speech. In H. Schaffer (Ed.), *Studies in mother-infant interaction.* New York: Academic Press.

Collis, G. (1979). Describing the structure of social interaction in infancy. In M. Bullowa (Ed.), *Before speech.* New York: Cambridge University Press.

Collis, G., & Schaffer, H. (1975). Synchronization of visual attention in mother-infant pairs. *Journal of Child Psychology and Psychiatry, 16,* 315–321.

Comrie, B. (1976). *Aspects.* Cambridge: Cambridge University Press.

Condon, W. (1979). Neonatal entrainment and enculturation. In M. Bullowa (Ed.), *Before speech.* New York: Cambridge University Press.

Condon, W., & Sanders, L. (1974). Neonate movement is synchronized with adult speech: Interactional participation and language acquisition. *Science, 183,* 99–101.

Conrad, R. (1972). The developmental role of vocalizing in short-term memory. *Journal of Verbal Learning and Verbal Behavior, 11,* 521–533.

Copple, C., & Suci, G. (1974). The comparative ease of processing standard English and Black nonstandard English by lower-class Black children. *Child Development, 45,* 1048–1053.

Cornell, E. (1978). Learning to find things: A reinterpretation of object permanence studies. In L. Siegel & C. Brainerd (Eds.), *Alternatives to Piaget.* New York: Academic Press.

Corrigan, R. (1975). A scalogram analysis of the development of the use and comprehension of "because" in children. *Child Development, 46,* 195–201.

Corrigan, R. (1976). *Patterns of individual communication and cognitive development.* Unpublished doctoral dissertation. University of Denver.

Corrigan, R. (1978a). Language development as related to stage 6 object permanence development. *Journal of Child Language, 5,* 173–189.

Corrigan, R. (1978b). Use of repetition to facilitate spontaneous language acquisition. *Journal of Psycholinguistic Research, 9,* 231–241.

Corsaro, W. (1979). Young children's conception of status and role. *Sociology of Education, 52,* 46–50.

Cotton, E. (1978). Noun-pronoun pleonasm: The role of age and situation. *Journal of Child Language, 5,* 489–499.

Cox, M. (1985). *The child's point of view: Cognitive and linguistic development.* Brighton, Eng.: Harvester Press.

Cox, M. (1989). Children's over-regularization of nouns and verbs. *Journal of Child Language, 16,* 203–206.

Cox, M., & Richardson, J. (1985). How do children describe spatial relationships? *Journal of Child Language, 12,* 611–620.

Craik, F. (1977). Age differences in human memory. In J. Birren & K. Schaie (Eds.), *Handbook of psychology of aging.* New York: Van Nostrand-Reinhold.

Cross, T. (1977). Mother's speech adjustments: The contribution of selected child listener variables. In C. Snow & C. Ferguson (Eds.), *Talking to children: Language input and acquisition.* New York: Cambridge University Press.

Cross, T. (1978). Mothers' speech and its association with rate of linguistic development in young children. In N. Waterson & C. Snow (Eds.), *The development of communication.* New York: Wiley.

Cruttenden, A. (1970). A phonetic study of babbling. *British Journal of Psychology, 61,* 397–408.

Cruttenden, A. (1974). An experiment involving comprehension of intonation in children from 7 to 10. *Journal of Child Language, 1,* 221–231.

Crystal, D. (1980). Neglected grammatical factors in conversational English. In S. Greenbaum, G. Leech, & J. Svartvik (Eds.), *Studies in English linguistics for Randolph Quirk.* London: Longman.

Crystal, D. (1986). Prosodic development. In P. Fletcher & M. Garman (Eds.), *Language acquisition* (2nd ed.). New York: Cambridge University Press.

Culp, R., & Boyd, E. (1975). Visual fixation and the effects of voice quality and content differences in 2-month-old infants. In F. Horowitz (Ed.), *Visual attention, auditory stimulation, and language discrimination in young infants. Monographs of the Society for Research in Child Development, 39.*

Cummins, J., & Das, J. (1977). Cognitive processing and reading difficulties. *Alberta Journal of Educational Research, 23,* 245–255.

Dale, P. (1976). *Language development: Structure and function.* New York: Holt, Rinehart & Winston.

Daniloff, R. (1973). Normal articulation processes. In F. Minifie, T. Hixon, & F. Williams (Eds.), *Normal aspects of speech, hearing, and language.* Englewood Cliffs, NJ: Prentice-Hall.

Daniloff, R., & Moll, K. (1968). Coarticulation of lip rounding. *Journal of Speech and Hearing Research, 11,* 707–721.

Danks, J., & Score, P. (1973). Imagery and deep structure in the prompted recall of passive sentences. *Journal of Verbal Learning and Verbal Behavior, 12,* 114–117.

Das, J. (1984). Simultaneous and successive processing in children with reading disability. *Topics in Language Disorders, 4*(3), 34–47.

Das, J., Kirby, J., & Jarman, R. (1979). *Simultaneous and successive cognitive processes.* New York: Academic Press.

Das, J., Snart, F., & Mulcahy, R. (1982). Reading disability and its relation to information-integration. In J. Das, R. Mulcahy, & A. Wall (Eds.), *Theory and research in learning disabilities.* New York: Plenum Press.

Davis, A. (1972). *English problems of Spanish speakers.* Urbana, IL: National Council of Teachers of English.

Davis, C., & Ball, H. (1989). Effects of age on comprehension of complex sentences in adulthood. *Journal of Speech and Hearing Research, 32,* 143–150.

Day, M. (1975). Developmental trends in visual scanning. In H. Reese (Ed.), *Advances in child development and behavior.* New York: Academic Press.

Dearden, R. (1967). The concept of play. In R. Peters (Ed.), *The concept of education*. London: Routledge & Kegan Paul.

deBoysson-Bardies, B., Halle, P., Sagart, L., & Durand, C. (1989). A crosslinguistic investigation of vowel formants in babbling. *Journal of Child Language, 16,* 1–17.

deBoysson-Bardies, B., Sagart, L., & Durand, C. (1984). Discernible differences in the babbling of infants according to target language. *Journal of Child Language, 11,* 1–15.

Deese, J. (1965). *The structure of associations in language and thought*. Baltimore: Johns Hopkins Press.

DeHart, G., & Maratsos, M. (1984). Children's acquisition of presuppositional usages. In R. Schiefelbusch & J. Pickar (Eds.), *The acquisition of communicative competence*. Baltimore: University Park Press.

DeLemos, C. (1981). Internal processes in the child's construction of language. In W. Deutsch (Ed.), *The child's construction of language*. New York: Academic Press.

Della Corte, M., Benedict, H., & Klein, D. (1983). The relationship of pragmatic dimensions of mothers' speech to the referential-expressive distinction. *Journal of Child Language, 10,* 35–43.

Demuth, K. (1989). Maturation, continuity and the acquisition of Sesotho passive. *Language, 65,* 56–80.

Demuth, K. (1990). Subject, topic and Sesotho passive. *Journal of Child Language, 17,* 67–84.

Dennis, M., Sugar, J., & Whitaker, H. (1982). The acquisition of tag questions. *Child Development, 53,* 1254–1257.

Derwing, B., & Baker, W. (1977). The psychological basis for morphological rules. In J. Macnamara (Ed.), *Language learning and thought*. New York: Academic Press.

Derwing, B., & Baker, W. (1986). Assessing morphological development. In P. Fletcher & M. Garman (Eds.), *Language acquisition* (2nd ed.). New York: Cambridge University Press.

Desor, J., Maller, O., & Andrews, K. (1975). Ingestive responses of human newborns to salty, sour, and bitter stimuli. *Journal of Comparative and Physiological Psychology, 24,* 966–970.

Dever, R. (1978). *Talk: Teaching the American language to kids*. Columbus, OH: Merrill.

de Villiers, J. (1984). Form and force interactions: The development of negatives and questions. In R. Schiefelbusch & J. Pickar (Eds.), *The acquisition of communicative competence*. Baltimore: University Park Press.

de Villiers, J. (1985). Learning how to use verbs: Lexical coding and the influence of the input. *Journal of Child Language, 12,* 587–595.

de Villiers, J., & de Villiers, P. (1973). Development of the use of word order in comprehension. *Journal of Psycholinguistic Research, 2,* 331–341.

de Villiers, J., & de Villiers, P. (1978). *Language acquisition*. Cambridge: Harvard University Press.

de Villiers, J., & de Villiers, P. (1979). *Early language*. Cambridge: Harvard University Press.

de Villiers, J., Tager-Flusberg, H., Hakuta, K., & Cohen, M. (1979). Children's comprehension of relative clauses. *Journal of Psycholinguistic Research, 8,* 499–518.

de Villiers, P. (1982). *Later syntactic development: The contribution of semantics and pragmatics*. Paper presented at the New York State Speech-Language-Hearing Association convention.

Devore, I., & Konner, M. (1974). Infancy in a hunter-gatherer life: An ethological perspective. In N. White (Ed.), *Ethology and psychiatry*. Toronto: University of Toronto Press.

deVries, J., & Vallee, F. (1980). *Language use in Canada*. Ottawa: Statistics Canada.

Dodd, B. (1972). Effects of social and vocal stimulation of infant babbling. *Developmental Psychology, 7,* 80–83.

Dodd, B. (1975). Children's understanding of their own phonological forms. *Quarterly Journal of Experimental Psychology, 27,* 165–172.

D'Odorico, L., & Franco, F. (1985). The determinants of baby talk: Relationship to context. *Journal of Child Language, 12,* 567–586.

Doehring, D. (1976). Acquisition of rapid reading responses. *Monographs of the Society for Research in Child Development, 41*(2).

Dollaghan, C. (1985). Child meets word: "Fast mapping" in preschool children. *Journal of Speech and Hearing Research, 28,* 449–454.

Donaldson, M., & McGarrigle, J. (1974). Some clues to the nature of semantic development. *Journal of Child Language, 1,* 185–194.

Donaldson, M., & Wales, R. (1970). On the acquisition of some relational terms. In J. Hayes (Ed.), *Cognition and the development of language*. New York: Wiley.

Dore, J. (1974). A pragmatic description of early language development. *Journal of Psycholinguistic Research, 3*, 343–350.

Dore, J. (1975). Holophrases, speech acts, and language universals. *Journal of Child Language, 2*, 21–40.

Dore, J. (1976). Children's illocutionary acts. In R. Freedle (Ed.), *Discourse production and comprehension* (Vol. 1). Hillsdale, NJ: Erlbaum.

Dore, J. (1977). "Oh them sheriff": A pragmatic analysis of children's responses to questions. In S. Ervin-Tripp & C. Mitchell-Kernan (Eds.), *Child discourse*. New York: Academic Press.

Dore, J. (1986). The development of conversational competence. In R. Schiefelbusch (Ed.), *Language competence: Assessment and intervention*. San Diego: College-Hill Press.

Dore, J., Franklin, M., Miller, R., & Ramer, A. (1976). Transitional phenomena in early language acquisition. *Journal of Child Language, 3*, 13–28.

Downey, R., & Hakes, D. (1968). Some psychological effects of violating linguistic rules. *Journal of Verbal Learning and Verbal Behavior, 7*, 158–161.

Downing, J., & Oliver, P. (1973/74). The child's conception of a word. *Reading Research Quarterly, 9*, 568–582.

Doyle, A., Champagne, M., & Segalowitz, N. (1978). Some issues in the assessment of linguistic consequences of early bilingualism. In M. Paradis (Ed.), *Aspects of bilingualism*. Columbia, SC: Hornbean Press.

Dreyfus-Brisac, C. (1966). The bioelectric development of the central nervous system during early life. In F. Falkner (Ed.), *Human development*. Philadelphia: Saunders.

Dromi, E., & Berman, R. (1982). A morphemic measure of early language development from Modern Hebrew. *Journal of Child Language, 9*, 403–424.

Duchan, J. (1986). Learning to describe events. *Topics in Language Disorders, 6*(4), 27–36.

Dulay, H., & Burt, M. (1974). Errors and strategies in child second language acquisition. *TESOL Quarterly, 8*, 129–138.

Dulay, H., Hernández-Chávez, E., & Burt, M. (1978). The process of becoming bilingual. In S. Singh & J. Lynch (Eds.), *Diagnostic procedures in hearing, language, and speech*. Baltimore: University Park Press.

Dunn, L. (1959). *Peabody Picture Vocabulary Test*. Minneapolis: American Guidance Service.

Durkin, K. (1978). *Spatial and temporal prepositions in the language of young school children*. Unpublished doctoral dissertation, Cambridge University.

Dyson, A. (1983). *Early writing as drawing: The developmental gap between speaking and writing*. Paper presented at the American Educational Research Association convention.

Edelsky, C. (1977). Acquisition of an aspect of communicative competence: Learning what it means to talk like a baby. In S. Ervin & C. Mitchell-Kernan (Eds.), *Child discourse*. New York: Academic Press.

Edmonds, M. (1976). New directions in theories of language acquisition. *Harvard Educational Review, 46*, 175–198.

Edwards, A. (1976). *Language in culture and class*. London: Heinemann Educational Books.

Edwards, M. (1974). Perception and production in child phonology: The testing of four hypotheses. *Journal of Child Language, 1*, 205–219.

Edwards, M., & Garnica, O. (1973). *Patterns of variation in the repetition of utterances by young children*. Unpublished paper, Stanford University.

Ehrenreich, B. (1981). The politics of talking in couples. *Ms, 5*, 43–45, 86–89.

Eibl-Eibesfeldt, I. (1971). *Love and hate*. New York: Holt, Rinehart & Winston.

Eilers, R., Oller, K., & Ellington, J. (1974). The acquisition of word meaning for dimensional adjectives: The long and short of it. *Journal of Child Language, 1*, 195–204.

Eimas, P. (1974). Linguistic processing of speech by young infants. In R. Schiefelbusch & L. Lloyd (Eds.), *Language perspectives—Acquisition, retardation and intervention*. Baltimore: University Park Press.

Eimas, P., Siqueland, E., Jusczyk, P., & Vigorito, J. (1971). Speech perception in infants. *Science, 171*, 303–306.

Eisenberg, A. (1982). *Language acquisition in cultural perspective: Talk in three Mexicano homes.* Unpublished doctoral dissertation, University of California, Berkeley.

Eisenberg, R. (1976). *Auditory competence in early life: The roots of communicative behavior.* Baltimore: University Park Press.

Elkind, D. (1970). *Children and adolescents.* New York: Oxford University Press.

Elliot, A. (1981). *Child language.* New York: Cambridge University Press.

Emerson, H. (1979). Children's comprehension of "because" in reversible and nonreversible sentences. *Journal of Child Language, 6,* 279–300.

Emerson, H., & Gekoski, W. (1976). Interactive and categorical grouping strategies and the syntagmatic-paradigmatic shift. *Child Development, 47,* 1116–1125.

Emslie, H., & Stevenson, R. (1981). Preschool children's use of the articles in definite and indefinite referring expressions. *Journal of Child Language, 8,* 313–328.

Erbaugh, M. (1980, December). *Acquisition of Mandarin syntax: 'Less' grammar isn't easier.* Paper presented at the meeting of the Linguistic Society of America, San Antonio, TX.

Erbaugh, M. (1982). *Coming to order: Natural selection and the origin of syntax in the Mandarin-speaking child.* Unpublished doctoral dissertation. University of California, Berkeley.

Erreich, A. (1984). Learning how to ask: Patterns of inversion in yes/no and wh- questions. *Journal of Child Language, 11,* 579–592.

Ervin, S. (1961). Changes with age in the verbal determinants of word-association. *American Journal of Psychology, 74,* 361–372.

Ervin, S. (1963). Correlates of associative frequency. *Journal of Verbal Learning and Verbal Behavior, 1,* 422–431.

Ervin, S. (1964). Imitation and structural change in children's language. In E. Lenneberg (Ed.), *New directions in the study of language.* Cambridge: MIT Press.

Ervin-Tripp, S. (1970). Discourse agreement: How children answer questions. In J. Hayes (Ed.), *Cognition and the development of language.* New York: Wiley.

Ervin-Tripp, S. (1971). Social backgrounds and verbal skills. In R. Huxley & E. Ingram (Eds.), *Language acquisition models and methods.* New York: Academic Press.

Ervin-Tripp, S. (1973a). *Language acquisition and communicative choice.* Stanford: Stanford University Press.

Ervin-Tripp, S. (1973b). Some strategies for the first two years. In T. Moore (Ed.), *Cognitive development and the acquisition of language.* New York: Academic Press.

Ervin-Tripp, S. (1977a). Wait for me roller-skate. In S. Ervin-Tripp & E. Mitchel-Kernan (Eds.), *Child discourse.* New York: Academic Press.

Ervin-Tripp, S. (1977b). From conversation to syntax. *Papers and Reports in Child Language Development, 13,* K1–21.

Ervin-Tripp, S. (1979). Children's verbal turn-taking. In E. Ochs & B. Schieffelin (Eds.), *Developmental pragmatics.* New York: Academic Press.

Ervin-Tripp, S. (1980). Lecture. University of Minnesota. May 14, 1980.

Ervin-Tripp, S., & Gordon, D. (1986). The development of requests. In R. Schiefelbusch (Ed.), *Language competence: Assessment and intervention.* San Diego: College-Hill Press.

Ervin-Tripp, S., O'Connor, M., Rosenberg, J., & O'Barr, A. W. (1984). Language and power in the family. In C. Kramerae & M. Schulz (Eds.), *Language and power* (4th ed.). Beverly Hills, CA: Sage.

Fagan, J. (1973). Infants' delayed recognition memory and forgetting. *Journal of Experimental Child Psychology, 16,* 424–450.

Fantz, R. (1963). Pattern vision in newborn infants. *Science, 140,* 296–297.

Fantz, R. (1964). Visual experience in infants: Decreased attention to familiar patterns relative to novel ones. *Science, 146,* 668–670.

Farb, P. (1973). *Word play: What happens when people talk.* New York: Knopf.

Farrar, M. (1990). Discourse and the acquisition of grammatical morphemes. *Journal of Child Language, 17,* 607–624.

Farwell, C. (1976). *Some ways to learn about fricatives.* Paper presented to the 8th Child Language Research Forum, Stanford University.

Fasold, R., & Wolfram, W. (1970). Some linguistic features of Negro dialect. In R. Fasold & R. Shuy (Eds.), *Teaching standard English in the inner city.* Washington, DC: Center for Applied Linguistics.

Feagans, L. (1980). Children's understanding of some temporal terms denoting order, duration, and simultaneity. *Journal of Psycholinguistic Research, 9,* 41–57.

Fenson, L., & Ramsey, D. (1980). Decentration and integration of the child's play in the second year. *Child Development, 51,* 171–178.

Ferguson, C. (1964). Baby talk in six languages. In J. Gumperz & D. Hymes (Eds.), *The ethnography of communication.* Menasha, WI: American Anthropology Association.

Ferguson, C. (1978). Learning to pronounce: The earliest stages of phonological development in the child. In F. Minifie & L. Lloyd (Eds.), *Communicative and cognitive abilities—Early behavioral assessment.* Baltimore: University Park Press.

Ferguson, C. (1979). Phonology as an individual access system: Some data from language acquisitions. In C. Fillmore, D. Kemper, & S.-Y. Wang (Eds.), *Individual differences in language ability and language behavior.* New York: Academic Press.

Ferguson, C., & Farwell, C. (1975). Words and sounds in early language acquisition: English initial consonants in the first fifty words. *Language, 51,* 419–439.

Ferguson, C., & Garnica, O. (1975). Theories of phonological development. In E. Lenneberg & E. Lenneberg (Eds.), *Foundations of language development* (Vol. 2). New York: Academic Press.

Ferguson, C., Peizer, D., & Weeks, T. (1973). Model-and-replica phonological grammar of a child's first words. *Lingua, 31,* 35–39.

Fernald, A. (1981). *Four-month-olds prefer to listen to "motherese."* Paper presented at a meeting of the Society for Research in Child Development.

Fernald, A., & Kuhl, P. (1981). *Fundamental frequency as an acoustic determinant of infant preference for motherese.* Paper presented at a meeting of the Society for Research in Child Development.

Fernald, A., Taeschner, T., Dunn, J., Papousek, M., deBoysson-Bardies, B., & Fukui, I. (1989). A cross-language study of prosody modifications in mothers' and fathers' speech to preverbal infants. *Journal of Child Language, 16,* 477–501.

Ferreiro, E. (1984). The underlying logic of literacy development. In H. Goelman, A. Oberg, & F. Smith (Eds.), *Awakening to literacy.* Exeter, NH: Heinemann.

Ferreiro, E., & Sinclair, H. (1971). Temporal relationships in language. *International Journal of Psychology, 6,* 39–47.

Ferreiro, E., & Teberosky, A. (1982). *Literacy before schooling.* Exeter, NH: Heinemann.

Ferrier, L. (1978). Some observations in error in context. In N. Waterson & C. Snow (Eds.), *The development of language.* New York: Wiley.

Fillmore, C. (1968). The case for case. In E. Bach & R. Harmas (Eds.), *Universals in linguistic theory.* New York: Holt, Rinehart & Winston.

Fillmore, L. (1976). *The second time around: Cognitive and social strategies in second-language acquisition.* Unpublished doctoral dissertation, Stanford University.

Flavell, J. (1970). Concept development. In L. Mussen (Ed.), *Handbook of child psychology.* New York: Wiley.

Flavell, J. (1977). *Cognitive development.* Englewood Cliffs, NJ: Prentice-Hall.

Flavell, J. (1981). Cognitive monitoring. In P. Dickson (Ed.), *Children's oral communication skills.* New York: Academic Press.

Flavell, J. (1982). On cognitive development. *Child Development, 53,* 1–10.

Flavell, J., & Wellman, H. (1977). Metamemory. In R. Kail & J. Hagen (Eds.), *Perspectives on the development of memory and cognition.* Hillsdale, NJ: Erlbaum.

Fodor, J., Bever, T., & Garrett, M. (1974). *The psychology of language.* New York: McGraw-Hill.

Fodor, J., Garrett, M., & Bever, T. (1968). Some syntactic determinants of sentential complexity II: Verb structure. *Perception and Psychophysics, 3,* 453–461.

Fogel, A. (1977). Tempo organization in mother-infant face to face interaction. In H. Schaffer (Ed.), *Studies on mother-infant interaction.* New York: Academic Press.

Fogel, A., Toda, S., & Kawai, M. (1988). Mother–infant face-to-face interaction in Japan and the United States: A laboratory comparison using 3-month-old infants. *Developmental Psychology, 24,* 398–406.

Folger, J., & Chapman, R. (1978). A pragmatic analysis of spontaneous imitations. *Journal of Child Language, 5,* 25–38.

Folger, M., & Leonard, L. (1978). Language and sensorimotor development during the early period of referential speech. *Journal of Speech and Hearing Research, 21,* 519–527.

Foss, D., & Hake, D. (1978). *Psycholinguistics: An introduction to the psychology of language.* Englewood Cliffs: NJ: Prentice-Hall.

Foster, S. (1981). The emergence of topic type in children under 2; 6: A chicken-and-egg problem. *Proceedings and Reports in Child Language Development, 20,* 52–60.

Foster, S. (1986). Learning topic management in the preschool years. *Journal of Child Language, 13,* 231–250.

Foulke, E., & Sticht, T. (1969). Review of research of the intelligibility and comprehension of accelerated speech. *Psychological Bulletin, 72,* 50–62.

Fourcin, A. (1978). Acoustic patterns and speech acquisition. In N. Waterson & C. Snow (Eds.), *The development of communication.* New York: Wiley.

Fowles, L., & Glanz, M. (1977). Competence and talent in verbal riddle comprehension. *Journal of Child Language, 4,* 433–452.

Fox, B., & Routh, D. (1975). Analyzing spoken language into words, syllables, and phonemes: A developmental study. *Journal of Psycholinguistic Research, 4,* 331–342.

Fox, B., & Routh, D. (1976). Phonemic analysis and synthesis as word-attack skills. *Journal of Educational Psychology, 68,* 70–74.

Francis, H. (1972). Toward an explanation of the syntagmatic-paradigmatic shift. *Child Development, 43,* 949–958.

Fraser, B. (1974). *The verb-particle combination in English.* Tokyo: Taishukan.

Frazer, C., Bellugi, U., & Brown, R. (1963). Control of grammar in imitation, comprehension and production. *Journal of Verbal Learning and Verbal Behavior, 2,* 121–135.

Frazer, C., & Roberts, N. (1975). Mothers' speech to children of four different ages. *Journal of Psycholinguistic Research, 4,* 9–16.

Freedle, R., & Lewis, M. (1977). Prelinguistic conversations. In M. Lewis & L. Rosenblum (Eds.), *Interaction, conversation, and the development of language.* New York: Wiley.

Freedman, D. (1964). Smiling in blind infants and the issue of innate vs. acquired. *Journal of Child Psychology and Psychiatry, 5,* 171–184.

Freedman, D. (1971). Behavioral assessment in infancy. In G. Stoelinga & J. Van Der Werff Ten Bosch (Eds.), *Normal and abnormal development of brain and behavior.* Leiden, Neth.: Leiden University Press.

Fremgen, A., & Fay, D. (1980). Overextensions in production and comprehension: A methodological clarification. *Journal of Child Language, 7,* 205–211.

French, A. (1989). The systematic acquisition of word forms by a child during the first-fifty-word-stage. *Journal of Child Language, 16,* 69–90.

French, L., & Brown, A. (1977). Comprehension of "before" and "after" in logical and arbitrary sequences. *Journal of Child Language, 4,* 247–256.

French, N., Carter, C., & Koenig, W. (1930). The words and sounds of telephone conversations. *Bell System Technical Journal, 9,* 290–324.

Frentz, T. (1971). Children's comprehension of standard and Negro nonstandard English sentences. *Speech Monographs, 38,* 10–16.

Friedlander, B. (1970). Receptive language development in infancy: Issues and problems. *Merrill-Palmer Quarterly, 16,* 7–51.

Frith, V. (1985). Beneath the surface of developmental dyslexia. In K. Patterson, J. Marshall, & M. Coltheart (Eds.), *Surface dyslexia: Neuropsychological and cognitive studies of phonological reading.* London: Erlbaum.

Fullard, W., & Reiling, A. (1976). An investigation of Lorenz's "Babyness." *Child Development, 47,* 1191–1193.

Furrow, D. (1984). Young children's use of prosody. *Journal of Child Language, 11,* 203–213.

Furrow, D., & Nelson, K. (1984). Environmental correlates of individual differences in language acquisition. *Journal of Child Language, 11,* 523–534.

Furrow, D., Nelson, K. & Benedict, H. (1979). Mothers' speech to children and syntactic development: Some simple relationships. *Journal of Child Language, 6,* 423–442.

Furth, H. (1966). *Thinking without language.* New York: Free Press.

Furth, H. (1971). Linguistic deficiency and thinking: Research with deaf subjects, 1964–1969. *Psychological Bulletin, 75,* 58–72.

Gainotti, G., Caltagirone, C., Miceli, G., & Masullo, C. (1981). Selective semantic-lexical impairment to language comprehension in right brain-damaged patients. *Brain and Language, 13,* 201–211.

Gale, D., Liebergott, J., & Griffin, S. (1981). *Getting it: Children's requests for clarification.* Paper presented at the American Speech-Language-Hearing Association Convention.

Gallagher, T. (1977). Revision behaviors in the speech of normal children developing language. *Journal of Speech and Hearing Research, 20,* 303–318.

Gallagher, T. (1981). Contingent query sequences within adult-child discourse. *Journal of Child Language, 8,* 51–62.

Galligan, R. (1987). Intonation with single words: Purposive and grammatical use. *Journal of Child Language, 14,* 1–21.

Garcia-Zamor, M. (1973). *Child awareness of sex-role distinctions in language use.* Paper presented at the Linguistic Society of America meeting.

Gardiner, M., & Walter, D. (1976). Evidence of hemispheric specialization from infant EEG. In S. Harnad, R. Doty, L. Goldstein, J. Jaynes, & G. Krauthmer (Eds.), *Lateralization in the nervous system.* New York: Academic Press.

Gardner, B., & Gardner, R. (1969). Teaching sign language to a chimpanzee. *Science, 165,* 664–672.

Gardner, B., & Gardner, R. (1971). Two way communication with a chimpanzee. In A. Schrier & F. Stollnitz (Eds.), *Behavior of nonhuman primates* (Vol 4). New York: Academic Press.

Gardner, H. (1974). Metaphors and modalities: How children project polar adjectives onto diverse domains. *Child Development, 45,* 84–91.

Gardner, H., Kircher, M., Winner, E., & Perkins, D. (1975). Children's metaphoric productions and preferences. *Journal of Child Language, 2,* 125–141.

Gardner, H., & Winner, E. (1979, May). The child is father to the metaphor. *Psychology Today,* 81–91.

Gardner, R., & Gardner, B. (1975). Early signs of language in child and chimpanzee. *Science, 187,* 752–753.

Gardner, R., Robey, B., & Smith, P. (1985). Asian Americans: Growth, change, and diversity. *Population Bulletin, 40*(4).

Garnica, O. (1973). The development of phonemic speech perception. In T. Moore (Ed.), *Cognition and the acquisition of language.* New York: Academic Press.

Garnica, O. (1977). Some prosodic and paralinguistic features of speech to young children. In C. Snow & C. Ferguson (Eds.), *Talking to children: Language input and acquisition.* New York: Cambridge University Press.

Garvey, C. (1975). Requests and responses in children's speech. *Journal of Child Language, 2,* 41–63.

Garvey, C. (1977). The contingent query. A dependent act of communication. In M. Lewis & L. Rosenblum (Eds.), *Interaction, conversation, and the development of language.* New York: Wiley.

Garvey, C., & Hogan, R. (1973). Social speech and social interaction: Egocentrism revisited. *Child Development, 44,* 562–568.

Gathercole, V. (1985). "Me has too much hard questions": The acquisition of the linguistic mass-count distinction in *much* and *many. Journal of Child Language, 12,* 395–415.

Gathercole, V. (1989). Contrast: A semantic constraint? *Journal of Child Language, 16,* 685–702.

Gearhart, M. (1978). *Social planning: Role play in a novel situation.* Paper presented at a Society for Research in Child Development meeting.

Gelman, R., & Shatz, M. (1977). Appropriate speech adjustments: The operation of conversational constraints on talk to 2-year-olds. In M. Lewis & L. Rosenblum (Eds.), *Interaction, conversation, and the development of language.* New York: Academic Press.

Genesee, F. (1978). Is there an optimal age for starting second language instruction? *McGill Journal of Education, 13*, 145–154.

Genesee, F. (1989). Early bilingual development: One language or two? *Journal of Child Language, 16*, 161–179.

Gentner, D. (1977). Children's performance on a spatial analogies task. *Child Development, 48*, 1034–1039.

Gentner, D. (1982). Why nouns are learned before verbs: Linguistic relativity versus natural partitioning. In S. Kuczaj (Ed.), *Language development: Vol 2. Language, thought, and culture.* Hillsdale, NJ: Erlbaum.

Geschwind, N. (1974). Selected papers on language and the brain. In R. Cohen & M. Wartofsky (Eds.), *Boston studies in the philosophy of science* (Vol 16). Dordrecht, Holland: Reidel.

Geschwind, N. (1979). Specializations of the human brain. *Scientific American, 241*(3), 180–199.

Geschwind, N., & Galaburda, A. (1985). Cerebral lateralization, biological mechanisms, associations and pathology: I. A hypothesis and a program for research. *Archives of Neurology, 42*, 428–459.

Gibbs, R. (1987). Linguistic factors in children's understanding of idioms. *Journal of Child Language, 14*, 569–586.

Gibson, E., & Levin, H. (1975). *The psychology of reading.* Cambridge: MIT Press.

Gillis, M., & Weber, R. (1976). The emergence of sentence modalities in the English of Japanese-speaking children. *Language Learning, 26*, 77–94.

Gilmore, L., Suci, G., & Chan, S. (1974). *Heart rate deceleration as a function of viewing complex visual events in 18-month-old infants.* Paper presented at a meeting of the American Psychological Association.

Ginsberg, G., & Kilbourne, B. (1988). Emergence of vocal alternation in mother–infant interchanges. *Journal of Child Language, 15*, 221–235.

Glanzer, D., & Dodd, D. (1975). *Developmental changes in the language spoken to children.* Paper presented at the biennial meeting of the Society for Research in Child Development.

Glass, A. (1983). The comprehension of idioms. *Journal of Psycholinguistics Research, 12*, 429–442.

Gleason, J. (1975). Fathers and other strangers: Men's speech to children. In D. Dato (Ed.), *Developmental psycholinguistics: Theory and application.* Washington, DC: Georgetown University Press.

Gleitman, L., & Gleitman, H. (1970). *Phrase and paraphrase: Some innovative users of language.* New York: Norton.

Gleitman, L., Gleitman, H., & Shipley, E. (1972). The emergence of the child as grammarian. *Cognition, 1*, 137–164.

Gleitman, L., Newport, E., & Gleitman, H. (1984). The current status of the motherese hypothesis. *Journal of Child Language, 11*, 43–79.

Gleitman, L., & Wanner, E. (1982). Language acquisition: The state of the state of the art. In E. Wanner and L. Gleitman (Eds.), *Language acquisition: The state of the art.* Cambridge: Cambridge University Press.

Glucksberg, S., Krauss, R., & Weisberg, R. (1966). Referential communication in nursery school children: Method and some preliminary findings. *Journal of Experimental Child Psychology, 3*, 333–342.

Goldfield, B., & Reznick, J. (1990). Early lexical acquisitions: Rate, content, and the vocabulary spurt. *Journal of Child Language, 17*, 171–183.

Goldfield, B., and Snow, C. (1985). Individual differences in language acquisition. In J. Berko Gleason (Ed.), *The development of language.* Columbus, OH: Merrill.

Goldin-Meadow, S., Seligman, M., & Gelman, R. (1976). Language in the two-year-old. *Cognition, 4*, 189–202.

Golinkoff, R. (1975). Semantic development in infants: The concept of agent and recipient. *Merrill-Palmer Quarterly, 21*, 181–193.

Golinkoff, R., & Kerr, L. (1978). Infants' perceptions of semantically defined action role changes in filmed events. *Merrill-Palmer Quarterly, 24*, 53–61.

Golinkoff, R., & Markessini, J. (1980). "Mommy sock": The child's understanding of possession as expressed in two-noun phrases. *Journal of Child Language, 7*, 119–136.

Goodenough, D., & Weiner, S. (1978). The role of conversational passing moves in the management of topical transitions. *Discourse Processes, 1*, 395–404.

Goodluck, H. (1986). Language acquisition and linguistic theory. In P. Fletcher & M. Garman (Eds.), *Language acquisition* (2nd ed.). New York: Cambridge University Press.

Goodman, K. (1976). Behind the eye: What happens in reading. In H. Singer & R. Ruddell (Eds.), *Theoretical models and processes of reading* (2nd ed.). Newark, DE: International Reading Association.

Goodman, Y. (1986). Children coming to know literacy. In W. Teale & E. Sulzby (Eds.), *Emergent literacy.* Norwood, NJ: Ablex.

Goossens, L. (1981). *On the development of the modals and of the epistemic function in English.* Paper presented at the Fifth International Conference on Historical Linguistics, Galway, Ireland.

Gopnik, A. (1982). Words and plans: Early language and the development of intelligent action. *Journal of Child Language, 9,* 308–318.

Gopnik, A., & Meltzoff, A. (1984). Semantic and cognitive development in 15- to 21-month-old children. *Journal of Child Development, 11,* 495–513.

Gopnik, A., & Meltzoff, A. (1986). Relations between semantic and cognitive development in the one-word stage: The specificity hypothesis. *Child Development, 57,* 1040–1053.

Gordon, D., & Ervin-Tripp, S. (1984). The structure of children's requests. In R. Schiefelbusch & J. Pickar (Eds.), *The acquisition of communicative competence.* Baltimore: University Park Press.

Gordon, P. (1982). *The acquisition of syntactic categories: The case of the count/mass distinction.* Unpublished doctoral dissertation. Massachusetts Institute of Technology.

Gordon, P. (1988). Count/mass category acquisition: Distributional distinctions in children's speech. *Journal of Child Language, 15,* 109–128.

Gorrell, P., Crain, S., & Fodor, J. (1989). Contextual information and temporal terms. *Journal of Child Language, 16,* 623–632.

Gourley, J., Benedict, S., Gundersheim, S., & McClellan, J. (1983). *Learning about literacy from children: An ethnographic study in a kindergarten classroom.* Paper presented at the American Educational Research Association convention.

Grace, J., & Suci, G. (1985). Attentional priority of the agent in the acquisition of word reference. *Journal of Child Language, 12,* 1–12.

Graves, D. (1979). What children show us about revision. *Journal of Language Arts, 56,* 312–319.

Greenberg, J., & Kuczaj, S. (1982). Towards a theory of substantive word-meaning acquisition. In S. Kuczaj (Ed.), *Language development: Vol. 1. Syntax and semantics.* Hillsdale, NJ: Erlbaum.

Greene, J. (1972). *Psycholinguistics: Chomsky and psychology.* Baltimore, Penguin Books.

Greenfield, P. (1978). Informativeness, presupposition, and semantic choice in single-word utterances. In N. Waterson & C. Snow (Eds.), *The development of communication.* New York: Wiley.

Greenfield, P., & Smith, J. (1976). *The structure of communication in early language development.* New York: Academic Press.

Greenlee, M. (1974). Interacting processes in the child's acquisition of stop-liquid clusters. *Papers and Reports on Child Language Development, 7,* 85–100.

Greenman, G. (1963). Visual behavior of newborn infants. In A. Solnit & S. Provence (Eds.), *Modern perspectives in child development.* New York: Hallmark.

Greenwald, C., & Leonard, L. (1979). Communicative and sensorimotor development in Down's syndrome children. *American Journal of Mental Deficiency, 84,* 296–303.

Greif, E., & Berko Gleason, J. (1980). Hi, thanks, and goodbye: Some more routine information. *Language and Society, 9,* 159–166.

Grice, H. (1975). Logic and conversation. In D. Davidson & G. Harmon (Eds.), *The logic of grammar.* Encina, CA: Dickenson Press.

Griffiths, P. (1974). *"That there" deixis: 1. That.* Unpublished paper, University of York.

Griffiths, P. (1986). Early vocabulary. In P. Fletcher & M. Garman (Eds.), *Language acquisition* (2nd ed.). New York: Cambridge University Press.

Griffiths, P., & Atkinson, M. (1978). A "door" to verbs. In N. Waterson & C. Snow (Eds.). *The development of communication.* New York: Wiley.

Grimm, H. (1975). *Analysis of short-term dialogues in 5–7 year olds: Encoding of intentions and modifications of speech acts as a function of negative feedback loops.* Paper presented at the Third International Child Language Symposium.

Grosjean, F. (1982). *Life with two languages.* Cambridge: Harvard University Press.

Gruber, J. (1967). Topicalization of child language. *Foundations of Language, 3,* 37–65.

Grunwell, P. (1981). The development of phonology. *First Language, 2,* 161–191.

Guerleu, D., & Renard, K. (1981). Les perceptions auditives du foetus humain. *Médecine et Hygiène, 39,* 2102–2110.

Guess, D., Sailor, W., & Baer, D. (1978). Children with limited language. In R. Schiefelbusch (Ed.), *Language intervention strategies.* Baltimore: University Park Press.

Guilford, J. (1967). *The nature of human intelligence.* New York: McGraw-Hill.

Guillaume, P. (1970). The emergence of the sentence. In A. Blumenthal (Ed.), *Language and psychology: Historical aspects of psycholinguistics.* New York: Wiley.

Gundloch, R. (1981). On the nature and development of children's writing. In C. Frederiksen & J. Dominic (Eds.), *Writing: The nature, development, and teaching of written communication* (Vol. 2). Hillsdale, NJ: Erlbaum.

Haaf, R., & Bell, R. (1967). A facial dimension in visual discrimination by human infants. *Child Development, 38,* 893–899.

Haas, A. (1979). The acquisition of genderlect. *Annals of the New York Academy of Sciences, 327,* 101–113.

Haas, A., & Owens, R. (1985). *Preschoolers' pronoun strategies: You and me make us.* Paper presented at the American Speech-Language-Hearing Association annual convention.

Haith, M. (1976). *Organization of visual behavior at birth.* Paper presented at the 22nd International Congress of Psychology.

Hakes, D. (1980). *The development of metalinguistic abilities in children.* Berlin: Springer-Verlag.

Hakes, D. (1982). The development of metalinguistic abilities: What develops? In S. Kuczaj (Ed.), *Language development: Vol. 2. Language, thought and culture.* Hillsdale, NJ: Erlbaum.

Hakuta, K. (1979). *Comprehension and production of simple and complex sentences by Japanese children.* Unpublished doctoral dissertation, Harvard University.

Hakuta, K., de Villiers, J., & Tager-Flusberg, H. (1982). Sentence coordination in Japanese and English. *Journal of Child Language, 9,* 193–207.

Halliday, M. (1975a). Learning how to mean. In E. Lenneberg & E. Lenneberg (Eds.), *Foundations of language development: A multidisciplinary approach.* New York: Academic Press.

Halliday, M. (1975b). *Learning how to mean: Explorations in the development of language.* New York: Arnold.

Halliday, M. (1979). One child's protolanguage. In M. Bullowa (Ed.), *Before speech.* New York: Cambridge University Press.

Halliday, M., & Hasan, R. (1976). *Cohesion in English.* London: Langman.

Handscombe, R. (1967). *The written language of eleven- and twelve-year-old children.* London: The Nuffield Foundation.

Harding, C., & Golinkoff, R. (1978). The origins of intentional vocalizations in prelinguistic infants. *Child Development, 49,* 33–40.

Harkness, S. (1977). Aspects of social environment and first language acquisition in rural Africa. In C. Snow & C. Ferguson (Eds.), *Talking to children.* New York: Cambridge University Press.

Harpin, W. (1976). *The second 'R'.* London: George Allen & Unwin.

Harris, M., Barrett, M., Jones, D., & Brooks, S. (1988). Linguistic input and early word meanings. *Journal of Child Language, 15,* 77–94.

Harris, P., Kruithof, A., Terwogt, M., & Visser, T. (1981). Children's detection and awareness of textual anomaly. *Journal of Exceptional Child Psychology, 31,* 212–230.

Harwood, F. (1959). Quantitative study of the speech of Australian children. *Language and Speech, 2,* 237–271.

Hatch, E. (1971). The young child's comprehension of time connectives. *Child Development, 42,* 2111–2113.

Haugan, G., & McIntire, R. (1972). Comparisons of vocal imitation, tactile stimulation and foods as reinforcers in infant vocalizations. *Developmental Psychology, 6*, 201–209.

Haugen, E. (1956). *Bilingualism in the Americas: A bibliography and research guide.* Montgomery: University of Alabama Press.

Haviland, S., & Clark, E. (1974). "This man's father is my father's son": A study of the acquisition of English kin terms. *Journal of Child Language, 1*, 23–47.

Haynes, H., White, B., & Held, R. (1965). Visual accommodation in human infants. *Science, 148*, 528–530.

Heath, S. (1983). *Ways with words: Language, life and work in communities and classrooms.* Cambridge: Cambridge University Press.

Heath, S. (1986a). Separating "things of the imagination" from life: Learning to read and write. In W. Teale & E. Sulzby (Eds.), *Emergent literacy.* Norwood, NJ: Ablex.

Heath, S. (1986b). Taking a cross-cultural look at narratives. *Topics in Language Disorders, 7*(1), 84–94.

Heras, I., & Nelson, K. (1972). Retention of semantic, syntactic, and language information by young bilingual children. *Psychonomic Science, 29*, 391–392.

Heringer, J. (1976). Idioms and lexicalization in English. In J. Kimball (Ed.), *Syntax and semantics: The grammar of causative constructions* (Vol. 9). New York: Academic Press.

Hernández-Chávez, E. (1972). *Early code separation in the second language speech of Spanish-speaking children.* Paper presented at Stanford Child Language Research Forum.

Hernández-Chávez, E. (1977a). *The acquisition of grammatical structures by a Mexican American child learning English.* Unpublished doctoral dissertation, University of California at Berkeley.

Hernández-Chávez, E. (1977b). The development of semantic relations in child second language acquisition. In M. Burt, H. Dulay, & M. Finnocchiaro (Eds.), *Viewpoints on English as a second language.* New York: Regents.

Hickman, M. (1986). Psychosocial aspects of language acquisition. In P. Fletcher & M. Garman (Eds.), *Language acquisition* (2nd ed.). New York: Cambridge University Press.

Hilke, D. (1988). Infant vocalizations and changes in experience. *Journal of Child Language, 15*, 1–15.

Hillenbrand, J. (1983). Perceptual organization of speech sounds by infants. *Journal of Speech and Hearing Research, 26*, 268–281.

Hirschman, R., & Katkin, E. (1974). Psychophysiological functioning, arousal, attention, and learning during the first year of life. In H. Reese (Ed.), *Advances in child development and behavior.* New York: Academic Press.

Hirsh-Pasek, K., Kemler Nelson, D., Jusczyk, P., Cassidy, K., Druss, B., & Kenedy, L. (1987). Clauses are perceptual units for young infants. *Cognition, 26*, 269–286.

Hirsh-Pasek, K., Treiman, R., & Schneiderman, M. (1984). Brown and Hamlon revisited: Mother's sensitivity to ungrammatical forms. *Journal of Child Language, 11*, 81–88.

Hladik, E., & Edwards, H. (1984). A comparative analysis of mother-father speech in the naturalistic home environment. *Journal of Psycholinguistic Research, 13*, 321–332.

Hockett, C. (1960). The origin of speech. *Scientific American, 203*, 88–95.

Hockett, C. (1967). Where the tongue slips, there slip I. In *To Honor Roman Jakobson: Essays on the occasion of his seventieth birthday.* The Hague: Mouton.

Hodgkinson, H. (1986). *Future search: A look at the present.* Washington, DC: National Education Association.

Hoff-Ginsberg, E. (1985). Some contributions of mothers' speech to their children's syntactic growth. *Journal of Child Language, 12*, 367–385.

Hoff-Ginsberg, E. (1986). Function and structure in maternal speech: Their relation to the child's development of syntax. *Developmental Psychology, 22*, 155–163.

Hoff-Ginsberg, E. (1990). Maternal speech and the child's development of syntax: A further look. *Journal of Child Language, 17*, 85–99.

Hoffman, P., & Norris, J. (1989). On the nature of phonological development evidence from normal children's spelling errors. *Journal of Speech and Hearing Research, 32*, 787–794.

Hoffner, C., Cantor, J., & Badzinski, D. (1990). Children's understanding of adverbs denoting degree of likelihood. *Journal of Child Language, 17,* 217–231.

Holden, M., & MacGinitie, W. (1972). Children's conceptions of word boundaries in speech and print. *Journal of Educational Psychology, 63,* 551–557.

Holdgrafer, G., & Sorenson, P. (1984). Informativeness and lexical learning. *Psychological Reports, 54,* 75–80.

Hollingshead, A. (1965). *Two factor index of social position.* Cambridge: Harvard University Press.

Holzman, M. (1972). The use of interrogative forms in the verbal interaction of three mothers and their children. *Journal of Psycholinguistic Research, 1,* 311–336.

Holzman, M. (1984). Evidence for a reciprocal model of language development. *Journal of Psycholinguistic Research, 13,* 119–146.

Hood, L., & Bloom, L. (1979). What, when, and how about why: A longitudinal study of early expressions of causality. *Monographs of the Society for Research in Child Development, 44.*

Hopmann, M., & Maratsos, M. (1978). A developmental study of factivity and negation in complex syntax. *Journal of Child Language, 5,* 295–309.

Horgan, D. (1978). The development of the full passive. *Journal of Child Language, 5,* 65–80.

Horgan, D. (1979). *Nouns: Love 'em or leave 'em.* Address to the New York Academy of Sciences.

Horstmeier, D., & MacDonald, J. (1978). *Ready, Set, Go—Talk to Me.* Columbus, OH: Merrill.

Horton, M., & Markman, E. (1979). *Children's acquisition of basic and superordinate level categories from intensional and extensional information.* Paper presented at the biennial meeting of the Society for Research in Child Development.

Howard, D. (1983). The effects of aging and degree of association on the semantic priming of lexical decisions. *Experimental Aging Research, 9,* 145–151.

Huerta-Macias, A. (1981). Codeswitching: All in the family. In R. Duran (Ed.), *Latino language and communicative behavior.* Norwood, NJ: Ablex.

Hunt, J. (1961). *Intelligence and experience.* New York: Ronald Press.

Hunt, K. (1965). *Grammatical structures written at three grade levels.* Urbana, IL: National Council of Teachers of English.

Hunt, K. (1970). Syntactic maturity in school children and adults. *Monographs of the Society for Research in Child Development, 35,* (1, Serial No. 134).

Husiam, J., & Cohen, L. (1981). Infant learning of ill-defined categories. *MPQ, 27,* 443–456.

Huttenlocher, J. (1974). The origins of language comprehension. In R. Solso (Ed.), *Theories in cognitive psychology: The Loyola symposium.* New York: Wiley.

Huttenlocher, J., Smiley, P., & Charney, R. (1983). Emergence of action categories in the child: Evidence from verb meaning. *Psychological Review, 90,* 72–93.

Huxley, R. (1970). The development of the correct use of subject personal pronouns in two children. In G. Flores d'Arcais & W. Levelt (Eds.), *Advances in psycholinguistics.* Amsterdam: North-Holland.

Hymes, D. (1972). Introduction. In C. Cazden, V. John, & D. Hymes (Eds.), *Functions of language in the classrooms.* New York: Teachers College, Columbia University.

Inglesias, A. (1986, May 3). *The cultural-linguistic minority student in the classroom: Management decisions.* Workshop presented at the State University College at Buffalo, NY.

Ingram, D. (1969). Language development in children. In H. Fraser & W. O'Donnell (Eds.), *Applied linguistics and the teaching of English.* London: Longmans.

Ingram, D. (1971). Transitivity in child language. *Language, 47,* 888–910.

Ingram, D. (1974a). Phonological rules in young children. *Journal of Child Language, 1,* 49–64.

Ingram, D. (1974b). The relationship between comprehension and production. In R. Schiefelbusch & L. Lloyd (Eds.), *Language perspectives—Acquisition, retardation, and intervention.* Baltimore: University Park Press.

Ingram, D. (1975). The acquisition of fricatives and affricates in normal and linguistically deviant children. In A. Carramazza & E. Zuriff (Eds.), *The acquisition and breakdown of lan-*

guage. Baltimore: Johns Hopkins University Press.

Ingram, D. (1976). *Phonological disability in children.* London: Arnold.

Ingram, D. (1979). *Early patterns of grammatical development.* Paper presented at the Conference on Language Behavior in Infancy and Early Childhood, Santa Barbara.

Ingram, D. (1986). Phonological development: Production. In P. Fletcher & M. Garman (Eds.), *Language acquisition* (2nd ed.). New York: Cambridge University Press.

Ingram, D., & Tyack, D. (1979). Inversion of subject NP and Aux in children's questions. *Journal of Psycholinguistic Research, 8,* 333–341.

Inhelder, B., & Piaget, J. (1969). *The early growth of logic in the child.* New York: Norton.

Ironsmith, M., & Whitehurst, G. (1978). The development of listener abilities in communication: How children deal with ambiguous information. *Child Development, 49,* 348–352.

Jaffe, J., Stern, D., & Peery, J. (1973). "Conversational" coupling of gaze behavior in prelinguistic human development. *Journal of Psycholinguistic Research, 2,* 321–329.

Jakobson, R., Fant, C., & Halle, M. (1951). *Preliminaries to speech analysis.* Cambridge: MIT Press.

James, S. (1980). *Language and sensorimotor cognitive development in the young child.* Paper presented at the New York Speech-Language-Hearing Association annual convention.

James, S., & Seebach, M. (1982). The pragmatic function of children's questions. *Journal of Speech and Hearing Research, 25,* 2–11.

Jenkins, J. (1969). Language and thought. In J. Voss (Ed.), *Approaches to thought.* Columbus, OH: Merrill.

Jenkins, J., & Palermo, D. (1964). Mediation processes and the acquisition of linguistic structure. In U. Bellugi & R. Brown (Eds.), *Monographs of the Society for Research in Child Development, 29.*

Jensen, P., Williams, W., & Bzoch, K. (1975). *Preference of young infants for speech vs. nonspeech stimuli.* Paper presented to the annual ASHA conference.

Jeremy, R. (1978). Use of coordinate sentences with the conjunction "and" for describing temporal and locative relations between events. *Journal of Psycholinguistic Research, 7,* 135–150.

Johnson, D., Toms-Bronowski, S., & Pittelman, S. (1982). Vocabulary development. *Volta Reviews, 84*(5), 11–24.

Johnson, H. (1975). The meaning of *before* and *after* for preschool children. *Journal of Exceptional Child Psychology, 19,* 88–99.

Johnson, H., & Chapman, R. (1980). Children's judgement and recall of causal connectives: A developmental study of "because," "so," and "and." *Journal of Psycholinguistic Research, 9,* 243, 260.

Johnston, J. (1982). Narratives: A new look at communication problems in older language disordered children. *Language, Speech, and Hearing Services in the Schools, 13,* 144–145.

Johnston, J. (1984). Acquisition of locative meanings: *Behind* and *in front of. Journal of Child Language, 11,* 407–422.

Johnston, J., & Slobin, D. (1979). The development of locative expressions in English, Italian, Serbo-Croatian, and Turkish. *Journal of Child Language, 6,* 531–547.

Juel, C. (1984). An evolving model of reading acquisition. In J. Niles & L. Harris (Eds.), *Changing perspectives on research in reading/language processing and instruction.* Newark, DE: National Reading Conference.

Jusczyk, P. (1977). Rhymes and reasons: Some aspects of the child's appreciation of poetic form. *Developmental Psychology, 13,* 599–607.

Kagan, J. (1970). The determinants of attention in the infant. *American Scientist, 58,* 298–306.

Kagan, J. (1972, March). Do infants think? *Scientific American, 226,* 74–82.

Kagan, J., & Lewis, M. (1965). Studies of attention. *Merrill-Palmer Quarterly, 11,* 92–127.

Kahn, J. (1975). Relationship of Piaget's sensorimotor period to language acquisition of profoundly retarded children. *American Journal of Mental Deficiency, 79,* 640–643.

Kaplan, E. (1969). *The role of intonation in the acquisition of language.* Unpublished doctoral dissertation, Cornell University.

Karmiloff-Smith, A. (1979). *A functional approach to child language: A study of determiners and reference.* New York: Cambridge University Press.

Karmiloff-Smith, A. (1981). The grammatical marking of thematic structure in the development of language production. In W. Deutsch (Ed.), *The child's construction of language*. New York: Academic Press.

Karmiloff-Smith, A. (1986). Some fundamental aspects of language development after age 5. In P. Fletcher & M. Garman (Eds.), *Language acquisition* (2nd ed.). New York: Cambridge University Press.

Katz, J. (1966). *The philosophy of language*. New York: Harper & Row.

Katz, J., & Fodor, J. (1963). The structure of a semantic theory. *Language, 39*, 170–210.

Katz, R., Shankweiler, D., & Liberman, I. (1981). Memory for item order and phonetic recoding in the beginning reader. *Journal of Exceptional Child Psychology, 32*, 474–484.

Kauffman, A. (1976). *Mothers' and fathers' verbal interactions with children learning language*. Unpublished master's thesis, Rutgers University.

Kaye, K. (1976). Infants' effects upon their mothers' teaching strategies. In J. Glidewell (Ed.), *The social context of learning and development*. New York: Gardner Press.

Kaye, K. (1977). Towards the origin of dialogue. In H. Schaffer (Ed.), *Studies in mother-child interaction*. London: Academic Press.

Kaye, K. (1979). Thickening thin data: The maternal role in developing communication and language. In M. Bullowa (Ed.), *Before speech*. New York: Cambridge University Press.

Kaye, K. (1980). Why we don't talk "baby talk" to babies. *Journal of Child Language, 7*, 489–507.

Kaye, K., & Charney, R. (1981). Conversational asymmetry between mothers and children. *Journal of Child Language, 8*, 35–49.

Kearsley, R. (1973). The newborn's response to auditory stimulation: A demonstration of orienting and defense behavior. *Child Development, 44*, 582–590.

Keenan, E. (1974). Conversational competence in children. *Journal of Child Language, 1*, 163–183.

Keenan, E. (1975). Evolving discourse—The next step. *Papers and Reports on Child Language Development, 10*, 80–87.

Keenan, E., & Schieffelin, B. (1976). Topic as a discourse notion: A study of topic in the conversation of children and adults. In C. Li (Ed.), *Subject and topic: A new typology of language*. New York: Academic Press.

Keller-Cohen, D. (1974). *The acquisition of temporal connectives in preschool children*. Unpublished doctoral dissertation, SUNY at Buffalo.

Keller-Cohen, D. (1980). *A view of child second language learning: Using experience with language to learn language*. Paper presented at the Language Development Conference, Boston University.

Kelly, C., & Dale, P. (1989). Cognitive skills associated with the onset of multiword utterances. *Journal of Speech and Hearing Research, 32*, 645–656.

Kemper, R. (1985). *Metalinguistic correlates of reading ability in second grade children*. Unpublished doctoral dissertation. Kent State University.

Kemper, S. (1984). The development of narrative skills: Explanations and entertainments. In S. Kuczaj (Ed.), *Discourse development: Progress in cognitive development research*. New York: Springer-Verlag.

Kemper, S., & Edwards, L. (1986). Children's expression of causality and their construction of narratives. *Topics in Language Disorders, 7*(1), 11–20.

Kent, L. (1979). *Programming a first language: Content and strategies*. Paper presented at the Capitol Area Speech and Hearing Association Spring Workshop, Albany, NY.

Kent, R. (1981). Articulatory-acoustic perspectives on speech development. In R. Stark (Ed.), *Language behavior in infancy and early childhood*. New York: Elsevier/North-Holland.

Keogh, B., & Kopp, C. (1978). From assessment to intervention: An elusive bridge. In F. Minifie & L. Lloyd (Eds.), *Communicative and cognitive abilities—Early behavioral assessment*. Baltimore: University Park Press.

Kessen, W., Haith, M., & Salapatek, P. (1970). Human infancy: A bibliography and guide. In P. Mussen (Ed.), *Carmichael's manual of child psychology*. New York: Wiley.

Kinsbourne, M., & Hiscock, M. (1977). Does cerebral dominance develop? In S. Segalowitz &

F. Gruber (Eds.), *Language development and neurolinguistic theory*. New York: Academic Press.

Kintsch, W. (1974). *The representation of meaning in memory*. Hillsdale, NJ: Erlbaum.

Kintsch, W. (1977). On comprehending stories. In M. Just & P. Carpenter (Eds.), *Cognitive processes in comprehension*. Hillsdale, NJ: Erlbaum.

Kintsch, W., & Kozminsky, E. (1977). Summarizing stories after reading and listening. *Journal of Educational Psychology, 69*, 491–499.

Kiparsky, P., & Menn, L. (1977). On the acquisition of phonology. In J. Macnamara (Ed.), *Language learning and thought*. New York: Academic Press.

Klatsky, R., Clark, E., & Macken, M. (1973). Asymmetries in the acquisition of polar adjectives: Linguistic conceptual? *Journal of Experimental Child Psychology, 16*, 32–46.

Klee, T. (1985). Role of inversion in children's question development. *Journal of Speech and Hearing Research, 28*, 225–232.

Klee, T., & Fitzgerald, M. (1985). The relation between grammatical development and mean length of utterance in morphemes. *Journal of Child Language, 12*, 251–269.

Klein, H. (1978). *The relationship between perceptual strategies and productive strategies in learning the phonology of early lexical items*. Unpublished doctoral dissertation, Columbia University.

Klein, H. (1981). Early perceptual strategies for the replication of consonants from polysyllabic lexical models. *Journal of Speech and Hearing Research, 24*, 535–551.

Klein, W. (1963). *An investigation of the spontaneous speech of children during problem solving*. Unpublished doctoral dissertation, University of Rochester.

Klima, E., & Bellugi, U. (1966). Syntactic regularities in the speech of children. In J. Lyons & R. Wales, *Psycholinguistic papers*. Edinburgh: Edinburgh University Press.

Klima, E., & Bellugi, U. (1973). Syntactic regularities in the speech of children. In C. Ferguson & D. Slobin (Eds.), *Studies of child language development*. New York: Holt, Rinehart & Winston.

Kloss, H., & McConnell, G. (1978). *Linguistic composition of the nations of the world: Vol. 2. North America*. Quebec: Les Presses de L'Université Laval.

Knafle, J. (1973). Auditory perception of rhyming in kindergarten children. *Journal of Speech and Hearing Research, 16*, 482–487.

Knafle, J. (1974). Children's discrimination of rhyme. *Journal of Speech and Hearing Research, 17*, 367–372.

Kohlberg, L., Yaeger, J., & Hjertholm, E. (1968). Private speech: Four studies and a review of theories. *Child Development, 39*, 691–736.

Konefal, J., & Fokes, J. (1984). Linguistic analysis of children's conversational repairs. *Journal of Psycholinguistic Research, 13*, 1–11.

Kosslyn, S., & Bower, G. (1974). The role of imagery in sentence memory: A developmental study. *Child Development, 45*, 30–38.

Koziol, S. (1973). The development of noun plural rules during the primary grades. *Research in the Teaching of English, 7*, 30–50.

Kramer, P., Koff, E., & Luria, Z. (1972). The development of competence in an exceptional language structure in older children and young adults. *Child Development, 43*, 121–130.

Krashen, S. (1973). Lateralization, language learning and the critical period: Some new evidence. *Language Learning, 23*, 63–74.

Krauss, R., & Glucksberg, S. (1967). The development of communication competence as a function of age. *Child Development, 40*, 255–260.

Kroll, B. (1981). Developmental relationships between speaking and writing. In B. Kroll & R. Vann (Eds.), *Exploring speaking–writing relationships: Connections and contrasts*. Urbana, IL: National Council of Teachers of English.

Kuczaj, S. (1978). Why do children fail to overgeneralize the progressive inflection? *Journal of Child Language, 5*, 167–171.

Kuczaj, S. (1983). "I mell a kunk!" Evidence that children have more complex representations of word pronunciations which they simplify. *Journal of Psycholinguistic Research, 12*, 69–73.

Kuczaj, S., & Brannick, N. (1979). Children's use of Wh question modal auxiliary placement rule. *Journal of Experimental Child Psychology, 28*, 43–67.

Kuczaj, S., & Maratsos, M. (1975). On the acquisition of front, back, and side. *Child Development, 46,* 202–358.

Kuhn, D., & Phelps, H. (1976). The development of children's comprehension of causal direction. *Child Development, 47,* 248–251.

LaBarbera, J., Izard, C., Vietze, P., & Parisi, S. (1976). Four- and six-month-old infants' visual responses to joy, anger, and neutral expression. *Child Development, 47,* 535–538.

LaBerge, D., & Samuels, S. (1974). Toward a theory of automatic information processing in reading. *Cognitive Psychology, 6,* 293–323.

Labov, W. (1970a). The logic of nonstandard English. In F. Williams (Ed.), *Language and poverty.* Chicago: Markham.

Labov, W. (1970b). Stages in the acquisition of standard English. In H. Hungerford, J. Robinson, & J. Sledd (Eds.), *English linguistics.* Atlanta: Scott Foresman.

Labov, W. (1971). Stages in the acquisition of standard English. In W. Labov (Ed.), *Readings in American dialectology.* New York: Appleton-Century-Crofts.

Labov, W. (1972). *Language in the inner city.* Philadelphia: University of Pennsylvania Press.

Labov, W. (1978). On the grammaticality of everyday speech. In W. Labov (Ed.), *Quantitative analysis of linguistic structure.* New York: Academic Press.

Labov, W., Cohen, P., Robins, C., & Lewis, J. (1968). *A study of the nonstandard English of Negro and Puerto Rican speakers in New York City* (Vol. 2). New York: Columbia University Press.

Lahey, M. (1974). The role of prosody and syntactic markers in children's comprehension of spoken sentences. *Journal of Speech and Hearing Research, 17,* 656–668.

Lakoff, G. (1971). On generative semantics. In D. Steinberg & L. Jakobovits (Eds.), *Semantics: An interdisciplinary reader in philosophy, linguistics and psychology.* London: Cambridge University Press.

Lakoff, G. (1972). Language in context. *Language, 48,* 907–927.

Lakoff, R. (1973). Language and woman's place. *Language and Society, 2,* 45–80.

Landberg, L., & Lundberg, L. (1989). Phonetic development in early infancy of four Swedish children during the first 18 months of life. *Journal of Child Language, 16,* 19–40.

Langlois, A., & Baken, R. (1976). Development of respiratory time factors in infant cry. *Developmental Medicine and Child Neurology, 18,* 732–737.

Lashley, K. (1951). The problem of serial order in behavior. In L. Jeffress (Ed.), *Cerebral mechanisms in behavior.* New York: Wiley.

Laufer, M., & Horii, Y. (1977). Fundamental frequency characteristics of infant nondistress vocalization during the first twenty-four weeks. *Journal of Child Language, 4,* 171–184.

Leach, E. (1972). Interrogation: A model and some implications. *Journal of Speech and Hearing Disorders, 37,* 33–47.

Lederberg, A., & Morales, C. (1985). Code switching by bilinguals: Evidence against a third grammar. *Journal of Psycholinguistic Research, 14,* 113–136.

Lee, V. (1981). Terminology and conceptual revision of the experimental analysis of language development: Why? *Behaviorism, 9,* 25–55.

Leech, G. (1970). *Towards a semantic description of English.* Bloomington: Indiana University Press.

Lefley, H. (1975). Differential self-concept in American Indian children as a function of language and examiner. *Journal of Personal and Social Psychology, 31,* 36–41.

Lemish, D., & Rice, M. (1986). Television as a talking picture book: A prop for language acquisition. *Journal of Child Language, 13,* 251–274.

Lemme, M., & Daves, N. (1982). Models of auditory linguistic processing. In N. Lass, L. McReynolds, J. Northern, & D. Yoder (Eds.), *Speech, Language and Hearing: Vol. 1. Normal Processes.* Philadelphia: Saunders.

Lempers, J. (1976). *Production of pointing, comprehension of pointing and understanding of looking behavior.* Unpublished doctoral dissertation, University of Minnesota.

Lempers, J., Flavell, E., & Flavell, J. (1977). The development in very young children of tacit knowledge concerning visual perception. *Genetic Psychology Monographs, 95,* 3–53.

Lenneberg, E. (1964). A biological perspective of language. In E. Lenneberg (Ed.), *New directions in the study of language.* Cambridge: MIT Press.

Lenneberg, E. (1967). *Biological foundations of language.* New York: Wiley.

Leonard, L. (1976). *Meaning in child language.* New York: Grune & Stratton.

Leonard, L., & Loeb, D. (1988). Government-binding theory and some of its applications: A tutorial. *Journal of Speech and Hearing Research, 31,* 515–524.

Leonard, L., Newhoff, M., & Mesalam, L. (1980). Individual differences in early child phonology. *Applied Psycholinguistics, 1,* 7–30.

Leonard, L., Wilcox, J., Fulmer, K., & Davis, A. (1978). Understanding indirect requests: An investigation of children's comprehension of pragmatic meanings. *Journal of Speech and Hearing Research, 21,* 528–537.

Lerner, A., & Loewe, F. (1956). *My fair lady.* New York: Chappell.

Levin, E., & Rubin, K. (1982). Getting others to do what you want them to: The development of children's requestive strategies. In K. Nelson (Ed.), *Children's language* (Vol. 4). New York: Gardner Press.

Levy, Y. (1983). It's frogs all the way down. *Cognition, 15,* 75–94.

Lewis, M. (1951). *Infant speech: A study of the beginnings of language.* New York: Humanities Press.

Lewis, M. (1969). Infants' responses to facial stimuli during the first year of life. *Developmental Psychology, 1,* 75–86.

Lewis, M. (1972). State as an infant-environment interaction: An analysis of mother-infant interaction as a function of sex. *Merrill-Palmer Quarterly, 18,* 95–121.

Lewis, M., & Ban, P. (1971). *Stability of attachment behavior: A transformational analysis.* Paper presented to the Society for Research in Child Development.

Lewis, M., & Cherry, L. (1977). Social behavior and language acquisition. In M. Lewis & L. Rosenblum (Eds.), *Interaction, conversation, and the development of language.* New York: Wiley.

Lewis, M., & Freedle, R. (1973). Mother-infant dyad: The cradle of meaning. In P. Pilner, L. Kranes, & T. Alloway (Eds.), *Communication and affect: Language and thought.* New York: Academic Press.

Lewis, M., & Wilson, D. (1972). Infant development in lower class American families. *Human Development, 15,* 112–127.

Lewis, M., Young, G., Brooks, J., & Michaelson, L. (1975). The beginning of friendship. In M. Lewis & L. Rosenblum (Eds.), *Friendship and peer relations.* New York: Wiley.

Liberman, I., Shankweiler, D., Fischer, F., & Carter, B. (1974). Explicit syllable and phoneme segmentation in the young child. *Journal of Experimental Child Psychology, 18,* 201–212.

Liebergott, J., Ferrier, L., Chesnick, M., & Menyuk, P. (1981). *Prelinguistic conversation in normal and at risk infants.* Paper presented to the American Speech-Language-Hearing Association convention.

Lieven, E. (1975). *Conversations between mothers and young children: Individual differences and their possible implications for the study of language learning.* Paper presented to the Third International Symposium on First Language Acquisition.

Lieven, E. (1978). Conversations between mothers and young children: Individual differences and their possible implications for the study of language learning. In N. Waterson & C. Snow (Eds.), *The development of communication: Social and pragmatic factors in language acquisition.* New York: Wiley.

Lieven, E. (1984). International style and children's language learning. *Topics in Language Disorders, 4*(4), 15–23.

Light, R. (1971). Some observations concerning black children's conversations. In R. Jacobson (Ed.), *The English Record* (Special Anthology Issue and Monograph), *14,* 155–167.

Limber, J. (1973). The genesis of complex sentences. In T. Moore (Ed.), *Cognitive development and the acquisition of language.* New York: Academic Press.

Lindholm, K., & Padilla, A. (1978). Language mixing in bilingual children. *Journal of Child Language, 5,* 327–335.

Lindsay, P., & Norman, D. (1977). *Human information processing* (2nd ed.). New York: Academic Press.

Lipsitt, L. (1966). Learning processes of human newborns. *Merrill-Palmer Quarterly, 12,* 45–71.

Lisker, L., & Abramson, A. (1965). Voice onset time in the production and perception of English stops. *Speech Research, Haskins Laboratories, 1.*

Litowitz, B. (1977). Learning to make definitions. *Journal of Child Language, 4,* 289–304.

Loban, W. (1976). *Language development: Kindergarten through grade twelve.* Urbana, IL: National Council of Teachers of English.

Locke, J. (1983). *Phonological acquisition and change.* New York: Academic Press.

Locke, J. (1986). Speech perception and the emergent lexicon: An ethological approach. In P. Fletcher & M. Garman (Eds.), *Language acquisition* (2nd ed.). New York: Cambridge University Press.

Lombardino, L. (1978). *Mothers' pragmatic functions in their verbal interactions with their non-delayed and Down's syndrome children.* Unpublished doctoral dissertation, The Ohio State University.

Longacre, R. (1983). *The grammar of discourse.* New York: Plenum Press.

Lord, C. (1975). *Is talking to baby more than baby talk?* Paper presented to the Society for Research in Child Development.

Lorenz, K. (1943). Die angeborenen möglicher Erfahrung. *Zeitschrift für Tierpsychologie, 5.*

Love, R. (1981). The forgotten minority: The communicatively disabled. *ASHA, 23,* 485–489.

Love, R., & Webb, W. (1986). *Neurology for the Speech-Language Pathologist.* Boston: Butterworths.

Lovell, K., & Dixon, E. (1967). The growth of the control of grammar in imitation, comprehension, and production. *Journal of Child Psychology and Psychiatry, 8,* 31–39.

Lowe, R., Knutson, P. & Monson, M. (1985). Incidence of fronting in preschool children. *Language, Speech, and Hearing Services in the Schools, 16,* 119–123.

Luria, A. (1970). The functional organization of the brain. *Scientific American, 222*(3), 66–78.

Lust, B., & Mervis, C. (1980). Development of coordination in the natural speech of young children. *Journal of Child Language, 7,* 279–304.

Lyons, J. (1975). Deixis as the source of reference. In E. Keenan (Ed.), *Formal semantics of natural language.* New York: Cambridge University Press.

MacDonald, J. (1978). *Environmental Language Inventory.* Columbus, OH: Merrill.

Macken, M., & Ferguson, C. (1983). Cognitive aspects of phonological development: Model, evidence and issues. In K. Nelson (Ed.), *Children's language.* Hillsdale, NJ: Erlbaum.

Macnamara, J. (1970). Comparative studies of reading and problem-solving in two languages. *TESOL Quarterly, 4,* 107–116.

Macnamara, J. (1972). Cognitive basis of language learning in infants. *Psychological Review, 79,* 1–13.

Macnamara, J. (1982). *Names for things: A study of human learning.* Cambridge, MA: MIT Press.

MacNeilage, P. (1970). Motor control of serial ordering in speech. *Psychological Review, 77,* 182–196.

Macrae, A. (1976a). *Meaning relations in language development: A study of some converse pairs and directional opposites.* Unpublished doctoral dissertation, University of Edinburgh.

Macrae, A. (1976b). Movement and location in the acquisition of deictic verbs. *Journal of Child Language, 3,* 191–204.

Macrae, A. (1978). *Natural descriptions and models of semantic development.* Paper presented at the Child Language Seminar, University of York.

MacWhinney, B. (1976). Hungarian research on the acquisition of morphology and syntax. *Journal of Child Language, 3,* 397–410.

MacWhinney, B. (1978). *The acquisition of morphology. Society for Research in Child Development Monograph, No. 43.*

MacWhinney, B. (1985). Acquisition of Hungarian. In D. Slobin (Ed.), *The crosslinguistic study of language acquisition.* Hillsdale, NJ: Erlbaum.

MacWhinney, B., & Bates, E. (1978). Sentential devices for conveying givenness and newness: A cross-cultural developmental study. *Journal of Verbal Learning and Verbal Behavior, 17,* 539–558.

Mahoney, G. (1975). An ethological approach to delayed language acquisition. *American Journal of Mental Deficiency, 80,* 139–148.

Mahoney, G., & Seely, P. (1976). The role of the social agent in language acquisition: Implications for language intervention programs. In N. Ellis (Ed.), *International review of research in mental retardation* (Vol. 8). New York: Academic Press.

Major, R. (1976). *One gramática or duas? Phonological differentiation of a bilingual child.* Paper presented at the Linguistic Society of America summer meeting.

Malzone, D., & Parker, E. (1979). Question form analysis in discourse agreement between a mother and a language-learning child. *Journal of Psycholinguistic Research, 8,* 21–28.

Mandler, J., & Johnson, N. (1977). Remembrance of things parsed: Story structure and recall. *Cognitive Psychology, 9,* 111–151.

Mann, V., Shankweiler, D., & Smith, S. (1984). The association between comprehension of spoken sentences and early reading ability: The role of phonetic representations. *Journal of Child Language, 11,* 627–643.

Maratsos, M. (1973). Decrease in the understanding of the word "big" in preschool children. *Child Development, 44,* 747–752.

Maratsos, M. (1974). When is a high thing the big one? *Developmental Psychology, 10,* 367–375.

Maratsos, M. (1976). *The use of definite and indefinite reference in young children: An experimental study of semantic acquisition.* Cambridge: Cambridge University Press.

Maratsos, M. (1983). Some current issues in the study of the acquisition of grammar. In P. Mussen (Ed.), *Carmichael's manual of child psychology* (Vol. III) (4th ed.). New York: Wiley.

Maratsos, M. (1988). The acquisition of formal word classes. In Y. Levy, I. Schlesinger, & M. Braine (Eds.), *Categories and processes in language acquisition.* Hillsdale, NJ: Erlbaum.

Maratsos, M., & Abramovitch, R. (1975). How children understand full, truncated and anomalous passives. *Journal of Verbal Learning and Verbal Behavior, 14,* 145–157.

Maratsos, M., Kuczaj, S., Fox, D., & Chalkley, M. (1979). Some empirical studies in the acquisition of transformational relations: Passives, negatives and the past tense. In W.

Collins (Ed.), *Children's language and communication.* Hillsdale, NJ: Erlbaum.

Marcos, H. (1987). Communicative function of pitch range and pitch direction in infants. *Journal of Child Language, 14,* 255–268.

Marsh, G., Friedman, M., Welch, V., & Desberg, P. (1981). A cognitive-developmental theory of reading acquisition. In G. McKinnon & T. Weller (Eds.), *Reading research: Advances in theory and practice.* New York: Academic Press.

Martlew, M. (1980). Mothers' control strategies in dyadic mother/child conversations. *Journal of Psycholinguistic Research, 9,* 327–347.

Maskarinec, A., Cairns, G., Butterfield, E., & Weamer, D. (1981). Longitudinal observations of individual infant's vocalizations. *Journal of Speech and Hearing Disorders, 46,* 267–273.

Mason, W. (1976). Environmental models and mental modes: Representational processes in the great apes and man. *American Psychologist, 31,* 284–294.

Masur, E. (1983). Gestural development, dual-directional signaling, and the transition to words. *Journal of Psycholinguistic Research, 12,* 93–110.

Mateer, C. (1983). Motor and perceptual functions of the left hemisphere and their interaction. In S. Segalowitz (Ed.), *Language functions and brain organization.* New York: Academic Press.

Matthei, E. (1987). Subject and agent in emerging grammars: Evidence for a change in children's biases. *Journal of Child Language, 14,* 295–308.

Maurer, D., & Salapatek, P. (1976). Developmental changes in the scanning of faces of infants. *Child Development, 47,* 523–527.

Maxwell, S., & Wallach, G. (1984). The language-learning disabilities connection: Symptoms of early language disability change over time. In G. Wallach & K. Butler (Eds.), *Language learning disabilities in school-age children.* Baltimore: Williams & Wilkins.

Maynard, D. (1980). Placement of topic changes in conversation. *Semiotica, 30,* 263–290.

McCabe, A., & Peterson, C. (1985). A naturalistic study of the production of causal connectives by children. *Journal of Child Language, 12,* 145–159.

McCall, R., Parke, R., & Kavanaugh, R. (1977). Imitation of live and televised models by children 1 to 3 years of age. *Monographs of the Society for Research in Child Development, 42.*

McCarthy, D. (1954). Language development in children. In L. Carmichael (Ed.), *Manual of child psychology.* New York: Wiley.

McClure, F. (1981). Formal and functional aspects of the codeswitched discourse of bilingual children. In R. Duran (Ed.), *Latino language and communicative behavior.* Norwood, NJ: Ablex.

McCormack, W., & Wurm, S. (Eds.), (1976). *Language and man: Anthropological issues.* The Hague: Mouton.

McCune-Nicolich, L. (1981). The cognitive bases of relational words in the single word period. *Journal of Child Language, 8,* 15–34.

McDermott, J. (1983, June). The solid-state parrot. *Science, 83,* 59–65.

McHale, C. (1973). *The development of the semantic concept of action role in preverbal and early verbal infants.* Unpublished doctoral dissertation, Cornell University.

McLaughlin, B. (1978). *Second-language acquisition in children.* Hillsdale, NJ: Erlbaum.

McLean, J., & Snyder-McLean, L. (1978). *A transactional approach to early language training.* Columbus, OH: Merrill.

McNeill, D. (1966). Developmental psycholinguistics. In F. Smith & G. Miller (Eds.), *The genesis of language.* Cambridge: MIT Press.

McNeill, D. (1970). *The acquisition of language: The study of developmental psycholinguistics.* New York: Harper & Row.

Mead, M., & Newton, N. (1967). Cultural patterning of perinatal behavior. In S. Richardson & A. Guttmacher (Eds.), *Childbearing: Its social and psychological aspects.* Baltimore: Williams & Wilkins.

Mehan, H. (1978). *Learning lessons.* Cambridge: Harvard University Press.

Mehler, J. (1971). Studies in language and thought development. In R. Huxley & E. Ingram (Eds.), *Language acquisition: Models and methods.* New York: Academic Press.

Meltzoff, A. (1988). Imitation, objects, tools, and the rudiments of language in human ontogeny. *Human Evolution, 3,* 45–64.

Meltzoff, A., & Moore, M. (1977). Imitation of facial and manual gestures by human neonates. *Science, 198,* 75–78.

Menig-Peterson, C. (1975). The modification of communicative behavior in preschool-age children as a function of the listener's perspective. *Child Development, 46,* 1015–1018.

Menn, L. (1971). Phonotactic rules in beginning speech. *Lingua, 26,* 225–251.

Menn, L. (1976). *Pattern, control and contrast in beginning speech: A case study in the development of word form and word function.* Unpublished doctoral dissertation, University of Illinois, Urbana-Champaign.

Menn, L. (1983). Development of articulatory, phonetic and phonological capabilities. In B. Butterworth (Ed.), *Language Production* (Vol. II). New York: Academic.

Menyuk, P. (1964). Syntactic rules used by children from preschool through first grade. *Child Development, 35,* 533–546.

Menyuk, P. (1965). *A further evaluation of grammatical capacity in children.* Paper presented to the Society for Research in Child Development.

Menyuk, P. (1969). *Sentences children use.* Cambridge: MIT Press.

Menyuk, P. (1971). *The acquisition and development of language.* Englewood Cliffs, NJ: Prentice-Hall.

Menyuk, P. (1974). Early development of receptive language: From babbling to words. In R. Schiefelbusch & L. Lloyd (Eds.), *Language perspectives—Acquisition, retardation and intervention.* Baltimore: University Park Press.

Menyuk, P. (1977). *Language and maturation.* Cambridge: MIT Press.

Menyuk, P., Menn, L., & Silber, R. (1986). Early strategies for the perception and production of words and sounds. In P. Fletcher & M. Garman (Eds.), *Language acquisition* (2nd ed.). New York: Cambridge University Press.

Mervis, C., & Mervis, C. (1988). Role of adult input in young children's category evolution: I. An observational study. *Journal of Child Language, 15,* 257–272.

Messer, D. (1980). The episodic structure of maternal speech to young children. *Journal of Child Language, 7,* 29–40.

Messer, S. (1967). Implicit phonology in children. *Journal of Verbal Learning and Verbal Behavior, 6,* 609–613.

Millar, J., & Whitaker, H. (1983). The right hemisphere's contribution to language: A review of the evidence from brain-injured subjects. In S. Segalowitz (Ed.), *Language functions and brain organization.* New York: Academic Press.

Miller, G., & Johnson-Laird, P. (1976). *Language and perception.* Cambridge: Harvard University Press.

Miller, J. (1981). *Assessing language production in children.* Baltimore: University Park Press.

Miller, J. (1985, January 13). Beaucoons of words. *New York Times Magazine,* p. 9.

Miller, J., & Chapman, R. (1981). The relation between age and mean length of utterance in morphemes. *Journal of Speech and Hearing Research, 24,* 154–161.

Miller, J., Chapman, R., Branston, M., & Reichle, J. (1980). Language comprehension in sensorimotor stages 5 and 6. *Journal of Speech and Hearing Research, 4,* 1–12.

Miller, J., & Yoder, D. (1974). An ontogenetic language teaching strategy for retarded children. In R. Schiefelbusch & L. Lloyd (Eds.), *Language perspectives—Acquisition, retardation and intervention.* Baltimore: University Park Press.

Miller, P., & Sperry, L. (1988). Early talk about the past: The origins of conversational stories of personal experience. *Journal of Child Language, 15,* 293–315.

Miller, W. (1971). Reported in S. Ervin-Tripp, *Some bases for early features of production.* Paper presented at Colloques Internationaux du Centre National de la Recherche Scientifique, 206.

Miller, W., & Ervin-Tripp, S. (1964). The development of grammar in child language. In U. Bellugi & R. Brown (Eds.), *The acquisition of language. Monographs of the Society for Research in Child Development,* 92.

Mishler, E. (1974). Studies in dialogue and discourse: 2. Types of discourse initiated and sustained through questioning. *Journal of Psycholinguistic Research, 3,* 99–123.

Mishler, E. (1976). Studies in dialogue and discourse: 3. Utterance structure and utterance function in interrogative sequences. *Journal of Psycholinguistic Research, 5,* 88–99.

Mitchell, P., & Kent, R. (1990). Phonetic variation in multisyllabic babbling. *Journal of Child Language, 17,* 247–265.

Mitchell-Kernan, C., & Kernan, K. (1977). Pragmatics of directive choice among children. In C. Mitchell-Kernan & S. Ervin-Tripp (Eds.), *Child discourse.* New York: Academic Press.

Mithum, M. (1989). The acquisition of polysynthesis. *Journal of Child Language, 16,* 285–312.

Moerk, E. (1972). Principles of dyadic interaction in language learning. *Merrill-Palmer Quarterly, 18,* 229–257.

Moerk, E. (1974). Changes in verbal child-mother interaction with increasing language skills of the child. *Journal of Psycholinguistic Research, 3,* 101–116.

Moerk, E. (1975). Verbal interactions between children and their mothers during the preschool years. *Developmental Psychology, 11,* 788–794.

Moerk, E. (1977). *Pragmatic and semantic aspects of early language development.* Baltimore: University Park Press.

Moerk, E. (1985). Analytic, synthetic, abstracting, and word-class-defining aspects of verbal mother-child interactions. *Journal of Psycholinguistic Research, 14,* 263–287.

Moffitt, A. (1971). Consonant cue perception by twenty to twenty-four week old infants. *Child Development, 42,* 717–731.

Molfese, D. (1972). *Cerebral asymmetry in infants, children and adults: Auditory evoked responses to speech and noise stimuli.* Unpublished doctoral dissertation, Pennsylvania State University.

Molfese, D., Freeman, R., & Palermo, D. (1975). The ontogeny of brain lateralization for speech and nonspeech stimuli. *Brain and Language, 2,* 356–368.

Molfese, V., Molfese, D., & Parsons, C. (1983). Hemisphere processing of phonological information. In S. Segalowitz (Ed.), *Language functions and brain organization.* New York: Academic Press.

Moore, K., & Meltzoff, A. (1978). Object permanence, imitation, and language development in infancy: Toward a neo-Piagetian perspective on communicative development. In F. Minifie & L. Lloyd (Eds.), *Communicative and cognitive abilities—Early behavioral assessment*. Baltimore: University Park Press.

Moore, M. (1973). *The genesis of object permanence*. Paper presented at the meeting of the Society for Research in Child Development.

Moore, T., & Harris, A. (1978). *Language and thought in Piagetian theory*. In L. Siegel & C. Brainerd (Eds.), *Alternatives to Piaget*. New York: Academic Press.

Morehead, D. (1971). Processing of phonological sequences by young children and adults. *Child Development, 42*, 279–289.

Morehead, D., & Ingram, D. (1973). The development of base syntax in normal and linguistically deviant children. *Journal of Speech and Hearing Research, 16*, 330–352.

Morehead, D., & Morehead, A. (1974). A Piagetian view of thought and language during the first two years. In R. Schiefelbusch & L. Lloyd (Eds.), *Language perspectives—Acquisition, retardation, and intervention*. Baltimore: University Park Press.

Morgan, J. (1978). Two types of convention in indirect speech acts. In P. Cole (Ed.), *Syntax and semantics: Vol. 9. Pragmatics*. New York: Academic Press.

Morgan, J., & Travis, L. (1989). Limits on negative information in language input. *Journal of Child Language, 16*, 531–552.

Morikawa, H., Shand, N., & Kosawa, Y. (1988). Maternal speech to prelingual infants in Japan and the United States: Relationships among functions, forms and referents. *Journal of Child Language, 15*, 237–256.

Morse, P. (1972). The discrimination of speech and nonspeech stimuli in early infancy. *Journal of Experimental Child Psychology, 14*, 477–492.

Morse, P. (1979). The infancy of infant speech perception: The first decade of research. *Brain, Behavior and Evolution, 16*, 351–373.

Morton, T., & Long, J. (1976). Effect of word transitional probability on phoneme identification. *Journal of Verbal Learning and Verbal Behavior, 15*, 43–52.

Moskowitz, A. (1973). On the status of vowel shift in the acquisition of English phonology. In

T. Moore (Ed.), *Cognitive development and the acquisition of language*. New York: Academic Press.

Moskowitz, B. (1978, November). The acquisition of language. *Scientific American, 239*, 93–108.

Moss, H. (1973). Communication in mother-infant interaction. In L. Krames, R. Pliner, & T. Alloway (Eds.), *Advances in the study of communication and affect* (Vol. 1). New York: Plenum Press.

Moss, H., & Robson, K. (1968). *The role of protest behavior in the development of mother-infant attachment*. Paper presented to the American Psychological Association.

Moulton, W. (1976). The sounds of Black English. In D. Harrison & T. Trabasso (Eds.), *Black English: A seminar*. Hillsdale, NJ: Erlbaum.

Mowrer, O. (1954). The psychologist looks at language. *American Psychologist, 9*, 660–694.

Mueller, E. (1972). The maintenance of verbal exchanges between young children. *Child Development, 43*, 930–938.

Mueller, E., Bleier, M., Krakow, J., Hegedus, K., & Cournoyer, P. (1977). The development of peer verbal interaction among two-year-old boys. *Child Development, 48*, 284–287.

Mulford, R. (1983). On the acquisition of derivational morphology in Icelandic: Learning about -ari. *Islenskt mal og almenn malfraedi, 5*.

Muma, J. (1978). *Language handbook*. Englewood Cliffs, NJ: Prentice-Hall.

Muma, J., & Zwycewicz-Emory, C. (1979). Contextual priority: Verbal shift at seven? *Journal of Child Language, 6*, 301–311.

Murillo, N. (1976). The Mexican American family. In C. Hernandez, M. Haug, & N. Wagner (Eds.), *Chicanos: Social and psychological perspectives*. St. Louis: Mosby.

Murray, A., Johnson, J., & Peters, J. (1990). Fine-tuning of utterance length to preverbal infants: Effects on later language development. *Journal of Child Language, 17*, 511–525.

Myers, F., & Myers, R. (1983). Perception of stress contrasts in semantic and nonsemantic contexts by children. *Journal of Psycholinguistic Research, 12*, 327–338.

Myers, N., & Perlmutter, M. (1978). Memory in the years from two to five. In P. Ornstein (Ed.), *Memory development in children*. Hillsdale, NJ: Erlbaum.

Myerson, R. (1975). *A developmental study of children's knowledge of complex derived words of English*. Paper presented to the International Reading Association.

Naigles, L. (1990). Children use syntax to learn verb meanings. *Journal of Child Language, 17*, 357–374.

Nakayama, M. (1987). Performance factors in subject–auxiliary inversion by children. *Journal of Child Language, 14*, 113–125.

Nakazima, S. (1962). A comparative study of the speech developments of Japanese and American English in children. *Studies in Phonology, 2*, 27–39.

Naremore, R. (1971). Teachers' judgements of children's speech: A factor analytic study of attitudes. *Speech Monographs, 38*, 17–27.

Nation, J., & Aram, D. (1977). *Diagnosis of speech and language disorders*. St. Louis: Mosby.

National Center for Health Statistics (1983). Births of Hispanic parentage, 1980. *Monthly Vital Statistics Report*. Washington, DC.

National Center for Health Statistics (1985). Advance report of final natality statistics, 1983. *Monthly Vital Statistics Report, 34*(6), Supplement [DHHS Pub. No. (PHS) 85–1120]. Hyattsville, MD: Public Health.

Naus, M., Ornstein, P., & Hoving, K. (1978). Developmental implications of multistore and depth-of-processing models of memory. In P. Ornstein (Ed.), *Memory development in children*. Hillsdale, NJ: Erlbaum.

Nayafuchi, M. (1970). Development of dichotic and monaural hearing abilities in young children. *Acta Otolaryngealogica, 69*, 409–415.

Nelson, D., Hirsh-Pasek, K., Jusczyk, P., & Cassidy, K. (1989). How the prosodic cues in motherese might assist language learning. *Journal of Child Language, 16*, 56–68.

Nelson, K. (1973a). Some evidence for the cognitive primacy of categorization and its functional basis. *Merrill-Palmer Quarterly, 19*, 21–39.

Nelson, K. (1973b). Structure and strategy in learning to talk. *Monographs of the Society for Research in Child Development, 38*.

Nelson, K. (1974). Concept, word, and sentence: Interrelations in acquisition and development. *Psychological Review, 81*, 267–285.

Nelson, K. (1977). The conceptual basis of naming. In J. Macnamara (Ed.), *Language learning and thought*. New York: Academic Press.

Nelson, K. (1978). Semantic development and the development of semantic memory. In K. Nelson (Ed.), *Children's language*. New York: Gardner Press.

Nelson, K. (1981b). Social cognition in a script framework. In L. Ross & J. Flavell (Eds.), *The development of social cognition in children*. Cambridge: Cambridge University Press.

Nelson, K., & Gruendel, J. (1977). Generalized event representation: Basic building blocks of cognitive development. In A. Brown & M. Lamb (Eds.), *Advances in developmental psychology*. Hillsdale, NJ: Erlbaum.

Newcombe, N., & Zaslow, M. (1981). Do 2 ½-year-olds hint? A study of directive forms in the speech of 2 ½-year-old children to adults. *Discourse Processes, 4*, 239–252.

Newport, E. (1976). Motherese: The speech of mothers to young children. In J. Castellan, D. Pisoni, & G. Potts (Eds.), *Cognitive theory* (Vol. 2). Hillsdale, NJ: Erlbaum.

Newport, E., Gleitman, A., & Gleitman, L. (1977). Mother I'd rather do it myself: Some effects and non-effects of maternal speech style. In C. Snow & C. Ferguson (Eds.), *Talking to children: Language input and acquisition*. New York: Cambridge University Press.

Newson, J. (1979). The growth of shared understandings between infant and caregiver. In N. Bullowa (Ed.), *Before speech*. New York: Cambridge University Press.

Nicolich, L. (1977). Beyond sensorimotor intelligence: Assessment of symbolic maturity through analysis of pretend play. *Merrill-Palmer Quarterly, 23*, 89–99.

Nietupski, J., Scheutz, G., & Ockwood, L. (1980). The delivery of communication therapy services to severely handicapped students: A plan for change. *Journal for the Association of the Severely Handicapped, 5*, 13–23.

Ninio, A., & Bruner, J. (1978). The achievement of antecedents of labelling. *Journal of Child Language, 5*, 1–15.

Ninio, A., & Snow, C. (1988). Language acquisition through language use: The functional sources of children's early utterances. In Y.

Levy, I. Schlesinger, & M. Braine (Eds.), *Categories and processes in language acquisition*. Hillsdale, NJ: Erlbaum.

Nippold, M., & Martin, S. (1989). Idiom interpretation in isolation versus context: A developmental study with adolescents. *Journal of Speech and Hearing Research, 32,* 59–66.

Nippold, M., Martin S., & Erskine, B. (1988). Proverb comprehension in context: A developmental study with children and adolescents. *Journal of Speech and Hearing Research, 31,* 19–28.

Nippold, M., & Sullivan, M. (1987). Verbal and perceptual analogical reasoning and proportional metaphor comprehension in young children. *Journal of Speech and Hearing Research, 30,* 367–376.

Nist, J. (1966). *A structural history of English.* New York: St. Martin's Press.

Nober, E., & Seymour, H. (1979). Speaker intelligibility of black and white school children for black and white adult listeners under varying listening conditions. *Language and Speech, 22,* 237–242.

Noff-Ginsberg, E. (1985). Some contributions of mothers' speech to their children's syntactic growth. *Journal of Child Language, 12,* 367–385.

Nold, E. (1981). Revising. In C. Frederiksen & J. Dominic (Eds.), *Writing: The nature, development, and teaching of written communication* (Vol. 2). Hillsdale, NJ: Erlbaum.

Norris, J., & Bruning, R. (1988). Cohesion in the narratives of good and poor readers. *Journal of Speech and Hearing Disorders, 53,* 416–423.

Obler, L. (1985). Language through the life-span. In J. Berko Gleason (Ed.), *The development of language.* Columbus, OH: Merrill.

O'Brien, M., & Nagle, K. (1987). Parents' speech to toddlers: The effect of play context. *Journal of Child Language, 14,* 269–279.

Ochs, E. (1982). Talking to children in Western Samoa. *Language and Society, 11,* 77–104.

Ochs, E., & Schieffelin, B. (1984). Language acquisition and socialization: Three developmental stories and their implications. In R. Shweder & R. LeVine (Eds.), *Culture and its acquisition.* New York: Cambridge University Press.

O'Donnell, R., Griffin, W., & Norris, R. (1967). *Syntax of kindergarten and elementary school children: A transformational analysis.* Urbana, IL: National Council of Teachers of English.

Oller, D. (1973). The effect of position in utterance on segment duration in English. *Journal of the Acoustical Society of America, 14,* 1235–1247.

Oller, D. (1974). Simplification as the goal of phonological processes in child speech. *Language Learning, 24,* 299–303.

Oller, D. (1976, November). *Analysis of infant vocalizations: A linguistic and speech scientific perspective.* Paper presented at the American Speech and Hearing Association Convention, Houston, TX.

Oller, D. (1978). Infant vocalization and the development of speech. *Allied Health and Behavior Sciences, 1,* 523–549.

Oller, D., & Eilers, R. (1982). Similarity of babbling in Spanish- and English-learning babies. *Journal of Child Language, 9,* 565–577.

Oller, D., & Eilers, R. (1983). Speech identification in Spanish and English-learning 2-year-olds. *Journal of Speech and Hearing Research, 26,* 50–53.

Oller, D., Eilers, R., Bull, D., & Carney, A. (1985). Prespeech vocalizations of a deaf infant: A comparison with normal metaphonological development. *Journal of Speech and Hearing Research, 28,* 47–62.

Oller, D., Wieman, L., Doyle, W., & Ross, C. (1976). Infant babbling and speech. *Journal of Child Language, 3,* 1–12.

Olmsted, D. (1971). *Out of the mouth of babes.* The Hague: Mouton.

Olson, D. (1970). Language and thought: Aspects of a cognitive theory of semantics. *Psychological Review, 77,* 257–273.

Olson, D. (1971). *Cognitive development: The child's acquisition of diagonality.* New York: Academic Press.

Olson, G. (1973). Developmental changes in memory and the acquisition of language. In T. Moore (Ed.), *Cognitive development and the acquisition of language.* New York: Academic Press.

Omar, M. (1973). *The acquisition of Egyptian Arabic as a native language.* The Hague: Mouton.

O'Neal, V., & Trabasso, T. (1976). Is there a correspondence between sound and spelling? Some implications for Black English speakers. In D. Harrison & T. Trabasso (Eds.), *Black English: A seminar.* Hillsdale, NJ: Erlbaum.

Osgood, C. (1963). On understanding and creating sentences. *American Psychologist, 18,* 735–751.

Oshima-Takane, Y. (1988). Children learn from speech not addressed to them: The case of personal pronouns. *Journal of Child Language, 15,* 95–108.

Osofsky, J., & Danzger, B. (1974). Relationships between neonatal characteristics and mother-infant interaction. *Developmental Psychology, 10,* 124–130.

Ostwald, R., & Peltzman, P. (1974). The cry of the newborn. *Scientific American, 230,* 84–90.

Otaki, M., Durrett, M., Richards, P., Nyquist, L., & Pennebaker, J. (1986). Maternal and infant behavior in Japan and America: A partial replication. *Journal of Cross-Cultural Psychology, 17,* 251–268.

Oviatt, S. (1982). Inferring what words mean: Early development in infants' comprehension of common object names. *Child Development, 53,* 274–277.

Owens, R. (1978). *Speech acts in the early language of non-delayed and retarded children: A taxonomy and distributional study.* Unpublished doctoral dissertation. The Ohio State University.

Owens, R. (1982). *Program for the acquisition of language with the severely impaired* (PALS). Columbus, OH: Merrill.

Owens, R. (1986). Communication, language and speech. In G. Shames & E. Wiig (Eds.), *Human communication disorders: An introduction.* Columbus, OH: Merrill.

Owens, R. (1991). *Language disorder: A functional approach to assessment and intervention.* Columbus, OH: Macmillan.

Owens, R., & MacDonald, J. (1982). Communicatives uses of the early speech of nondelayed and Down syndrome children. *American Journal of Mental Deficiency, 86,* 503–511.

Oyama, S. (1976). A sensitive period for the acquisition of a non-native phonological system. *Journal of Psycholinguistic Research, 5,* 261–285.

Oyama, S. (1978). The sensitive period and comprehension of speech. *Working Papers in Bilingualism, 16,* 1–17.

Padilla, A., & Liebman, E. (1975). Language acquisition in the bilingual child. *The Bilingual Review, 2,* 34–55.

Padilla, A., & Lindholm, K. (1976). Acquisition of bilingualism: A descriptive analysis of the linguistic structures of Spanish/English speaking children. In G. Keller (Ed.), *Bilingualism in the bicentennial and beyond.* New York: Bilingual Review Press.

Palermo, D. (1982). Theoretical issues in semantic development. In S. Kuczaj (Ed.), *Language development: Vol. 1. Syntax and semantics.* Hillsdale, NJ: Erlbaum.

Palermo, D., & Molfese, D. (1972). Language acquisition from age five onward. *Psychological Bulletin, 78,* 409–428.

Palmer, F. (1965). *The English verb.* New York: Longmans.

Palmer, S. (1978). Fundamental aspects of cognitive representation. In E. Rosch & B. Lloyd (Eds.), *Cognition and categorization.* Hillsdale, NJ: Erlbaum.

Paris, S., & Mahoney, G. (1974). Cognitive integration in children's memory for sentences and pictures. *Child Development, 45,* 633–642.

Parker, E. (1976). *Verbal and non-verbal interaction between mothers and young children.* Unpublished doctoral dissertation, City University of New York.

Parlee, M. (1979). Conversational politics. *Psychology Today, 5,* 48–56.

Parnell, M., Patterson, S., & Harding, M. (1984). Answers to *Wh-* questions: A developmental study. *Journal of Speech and Hearing Research, 27,* 297–305.

Parner, J., & Leekam, S. (1976). Belief and quantity: Three-year-olds' adaptation to listener's knowledge. *Journal of Child Language, 13,* 305–315.

Parsons, C. (1980). *The effect of speaker age and listener compliance and noncompliance on the politeness of children's request directives.* Unpublished doctoral dissertation, Southern Illinois University.

Pawlby, S. (1977). Imitative interaction. In H. Schaffer (Ed.), *Studies in mother-infant interaction.* New York: Academic Press.

Pea, R. (1979). The development of negation in early child language. In D. Olson (Ed.), *The social foundations of language and thought: Essays in honor of Jerome S. Bruner*. New York: Norton.

Pea, R., & Mawby, R. (1981, August). *Semantics of modal auxiliary verb uses by preschool children*. Paper presented at the Second International Congress for the Study of Child Language, Vancouver, Canada.

Pease, D., & Berko Gleason, J. (1985). Gaining meaning: Semantic development. In J. Berko Gleason (Ed.), *The development of language*. Columbus, OH: Merrill.

Penman, R., Cross, T., Milgrom-Friedman, J., & Meares, R. (1983). Mothers' speech to prelingual infants: A pragmatic analysis. *Journal of Child Language, 10*, 17–34.

Perera, K. (1984). *Children's writing and reading*. Oxford: Blackwell.

Perera, K. (1986). Language acquisition and writing. In P. Fletcher & M. Garman (Eds.), *Language acquisition* (2nd ed.). New York: Cambridge University Press.

Perfetti, C. (1984). Reading acquisition and beyond: Decoding includes cognition. *American Journal of Education, 93*, 40–60.

Perfetti, C., Finger, E., & Hogoboam, T. (1978). Sources of vocalization latency differences between skilled and less skilled young readers. *Journal of Educational Psychology, 5*, 730–739.

Perfetti, C., & Goodman, D. (1970). Semantic constraint on the decoding of ambiguous words. *Journal of Experimental Psychology, 86*, 420–427.

Perlmutter, M., & Lange, G. (1978). A developmental analysis of recall-recognition distinctions. In P. Ornstein (Ed.), *Memory development in children*. Hillsdale, NJ: Erlbaum.

Peters, A. (1983). *The units of language acquisition*. New York: Cambridge University Press.

Peters, A. (1986). Early syntax. In P. Fletcher & M. Garman (Eds.), *Language acquisition* (2nd ed.). New York: Cambridge University Press.

Peterson, C. (1990). The who, when and where of early narratives. *Journal of Child Language, 17*, 433–455.

Peterson, C., & McCabe, A. (1983). *Developmental psycholinguistics: Three ways of looking at a child's narrative*. New York: Plenum Press.

Peterson, C., & McCabe, A. (1987). The connective "and": Do older children use it less as they learn other connectives? *Journal of Child Language, 14*, 375–381.

Petretic, P., & Tweney, R. (1977). Does comprehension precede production? The development of children's responses to telegraphic sentences of varying grammatical adequacy. *Journal of Child Language, 4*, 201–209.

Petrovich-Bartell, N., Cowan, N., & Morse, P. (1982). Mothers' perceptions of infant distress vocalizations. *Journal of Speech and Hearing Research, 25*, 371–376.

Pflaum, S. (1986). *The development of language and literacy in young children* (3rd ed.). Columbus, OH: Merrill.

Phillips, J. (1973). Syntax and vocabulary of mothers' speech to young children: Age and sex comparisons. *Child Development, 44*, 182–185.

Piaget, J. (1926). *Language and thought of the child*. London: Routledge & Kegan Paul.

Piaget, J. (1950). *The psychology of intelligence*. London: Routledge & Kegan Paul. (Orig. pub. in 1947)

Piaget, J. (1952). *The origins of intelligence in children*. New York: International Universities Press.

Piaget, J. (1954). *The construction of reality in the child*. New York: Basic Books.

Piaget, J. (1964). Three lectures. In R. Ripple & U. Rockcastle (Eds.), *Piaget rediscovered*. Ithaca, NY: Cornell University Press.

Piaget, J. (1966). Time perception in children. In J. Frazer (Ed.), *The voices of time*. New York: Braziller.

Piaget, J., & Inhelder, B. (1958). *The growth of logical thinking from childhood to adolescence*. New York: Basic Books. (Orig. pub. in 1955)

Piaget, J., & Inhelder, B. (1964). *The early growth of logic in the child*. New York: Harper & Row. (Orig. written in 1959)

Piaget, J., & Inhelder, B. (1969). *The psychology of the child*. New York: Basic Books.

Pine, J., & Lieven, E. (1990). Referential style at thirteen months: Why age-defined cross-sectional measures are inappropriate for the study of strategy differences in early language development. *Journal of Child Language, 17,* 625–631.

Pinker, S. (1982). A theory of the acquisition of lexical interpretive grammars. In J. Bresnan (Ed.), *The mental representation of grammatical notions.* Cambridge, MA: MIT Press.

Pinker, S. (1984). *Language learnability and language development* Cambridge, MA: Harvard University Press.

Pinker, S. (1989). Resolving a learnability paradox in the acquisition of the verb lexicon. In M. Rice & R. Schiefelbush (Eds.), *The teachability of language.* Baltimore: Brookes.

Poole, I. (1934). Genetic development of articulation of consonant sounds in speech. *Elementary English Review, 11,* 159–161.

Poplack, S. (1981). Syntactic structure and social function of codeswitching. In R. Duran (Ed.), *Latino language and communicative behavior.* Norwood, NJ: Ablex.

Posner, M. (1973). *Cognition: An introduction.* Glenview, IL: Scott, Foresman.

Prather, E., Hedrick, D., & Kern, C. (1975). Articulation development in children aged two to four years. *Journal of Speech and Hearing Disorders, 40,* 179–191.

Pratt, K. (1954). The neonate. In L. Carmichael (Ed.), *Manual of child psychology.* New York: Wiley.

Pratt, M., Scribner, S., & Cole, M. (1977). Children as teachers: Developmental studies of instructional communication. *Child Development, 48,* 1475–1481.

Preese, A. (1987). The range of narrative forms conversationally produced by young children. *Journal of Child Language, 14,* 353–373.

Preisser, D., Hodson, B., and Paden, E. (1988). Developmental phonology: 18–29 months. *Journal of Speech and Hearing Disorders, 53,* 125–130.

Premack, D. (1970). The education of Sarah. *Psychology Today, 4,* 54–59.

Premack, D. (1971). Language in chimpanzee? *Science, 172,* 808–822.

Premack, D. (1972). Teaching language to an ape. *Scientific American, 227,* 92–99.

Premack, D. (1986). *Gavagai! or the future of the animal language controversy.* Cambridge: MIT Press.

Preston, M., & Lambert, W. (1969). Interlingual interference in a bilingual version of the Stroop Color-Word Task. *Journal of Verbal Learning and Verbal Behavior, 8,* 295–301.

Priestley, T. (1977). One idiosyncratic strategy in the acquisition of phonology. *Journal of Child Language, 4,* 45–61.

Prinz, P. (1983). The development of idiomatic meaning in children. *Language and Speech, 26,* 263–272.

Prinz, P., & Prinz, E. (1979). Simultaneous acquisition of ASL and spoken English. *Sign Language Studies, 25,* 283–296.

Prorok, E. (1980). Mother–child verbal interchange: A descriptive study of young children's verbal behavior. *Journal of Psycholinguistic Research, 9,* 451–471.

Prutting, C. (1979). Process /Prá, ses/n: The action of moving forward progressively from one point to another on the way to completion. *Journal of Speech and Hearing Disorders, 44,* 3–30.

Pye, C. (1988). *Precocious passives (and antipassives) in Quiche Mayan.* Paper presented at the Child Language Research Forum, Stanford University, Stanford, CA.

Pye, C., & Ratner, N. (1984). Higher pitch in BT is not universal: Acoustic evidence from Quiche Mayan. *Journal of Child Language, 11,* 515–522.

Pye, C., Wilcox, K., & Siren, K. (1988). Refining transcription: The significance of transcription "errors." *Journal of Child Language, 15,* 17–37.

Quirk, R., Greenbaum, S., Leech, G., & Svartvik, J. (1972). *A grammar of contemporary English.* London: Longman.

Raghavendra, P., & Leonard, L. (1989). The acquisition of agglutinating languages: Converging evidence from Tamil. *Journal of Child Language, 16,* 313–322.

Ramey, C., Farran, D., Campbell, F., & Finkelstein, N. (1978). Observations of mother-infant interactions: Implications for development. In F. Minifie & L. Lloyd (Eds.), *Communicative and cognitive abilities—Early behavioral assessment.* Baltimore: University Park Press.

Ramirez, A. (1981). Language attitudes and the speech of Spanish-English bilingual pupils. In R. Duran (Ed.), *Latino language and communication behavior.* Norwood, NJ: Ablex.

Ramsay, D. (1977). *Object word spurt, handedness, and object permanence in the infant.* Unpublished doctoral dissertation, University of Denver.

Rasmussen, T., & Milner, B. (1976). Clinical and surgical studies of the cerebral speech areas in man. In K. Zülch, O. Creutzfeldt, & G. Galbraith (Eds.), *Otfrid Foerster Symposium on cerebral localization.* Heidelberg: Springer.

Ratner, N. (1988). Patterns of parental vocabulary selection in speech to very young children. *Journal of Child Language, 15,* 481–492.

Ratner, N., & Bruner, J. (1978). James, social exchange, and the acquisition of language. *Journal of Child Language, 5,* 391–401.

Ravem, R. (1974). The development of "wh-" questions in first and second language learners. In J. Richards (Ed.), *Error analysis: Perspectives on second language learning.* London: Longman Group.

Read, C. (1971). Pre-school children's knowledge of English phonology. *Harvard Educational Review, 41,* 1–34.

Read, C. (1981). Writing is not the inverse of reading for young children. In C. Frederiksen & J. Dominic (Eds.), *Writing: The nature, development, and teaching of written communication.* Hillsdale, NJ: Erlbaum.

Reber, A. (1973). On psycho-linguistic paradigms. *Journal of Psycholinguistic Research, 2,* 289–319.

Redlinger, W., & Park, T. (1980). Language mixing in young bilinguals. *Journal of Child Language, 7,* 337–352.

Reeder, K. (1980). The emergence of illocutionary skills. *Journal of Child Language, 7,* 13–28.

Rees, N. (1972). The role of babbling in the child's acquisition of language. *British Journal of Disorders in Communication, 4,* 17–23.

Rees, N. (1975). Imitation and language development: Issues and clinical implications. *Journal of Speech and Hearing Disorders, 40,* 339–350.

Rees, N. (1978). Pragmatics of language. In R. Schiefelbusch (Ed.), *Bases of language intervention.* Baltimore: University Park Press.

Rees, N., & Wollner, S. (1981). *An outline of children's pragmatic abilities.* Paper presented at the American Speech-Language-Hearing Association annual convention, Detroit.

Reich, P. (1986). *Language development.* Englewood Cliffs, NJ: Prentice-Hall.

Reichle, J. (1990 April). *Intervention with presymbolic clients: Setting up an initial communication system.* Paper presented at the New York State Speech-Language-Hearing Association Annual Convention, Kiamesha Lake, New York.

Reichle, J., & Yoder, D. (1979). Communication behavior of the severely and profoundly mentally retarded: Assessment and early stimulation strategies. In R. York & E. Edgar (Eds.), *Teaching the severely handicapped* (Vol. 4). Seattle: American Association for the Education of the Severely/Profoundly Handicapped.

Rembold, K. (1980). *An examination of the effects of verbal and non-verbal feedback in maternal speech to two-and-one-half-year-old children.* Unpublished manuscript, University of Wisconsin.

Remick, H. (1976). Maternal speech to children during language acquisition. In W. von Raffler-Engle & Y. Lebrun (Eds.), *Baby talk and infant speech.* Amsterdam: Swets & Zeitlinger.

Rescorla, L. (1976). *Concept formation in word learning.* Unpublished doctoral dissertation, Yale University.

Rescorla, L. (1980). Overextension in early language development. *Journal of Child Language, 7,* 321–335.

Rheingold, H., Gewirtz, J., & Ross, H. (1959). Social conditioning of vocalizations in the infant. *Journal of Comparative and Physiological Psychology, 52,* 68–73.

Rice, M. (1978). *The effect of children's prior nonverbal color concepts on the learning of color words.* Unpublished doctoral dissertation, University of Kansas.

Rice, M. (1984). Cognitive aspects of communicative development. In R. Schiefelbusch & J. Pickar (Eds.), *The acquisition of communicative competence.* Baltimore: University Park Press.

Richards, M. (1974). *The integration of a child into a social world.* New York: Cambridge University Press.

Richards, M. (1980). Adjective ordering in the language of young children: An experimental investigation. *Journal of Child Language, 6,* 253–277.

Ricks, D. (1979). Making sense of experience to make sensible sounds. In M. Bullowa (Ed.), *Before speech*. New York: Cambridge University Press.

Roberts, K., & Horowitz, F. (1986). Basic level categorization in seven- and nine-month-old infants. *Journal of Child Language, 13*, 191–208.

Robertson, S. (1975). *The cognitive organization of action events: A developmental perspective*. Paper presented to the American Psychological Association.

Robertson, S., & Suci, G. (1980). Event perception by children in the early stages of language production. *Child Development, 51*, 89–96.

Robey, B. (1985). America's Asians. *American Demographics, 53*, 22–29.

Robey, B. (1987). Locking up heaven's door. *American Demographics, 55*, 24–29.

Robinson, I. (1986). Blacks move back to the South. *American Demographics, 54*, 40–43.

Robson, K. (1967). The role of eye-to-eye contact in maternal-infant attachment. *Journal of Child Psychology and Psychiatry, 8*, 13–25.

Rodd, L., & Braine, M. (1971). Children's imitations of syntactic constructions as a measure of linguistic competence. *Journal of Verbal Learning and Verbal Behavior, 10*, 430–443.

Rodgon, M. (1976). *Single-word usage, cognitive development and the beginnings of binatorial speech*. New York: Cambridge University Press.

Rodgon, M. (1977). Situation and meaning in one- and two-word utterances: Observations on Howe's "The meanings of two-word utterances in the speech of young children." *Journal of Child Language, 4*, 111–114.

Rodgon, M., Jankowski, W., & Alenskas, L. (1977). A multifunctional approach to single word usage. *Journal of Child Language, 4*, 23–45.

Rondal, J. (1980). Fathers' and mothers' speech in early language development. *Journal of Child Language, 7*, 353–369.

Rondal, J., & Cession, A. (1990). Input evidence regarding the semantic bootstrapping hypothesis. *Journal of Child Language, 17*, 711–717.

Rondal, J., Ghiotto, M., Bredart, S., & Bachelet, J. (1987). Age-relation, reliability and grammatical validity of measures of utterance length. *Journal of Child Language, 14*, 433–446.

Rosch, E. (1973). On the internal structure of perceptual and semantic categories. In T. Moore (Ed.), *Cognitive development and the acquisition of language*. New York: Academic Press.

Ross, E. (1981). The aprosodias. *Archives of Neurology, 38*, 561–569.

Ross, G. (1980). Categorization in 1- to 2-year-olds. *Developmental Psychology, 16*, 391–396.

Roth, F. (1986). Oral narrative abilities of learning-disabled students. *Topics in Language Disorders, 7*(1), 21–30.

Roth, F., & Davidge, N. (1985). Are early verbal communicative intentions universal? A preliminary investigation. *Journal of Psycholinguistic Research, 14*, 351–363.

Roth, F., & Spekman, N. (1981). *Preschool children's comprehension and production of directive forms*. Paper presented at the American Speech-Language-Hearing Association annual convention.

Roth, F., & Spekman, N. (1985, June). *Story grammar analysis of narratives produced by learning disabled and normally achieving students*. Paper presented at the Symposium on Research in Child Language Disorders, Madison, WI.

Rūkė-Draviņa, V. (1981). In P. Dale & D. Ingram (Eds.), *Child language—An international perspective*. Baltimore: University Park Press.

Rummelhart, D. (1975). Notes on a schema for stories. In D. Brown & A. Collins (Eds.), *Representation and understanding: Studies in cognitive science*. New York: Academic Press.

Rummelhart, D. (1977). Toward an interactive model of reading. In S. Dornic (Ed.), *Attention and performance* (Vol. 1). Hillsdale, NJ: Erlbaum.

Russell, C. (1982). Coming alive down South. *American Demographics, 50*, 19–23.

Russell, C. (1983). The news about Hispanics. *American Demographics, 51*, 14–25.

Ryan, J. (1973). Interpretation and imitation in early language development. In R. Hinde & S. Stevenson-Hinde (Eds.), *Constraints on language*. London: Academic Press.

Ryan, J. (1974). Early language development: Towards a communicational analysis. In P. Richards (Ed.), *The integration of a child into a social world.* London: Cambridge University Press.

Sachs, J. (1967). Recognition memory for syntactic and semantic aspects of connected discourse. *Perception and Psychophysics, 2,* 437–442.

Sachs, J. (1972). On the analyzability of stories by children. In J. Gumperz & D. Hymes (Eds.), *Directions in sociolinguistics: The ethnography of communication.* New York: Holt, Rinehart & Winston.

Sachs, J. (1977). The adaptive significance of linguistic input to prelinguistic infants. In C. Snow & C. Ferguson (Eds.), *Talking to children: Language input and acquisition.* New York: Cambridge University Press.

Sachs, J. (1984). Children's play and communicative development. In R. Schiefelbusch & J. Pickar (Eds.), *The acquisition of communicative competence.* Baltimore: University Park Press.

Sachs, J. (1985). Prelinguistic development. In J. Berko Gleason (Ed.), *The development of language.* Columbus, OH: Merrill.

Sachs, J., & Devin J. (1976). Young children's use of age-appropriate speech styles in social interaction and role-playing. *Journal of Child Language, 3,* 81–98.

Sachs, J., & Truswell, L. (1978). Comprehension of two-word instructions by children in the one-word stage. *Journal of Child Language, 5,* 17–24.

Salapatek, P., & Kessen, W. (1966). Visual scanning of triangles by the human newborn. *Journal of Experimental Child Psychology, 3,* 155–167.

Salus, P., & Salus, M. (1974). Developmental neurophysiology and phonological acquisition order. *Language, 50,* 151–160.

Sander, L., Stechler, G., Burns, P., & Julia, H. (1970). Early mother–infant interaction and 24-hour patterns of activity and sleep. *Journal of the American Academy of Child Psychiatry, 9,* 103–123.

Sanders, E. (1972). When are speech sounds learned? *Journal of Speech and Hearing Disorders, 37,* 55–63.

Satz, P. (1975). Cerebral dominance and reading disability: An old problem revisited. In R. Knights & D. Bakker (Eds.), *The neuropsychology of learning disorders: Theoretical approaches.* Baltimore: University Park Press.

Sause, E. (1976). Computer content analysis of sex differences in the language of children. *Journal of Psycholinguistic Research, 5,* 311, 324.

Saville-Troike, M. (1988). Private speech: Evidence for second language learning strategies during the "silent" period. *Journal of Child Language, 15,* 567–590.

Sawyer, J. (1973). Social aspects of bilingualism in San Antonio, Texas. In R. Bailey & J. Robinson (Eds.), *Varieties of present-day English.* New York: Macmillan.

Saywitz, K., & Cherry-Wilkinson, L. (1982). Age-related differences in metalinguistic awareness. In S. Kuczaj (Ed.), *Language development: Vol. 2. Language, thought and culture.* Hillsdale: NJ: Erlbaum.

Scaife, M., & Bruner, J. (1975). The capacity of joint visual attention in the infant. *Nature, 253,* 265–266.

Scarborough, H., & Dobrich, W. (1990). Development of children with early language delay. *Journal of Speech and Hearing Research, 33,* 70–83.

Scarborough, H., Wyckoff, J., & Davidson, R. (1986). A reconsideration of the relationship between age and mean utterance length. *Journal of Speech and Hearing Research, 29,* 394–399.

Schaffer, H., Collis, G., & Parsons, G. (1977). Vocal interchange and visual regard in verbal and pre-verbal children. In H. Schaffer (Ed.), *Studies in mother-infant interaction.* New York: Academic Press.

Schaffer, H., & Emerson, P. (1964). The development of social attachments in infancy. *Monographs of the Society for Research in Child Development, 29.*

Schaffer, H., Hepburn, A., & Collis, G. (1983). Verbal and nonverbal aspects of mothers' directives. *Journal of Child Language, 10,* 337–355.

Schaffer, R. (1977). *Mothering.* Cambridge: Harvard University Press.

Schane, S. (1973). *Generative phonology.* Englewood Cliffs, NJ: Prentice-Hall.

Schank, R. (1972). Conceptual dependency: A theory of natural language understanding. *Cognitive Psychology, 3,* 552–631.

Schank, R., & Abelson, R. (1977). A case study in the development of knowledge structures. In R. Schank & R. Abelson (Eds.), *Scripts, plans, and goals for understanding.* Hillsdale, NJ: Erlbaum.

Schegloff, E., & Sacks, H. (1973). Opening up closings. *Semiotica, 4,* 289–327.

Scherer, N., & Olswang, L. (1984). Role of mothers' expansions in stimulating children's language production. *Journal of Speech and Hearing Research, 27,* 387–396.

Schiefelbusch, R. (1978a). Introduction. In R. Schiefelbusch (Ed.), *Base of language intervention.* Baltimore: University Park Press.

Schiefelbusch, R. (1978b). Summary and interpretation. In R. Schiefelbusch (Ed.), *Bases of language intervention.* Baltimore: University Park Press.

Schiefelbusch, R. (Ed.) (1979). *Language intervention from ape to child.* Baltimore: University Park Press.

Schieffelin, B. (1982). Cross-cultural perspectives on the transition: What differences do the differences make? In R. Golinkoff (Ed.), *The transition from prelinguistic communication: Issues and implications.* Hillsdale, NJ: Erlbaum.

Schieffelin, B., & Eisenberg, A. (1984). Cultural variation in children's conversations. In R. Schiefelbusch & J. Pickar (Eds.), *The acquisition of communicative competence.* Baltimore: University Park Press.

Schiff, N. (1979). The influence of deviant maternal input on the development of language during the preschool years. *Journal of Speech and Hearing Research, 22,* 581–603.

Schlesinger, I. (1971). Production of utterances and language acquisition. In D. Slobin (Ed.), *The ontogenesis of grammar.* New York: Academic Press.

Schlesinger, I. (1977). The role of cognitive development and linguistic input in language acquisition. *Journal of Child Language, 4,* 153–169.

Schnur, E., & Shatz, M. (1984). The role of maternal gesturing in conversations with one-year-olds. *Journal of Child Language, 11,* 29–41.

Schober-Peterson, D., & Johnson, C. (1989). Conversational topics of 4-year-olds. *Journal of Speech and Hearing Research, 32,* 857–870.

Schumaker, J. (1976). *Mothers' expansions: Their characteristics and effects on child language.* Unpublished doctoral dissertation, University of Kansas.

Schwartz, J., & Tallal, P. (1980). Rate of acoustic change may underlie hemispheric specialization for speech perception. *Science, 207,* 1380–1381.

Schwartz, R., Chapman, K., Prelock, P., Terrell, B., & Rowan, L. (1985). Facilitation of early syntax through discourse structure. *Journal of Child Language, 12,* 13–25.

Schwartz, R., & Leonard, L. (1984). Words, objects, and actions in early lexical acquisition. *Journal of Speech and Hearing Research, 27,* 119–127.

Schwartz, R., & Terrell, B. (1981). *The role of input frequency in lexical acquisition.* Paper presented at the American Speech-Language-Hearing Association annual conference.

Schweigert, W. (1986). The comprehension of familiar and less familiar idioms. *Journal of Psycholinguistic Research, 15,* 33–45.

Scollon, R. (1974). A real early stage: An unzippered condensation of a dissertation on child language. *University of Hawaii Working Papers in Linguistics, 6,* 67–81.

Scollon, R., & Scollon, S. (1981). *Narrative, literacy and face in interethnic communication.* Norwood, NJ: Ablex.

Scopesi, A., & Pellegrino, M. (1990). Structure and function of baby talk in a day-care center. *Journal of Child Language, 17,* 101–114.

Scott, C. (1984a). Adverbial connectivity in conversations of children 6 to 12. *Journal of Child Language, 11,* 423–452.

Scott, C. (1984b, November). *What happened to that: Structural characteristics of school children's narratives.* Paper presented at the annual convention of the American Speech-Language-Hearing Association, San Francisco.

Scott, C. (1987). *Summarizing text: Context effects in language disordered children.* Paper presented at the First International Symposium, Specific Language Disorders in Children, University of Reading, England.

Scott, C. (1988). Producing complex sentences. *Topics in Language Disorders, 8*(2), 44–62.

Scoville, R. (1983). Development of the intention to communicate: The eye of the beholder. In L. Feagans, C. Garvey, & R. Golinkoff (Eds.), *The origins and growth of communication.* Norwood, NJ: Ablex.

Scribner, S., & Cole, M. (1981). *The psychology of literacy.* Cambridge, MA: Harvard University Press.

Searle, J. (1965). What is a speech act? In M. Black (Ed.), *Philosophy in America.* New York: Allen & Unwin; Cornell University Press.

Searle, J. (1972, June 29). Chomsky's revolution in linguistics. *New York Review of Books, 18,* 16–24.

Searlman, A. (1977). A review of right hemisphere linguistic capabilities. *Psychological Bulletin, 84,* 503–528.

Seliger, H. (1978). Implications of a multiple critical periods hypothesis for second language learning. In W. Ritchie (Ed.), *Second language acquisition research.* New York: Halsted Press.

Sengoku, T. (1983). Mother–child relationship in Japan and the United States through behavioral observation. *Journal of Perinatal Medicine, 13,* 126–141.

Sexton, H. (1980). *The development of understanding of causality in infancy.* Paper presented at the International Conference on Infant Studies, New Haven.

Seymour, H., & Seymour, C. (1981). Black English and Standard American English contrasts in consonantal development of four and five-year old children. *Journal of Speech and Hearing Disorders, 46,* 274–280.

Shand, N., & Kosawa, Y. (1985). Japanese and American behavior types at three months: Infants and infant–mother dyads. *Infant Behavior and Development, 8,* 225–240.

Shankweiler, D., Liberman, I., Mark, L., Fowler, C., & Fischer, F. (1979). The speech code and learning to read. *Journal of Experimental Psychology: Human Learning and Memory, 5,* 531–545.

Shankweiler, D., & Studdert-Kennedy, M. (1975). A continuum of lateralization for speech perception? *Brain and Language, 2,* 22–225.

Shannon, C., & Weaver, W. (1949). *The mathematical theory of communication.* Urbana: University of Illinois Press.

Shapiro, B., & Danley, M. (1985). The role of the right hemisphere in the control of speech prosody in propositional and affective contexts. *Brain and Language, 25,* 19–36.

Sharpless, E. (1974). *Children's acquisition of personal pronouns.* Unpublished doctoral dissertation, Columbia University.

Shatz, M. (1975). How young children respond to language: Procedures for answering. *Papers and Reports in Child Language Development, 10,* 97–110.

Shatz, M. (1978a). Children's comprehension of their mothers' question-directives. *Journal of Child Language, 5,* 39–46.

Shatz, M. (1978b). The relationship between cognitive processes and the development of communication skills. In B. Keasey (Ed.), *Nebraska symposium on motivation.* Lincoln: University of Nebraska Press.

Shatz, M. (1987). Bootstrapping operations in child language. In K. Nelson & A. VanKleeck (Eds.), *Children's Language* (Vol. 6). Hillsdale, NJ: Erlbaum.

Shatz, M., & Gelman, R. (1973). The development of communication skills: Modifications in the speech of young children as a function of the listener. *Monograph of Society for Research in Child Development, 38.*

Shatz, M., Hoff-Ginsberg, E., & MacIver, D. (1989). Induction and the acquisition of English auxiliaries: The effects of differential enriched input. *Journal of Child Language, 16,* 121–140.

Shatz, M., & O'Reilly, A. (1990). Conversational or communicative skill? A reassessment of two-year-olds' behavior in miscommunication episodes. *Journal of Child Language, 17,* 131–146.

Shatz, M., Wellman, H., and Silber, F. (1983). The acquisition of mental verbs: A systematic investigation of the first reference to mental state. *Cognition, 14,* 301–321.

Shaw, G. (1916). *Pygmalion.* New York: Brentano's.

Sheldon, A. (1974). The role of parallel function in the acquisition of relative clauses in English. *Journal of Verbal Learning and Verbal Behavior, 13,* 272–281.

Shibamoto, J., & Olmstead, D. (1978). Lexical and syllabic patterns in phonological acquisition. *Journal of Child Language, 5*, 417–456.

Shipley, E., Smith, C., & Gleitman, L. (1969). A study in the acquisition of language free response to commands. *Language, 45*, 322–342.

Shorr, D., & Dale, P. (1981). Prepositional marking of source-goal structure and children's comprehension of English passives. *Journal of Speech and Hearing Research, 24*, 179–184.

Shultz, T. (1974). Development of the appreciation of riddles. *Child Development, 45*, 100–105.

Shurger, G. (1975). *Text analysis as an approach to the study of early linguistic operations.* Paper presented to the Third International Symposium on First Language Acquisition.

Shute, B., & Wheldall, K. (1989). Pitch alteration in British motherese: Some preliminary acoustic data. *Journal of Child Language, 16*, 503–512.

Siegel, L. (1977). The cognitive basis of the comprehension and production of relational terminology. *Journal of Experimental Child Psychology, 24*, 40–52.

Siegel, L. (1979). Infant perception, cognitive and motor behaviors as predictors of subsequent cognitive and language development. *Canadian Journal of Psychology/Review of Canadian Psychology, 33*, 382–395.

Sinclair, H. (1967). *Acquisition de langage et développement de la pensée.* Paris: Dunod.

Sinclair, H. (1970). The transition from sensorimotor to symbolic activity. *Interchange, 1*, 119–126.

Sinclair, H. (1976, March 30). *Comprehension of linguistic structures and their acquisition in different languages.* Paper presented at Barnard College.

Sinclair, H., & Ferreiro, E. (1970). Etude génétique de la compréhension, production et répétition de phrases au mode passif. *Archives de Psychologie, 40*, 1–42.

Sinclair-DeZwart, H. (1973). Language acquisition and cognitive development. In T. Moore (Ed.), *Cognitive development and the acquisition of language.* New York: Academic Press.

Singh, S., Woods, D., & Becker, G. (1972). Perceptual structure of 22 prevocalic English consonants. *Journal of the Acoustical Society of America, 52*, 1698–1713.

Skinner, B. F. (1957). *Verbal behavior.* New York: Appleton-Century-Crofts.

Slater, C. (1986). Don't knock immigration. *American Demographics, 54*, 4–7, 50–51.

Slayton, D., & Ainsworth, M. (1973). Individual differences in infant responses to brief everyday separations as related to other infant and maternal behaviors. *Developmental Psychology, 9*, 226–235.

Slobin, D. (1968). Imitation and grammatical development in children. In N. Endler, L. Boulter, & H. Osser (Eds.), *Contemporary issues in developmental psychology.* New York: Holt, Rinehart & Winston.

Slobin, D. (1971). *Psycholinguistics.* Glenview, IL: Scott, Foresman.

Slobin, D. (1973). Cognitive prerequisites for the development of grammar. In C. Ferguson & D. Slobin (Eds.), *Studies of child language development.* New York: Holt, Rinehart & Winston.

Slobin, D. (1978). Cognitive prerequisites for the development of grammar. In L. Bloom & M. Lahey (Eds.), *Readings in language development.* New York: Wiley.

Slobin, D. (1982). Universal and particular in the acquisition of language. In E. Wanner & L. Gleitman (Eds.), *Language acquisition: The state of the art.* New York: Cambridge University Press.

Slobin, D. (1985). *The crosslinguistic study of language acquisition.* Hillsdale, NJ: Erlbaum.

Slobin, D., & Aksu, A. (1982). Tense, aspect, and modality in the use of the Turkish evidential. In P. Hopper (Ed.), *Tense-aspect: Between semantics and pragmatics.* Amsterdam: Benjamins.

Slobin, D., & Welsh, C. (1971). Elicited imitation as a research tool in developmental psycholinguistics. In C. Lavatelli (Ed.), *Language training in early childhood education.* Urbana: University of Illinois Press.

Smith, B. (1978). Temporal aspects of English speech production: A developmental perspective. *Journal of Phonetics, 6*, 37–67.

Smith, C. (1970). An experimental approach to children's linguistic competence. In J. Hayes (Ed.), *Cognition and the development of language.* New York: Wiley.

Smith, E., Shoben, E., & Rips, L. (1974). Structure and process in semantic memory: A feature model for semantic decisions. *Psychological Review, 81,* 214–241.

Smith, F. (1971). *Understanding reading: A psycholinguistic analysis of reading and learning to read.* New York: Holt, Rinehart & Winston.

Smith, M. (1933). Grammatical errors in the speech of preschool children. *Child Development, 4,* 183–190.

Smith, N. (1973). *The acquisition of phonology: A case study.* New York: Cambridge University Press.

Smith, P. (1986). The development of reading: The acquisition of a cognitive skill. In P. Fletcher & M. Garman (Eds.), *Language acquisition* (2nd ed.). New York: Cambridge University Press.

Smolak, L. (1987). Child character and maternal speech. *Journal of Child Language, 14,* 481–492.

Smolak, L., & Weinraub, M. (1983). Maternal speech: Strategy or response? *Journal of Child Language, 10,* 369–380.

Snow, C. (1972). Mother's speech to children learning language. *Child Development, 43,* 549–566.

Snow, C. (1977a). The development of conversation between mothers and babies. *Journal of Child Language, 4,* 1–22.

Snow, C. (1977b). Mothers' speech research: From input to interaction. In C. Snow & C. Ferguson (Eds.), *Talking to children: Language input and acquisition.* New York: Cambridge University Press.

Snow, C. (1978). The conversational context of language acquisition. In R. Campbell & P. Smith (Eds.), *Recent advances in the psychology of language: Language development and the mother-child interaction* (Vol. 4). New York: Plenum.

Snow, C. (1983). Literacy and language: Relationships during the preschool years. *Harvard Educational Review, 53,* 165–189.

Snow, C. (1984). Parent-child interaction and the development of communicative ability. In R. Schiefelbusch & J. Pickar (Eds.), *The acquisition of communicative competence.* Baltimore: University Park Press.

Snow, C. (1986). Conversations with children. In P. Fletcher & M. Garman (Eds.), *Language acquisition* (2nd ed.). New York: Cambridge University Press.

Snow, C. (1990). The development of definitional skill. *Journal of Child Language, 17,* 697–710.

Snow, C., Arlmann-Rupp, A., Hassing, Y., Jobse, J., Jootsen, J., & Vorster, J. (1976). Mother's speech in three social classes. *Journal of Psycholinguistic Research, 5,* 1–20.

Snow, C., DeBlauw, A., & Van Roosmalen, G. (1979). Talking and playing with babies: The role of ideologies in child-rearing. In M. Bullowa (Ed.), *Before speech.* New York: Cambridge University Press.

Snow, C., & Hoefnagel-Hohle, M. (1978). The critical period for language acquisition: Evidence from second language learning. *Child Development, 49,* 1114–1128.

Snow, C., & Ninio, A. (1986). The contracts of literacy: What children learn from learning to read books. In W. Teale & E. Sulzby (Eds.), *Emergent literacy: Writing and reading.* Norwood, NJ: Ablex.

Snyder, A. (1914). Notes on the talk of a two-and-a-half year old boy. *Pedagogical Seminary, 21,* 412–424.

Snyder, L. (1978). Communicative and cognitive abilities and disabilities in the sensorimotor period. *Merrill-Palmer Quarterly, 24,* 161–180.

Snyder, L., & Downey, D. (1983). Pragmatics and information processing. *Topics in Language Disorders, 4*(1), 75–86.

Snyder-McLean, L., & McLean, J. (1978). Verbal information gathering strategies: The child's use of language to acquire language. *Journal of Speech and Hearing Disorders, 43,* 306–325.

Spencer, G. (1984). *Projections of the population of the United States by age, sex, and race: 1983–2080 [Current Population Reports, series P–25, No. 952].* Washington, DC: U.S. Department of Commerce, Bureau of the Census.

Spilich, G. (1983). Life-span components of text processing: Structural and procedural differences. *Journal of Verbal Learning and Verbal Behavior, 22,* 231–244.

Sroufe, L., & Waters, E. (1976). The ontogenesis of smiling and laughter: A perspective on the organization of development in infancy. *Psychological Review, 83,* 173–189.

Staley, C. (1982). Sex-related differences in the style of children's language. *Journal of Psycholinguistic Research, 11,* 141–158.

Stanovich, K. (1980). Toward an interactive-compensatory model of individual differences in the development of reading fluency. *Reading Research Quarterly, 16,* 32–71.

Stark, R. (1978). Features of infant sounds: The emergence of cooing. *Journal of Child Language, 5,* 1–12.

Stark, R. (1979). Prespeech segmental feature development. In P. Fletcher & M. Garman (Eds.), *Language acquisition.* New York: Cambridge University Press.

Stark, R. (1986). Prespeech segmental feature development. In P. Fletcher & M. Garman (Eds.), *Language acquisition* (2nd ed.). New York: Cambridge University Press.

Stark, R., & Nathanson, S. (1974). Spontaneous cry in the newborn infant: Sounds and facial gestures. In J. Bosma (Ed.), *Fourth symposium on oral sensation and perception: Development in the fetus and infant.* Bethesda, MD: U.S. Government Printing Office.

Starr, S. (1975). The relationship of single words to two-word sentences. *Child Development, 46,* 701–708.

Steffenson, M. (1978). Satisfying inquisitive adults: Some simple methods of answering yes/no questions. *Journal of Child Language, 5,* 221–236.

Stein, N., & Glenn, C. (1979). An analysis of story comprehension in elementary school children. In R. Freedle (Ed.), *New directions in discourse processing* (Vol. 2). Norwood, NJ: Ablex.

Stein, N., & Policastro, M. (1984). The concept of story: A comparison between children's and teachers' viewpoints. In H. Mandler, N. Stein, & T. Trabasso (Ed.), *Learning and comprehension of text.* Hillsdale, NJ: Erlbaum.

Steinschneider, A., Lipton, E., & Richmond, J. (1966). Auditory sensitivity in the infant: Effect of intensity on cardiac and motor responsivity. *Child Development, 37,* 233–252.

Stephany, U. (1986). Modality. In P. Fletcher & M. Garman (Eds.), *Language acquisition* (2nd ed.). New York: Cambridge University Press.

Stern, A. (1973). *An analysis and comparison of mothers' and fathers' speech to children in a story-telling situation.* Unpublished paper, Boston University.

Stern, D. (1977). *The first relationship.* Cambridge: Harvard University Press.

Stern, D., Beebe, B., Jaffe, J., & Bennett, S. (1977). The infant's stimulus world during social interaction: A study of caregiver behaviors with particular reference to repetition and timing. In H. Schaffer (Ed.), *Studies in mother-infant interaction.* London: Academic Press.

Stern, D., Jaffe, J., Beebe, B., & Bennett, S. (1975). Vocalizing in unison and in alternation: Two modes of communication within the mother-infant dyad. In D. Aaronson & R. Rieber (Eds.), *Developmental psycholinguistics and communication disorders.* New York: New York Academy of Science.

Stern, D., Spieker, S., Barnett, R., & MacKain, K. (1983). The prosody of maternal speech: Infant age and context related changes. *Journal of Child Language, 10,* 1–15.

Stern, D., Spieker, S., & MacKain, K. (1982). Intonation contours as signals in maternal speech to prelinguistic infants. *Developmental Psychology, 18,* 727–735.

Stern, D., & Wasserman, G. (1979). *Maternal language to infants.* Paper presented at the Society for Research in Child Development meeting.

Stoel-Gammon, C. (1988). Prelinguistic vocalizations of hearing-impaired and normally hearing subjects: A comparison of consonantal inventories. *Journal of Speech and Hearing Disorders, 53,* 302–315.

Stoel-Gammon, C., & Cooper, J. (1984). Patterns of early lexical and phonological development. *Journal of Child Language, 11,* 247–271.

Stoel-Gammon, C., & Otomo, K. (1986). Babbling development of hearing-impaired and normally hearing subjects. *Journal of Speech and Hearing Disorders, 51,* 33–41.

Stone, L., Smith, H., & Murphy, L. (Eds.) (1973). *The competent infant: Research and commentary.* New York: Basic Books.

Stotsky, S. (1983). Research on reading/writing relationships: A synthesis and suggested directions. *Language Arts, 60,* 627–642.

Strain, B. (1974). *Early dialogues: A naturalistic study of vocal behavior in mothers and three-month-old infants.* Unpublished doctoral dissertation, George Peabody College.

Strand, K., & Fraser, B. (1979). *The comprehension of verbal idioms by young children.* Unpublished paper, Boston University, School of Education.

Streissguth, A., & Bee, H. (1972). Mother-child interactions and cognitive development in children. In W. Hartup (Ed.), *The young child: Review of reviews* (Vol. 2). Washington, DC: National Association for the Education of Young Children.

Strohner, H., & Nelson, K. (1974). The young child's development of sentence comprehension: Influences of event probability, nonverbal context, syntactic form, and strategies. *Child Development, 45,* 567–576.

Studdert-Kennedy, M., & Shankweiler, D. (1970). Hemispheric specialization for speech perception. *Journal of the Acoustical Society of America, 48,* 579–594.

Sugarman, S. (1978). A description of communicative development in the prelanguage child. In I. Markova (Ed.), *The social context of language.* New York: Wiley.

Sugarman, S. (1984). The development of preverbal communication. In R. Schiefelbusch & J. Pickar (Eds.), *The acquisition of communicative competence.* Baltimore: University Park Press.

Sulzby, E. (1981). *Kindergartners begin to read their own compositions.* Final report to the Research Foundation of the National Council of Teachers of English.

Sulzby, E. (1985). Kindergartners as writers and readers. In M. Farr (Ed.), *Advances in writing research* (Vol. 1). Norwood, NJ: Ablex.

Sulzby, E. (1986). Writing and reading: Signs of oral and written language organization in the young child. In W. Teale & E. Sulzby (Eds.), *Emergent literacy: Writing and reading.* Norwood, NJ: Ablex.

Sund, R. (1976). *Piaget for educators: A multimedia approach.* Columbus, OH: Merrill.

Sussman, H., Franklin, P., Simon, T. (1982). Bilingual speech: Bilateral control? *Brain and Language, 15,* 125–142.

Sutter, J., & Johnson, C. (1990). School-age children's metalinguistic awareness of grammaticality in verb form. *Journal of Speech and Hearing Research, 33,* 84–95.

Sutton-Smith, B. (1981). *The folkstories of children.* Philadelphia: University of Pennsylvania Press.

Sutton-Smith, B. (1986). The development of fictional narrative performances. *Topics in Language Disorders, 7*(1), 1–10.

Suzman, S. (1987). Passives and prototypes in Zulu children's speech. *African Studies, 46,* 241–254.

Swacher, M. (1975). The sex of the speaker as a sociolinguistic variable. In B. Thorne & N. Henley (Eds.), *Language and sex: Difference and dominance.* Rowley, MA: Newbury House.

Swain, M. (1972). *Bilingualism as a first language.* Unpublished doctoral dissertation, University of California at Irvine.

Swinney, D., & Cutler, A. (1979). The access of processing of idiomatic expressions. *Journal of Verbal Learning and Verbal Behavior, 18,* 523–534.

Tannen, D. (1990). *You just don't understand: Talk between the sexes.* New York: Ballantine.

Tanouye, E. (1979). The acquisition of verbs in Japanese children. *Stanford Papers and Reports on Child Language Development, 17,* 49–56.

Tanternannova, M. (1973). Smiling in infants. *Child Development, 44,* 701–704.

Tanz, C. (1976). *The acquisition of deictic terms.* Unpublished doctoral dissertation, University of Chicago.

Tanz, C. (1980). *Studies in the acquisition of deictic terms.* New York: Cambridge University Press.

Tanz, C. (1983). Asking children to ask: An experimental investigation of the pragmatics of relayed questions. *Journal of Child Language, 10,* 187–194.

Taylor, D. (1969). Differential rates of cerebral maturation between sexes and between hemispheres. *Lancet, 12,* 140–142.

Taylor, I. (1980). The Korean writing system: An alphabet? A syllabary? A logography? In P. Kolers, M. Wrolstad, & H. Bouma (Eds.), *Processing of visible language* (Vol. II). New York: Plenum Press.

Taylor, O. (1986). Language and communication differences. In G. Shames & E. Wiig (Eds.), *Human Communication Disorders, An Introduction*. Columbus, OH: Merrill.

Teale, W. (1984). Reading to young children: Its significance for literacy development. In H. Goelmann, A. Oberg, & F. Smith (Eds.), *Awakening to literacy*. Exeter, NH: Heinemann.

Temple, C., Nathan, R., & Burris, N. (1982). *The beginnings of writing*. Boston: Allyn & Bacon.

Templin, M. (1957). *Certain language skills in children*. Minneapolis: University of Minnesota Press.

Terrance, H., Petitto, L., Saunder, R., & Bever, J. (1979). Can an ape create a sentence? *Science, 206*, 891–902.

Terrell, S., & Terrell, F. (1983). Effects of speaking Black English upon employment opportunities. *ASHA, 25*, 27–29.

Tfouni, L., & Klatsky, R. (1983). A discourse analysis of deixis: Pragmatic, cognitive and semantic factors in the comprehension of "this," "that," "here," and "there." *Journal of Child Language, 10*, 123–133.

Thatcher, R., & John, E. (1977). *Functional neuroscience: Vol. 1. Foundations of cognitive processes*. Hillsdale, NJ: Erlbaum.

Thomas, E., & Martin, J. (1976). Analysis of parent-infant interaction. *Psychological Review, 83*, 141–156.

Thomson, J., & Chapman, R. (1977). Who is "Daddy" revisited: The status of two year olds' overextended words in use and comprehension. *Journal of Child Language, 4*, 359–375.

Thorndyke, P. (1977). Cognitive structures in comprehension and memory of narrative discourse. *Cognitive Psychology, 9*, 77–110.

Thorne, B., Kramerae, C., & Henley, N. (Eds.) (1983). *Language, gender, and society*. Rowley, MA: Newbury House.

Thorne, J. (1972). On the notion "definite." *FL, 8*, 562–568.

Thorum, A. (1980). *The Fullerton Language Test for Adolescents: Experimental Edition*. Palo Alto, CA: Consulting Psychologists Press.

Tibbits, D. (1980). Oral production of linguistically complex sentences with meaning relationships of time. *Journal of Psycholinguistic Research, 9*, 545–564.

Toda, S., Fogel, A., & Kawai, M. (1990). Maternal speech to three-month-old infants in the United States and Japan. *Journal of Child Language, 17*, 279–294.

Todd, G., & Palmer, B. (1968). Social reinforcement of infant babbling. *Child Development, 39*, 591–596.

Tognola, G., & Vignolo, L. (1980). Brain lesions associated with oral apraxia in stroke patients: A cliniconeuroradiological investigation with the CT scan. *Neuropsychologia, 18*, 257–272.

Tomasello, M., Conti-Ramsden, G., & Ewert, B. (1990). Young children's conversations with their mothers and fathers: Differences in breakdown and repair. *Journal of Child Language, 17*, 115–130.

Tomasello, M., & Farrar, M. (1984). Cognitive bases of lexical development: Object permanence and relational words. *Journal of Child Language, 11*, 477–493.

Torrey, J. (1979). Reading that comes naturally: The early reader. In T. Waller & G. MacKinnon (Eds.), *Reading research: Advances in theory and practice*. New York: Academic Press.

Trantham, C., & Pedersen, J. (1976). *Normal language development*. Baltimore: Williams & Wilkins.

Trehub, S., & Abramovitch, R. (1978). Less is not more: Further observations on nonlinguistic strategies. *Journal of Experimental Child Psychology, 25*, 160–167.

Trevarthen, C. (1974). Prespeech in communication of infants with adults. *Journal of Child Language, 1*, 335–337.

Trevarthen, C. (1979). Communication and cooperation in early infancy: A description of primary intersubjectivity. In M. Bullowa (Ed.), *Before speech*. New York: Cambridge University Press.

Trevarthen, C., & Hubley, P. (1978). Secondary intersubjectivity: Confidence, confiding and acts of meaning in the first year. In A. Lock (Ed.), *Action, gesture and symbol: The emergence of language*. New York: Academic Press.

Tronick, E., Adamson, L., Wise, S., & Brazelton, T. (1975). *Infant emotions in normal and perturbated interactions.* Paper presented to the Society for Research in Child Development.

Tronick, E., Als, H., & Adamson, L. (1979). Structure of early face-to-face communicative interactions. In M. Bullowa (Ed.), *Before speech.* New York: Cambridge University Press.

Trotter, R. (1983, August). Baby face. *Psychology Today, 17*(8), 14–20.

Tuaycharoen, P. (1978). The babbling of a Thai baby: Echoes and responses to the sounds made by adults. In N. Waterson & C. Snow (Eds.), *Development of communication: Social and pragmatic factors in language acquisition.* New York: Wiley.

Tulving, E. (1972). Episodic and semantic memory. In E. Tulving & W. Donaldson (Eds.), *Organization in memory.* New York: Academic Press.

Turnure, C. (1971). Response to voice of mother and stranger by babies in the 1st year. *Developmental Psychology, 4,* 182–190.

Tyack, D., & Gottsleben, R. (1986). Acquisition of complex sentences. *Language, Speech, and Hearing Services in Schools, 17,* 160–174.

Tyack, D., & Ingram, D. (1977). Children's production and comprehension of questions. *Journal of Child Language, 4,* 211–224.

U.S. Department of Health and Human Services. (1985). *Report of the Secretary's Task Force on Black and Minority Health, Vol. I: Executive Summary* [Pub. No. 491–313/44706]. Washington, DC.

U.S. Department of Health and Human Services. (1986). *Report of the Secretary's Task Force on Black and Minority Health, Vol. IV: Cardiovascular and Cerebrovascular Disease, Part I* [1986–62038:40716]. Washington, DC.

Uzgiris, I. (1972). Patterns of vocal and gestural imitation in infants. In *Proceedings of the symposium on genetic and social influences.* Basle: Karger.

Uzgiris, I. (1976). Organization of sensori-motor intelligence. In M. Lewis (Ed.), *Origins of intelligence.* New York: Plenum Press.

Vaid, J. (1983). Bilingualism and brain lateralization. In S. Segalowitz (Ed.), *Language functions and brain organization.* New York: Academic Press.

Vaidyanathan, R. (1988). Development of forms and functions of interrogatives in children: A language study of Tamil. *Journal of Child Language, 15,* 533–549.

Vanevery, H., & Rosenberg, S. (1970). Semantics, phrase structure and age as variables in sentence recall. *Child Development, 41,* 853–859.

VanHekken, S., Vergeer, M., & Harris, P. (1980). Ambiguity of reference and listeners' reaction in a naturalistic setting. *Journal of Child Language, 7,* 555–563.

Van Kleek, A. (1982). The emergence of linguistic awareness: A cognitive framework. *Merrill-Palmer Quarterly, 28,* 237–265.

Venable, G. (1974). *A study of second-language learning in children.* Unpublished masters thesis, McGill University.

Vietze, P., & Strain, B. (1975). *Contingent responsiveness between mother and infant: Who's reinforcing whom?* Paper presented at SEPA.

Vihman, M. (1985). Language differentiation by the bilingual infant. *Journal of Child Language, 12,* 297–324.

Vihman, M., & Greenlee, M. (1987). Individual differences in phonological development: Ages one and three years. *Journal of Speech and Hearing Research, 30,* 503–521.

Vogel, I. (1975). One system or two: An analysis of a two-year-old Romanian-English bilingual's phonology. *Papers and reports on Child Language Development, 9,* 43–62.

Volterra, V., & Taeschner, T. (1978). The acquisition and development of language by bilingual children. *Journal of Child Language, 5,* 311–326.

Von Frisch, K. (1950). *Bees, their vision, chemical senses, and language.* Ithaca, NY: Cornell University Press.

Vygotsky, L. (1962). *Thought and language.* Cambridge: MIT Press. (Orig. pub. in 1934)

Vygotsky, L. (1978). *Mind in society* Cambridge, MA: Harvard University Press.

Wadsworth, B. (1979). *Piaget's theory of cognitive development.* New York: Longman.

Wales, R. (1979). Deixis. In P. Fletcher & M. Gorman (Eds.), *Language acquisition: Studies in first language development.* Cambridge: Cambridge University Press.

Wales, R. (1986). Deixis. In P. Fletcher & M. Garman (Eds.), *Language acquisition* (2nd ed.). New York: Cambridge University Press.

Wanska, S., & Bedrosian, J. (1985). Conversational structure and topic performance in mother-child interaction. *Journal of Speech and Hearing Research, 28,* 579–584.

Ward, M. (1971). *Them children: A study in language learning.* New York: Holt, Rinehart & Winston.

Warden, D. (1976). The influence of context on children's use of identifying expressions and references. *British Journal of Psychology, 67,* 101–112.

Warren-Leubecker, A. (1982). *Sex differences in speech to children.* Unpublished master's thesis, Georgia Institute of Technology.

Waryas, C. (1973). Psycholinguistic research in language intervention programming: The pronoun system. *Journal of Psycholinguistic Research, 2,* 221–237.

Washington, D., & Naremore, R. (1978). Children's use of spatial prepositions in two- and three-dimensional tasks. *Journal of Speech and Hearing Disorders, 21,* 151–165.

Wasz-Hockert, O., Lind, J., Vuorenkoski, V., Partanen, T., & Valanne, E. (1968). *The infant cry.* London: Heinemann Medical Publications.

Waterman, P., & Schatz, M. (1982). The acquisition of personal pronouns and proper names by an identical twin pair. *Journal of Speech and Hearing Research, 25,* 149–154.

Waterson, N. (1978). Growth of complexity in phonological development. In N. Waterson & C. Snow (Eds.), *The development of communication.* New York: Wiley.

Watson, R. (1985). Towards a theory of definition. *Journal of Child Language, 12,* 181–197.

Webb, P., & Abrahamson, A. (1976). Stages of egocentrism in children's use of "this" and "that": A different point of view. *Journal of Child Language, 3,* 349–367.

Wehrabian, A. (1970). Measures of vocabulary and grammatical skills for children up to age six. *Developmental Psychology, 2,* 439–446.

Wehren, A., DeLisi, R., & Arnold, M. (1981). The development of noun definition. *Journal of Child Language, 8,* 165–175.

Weiner, F., & Lewnau, L. (1979). *Nondiscriminatory speech and language testing of minority children: Linguistic interferences.* Paper presented at the American Speech and Hearing Association annual conference.

Weiner, P. (1985). The value of follow-up studies. *Topics in Language Disorders, 5*(3), 78–92.

Weist, R. (1986). Tense and aspect. In P. Fletcher & M. Garman (Eds.), *Language acquisition* (2nd ed.). New York: Cambridge University Press.

Wellen, C. (1985). Effects of older siblings on the language young children hear and produce. *Journal of Speech and Hearing Disorders, 50,* 84–99.

Wellman, B., Case, I., Mengert, I., & Bradbury, D. (1931). Speech sounds of young children. *University of Iowa Studies in Child Welfare, 5.*

Wellman, H., & Lempers, J. (1977). The naturalistic communicative abilities of two-year-olds. *Child Development, 48,* 1052–1057.

Wells, G. (1974). Learning to code experience through language. *Journal of Child Language, 1,* 243–269.

Wells, G. (1979). Learning and using the auxiliary verb in English. In V. Lee (Ed.), *Language development.* New York: Wiley.

Wells, G. (1980). Adjustments in adult-child conversation: Some effects of interaction. In H. Giles, W. Robinson, & P. Smith (Eds.), *Language: Social psychological perspective.* Oxford: Pergamon Press.

Wells, G. (1985). *Language development in the preschool years.* New York: Cambridge University Press.

Wells, G., Barnes, S., Gutfreund, M., & Satterly, D. (1983). Characteristics of adult speech which predict children's language development. *Journal of Child Language, 10,* 65–84.

Werner, H., & Kaplan, B. (1963). *Symbol formation: An organismic developmental approach to language and the expression of thought.* New York: Wiley.

Westermeyer, R., & Westermeyer, J. (1977). Tonal language acquisition among Lao children. *Anthropological Linguistics, 19,* 260–264.

Wetstone, H., & Friedlander, B. (1973). The effects of word order on young children's responses to simple questions and commands. *Child Development, 44,* 734–740.

Whaley, J. (1981). Readers' expectation for story structure. *Reading Research Quarterly, 17*. 90–114.

Whitaker, H. (1970). *A model of neurolinguistics.* Occasional papers, No. 10, Language Center, University of Essex, Colchester, England.

Whitaker, H. (1973). Comments on the innateness of language. In R. Shuy (Ed.), *Some new directions in linguistics.* Washington, DC: Georgetown University Press.

White, B. (1971). *Human infants: Experience and psychological development.* Englewood Cliffs, NJ: Prentice-Hall.

White, B. (1975). Critical influences in the origins of competence. *Merrill-Palmer Quarterly, 22*, 243–266.

Whitehurst, G., Kedesdy, J., & White, T. (1982). A functional analysis of meaning. In S. Kuczaj (Ed.), *Language development: Vol. 1. Syntax and semantics.* Hillsdale, NJ: Erlbaum.

Whorf, B. (1956). *Language, thought, and reality.* New York: Wiley.

Wieman, L. (1976). Stress patterns of early child language. *Journal of Child Language, 3*, 283–286.

Wiig, E., & Semel, E. (1984). *Language assessment and intervention for the learning disabled* (2nd ed.). Columbus, OH: Merrill.

Wilcox, S., & Palermo, D. (1974/75). "In," "on" and "under" revisited. *Cognition, 3*, 245–254.

Wilkinson, A. (1971). *The foundations of language: Talking and reading in young children.* Oxford: Oxford University Press.

Wilkinson, A., Barnsley, G., Hanna, P., & Swan, M. (1979). Assessing language development: The Crediton Project. *Language for Learning, 1*, 59–76.

Wilkinson, L., Calculator, S., & Dollaghan, C. (1982). Ya wanna trade—just for awhile: Children's requests and responses to peers. *Discourse Processes, 5*, 161–176.

Wilkinson, L., Hiebert, E., & Rembold, K. (1981). Parents' and peers' communication to toddlers. *Journal of Speech and Hearing Research, 24*, 383–388.

Wilkinson, L., & Rembold, K. (1982). The communicative context of early-language development. In S. Kuczaj (Ed.), *Language development: Vol. 2. Language, thought and culture.* Hillsdale, NJ: Erlbaum.

Williams, F., Cairns, H., & Cairns, C. (1971). *An analysis of the variations from standard English pronunciation in the phonetic performance of two groups of nonstandard-English-speaking-children.* Center for Communication Research, University of Texas.

Williams, F., Hewitt, N., Miller, L., Naremore, R., & Whitehead, J. (1976). *Explorations of the linguistic attitudes of teachers.* Rowley, MA: Newbury House.

Williams, F., & Naremore, R. (1969). On the functional analysis of social class differences in modes of speech. *Speech Monographs, 36*, 77–102.

Williams, R., & Wolfram, W. (1977). *Social dialects: Differences vs. disorders.* Washington, DC: American Speech and Hearing Association.

Willis, F., & Williams, S. (1976). Simultaneous talking in conversation and the sex of the speakers. *Perceptual and Motor Skills, 43*, 1067–1070.

Wing, C., & Scholnick, E. (1981). Children's comprehension of pragmatic concepts expressed in "because," "although," "if" and "unless." *Journal of Child Language, 8*, 347–365.

Winitz, H. (1983). Use and abuse of the developmental approach. In H. Winitz, *Treating language disorders.* Baltimore: University Park Press.

Winograd, T. (1972). Understanding natural language. *Cognitive Psychology, 3*, 1–19.

Wolf, M., Bally, H., & Morris, R. (1984). *Automaticity, retrieval processes, and reading: A longitudinal investigation of average and impaired readers.* Manuscript submitted for publication.

Wolff, P. (1963). Observations on the early development of smiling. In B. Foss (Ed.), *Determinants of infant behavior II.* New York: Wiley.

Wolff, P. (1966). The causes, controls and organization of behavior in the neonate. *Psychological Issues, 5*, 1–99.

Wolff, P. (1969). The natural history of crying and other vocalizations in early infancy. In B. Foss (Ed.), *Determinants of infant behavior IV.* London: Methuen.

Wolfram, W., & Fasold, R. (1974). *The study of social dialects in American English.* Englewood Cliffs, NJ: Prentice-Hall.

Woll, B. (1978). Structure and function in language acquisition. In N. Waterson & C. Snow (Eds.), *The development of communication.* New York: Wiley.

Wootten, J., Merkin, S., Hood, L., & Bloom, L. (1979). *Wh- questions: Linguistic evidence to explain the sequence of acquisition.* Paper presented at the biennial meeting of the Society for Research in Child Development.

Yeni-Komshian, G., & Rao, P. (1980). *Speech perception in right and left CVA patients.* Paper presented at the International Neuropsychological Society meeting.

Yoder, P., & Kaiser, A. (1989). Alternative explanations for the relationship between maternal verbal interaction style and child language development: *Journal of Child Language, 16,* 141–160.

Zachary, W. (1978). Ordinality and interdependence of representation and language development in infancy. *Child Development, 49,* 681–687.

Zaidel, E. (1977). Unilateral auditory language comprehension on the Token test following cerebral commissurotomy and hemispherectomy. *Neuropsychologia, 15,* 1–18.

Zarebina, M. (1965). *The formation of the language system of a child.* Krakow: Wydawnictwo Polskiej Akademii Nauk.

Zhurova, L. (1973). The development of analysis of words into their sounds by preschool children. In C. Ferguson & D. Slobin (Eds.), *Studies of child language development.* New York: Holt, Rinehart & Winston.

Glossary

Accommodation Process of reorganizing cognitive structures or schemata or creating new schemata in response to external stimuli that do not fit into any available schema. Piagetian concept.

Account A type of narrative in which the speaker relates a past experience in which the listener did not share.

Action relational words Words that define the manner in which objects are related through movement; semantic category.

Adaptation Process by which an organism adapts to the environment; occurs as a result of two complementary processes, assimilation and accommodation. Piagetian concept.

Adjective A syntactic unit used to modify a noun, including possessive nouns (*mom's*), ordinals (*first*), adjectives (*blue, old*), and descriptors (*shopping* center).

Adverb A syntactic unit used to modify a word or phrase other than a noun or pronoun, such as a verb (ran *quickly*), an adjective (*extremely* old man), another adverb (*very* quickly), or a whole clause (*Obviously* you do not understand). Adverbs may indicate the time (*later, today, previously*), place (*here*), manner (*quietly, slowly*), or degree (*overly, last*).

Allophone Perceptual grouping of phones of similar speech sounds.

Anaphoric reference Grammatical mechanism that notifies the listener that the speaker is referring to a previous reference. Pronouns are one type of word used in anaphoric reference.

Angular gyrus Association area of the brain, located in the posterior portion of the temporal lobe, responsible for linguistic processing, especially word recall.

Antonyms Words that differ only in the opposite value of a single important feature.

Archiform One member of a word class used to the exclusion of all others. For example, *a* may be used for all articles or *he* for all third person pronouns.

Arcuate fasciculus White, fibrous tract of axons and dendrites underlying the angular gyrus in the brain. Language is organized in Wernicke's area and transmitted through the arcuate fasciculus to Broca's area.

Article A syntactic unit that precedes a noun or noun equivalent, marking definite (*the*) or indefinite (*a, an*) references or new (*a, an*) or old (*the*) information.

Articulation Dynamic process of producing speech sounds by movement of speech organs and the resultant modification of the laryngeal tone.

Aspect The dynamics of an event, noted by the verb, relative to the event's completion, repetition, or continuing duration.

Assimilation Process by which external stimuli are incorporated into existing cognitive structures or schemata. Piagetian concept.

Associative complex hypothesis Theory that each example of a meaning category shares something with a core concept. In other words, there are common elements in the meanings of *pants*, *shirt*, *shoes*, and *hat* that classify each as clothing. Vygotskyan concept.

Attribution relational words Words that mark the attributes, characteristics, or differences between two objects; semantic category.

Auxiliary verb A "helping" or nonprimary verb used to form tenses (*do* want, *did* read, *am* going, *was* eating, *have been* running) and to express mood or intention (*can, could, may might, must, shall, should*). The latter type are called **modals**.

Babbling Long strings of sounds that children begin to produce at 4 months of age.

Backward reduction Syntactic process of phrasal coordination in which common elements within two main clauses of a compound sentence are deleted from the initial clause. For example, "Joe ran and Ron ran" becomes "Joe and Ron ran." The full clause follows the conjunction.

Bilingual Fluent in two languages; uses two languages on a daily basis.

Bootstrapping Process of learning language in which the child uses what he or she knows to decode more mature language. For example, the child may use semantic knowledge to aid in decoding and learning syntax.

Bound morpheme Meaning unit that cannot occur alone but must be joined to a free morpheme; generally includes grammatical tags or markers that are derivational, such as *-ly, -er,* or *-ment,* or inflectional, such as *-ed* or *-s.*

Broca's area Cortical area of the left frontal lobe of the brain responsible for detailing and coordinating the programming of speech movements.

Case A distinct semantic role such as *agent* or *location*.

Centering The linking of entities in a narrative to form a story nucleus. Links may be based on similarity or complementarity of features, sequence, or causality.

Central nervous system (CNS) Portion of the nervous system consisting of the brain and spinal cord.

Cephalocaudal Head-to-foot developmental progression.

Cerebrum Upper brain, consisting of the cortex and the subcortical structures.

Chaining Narrative form consisting of a sequence of events that share attributes and lead directly from one to another.

Clause Group of words containing a subject and the accompanying verb, and used as a sentence (independent clause) or attached to an independent clause (dependent clause).

Coarticulation Co-occurrence of the characteristics of two or more phonemes as one phoneme influences another in perception or in production; may be forward (anticipatory) or backward (carryover).

Code switching Process of varying between two or more languages.

Cognates Phoneme pairs that differ only in voicing; manner and place of articulation are similar. For example, /f/ and /v/ are cognates, as are /s/ and /z/.

Cognitive determinism Theoretical construct that considers linguistic content to reflect the developmental order of cognitive structures.

Cognitive knowledge Individual's knowledge of reality gained through experiences and perceptions, in contrast to semantic knowledge.

Cognitive stimulation   Process of providing stimuli for comparison to stored referents, thus requiring evaluation and comparison.

Communication   Process of encoding, transmitting, and decoding signals in order to exchange information and ideas between the participants.

Communication competence   Degree of success in communicating, measured by the appropriateness and effectiveness of the message.

Communication functions   Uses or purposes of communication, such as requesting information or replying.

Complex sentence   Sentence consisting of a main clause and at least one subordinate clause.

Compound sentence   Sentence consisting of two or more main clauses.

Conjunction   A syntactic unit used to connect words, phrases, or clauses, such as *and, but, or, if, so, since, because, therefore, though, although,* and so on.

Consonant cluster reduction   Phonological process seen in preschool children in which one or more consonants are deleted from a cluster of two or more (*/tr, str, sl, kr/*) in order to simplify production.

Constituent   Unit, or component, of a sentence.

Contingent query   Request for clarification, such as "What?" or "Huh?"

Convergent semantic production   Process of recalling or producing a unique semantic unit, such as a word, phrase, or sentence, to fit a given linguistic restriction, such as the meaning of a stimulus. For example, convergent abilities are needed in completing crossword puzzles.

Copula   Form of the verb *to be* as a main verb. Signifies a relationship between the subject and a predicate adjective (*fat, tired, young*) or another noun (*teacher, farmer, pianist*).

Corpus callosum   Main transverse tract of neurons running between the two hemispheres of the brain.

Cortex   Outermost gray layer of the brain, made up of neuron cell bodies.

Count noun   A noun that can be singular (*cat*) or plural (*cats*), regular (*dog–dogs*) or irregular (*woman–women*) and can be preceded by a numerical term (*two rabbits*) or by *many* (*many cars*).

Critical period   Hypothesized period, prior to age 5, in which language learning must occur.

Deep structure   Basic structure or meaning that underlies a sentence; generated through the use of phrase structure rules. Chomskyan concept.

Deficit approach   Notion that only one dialect of a language is inherently correct or standard and that others are substandard or exhibit some deficit.

Deictic gaze   Gaze directed at a referent rather than a communication partner.

Deixis   Process of using the speaker's perspective as a reference. For example, deixis can be seen in words such as *this, that, here, there, me,* and *you.*

Demonstratives   Articles that indicate, from the speaker's perspective, to which entity the speaker is referring. Examples include *this, that, these,* and *those.*

Dialect   Language rule system of an identifiable group that varies from the rule system of an ideal standard.

Diminutive   Form of the noun used to denote that it refers to something small, as in *dog–doggie,* and *cat–kittie.*

Diphthong   Vowellike speech sound produced by blending two vowels within a syllable.

Direct object   A noun or noun equivalent, such as a phrase or clause, that answers the question *what?* or *whom?* following a transitive verb [He threw the *ball* (noun). She likes *to fish* (infinitive phrase). I know *where you went* (clause).]. Direct objects receive or are affected by the action of the verb.

Distancing   Gradual increase in the perceptual distance of infants and the accompanying shift from the senses of touch, taste, and smell to vision and hearing.

Distinctive features   Significant acoustic or articulatory characteristics of a phoneme that distinguish it from other phonemes.

Divergent semantic production   Process of recalling or producing a variety of words, phrases, or sentences on a topic. Divergent semantic abilities give language its originality, flexibility, and creativity.

Echolalia   Immediate, whole or partial vocal imitation of another speaker; characterizes the child's speech beginning at about 8 months.

Ellipsis   Conversational device of omitting redundant information. For example, when asked "Who saw the movie?" we reply "I did," not "I saw the movie."

Entrainment   Interactional synchronization or movement to speech.

Epenthesis   Process of inserting a vowel sound where none is required.

Episodic memory   Autobiographical and experiential memory of particular events.

Equilibrium   State of cognitive balance or harmony between incoming stimuli and cognitive structures. Piagetian concept.

Eventcast   A type of narrative that explains some current or anticipated event. Eventcasts often accompany the play of young children.

Evocative utterance   Toddler language-learning strategy in which the child names an entity and awaits adult evaluative feedback as to the correctness of the name or label.

Expansion   Adult's more mature version of a child utterance that preserves the word order of the original child utterance. For example, when a child says "Doggie eat," an adult might reply, "The doggie is eating."

Extension   Adult's semantically related comment on a topic established by a child. For example, when a child says "Doggie eat," an adult might reply, "Yes, doggie hungry."

Extinction   Behavioral concept of removing all reinforcement until a behavior decreases or ceases.

Fast mapping   Word-learning strategy in which the child infers a connection between a word and its referent after only one exposure.

Figurative language   Expressions that use words or phrases in an impression or represent an abstract concept; cannot be interpreted literally. For example, "My father *hit the roof*" cannot be explained at a syntactic level. Types of figurative language include idioms, metaphors, similes, and proverbs.

Fissure   A valley, or depression (also called a *sulcus*), between two gyri on the surface, or cortex, of the brain.

Forward reduction   Syntactic process of phrasal coordination in which common elements within two main clauses of a compound sentence are deleted from the second clause. For example, "Lynn laughed and Lynn cried" can be reduced to "Lynn laughed and cried."

Free alternation   Variable use of members of a word class without consideration of different meanings. For example, *the* and *a* may be used randomly.

Free morpheme   Meaning unit that can occur alone, such as *dog, chair, run,* and *fast*.

Fully resonant nuclei (FRN)   Vowellike sounds that are fully resonated laryngeal tones.

Functional-core hypothesis   Theory that word meanings represent dynamic relationships, such as actions or functional uses, rather than static perceptual traits. Concept usually associated with Nelson.

Gerund A verb (*swim*) plus -*ing* that functions as a noun in the subject (*Swimming* is great exercise) or object (I like *swimming*) position of a sentence or as the object of a preposition (By *swimming* for shore, he saved himself). Gerunds can be modified by adjectives (*graceful* swimming) or adverbs (swimming *gracefully*).

Government-binding theory Linguistic theory that attempts to describe the way in which the human mind represents an autonomous system of language that is diverse and flexible and yet learned from limited input.

Grammars Systems of rules or underlying principles that describe the five aspects of language.

Gyrus Hill between two fissures, or sulci, on the surface, or cortex, of the brain.

Habituation Expectation of occurrence formed for frequently occurring stimuli. Habituation is one method of testing infants' perceptions of changing stimuli.

Heschl's gyrus Area located in the auditory cortex of each hemisphere of the brain that receives incoming auditory signals from the inner ear.

Hypothesis testing utterance Toddler language-learning strategy in which the child seeks confirmation of the name of an entity by naming it with rising intonation, thus posing a yes/no question.

Idiom Short, figurative expression, such as *blow your mind, hit the roof,* or *split my sides.*

Illocution Intention of an utterance.

Illocutionary force Speaker's intention or attitude toward his or her utterance.

Index Shared property of a motor act that indicates recognition by an infant.

Indicating Following a line of regard by commenting. Mothers follow their infant's line of regard and comment on the object or event that is the focus of the child's attention.

Indirect object A noun or noun equivalent that is indirectly affected by the verb in that the action is performed for the indirect object (Give the notes to *her*. She gave *me* a gift.). Indirect objects usually are preceded by or can be rewritten to be preceded by *for* or *to*.

Infinitive A verb (*swim*) preceded by *to* that functions as a noun (I love *to swim*. To swim is such a joy.) and occasionally as an adjective (I have a project *to finish*.) or adverb (She worked *to become* a teacher.). The *to* may be omitted following certain words, such as *help, dare,* and *let* (He helped *fix* my bike. We dared not *tell* our secret. Let's *go* now.).

Information processing Theoretical model of brain function that stresses methods employed in dealing with information.

Integrative rehearsal Use of repetition or rehearsal to transfer information to long-term memory. Information-processing concept.

Interrogative utterance Toddler language-learning strategy in which the child attempts to learn the name of an entity by asking *What?, That?,* or *Wassat?*. Not to be confused with adultlike interrogative sentences, which are more varied (*what, where, who, why, how, when*).

Intransitive verb A verb that does not take a direct object (I *waited* quietly for hours) and is not able to be made passive.

Irregular past tense verb A verb that takes a marker other than the -*ed* past tense marker (*eat–ate, stand–stood, throw–threw*).

Jargon Strings of unintelligible speech sounds with the intonational pattern of adult speech.

Joint (shared) reference   Process of differentiating or noting a particular object, action, or event for the purpose of communication.

Language   Socially shared code or conventional system for representing concepts through the use of arbitrary symbols and rule-governed combinations of those symbols.

Larynx   Anatomical structure that surmounts the trachea and houses the vocal folds. Made of several separate cartilaginous elements, the larynx's primary function is to protect the lungs from the entrance of foreign material.

Lexicon   Individual dictionary of each person containing words and the underlying concepts of each. The lexicon is dynamic, changing with experience.

Linguistic competence   Native speaker's underlying knowledge of the rules for generating and understanding conventional linguistic forms.

Linguistic determinism   Theory that language determines thought; all higher thought is dependent upon language. Whorf hypothesis.

Linguistic performance   Actual language use, reflecting linguistic competence and the communication constraints.

Linguistic relativism   Theory that the experiences of speakers of different languages vary; that groups with the same language think in the same manner. Whorf hypothesis.

Location relational words   Words that define the geographic, physical, directional, or spatial relationship of two objects; semantic category.

Locution   Meaning or proposition expressed in a speech act.

Main clause   Clause within a multiclause sentence that can occur alone.

Marking   Process a mother uses to attract her infant's attention. For example, the mother could shake an object or exaggerate an action.

Mass noun   Noun referring to homogeneous, nonindividual substances (*water, sand, sugar, salt, milk*) that cannot take a numerical term (*one, 300*). Unlike count nouns, mass nouns take *much* (*much sand*) rather than *many*.

Mean length of utterance (MLU)   Average number of morphemes per utterance.

Metalinguistic cues   Linguistic intuitions on the acceptability of communication.

Metaphor   Figure of speech in which a comparison or resemblance is implied between two entities. Meaning is extended on the basis of some natural relationship, such as *mouth of a bottle*.

Modal auxiliary   Auxiliary verb used to express mood or attitude, such as ability (*can*), permission (*may*), intention (*will*), possibility (*might*), and obligation (*must*).

Morpheme   Smallest unit of meaning; indivisible (*dog*) without violating the meaning or producing meaningless units (*do, g*). There are two types of morphemes, free and bound.

Morphology   Aspect of language concerned with rules governing change in meaning at the intraword level.

Motherese   Style of talking used most often by white middle-class American mothers when addressing their 18- to 24-month-old toddlers.

Mutual gaze   Eye contact with a communication partner; used to signal intensified attention.

Myelination   Process of maturation of the nervous system in which the nerves develop a protective myelin sheath, or sleeve.

Narrative level   Overall organization of a narrative.

Nasal cavity   Nose; cavity between the pharynx and the nares, separated from the oral cavity by the palate.

Neonate   Newborn.

Neurolinguistics   Study of the anatomy, physiology, and biochemistry of the brain responsible for language processing and formulation.

Neuron   Nerve cell; basic unit of the nervous system.

Nonegocentrism   Ability to take another person's perspective.

Nonlinguistic cues   Coding devices that contribute to communication but are not a part of speech. Examples include gestures, body posture, eye contact, head and body movement, facial expression, and physical distance or proxemics.

Noun   A syntactic unit noting a person, place, thing, quality, or activity (*Juan, New York, automobile, courage, departure*) that can usually be made possessive and plural (*woman's, women*). Nouns can serve as the subject, object, or indirect object of a sentence [*Mary* (subject) gave the *ball* (object) to *John* (indirect object)] or as the object of a preposition (to *school,* at the old *mill*). The noun is the only element required in a noun phrase.

Noun phrase   A noun element consisting of a noun, pronoun, or phrasal noun substitute, such as an infinitive or gerund, and the associated words that describe or modify that element. The noun element is the only obligatory portion.

Object   A sentence element filled by a noun or noun substitute upon which the action is performed, as in "She threw the *ball*" (direct object), or for whom the action is performed, as in "She bought the flowers for *him*" (indirect object).

Object noun phrase complement   Subordinate clause that serves as the object of the main clause, as in "I remember *what you did to me*."

Operant conditioning   Behavioral training as a result of reinforcement and punishment.

Oral cavity   Mouth; cavity between the pharynx and the lips, bounded below by the tongue, and above by the palate.

Organization   Tendency for all living things to systemize or organize behaviors. Piagetian concept.

Overextension   Process in which a child applies a word's meaning to more exemplars than an adult would. The child's definition is too broad and is thus beyond acceptable adult usage.

Paralinguistic codes   Vocal and nonvocal codes that are superimposed on a linguistic code to signal the speaker's attitude or emotion or to clarify or provide additional meaning.

Participle   A verb (*swim*) plus *-ing, -ed, -t,* or *-en* used as an adjective (Let's go to the *swimming* pool. He had a *concealed* weapon. It was a *lost* cause. He was a *broken* man.).

Perceptual (or sensory) stimulation   Reception of stimuli and recognition of their parameters.

Peripheral nervous system   All elements of the nervous system outside of the skull and spinal cord.

Perlocution   Aspect of speech acts related to the listener's interpretation of the speaker's message.

Pharynx   Cavity extending from the larynx to the nasal cavity.

Phonation   Process of producing a low-pitched hum or buzz from the vibration of the vocal folds.

Phone   Actual produced speech sound.

Phoneme   Smallest linguistic unit of sound, each with distinctive features, that can signal a difference in meaning when modified.

Phonetically consistent forms (PCFs)   Consistent vocal patterns that accompany gestures prior to the appearance of words.

Phonology   Aspect of language concerned with the rules governing the structure, distribution, and sequencing of speech sound patterns.

Phrasal coordination   Process of conjoining clauses and deleting common elements.

Phrase   Group of words that does not contain a subject or predicate and is used as a noun substitute or as a noun or verb modifier.

Phrase structure rules   Rules that delineate basic relationships underlying sentence organization. Chomskyan concept. Chomsky found the phrase structure rules to be universal and thus concluded that they were innate.

Possession relational words   Words that recognize an association between an object and a particular person; semantic category.

Pragmatics   Aspect of language concerned with language use within a communication context.

Preposition   A syntactic unit noting the relation—usually in space or time—of a noun or its equivalent to some other word in the sentence (*on* the dresser, *in* my heart, *at* five o'clock). Common prepositions include *after, at, before, between, by, for, from, in, of, on, over, to, under,* and *with*.

Present progressive   A verb tense consisting of *be* + *Verb-ing* and used to express a continuous action occurring at the present time (*am eating, are running*).

Presupposition   Process of assuming which information a listener possesses or may need.

Primitive speech act (PSA)   Act, prosodic pattern, or word that conveys the early intentions of children. Term coined by Dore.

Pronominal   Adjective form of the word *pronoun*, as in *This sentence uses a pronominal form*.

Pronoun   A syntactic unit that can take the place of a noun. Pronouns may fulfill syntactic functions such as subject (*I, you, he, she, it, we, they*), object (*me, you, him, her, it, us, them*), possessive (*my, your, his, her, its, our, their*), and reflexive (*myself, yourself, himself, herself, itself, ourselves, yourselves, themselves*). In addition, pronouns may be classified as interrogative (*Who* is she?), relative (The girl *who* sits behind me never does her homework), and indefinite (*all, any, anyone, each, either, everyone, few, no one, one, some, someone*).

Propositional force   Conceptual content or meaning of speech acts.

Protoconversation   Vocal interactions between mothers and infants that resemble the verbal exchanges of more mature conversations.

Prototypic complex hypothesis   Theory that word meanings represent an underlying concept exemplified by a central referent, or prototype, that is a best exemplar or a composite of the concept.

Proverb   Figure of speech that often gives advice or states some folk wisdom, such as "Don't put all your eggs in one basket."

Psycholinguistics   Study of the psychological aspects of language, especially as they apply to the psychological processes involved in learning, processing, and using language.

Punishment   Response that follows a behavior and decreases the probability of recurrence of that behavior.

Quasi-resonant nuclei (QRN)   Partial resonance of speech sounds found in neonates.

Recount   A type of narrative that relates past experiences of which the child and the listener partook, observed, or read.

Reduplicated babbling   Long strings of consonant-vowel syllable repetitions, such as *ba-ba-ba-ba-ba*, which appear in the vocal play of 6- to 7-month-old infants.

Referencing   Differentiation of one entity from many; noting the presence of a single object, action, or event for one's communication partner.

Reflexes   Automatic, involuntary motor patterns. Although many neonatal behaviors are reflexive, this condition changes quickly with maturity.

Reflexive relational words   Words that relate objects to themselves in such ways as existence, nonexistence, disappearance, and recurrence; semantic category.

Register   Situationally influenced language variations, such as motherese.

Regular past tense verb   A verb that takes the *-ed* marker for the past tense (*walked, jumped, typed*).

Rehearsal   Process of maintaining information within long-term memory; repetition, drill, or practice.

Reinforcement   Response that follows a behavior and increases the probability of recurrence of that behavior.

Relational words   Words that refer across entities, including action, location, appearance, disappearance, and possession; semantic category.

Relative clause   Subordinate clause that follows and modifies a noun, as in "I really like the car *that we test-drove last night.*"

Request for clarification   Request from the listener for restatement of or additional information on some unclear utterance of the speaker.

Resonation   Process of modifying the laryngeal tone by altering the shape of the pharyngeal, oral, and nasal cavities.

Respiration   Process of inhalation and exhalation, plus the resultant gas exchange.

Reticular formation   Unit of neurons within the brain stem responsible for sensory integration and for inhibition or facilitation of sensory information.

Rich interpretation   Process of interpreting child language by considering both the linguistic and nonlinguistic contexts.

Schemata (sing. schema)   Cognitive structures or concepts that an individual uses to process incoming sensory information; manifested as an organized pattern or reaction to stimuli. Piagetian concept.

Segmentation   Process of dividing conversation so that utterances encode the relevant dynamic elements of a situation; accompaniment to joint action.

Selection restrictions   Constraints of specific word meanings that govern possible word combinations.

Selective imitation   Toddler language-learning strategy in which the child imitates those language features that he or she is in the process of learning. Toddlers do not imitate randomly.

Semantic features   Perceptual or functional aspects of meaning that characterize a word.

Semantic-feature hypothesis   Theory that word meanings represent universal semantic features or attributes, such as animate/inanimate and male/female. For young children, meanings represent perceptual attributes. Hypothesis usually associated with Clark.

Semantic knowledge   Word or linguistic structure meanings, in contrast to cognitive knowledge.

Semantic memory   Individual's internal thesaurus of word and symbol knowledge and of the rules for relations between them.

Semantics   Aspect of language concerned with rules governing the meaning or content of words or grammatical units.

Semantic-syntactic rules Word order rules that describe the early multiword utterances of young children. Examples include *agent + action* and *negative + X*.

Sensorimotor Stage of cognitive development (approximately from birth to 2 years) in which a child acquires knowledge of actions and objects through sensory and motor input. Piagetian concept.

Sentence An independent clause (*subject + verb* that can stand alone) that may be classified as simple (independent clause alone), compound (two or more independent clauses joined together), complex (an independent clause plus one or more dependent clauses), or compound-complex (two or more independent clauses plus one or more dependent clauses).

Sentential coordination Conjoining of full clauses.

Sibilants Sounds produced by forcing air through a narrow constriction formed by the tongue and palate. The turbulence produced results in a hissing sound. Examples include /s/, /z/, /ʃ/, and /ʒ/.

Sign Symbol that represents a cognitive structure; denotes thought about some entity or event. A word is an example.

Signal Indicator that elicits an action schema and in which there is no differentiation between the form of the action (signifier) and the content (significant). An example is maternal posturing for "I'm going to get you."

Simile Figure of speech that states an explicit comparison, such as *eats like a pig* or *lovely as a flower*.

Simple sentence Linguisitc structure that contains one full clause.

Social smile Infant's smile in response to an external social stimulus.

Sociolinguistics Study of the sociological influence on language learning and use, especially cultural and situational variables, including dialects, bilingualism, and parent–child interactions.

Speech Dynamic neuromuscular process of producing speech sounds for communication; a verbal means of transmission.

Speech act Basic unit of communication; an intentional, verbally encoded message that includes the speaker's intentions, the speaker's meaning, the message's meaning, and the listener's interpretation. Concept specified by Searle.

Stories Fictionalized narratives.

Story grammar Narrative framework that specifies the underlying relationship of the story components.

Subordinate clause Clause that cannot occur alone but functions in support of the main clause.

Sulcus *See* Fissure.

Supramarginal gyrus Association area of the brain, located in the posterior portion of the temporal lobe, responsible for linguistic processing, especially of longer syntactic units such as sentences.

Suprasegmental devices Paralinguistic mechanisms superimposed on the verbal signal to change the form and meaning of the sentence by acting across the elements or segments of that sentence. Examples include intonation, stress, and inflection.

Surface structure Structural characteristics of the actual spoken message; result of application of the phrase structure and transformational rules to the deep structure.

Symbol Entity that represents another entity containing similar features. For example, a word is a symbol for the entity it represents.

Synapse Miniscule space between the axon of one neuron and the dendrites of another.

Synonym Word that shares the same or a similar meaning with another word.

Syntagmatic-paradigmatic shift   Change in word associational behavior from a syntactic to a semantic basis; occurs during the school-age years.

Syntax   Organizational rules specifying word order, sentence organization, and word relationships.

Tense   A marking of the verb, such as past or future, that relates the speech time in the present to the event time or time when the event occurs.

Thalamus   Organ located in the higher brain stem that receives incoming sensory information, except smell, and relays this information to the appropriate portion of the brain for analysis.

Topic   Content or subject about which conversational partners speak.

Topic-comment   Process by which a topic is established and then elaborated upon. The infant may establish a topic by a look, gesture, or word; the infant or mother may then elaborate.

Transactional model   Communication-first model of language development, evidenced in the give and take of early child–parent dialogues.

Transformational rules   Rules that operate on strings of symbols, rearranging phrase structure elements to form an acceptable sentence for output. There are rules for negatives, passive voice, interrogatives, and so on. Chomskyan concept.

Transitive verb   A verb that must take a direct object to complete its meaning (The woman *sold* his books). Transitive verbs can be made into passive voice (The books *were sold* by the woman).

Turnabout   Conversational device used by a mother with a preschooler to maintain the conversation and aid the child in making on-topic comments. In its usual form, the turnabout consists of a comment on or reply to the child's utterance followed by a cue, such as a question, for the child to reply.

Underextension   Process in which a child applies a word meaning to fewer exemplars than an adult would. The child's definition is too restrictive and more limited than in adult usage.

Uninflected verb   Verb containing no marking for person (*runs, eats, jumps*) or for tense (*will run, has been eating, jumped*), as in *run, eat,* and *jump.*

Variegated babbling   Long strings of nonidentical syllables that appear in the vocal play of some 8- to 10-month-old infants.

Verb   A syntactic unit noting action (*run, jump, eat*) or being/state (*be, want, feel*) that changes form to indicate time or tense (*go, went, will go, is going*), person (*am–is, run–runs*), number (*is–are*), mood (*could, might*), and aspect. Verbs can be classified as transitive, intransitive, or equative.

Verb phrase   Verb and the words or phrases, such as prepositional phrases, that accompany it.

Vernacular   Casual, informal, or intimate language register or style.

Vocal folds   Laryngeal vibrators responsible for phonation.

Vocal play   Long strings of consonant-vowel syllables produced in self-imitation, such as *ba-ba-ba-ba;* appears at about 6 months of age.

Voice   Change made in the verb to indicate whether the subject of the sentence acts (**active voice**), e.g., *The cat chases the dog,* or is acted upon (**passive voice**), e.g., *The dog is chased by the cat.*

Voiced phonemes   Phonemes that are produced with vibration at the level of the larynx.

Voiceless phonemes Phonemes that are produced without vibration at the level of the larynx.

Voice onset time (VOT) Interval between the burst of a voice plosive and the commencement of phonation.

Wernicke's area Language-processing area of the brain, located in the left temporal lobe; responsible for organizing the underlying structure of outgoing messages and analyzing incoming linguistic information.

Author Index

Subject Index